Cognition, Evolution, and Behavior

Cognition, Evolution, and Behavior

98,510 -

Sara J. Shettleworth

New York   Oxford

Oxford University Press

1998

Oxford University Press

Oxford   New York
Athens   Auckland   Bangkok   Bogotá   Buenos Aires   Calcutta
Cape Town   Chennai   Dar es Salaam   Delhi   Florence   Hong Kong   Istanbul
Karachi   Kuala Lumpur   Madrid   Melbourne   Mexico City   Mumbai
Nairobi   Paris   São Paulo   Singapore   Taipei   Tokyo   Toronto   Warsaw

and associated companies in
Berlin   Ibadan

Copyright © 1998 by Oxford University Press

Published by Oxford University Press, Inc.
198 Madison Avenue, New York, New York 10016

Oxford is a registered trademark of Oxford University Press

Library of Congress Cataloging-in-Publication Data
Shettleworth, Sara J.
    Cognition, evolution, and behavior / by Sara J. Shettleworth.
        p.   cm.
    Includes bibliographical references and index.
    ISBN 0-19-511047-1; 0-19-511048-X (pbk.)
    1. Cognition in animals.   2. Animal behavior—Evolution.
3. Animal ecology.   I. Title.
    QLZ85.S44   1998
    591.5—dc21   98-23516

9 8 7 6

Printed in the United States of America
on acid-free paper

The role of psychology, then, is to describe the innate features of the minds of different organisms which have evolved to match certain aspects of that physical external universe, and the way in which the physical universe interacts with the mind to produce the phenomenal world.

O'Keefe & Nadel,
The Hippocampus as a Cognitive Map

Preface

The evolution of the animal mind is one of the most exciting problems in the cognitive sciences. The feats of navigation performed by bees and pigeons, tales of talking parrots and counting rats, self-aware chimpanzees and deceiving plovers not only fascinate the nonspecialist but also raise important issues in psychology and biology. How do bees or pigeons find their way home? Can other animals navigate as well as they do, and if not, why not? Do parrots *really* talk? What use would counting be to rats in the wild anyway? Do monkeys and apes, which look so much like us, think like us too? What is the relationship between the human mind and the minds of other species?

Questions like these raise issues that are intrinsically interdisciplinary. Because of this they are covered inadequately in most textbooks, although they are increasingly the subject of popular and semipopular treatments (e.g., Barber, 1994; M. S. Dawkins, 1993; Gould & Gould, 1994) . On the one hand most introductions to animal cognition for psychology students review laboratory studies on rats, pigeons, and monkeys from an anthropocentric point of view. Evolutionary issues or descriptions of behavior outside the laboratory are oversimplified and kept in the background, if they are discussed at all. On the other hand, introductions to animal behavior or behavioral ecology include at most a one-chapter survey, usually sketchy and outdated, of research on animal learning and cognition, even though the authors may point out that the sorts of cognitive processes generally studied by psychologists play a role in ecologically relevant behavior. A zoologist wishing to know more soon feels mired in the psychologist's specialist terminology. Equally specialized terms await the psychology student wanting to know more about evolution and behavioral ecology. *Phylogeny*, *MVT*, and *ESS* are just as baffling to the uninitiated as *US*, *RI*, and *fixed interval schedule*.

I wrote this book in the belief that the future of research on comparative cognition, behavioral ecology, and behavioral neuroscience lies in increased interdisciplinary training and communication. I have tried to capture a vision of an approach to the evolution of the mind in which it is natural, indeed necessary, to integrate the answers to questions traditionally asked in psychology laboratories with the answers to questions about ecology and evolution. I have tried to make it accessible to students and researchers from both psychology and biology, or with backgrounds in neither. It is for the increasing numbers of people trained in the cognitive sciences who feel that the study of cognition in animals, including ourselves, is incomplete without consideration of evolution and ecology. Equally, it is for the increasing numbers of behavioral ecologists and ethologists who find themselves wanting to answer essentially psychological questions about behavior. If this book increases research and understanding in these areas, it will have done its job.

The issues discussed here are diverse, from the nature of habituation to whether chimpanzees have a theory of mind. This diversity reflects the fact that research on animal cognition is currently being done by at least three somewhat independent groups of scientists, and the problems and species they work on differ accordingly. Psychologists trained in so-called animal learning tend to study conditioning and cognitive problems such as timing, counting, and spatial orientation in the laboratory, primarily using rats, pigeons, and a few other readily available species. Meanwhile, a group of people with backgrounds in anthropology and child development are attempting to gain insight into the commonalities between humans and other primates by studying apes and monkeys, both in the field and in a variety of laboratory situations. And at the same time, biologists of many stripes, working on insects, mammals, fish, and birds, find themselves confronted with questions about cognitive mechanisms in their animals' natural environments, from how birds perceive and remember song to whether fish copy one another, and how bees and voles encode spatial information. Primarily because of poor communication, the insights acquired by these different groups of researchers are not always well integrated with one another. Furthermore, people with interests of one sort may tend to be uninterested in or dismissive of research of another sort. For instance, someone interested in theory of mind in primates may think the study of conditioning is about boring mechanical processes that were well understood long ago, whereas someone studying conditioning may see theory of mind, intentionality, and the like as not amenable to rigorous experimental analysis. In fact, however, much can be learned by bringing together data, methods, and/or theory even from areas as disparate as these.

Most texts on behavioral ecology (e.g., Krebs & Davies, 1993) are organized by adaptive problem: how to find food, choose mates, form groups, and so on. Texts on cognition are generally organized by cognitive process: attention, short-term memory, long-term memory. Similarly, texts on learning and memory in animals are organized according to traditional kinds of learning, usually starting with habituation, then classical and instrumental conditioning, and finally more "cognitive" processes such as timing, spatial orientation, and concept formation. The ecological problems animals solve do not have a one-to-one correspondance with the cognitive mechanisms used to solve them (see also Cosmides & Tooby, 1995) . Consider parental care. The digger wasp provisions her young by bringing caterpillars to the nest in response to a series of sign stimuli. One of the most striking features of the wasp's parental care is the apparent ability to keep track of the locations and state of provisioning of several nests concurrently. Starlings bring food to their young, too, but all their offspring are in the same place. Unlike wasps, starlings respond to the babies' hunger as communicated by begging. As the nestlings develop, the parents learn to recognize them individually, enabling them to locate their own offspring after the young have left the nest but still need parental feeding. In contrast to wasps and starlings, chimpanzees' parental care extends over several years and involves much learning about the social and physical world by the young while in the company of their mother and older siblings. At the same time, however, since the chimpanzee baby clings to its mother, no special feats of spatial memory are required to ensure that the mother provides food for her offspring. For understanding how the mind works, it does not make sense to group wasp, starling, and chimpanzee together and expect to find common cognitive mechanisms for parental care.

Because this book is about understanding cognition, chapters 2 through 11 are organized largely in terms of categories of information processing rather than ecological problems. Nevertheless, the organization follows functional principles. The traditional categories of cognitive mechanism are in fact defined by the jobs they do. *Attention* refers to selective processing of information. *Memory* is retention of information. *Spatial cognition* refers to processing and acting on information about places. These information-processing problems cut across ecological problems like mate choice and foraging, although some may be unique to specific ecological problems. For instance, theory and data about how animals assess rates of occurrence (chapter 9) come primarily from foraging behavior. Imprinting (chapter 4) has been studied most as a process by which young birds recognize their parents. Nevertheless, many cognitive mechanisms solve problems that are important in a number of ecological contexts. Recognizing and classifying objects is important whether those objects are food, mates, offspring, parents, or enemies. One can therefore ask, as we do in chapters 4 and 5, whether recognizing all of them obeys similar principles. And in one of the chapters that is an exception to this scheme, chapter 12 (Communication and Language), we will find ourselves recapitulating many issues introduced elsewhere.

A major aim of this book is to argue for an adaptationist or ecological approach to cognition. To set the stage, a large part of chapter 1 is devoted to discussing adaptation, how hypotheses about adaptation can be tested, and how adaptationist and psychological explanations can be related to each other. That chapter also makes the important distinction between *cognition* and *consciousness* and introduces some other key ideas in the study of cognition, evolution, and behavior. The titles of chapters 2 through 12 are much like the chapter titles in any text about animal learning and cognition, starting with perception and "simple" forms of learning like habituation and Pavlovian conditioning, then moving on to category learning, spatial behavior, counting, timing, "reasoning," communication, and various forms of social cognition. But each chapter synthesizes laboratory analyses of cognitive mechanisms with related theory and data from behavioral ecology. For example, how does understanding species-specific perceptual mechanisms help to explain the evolution of mate choice, and vice versa (chapter 2)? Can imprinting and kin recognition be accounted for by the mechanisms of simple recognition learning revealed in studies of habituation and perceptual learning (chapter 4)? How animals classify complex stimuli has been studied using untrained responses to species-specific signals in the field and highly trained responses to artificial stimuli in the laboratory. Can all these phenomena be accounted for in the same way, and if not, why not (chapter 5)? How are models of optimal foraging related to principles of reinforcement and choice (chapter 9)? Are there special forms of uniquely social learning and understanding, and if so are they especially well developed in species with complex social lives (chapters 10 and 11)? Those who have already studied the psychology of animal cognition or behavioral ecology will find some familiar material, but juxtaposed with much that is new, some of it interpreted in new ways. The usefulness of this kind of integration is reevaluated in chapter 13 in the light of the examples in earlier chapters.

Acknowledgments

This book might never have been begun without the opportunity provided by a Visiting Fellowship at Magdalen College, Oxford, in Hilary Term, 1995, and for that transforming experience I am deeply grateful to the President and Fellows of Magdalen. For welcoming a psychologist into their midst during that and many other visits over the past 18 years and for making those visits endlessly rewarding, I thank members of the Department of Zoology, Oxford, particularly John Krebs and also Alex Kacelnik. My research has been funded continuously for over 25 years by the Natural Sciences and Engineering Research Council of Canada, through its enlightened policy of support for individual scientists' research programs, and I am grateful for having been able to work in the environment that policy made possible.

Special thanks to all those who helped with the more tedious aspects of preparing the manuscript: to Tim Jarsky, Laura Mulcaster, Leslie Sole, and Jennifer Waring for inputting seemingly endless piles of references; to Alana Balaban for scrupulously checking the formating in between trips to the library; Stuart Marcovitch for the massive job of collecting permissions to reproduce previously published material; and especially Rick Westwood not only for help with the manuscript but also for keeping the lab running so I could concentrate on writing. For reading chapters and contributing to making them better, I am grateful to Alison Sekuler, Pat Bennett, and students in their lab during the summer of 1996 for comments on chapter 2; Melissa Bateson for straightening me out on some issues in chapter 9; Rob McDonald for reading chapter 7; and Marc Hauser and several anonymous reviewers who read early drafts of chapters for their comments and encouragement. David Kabelik gave invaluable help with the page proofs. Members of graduate courses in three different places put up with absent boxes and missing or unreadable figures in order to provide the students' point of view; to Lucy Jacobs's animal cognition seminar at Berkeley, Al Kamil's joint biology-psychology course at the University of Nebraska, and Psy 2205 at the University of Toronto, thanks for your help. Al Kamil, Lucy Jacobs, and Nick Mackintosh all read the manuscript for Oxford, and Judy Stamps read the whole thing for the fun of it. All contributed constructive and illuminating comments and corrections that are much appreciated even if I did not act on all of them. Finally, it is a pleasure to thank the two people who contributed the most to the making of this book: Dr. Margaret C. Nelson for patiently turning shipment after shipment of almost illegible scribbles into such wonderful illustrations and Joan Bossert of Oxford University Press for unfailing enthusiasm, support, and editorial advice. This book is dedicated to all past and future students of comparative cognition, especially Catherine Plowright, Pam Reid, Jeff Dickinson, Dave Brodbeck, Rob Hampton, Jon Crystal, and the late Shannon Hamm.

Sara J. Shettleworth

Toronto
January 1998

Contents

Cognition, Evolution, and Behavior

Cognition, Evolution, and the Study of Behavior

Along the streets of Davis, California, walnut trees have been planted for shade. They also provide food for the many crows that roost near Davis. Crows crack walnuts by dropping them from heights of 5–10 meters or more onto sidewalks, roads, and other hard surfaces. Occasionally, crows are seen dropping walnuts in front of approaching cars, as if using the cars to crush the nuts for them. Do crows intentionally use cars as nutcrackers? Some of the citizens of Davis, as well as some professional biologists (Grobecker & Pietsch, 1978), were convinced that they do, at least until a team of young biologists at University of California, Davis decided to put this anecdote to the test (Cristol, Switzer, Johnson, & Walke, 1997). They reasoned that if crows were using cars as tools, the birds would be more likely to drop nuts onto the road when cars were coming than when the road was empty. Furthermore, if a crow was standing in the road with an uncracked walnut as a car approached in the same lane, it should leave the nut in the road to be crushed rather than carry it away.

Cristol and his collaborators stationed themselves in various places in Davis where crows were feeding on walnuts and recorded what the birds did when cars were approaching and when the road was empty. Their data provided no support for the notion that crows were using automobiles as nutcrackers (figure 1.1). In other respects, however, the birds' behavior with walnuts was quite sophisticated (Cristol & Switzer, in press). For example, by dropping nuts from buildings on the Davis campus, Cristol and Switzer ver-

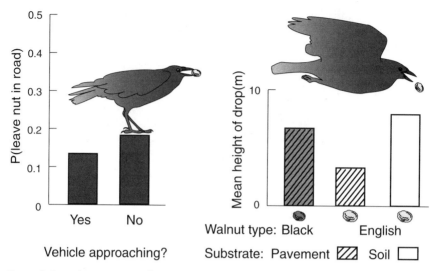

Figure 1.1. *Left:* Proportion of crows dropping a walnut in the road when flying away as a function of whether or not a vehicle was approaching (Cristol, Switzer, Johnson, & Walke, 1997). *Right:* Mean height to which crows carried black or English walnuts before dropping them onto pavement (cross-hatched bars) or onto soil (English walnuts only) (Cristol & Switzer, in press)

ified that English walnuts did not have to be carried so high before breaking as the harder black walnuts that are also found in Davis. They also determined, not surprisingly, that walnuts broke more easily when dropped onto pavement than when dropped into soil. The crows' behavior reflected these facts (figure 1.1). Moreover, a crow dropping a nut took into account the likelihood that a greedy fellow crow might steal a dropped nut before it could be retrieved: the fewer crows waiting on the ground nearby, the higher they took walnuts before dropping them.

The story of the nutcracking crows encapsulates some important issues in the comparative study of cognition. Foremost is how to translate a hypothesis about essentially unobservable internal processes into hypotheses about observable behavior in a way that permits different possible explanations to be distinguished unambiguously. Here, this meant asking, "What will crows do if they are using cars as tools that they will not do if they are merely dropping nuts onto the road as a car happens by?" A second issue has to do with the kinds of hypotheses people are willing to entertain about the processes underlying animal behavior. The citizens of Davis who saw nutcracking as an expression of the clever crows' ability to reason and plan were engaging in an anthropomorphism that is common even among professional students of animal behavior (Blumberg & Wasserman, 1995; Kennedy, 1992). As we will see, such thinking can be a fertile source of ideas, but research often reveals that simpler, more mechanical-seeming processes are doing surprisingly complex jobs. Free-living crows were observed doing something suggestive of interesting kinds of information processing and decision making. Their behavior was then examined with more controlled observations and experiments. Among other things, these revealed how closely the crows' behavior matched the environmental requirements. Numerous processes of perception, learning, and decision making underlie the crows' nutcracking, and each of these could be analyzed further. For example, how do crows judge the height from which they drop nuts? Do they have to learn to adjust their behavior to the kind of nut, the kind of substrate, and the number of nearby crows? Several species of crows, gulls, and other birds break hard-shelled prey by dropping them (review in Switzer & Cristol, in press), and one might also ask what kind of environmental conditions or evolutionary history favors this behavior.

1.1 Cognition and Consciousness

1.1.1 What Is Cognition?

Cognition refers to the mechanisms by which animals acquire, process, store, and act on information from the environment. These include perception, learning, memory, and decision making. The study of comparative cognition is therefore concerned with how animals process information, starting with how information is acquired by the senses. The behavior examined for evidence of cognition need not be learned, and it need not be studied in the laboratory by psychologists. In this book, for example, how birds classify songs or potential mates in the field will be considered alongside how animals can be taught to classify artificial stimuli in the laboratory (see chapter 5). Possible examples of tool use in the field, like the crows' nutcracking, will be examined along with tests of what captive monkeys understand when they learn to use tools (see chapter 10). The dance communication of bees and the alarm calling of chickens will be considered alongside the use of human gestures, words, and symbols by parrots and chimpanzees (see chapter 12). How ants find their way in the desert and how rats find their way in mazes will both be examined, among other examples, for what they reveal about the principles of spatial cognition (see chapter 7).

Not all would agree on the usefulness of a broad definition of cognition as information processing. McFarland (1991) proposes that *cognitive* should be reserved for the manipulation of *declarative* rather than *procedural* knowledge. Declarative knowledge is "knowing that" whereas procedural knowledge is "knowing how," or knowing what to do, as in a stimulus-response connection. The declarative knowledge that a chipmunk might gain from moving about its territory could contain maplike information like "home burrow is south of that big rock." Or the chipmunk might instead store information about its territory as procedural knowledge like "turn left at the rock." The first kind of representation implies a degree of flexibility in decision making and behavior that the second does not (see chapter 7). However, in both cases behavior results from the ability to process and store information about the world. In this book, we will be concerned in a broad way with how animals do this.

For many psychologists, mental representations of the world are the essence of cognition. Gallistel (1990) has developed at length a "computational-representational" approach to animal cognition. He suggests that experience results in the establishment in the brain of *functioning isomorphisms* between brain processes and events in the world. Adaptive behavior arises because, in effect, brain processes perform computations on incoming information that transform it to appropriate behavioral output. This must be true in some sense, but it is easy to overemphasize the richness and detail of animals' representations and the complexity of the processes operating on them. For instance, Gallistel suggests that an animal assessing the availability of food stores information about the time at which it finds each food item as it searches. Separate stores of information about numbers of items and times are converted, by a brain process isomorphic to division, into a representations of the rate of food available. As we will see, the richness of representations underlying behavior varies considerably across species and behavior systems. Much interesting adaptive behavior is based on processing limited information in simple ways.

At the beginning of the 1900s psychologists' study of cognitive processes in animals narrowed into the study of associative learning (see Boakes, 1984). The subfield of animal cognition arose in the 1970s (Hulse, 1993; Wasserman, 1993). Its practitioners were concerned to distinguish themselves from S-R psychologists, who explained behavior in terms of connections between stimuli and responses and eschewed speculation about unobservable processing of information. Psychologists studying animal cognition, in contrast, use behavior as a window onto processes of memory and representation (Wasserman, 1984). Much of their research uses learned behavior of rats and pigeons in the laboratory to analyze processes that have been successfully studied in people, such as memory for lists of items, concept formation, and attention. The distinguishing feature of such problems is that behavior appears to be based not on immediate stimulation but on stored representations of events and their significance (Terrace, 1984). However, the line between behavior resulting from associations and that reflecting "representational" processes is not always easy to draw, and it cannot necessarily be drawn in advance of detailed experimental analysis. Moreover, functionally similar behavior, such as communicating, recognizing neighbors, or way finding, may be accomplished in different ways by different kinds of animals (Dyer, 1994). Comparing the ways in which different species solve similar information-processing problems and the kinds of representations different species have is an important part of the study of comparative cognition.

1.1.2 The Role of Consciousness in Animal Cognition

Most people think they know what it means to be *conscious* of events. We commonly distinguish between merely responding to events and being *aware* of them, as when someone driving along a busy highway while deep in conversation says, "I wasn't conscious of the passing miles." Within psychology, the rise of behaviorism in the early 1900s threw into disrepute any attempt to study people's introspection about their conscious states, and the cognitive revolution of the 1960s and 1970s continued this tradition. Studying cognition meant, as it does in this book, inferring how information is processed from analyzing input-output relations. The quality of awareness or consciousness accompanying the processing of information was not studied. More recently, however, several striking phenomena have come to light in which people apparently process and retain information without awareness. The discovery of "blindsight" (see box 1.1), priming in memory (see chapter 6), and related phenomena have made the study of consciousness scientifically respectable (Schacter, 1995a). The essence of all these phenomena is that people may deny seeing or remembering something—that is, be unaware of it—while at the same time showing through their behavior that they do see or remember the thing in question. Thus, in these situations verbal report of subjective conscious awareness has been dissociated from other behavior. This means that to ask whether similar dissociations exist in animals, it is necessary to accept some piece of the animal's behavior as the equivalent of the person's verbal report. But this is where the problems lie. Even if, as in the experiment described in box 1.1, we can experimentally dissociate two responses to the same stimulus, we have to be willing to accept that one of those responses indexes a subjective state of the animal equivalent to our own experience. Clearly, we can never know whether this is correct or not, since we can never know the animal's private state. How animals process information—including under what conditions, if any, they show the kinds of dissociations just described—can be analyzed without making any assumptions about what their private experiences are like. Those could be like anything from the private experiences of plants or robots (nonexistent, we assume) to those of the most sensitive and thoughtful human beings, but on the whole this book will not be concerned with trying to find out.

This point of view is emphatically rejected by scientists calling themselves *cognitive ethologists* (Ristau, 1991a), as well as by some best-selling popular authors (e.g., Barber, 1994; Masson & McCarthy, 1995). Cognitive ethologists, stimulated by the writings of the distingushed biologist Donald Griffin (1976), claim that behaviorism has unduly inhibited investigation of the nature of consciousness in animals. They claim that much behavior suggests that animals have intentions, beliefs, and self-awareness and that they consciously think about alternative courses of action and make plans. Evidence for this position has been drawn from a wide variety of species and behaviors. Some of it is discussed in chapter 11. Studies of communication and of animals apparently deceiving one another are particularly prominent because they seem to reveal flexible behaviors governed by intentions to achieve certain goals. However, it has proved extremely difficult to find a situation for which the notion that an animal is consciously thinking or manipulating information unambiguously predicts what it does (Dawkins, 1993).

This is not to say, however, that mentalistic terms are not sometimes used legitimately to refer to processes underlying animal behavior. Consider, for

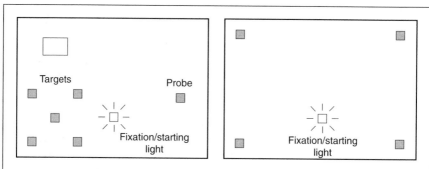

Figure B1.1. Stimulus displays for testing blindsight in monkeys. Redrawn from Cowey and Stoerig (1995) with permission.

Box 1.1. Vision Without Awareness

Neurological patients with "blindsight" react to objects in the visual field without being able to report awareness of them (Weiskrantz, 1986). If such patients, who have damage in area V1 of the visual cortex, are shown an object in the affected part of the visual field and asked where it is, what it is, and so on, they report seeing nothing. However, when they are forced to point to the object's location or guess its characteristics, they perform above chance. Thus, these people seem to have vision without awareness. Visual detection apparently can be dissociated from visual awareness in monkeys, too (Cowey & Stoerig, 1995, 1997). Three monkeys with lesions to area V1 were trained in two different tasks (figure B1.1). One was analogous to asking them "Is anything there?" and the other, to asking them "Where is it?" The lesions affected only the right half of each monkey's visual field, so each monkey's performance to stimuli there could be compared to its performance with stimuli in the field with normal vision. To control the part of the retina stimulated, displays were presented briefly while the monkey was fixating a spot in the middle of a computer screen.

To train the monkeys to report "Is anything there," a stimulus was presented in any of five positions in the lower part of the normal field, and on some trials no stimulus was presented (figure B1.1, left). In the former case, the monkey was rewarded for touching the location where the stimulus had appeared. In the latter, it was rewarded for reporting no by touching a white rectangle at the top of the screen. When the monkeys were reporting presence or absence correctly on about 95% of the trials, they were tested with occasional probes in the "blind" half of the visual field. They reported "no stimulus" about 95% of the time. Importantly, a normal control monkey transferred correct responding to this novel location. In the other task, a brief flash appeared in one of the four corners of the screen on every trial (figure B1.1, right). The monkeys had simply to touch the location where it had appeared, in effect reporting where they saw it. In this task, performance was highly accurate whether a stimulus was presented in the normal or the "blind" visual field. These data are consistent with other evidence that primates have separate visual pathways for perception and action (Goodale & Milner, 1992). Like people with comparable brain damage, the monkeys appear to have vision without awareness, suggesting that their normal vision is accompanied by awareness.

example, a rat trained to run out of a dark compartment into a lighted one by shocking it in the dark compartment. This kind of training is usually referred to as fear conditioning. The rat is said to fear the place where it was shocked, and indeed, it may show physiological symptoms similar to those shown by a person describing himself as fearful. Similarly, as discussed in chapter 11, a hungry rat trained to press a lever for food reward could be said to be doing so because it desires food and believes that lever pressing will give it food. Belief, desire, fear, or other mental states may be ascribed to animals in such cases on the basis of well-defined behavioral criteria without necessarily implying that the animals must be undergoing the same kinds of conscious experiences that a person would have. As the research mentioned earlier (see also chapter 6) has revealed, people can perceive, remember, and act on information either with or without the kind of awareness that underlies explicit verbal reports of consciousness. Most or all of the behavior of other species might be occurring in the absence of that conscious awareness.

Cognitive ethology founders on the problem of specifying behavioral evidence of consciousness that cannot unambiguously be explained otherwise. But if we accept that human beings are conscious (a not insignificant philosophical problem in its own right; Farber & Churchland, 1995), it seems that some other species, perhaps among primates, must have at least a rudimentary form of consciousness. Even though no living primates are our direct ancestors (see figure 1.8), saying that only humans are conscious seems like rejecting evolutionary continuity. On the other hand, if consciousness has evolved, it must be adaptive for something. That is, there must be something promoting survival and reproduction that a conscious animal can do and one lacking consciousness cannot (M. S. Dawkins, 1993). Once again, the argument for animal consciousness founders on the difficulty of specifying what a conscious animal can uniquely do.

So are there no precursors of consciousness in other species? This same problem of an apparent evolutionary gap between humans and other species arises in discussions of the evolution of human language. Despite the apparent successes of teaching aspects of language to apes, most would now conclude that language is unique to humans (see chapter 12). Moreover, some suggest that conscious thought is necessarily tied to language. It follows from these two suppositions that neither animals nor preverbal children can possibly be conscious (Macphail, 1998). Anthropological studies of human evolution and of primate behavior in the wild are likely to add fuel to these discussions for some time to come. There is a variety of philosophical views about the nature of consciousness, and recent years have seen increasing dialogue among philosophers and scientists studying animal behavior and artificial intelligence (see Further Readings at the end of this chapter). Current developments in cognitive neuroscience are not irrelevant, either (see box 1.1; see also Clark & Squire, 1998 and this book section 6.5.4). If some pattern of brain activity turns out to be uniquely associated with verbal reports of conscious awareness, thinking, remembering, or the like, what if this same pattern can be identified in a nonverbal animal?

In summary, there are three sorts of views about animal consciousness.

1. Animals are not conscious in any interesting sense of the term (Macphail, 1998).
2. Some animals may be conscious in some sense, but we cannot know because *consciousness* refers to a private subjective state. Furthermore, it does not seem possible to specify any behavior uniquely resulting from consciousness. How animals process information and behave adaptively can be understood, and, on the whole, should be studied, without reference to consciousness (M. S. Dawkins, 1993; Yoerg & Kamil, 1991).
3. Some animals are undoubtedly conscious, and scientists should be trying to understand the nature of their conscious states (Griffin, 1981; Griffin, 1992; Ristau, 1991a).

The second of these viewpoints is implicit in most of this book, but chapter 11 considers some research resulting from the third.

1.1.3 A Word about *Intelligence*

It is sometimes said by cognitive ethologists (Griffin, 1992) and popular writers (e.g., Barber, 1994) that animals must be thinking because they behave so intelligently. Indeed, to the nonspecialist one of the most persuasive arguments that animals think as we do is that it is impossible to imagine another explanation for their intelligent behavior (Blumberg & Wasserman, 1995). On the whole, however, *intelligence* in this sense is not a useful term for describing animal behavior, for two reasons (Mackintosh, 1988; Mackintosh, 1994a). First, intelligence is generally used to describe global ability in people, whereas the cognitive abilities of animals (and perhaps people as well) are modular (see section 1.5). For instance, a Clark's nutcracker that can retrieve thousands of pine seeds months after caching them (see box 1.4) is not necessarily "smart." It is particularly good at encoding and retaining certain kinds of spatial information, but it may remember other kinds of information no better than other birds. Natural selection selects for very restricted kinds of abilities. Second, intelligence should be defined formally with respect to a specified goal (McFarland & Bösser, 1993). A robot is intelligent with respect to a goal of efficiency if it minimizes use of its battery when crossing a room. It is intelligent with respect to the goal of remaining intact if it avoids collisions. In this view, animal intelligence should ultimately be defined in terms of *fitness* (box 1.2). It can also be defined in terms of some intermediate goal that increases fitness, such as maximizing rate of food intake or minimizing risk of predation. Sometimes, intelligent behavior may be produced by very "unintelligent" means.

1.2 Kinds of Explanation of Behavior

1.2.1 Tinbergen's Four Whys

The pioneering ethologist Niko Tinbergen (1963) pointed out that the question, "Why does the animal do that?" can mean four different things, some-

---

Box 1.2. Natural Selection and Fitness

Evolution, the change in the characteristics of organisms over generations, occasioned much debate before Charles Darwin (1859) and Alfred Russell Wallace explained how it happens. Fossils indicated that very different kinds of animals and plants had existed in the past. Explorers, including Darwin and Wallace themselves, documented how animals and plants in different parts of the world are both similar and different. What Darwin and Wallace did, independently at about the same time, was to show that the process of evolution has an inevitable natural cause in the most basic characteristics of living things. This cause is *natural selection*, and it occurs because of the following:

1. Offspring inherit their parents' characteristics. Bean seeds produce more bean plants, robin eggs produce more robins. At a more detailed level, too, parents pass on their characteristics to their children. We now know a great deal about the genetic mechanisms involved, but the principle of *inheritance* is independent of any knowledge about genes, which Darwin and Wallace lacked.
2. There is *variation* among individuals within the same species, even among closely related individuals within a species.
3. *Selection* takes place. A sea turtle lays hundreds of eggs, an oak tree drops hundreds of acorns, yet the world is not overrun with sea turtles or oak trees. Only those best equipped to survive in the current environment will be the ones that live to reproduce. This principle is sometimes summarized as "the survival of the fittest." In technical terms, however, *fitness* refers to an organism's ability to leave copies of its genes in the next generation, not what people get at the gym. A male who sires 10 healthy offspring is fitter than one who sires 2. As discussed in chapter 4, fitness can be enhanced through helping genetic relatives as well as direct offspring.

As an inevitable consequence of inheritance, variation, and selection, evolution will occur. Gradually, over many generations, the individuals with characteristics that made their ancestors best able to survive and reproduce in the current environment will come to predominate. A modern way of viewing natural selection is that the *genes* best able to program the organisms bearing them to propagate successfully will be the ones that persist over generations (R. Dawkins, 1976, 1995).

---

times referred to as "Tinbergen's four whys." "Why?" can mean "How does it work?" in the sense of "What events inside and outside the animal cause it to behave as it does at this moment?" This is the question of the *proximate cause* (or simply cause) of behavior. Perceptions, representations, and decisions, as well as the neural events that accompany them, are all possible proximate causes of behavior. One might also ask about *development* in the individual—that is, "What experiences and genetic makeup cause the animal to behave as it does?" "Why" might also mean "What is the behavior good for; what is its survival value?" This is the question of *function* or *adaptive value*. Finally, one may ask how a particular behavior *evolved*, as inferred from its phylogenetic history (section 1.4.3), which indicates what the behavior of ancestral species was like and how and why it changed over generations. Causation, development, function, and evolution are often referred to as levels of explanation, but that should not be taken to imply that one is primary or more important than others. They are complementary accounts that can be given of any behavior. As Tinbergen emphasized (see also M. S. Dawkins, 1989), a complete understanding of behavior includes answers to all of them. However, it is very important to be clear on how they differ from one another and to avoid confusing the answer to one question with the answer to another.

Consider as an example some possible answers to the question raised at the beginning of the chapter, "Why do crows drop walnuts?" The proximate cause of nut dropping would be sought in some interaction of the bird's internal state, most likely hunger, with external stimuli like the presence of walnuts, other crows, and hard surfaces. Proximate causes can be specified at various levels of detail. A description of the firings of all the neural circuits between reception of the relevant external stimuli and movements of the muscles is the most complete causal explanation of any behavior. Explaining why a crow carries walnuts into the air and drops them in these terms would include such things as explaining how hunger changes the threshold for approaching and picking up nuts and how the crow's visual system processes information about heights and translates this into flying and dropping instructions. Often, however, causal mechanisms—and these may include cognitive processes—are inferred from input-output relations at the level of the whole animal.

Explanations of the immediate causes of behavior do not include teleology, or reference to conscious purposes or goals (for further discussion see Hogan, 1994a). The future cannot cause what is happening in the present. The crow does not drop walnuts "to get food," though it is possible that she does so because similar behavior in the past was followed by access to a tasty snack—that is, because of past experience of reinforcement. Examining the bird's history of reinforcement would be part of a developmental explanation, as would an account of any other factors within the individual's lifetime that affected its nut-dropping behavior. Like causal explanations, developmental explanations can vary in detail. A complete developmental explanation of behavior would include describing how the animal's genes in interaction with its environment direct development of the nervous system and muscles—indeed, the whole animal.

The immediate function, or adaptive value, of behavior is what it is good for in the life of the individual. Cracking walnuts clearly functions in obtaining food, but questions about the function of the crow's behavior can also be asked at finer levels of detail. For instance, the functional question, "Why carry a nut so high and no higher?" was tackled by testing whether the height to which a nut was carried was matched to the type of nut and where it was dropped (see figure 1.1; see also Zach, 1979).

Tinbergen's fourth question, "How did it evolve?" usually has to be tackled by trying to look at the behavior's phylogenetic history using methods described in section 1.4. For the crow's nutcracking, this would include surveying the literature to discover whether close relatives of American crows also drop hard-shelled food items and whether specific ecological conditions are associated with such behavior (Switzer & Cristol, in press). Evolution can rarely be studied directly because it takes place on a time scale much longer than a scientist's life span, but there are a few examples in which natural populations have been observed to change relatively rapidly in response to changes in selection pressures. Some of these examples involve behavior either explicitly or implicitly (Endler, 1986; Weiner, 1995). For instance, in the last 20 years or so, the beaks of seed-eating finches on the Galápagos Islands have changed in response to drastic changes in rainfall (Grant, 1986; Weiner, 1994). In years of drought, only the birds most skilled at finding and cracking the few remaining seeds could survive and reproduce. Beak depth, an indication of seed-cracking power, contributed importantly to survival in the medium ground finch (*Geospiza fortis*). Because beak depth is heritable, changes in the population's distribution of beak depths could be detected in a few generations (figure 1.2). The birds' behavior must have changed, too, perhaps through learning. Rather than ignoring the seeds most difficult to crack, as they did in times of plenty, the successful individuals needed to become good at finding and processing them.

In terms of Tinbergen's four questions, cognition—defined as information processing—is one of the proximate causes of behavior. Because studying cognition may include analyzing how information and ways of responding to it are acquired, studying cognition may also involve studying aspects of development. Throughout this book we will be concerned with the adaptive value and evolution of cognitive mechanisms. But speaking of cognition doesn't imply that animals are aware of the effects that their actions have on fitness. Evolution produces machines that reproduce themselves (see box 1.2). A robin builds a nest and lays eggs. It responds to eggs by incubating them. As a result of the parents keeping the eggs at a temperature they have evolved to develop at, young robins hatch with nervous systems so constructed that they open their beaks and beg when an adult approaches the nest. The adult's nervous system responds to gaping by inserting food, and so on. The bird isn't responding to "my young," let alone planning to have lots of grandchildren, but to stimuli that are generally reliable correlates of offspring, like gaping mouths in its nest. Behavioral mechanisms, including cognitive processes such as memory for the location of the nest and tuning of the adults' perception to the signals emitted by the young, are selected if they increase their bearer's representation in future generations, but such mechanisms need not include conscious foresight into the outcomes of behavior.

1.2.2 "Learned" and "Innate" Behavior

In discussions of development, *learning* is often contrasted with genetic or *innate* control of behavior. What this dichotomy overlooks is that learning is possible only if the animal is already programmed by its genes, together with whatever experience it has already had, to be affected by experience in a cer-

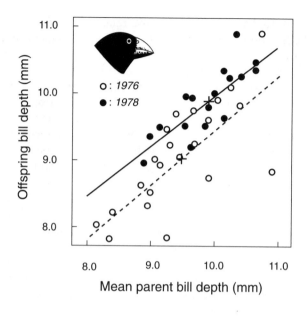

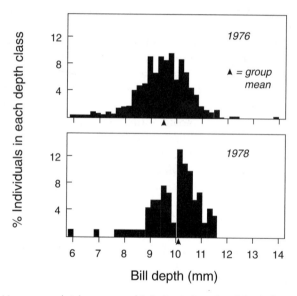

Figure 1.2. *Upper panel:* Inheritance of bill depth (height of the bill in the drawing) in medium ground finches in two different years. Slope of the line relating offspring to parent bill depth—heritability—was almost the same in both years. Variation and selection of bill depth are illustrated in the two lower panels. In 1978 there was a drought, and the finches could subsist only by cracking the hardest seeds. Redrawn from Boag and Grant (1984) and Boag (1983) with permission.

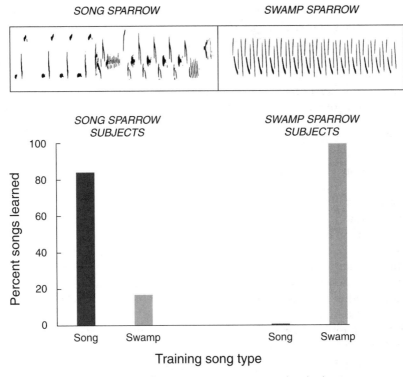

Figure 1.3. Song sparrows and swamp sparrows exposed to both song sparrow and swamp sparrow songs when young learn primarily the songs of their own species. Top panel shows sonagrams (sound frequency vs. time) of songs from normal adults of the two species. Redrawn from Marler and Peters (1989) with permission.

tain way. No behavior is either strictly learned or entirely innate. An excellent illustration of how preexisting selective processes in the animal interact with experience to produce learning comes from comparisons of song learning in two species of sparrows (Marler & Peters, 1989). Along with many other species of songbirds (see chapter 10), male song sparrows (*Melospiza melodia*) and swamp sparrows (*Melospiza georgiana*) need to hear species-specific song early in life in order to sing it when they mature. Despite being closely related to song sparrows, swamp sparrows have a much simpler song.

In the course of their investigations of when and what the two species learn during early exposure to song, Marler and Peters played songs of both song sparrows and swamp sparrows to isolated young of both species in the laboratory. Thus, all the young males had the same acoustic experience. But their behavior as adults revealed that they had learned different, species-appropriate things from it (figure 1.3). Swamp sparrows learned only swamp sparrow songs, and song sparrows had a strong preference to learn song sparrow songs. The interaction of species with experience is evident in birds raised in the laboratory from the egg or very early nestling stage, indicating that it probably does not result from birds hearing their father's song. Because birds of each species sometimes do produce sounds characteristic of the other species, it seems unlikely that the species difference in song production results from a motor constraint. In the wild, these two species may live within earshot of each other, so genetically programmed selectivity in perception and/or learning likely functions to ensure that each one learns only its own species' song. In fact, young birds still in the nest are selectively responsive to their own species' song, as shown by the way heart rate changes when they are played different kinds of sounds (Marler & Peters, 1989).

This example comes from a specialized behavior shown by only a few of the world's species, but it makes a very important general point: cognitive mechanisms are adaptations to process and use certain kinds of information in certain ways, not general information-processing mechanisms. This statement is just as true of apparently species-general processes, such as associative learning, spatial memory, or social learning, as it is of song learning (Gallistel, 1995; Tooby & Cosmides, 1995). In section 1.4 we look more closely at what it means to say something is an adaptation and how this notion can be tested. Then we will return to the notion that cognition is a set of adaptations and ask whether it can tell us anything about how cognitive mechanisms work or how they should be studied.

Returning to the theme of this section for a moment, some may have noticed that *genetically programmed* seems to have been substituted for the term *innate*. Of course, this is not really an acceptable substitute if it implies that genes can work without an environment to work in. However, we do sometimes need a term for the many behaviors that appear in development ready to serve their apparent function before they can have done so. For instance, selecting the species-typical song for learning clearly serves the function of allowing the adult male, many months later, to sing in a way that his conspecifics are most responsive to. Hogan (1994b) has suggested the term *prefunctional* for such cases, because it does not imply that the genes have worked in isolation nor that prior experience is irrelevant.

Finally, to say that some behavior or cognitive process has a genetic basis is not to say that it is unmodifiable (for discussion see M. S. Dawkins, 1995). As in the comparison of song and swamp sparrows, how much and in what ways behavior can be modified is itself influenced genetically. The extent to which behavior patterns or cognitive capacities are modifiable by experience varies greatly. Some motor patterns are so much the same in all members of a species that they can be used as reliably as body structure to diagnose species membership. Others are more labile.

1.3 Approaches to Comparative Cognition

This book synthesizes the approaches to animal cognition taken by psychologists, on the one hand, and biologists, on the other. The two traditions being contrasted here have also been called the study of general processes and the study of adaptive specializations (Riley & Langley, 1993) or the General Social Science Model and evolutionary psychology (Cosmides & Tooby, 1992). Because psychologists have traditionally been most interested in the capacities shown by humans, psychologists working with animals have approached cognition in animals from an anthropocentric point of view (Shettleworth, 1993b; Staddon, 1989). Biologists, in contrast, are more interested in cognition—if they are interested in it at all—as it functions in species-specific ecological contexts. Psychologists tend to ask, "Can animals do what people do, and if so how?" whereas biologists tend to ask, "How and why do animals do what they do in the wild?" Thus the contrast between traditional psychological and biological approaches is one between anthropocentric, or human-centered, and ecological, animal-centered, approaches. (*Anthropocentrism* in comparative psychology is not the same as *anthropomorphism*. Anthropocentrism refers to choosing problems to study with reference to—that is, centered on—human psychology. Anthropomorphism refers to accounting for behavior by imputing humanlike characteristics such as conscious thought to other species. The problem with anthropomorphism is that it too often masquerades as explanation. As we have seen in the case of the nut-cracking crows, just because an animal's behavior looks to the casual observer like what a person would do in a similar-appearing situation, it does not mean it can be explained in the same way. Experiments are generally needed to find out.)

1.3.1 The Anthropocentric Approach

Comparative psychology began with Darwin's claim—profoundly shocking at the time—that humans are similar to other species in mental as well as physical characteristics. Chapter 3 of his second major book on evolution, *The Descent of Man and Selection in Relation to Sex* (Darwin, 1871), outlines a research program for testing this claim. In it, Darwin suggested that other animals share with humans cognitive abilities such as reasoning, memory, language, and aesthetic sensibility. His emphasis was on continuity among species rather than diversity, the other side of the evolutionary coin (Rozin & Schull, 1988). Acceptance of continuity has led to using animals in psychology primarily as little furry or feathery people, model systems for studying general processes of learning, memory, decision making, even psychopathology. Such work has been of great practical value (Miller, 1985). It also provides an essential underpinning for behavioral brain research using animal subjects because it make sense to look for the neural bases of learning and memory in humans by studying animals only on the assumption that basic behavioral and brain processes are the same across the species being compared (Preuss, 1995).

Research on animal cognition based on the anthropocentric approach has three important characteristics. First, anthropocentric research focuses on memory, representation, and other kinds of information processing that can be identified in people. Second, although such research is implicitly comparative, in that other species like parrots or pigeons are compared with humans, the choice of species to compare is often based more on convenience than on sound evolutionary considerations. Finally, traditionally, though perhaps less so today, discussions of anthropocentric research were pervaded by the incorrect and misleading notion of a *phylogenetic scale* (Campbell & Hodos, 1991; Hodos & Campbell, 1969) This is the idea that evolution is a continuous ladder of improvement, from "lowly" worms and slugs, through fish, amphibians and reptiles, to birds and mammals. Humans, needless to say, are the pinnacle of evolution in this scheme. But, as discussed in section 1.4, present-day species cannot be lined up in this way. People are not just highly evolved, more complex, "better," fish, birds, rats, or even monkeys. Correct inferences about the relationship between cognitive or brain processes in humans and those in nonhumans may depend on a more detailed appreciation of the biology of "animal models" than is commonly shown (Deacon, 1990; Preuss, 1995).

These problems notwithstanding, psychological research on animal cognition has produced much of interest and value, as we will see throughout this book. Studying a few very diverse species, it could be argued, is the best way to reveal processes general to all species (box 1.3). For example, the fact that people, monkeys, rats, pigeons, fish, bees, and sea slugs all show Pavlovian conditioning means that someone wishing to explain associative learning in another species would be pretty safe in hypothesizing that it reflects the same process.

1.3.2 Biological Approaches to Animal Behavior

While experimental animal psychology was flourishing in North America, *ethology* was developing in departments of zoology in Europe. Guided by Tinbergen's four questions, ethologists emphasized the apparently unlearned behavior of animals in the wild. They studied a wide range of species, including insects, birds, and fish. Behavior was seen to be as much a characteristic of a given species as its coloration or the structure of its body (Lorenz, 1941/1971; Tinbergen, 1959). In the 1960s and '70s the ethological study of the adaptive value and evolution of behavior developed into the field of *behavioral ecology*

Box 1.3. Traditional Comparative Psychology: An Example

In the 1960s and '70s, M. E. Bitterman and his associates carried out an extensive program of research comparing the performance of goldfish, painted turtles, pigeons, laboratory rats, and monkeys on a number of standard laboratory tasks (Bitterman, 1965, 1975). Their overall aim was to test the assumption that the "intelligence" of "lower" animals differed only in degree and not in kind from that of "higher" animals. Of course, as Bitterman (1975) recognized, these species are not on an evolutionary ladder but at the ends of separate branches of the bush of life (figure B1.3).

Bitterman employed ingenious variations on standard apparatus to present the

⟶

Box 1.3. (*continued*)

same kinds of tasks to these very different species. Fish pushed paddles inserted into their tanks for a reward of worms; pigeons pecked lighted disks for a few grains of corn; turtles crawled down small runways. In one series of experiments, the animals were compared on their ability to learn *successive reversals* of simple visual and spatial discriminations. In successive reversal (see chapter 5), an animal is first rewarded for choosing a certain one of two simultaneously presented stimuli — say, red rather than green. After a number of trials of this kind, the rewarded stimulus is reversed — for example, the animal must choose green rather than red, and so on. "Intelligent" behavior is to improve over successive reversals, eventually performing perfectly after just one trial on each new problem. Within each species, performance on visual discriminations (e.g., red vs. green for species with color vision or black vs. white for those without) was also compared to performance on spatial (e.g., left vs. right) discriminations. Monkeys, rats, and pigeons improved on both visual and spatial reversals; fish improved on neither; and turtles improved on spatial but not visual reversals. Much can be disputed about whether these species do differ in this way in general (see chapter 5). More important is to ask what, if anything, results from this kind of selection of species and problems can reveal about "the evolution of intelligence."

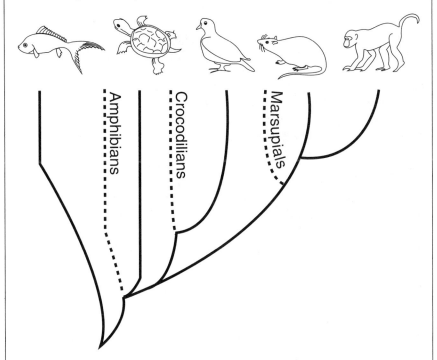

Figure B1.3. A simple phylogeny of the species tested by Bitterman and his colleagues in comparative studies of learning. Neither the recency with which one group is thought to have diverged from another nor its left-right arrangement in such a diagram necessarily implies anything about "intelligence." Redrawn from Bitterman (1975) with permission.

(Krebs & Davies, 1993). Behavioral ecology, or sociobiology (Wilson, 1975), is characterized by an attempt to predict behavior from first principles of evolutionary biology using explicit models of the consequences of behavior for fitness. Like ethologists, behavioral ecologists focus on the behavior of animals in the field and study a wide variety of species, but until recently they were concerned almost exclusively with the functional and evolutionary "why" questions. Early research in behavioral ecology aimed to discover simply whether or not behavior had the properties predicted by evolutionary models. For example, did a redshank or some other bird choose food items optimally? More recently, behavioral ecologists have begun to appreciate the role of cognitive mechanisms in producing or failing to produce the predicted behavior (e.g., Dukas, 1998; Krebs & Davies, 1997; Stamps, 1991). They might ask now, for example, about the processes of perception, learning, and choice that lead the redshank to select its prey and how these play a role in the bird's making, or failing to make, optimal choices. Particular attention is given to such questions in chapters 2 and 9.

1.3.3 Synthesis

Ethologists, behavioral ecologists, and traditional comparative psychologists emphasize different questions about animal behavior, but their fields are all interrelated. Some people have realized that the data or theory of one field can illuminate issues being studied by the others. Thus it seems reasonable to try to develop an approach that combines these traditions. Within psychology, this point of view has led to what has been called the *ecological* or *synthetic approach* to comparative cognition (Kamil, 1988, 1998; Shettleworth, 1993b). Unlike the anthropocentric or general process approach, the ecological approach emphasizes analyzing how animals use cognition in the wild—for example, in foraging or finding their way around. Species are chosen on the basis of behavior indicating some particularly interesting cognitive processing, such as the ability to home over large distances or remember the locations of large numbers of food items (box 1.4). The ecological approach includes explicitly comparative studies designed to analyze the evolution and adaptive value of particular cognitive abilities. The species compared may be

---

Box 1.4. Food Storing Birds and the Ecological Approach

Some species of birds store food in the wild and use memory to find it again. One of the most remarkable is the Clark's nutcracker (*Nucifraga columbiana*) of the American West. Nutcrackers bury thousands of caches of pinyon pine seeds in the late summer and dig them up from beneath the snow throughout the winter and into the next spring (figure B1.4). Early observers of food-storing in corvids (jays, crows, and nutcrackers) and parids (chickadees and titmice) found it incredible that these birds

⟫

Box 1.4. (*continued*)

might be able to remember the locations of caches. Perhaps they were just raising the general level of availability of food for all birds in the area. But modern thinking about natural selection (see box 1.2) makes clear that food-storing behavior could not evolve unless the individuals doing the storing benefit more from their investments of time and energy than lazy individuals which simply eat the food stored by others (Andersson & Krebs, 1978). As this argument suggests, food-storing birds do retrieve their own caches, and they use memory to do it (Shettleworth, 1995).

The fact that food-storers must remember the locations of a large number of items for days, weeks, or months suggests that, along with the specialized behavior of caching food, they may have evolved a specialized memory. Maybe they can remember more items of spatial information for longer than other birds. Within both the corvids and the parids, some species store more food than others, so the hypothesis about adaptive specialization of memory can be tested by looking for divergence in memory abilities within families and convergence across families. There is now considerable data indicating that corvids or parids that store more have better spatial memory. Some of it is discussed in chapter 6. Moreover, the hippocampus, a part of the brain involved in spatial memory, is bigger relative to brain and body size in food-storers than in nonstoring species (see figure 1.6). Research on food-storing birds is a good example of how evolutionary biology, field studies, neurobiology, psychological theories about memory, and techniques for testing memory in the laboratory can be synthesized to provide insights into how memory evolves. Related research on the relationship among space use, memory, and brain in rodents is discussed in section 1.5.

Figure B1.4. A Clark's nutcracker burying a seed. A bird generally caches several seeds in each site. From a photograph by R. P. Balda.

close relatives that face different cognitive demands in the wild and therefore are expected to have *diverged* in cognitive ability. For example, one species may defend a large territory and one a small one. Alternatively, species may be compared that are not very close relatives but face similar cognitive demands in the wild. Such species are expected to have *converged* in the ability of interest. Data about natural history and evolution are an integral part of this kind of comparative psychology, but so are theories and methods developed with the anthropocentric approach.

Social scientists' interest in the evolution of cognition is no longer confined to researchers working with animals. *Evolutionary psychologists* have begun to explore the notion that basic principles of cognition in humans reflect social and environmental demands throughout evolution (Barkow, Cosmides, & Tooby, 1992; Crawford, 1993). Processes of generalization and discrimination in visual perception, for example, reflect the structure of the physical world (Shepard, 1994). Reasoning ability, it has been suggested, evolved at least in part to deal with the complexities of social structure and social obligations in early hominid groups (Cosmides, 1989). Evolutionary psychology has generated some provocative findings, but some aspects of it have the weakness of having to base hypotheses on conjectures about the conditions present early in human evolution. In this respect, research on the evolution of cognition in other animals is on much firmer ground because their present-day environments have likely changed much less than that of the human species. Hypotheses about evolution and adaptation can also be tested more directly in other species than in humans by comparing groups of present-day species. Thus research with nonhuman species can provide well-grounded hypotheses for testing in humans, as well as a model for how such hypotheses should be tested.

While some psychologists have been advocating a more biological approach to cognition, some behavioral ecologists have been pointing out that it is important to take into account motivational, cognitive, and neural mechanisms when testing ideas in behavioral ecology (Dukas, 1998; Huntingford, 1993; Krebs & Davies, 1997; Real, 1993; Yoerg, 1991). For example, the evolution of social signals is likely to reflect and be reflected in the nature of perceptual systems (see chapter 2). The attempt to integrate information from cognitive psychology with the study of how animals solve ecologically important problems has been referred to as *cognitive ecology* (Dukas, 1998; Real, 1993). Cognitive ecology, cognitive ethology, evolutionary psychology, ecological comparative psychology—whatever these enterprises are called, they all have in common the conviction that cognition is best understood by being studied in the context of evolution and ecology.

1.4 Testing Adaptive/Evolutionary Explanations

"Drab coloration is an adaptation for reducing detection by visual predators." "Bats' sonar is an adaptation for detecting flying insects in the dark." "Reasoning ability is an adaptation to conditions in early hunter-gatherer soci-

eties." For most biologists, to say that some characteristic of an animal's structure, behavior, or cognition is an *adaptation* is to assert that it has evolved
through natural selection (but see Reeve & Sherman, 1993). But selection has
occurred in the past, so how can we ever test such a statement? Aren't hypotheses about adaptation no better than Kipling's *Just So Stories* (Gould &
Lewontin, 1979) like "The Elephant's Child," which explains that elephants
have long trunks because a curious young elephant once stretched his nose
while pulling it from a crocodile's jaws? This issue has attracted a lot of discussion in the last 20 years or so (see Dennett, 1995), but many biologists
would now agree that, even though we can seldom observe evolution directly,
there are nevertheless several rigorous ways to test ideas about adaptation. It
is important to be aware of them when attempting to evaluate adaptationist
accounts of cognition. Rarely is the kind of evidence available that would
allow more than a tentative hypothesis about the evolutionary history and
adaptive value of any cognitive mechanism.

   Tinbergen's four questions distinguish present-day function from evolution. This is an important distinction because a character can serve a function
in the present without having been selected for that function. Function may
change over evolutionary time (Williams, 1966). To take a nonevolutionary
analogy, in big tourist centers like Rome or New York one sometimes sees
groups of visitors all wearing identically colored hats. Hats are designed
(adapted) to protect the head. Originally, tour organizers giving out souvenir
hats may just have found it convenient to give out hats that were all the same.
But, that having happened, the hats now serve the new function of allowing
members of a group to identify one another and avoid getting separated.

   Evolution and present-day function are not unrelated, however. Demonstrations that a behavior serves a particular function can increase confidence
in the hypothesis that that function has contributed to its evolution. This is
particularly so when other kinds of evidence point to the same conclusion. A
good example is Tinbergen's own classic studies of eggshell removal in gulls
(Tinbergen et al., 1963). Soon after their eggs hatch, black-headed gulls
(*Larus ridibundus*) pick up the empty eggshells, fly off, and drop them some
way from the nest. Why should a bird leave its vulnerable chicks for even a few
seconds to engage in this behavior? One possibility was that white insides of
broken shells attract predators. To test this hypothesis, Tinbergen and his colleagues distributed single gull eggs around the dunes where the black-headed
gulls nest. Some of these decoy eggs had broken eggshells nearby; others were
isolated. The eggs with broken shells close by disappeared sooner, eaten by
crows and herring gulls, than the isolated, less conspicuous, eggs (figure 1.4).
Thus, removing broken eggshells from the nest functions to reduce predation
by the sorts of predators found on the dunes where the gulls nest. This suggests a comparative hypothesis: gull species nesting in areas without this same
predation pressure should not remove empty shells from their nests. The kittiwake (*Rissa tridactyla*) provides a natural test of this hypothesis. This is a
species of gull that nests on small ledges on steep cliffs, inaccessible to most
predators. Kittiwakes differ behaviorally from ground-nesting gull species in

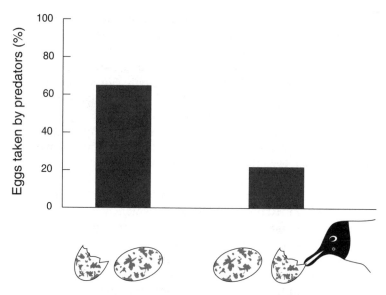

Figure 1.4. Proportion of 60 black-headed gull eggs taken by predators when the eggs were placed in the dunes near a broken eggshell (left bar) or alone, mimicking the situation in a nest from which the owner had removed broken shells (Tinbergen et al., 1963, table 16).

a number of ways that can be seen as adaptations to their different nesting habitats (Cullen, 1957). Among other things, they do not remove broken eggshells from their nests.

1.4.1 Adaptation as Design

Many features of animals' structure and behavior seem so perfectly suited to their function that they appear unlikely to have arisen merely by chance. The eyes of vertebrates, the sonar of bats, the nestbuilding and parental behavior of birds all seem to be designed to accomplish their ends. Often, designs in biology are remarkably like what engineers would build to achieve the same goals. These considerations seem to compel the conclusion that intricate structures and behaviors like eyes, ears, and eggshell removal must be evolved adaptations. In pre-Darwinian days, however, the argument from design was used as evidence for a divine creator (see R. Dawkins, 1986; Dennett, 1995). Darwin's genius lay in deducing how natural causes produce the same end (see box 1.2). This goes to show that when the alternatives are not obvious, it is easy to be taken in by the argument, "This is so well suited to its function, it must have evolved to serve that function."

A major contribution of behavioral ecology has been the use of formal optimality arguments to study adaptation (see chapter 9). Working out the optimal behavior for a given situation is a way of specifying the best design. One beauty of precise optimality arguments is that in principle they can be shown to be false. For example, the schooling behavior of fish had been thought to save energy for each individual by allowing it to swim in the eddies from its neighbors. However, detailed consideration of the hydrodynamics of swimming fish shows that, in fact, individuals of some species do not position themselves so as to benefit as much as they could from the way the water is moved by other fish in the school (Partridge & Pitcher, 1979). Thus, although hydrodynamic advantage may have contributed to the evolution of schooling behavior, other selective forces need to be sought to explain it fully (see M. S. Dawkins, 1995).

1.4.2 The Comparative Method

We have already met the comparative method at the beginning of this section: the hypothesis that removing empty eggshells evolved because nests without empty shells suffer less predation was tested, in part, by comparing species subject to different predation pressures. In general, a comparative test of the adaptive value of a character consists of obtaining data from a large number of species and relating the degree to which they display the character with the degree to which the hypothesized selection pressure is present (for an introduction see Harvey & Purvis, 1991; a more technical treatment is Harvey & Pagel, 1991).

Animals live in all sorts of places and in an amazing variety of kinds of social groups. Some are solitary and cryptic except during mating. Others, like the wildebeest of the African plains, form enormous herds. Breeding may take place between members of monogamous pairs or, among other possibilities, a few males may each control access to a harem of many females, in a *polygynous* mating system. In some species, mating is completely promiscuous. Why have all these different social arrangements evolved? Some of the earliest work in what came to be called behavioral ecology consisted of attempts to answer this question by relating social structure to ecology (for a review see Krebs & Davies, 1993, chapter 2). Vulnerability to predators, what kind of food a species eats and its spatial and seasonal distribution, the availability of sites for raising young—all of these and other variables predict social organization in a variety of animal groups. For example, in African ungulates, body size, habitat, group size, and mating system are related in the way shown in table 1.1 (Jarman, 1974). Smaller species need high-quality food because they have a high metabolic rate. They primarily seek fruits and buds in the forest. Because these foods are relatively sparse, the animals cannot form large groups, and there is no opportunity for one male to monopolize many females. Rather, the small-bodied forest species are found alone or in pairs. The large-bodied species graze relatively unselectively on the plains, on food that is locally very abundant but which varies seasonally in distribution. Thus species like wildebeest tend to form large herds that migrate long distances with the seasons. Being in a group opens the opportunity for one male to monopolize several females. Hence, polygyny rather than monogamy tends to be found in the large grassland species.

Table 1.1. Relationship between ecology and social behavior in African ungulates

	Exemplary species	Body weight (kg)	Habitat	Diet	Group size	Reproductive unit	Anti-predator behaviour
Group I	Dikdik Duiker	3–60	Forest	Selective browsing; fruit, buds	1 or 2	Pair	Hide
Group II	Reedbuck Gerenuk	20–80	Brush, riverine grassland	Selective browsing or grazing	2 to 12	Male with harem	Hide, flee
Group III	Gazelle Kob Impala	20–250	Riverine, woodland dry grassland	Graze or browse	2 to 100	Males territorial in breeding season	Flee, hide in herd
Group IV	Wildebeest Hartebeest	90–270	Grassland	Graze	Up to 150 (thousands on migration)	Defence of females within herd	Hide in herd, flee
Group V	Eland Buffalo	300–900	Grassland	Graze unselectively	Up to 1000	Male dominance hierarchy in herd	Mass defence against predators

Reproduced from Krebs & Davies, 1981; data from Jarman, 1974.

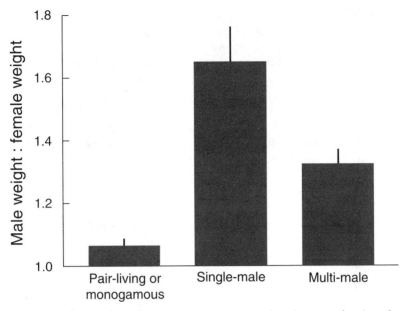

Figure 1.5. Body size dimorphism in primates, measured as the ratio of male to female body weight, as a function of whether the breeding group has a single male and female, a single male defending a group of females, or multiple males and females. Redrawn from Clutton-Brock & Harvey (1984) with permission.

By itself, especially as summarized in a paragraph, this account has all the marks of a "Just-so Story." Several things make it much more than that. For one, a similar account can be given of social structure in other animal groups, including birds and primates (Krebs & Davies, 1993). This is what would be expected if social structure is the outcome of fundamental selection pressures like the distributions of food and predators and not just associated with ecology in ungulates by chance. For another, more detailed comparative analyses have tended to uphold the conclusions from the kinds of categorical analyses summarized in table 1.1. Consider one correlate of social structure, *sexual dimorphism* in body size—that is, the degree to which males and females are different sizes (Clutton-Brock & Harvey, 1984). In a variety of animal groups, males tend to be about the same size as females in species that form breeding pairs, whereas males tend to be larger than females in polygynous species. One possible explanation of this relationship is that male size is related to the need to defend females from rival males. Among primates, polygynous species are also distinguished by whether they live in one-male groups or multi-male groups. Each male dominates more females in one-male groups. Sexual dimorphism in primates, measured as ratio of male weight to female weight, can be related to mating system in the categorical way just described, with species divided into three classes (figure 1.5) or with polygyny described as a continuous variable, the ratio of males to females in species-typical breeding groups (Clutton-Brock & Harvey, 1977).

Results like those shown in figure 1.5 and table 1.1 must not be distorted by unequal degrees of relatedness among the species being considered. If the species within each ecological category are more closely related to each other than they are to species in other ecological categories, differences among categories could reflect common descent as much as common selection pressure. One way to deal with this problem is to look at different kinds of species. For instance, the same relationship between sexual dimorphism and breeding system is found in several independent animal groups, suggesting that it does indeed reflect the degree to which males compete for females. In general, a good way to distinguish similarity owing to common descent from similarity owing to common ecological conditions is to test for the same kind of relationship, that is, convergence, in different animal groups that face similar selection pressures, as well as divergence between closely related species with different ecologies. This implies that the conclusions of a comparative analysis will depend on the quality of information available about phylogeny, or relatedness, of the species being compared (see next section).

Although figure 1.5 shows a significant positive relationship between sexual dimorphism in body size and number of females per male in the breeding group, the error bars indicate that considerable variation is still unaccounted for. Correlations between characters and ecology across large numbers of species almost always use data from many sources, and inevitably some data points will represent larger numbers of more careful observations than others. However, if enough species are sampled, random errors should balance each other out and any genuine relationship reveal itself. The variables examined also need to be good measures of the ecological factors being considered. For instance, ratio of females to males in the breeding group might not be the best measure of intermale competition, the factor hypothesized to favor large-bodied males. Furthermore, social structure is unlikely to be the only variable relevant to sexual dimorphism. In primates, smaller species tend to be arboreal, and life in trees might constrain the males from getting too big (Clutton-Brock & Harvey, 1977).

Obvious exceptions to an overall relationship can be instructive. Figure 1.6 shows an example based on the *allometric* relationship among the sizes of body parts. Animals with bigger bodies have, on average, bigger brains, eyes, teeth, and so on. The regression of the size of any structure against a measure of total body size has a characteristic slope, with most points clustered close to the overall regression line. In figure 1.6, volume of the hippocampus, a brain structure important for spatial memory, is plotted against body weight and against volume of the telencephalon (most of the rest of the brain) for a large number of genera of birds. Three points stand out as being substantially above the overall regression lines—that is, birds in three genera have larger hippocampi than expected for their body and brain sizes. These all contain species that store food for the winter and retrieve it using long-lasting spatial memory (see box 1.4). These data are consistent with the hypothesis that species facing extra demands on spatial memory have evolved an extra-large hippocampus.

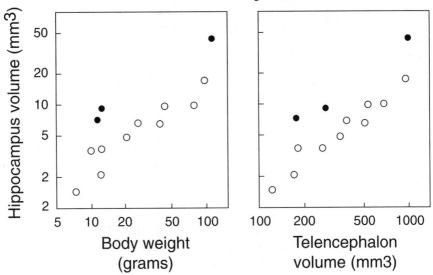

Figure 1.6. Hippocampal volume correlated with body weight (left panel) and volume of the telencephalon in birds. Redrawn from Sherry et al. (1989) with permission.

1.4.3 Mapping Phylogeny

If a character is consistently associated with an ecological condition it seems likely that the character evolved in response to that condition. But of course correlation is not evolutionary causation. For example, maybe food-storing species evolved an unusually large hippocampus for some unknown reason and that structural modification then allowed them to benefit from storing food. Or maybe, rather than ask why some birds have such a large hippocampus relative to brain and body size, we should be asking why other birds have such a small one (Deacon, 1995). Such questions have to do with the sequence of events in evolution, with what ancestral species were like, and how and why they changed. Although these are all questions about the past, it is possible to find surprisingly detailed answers to them by looking at present-day species, given some reasonable assumptions about how evolution works. This is the study of *phylogeny*, or the reconstruction of the tree of life, the branching relationships among species during evolution (Brooks & McLennan, 1991; Ridley, 1993).

Suppose we have a bat, a bird, and a chimpanzee. The bat is like the bird in having wings, but it is like the chimpanzee in having fur instead of feathers, lactating, and giving birth to live young instead of laying eggs (table 1.2). On the basis of these four characters, we would classify bats and chimpanzees as more closely related—having a more recent common ancestor—than bats and birds because bats and chimpanzees have more characters in common.

Table 1.2. A simple example of biological classification based on four characters

	Bird	Bat	Chimpanzee
Wings?	Yes	Yes	No
Body Covering	Feathers	Fur	Fur
Reproduction	Lays eggs	Live young	Live young
Feeding of Young	No lactation	Lactation	Lactation

Moreover, the wings of birds and bats develop differently embryologically and differ in details of structure. Thus they are *homoplasies*, not *homologies*—that is, they have evolved independently from the primitive vertebrate forelimb rather than being similar by virtue of descent from a winged ancestral bird/bat.

Biological classification is hierarchical. Figure 1.7 shows three common ways of representing the nested relationships among species. A *phylogenetic tree* represents the divergence among species over time. The times at which species diverged from an ancestral state can be tied down by examining the fossil record or from molecular evidence based on the difference in the DNA between species and the rate of random mutation of DNA. Figure 1.8 shows the phylogeny of primates based on molecular evidence. Characters of present-day species alone can be used in *cladistic* classification. Without knowing anything about the fossil record, we can infer that bats, birds, and chimpanzees share a common vertebrate ancestor and that bats and chimpanzees share a mammalian ancestor (one that had fur, gave birth to live young, and lactated) that they do not share with birds. These inferences are based in part on the notion that any particular evolutionary change is improbable. For a new species to evolve, an advantageous rather than deleterious or lethal mu-

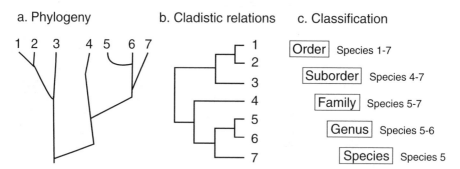

Figure 1.7. For seven fictitious species, the relationship between a phylogenetic tree (divergence as a function of time), a cladistic classification, and—for species 5—the traditional classification in terms of species, genus, etc. As an example of how to read panel b, species 1 and 2 share a character they do not share with species 3, while all three of them share a character not shared with species 4–7. Redrawn from Ridley (1993) with permission.

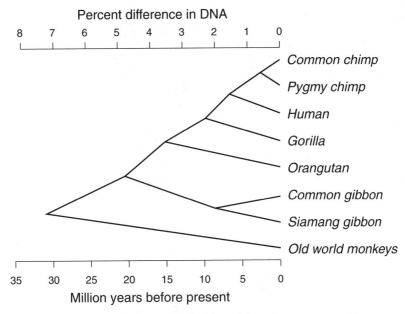

Figure 1.8. Phylogenetic relationships of Old World monkeys, apes, and humans as revealed by DNA hybridization. Greater similarity in DNA (top axis) indicates more recent divergence (bottom axis). Redrawn from Ridley (1993) with permission.

tation has to occur, and it has to spread. It is therefore more likely that shared characteristics were present in a common ancestor than that they evolved several times independently. Representations of cladistic classification can show the characters that have changed in the evolution of each new species, as in the example in figure 1.9. Finally, a cladistic classification corresponds to the traditional hierarchical classification of organisms into species, genera, families, and so on, as indicated in figure 1.7.

1.4.4 Testing Adaptive/Evolutionary Explanations: Summary

Three kinds of methods for testing hypotheses about adaptation have been discussed in this part of the chapter (Ridley, 1993): model building, direct observation and experiment, and the comparative method. Model building is a sophisticated approach to the argument from design, which is at the core of the notion of adaptation. If organisms were not so intricate and did not seem so beautifully suited to their niches, questions about how and why they got that way might not be so central in biology. Mathematical optimality models, of which we will examine some examples in chapter 9, can specify precisely what "good design" is. Thus they permit better tests of hypotheses about adaptive value than less formal arguments, which are more difficult to falsify. A model's predictions can fail because the modeler failed to take into account

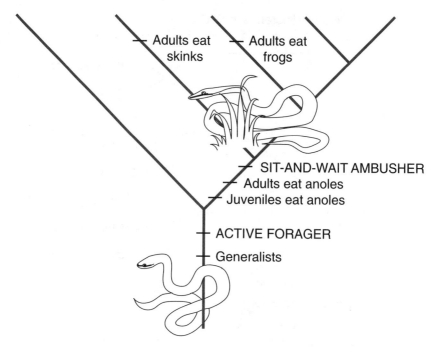

Figure 1.9. Cladogram for colubrid snakes on the island of Hispanola based on their feeding behavior. The species of interest (the 4 rightmost branches) and a comparison group of close relatives (the outgroup, left branch) all evolved from active generalist foragers. Evolutionary changes inferred from shared characters are indicated along the branches. Time is not explicitly represented in this type of diagram, unlike that in figure 1.8. Redrawn from Brooks & McLennan (1991) with permission.

all the relevant factors, and this may lead to more complex models incorporating tradeoffs among competing selection pressures. It is also important to be aware that evolution has not necessarily always produced the absolute optimum.

Not all questions about adaptation lend themselves to formal modeling. For instance, we simply do not know enough about avian hippocampal function and anatomy to construct a model predicting how big a hippocampus should be associated with how strong a dependence on stored food. In any case, an important second approach is direct observation of the fitness consequences of behavior. This includes experimental tests of the hypothesized function, as in Tinbergen's experiments on eggshell removal. Sometimes environmental conditions change quickly enough that corresponding evolutionary changes can be observed, as in the changes in Galápagos finches' beak size and feeding behavior with changes in rainfall (see figure 1.2). Different populations of the same species may show instructive adaptions to local conditions of predation or food availability. For instance, in Trinidad different populations of guppies differ in coloration as a function of the visual sensitivies of the local predators (Endler, 1991; see also chapter 2).

At best, experimental tests of function or observations of natural selection in action can be done on only a few species. For a look at the broad sweep of evolution, at whether an important selection pressure has produced similar patterns across many species, the comparative method is essential. It must be applied together with good information about phylogeny so similarity owing to common adaptation can be distinguished from similarity owing to common descent. Conclusions about adaptation may therefore change with changes in the amount and quality of information used to construct the associated phylogeny (Ryan, 1996). We will see an example in chapter 2. A major constraint on the use of the comparative method is the availability of comparable data from a sufficiently large number of species.

Clearly, each method for studying adaptation is better suited to some kinds of questions and bodies of data than others. In the best possible case, all of them can be used in a complementary way. What we need to ask when confronted with an adaptationist argument about some aspect of cognition is, "On what method for testing adaptation is this argument based, and how rigorously was that method applied?"

1.5 Evolution and Cognition

So far, this chapter has consisted of a lightning survey of some big questions surrounding the study of animal cognition. What are we going to mean by *cognition* anyway (section 1.1)? What kinds of explanation can be given of cognition and behavior (section 1.2)? How should cognitive processes of different species be compared, ecologically or anthropocentrically (section 1.3)? How can adaptive or evolutionary explanations be tested (section 1.4)? This section brings together all these issues to ask whether there are any special problems with testing adaptive or evolutionary accounts of cognition. To discuss this question, we need to step back briefly and consider a framework for analyzing the organization of behavior.

1.5.1 Evolution and the Structure of Behavior

Studying cognition by looking at behavior means inferring mental organization from observing input-output relations. The input comes through the animal's senses. The output is the animal's actions. This description also applies to the study of motivation—that is, to studying how behavior is organized into systems like hunger, fear, and sexual behavior. Behavior systems, called *instincts* by Tinbergen and other classical ethologists, are hierarchical organizations of motor patterns that share some proximate causal factors (Hogan, 1994b; Shettleworth, 1994a; Timberlake, 1994). For example, an animal's hunger system includes the behavior patterns that change in frequency, intensity, or probability when it has been deprived of food and/or is in the presence of food. For a chicken, these might be walking around, scratching the ground, and pecking. A behavior system also includes relevant stimulus pro-

Central mechanisms

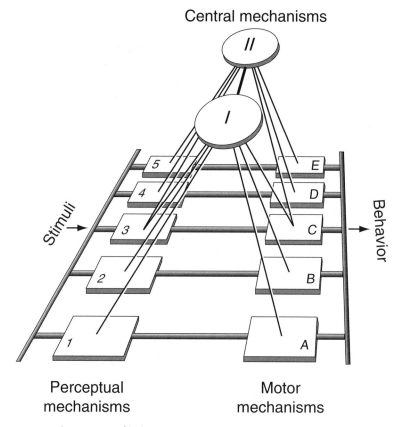

Perceptual
mechanisms

Motor
mechanisms

Figure 1.10. The structure of behavior systems. Stimuli are processed by perceptual mechanisms (1–5) and may affect motor mechanisms directly, as in reflexes (horizontal lines) or through the mediation of central mechanisms, of which two (I and II) are indicated. Each interconnected set of perceptual, central, and motor mechanisms forms a behavior system, so two behavior systems are shown here. Some motor mechanisms, such as C, which might be walking or pecking, may belong to more than one behavior system. Redrawn from Hogan (1988) with permission.

cessing (perceptual) mechanisms and central mechanisms that coordinate external and internal inputs (figure 1.10). In the case of the hunger system in a chicken, a central motivational mechanism integrates the bird's state of depletion or satiation with visual information to determine whether or not it will peck at what it sees (Hogan, 1994b). Cognitive mechanisms are part of this organization, too. Whether or not the chicken pecks at a grain may be influenced by how easy the grain is to see, by past learning about the consequences of pecking, and by what the bird ate recently.

As just described, behavior systems are defined causally (Hogan, 1994b), not in terms of immediate outcome or apparent goal. The behaviors in the hunger system, for example, are not necessarily identical with behavior that

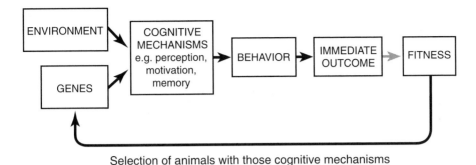

Figure 1.11. How cognition and behavior are shaped by natural selection. Adapted from Shettleworth (1987) with permission.

functions to get food. Nevertheless, to a large extent the causal organization of behavior must make functional sense. An animal that ignored food while starving or that approached predators rather than hiding or running away would probably not leave as many offspring as one that ate when hungry and fled from danger. Animals that ignore food when deprived or behave in a friendly manner toward predators have been weeded out by natural selection, not because they are "too stupid" to foresee the dire consequences of their acts but because they leave fewer copies of their genes than do individuals whose motivational and cognitive mechanisms result—*blindly*—in their being better nourished and less preyed upon. This relationship is depicted in figure 1.11. As the figure indicates, natural selection shapes cognition in an indirect way. Cognition—processing of environmental information—results in behavior. That behavior has an immediate consequence, such as ingesting food, depositing sperm in a fertile female, strengthening a nest. In the long run, such consequences have a measurable impact on the individual's fitness and thereby on the representation of genes contributing to the mechanisms that generate that behavior.

With few exceptions, like nestbuilding and burrowing, behavior does not leave fossils. But the evolution of behavior can nevertheless be inferred from phylogeny. One example was given in figure 1.9. In terms of the organization of behavior systems shown in figure 1.10, species differences could evolve in sensory, motor, or central mechanisms. For instance, the range of energies detectable by the senses could expand or contract, new motor patterns could appear, and/or the central coordination of input and output could change. The evolution of behavior can be traced at a more detailed level, too. For instance, species differences in motor patterns may be analyzed into differences in muscular and skeletal anatomy and patterns of firing in nerve cells (Lauder & Reilly, 1996). Species differences in visual sensitivity related to differences in the pattern of wavelengths prevalent in different environments might be attributable to differences in photopigments (see chapter 2). At a more molecular level still, the activity of genes responsible for production of the photopigments could be analyzed.

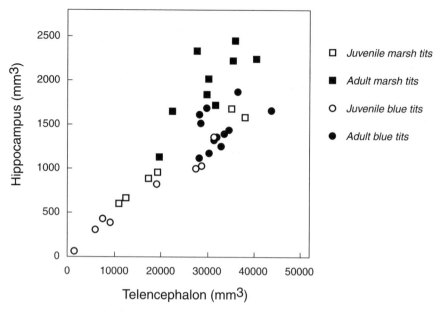

Figure 1.12. Growth of hippocampus and telencephalon (most of the rest of the brain) in marsh tits, a food-storing species, and blue tits, which do not store food. Redrawn from Healy et al. (1994) with permission.

Many *morphological* (i.e., structural) differences among species result from relatively small changes in developmental programs (Ridley, 1993). A speeding up or slowing down of growth in one part relative to others can result in dramatic changes in shape. The brains of food-storing birds provide one example related to cognition (figure 1.12). In baby marsh tits (food-storers) and baby blue tits (nonstorers), the whole brain grows rapidly in the first few weeks after hatching. At this stage, the hippocampus develops relative to the rest of the brain in the same way in both species. By around 6 weeks after hatching, when the babies are feeding themselves and the marsh tits are starting to store food, brain growth has slowed down. However, the marsh tits' hippocampus continues to grow, so that the typical food-storers' superiority of hippocampal size relative to the rest of the brain appears by the time memory for storage sites is needed (Healy, Clayton, & Krebs, 1994). Magpies (food-storing birds) and jackdaws show the same pattern (Healy & Krebs, 1993). In the case of marsh tits, experience using spatial memory also contributes to the species difference in hippocampus, but blue tits are not influenced by experience in the same way as marsh tits (Clayton, 1995).

Darwin was deeply impressed by how behavior as well as structure could be artificially selected by animal breeders. And in chapter 8 of *The Origin of Species,* he speculated on how complex and intricate behaviors like the comb-building behaviors of honeybees could have evolved in small steps. Nowadays, genetic engineering is used to demonstrate that particular genes contribute to particular behaviors or cognitive processes and to analyze the mechanisms by

A Typical Polygynous Mammal   A Typical Monogamous Mammal

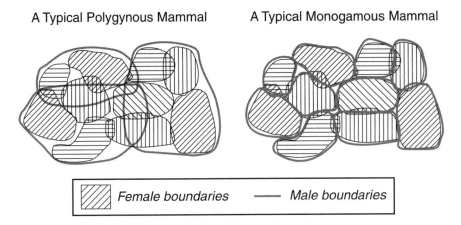

Female boundaries   —— Male boundaries

Figure 1.13. Relative territory sizes in males vs. females of polygynous vs. monogamous mammals. Redrawn from Gaulin (1995) with permission.

which they do so (Gerlai, 1996; Mayford, Abel, & Kandel, 1995). For example, mice can be created that lack a particular neurotransmitter important for spatial memory. Natural selection can provide molecular geneticists with opportunities to dissect how genetic changes have produced species differences, including differences in cognition and behavior. Bringing together information derived from genetic engineering with phylogenies of real species offers exciting possibilities for future research on the mechanisms of evolutionary change.

1.5.2 Adaptation and Cognition

In many monogamous species, the male and female occupy a territory together. In contrast, in some polygynous animals females have relatively small territories where they rear their young, while males range over larger areas, visiting several different females for mating (figure 1.13). These observations suggest that in monogamous species, males and females need similar abilities to find their way around and remember the locations of resources in the pair's territory, whereas in polygynous species males need a better developed ability to process and remember spatial information than females. This hypothesis about the relationship between spatial cognition and mating system has inspired research on sex differences in brain and spatial cognition in rodents (Gaulin, 1995; Jacobs, 1995), currently one of the best developed programs relating natural behavior, memory, and brain. Like any tests of adaptationist hypotheses about cognition, this research has had to confront a series of problems.

The specific hypothesis here is that males and females do not differ in spatial ability in monogamous species while there is a difference in favor of males in polygynous species. Research designed to test such a hypothesis should begin by asking, "*What method can be used: modelling, experiment, or the com-*

parative method?" Modeling and experiment seem unlikely to be useful or practical here, but the comparative method is appropriate because there are a large number of species of small rodents such as mice, voles, and kangaroo rats whose behavior is relatively well studied. This method has been adopted by Gaulin and others working on this problem (Gaulin, 1995; Jacobs, 1995), who have compared males and females of monogamous vs. closely related polygynous species in tests of "spatial ability." To evaluate such a program we can ask a series of four questions. Two are general to any application of the comparative method; the other two are specific to testing hypotheses about cognition.

1. *How good are the data on which the hypothesis is based?* Is it really the case that males in monogamous species use space in the same way as females whereas males in polygynous species use, and therefore must process information about, bigger areas than females? In the field, an animal's use of space is assessed by the size of its home range. Home range can be measured by radio tracking or by setting out extensive grids of traps and recording where an individual is found each time it is captured. Ideally, conclusions about what is typical of a species should be based on adequate amounts of data from several populations of that species. Such data can be hard to get, and in fact some have questioned whether the data about species-typical ranging patterns used by Gaulin and others are representative of the species they studied (Sawrey, Keith, & Backes, 1994). Even if the data are representative, a further issue is in what sense a larger territory requires "more" or "better" spatial ability. For instance, do males and females know their territories with the same degree of spatial resolution? There seem to be few, if any, data on what sorts of spatial knowledge the species being compared exhibit in the field.

2. *Are there enough independent comparisons?* This is a question about how many species are available for comparison and their phylogeny. One solution to the practical difficulties of doing behavioral tests in the laboratory on large numbers of species is to compare two species at a time, in this case one monogamous species with one closely related polygynous species. Five such comparisons are required, all coming out in the predicted direction, to achieve statistical significance at the .05 level (Kamil, 1988). (This argument assumes that if sex differences in spatial ability are not associated with mating system, there is a 50% chance of each independent set of results being consistent with the hypothesis.) So we need at least five pairs of species to study, and they should represent *independent* evolution of monogamy vs. polygyny— that is, cases in which ancestral species diversified and monogamy arose separately in several lineages. Research on spatial ability and mating systems has been done on, among other rodents, voles (*Microtus*) and mice (*Peromyscus*), although only three or four pairs of species have been sampled so far.

Using evolutionarily independent comparisons to test this adaptationist hypothesis about cognition is not without problems, however. Differences in the use of space might inevitably be associated with some noncognitive species differences—for instance, in motor ability. In some species, however, sex differences in space use are seasonal, presenting an opportunity to test for seasonal changes in cognition, brain, and behavior within the same individuals (Gaulin, 1995). And of course the hypothesis that male-female differences in ranging behavior are associated with sex differences in spatial ability can be tested with any animal, not just rodents.

3. *Is the test of cognition appropriate?* Do we have a good test of the ability hypothesized to differ adaptively in the field? It is a bit vague how possessing a large territory is supposed to make greater demands on spatial cognition than possessing a small one. Is it that the large-territory holder can find his way accurately over bigger distances? Does it mean the holder of a large territory can memorize more spatial information—remember the locations of more objects, for example? How does any of this translate into quantifiable performance in the laboratory?

As we will see in chapter 7, many tests of spatial cognition have been devised, and performance in most of them appears to depend on a single area of the brain, the hippocampus (in birds and mammals, anyway). The hippocampus shows sex differences associated with mating systems (Gaulin, 1995). The neuroanatomical evidence suggests that performance in a wide variety of tasks is subserved by a unitary "spatial ability," and therefore almost any spatial task can be used to compare species. In fact, however, while the predicted pattern of sex differences appears in voles learning complex mazes, that pattern has failed to appear in a test of the same species' ability to learn to swim quickly to the single dry place in a swimming pool (Sawrey, Keith, & Backes, 1994). Negotiating a large and complex space may seem more like what animals do in the field than the swimming pool task. However, contrary to what this notion suggests, performance in the swimming pool *is* correlated with seasonal sex differences in space use in deer mice (Galea, Kavaliers, Ossenkopp, Innes, & Hargreaves, 1994). Males perform better than females when the animals are in reproductive condition, but this sex difference disappears outside of the breeding season, when the two sexes are assumed to be using space in the same way.

Another issue is how sensitive the tests are. All animals may perform equally well on a very easy test and equally poorly on a very difficult test; what is needed is a test of intermediate difficulty. Tests of comparable difficulty should be used for all the species pairs considered. For instance, if very easy tasks were used for voles and tasks of intermediate difficulty for kangaroo rats, one might conclude from the limited evidence reviewed here that kangaroo rats but not voles show sex differences in spatial cognition associated with mating system. These kinds of considerations bring us to the fourth question.

4. *Do differences in performance represent differences in cognition?* Sexual dimorphism, group size, or hippocampal volume are defined by straightforward physical measurements. Although people may debate whether such measurements are appropriate for testing particular comparative hypotheses, at least they refer to things one can see. But a character like "spatial ability" is invisible. It has to be inferred from measurements of behavior, and behavior can be affected by many things other than cognition. (This is the distinction between *learning* and *competence* or *performance*, discussed further in chapter 3.)

We cannot just test males and females of a number of different species, all in the same way, and conclude that the results answer the question of whether there are sex differences in cognition associated with ecology. There is no guarantee that a test standardized in terms of physical variables affects all the species in the same way. For instance, animals that become frightened and stay close to the walls in a big open space might take a long time to learn to swim straight to the dry platform in the middle of a pool of water. If the animals are rewarded with food, we need to be sure all species are equally hungry and equally fond of the reward provided. Although searching for food in a maze and escaping from a pool of water both require spatial cognition, they also rely on different motivational systems (Dudchenko, Goodridge, Seiterle & Taube, 1997; Martin, Harley, Smith, Hoyles, and Hynes, 1997). Such considerations underline the importance of what Macphail (1982, 1987) calls *contextual variables.* Within any species, numerous features of the experimental context, some much less obvious than timidity or size and type of reward, can affect what animals do. Therefore, if species are compared in a single task, any differences among them could be the result of contextual variables rather than species differences in the cognitive ability that performance is supposed to measure.

Several solutions to this problem have been suggested. One is *systematic variation* (Bitterman, 1965). This means testing the animals under several values of relevant contextual variables. For instance, the difficulty of the task should be varied over a wide range. Gaulin and Fitzgerald (1989) did just that by using seven different mazes to compare spatial learning in monogamous prairie voles (*Microtus ochorogaster*) and polygynous meadow voles (*M. pennsylvanicus*). Meadow vole males performed better than meadow vole females on all the mazes, but, as predicted, there was no sex difference in the prairie voles (figure 1.14). Notice that the mazes seem to be a fair test of species differences in that both species score about the same on any given maze.

Systematic variation amounts to trying to reject the null hypothesis that no factor other than differences in cognition is responsible for differences in performance (Kamil, 1988). For instance, it might be suggested that sex differences in activity are responsible for sex differences in performance in spatial tasks. This possibility has been rendered implausible by showing that males' and females' activity levels are similar under a range of conditions (Gaulin, FitzGerald, & Wartell, 1990). But a sceptic might then suggest another confounding factor, further systematic variation would have to be done, and so on *ad infinitum.* Kamil's proposed solution to this problem is, instead of systematically varying factors within a given task, to vary the tasks. For instance, if different groups of animals really differ in ability to process and remember spatial information, differences among them ought to be detectable in a variety of different spatial tasks. There may, of course, be tasks or species for which contextual variables are overwhelmingly important, but if enough tasks are used, they should converge on a single conclusion. Kamil and his colleagues have used this approach with considerable success to compare mem-

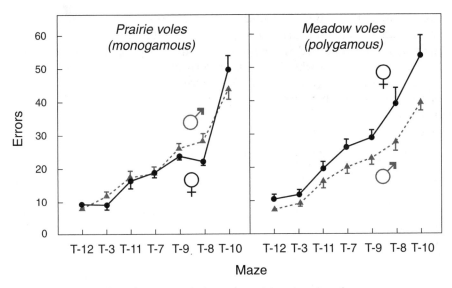

Figure 1.14. Number of errors made by male and female voles of two species in a series of increasingly difficult mazes. Data from Gaulin and Fitzgerald (1989) redrawn from Gaulin (1995) with permission.

ory for spatial information in food-storing vs. nonstoring species of birds (see box 1.4; see also chapter 6).

Ideally, a thorough comparative program of this sort includes tests on which the species are predicted not to differ, or—even better—to differ in the opposite direction. For instance, the species predicted to perform best on tests of spatial memory should not also do best on tests of memory for non-spatial information. In food-storing species of corvids (the crow family, including jays and nutcrackers; see box 1.4), some species are highly social while others are not. Therefore, the pattern of species differences in social cognition may differ from that in spatial cognition (Balda, Kamil, & Bednekoff, 1996). Dissociating performance on two kinds of tasks rules out the possibility that one group of animals simply performs better than another because of general contextual variables such as how well they adapt to the laboratory. In species exhibiting a sex difference in spatial behavior hypothesized to be related to space use in the wild, the sex difference may be present only in the breeding season (Galea et al., 1994). Such seasonal or developmental changes within individuals of the same species offer perhaps the best opportunities for testing adaptive relationships among cognition, brain, and natural behavior with minimal confounds from contextual variables.

In addition to testing comparative hypotheses about cognition with a number of convergent operations, other kinds of tests of adaptation might be considered. Just as with eggshell removal, an experimental demonstration of function in one or two species can be combined with a broad comparative correlation of the character with purportedly important ecological factors.

For instance, the notion that a larger hippocampus is part of food-storing species' adaptation for retrieving stored food (see figure 1.6) is supported by demonstrations that food-storing birds with hippocampal lesions store food but cannot remember where they put it (Krushinskaya, 1966; Sherry & Vaccarino, 1989). However, it is not always apparent how cognitive abilities or the opportunity to use them can be manipulated to test whether they serve their hypothesized function in the field.

1.5.3 Can Function Explain Mechanism?

If an ability is an adaptation to certain ecological requirements, it should vary quantitatively across species with the severity of those requirements. More spatial information to process means more spatial memory; greater reliance on accurate visual localization of prey means better stereoscopic vision (chapter 2); more complex social groups means better-developed social cognition (chapter 10). These statements describe *adaptative specializations* of characters that species share. Such variations are readily observed in characters like beaks in birds (figure 1.15). A bird that drinks nectar needs a long narrow beak, one that lives on hard seeds needs a beak like a nutcracker, one that tears flesh needs a sharp hooked beak. Can we use notions about adaptation in a similar way to make predictions about how cognitive mechanisms work? Can we say something like, "This species needs to solve this information-processing problem in the wild, therefore its mental equipment must include mechanisms with the following properties"? To suggest that we can is to suggest that Tinbergen's four whys are not just complementary questions about behavior but rather that answering the functional why question can help to reveal the answer to the causal why.

Among the most prolific and eloquent proponents of the view that thinking about cognition as an adaptation is the best way to understand how it works are the evolutionary psychologists Leda Cosmides and John Tooby (e.g., Cosmides & Tooby, 1995; Tooby & Cosmides, 1995), but it has also been explored by others (e.g., Rozin & Schull, 1988; Sherry & Schacter, 1987; Shettleworth, 1983). If cognition is an adaptation to solve ecologically important problems, we should expect to find a collection of specialized computational devices designed for special purposes rather than a single general-purpose problem-solving mechanism. Perception provides many examples: animals do not have a single generalized sensory system for detecting all kinds of physical energies. Vision, hearing, olfaction, and so on are each specialized for a different kind of energy detection. As we will see in chapter 2, the senses are also further specialized within each species in a way that reflects its lifestyle and the information available in its habitat. The idea that cognitive science can advance by analyzing the information-processing tasks that organisms are designed to do has been profitably applied to the study of perception (Marr, 1982; Shepard, 1994). Described from an adaptationist point of view, distinguishable cognitive mechanisms or *modules* (Fodor, 1983) will evolve whenever the information-processing problems a species has to solve

Figure 1.15. Some adaptations of birds' bills for different modes of feeding. From left to right, a seed cracker, nut cracker, meat tearer, generalized forager, flower prober, and earth prober. After Welty (1963) with permission.

require different, *functionally incompatible*, kinds of computations (Sherry & Schacter, 1987). These modules will be *domain-specific*—that is, each one will operate only on a restricted, appropriate, set of inputs. For instance, in birds, the ability to memorize something and imitate it months later is confined to certain species and certain kinds of input—namely, sounds likely to be species-typical song (chapter 10). Returning to the locations of stored food items requires a different kind of memory. Of course this same approach predicts that, unlike song learning, some cognitive modules will be found in most species and will be able to process many kinds of input because they deal with information of widespread importance. The generality of associative learning (see chapter 3) can be understood if it is seen as an adaptation for learning about physical causal relationships among all kinds of objects and events in the world. Similarly, some properties of memory (see chapter 6), such as the fact that it fades with time, would be expected to be the same regardless of the events remembered because they are adaptations for making available the information that is most likely to be needed again. In chapter 13, after surveying how animals process and act on a variety of kinds of information, including information about physical causation, time, space, and social relationships, we will be equipped for more detailed consideration of cognitive modularity.

A second key prediction of the adaptationist viewpoint is that information processing should reflect "innate knowledge." An organism is not the proverbial *tabula rasa*, or blank slate. Rather, animals' nervous systems are preorganized to process information in species-appropriate ways. Not only such obviously specialized learning abilities as bird song but also associative learning, mechanisms of memory storage, attention, and problem solving all reflect environmental requirements. Thus, cognitive scientists should be seeking to understand how the structure of information-processing devices mirrors the structure of the world. Not only does an adaptationist approach predict that the human or nonhuman mind is organized into domain-specific information-processing modules, but evolutionary psychologists claim it also predicts the details of how these modules work. For example, Cosmides (1989) claims that the ability to solve the Wason selection task, a logical problem, reflects an adaptation for detecting cheaters on social contracts. This notion predicts that people should reach the logically correct solution more often with problems about detecting cheaters than with formally identical problems about other material. Although the results of a number of experiments are consistent with this hypothesis, it has not gone unchallenged (see chapter 11). The same kind of argument has been applied to experimental tests of the adaptive value of Pavlovian conditioned responding (see chapter 3). Such research is implicitly based on the argument from design: "X appears to be designed specifically to do Y; if it is, then animals with X should be better at Y than at some superficially similar but adaptively irrelevant task, Z."

The evolutionary psychologists' approach is essentially the same as the approach to cognition taken in this book. However, it faces several problems. Some stem from the indirectness of the relationship between cognition and fitness depicted in figure 1.11. As Lehrman put it, "Nature selects for outcomes, not processes of development" (Lehrman, 1970; Rozin & Schull, 1988; Shettleworth, 1983). The answers to Tinbergen's four questions are complementary: function does not uniquely determine the details of causation (Hogan, 1994a). For instance, if the adaptive problem solved by eggshell removal is reducing predation, why didn't gulls evolve eggshells that were cryptically colored inside? The answer to this sort of question may lie in *constraints* from other aspects of the species' biology. The way in which eggshells are produced in the gull's oviduct may not readily allow for a change in the color of their interior, whereas gulls need to be equipped with motor patterns for picking things up and carrying them in foraging and nestbuilding, and these could be used equally well to carry eggshells. To take an example from cognition, many animals need to be able to return to a home to care for their young or to gain protection from predators. Thus they need a cognitive device for remembering and relocating places. But the mechanism that does this job differs from species to species (chapter 7). Nevertheless, details of ecology, behavior, and sensory or neural equipment may adaptively determine how a certain function is achieved. For instance, animals should evolve to care for their own offspring in preference to unrelated young (see chapter 4). Therefore, species that engage in parental care must have mechanisms for recognizing their own offspring, in some sense. This can mean nothing more sophisticated than spending a couple of weeks stuffing food into any gaping mouth in your nest, but another mechanism would be needed in a species with young that run around while their parents are still feeding them. Even though the prediction that offspring should be favored does not tell us how a particular species recognizes its young, a closer look at the species' biology may make adaptive sense of the mechanisms by which it does so.

1.5.4 Conclusions and Implications

By now, some readers may be saying to themselves, "Surely we know all living things are the products of evolution, so what's new about an adaptationist approach to cognition?" As behavioral ecologists have discussed many times (see Parker & Maynard Smith, 1990), the aim of investigations of adaptation is generally not to prove adaptations exist. The last section has suggested that studying cognitive mechanisms as adaptations may help understand how they work. Studying cognition in humans and other species as an adaptation has three other practical implications.

First, it determines what phenomena are studied. For example, a psychologist interested in some aspect of cognition as an adaptation is more likely to take the ecological than the anthopocentric approach to species comparison, more likely to study how animals detect cryptic prey than how they learn lists of items, more likely to select species to study on the basis of their using a particular ability in nature than on the basis of their convenience for laboratory research. Such a scientist is more likely to expect to find species- and problem-specific cognitive modules than generalized capacities.

Second, a thoroughgoing evolutionary approach to psychology is likely to have an effect on research in cognitive neuroscience (Francis, 1995). Much research on the neural basis of cognition is implicitly based on the ancient pre-Darwinian assumption of the phylogenetic ladder (Deacon, 1990; Preuss, 1995). For example, using the Norway rat as an "animal model" of spatial orientation or eating seems to assume that rats are in some sense simplified humans. If the aim of research is to answer questions about specific aspects of human function, "model" species should be chosen for similarity to humans in those aspects of adaptation. Human brain anatomy may be better understood by taking the phylogeny of primates into account than by assuming human brains are rat brains with some new pieces added (Preuss, 1995). Understanding the function of specific parts of the brain can be aided by the comparative method, as in the study of hippocampus and memory in food-storing birds mentioned earlier in this chapter (Harvey & Krebs, 1990).

Finally, as has happened repeatedly in behavioral ecology, the results of adaptationist studies of nonhuman species invite extrapolation to humans.

Some of these extrapolations are both controversial and misguided. Therefore, it is important that studies with nonhumans be done with utmost care. For example, consider the possible association of sex differences in rodents' spatial cognition with their breeding system. Because humans are thought to have evolved as a mildly polygynous species and because cognitive differences between men and women are well documented (Voyer, Voyer, & Bryden, 1995), such research tempts generalization beyond rodents. One recent manifestation of this tendency to overgeneralize is an "explanation" of the pattern of sex differences in mathematical performance based on the purported function of various computational abilities (Geary, 1996). A thoughtful reader of this chapter will already be equipped with several objections to such facile extrapolation. First, not enough rodent species have been studied yet to be sure that polygyny and superior male spatial ability go together, even among rodents. Second, the hypothesis that mating system is associated with male spatial ability applies only to cases in which polygynous males hold bigger territories than females, and this is not a necessary attribute of polygyny. For example, a male hamadryas baboon controls access to several females, but the whole group travels around together (Kummer, 1995; see also chapter 11). Males with a harem like this would not be expected to have better spatial ability than females. One therefore needs to know something about early hominid social systems to know whether the hypothesis is appropriate for humans at all. This is not to say that adaptationist hypotheses cannot provide stimulating and powerful ways of understanding many aspects of human behavior and cognition (Barkow, Cosmides, & Tooby, 1992), but only that they must be applied carefully. Because the processes involved are generally simpler and more obvious in other species than in humans and more relevant comparative data are available, studies of nonhumans can provide a good model of how an adaptionist approach to cognition can work.

1.6 Summary

The study of cognition consists of analyzing how animals acquire, process, and use information from the environment. Most people who study comparative cognition remain agnostic as to whether animals process information consciously or not. In contrast, cognitive ethologists recommend trying to study conscious processes such as beliefs and intentions in animals, but it is difficult, if not impossible, to obtain unambiguous evidence that animals are conscious.

Four questions, often referred to as Tinbergen's four whys, can be asked about any behavior. These are questions about immediate causation, development in the individual, present-day function, and evolution. The four questions are complementary; each contributes to a complete understanding of behavior. Cognitive mechanisms such as perception and memory are among the immediate causes of behavior; learning is part of behavioral development. Cognitive processes also play a role in an animal's adaptation to its environment.

Cognition in nonhuman species has been studied from two distinct points of view. The anthropocentric approach seeks to understand the evolution of human cognitive capacities by reference to an assumed phylogenetic scale. However, present-day species represent the ends of a multitude of branches on the evolutionary tree of life, not stages in a linear progression to humans. Therefore, comparative data from widely divergent species must be interpreted cautiously. The ecological approach to cognition consists of analyzing the kinds of information processing animals do in situations of ecological importance like foraging, choosing mates, or finding their way home. With this approach, species are compared with reference to evolutionary and ecological relationships.

A claim that any character is adaptive can be tested in three ways: by modeling, to discover whether the character is indeed well designed for its function; with the comparative method, to test whether variations in the character across many species are related to variations in ecology; and by experiment. Ideally two or more of these methods can be used together. Using the comparative method requires good inferences about the phylogeny of the species being compared. Information about the distribution of different character states in present-day species can be used to infer how they evolved. Evolutionary psychologists claim that understanding how cognitive mechanisms evolved and what they are for can help us to understand how they work. However, testing adaptationist hypotheses about cognition can be difficult because cognitive processes do not affect fitness directly but only through the medium of behavior.

Most of these ideas will surface again and again in discussions of specific examples thoughout the book. When we get to the end, in chapter 13, we will look once more at some of the issues raised in this chapter.

Further Reading

Ethology (Hinde, 1982), *From Darwin to Behaviorism* (Boakes, 1984) and the book by Richards (1987) are recommended for historical background. Many of the issues introduced in this chapter, including adaptation, Tinbergen's four questions, the meaning of *innate*, and the question of animal consciousness are analyzed briefly and lucidly by Marian Dawkins in *Unravelling Animal Behaviour* (1995). The present brief discussion does not begin to do justice to philosophical views on the nature of consciousness. The writings of Searle (1980), Dennett (1996), P. M. Churchland (1995), Chalmers (1995), and Allen and Bekoff (1997) are especially relevant here. Kennedy's (1992) little book is a stimulating analysis of what he saw as the insidious influence of anthropomorphism in the study of animal behavior. Fisher (1995) presents a contrary view. A further sense of the controversy in this area can be gotten from the correspondance in the January 1996 *American Psychologist* that deals with Blumberg and Wasserman's (1995) insightful discussion of anthropomorphism in comparative cognition.

For understanding the theory of evolution, there is no substitute for reading at least part of *The Origin of Species* (Darwin, 1859) or *The Descent of Man and Selection in Relation to Sex* (Darwin, 1871). For a current text, Ridley (1993) is highly recommended. *Behaviour and Evolution* (Slater & Halliday, 1994) contains useful reviews on all aspects of the topic. Evolutionary theory and its application to behavior have been the subject of some outstanding books for the general reader. Richard Dawkins's *The Selfish Gene* (1976) is already a classic exposition of the basics of behavioral ecology. *The Blind Watchmaker* (R. Dawkins, 1986) is equally clear and readable. *Darwin's Dangerous Idea* (Dennett, 1995) is a philosopher's discussion of evolutionary theory and its wider implications. *The Beak of the Finch* (Weiner, 1994) is a very readable account of studies of evolution in action on the Galápagos.

2

Perception and Attention

To a bat or an owl, a summer evening is full of sounds of which we are only dimly aware. A honeybee sees patterns on flowers that are invisible to us. The idea that every kind of animal has its own *umwelt*, or self-world, formed by the kinds of information its senses can process, was one of the fundamental insights of the founders of ethology. The ethologist von Uexküll (1934/1957) attempted to picture how the world might look to other species (figure 2.1), and in a famous essay on the nature of consciousness, the philosopher Nagel (1974) discussed whether it is possible to know "What is it like to be a bat?" Although most behavioral scientists do not attempt to study animals' subjective experiences (see chapter 1), a great deal is known about how different kinds of animals process sensory information. We begin our discussion of comparative cognition at this basic level for two reasons. First, it is important to keep in mind that adaptive behavior can result from specializations in perception as much as from higher level learning or decision processes. Second, perception provides some excellent examples of modularity and adaptation in information processing. This chapter begins with a few illustrative examples of sensory specializations and then looks at how perception can be studied in animals and introduces the important ideas of signal detection theory. Armed with this information, we can see how "receiver psychology" (Guilford & Dawkins, 1991) may have shaped evolution of sexual displays and other animal signals. And at the end of the chapter we look at how sensory information is filtered by attention, how it is put together into perceptions of objects and

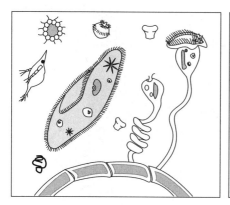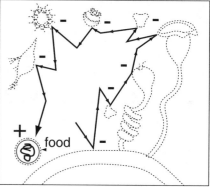

Figure 2.1. Von Uexküll's conception of the *umwelt* of a paramecium (the gray single-celled organism in the center of the left panel). The environment in all the complexity perceived by humans is depicted on the left, the same environment as perceived by the paramecium on the right. Redrawn from von Uexküll (1934/1957) with permission.

situations, and how attentional processes can explain the classical ethological phenomenon of search image formation.

2.1 Specialized Sensory Systems

Every animal must be able to respond appropriately to its own food, mates, young, and predators. The cues that it can use to do so are determined by the environment characteristic of its species (Dusenbery, 1992). Species active at night have a different set of cues available to them from those active during the day; those that live underground, different cues from those that live in the treetops; creatures of the deep sea, different cues again from creatures of clear streams. Thus we might expect sensory systems and their sensitivities to be matched to lifestyle and environment.

The sensory specializations we find most impressive are those in which animals respond to forms of energy that an unaided human cannot detect. The ultrasonic hearing of bats is one well-studied example (see figure 2.5). Many bat species detect prey in the dark by using a kind of sonar. They continually emit ultrasonic cries, and the echoes from flying insects enable the bats to locate their prey in complete darkness. Some snakes locate live prey by homing in on warm objects, using infrared detectors in their snout. The platypus feeds underwater at night using sensitive receptors in its bill to detect the electric fields generated by movements of its prey (Manger & Pettigrew, 1995). Fish of the genus *Gymnotus* communicate with one another using weak electric pulses. Just as some birds mark their territories with individually recognizable songs, some electric fish have individual electric "signatures" (McGregor & Westby, 1992).

Color resides not in objects but in the observer's perception of wavelength differences or similarities (Goldsmith, 1990, 1994; Thompson, Palacios, & Varela, 1992). To a color-blind animal, objects differ visually only in brightness. Because both bees and birds evidently use the wavelengths visible to humans in foraging, mating, and orienting, it is easy to assume that they see the world the way we do. But the differences in their wavelength sensitivity may need to be taken into account in deciding how they see prey items or potential mates. For instance, bees have visual receptors for ultraviolet (UV) light. Two flowers that look the same color to us look quite different to bees if they have different UV reflectances (Chittka, Shmida, Troje, & Menzel, 1994). Many species of birds also have UV vision, and some feathers reflect UV light, suggesting that UV vision might play a role in intra-species communication (Bennett & Cuthill, 1994; Finger & Burkhardt, 1994). Consistent with this suggestion, the behavior of female zebra finches in laboratory tests of mate choice is influenced by whether or not they can see the UV wavelengths reflected by stimulus males (Bennett, Cuthill, Partridge, & Maier, 1996). And kestrels use the UV reflectance of vole urine to locate places where voles can be found, areas that are indistinguishable to humans (Viitala, Korpimaki, Palokangas, & Koivula, 1995).

The foregoing are but a few examples of striking differences in the energies different species can sense. Less obvious are differences among closely related species in the sensitivity of particular systems. For example, because sunlight is filtered by seawater, the distribution of wavelengths illuminating objects changes with depth. This means that optimal visual sensitivity is different for fish dwelling at different depths. It may even change with age if the same fish lives at different depths at different stages of its life cycle (Lythgoe, 1979). As shown in figure 2.2, the light environment is also very different in different parts of the forest and at different times of day. The nuptial plumage of male forest birds and the times and places at which they display may be matched to the available light in such a way as to maximize the males' conspicuousness (Endler & Théry, 1996). In a group of closely related Himalayan warbler species, males had brighter colors the darker the habitat in which they displayed (Marchetti, 1993). The sound frequencies that travel farthest are determined by features of the environment like atmospheric conditions and kind of vegetation (Wiley & Richards, 1982). These physical constraints have affected the evolution of animal sound production and reception mechanisms (Gerhardt, 1983). For example, the songs of forest birds tend to have a different distribution of frequencies than the songs of birds from more open habitats (see Catchpole & Slater, 1995).

How much of the environment an animal can see at once depends on where its eyes are. Animals with eyes on the sides of their heads can see a wider arc of their surroundings than animals like humans and many other primates with frontally placed eyes. The placing of the eyes also reflects the extent of binocular vision required by the species diet and the extent to which the animal is predator as opposed to prey (figure 2.3). The most important things may be near the horizon or above or in front of the animal. This feature of ecology may be matched by greater visual acuity in some parts of the visual field than others. For example, pigeons view a small area in front of them binocularly. Binocular vision, and concomitantly good depth perception, are important

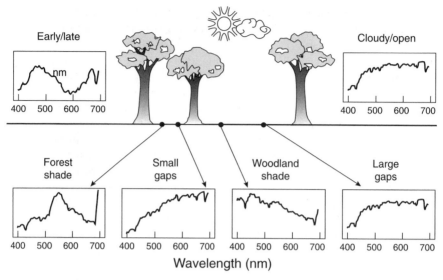

Figure 2.2. The relative intensities of different wavelengths of light in different parts of a forest and under different conditions. Forest shade, for instance, is greenish, whereas small gaps are rich in longer (redder) wavelengths. Redrawn from Endler (1992) with permission.

for accurate pecking at seeds, whereas the lateral field of view is important for detecting predators. Accordingly, pigeons have two "foveas," or areas of max-imally dense photoreceptors, one in the binocular field and one on which ob-jects to the side are focused. Information does not transfer perfectly between the frontal and lateral fields (Roberts, Phelps, Macuda, Brodbeck, & Russ, 1996). Species of birds with different lifestyles also have different retinal dis-tributions of photoreceptors (Nalbach, Wolf-Oberhollenzer, & Remy, 1993). For example, seabirds tend to have a central horizontal strip of high-density photoreceptors. Owls and other birds of prey have the densest photoreceptors in the part of the retina that views the ground. They may have to turn their heads almost upside down to see something approaching from above. Al-though their eyes are structured very differently from the eyes of vertebrates, insects also have the densest photoreceptors placed to receive the most im-portant information (Land, 1990).

In many situations animals respond to a very narrow range of stimuli. For example, male moths of species like *Bembyx mori* are sexually attracted to a particular molecule, one contained in a pheromone emitted by the female of their own species (see Hopkins, 1983). A hungry baby herring gull pecks at a red spot near the end of its parent's beak and less at other colors in other lo-cations (Tinbergen & Perdeck, 1950). The first step in analyzing such an ex-ample of selective behavior is to find out whether it can be explained by the responsiveness of the sensory system involved. In the case of the moth, the characteristics of the olfactory system completely account for the male's se-lective sensitivity. The male moth's antennae are covered with receptors se-

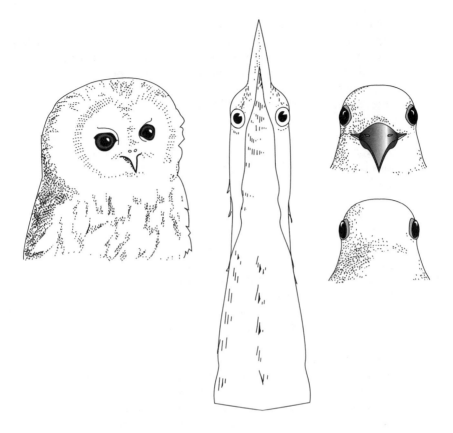

Figure 2.3. Differences in the placement of the eyes for different lifestyles, illustrated by an owl, a bittern, and a yellow-billed cuckoo. The bittern is able to look binocularly for fish in shallow water as well as keep both eyes on a predator when it "freezes" with its bill pointed upward. The cuckoo can converge on objects both in front and behind, a different visual adaptation for predator detection. Redrawn from Welty (1963) with permission.

lective for the female's sexual pheromone. In contrast, the herring gull's selective pecking at red spots on beaklike objects reflects processing at a higher level (Delius, Thompson, Allen, & Emmerton, 1972). Both the female pheromone and the red spot would be be classified as *sign stimuli* (see chapter 5), but one reflects a purely sensory filter, the other a more central processing mechanism.

2.2 How Can We Find Out What Animals Perceive?

2.2.1 Studying Perception in Animals

Three approaches can be taken to analyzing perception in animals: (1) electrophysiology and related methods of neuroscience, (2) studying how natural behavior changes with changes in stimulation, and (3) testing learned behavior with the methods of animal psychophysics. Each one of these approaches has its advantages and disadvantages. Two or three of them can be used together to reach an understanding of why an animal responds selectively to stimuli in a natural situation.

Recording the electrical responses of sensory neurons to controlled stimuli (*electrophysiology*) is the most direct way to find out what sensory information is potentially available to an animal. In the case of the moths described in the previous section, such methods make clear that the "decision" whether sexual pheromones belong to the right species is reached by the receptors. In other cases, recording at different points in the pathway from the receptors can reveal how a sensory system analyzes and classifies stimuli before they reach central decision-making mechanisms (see Moss & Shettleworth, 1996, for some examples).

Recording nervous activity in the sensory pathways is more direct and in some ways easier than testing behavior, but to find out what features of the world are behaviorally significant it may be more meaningful to look directly at behavior. The first thing that comes to mind in this regard is to observe natural behavior. For example, hamsters, like many other mammals, mark their territories with secretions from special glands. To find out whether they can discriminate among the scent marks of different individuals, Johnston, Derzie, Chiang, Jernigan, & Lee (1993) made use of the fact that a hamster spends a great deal of time sniffing a glass plate scent-marked by another hamster. This response decreases as the hamster encounters successive marks of the same kind from the same hamster—that is, the response *habituates* (see chapter 4). However, once the subject hamster has habituated to the scent from one hamster, it still vigorously investigates scent from a second hamster (figure 2.4). This *dishabituation* of investigation shows that the animal can discriminate the second scent from the first. As we will see in later chapters, the habituation/dishabituation method is a powerful one for discovering what stimuli all kinds of subjects, including humans, discriminate.

The differences animals perceive among behaviorally relevant stimuli can be studied in the field as well as in the laboratory. For example, many territorial songbirds learn the characteristics of their neighbor's songs and where those neighbors typically sing (see box 4.4). A familiar neighbor singing from a new location is treated as a threat and attacked. A novel conspecific song from a loudspeaker is also attacked (Falls, 1982), making it possible to present songs in a controlled way in the field to find out what aspects of this complex auditory stimulus birds are sensitive to. Experiments of this kind have shown, for example, that great tits can discriminate the individual voices of their neighbors. They respond differently to the same song sung by two different birds (Weary, 1996).

One problem with using natural responses to natural stimuli is that there are at least two reasons why an animal may respond in the same way to two or more stimuli. It may not be able to discriminate among them or the differences it discriminates may have no behavioral significance for it. In the ex-

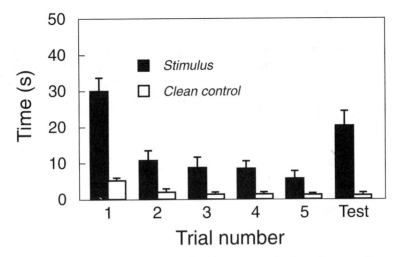

Figure 2.4. Data from the habituation/dishabituation method used to test olfactory discrimination in male golden hamsters. Time spent sniffing the scented half of a glass plate is compared to time spent sniffing the clean half. A different odor is presented in the test than in the first 5 trials. Redrawn from Johnston et al. (1993) with permission.

ample above, for instance, a territorial male bird might be equally aggressive toward two very different novel songs, but he might later show that he could discriminate them if one was the song of a neighbor while the other remained relatively novel (see Weary, 1996, for further discussion). Late in the breeding season, when sex hormone levels are lower, he might respond equally little to all songs. A good understanding of the behavior of the species being tested is clearly necessary to ensure that tests of discrimination are being done in a meaningful way.

A second problem with the habituation method is that it can be used only with stimuli that already evoke an identifiable behavior. Often, as in the case of bird song, these stimuli are quite complex, and it may be difficult to relate the animal's response to them to simple sensory abilities like the ability to discriminate wavelength or intensity. An important question about the evolution of sensory systems and their impact on intra-specific signaling systems is whether the sensory system's sensitivity and the characteristics of signals are matched to one another (see section 2.5). This question cannot be answered by looking only at responses to natural signals. Electrophysiological or psychophysical methods must be used to study sensory ability separately from the behavior evoked by the signals of interest.

2.2.2 Animal Psychophysics

One of the oldest areas of experimental psychology is *psychophysics*, the study of how information is processed by the senses. For example, what is the smallest amount of light energy, at each wavelength, that can be seen in total darkness? Or, with a given background sound, what increase in sound pressure level is required for subjects to report an increase in loudness? The former is a question about the *absolute threshold*; the latter, about the *relative* or *difference threshold*. Data from psychophysical investigations typically consist of plots of absolute or relative thresholds as a function of a physical stimulus dimension.

A psychophysicist interested in absolute auditory thresholds can tell a human subject, "Press this button whenever you hear a tone." Visual acuity can be tested by instructing a person, "Press the left button when you see stripes; press the right when you see a gray patch." Animals, in contrast, have to be given their instructions by careful training, using the methods of operant or classical conditioning. Figuring out how to ask nonverbal subjects the questions one wants to ask in a way that yields unambiguous answers is one of the biggest challenges in any area of comparative cognition. With operant methods, the animal is placed in a situation where it can obtain reward or avoid punishment *only* by using as a cue the stimulus the experimenter is interested in. Since animals seem to have an uncanny knack of latching onto subtle irrelevant cues, being sure the animal responds only to the dimension of interest is not as easy as it sounds. Well-designed psychophysical experiments must include controls for the possible influence of extraneous cues.

A typical procedure for investigating animal sensory abilities is one used for testing bats' ability to discriminate distances by echolocating (figure 2.5). The basic idea is to reward a bat for making one response when it detects an object moving rapidly back and forth (a "jittering" target) and another response when the target is stationary. As long as the bat can make the correct choice at above the chance level of 50%, it must be discriminating between the two distances from which it hears the jittering target's echoes — that is, between the two echo delays. Since all bats are not really "as blind as a bat," the experiment depicted in figure 2.5 had to control for the possibility that the bats saw the targets as moving vs. stationary rather than detecting their echoes. The bat's cries were picked up by a microphone near its mouth and broadcast back to it either with a fixed delay, as if reflected by a stationary object, or with alternating short and long delays, as if coming from a jittering target. The bat sat on a Y-shaped platform and was rewarded with a mealworm for crawling onto the left arm when a jittering target was presented and onto the right arm for a stationary one. To ensure that the animal learned the required discrimination, training began with large movements of the jittering target. When the animal performed correctly a large proportion of the time on this easy task, the task was made more difficult, and so on. The bats were eventually making extremely fine discriminations.

This elaborate instrumentation and training procedure may suggest that psychophysical experiments can be done only in the laboratory, but this is not so. Classic field studies of bees' color and shape perception were done by von Frisch (1967), using methods described in chapter 12 (see also Gould & Gould, 1988). Animals that return repeatedly to one food source as bees do are particularly good candidates for field tests of their discrimination abilities. As another example, Goldsmith, Collins, and Perlman (1981) tested black-

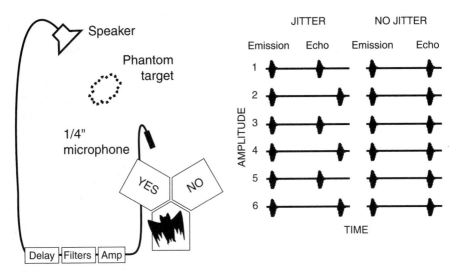

Figure 2.5. Schematic view of a setup for testing temporal discrimination in bats. The bat was reinforced for moving onto the left platform for a jittering target ("yes, jitter present") and onto the right platform when no jitter was present. Redrawn from Moss and Schnitzler (1989) with permission.

chinned hummingbirds' color vision in the field by attracting free-flying hummingbirds to feeders containing sugar water. This artificial nectar was available from feeders illuminated with one wavelength of light but not another one 10 nm longer or shorter. By counting the number of correct choices in a fixed number of trials with different pairs of wavelengths, Goldsmith et al. were able to compute the birds' relative wavelength sensitivity across the spectrum.

The tests of bats', bees', and hummingbirds' discrimination abilities are based directly on the animals' natural feeding behaviors. The bats receive food when they approach an object detected by echolocating. The hummingbirds and bees extract nectar from "flowers" of different colors and shapes. Natural contingencies such as these may be best for exploring the limits of an animal's sensory abilities because the animal is using the sense for the job it has most likely evolved to do. Not all training methods used in animal psychophysics are so obviously related to the subjects' natural behaviors. If a response selected for convenience can be connected to the stimulus of interest by some sort of training procedure, it might be assumed that the motivational and response system used is not important—that is, that any arbitrary response and motivation may be used to tap the capabilities of any sensory system. However, this may not always be true. Figure 2.6 shows an example in which a fish, the rudd (*Scardinius erythropthalmus*), displays different relative sensitivity to wavelength in food-rewarded discrimination training from that in classical conditioning with shock. The motivational state related to the reinforcer may have more subtle effects as well. For example, pigeons are more likely to attend to lights than tones when working for food, but the reverse is true

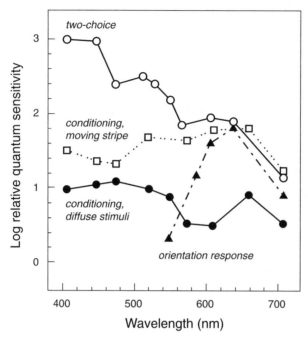

Figure 2.6. Performance of rudd in four tests of wavelength sensitivity. In the two-choice discrimination, the fish had to choose an aperture where a monochromatic light had been added to the background white light; in conditioning, moving stripes or a diffuse stimulus signaled shock; the orientation response consisted of the fish diving to the bottom of the tank when a simulated predator was moved overhead. Redrawn from Muntz (1974) with permission.

when they are avoiding shock (Foree & LoLordo, 1973). This could mean that subtle auditory discriminations are easier to teach to frightened than to hungry pigeons, but subtle visual ones are easier if the bird is hungry rather than frightened. On the other hand, in chapter 5 we will see that hungry animals performing food-rewarded discriminations may categorize social signals in the same way they would be expected to if they were in a social situation rather than "foraging." There may be no general way of predicting how the motivational and response system used in psychophysical experiments will affect the results.

2.3 Some Psychophysical Principles

All sensory systems that have been studied have some basic properties in common (Barlow, 1982). Many of these properties are shared by instruments designed to discover the physical energies detected by animal senses. As we have already seen, the senses are characterized by specificity in the kinds of energies they detect: the visual system is specific for electromagnetic radiation in a certain range of wavelengths, the auditory system for changes in sound pressure, the olfactory system for airborne chemicals. Moreover, most sensory systems are not equally sensitive to everything they can detect. Rather, each system can be characterized electrophysiologically and behaviorally by a tuning curve. The plots of visual sensitivity as a function of wavelength in figure 2.6 are examples.

In addition to quality ("what is it?"), an important feature of stimuli is intensity ("how much is it?"). Brightness, sweetness, and loudness are examples of perceptual intensity continua. An important psychophysical principle that emerges from research on perception of such stimulus dimensions is *Weber's law*, which describes the difference threshold (or *just noticeable difference* between two stimuli, the *JND*) as a function of their magnitude. The JND, the amount that has to be added to a given stimulus in order for a difference in intensity (or size, etc.) to be perceived, is a constant proportion across a wide range of base values. This proportion, the *Weber fraction*, is a function of the particular species and sensory channel. For example, suppose a 10-gram weight has to be increased by .5 grams in order for a person consistently to detect the difference. Weber's law says that if we now ask for the same judgment but start with a 20-gram weight, the difference threshold will be 1 gram, whereas it would be .25 grams if we started with a 5-gram weight. Examples of Weber's Law in animals' timing behavior are presented in chapter 8.

Three other psychophysical principles have important implications for systems in which one animal provides the stimulus for responses by another. First, sensory neurons tend to respond more to physically intense stimuli. Therefore, more intense or reliable behavioral responses can be expected to stimuli that are brighter, louder, or bigger in some other way. This seems so obvious and right as hardly to need stating, but animals need not have been designed this way. One could build, say, a sound meter that gave large readings to quiet sounds, and none at all to loud ones. An animal built that way would react to things far away from it and ignore predators or food items close by. In fact, the opposite is generally the case, and it does make functional sense that animals should react more intensely to things that are larger and/or closer. As we will see in section 2.5, this fact has evidently influenced the evolution of sexual displays and communication systems.

A second general feature of sensory or perceptual systems is a tendency to *habituate* (or show *adaptation*) to prolonged unchanging stimulation. We have seen in the last section how this feature has been put to use to discover what differences among odors hamsters can detect. It has been suggested that the tendency for listeners to habituate explains why some bird species have repertoires of many different songs. Females, it is suggested, will be more stimulated by a constantly changing series of songs than by one song type sung monotonously over and over. This account of repertoire size is controversial, but in some species males that sing more different songs are more successful in obtaining mates (see Catchpole & Slater, 1995)

Finally, in many systems, response to a given stimulus depends on its contrast with the background. A quiet tone is more easily heard in silence

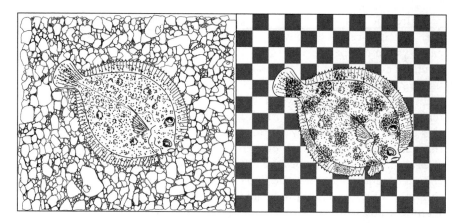

Figure 2.7. Examples of camouflage, showing how a tropical flounder changes its pattern to match the substrate on which it is placed. Even though its eyes are on the top of its head, the flounder must somehow perceive the color and pattern of the substrate. From photographs in Ramachandran et al. (1996) with permission.

than in soft noise. To a person with normal color vision, a red spot looks redder on a green than on an orange background. The tendency of sensory systems to respond more strongly to stimuli that contrast with what surrounds them in time or space appears to have shaped the evolution of animal color patterns, auditory signals, and the like. For example, many animals that are food for other animals resemble the substrate on which they typically rest—that is, they minimize contrast. Such animals sometimes behave so as to enhance their resemblance to their surroundings. For instance, moths that resemble birch bark not only choose birch trees to rest on but also rest so that their stripes are in the same orientation as the black patches on the bark (Pietrewicz & Kamil, 1981; see figure 2.19). Flounders, fish which lie flat on the bottom of the sea, provide one remarkable example of how animals can change their appearance to match the substrate (figure 2.7).

Far from being cryptic, some animals have what would appear to be the maximum possible contrast with their typical backgrounds. Red rain forest frogs and bright yellow-and-black striped caterpillars seem to be advertising their presence to predators. However, many such *aposematically* or warningly colored species are actually not very good meals. They may sting, prickle, taste bad, or otherwise cause their attackers to reject them. In chapter 5 we will see how their bright colors may help predators to learn to avoid attacking them and others like them. Contrast with the background is also important in effective intra-specific communication. The colorful nuptial plumage and loud songs of many male birds testify to this. There are many other examples of how animal signals seem to have evolved in a direction that increases contrast with the background (see section 2.5).

2.4 Signal Detection Theory

2.4.1 Detecting Signals in Noise: Theory

In section 2.3, threshold was mentioned as if it were a definite quantity above which a stimulus is always detected and below which it never is. Even in the best-controlled psychophysical experiment, however, this is not what happens. Observers report detecting a constant stimulus only a proportion of the time. Threshold is calculated as the value detected a fixed proportion of the time. Often 75 or 80% is used. Variation in response to a constant stimulus is thought to be due to inevitable changes in the observer's state, perhaps lapses in attention or spontaneous firing of sensory nerves, and to uncontrollable fluctuations in the stimulus. In addition, observers vary in how conservative or liberal they are about saying "it's there" when they are unsure. Thus in recent times the idea of an observer with an absolute threshold has been replaced by the idea that the stimulus has a distribution of effects. The observer's problem is to detect that *signal* against a fluctuating background with which the signal can be confused (*noise*). An animal's problem outside the laboratory is essentially the same: to detect biologically important signals in an environment filled with unimportant stimuli. For both the psychophysical observer and the animal in the field, a certain proportion of mistakes is inevitable. The problem for both is how to respond so as to keep the cost of mistakes to a minimum. Signal detection theory quantifies this fundamental tradeoff.

Signal detection theory (figure 2.8) was originally developed to guide radar operators in the best way to decide which blobs to treat as planes on a noisy radar screen. It has been used extensively in the analysis of human psychophysical data (Macmillan & Creelman, 1991) but the ideas it embodies can be applied to any difficult discrimination performed by any creature. Signal detection theory conceptualizes the perceiver as faced with the task of discriminating some signal from a noisy background. Signal and noise both have a distribution of effects because they vary randomly and/or because the receiver's state varies from moment to moment. The computations are simplest if these distributions are normal with the same variance, as in figure 2.8. The essential features of these distributions, regardless of their shape, are that (1) they overlap, more so the more similar are signal and noise; and (2) the value along the stimulus input continuum represents the only information about the signal that is available to the perceiver. Thus, many values along the sensory continuum are inherently ambiguous: the perceiver cannot *know* whether they represent the noise alone or the signal. All the perceiver can do is to set a decision criterion, a value along the stimulus dimension above which to say "signal" and below which to say "no signal." Once the criterion is set, any of four things can happen: the observer can say "signal" when there is in fact a signal; these responses are termed *correct detections* or *hits*. Inevitably, however, the observer will sometimes say "signal" when there is no signal; such responses are *false alarms*. Saying "no signal" when the signal is in fact absent

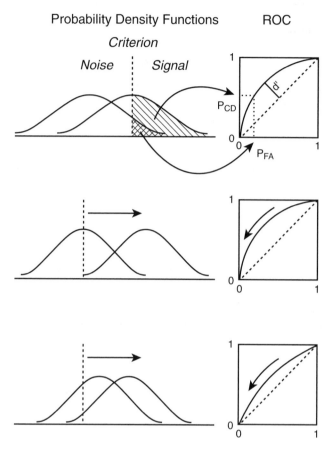

Figure 2.8. The elements of signal detection theory. Hypothetical normal probability distributions of the effect of signal and of noise along some stimulus dimension together with the placement of the criterion for classifying stimuli as "signal" vs. "noise" translate into ROC curves. As the criterion moves from left to right, as shown in the two lower panels, correct detections (CD) and false alarms (FA) move along the ROC curve in the direction of the curved arrows. As signal and noise become less discriminable, in the bottom panel, performance moves onto an ROC curve with a smaller d'. After Wiley (1994) with permission.

is a *correct rejection*; "no signal" when a signal is there is a *miss*. Thus there are two kinds of correct responses, and two kinds of errors (table 2.1). The probability of each is related to the location of the criterion and the overlap between the two distributions as shown in figure 2.8.

With given distributions (i.e., fixed characteristics of the signal, the background, and the sensory system), correct detections and false alarms change together in a way described by the receiver operating characteristic, or ROC curve (figure 2.8). ROC curves are characterized by their distance from the diagonal that bisects the plot of p (correct detection) vs. p (false alarm), rep-

Table 2.1. Classification of responses in a signal detection task

Response	Signal	
	Present	Absent
Yes ("Signal there")	Correct Detection (Hit)	False Alarm
No ("No signal")	Miss	Correct Rejection

resented by the parameter d' ("dee prime"). A perceiver with a lower criterion, saying "signal" more often, has more correct detections but necessarily more false alarms (and concomitantly fewer correct rejections) as well. A conservative observer will make few false alarms but concomitantly fewer correct detections. The optimal location of the criterion depends on the relative payoffs for the four possible outcomes described above. For instance, as the payoff for correct detections rises relative to the penalty for false alarms, the criterion should be lower—that is, the observer should respond more often as if the signal is present. It is possible to move onto a ROC curve further from the diagonal, with higher d' and higher sensitivity, only if the stimuli become more discriminable. This can happen because of changes in the signal, the noise, or the observer's sensory system.

2.4.2 Data

Humans and other species do perform in psychophysical experiments as predicted by signal detection theory. For example, Wright (1972) tested pigeons' ability to discriminate wavelengths in the way depicted in figure 2.9a. The idea behind this two-alternative forced-choice experiment was to ask the bird whether it perceived both halves of a central pecking as the same color or as different colors. It pecked a left side key to report "same" and the right side key to report "different." If the bird reported "same" or "different" correctly, it was occasionally rewarded with food. Feedback was always given by briefly turning on a light above the feeder after a correct response but extinguishing all lights in the test chamber after an incorrect response. The bird's criterion for pecking left vs. right was manipulated by varying the probability of reward for correct left vs. right responses. Thus, on some sessions it was more profitable to report "same" correctly than it was to report "different," and on other sessions the opposite was true. The pattern of results was exactly as predicted by a signal detection analysis. For each pair of wavelengths, plotting the probability of correctly reporting "different" vs the probability of incorrectly reporting "different" traced out a single ROC ve as the payoffs were varied. For example, when the probability of r .orcement for reporting "different" (pecking the right key) was relatively high, the birds behaved as if adopting a liberal criterion, with a relatively high p (correct detection) accompanied by relatively high p (false alarm). As indicated in figure 2.9a, the more different the wavelengths were, the further from the diagonal was the ROC plot (i.e., the higher the d').

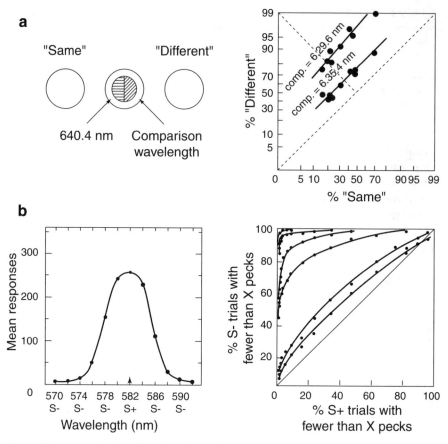

Figure 2.9. a. Method and results of Wright's (1972) experiment on wavelength discrimination in pigeons. The ROC curves described by the results are plotted as straight lines on logarithmic coordinates. b. Pigeons' wavelength generalization gradient and derived ROC curves from D. S. Blough (1967). Redrawn with permission.

Wright's procedure for varying the birds' criterion or bias was very time-consuming because each bird had to complete many trials at each combination of wavelengths and reinforcement probability. In experiments with human observers, the observer can be asked, in effect, to apply several criteria simultaneously. On each trial, the observer is asked not only to make a decision about which stimulus was present but also to report the certainty with which he or she has made that choice. Responses given with high certainty are assumed to have exceeded a more stringent criterion than those given with lower certainty. Animals can also reveal their "certainty" about their choices by how quickly or how much they respond. If the choice keys in a psychophysical experiment are lit for a fixed amount of time on each trial, the number of responses made to the chosen alternative in that time behaves like the human observers' report of subjective certainty. For example, D. S. Blough

(1967) trained pigeons on a difficult wavelength discrimination. A central pecking key lit up for 30-second trials with one of 13 wavelengths. Pecks at 582 nm were reinforced but pecks at any of 12 other wavelengths ranging between 570 and 590 nm were never reinforced. The birds' rates of pecking traced out a typical *generalization gradient*, with more pecking to stimuli closest to the positive or reinforced stimulus (figure 2.9b). One way to interpret these data is to say that the lower the rate, the more certain the bird was that the stimulus was not 582 nm. For each nonreinforced stimulus, the proportion of trials with fewer pecks than each of a series of criteria did trace out a ROC curve, just as this notion suggests, with stimuli further from 580 nm giving ROC curves of higher d' (figure 2.9b).

2.4.3 Implications for the Evolution of Animal Signals

The examples presented so far have been framed in terms of psychophysical experiments, but signal detection theory applies to any decision whether or not to respond to a signal. The "decision" need not involve performing a learned response for reward. The criterion can represent the threshold for attacking a rival or a prey item or displaying sexual behavior. The threshold might be adjusted through evolution or through individual experience. Likewise, evolution and/or experience might adjust the distributions of signal or noise effects by altering some aspect of the signaler or the sensitivity of the receiver. The payoffs may be in terms of energy wasted, injury risked, food items or mating opportunities gained or lost. Elsewhere, we will see how signal detection theory can be applied to egg recognition, memory, predator-prey interactions, alarm calling, and other animal decisions. Here, we consider an example from animal signaling systems (for further discussion and related models see Getty, 1995; Reeve, 1989; Sherman, Reeve, & Pfennig, 1997; Wiley, 1994).

Suppose the perceiver is a female bird in the spring, living in an area inhabited not only by males of her own species but also by males of another species that look and sound very similar to males of her species. Natural selection will have provided her with some mechanism ensuring that she is more likely to mate with a male of her own species than with males of other species—otherwise her species would already be extinct. To make clear the applicability of signal detection theory to this problem, the following discussion refers to the female's *decision* to mate or not to mate. Bear in mind that this means only that the female performs or does not perform some behavior leading to successful copulation and production of young. It does not mean that she decides in the same way a human observer in a psychophysical experiment decides how to classify a light or a tone. The female's decision mechanism might be as simple as the evolutionarily determined threshold for release of a display that in turn releases copulation by the male.

The female's problem can be translated into the language of signal detection theory as shown in figure 2.10. The signal and noise distributions now represent the distributions of sensory effects of some male feature or features

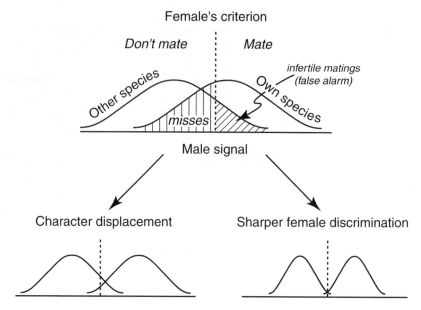

Figure 2.10. Signal detection theory applied to mate choice, showing how false alarms (infertile matings) can be reduced either by males evolving more discriminable characteristics or by females evolving better discrimination.

such as plumage color or song. The "signal" is the distribution from males of the female's own species; "noise" is signals from the other species. The criterion represents the female's threshold for mating with a male, although in fact successful copulation is not usually the result of a single response on the part of either male or female. Correct detections result in viable, fertile offspring, the ultimate evolutionary payoff. False alarms result in wasted reproductive effort. Because many birds lay just one clutch of eggs in a season and may not live long past their first breeding season, incubating eggs and feeding young that do not eventually put their parents' genes into succeeding generations does represent a considerable cost, adding pressure on females to adopt high criteria. On the other hand, too many missed detections of conspecific males means that the breeding season may pass, or all males become mated, before the female mates at all, so some false alarms may be worth the risk.

Two kinds of insights follow from this analysis (Wiley, 1994). First, females are stuck with a certain probability of false alarms and missed detections unless something happens to reduce the overlap of the signal and noise distributions—that is, to move the female onto an ROC curve of higher d'. This can occur in two different ways. On the one hand, the two distributions can stay the same shape while their means move further apart (figure 2.10). This might represent the case of males of the two species in our example evolving more differentiated songs or displays, a phenomenon referred to as *character displacement*. The female's discrimination will also improve if the distributions become narrower while the means remain the same. This might represent the case of changes in the female's sensory system that, for example, sharpen her sound or color discrimination ability. She might also pay more attention to the parts of the signal that best differentiate the species. The distributions of sensory effects from the males could also be sharpened if the males evolve so as to broadcast their signals more effectively. For example they might sing from more exposed perches so their songs are degraded less before reaching the female.

The second insight afforded by a signal detection analysis of mating signals is seen in a situation like that depicted in figure 2.10: where the signals of two species overlap, the males successful in achieving matings will have a more extreme distribution of signal characteristics than the distribution in the population. That is to say, they will have exaggerated signals, and, in fact, a review of the literature suggests that this is often true (Ryan & Keddy-Hector, 1992). As long as the male features that release female sexual behavior are at all similar between species, the typical payoff matrix for this situation means that females should reject the conspecific males most similar to males of the other species. Therefore the average acceptable male will differ more from males of the other species (or from background noise of whatever sort) than the average male of the species. If the male characteristics that elicit sexual responses in females are heritable, over generations this process will cause the average male to differ in a more and more extreme way from males of sympatric species and/or from the environmental background.

Exaggerated features elicit greater than normal responses in systems other than sexual behavior. Egg retrieving in the herring gull provides a classic example. Like many other birds that nest on the ground, an incubating herring gull that sees an egg placed just outside its nest uses its beak and neck to roll the egg into the nest. The Dutch ethologist Baerends and his colleagues (Baerends & Kruijt, 1973) presented gulls with pairs of artificial eggs differing in size, color, or speckling and recorded which one of each pair was chosen. The preferred size and number of speckles were both greater than the values typical of the study population. The preferred values were combined in a single giant, densely speckled egg to create a *supernormal releaser* of retrieval behavior, an egg that the gulls preferred to a normal egg. One might speculate that this kind of response is generated when selection pressure works to sharpen a discrimination in only one direction. For example, presumably it is important not to retrieve a lot of noneggs. The activity wastes energy (gulls' beaks not being very efficient retrieval tools) and extra objects cluttering the nest mean less room for eggs and chicks. The gulls' discrimination in favor of supernormal eggs may indicate that, over evolutionary time, their typical nesting habitat contained more small, plain, dull than large, colorful, speckly noneggs, leading to a bias in favor of retrieving the largest, most speckly object in sight. An analogous phenomenon in discrimination learning is *peak shift* (Arak & Enquist, 1993; Hogan, Kruijt, & Frijlink, 1975; see also chapter 5).

2.5 Perception and Evolution

Some of the most important sensory information animals have to process comes from other animals. Interactions between predators and prey, parents and offspring, males and females both shape and are shaped by the characteristics of sensory systems. Together with the characteristics of the environment that determine the most effective channels for communication, the properties of their conspecifics' and predators' senses create selection pressures on animals' behavior, appearance, and lifestyle. At the same time, unrelenting competition to detect the best habitat, food, and mates constantly selects for animals able to make sharp discriminations.

In recent years, studies in several areas of behavioral ecology have been concerned with the way general properties of sensory systems have apparently shaped the evolution of animal signaling systems. To take a simple example, some signals are most effective if they can be broadcast over long distances. A male bird singing loudly or a male fish sporting bright colors will be heard or seen by more potential mates than will less conspicuous males. In contrast, some sexual signals work best if they can be detected only from close by. For example, some male bluehead wrasse (*Thalassoma bifasciatum*) hold territories and attract females into them for spawning. Once the female enters the territory, the two fish engage in an elaborate sequence of behavior leading up to simultaneous release of eggs and sperm. There are also "sneaky" males who, rather than wasting effort holding territories, search for courting couples and dart in and release their sperm just as the female is ready to release eggs. This creates a pressure against the territorial male making his readiness to mate too conspicuous. When he is advertising his territorial status and attacking other males, his body is bright green and blue, reflecting wavelengths that are transmitted well through seawater. In contrast, when he is about to mate, his colors are muted and a small dark spot appears on his fins (figure 2.11). These signals will be visible to a nearby female but relatively inconspicuous to males waiting to dash into the territory (M. S. Dawkins & Guilford, 1994).

The rest of this section discusses three other kinds of examples of the interrelationship between perception and the evolution of signals. Some of them are relatively new and the conclusions are still disputed. Each example illustrates a different kind of behavioral interaction. The examples also illustrate how experimental and comparative methods, laboratory and field studies, sensory psychology, and behavioral ecology can all be integrated to shed light on the evolution of animal signaling systems.

2.5.1 Predators and Prey

Most animals are subject to two conflicting selection pressures: be as inconspicuous as possible to predators but be as conspicuous as possible to selected conspecifics. One of the best illustrations of how the sensory systems of predators and prey have influenced signals and behavior involves the color patterns

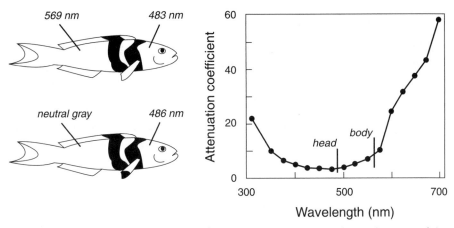

Figure 2.11. Colors of the male bluehead wrasse when chasing other males (upper fish) and when courting females (lower fish) related to the wavelength-attenuating effects of Carribbean sea water. Redrawn from M. S. Dawkins and Guilford (1994) with permission.

and mating behavior of guppies (Endler, 1991). Guppies (*Poecilia reticulata*) are small South American fish that live in clear tropical streams. Mature males sport colored spots and patches that are used in courtship behavior. Male color pattern is heritable, and varies in different populations. In experimental tests of the effectiveness of these patches, females are more likely to mate with males that have larger and brighter blue and orange, red, or yellow patches. Thus female choice creates sexual selection pressure for conspicuous coloration. In contrast, predators create selection pressure for cryptic coloration: duller, smaller, color patches, and patterns that match the background.

The effects of predation have been established in several ways. In the field, guppies may be found in streams that have different numbers and kinds of visually hunting, diurnal predators. Males from populations with more predators are more cryptically colored. Prawns are thought to see poorly in the red end of the spectrum; as might be expected, guppies in areas with heavy predation by prawns have more orange than guppies subject to predators with better red-orange vision. The predicted effects of predation have also been observed directly by establishing guppies from a single genetic background and distribution of color patterns in artificial laboratory streams and exposing them to different numbers and kinds of predators. In guppies' natural habitat in forest streams, the intensity and wavelength of light varies with the time of day (see figure 2.2). Visually hunting predators are most active in the middle of the day, but in both the laboratory and the field, guppies engage in more sexual display early and late in the day—that is, in relatively dim light. Taken all together, the transmission characteristics of tropical streams and the visual capabilities of guppies and their most common predators indicate that, at the times of day when they are most likely to be courting, guppies' colors are relatively more conspicuous to other guppies than to guppy predators (Endler, 1991).

2.5.2 Parents and Offspring

Animals need mechanisms that ensure they direct parental care to their own offspring and not to unrelated young. Such mechanisms need not involve recognition of offspring as such. For example, if a bird establishes a nest and sits on it for two or three weeks before producing a family of helpless nestlings, she must have learned its location. She does not need to learn anything new when the babies hatch in order to be sure of feeding only her own offspring. This is particularly likely to be true if each pair of birds nests separately from nearby conspecifics. Birds that nest in colonies have more of a problem, however. If nests are close together and the young start to move around before parental care ceases, parents and offspring need a way to get together whenever the adult returns home with food. This formulation suggests that mechanisms of offspring recognition may be different in colonial as opposed to solitary nesting species. Beecher and his colleagues (Beecher & Stoddard, 1990) have tested this prediction for closely related species of swallows.

Like many other altricial birds, baby swallows emit begging calls when the parent arrives at the nest. By the age of 17 days, young swallows change from the infantile begging call to a more individually distinctive signature call. Beginning at this age, too, alien young placed in a nest will be rejected. Thus the signature calls appear to be the means by which the parent recognizes his or her own offspring. Playback studies in the field showed that colonial cliff swallows (*Hirundo pyrrhonata*) discriminated quite well between the signature calls of their own and alien young. When two speakers were placed equidistant from the nest, cliff swallows approached the one playing their own nestlings' calls rather than the one playing the calls of other young. In contrast, barn swallows (*H. rustica*), which do not nest in colonies, approached signature calls of their own and another barn swallow's young about equally. Similar evidence indicating that nestling recognition is better developed in colonial species were obtained from another pair of species, the colonial bank swallow (*Riparia riparia*) and the noncolonial rough-winged swallow (*Stelgidopteryx serripennis*).

Colonial species might differ from solitary nesters in at least three ways relevant to offspring recognition: (1) the young of colonial species might give more variable and individually distinctive calls, making it easier for adults to learn them; (2) adults of colonial species might be better able to perceive differences among signature calls; and (3) adults of colonial species might be better able to learn to distinguish among signature calls—that is, there might be adaptations in signals, perception, or learning. In addition, behavior toward alien young could differ between species in the absence of differences in signals or cognition. Of course, all of these mechanisms might contribute to enhanced individual recognition in colonial species. They are not mutually exclusive but complementary.

Analysis of their structure indicates that the calls of the colonial bank swallow chicks are more individually distinctive and carry more information about individual identity than do those of barn swallows. This provides evidence consistent with possibility (1). For evidence relevant to possibilities (2) and (3), Loesche, Stoddard, Higgins and Beecher (1991) turned to tests of discrimination learning in the laboratory. Cliff swallows and barn swallows were trained on discriminations between several pairs each of cliff swallow or barn swallow calls. Consistent with the finding that cliff swallow calls differ more from one another than do barn swallow calls, birds of both species, as well as a starling, an unrelated bird, found the discrimination between cliff swallow calls easier to learn. Moreover, although only a few birds of each species were tested, there was no indication that the cliff swallows learned the discrimination faster. Thus, unlike other cases to be considered later, there is no evidence in this system for specialization in the adults' perceptual or learning abilities. The job is being done by specialization in the signals alone.

2.5.3 Sensory Bias: Frog Calls and Swallow Tails

Darwin (1871) was the first to discuss an evolutionary problem that is still being debated today: why do males of some species have secondary sexual characters so large or conspicuous that they must surely be detrimental to survival? Natural selection would be expected to mitigate against cumbersome antlers and extraordinarily long brightly colored tails, so why do such exaggerated characters persist? Darwin's answer was that such ornaments evolved because females prefer them: the force of sexual selection outweighs the forces of natural selection. In recent years, sexual selection has become the subject of very active experimentation and theorizing (Andersson, 1994; Johnstone, 1995; Krebs & Davies, 1993). A central question in this area is "What is the evolutionary cause of the observed patterns of female choice—in particular, females' preference in many species for exaggerated male characters?" Three general classes of answers have been suggested, and each of them seems to be correct for some situations. The first, now referred to as the "runaway" hypothesis, is essentially Darwin's, buttressed by mathematical modeling. If, at some stage in evolution, females began by chance to prefer an arbitrary male character, under certain conditions females with the preference and males with the character would come to dominate the gene pool, in a runaway positive feedback process. On this scenario, then, the female preference and the male character evolved together, and the preferred male character need not be beneficial to male survival. On the second or "good genes" hypothesis, females prefer male characteristics correlated with large size or good health because they predict the male's ability to provide resources for her and her offspring. It is easy to see how genes for preferring males that are better fathers would spread: by hypothesis, daughters of females with these genes would inherit preference for better fathers, and sons, the genes for being better fathers, and by definition better fathers have more descendents than poor fathers. On this hypothesis, the preferred character might become exaggerated through evolution, but it existed before the female preference evolved.

The currently most-discussed hypothesis about sexual selection is the sensory drive or sensory bias hypothesis (Endler, 1992; Ryan, 1994; Endler & Basolo, in press, review the many different terms and ideas in this area). Male secondary sexual characters could evolve not because of a specifically sexual preference on the part of females but because preexisting features of sensory systems or perceptual preferences make such characters especially stimulating. Of course, sensory bias could get runaway selection started, but the sensory bias theory has been thought to make at least two unique kinds of predictions. First, female sexual preferences can evolve before male characters. Comparative data can be used to examine this possibility. Second, a preference expressed in a sexual context may have a function in another context, such as feeding or predator avoidance. For instance, male lizards of the species *Anolis auratus* start their sexual display with a rapid up and down motion of the head (Fleishman, 1988). Sudden motion attracts attention in many contexts, and for good reason, as it could indicate a live prey item or an approaching predator. The sexual display of the male water mite (*Neumania papillator*) includes waving his appendages in a way that mimics the motion of prey items, and in fact hungry females are more likely than sated ones to repond to displaying males (Proctor, 1992). By implication, in both of these cases female responsiveness evolved first in the nonsexual context and males have been selected to exploit it in the sexual context. Cladistic analysis (see chapter 1) has supported this conclusion for water mites.

The call of the male túngara frog (*Physalaemus pustulosus*) is another mating signal that may have evolved through exploiting the sensory bias of females (Ryan & Rand, 1993). The call contains a whine followed by a number of lower pitched chucks. The whine is necessary and sufficient for mate recognition, but the addition of chucks enhances the attractiveness of the call to females in choice tests in the laboratory. What is interesting about the chucks is that they contain predominantly the frequencies to which the basilar papillae of the female frog's inner ear are most sensitive. This suggests that chucks might be quite stimulating to females generally, even though males of closely related species do not add chucks to their calls, and this proves to be the case. Females of the closely related species *P. coloradorum* respond more to *P. coloradorum* calls with added chucks than to unaltered calls. Thus, they have a preference for calls with chucks, which they normally do not express because males of their species do not chuck. A similar bias is found in other *Physalaemus* species. In principle, phylogenetic analysis based on characters other than male mating calls can answer the question of whether the chucks are recently evolved, as the sensory bias hypothesis suggests. One such analysis (Ryan & Rand, 1993) has supported the sensory bias hypothesis; however, another one (Pomiankowski, 1994; Ryan, 1996; Shaw, 1995) indicates that chucks are an ancestral character that has recently been lost in some species.

Ryan and Rand's work on the frogs' calls is a model research program in the way it combines studies of sensory systems, behavior, and phylogeny in a whole group of related species. However, the continual appearance of new methods for investigating phylogenies can make it difficult to draw firm con-

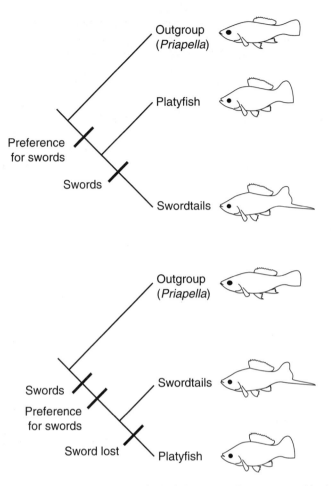

Figure 2.12. Possible alternative swordtail phylogenies. These are simplified, since each branch actually contains numerous species, and within each branch only one or two species have been tested. Adapted from Basolo (1995a) with permission.

clusions in this area (Martins & Hansen, 1996). The difficulties are well illustrated by research on female swordtail fishes' preferences for males with swordlike extensions to their tails (see Ryan & Rand, 1995). By experimentally lengthening or shortening males' swords, Basolo (1990a, 1990b) showed that female swordtails prefer longer swords. Platyfish are a group of swordless species that share a common ancestor with swordtails (figure 2.12). It turns out that, as sensory bias predicts, females of a swordless platyfish species also prefer males with swords. These behavioral data are not disputed, but conclusions about the role of sensory bias in evolution also depend on phylogenetic data. In this case, the question is whether the most recent common ancestor of swordtails and platyfish had a sword or not. The best phylogeny available when Basolo made her discovery (figure 2.12 top) indicates that swordlessness is ancestral, and therefore preference for swords must have evolved before swords. However, a newer phylogeny based more heavily on similarities in DNA (figure 2.12 bottom) seems to indicate that swords were ancestral and have been gained and lost several times within the swordtail-platyfish group (Meyer, Morrissey, & Schartl, 1994). Even newer behavioral data, though, reveals that in a species in the outgroup for this phylogeny—that is, the closest relative of both swordtails and platyfish—females also prefer males with swords (Basolo, 1995b). This indicates that preference for swords predated any evolution of swords. Most likely this tale is not all told yet. Among other things, for most species it is not known what the females actually prefer about males with long swords (see Basolo, 1995a). It may not be a sword per se that is stimulating but larger total size (Ryan, 1994). For instance, male sticklebacks prefer model females that appear larger, regardless of whether they have the shape typical of an egg-bearing female stickleback (Rowland, 1989). Nevertheless, research bearing on the evolution of female swordtails' sexual preferences underlines the general point that ideas about relationships among species are not based on a cut-and-dried body of data and theory. As this changes, so too may ideas about the evolution of cognition and/or the role of cognition in evolution.

The possibility that animals may respond more strongly to stimuli that never occur in nature than to natural stimuli was already discussed in section 2.4.2. The sensory bias hypothesis suggests that this could occur because of the way sensory systems work. Another possibility is that as a system evolves to make particular natural discriminations, strong responses to stimuli that never occur evolve as a by-product. Females often respond best to more extreme characters than those typical of normal males of their species (Ryan & Keddy-Hector, 1992). In the majority of such cases, characters with *more* of some feature than the mean—louder, bigger, brighter—are preferred. The sensory bias and the good genes hypotheses would both predict this: sensory bias because bigger, louder, or brighter is more easily detected or more stimulating; good genes because the bigger, louder, brighter males are probably those in better condition, better able to obtain and hold resources. Preference for mates with symmetrical structures, discussed in box 2.1, is another case in which general principles of perception predict the same sexual preferences as "good genes."

2.6 Perceiving Objects

2.6.1 Features and Objects

Ordinarily, animals react to objects, not isolated features of objects. Red has a different significance for a male stickleback on a rival's belly than on a piece of food. How is perception of individual features related to perception of objects? To discuss the answer to this question, we need a few terms. The first is stimulus *modality*. Vision, hearing, touch, taste, olfaction—the different sensory systems are each sensitive to a certain stimulus modality, or type of physical energy. Within each sensory modality, stimuli have various *dimensions*. For example, the dimensions of visual stimuli include intensity, wavelength, shape, and motion. Discussions of the processing of dimensions within a modality often assume that the perceptual system includes a stimulus *analyzer* for each dimension a species is sensitive to. Paying attention to a specific stimulus dimension is then referred to as switching in the analyzer for that dimension. Objects are defined by particular values of stimulus dimensions such as round and red, the object's *features*.

Much of this and the next section are devoted to what happens in a very simple task known as *visual search* (Schiffrin, 1988; Treisman, 1988). In visual search, as the name implies, the subject searches for something by looking for it, as opposed, for example, to listening or feeling for it. The thing being searched for is referred to as the *target*. It is embedded among *distractors*. Figure 2.13a shows a typical example for a human subject, a target X among distracting Os, and one that might confront a visual granivorous predator, a black seed among white pebbles. No one reading this book would fail to find the X or the seed in figure 2.13a, but suppose the figure had been flashed for a fraction of a second or the distractors were much more similar to the tar-

---

Box 2.1. Symmetrical Is Beautiful

All vertebrates, and many invertebrates and plants too, have bilaterally symmetrical structures. *Fluctuating asymmetry* (FA) refers to the fact that when the sizes of the structures on left and right are compared, a population of organisms generally exhibits a normal distribution of size differences around perfect equality. In structures that exhibit fluctuating asymmetry, the most extreme deviations from perfect symmetry tend to occur in individuals that have developed under relatively unfavorable conditions. Thus FA might reflect the ability of an individual or its parents to locate essential resources— that is, it might be a sign of gene quality. On the "good genes" hypothesis of sexual selection, then, mates with symmetrical structures should be preferred. Male sexual ornaments like long tails or horns tend to have greater FA than other morphological characters like legs or wings, but bigger ornaments may show less FA. This pattern would result from sexual selection for big symmetrical ornaments (Møller & Pomiankowski, 1993a; Watson & Thornhill, 1994).

Ornament symmetry does influence breeding success in a number of species. One well-studied case involves the outermost tail feathers of male swallows (*Hirundo rustica*), known as barn swallows in North America. Møller (1992) independently changed the mean length and symmetry of males' tails by cutting and/or glueing pieces of feather on males in the field. Importantly, such a manipulation decouples the features of a male's tail from other characteristics that may make him attractive or a good father. Females evidently found males with the longest and most symmetrical tails most stimulating, since those males were mated soonest and became fathers of the most fledglings (figure B2.1). Remarkably, preference for males with symmetrical characters can extend to arbitrary features that could not have been sexually selected. Female zebra finches prefer males wearing plastic leg rings arranged symmetrically on

⠀⠀▥➡

Box 2.1. Symmetrical Is Beautiful (*continued*)

both legs—for example, a green one above an orange one on each leg vs. two green rings on one leg and two orange rings on the other (Swaddle, 1996; Swaddle & Cuthill, 1994).

Just as with preference for large or conspicuous ornaments, the issue arises whether preference for symmetry is specifically selected or whether it is the outcome of selection for something else. Two simple neural network models support the latter possibility (Enquist & Arak, 1994; Johnstone, 1994). For instance, a simulated network evolving to prefer (give a large response to) a character such as a tail rather than random patterns showed the largest response to a symmetrical "tail" even though it had not been explicitly trained to do so. Such models can be criticized as too simplistic (Dawkins & Guilford, 1995), but the conclusion they suggest nevertheless seems intuitively plausible.

Humans, too, find symmetry beautiful in the faces of potential mates and in other things (see Grammer & Thornhill, 1994). We find vertical symmetry a very salient, easily detectable attribute of objects, as might be expected of a species that conducts most of its social interactions in the upright position (Corballis & Roldan, 1975). Bees, too, easily classify patterns as symmetrical or not, an ability that could be useful in detecting the most productive flowers to visit (Giurfa, Eichmann, & Menzel, 1996). Studies of the role of symmetry perception in sexual selection and of sexual selection in symmetry perception provide a good example of the rich and wide-ranging implications of integrating models in behavioral ecology with analyses of cognitive mechanisms.

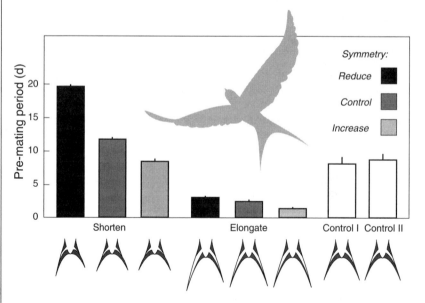

Figure B2.1. Effects of the length and symmetry of male swallows' tails on the number of days before a female mated with them. Tails were shortened by cutting pieces off the male's outer tail feathers or lengthened by glueing pieces on. The two control groups (white bars) either had their tails untouched or had pieces cut off and glued back on. Adapted from Møller (1992) with permission.

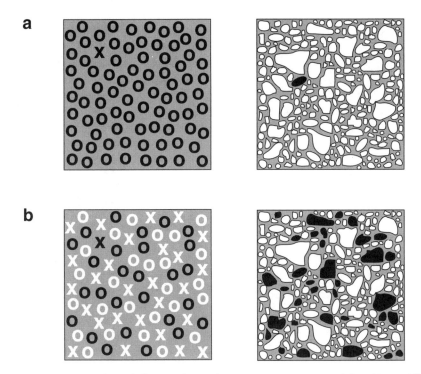

Figure 2.13. Typical stimuli for visual search experiments. a. Targets defined by a difference in one feature (shape or color) "pop out" from the background. b. Conjunctively defined targets, the black X and the black grain, take longer to find. Panels on the right adapted from M. Dawkins (1971a) with permission.

get, say Ys instead of Os surrounding the target X. Now the results would start to be interesting. Under these sorts of conditions, with limited viewing time or high similarity between target and distractors, subjects may make mistakes and/or take longer to find the target.

In figure 2.13a, the target X seems to "pop out" from the background of Os. The same would be true if the target were a yellow X among red Xs or a moving dot among stationary ones. The pop-out effect is evident in data from visual search tasks in the fact that *reaction time* (latency to detect the target) increases only slightly with the number of distractors (figure 2.14). In contrast, when the target is defined by the conjunction of two features, for example a black X or among black Os and white Xs and Os (figure 2.13b), reaction time increases sharply with the number of distractors. One interpretation of this pattern of data is that when target and distractors differ in just one feature, the objects in the display are processed *in parallel*—that is, all at the same time. Hence, the number of items being processed does not influence reaction times when a target is present. When the target is defined by a conjunction of features, the items have to be processed *serially*—that is, one by one. Thus, the more items there are, the longer the reaction time. With

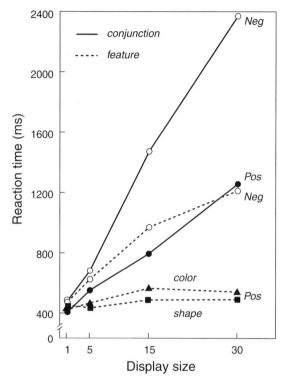

Figure 2.14. Human subjects' latencies to respond correctly in visual search experiments with a target defined by a single feature or by a conjunction of features. On positive trials (Pos) the target was present; it was absent on negative (Neg) trials. Redrawn from Treisman and Gelade (1980) with permission.

conjunctive targets, the times taken to decide "no, the target is not there" support this interpretation. Every item in the display must be mentally inspected in order to decide the target is absent. If the items are being processed serially, it will take twice as long on average to say (correctly) "no target" than to locate the target (figure 2.14). The fact that the functions relating reaction time to number of distractors are straight lines indicates that processing each additional item takes a constant amount of time (Treisman & Gelade, 1980).

2.6.2 Feature Integration Theory

Treisman's (1988) interpretation of results like those just described is that elementary features of objects such as shape, color, and motion are registered automatically and immediately, without needing attention (*preattentively*). Identifying visual objects consisting of a conjunction of features requires that the object's location in space become the focus of attention. As discussed further below, attention is sometimes thought of as a spotlight that sweeps across a scene, taking in one part at a time. Some of the evidence in support of Treisman's *feature integration theory* comes from experiments in which subjects are briefly shown a circular display of colored letters and asked to report the color, the shape, or both the color and shape of the letter in one location. The probability of correctly reporting the conjunction of features is predicted almost perfectly by the probabilities of correctly reporting color and shape separately (Treisman, 1988). This pattern of data is consistent with the notion that the object's features are first processed independently rather than as a unit. In related experiments, identifying a conjunctive target was strongly associated with being able to report its location correctly. Identification was at chance when the location was reported incorrectly, as would be predicted on the theory that objects are perceived as a spatial conjunction of independently processed features.

Although some animals have been tested extensively in visual search tasks, no experiment reported so far has directly compared searches for simple vs. conjunctive targets using exactly the same sorts of features used for human subjects (but see D. S. Blough, 1992). However, another experimental test of feature integration theory known as *texture segregation* has been used with both humans and other animals. The idea behind texture segregation is that a cluster of identical objects is perceived as a distinct object in itself. The examples in figure 2.15 suggest that the distinction between elemental and conjunctive targets is just as evident here as when individual targets are being detected: areas defined by a difference in one element, such as a cluster of white objects among black ones, pop out. Areas defined by a conjunction of elements, such as a cluster of white squares and black circles among white circles and black squares, take time to detect. Data from humans support this conclusion (Treisman & Gelade, 1980). Comparable data from pigeons suggest that the same kind of process governs pigeons' object perception.

In the experiments with pigeons (Cook, 1992a, 1992b; Cook, Cavoto, & Cavoto, 1996), birds were trained to peck at displays on a video monitor that was surrounded by an array of infrared emitters and detectors connected to a computer. This "touch frame" was positioned so that when the bird pecked at the TV screen, its beak broke two infrared beams crossing the screen at right angles. The computer converted information about which beams were broken into a map of the locations pecked and related this to the positions of displays on the screen. The screen was covered with rows of small shapes, with a rectangle about a quarter of the screen's area having different shapes from the rest (figure 2.15). The birds were reinforced with food for pecking five times anywhere on this rectangle; one peck elsewhere caused the screen to go dark and postponed the next trial. The pigeons were trained at first with a relatively small number of different small shapes and colors defining the target rectangle and just a few target positions, but they continued to perform well above chance when novel shapes, colors, and positions were introduced. These data alone suggest that, like humans, the pigeons perceived the cluster of distinctive items as "an object" and that they had learned "peck the object," not "peck the training items." Most important, however, targets defined by a difference in a single feature were consistently detected more accurately

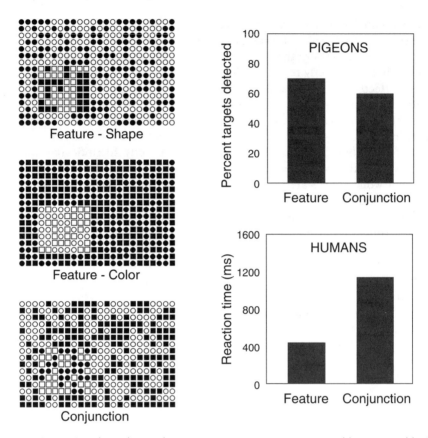

Figure 2.15. Stimuli used to study texture segregation in pigeons and humans and both species' performance with simple and conjunctive targets. Data from Cook (1992a); stimuli reproduced from the same article with permission.

than targets defined by a conjunction of features. Cook (1992b) tested humans with the same displays as the pigeons. The pattern of results was the same, except that whereas the pigeons showed differences mainly in accuracy of detecting the target areas, people showed differences in reaction time (figure 2.15). Nevertheless, these data compellingly indicate that at least this one animal species, evolutionarily and neurologically very different from us, shares the same kind of elemental processing in the early stages of vision (review in Blough & Blough, 1997).

Feature integration can be contrasted with the Gestalt approach to perception, in which perception of the whole is primary and analysis into parts comes later. It also contrasts with the influential approach of J. J. Gibson (1979), which emphasizes the importance of ecologically relevant wholes. For instance, the spatial structure of the environment is immediately evident in the way objects move relative to each other when the observer moves: nearby objects move across the visual field faster than those farther away. The contrast between elemental and holistic approaches pervades theoretical debates about a range of cognitive processes. Fetterman (1996) and D. S. Blough (1992) discuss it in the context of comparative cognition. Feature integration theory assumes a modular organization of perception in that there is a separate module for processing each stimulus dimension. In evolution, modular organization would permit the ability to process additional dimensions to be added onto an initially simple perceptual system. Similarly, in a modular system, the ability to process a feature of particular importance for a given species could be fine-tuned without affecting processing of other features (for a classic discussion of modularity in vision, see Marr, 1982).

2.7 Attention

At any given moment, most of the surrounding is irrelevant for current behavior. For example, as you read this text, you may be drinking a cup of coffee and playing your stereo, but neither the taste of coffee nor the sound of music is relevant for the task at hand. For some species, like the *Bembyx* moth, the problem of selecting what parts of the world to respond to has been solved by the evolution of specialized sensory channels and stimulus coding mechanisms that ensure that only the few things in the world that matter for survival and reproduction can evoke behavior. But such reliable stimulus-response coding limits flexibility and breadth of sensitivity. Worms and moths differ from birds and monkeys in the number and kind of different states of the world they can discriminate (see Staddon, 1983). Animals like birds, monkeys, and human beings, which can perceive a wide range of stimuli in several modalities, need a mechanism for selecting what to respond to from moment to moment. *Attention* is the process that does this selecting. It has been studied extensively in humans (Schiffrin, 1988) using visual search tasks as well as tests of divided attention, in which people are asked to process more than one kind of information at a time. As with object perception, the processes revealed by such experiments seem to be shared by the few other species that have been tested. Indeed, attentional processes may even play a role in allowing some insects to locate food efficiently (Bernays & Wcislo, 1994)

2.7.1 Attention in Visual Search

In experiments like those described in section 2.6, visual search is used as a test of *focused attention*—that is, the subject searches for one thing at a time. The question being investigated is how the distractors in the visual display do just what their name implies—that is, distract the subject from finding the target as rapidly and accurately as possible. When the subject is given just one target to search for, reaction times increase (or accuracy decreases) as the number of distractors (the *display size*) or the similarity of the distractors to the target increases. The data from search for conjunctive targets in figure 2.14 illustrate effects of display size in humans. Figure 2.16 shows data from pigeons illustrating comparable effects of similarity and display size. Notice

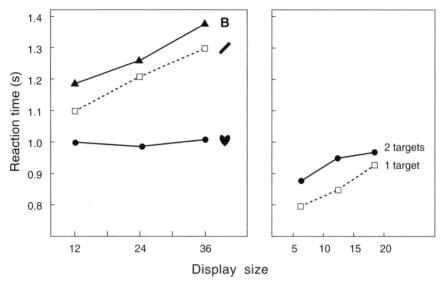

Figure 2.16. Effects of display size and target-distractor similarity (left) or memory set size (right) on visual search in pigeons, as measured by time taken to locate the target. Left panel redrawn from P. M. Blough (1992) with permission; the distractors were standard alphanumeric characters, hence the heart shape was the least similar and "popped out." Right panel, one pigeon's data from P. M. Blough (1989), redrawn with permission.

that with low similarity between target and distractors, display size has almost no effect, just as in the pop-out effect in human subjects.

Figure 2.16 also illustrates the effects of number of possible targets used in a series of trials, the *memory set size*. In human subjects, too, search slows as the number of potential targets increases. Subjects searching for just one sort of target are like specialist foragers, animals that eat only one kind of thing, whereas subjects for which targets are mixed unpredictably are like generalists, foragers that can eat several kinds of prey. Decreased performance with a larger memory set size is a cost of being a generalist. If the targets were food items, the benefit to generalists of being able to eat more of what is encountered might have to be traded off against this cost. However, the detrimental effect of memory set size diminishes with extended practice. That is, search becomes *automatized*, as if attention is automatically drawn to items that have frequently been attended to (Schiffrin, 1988). Very experienced pigeons in the laboratory are also unaffected by changes in memory set size (P. M. Blough, 1984). These findings suggest that generalizing might not have a cost in the wild when animals are foraging on very familiar items.

The effect of memory set size means that a given target is found more quickly or accurately when it is the only one presented over a series of trials than when it is unpredictably mixed with one or more other targets. This effect can also be seen when there are several possible targets and the same one occurs several times in succession. Finding one target of a given type *primes* attention to targets of that type. Priming is thought of as a transitory activation or facilitation of processing of the target's features. Priming can occur in either of two ways: *sequentially*, as just described, or *associatively.* In associative priming, performance is facilitated by presenting a cue that has been associated with the target, either just before or during presentation of the target. For example, in a further part of the study whose results are displayed in figure 2.16, distinctive borders were added to the stimulus displays. Black and white were paired with A and L, respectively; a striped border, paired equally often with A and L, served as an ambiguous cue (D. S. Blough, 1991; P. M. Blough, 1989). Performance with each letter was better when it was cued than otherwise. If each target is paired consistently with a particular distractor, the distractors themselves may also serve as associative priming cues (D. S. Blough, 1993a). Pigeons show both associative and sequential priming. In both humans and pigeons, priming seems not only to facilitate processing of the primed target, but to inhibit processing of unprimed targets. In P. M. Blough's (1989) experiments, performance on occasional test trials in which A appeared when L was cued or vice versa was worse than on trials with the ambiguous cue. Pigeons can also be primed to attend to particular areas of a display (D. S. Blough, 1993b). These data on priming seem to suggest that, if foraging is like visual search for prey scattered on a substrate of distractors, as figure 2.13 was made to suggest, any source of information about the identity of the prey will be used to aid search (D. S. Blough, 1993a). These include what prey have been found recently (sequential priming), where they have been found (priming of locations), and what substrate they were found on (associative priming).

2.7.2 Attention and Foraging: Search Images

By comparing the kinds of insects birds brought to their young with the kinds available in the trees where the birds foraged, Luc Tinbergen (1960) discovered that insects are not preyed on when they first appear in the environment. Instead, a new prey type such as a freshly hatching species of caterpillar will suddenly begin to be taken when its abundance increases. This sudden increase in predation, Tinbergen suggested, reflects the predators adopting a *specific searching image* for that prey type after a few chance encounters. "The birds perform a highly selective seiving operation on the stimuli reaching the retina" (p. 333). Described in this way, adopting a searching image (nowadays *search image*) sounds like an attentional process. Recent experiments have supported this conclusion.

The idea that animals might search selectively, ignoring items that do not match a mental representation of desired prey, is appealing because it agrees so well with introspection. Most people have had the experience of not seeing what is right in front of their noses. Indeed, perhaps the earliest reference to search images in animal behavior is von Uexküll's (1934/1957) description of looking for a familiar earthenware water jug and not seeing the glass one that had replaced it (figure 2.17). Animals, too, von Uexküll suggested, could have

Figure 2.17. Von Uexküll's depiction of his own search image of an earthen water jug and of a frog's search image of a worm. After von Uexküll (1934/1957) with permission.

a mental image of a prey item that enhances their ability to detect matching items (figure 2.17). Although Tinbergen himself was somewhat tentative about the properties of a search image, it has generally been assumed that an animal can have only one search image at a time—that is, predation on one cryptic prey type is temporarily enhanced while detection of other types is inhibited. Crypticity is important because search images presumably are useful only for prey that are difficult to find in the first place. Conspicuous items do not require a search image.

By themselves, Tinbergen's field data can be explained in a number of ways. If the birds he observed were relatively young, they could have been learning that particular insects were suitable as prey or where or how to hunt for them (M. Dawkins, 1971a). Learning the characteristics of novel prey in the first place is probably a kind of perceptual learning (see chapter 4; de Ruiter, 1952; Pietrewicz & Kamil, 1981). It is not the same as selectively attending to a known prey type. To separate these processes, most recent experiments on search images have been done by varying the abundance and/or crypticity of items that are familiar to the animals being tested. For example, Bond (1983; Langley, Riley, Bond, & Goel, 1996) studied pigeons searching for two kinds of grains, black gram and wheat, scattered over multicolored gravel. Because the grains were the same color as some of the gravel, they were more difficult for the birds to detect on this background than on a plain gray one. After the birds were familiar with feeding on these grains on the gravel backgrounds, the relative proportions of black gram and wheat were varied randomly between 100% black gram and 100% wheat. The birds behaved consistently with Tinbergen's observations, taking proportionately less of the minority type rather than matching the proportion taken to the proportion available (see figure 2.18). However, pigeons do match the propor-

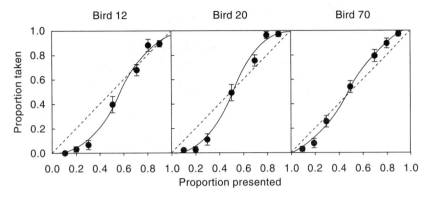

Figure 2.18. Proportion of cryptic grains of one type taken by each of three pigeons as a function of its proportion in a mixture of two types of cryptic grains in the study by Bond (1983). Redrawn with permission.

tion taken to the proportion available when the prey items are conspicuous, showing that crypticity is important, not just variations in relative proportion (Langley et al., 1996).

One way to find more prey that are difficult to see is to search more slowly, spending longer scanning each section of the substrate (Gendron & Staddon, 1983; Guilford & Dawkins, 1987). For each degree of crypticity, there is a search rate that optimally balances the potential benefit of searching more quickly and thereby encountering more prey against the cost of missing cryptic items by going too fast (Gendron & Staddon, 1983)—that is, there is a tradeoff between speed and accuracy. According to this *search rate hypothesis*, a predator searching slowly should detect all equally cryptic prey equally well. In contrast, an animal with a search image should take one type and ignore the other, even if both types are equally cryptic. The data in figure 2.18 are consistent with Bond's birds having a search image. The two grains must have been equally cryptic because when equal numbers were presented (proportion presented = 50%), equal numbers were taken. The search rate hypothesis predicts that the proportion taken should equal the proportion presented under all conditions, but this is not what happened. Disproportionate predation on the more abundant type seems to imply that the birds were using a search image for the more frequently encountered grain.

Allowing an animal to search freely for prey items has some drawbacks as an experimental technique. The animal, rather than the experimenter, controls the rate and sequence of encounters, and the relative proportion of different items changes as the food depletes. To test the effect of recent experience on choice or detectability of prey, it is necessary to present a standard test after differing experiences (see chapter 3). One way to do this is to present prey items one at a time. For example, Pietrewicz and Kamil (1981) tested blue jays (*Cyanocitta cristatta*) in an operant task in which they pecked at slides showing two species of moths (blue jays' natural prey items) resting against tree trunks on which they were relatively cryptic. The birds were rewarded with mealworms for indicating correctly whether or not a moth was present on each slide. The critical data came from comparing performance in trials following runs of moths of the same type with performance in mixed trials with both species (figure 2.19). Performance improved within runs as compared to mixed trials. Notably, the birds' accuracy at detecting the absence of a moth improved as well as their accuracy at detecting the presence of a moth, consistent with the notion that attention enhances detection of attended features and inhibits detection of nonattended features.

These data appear to show that the bluejays had a search image for the moth species they had encountered most recently. Because the moths were depicted as they would appear in nature, one species on birch tree trunks and the other on oak trunks, the situation was like that in studies of associative priming. However, the effect of runs of item evident in figure 2.19 means that sequential priming was also occurring, over and above any associative priming. In the kind of situation studied by Bond, with several kinds of prey items on the same substrate, a search image is presumably invoked as a result of finding several items of the same type in succession. This kind of situation has been analyzed in two series of experiments in which pigeons searched for grains among gravel (Langley, 1996; Langley et al., 1996; Reid & Shettleworth, 1992). In each case, free search and controlled presentations of single grains have been combined in a revealing way.

Pamela Reid (Reid & Shettleworth, 1992) used wheat dyed yellow, green, or brown on a background of glued-down aquarium gravel. The gravel had many green and brown stones but few yellow ones. An experiment like Bond's with the dyed wheat gave results similar to those in figure 2.18 and established that brown and green were equally cryptic while yellow grains were highly conspicuous to the pigeons. To control the birds' experience, Reid used the apparatus shown in figure 2.20. Small plaques of gravel, each holding one or two grains, were presented one at a time, and the birds were allowed a single peck at each one. In a run of green or brown after a run of conspicuous yellow grains, the birds' accuracy was relatively low and gradually increased, consistent with their forming a search image for the new cryptic type, just as when they searched freely for grains. However, when the birds were switched from a run of one cryptic type to a run of the other, they performed just as well as if they had a single cryptic type all along (figure 2.20). This seems to mean that although the birds have to form a search image for cryptic grain, it is not specific to the grain's color. However, when Reid's pigeons had a choice between brown or green, the two cryptic types, after a run of one of them, they tended to choose the type they had just been having. This was not just a general preference for what they had been eating most recently, because the effect depended on the grains being cryptic. Thus the "search image" seems to include information about the grain's color.

The birds in these experiments are clearly engaged in visual search, so it should not be surprising if the notions about feature detection and priming in the last section explain what is going on. Easy detection of the conspicuous

Correct Detections

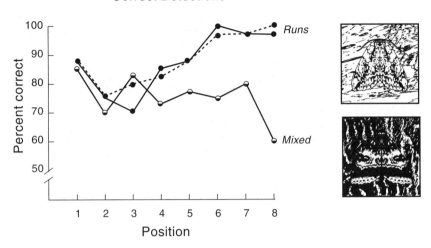

Correct Rejections

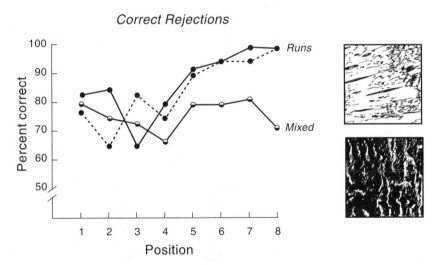

Figure 2.19. Performance of blue jays reinforced for reporting the presence (top panel) or absence (lower panel) of moths in slide images like those on the right in runs of the same moth species or trials with a mixture of two species. Adapted from Pietrewicz and Kamil (1981) with permission.

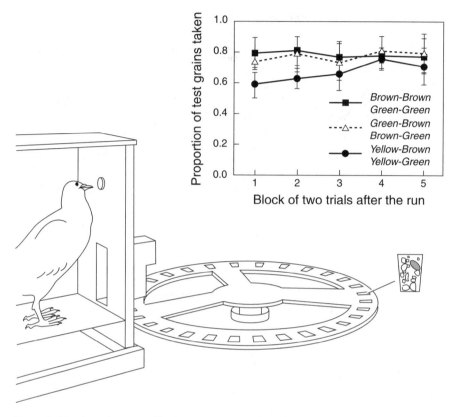

Figure 2.20. Search image effects in pigeons searching for cryptic brown or green or conspicuous yellow grains. Data from a test run of 10 grains after a run of the same or a different color, as indicated. Adapted from Reid and Shettleworth (1992) with permission.

yellow grains is an instance of the pop-out effect because the target (the grain) differs from the distractors (the bits of gravel) in a single feature (color). The cryptic grains are difficult to detect because they share the salient feature of color with the distractors and can be distinguished from distractors only by a conjunction of features like shape and texture. Because the cryptic items were all grains of wheat, priming with grains dyed one color might be expected to enhance detection of other grains with the same shape, size, and texture. The effect on choice shows that the specific color was also primed to some extent. Priming occurs even if the priming grains are conspicuous, but it is detected only in a test with cryptic grains (Langley et al., 1996). Thus, contrary to the depictions in figure 2.17, the "search image" is not a whole image of the prey item. As suggested by feature integration theory, it may be a collection of independently primed features of the prey. Thus, when, unlike the case in Reid's experiments, two cryptic items do not share the features allowing them to be detected against their background, the search image/priming effect should be truly specific, with enhanced detection of one item accompanied by reduced detection of the other. This was likely true in Pietrewicz and Kamil's experiments, since they had different backgrounds for their two cryptic items (see also Plaisted & Mackintosh, 1995).

In the experiments discussed so far, items in runs were presented with the same inter-item interval as items in random mixtures. This means that, for instance, two green grains were separated by twice as long on average in mixed trials as in green-only trials. Plaisted (1997) tested whether this difference in presentation rate can by itself produce differences in discrimination accuracy. She studied pigeons detecting two small black-and-white patterns against black-and-white checkered backgrounds on a computer screen. When items in runs were presented at a rate that matched the rate at which items of a single type occurred in mixed trials, accuracy was no greater than in the matched mixed trials. This result means that, at least with the type of stimuli used in these experiments, items do not interfere with one another in mixed sessions. Plaisted (1997) therefore proposes that search images reflect a short-lived priming of independent memory traces for recent items rather than priming of attention to particular item features. It remains to be seen whether this proposal can account completely for the results of experiments using different types of items, such as those discussed next.

In Langley's (1996) experiments, pigeons saw computer images of two patches of multicolored gravel, one of which had a bean or a grain of wheat on it. They were reinforced for pecking at the bean or the wheat. Here, detection of one cryptic type was clearly inhibited by priming with another cryptic type (figure 2.21). A unique feature of Langley's work was that she manipulated features of the imaged grains to find out which ones were part of the "search image." For instance, a gray test bean might be presented after a run of normal black beans or a rounded grain of wheat after a run of normal oval wheat grains. For beans, both color and shape were important (figure 2.21), whereas for wheat color was more important than shape. Computer manipulation of images is a powerful technique that will likely be used more often in future investigations of visual search for cryptic prey (Plaisted & Mackintosh, 1995, is another example). Predators and prey are engaged in an arms race, with the predator's cognitive mechanisms pitted against the prey's ability to evade detection. Details of the way detection is primed have implications for the evolution of prey species. For example since, as Tinbergen (1960) hypothesized, search image effects are short lived (Langley, 1996; Plaisted & Mackintosh, 1995; Plaisted, 1997), cryptic prey of a single species should spread themselves out in the environment to reduce the frequency with which predators are exposed to their features. *Polymorphism*—that is, a tendency for different individuals of the same species to have markedly different colors or patterns, would have the same effect (Croze, 1970).

2.7.3 Divided Attention

In tests of *divided attention*, in contrast to tests of focused attention, subjects are instructed to report on two or more sources of information at once. The

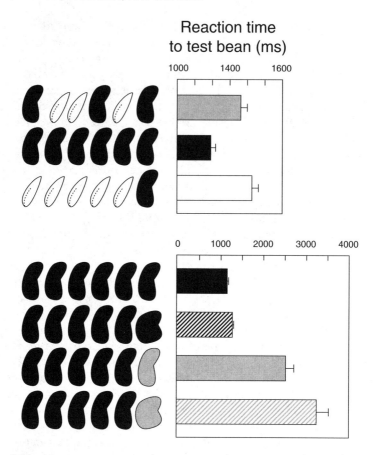

Figure 2.21. Mean reaction times of pigeons searching computer displays for images of wheat grains or beans (top panel) or beans with altered color and/or shape (lower panel). Data redrawn from Langley (1996) with permission.

classic illustration of how hard it is for people to divide attention is the situation at a cocktail party: many conversations are going on simultaneously, but it is very difficult to follow more than one of them at a time. In this case several sources of information compete for attention in the same modality—that is, audition. Attention may also have to be divided between channels within the same modality, as when different information is fed to each ear through headphones, or between modalities, as when reading while listening to the radio. In general, performance on a given task falls when attention must be shared between it and another task, but, just as in focused attention, this effect may diminish as practice leads to automatization (Schiffrin, 1988). The difficulty of dividing or sharing attention is generally interpreted as a limitation on information-processing capacity. Hence, the effect diminishes with automatization because well-learned tasks demand fewer processing resources. The detrimental effect of attention sharing may be asymmetrical—

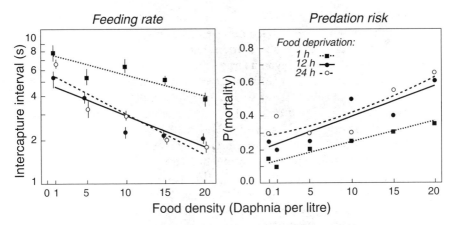

Figure 2.22. Effects of guppies' feeding rate (the inverse of the interval between prey captures, left panel) on predation risk, the number of guppies caught by a predator. Redrawn from Godin and Smith (1988) with permission.

that is, one modality or feature may dominate. In humans, *visual dominance* is the rule (Posner & Nissen, 1976).

Any animal that can be prey for other animals must be ever attentive to the possible approach of a predator. A forager cannot wait until it is satiated to check for predators but must continuously divide attention between foraging and vigilance. For instance, members of a flock of starlings walking across a field probing the ground for leatherjackets raise their heads between pecks and scan the sky and the bushes for predators. The smaller the flock, the more time each individual spends scanning (review in Elgar, 1989; Powell, 1974). More demanding foraging tasks leave less time for vigilance. For example, when blackbirds are foraging on cryptic baits they take longer between scans and spend a smaller proportion of the time scanning than when they are feeding on conspicuous baits (Lawrence, 1984). The optimal tradeoff between feeding and vigilance obviously depends on such things as the likelihood of attack and the animal's hunger level. Behavior tends to reflect this tradeoff. For example, sticklebacks recently exposed to a model predator, a kingfisher flying overhead, feed more slowly than fish not so exposed, suggesting that the frightened fish are devoting more time to vigilance (Milinski & Heller, 1978). This conclusion is supported by evidence that stickleback feeding slowly detect overhead predators more quickly than fish feeding fast (Milinski, 1984). The most direct evidence for a tradeoff between feeding rate and risk of predation comes from an experiment in which guppies feeding on water fleas (*Daphnia*) were exposed to predation by a cichlid fish (figure 2.22; Godin & Smith, 1988). The amount of attention devoted to foraging, as reflected in the interval between prey captures, was manipulated by varying both the density of *Daphnia* and the guppies' hunger level. The faster the guppies were feeding (i.e., at shorter intercapture intervals in the figure), the more likely one was to be captured by the cichlid.

The *confusion effect* may have been one reason why the guppies confronted with larger numbers of prey were more easily captured by the cichild. The confusion effect refers to the observation that many species of predators have more difficulty capturing prey in a large school, swarm, or flock of similar individuals than single prey or individuals in a small group (Krakauer, 1995; Miller, 1922). The probability of an attack ending in prey capture once it has been initiated can decline dramatically with increases in the number of individuals in the group being attacked (Landeau & Terborgh, 1986; review in Magurran, 1990). However, because prey are encountered more often when they are aggregated, feeding rate may still be higher with aggregated than dispersed prey, as illustrated in figure 2.22. Interestingly, sticklebacks that are not hungry choose to feed on sparser prey aggregations than do hungry sticklebacks. This suggests that overcoming the confusion effect may be aversive, but that hunger can overcome the fishes' aversion. Thus motivational interactions appear to reflect the evolutionary tradeoff between the benefits of foraging and the costs of vigilance (Dukas & Clark, 1995 for more on the cost of vigilance; Milinski, 1984).

The confusion effect has generally (cf. Krakauer, 1995) been interpreted as caused by the predator's dividing its attention among the prey rather than focusing on one until capturing it. The individual in a school of identical conspecifics is the limiting case of a cryptic prey item because it is identical to the "background" of surrounding individuals. On this view it is not surprising that odd individuals or stragglers in a group tend to be the ones captured. Just as in visual search (e.g., D. S. Blough, 1979), the larger the group, the more detectable an odd individual seems to be (Milinski, 1990). Notice that the predator confronted with a dense school of prey is assumed to be dividing attention among two or more spatial locations, perhaps because the motion it perceives at each one automatically attracts attention. Intuitively, if attention is like a spotlight, it may be harder to track just one item if several of them are within the "spotlight." There has been little or no research on humans' abilities to localize a single target within different sizes and densities of "schools" of identical distractors (A. S. Sekuler & P. J. Bennett, personal communication, 1996), and it could be instructive to see what people do, how contemporary detailed theories of attention account for it, and whether the same mechanisms are at work in other species.

The evolutionary determinants of group living and group size are important topics in behavioral ecology (chapter 10). The material in this section suggests that the difficulty of effectively dividing attention confers at least two benefits of living in groups. One is that each individual prey animal forming a group does not have to take so much attention away from foraging for vigilance because others can warn it of approaching predators. The other is that by being in a group of similar-looking individuals the potential prey animal benefits from the ability of the swarm to confuse a predator. The confusion effect may account for several features of swarming or schooling species, such as the fact that they tend not to show sexual dimorphism (i.e., males and females look the same), that they crowd together more when threatened, and that mixed species groups tend either to consist of species that look similar or to break up into same-species groups in the presence of a predator (Landeau & Terborgh, 1986; Tegeder & Krause, 1995).

2.8 Summary

Many universals in perception like those reviewed in sections 2.3 and 2.4 can be understood in the view that the principles of perception reflect the organization of the physical world (Shepard, 1994). Paradoxically, some of the best support for such an adaptationist view of perception comes from evidence that general mechanisms have been tweaked by evolution in an adaptive way for each species. To begin with, species differ dramatically in the sensory channels they use and in the patterns of sensitivity of those channels. Differences in sensory systems among species can be related to differences in their habitat and lifestyle. Nevertheless, all sensory systems that have been studied share some features, such as greater response to more intense stimuli, sensitivity to contrast, Weber's law, and a tendency to habituate.

Behavioral methods for discovering what animals perceive include testing natural behavior to the stimuli of interest and testing learned behavior using the methods of animal psychophysics. Signal detection theory is a general model of the discrimination of signals from background noise that can be applied to data from psychophysical experiments with any species. It can also be applied to any situation where an animal has to make a difficult discrimination, and it has implications for the evolution of animal signals. In animal signaling systems, one animal provides a signal to which another animal, of the same or a different species, responds. Perception and the evolution of signals are, therefore, inextricably linked. Several issues in behavioral ecology cannot be resolved without considering the perceptual systems of the species involved.

To understand how objects are perceived we have to go beyond sensitivities to individual stimulus modalities to ask how features are combined. One influential theory states that objects are perceived as the sum of individual primary features, such as color and shape, that occur at the same time and place. This feature integration theory is supported primarily by the performance of humans in visual search tasks, but some similar data have been reported from other species. To understand how behavior is controlled selectively by only some parts of the environment at any given time, it is necessary to understand the process of attention. Characteristics of attention such as its susceptibility to priming have also been revealed by visual search tasks in humans and other animals. The apparent ability of foragers to form a search image, enabling them better to detect cryptic prey, may be accounted for by priming of attention to the features of the prey that best distinguish it from the background. Dividing attention between two or more tasks causes performance on each one to fall. The effects of divided attention can be seen in the tradeoff between foraging and vigilance and in the confusion effect, both of which create a selection pressure for animals to live in groups.

The story of research on search images is a good example of how observations in the field can suggest that animals are using a certain kind of cognitive mechanism that can then be analyzed in the laboratory. Attempts to do so have included a whole range of tests from the "naturalistic" to the "artificial." Tests in which animals searched freely for familiar prey with controlled characteristics (e.g., Bond, 1983; M. Dawkins, 1971a) showed that disproportionate predation on more common items and relative neglect of less common ones can be observed in the laboratory. Studies with items presented in an even more controlled way (M. Dawkins, 1971b; Langley et al., 1996; Pietrewicz & Kamil, 1981; Reid & Shettleworth, 1992) bridge the gap between studies of search image and those of visual search for abitrary targets like letters and shapes (e.g., P. M. Blough, 1992; Plaisted & Mackintosh, 1995). While the results indicate that short-lived priming of feature detection is likely responsible for effects originally attributed to activation of a complete representation or image of a prey item, they do not mean that attentional priming is the only mechanism responsible for observations like Tinbergen's (1960). When animals first encounter novel prey items, they must learn to recognize them as prey and learn where to find them and how to capture and handle them, among other things. Each of these processes can be isolated and analyzed experimentally, as we will see in the next two chapters.

Further Reading

Dusenbery's (1992) *Sensory Ecology* is a comprehensive overview of the principles of information transmission, emphasizing physical principles. Lythgoe's (1979) *The Ecology of Vision* is a rich source of information about adaptations in animal visual systems. Barlow and Mollon (1982) is a useful general introduction to sensory systems, emphasizing mammals. A brief overview of methods in animal psychophysics is provided by Blough and Blough (1977). The two volumes of *Comparative Perception* (Berkley & Stebbins, 1990) survey more recent work on a wide range of systems, mainly in birds and mammals, and Moss and Shettleworth (1996) contains several examples integrating neural and behavioral investigations of ethologically meaningful perceptual mechanisms.

The chapters in Halliday and Slater (1983) are a good general introduction to animal communication, including sensory specializations. Krebs and Davies (1993) can be consulted for more up-to-date treatment of the evolution of communication systems, and Hauser (1996) provides a thorough review and discussion of most of the issues covered here. Noteworthy reviews of issues in this area are those by Guilford and Dawkins (1991), Endler (1992), and Ryan (1994). Wiley (1994) is an excellent introduction to signal detection theory with an analysis of its implications for issues in animal communication. A widely praised comprehensive review of sexual selection is the book by Andersson (1994).

Treisman & Gelade's (1980) classic discussion of feature integration theory is highly recommended. Treisman (1988) reviews more recent developments. Schiffrin's (1988) chapter is a very thorough review of attention. Blough and Blough (1997) is a thorough, up-to-date review of research on form perception and attention in pigeons. Guilford and Dawkins (1987) is a good review of the early work on search images. The confusion effect and experiments on the tradeoff between foraging and vigilance are reviewed by Milinski (1990).

3

Learning

A Framework and Its Application to Pavlovian Conditioning

A snail crawls along a leaf. A sudden breeze shakes the leaf, and the snail withdraws into its shell. A few seconds later the snail is out again. Another gust sends it back, but this time the snail is almost immediately on its way.

A hen and her chicks move slowly around the farmyard, scratching and pecking. They come upon a corncob bright with yellow kernels. The hen calls, and the chicks gather around the corn, pecking with the hen. A fuzzy black and orange caterpillar crawls across the hen's path. She fixates on it briefly, shakes her head, and walks away. A sharp-eyed chick gives the caterpillar a forceful peck, then wipes his bill vigorously on the ground.

On a spring morning in England, a male great tit flies from tree to tree, pausing to sing at the boundaries of his territory. Although he can hear other males singing nearby, he does not pause in his patrolling until here, in the oak, he hears a male who was not there yesterday. He lowers the black feathers on the top of his head and flies toward the strange male, prepared for a fight.

Sitting at dinner one winter evening, I hear a clatter at the back door. A raccoon has just tipped over the garbage can again—rearing up, pulling at the edge, and jumping neatly away as it falls.

None of these animals could behave as they do without the ability to learn. But their behavior seems to represent a number of different kinds of learning. What does the snail's learning that the rhythmically shaking leaf is not a sign of danger have in common with the hen's recognizing the noxious caterpillar or the racoon's finding the garbage can night after night? What process is responsible for the chicks' following their mother and not another hen on the other side of the barnyard? Does it have anything in common with the way the great tit learns to recognize his neighbors' songs? What does either of these processes have in common with the process by which the great tit comes to sing his song in the first place? What makes the snail's ability to reduce its reaction to harmless shaking seem to represent one kind of learning and the chicks' ability to identify the hen another?

This chapter outlines a framework for answering these and other questions about learning. We begin with a brief review of the history of research on learning and then consider a general way of thinking about learning and some ideas about its evolution. The longest part of the chapter discusses associative learning, primarily Pavlovian conditioning. Armed with the general framework and some facts about associative learning, we will be better able to analyze other examples of learning in future chapters. We will also be equipped to assess claims in chapters 10 through 12 that some animals sometimes behave in ways that cannot be the products of associative learning but rather require self-consciousness, a theory of mind, or the like.

3.1 General Processes and Adaptive Specializations

3.1.1 "Constraints on Learning"

Experimental studies of learning were stimulated by Darwin's (1859) claim that animal minds should share properties with human minds. As studies of learning came to focus more and more on simple associative processes (Boakes, 1984; Jenkins, 1979), the possibility that there could be diverse kinds of learning within each individual or in different species tended to be overlooked. The result was an approach that has come to be known as general process learning theory (Seligman, 1970), an attempt to account for all learning with the same set of principles. These were principles of associative learning, as studied in instrumental (operant) and Pavlovian (classical) conditioning. General process learning theory had its heyday in the 1940s and '50s. Although there were a few dissenters (e.g., Tolman, 1949), even now most texts on learning in animals devote the majority of their pages to associative learning, with perhaps an introductory chapter on habituation and sensitization and a concluding mention of "special" learning processes like imprinting and imitation.

Relatively recently, however, there have been a number of stimuli to considering a wider range of kinds and aspects of learning. In the mid-1960s, psychologists discovered several puzzling phenomena that seemed to be evidence of "constraints on learning," cases in which the supposedly general principles of conditioning ought to apply but do not seem to (Rozin & Kalat, 1971; Seligman, 1970; Shettleworth, 1972). The most important examples of "constraints" were conditioned taste aversion, or poison avoidance learning (box 3.1), and autoshaping. In autoshaping (Brown & Jenkins, 1968), pigeons are placed in an operant chamber and a disk on the wall (the pecking key) is

Box 3.1. Flavor Aversion Learning

When rats (and many other vertebrates) sample a flavor and become ill later on, they learn to avoid consuming that flavor. As first described by John Garcia and his colleagues in 1966, flavor aversion learning has two remarkable properties. First, it takes place even with delays of hours between sampling the flavor (the CS in this Pavlovian paradigm) and becoming ill (the US) (Garcia, Ervin, & Koelling, 1966). Second, in rats, learning with illness as a US is specific to flavors. Garcia and Koelling (1966) had rats drink from a tube of flavored solution and also exposed them to a noise and a light each time they licked ("bright noisy tasty water"). Some of the rats were made ill after drinking, whereas some were shocked through the feet while they drank. When tested with the light plus the noise or the flavor alone after conditioning, the poisoned rats avoided drinking the "tasty water" while the rats that had been shocked avoided drinking the "bright noisy water." Figure B3.1 displays data from a later experiment with this basic design but with the mode of presentation of the various CSs and USs better controlled than in the original experiment (Domjan & Wilson, 1972).

When they were first reported, these findings attracted tremendous attention because long-delay learning and CS-US specificity seemed to contradict then-current assumptions about the generality of the laws of learning. Some investigators rushed to test hypotheses that various uninteresting "general process" factors might have been responsible, while others were equally quick to claim far-reaching implications for them (Domjan, 1983). As discussed later in this chapter, the idea that learning might

➧

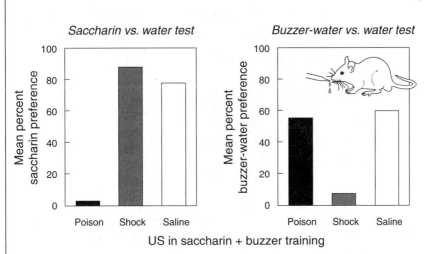

Figure B3.1. Test performance of three groups of rats that had experienced saccharin-flavored water infused into their mouths while hearing the sound of a buzzer and had then been shocked, injected with lithium chloride to produce illness, or given a control saline injection. In the test rats could drink plain water and either saccharin (left panel) or water in a bottle that produced a buzzing sound when licked. Conditioning is evident in reduced preference relative to controls. Redrawn from Domjan and Wilson (1972) with permission.

Box 3.1. Flavor Aversion Learning (*continued*)

---

be especially fast with certain functionally appropriate combinations of events is now generally accepted. However, it is still controversial whether the change in behavior that occurs when a flavor is followed many hours later by poison actually represents associative learning. Although the overall form of the function relating performance to the delay between CS and US is the same in flavor aversion learning as in other conditioning preparations (see figure 3.11), the aversions that develop with delays of hours may represent a nonassociative effect, namely reduced habituation of neophobia (i.e., avoidance of novel flavors) brought about by the poisoning (DeCola & Fanselow, 1995).

---

repeatedly lit for a few seconds and followed by presentations of food. There is no requirement for the pigeon to peck the key, but neverthless pecking reliably develops and persists. This finding seemed related to the Brelands' (Breland & Breland, 1961) reports that animals being reinforced with food engaged in species-specific food-related behaviors that were counterproductive in the experimental situation. For instance, a racoon rewarded for depositing coins in a bank began to delay reinforcement by "washing" and rubbing the coins together in its paws. Attention was also drawn to the difficulty of training rats to perform anything other than defensive behaviors in avoidance experiments with shock (Bolles, 1970). To such observations of constraints on what animals could learn (or at least, do) in laboratory paradigms was added information about song learning, imprinting, and other "unusual" examples of learning observed by ethologists.

Around 1970 a small flood of articles appeared on the theme that general process theory had overlooked the biological aspects of learning (Bolles, 1970; Garcia, McGowan, & Green, 1972; Rozin & Kalat, 1971; Seligman, 1970; Shettleworth, 1972). Animals had learning mechanisms adaptively specialized for solving problems they face in nature. The narrow psychological approach to learning had overlooked these, but the newly discovered phenomena could be understood by thinking about the functions that learning had evolved to serve. However, despite proclamations that a revolution in the study of learning was on its way, in the ensuing years the original candidates for "biological constraints" and "adaptive specializations" were absorbed into a liberalized general theory of associative learning (Domjan, 1983). At the same time, by not formulating a clear research program with testable predictions, proponents of the "biological constraints" approach failed to stimulate research into other, related, phenomena that might have provided better evidence for adaptively specialized learning processes (Domjan & Galef, 1983). The term "constraints" in itself seems to assume a general process that is constrained in particular species and situations. However, consistent with the viewpoint presented in chapters 1 and 2, it is more appropriate to think in terms of evolved predispositions than in terms of constraints (Hinde & Stevenson-Hinde, 1973).

3.1.2 "Constraints," Modularity, and Other Areas of Psychology

At about the same time as these views about learning in animals were starting to be expressed, similar ideas were arising about cognition in humans. Some cognitive psychologists, most notably Neisser (1978), were discontented with a science of the human mind built almost exclusively on laboratory studies using such "unnatural" materials as nonsense syllables and lists of words. They advocated a more "ecologically valid" approach. Experimenters began to study peoples' memory for events in their own personal past, material learned at school, or events of public importance. Whether such research adds new theoretical insights into cognition is debatable (Banaji & Crowder, 1989; Bruce, 1985; Loftus, 1991).

The ecological approach to perception was better developed. As we saw in chapter 2, perceptual systems have evolved for responding to ecologically relevant stimuli. Some psychologists have argued that laboratory studies with simplified, abstracted stimuli fail to capture important functions of the system as a whole (Gibson, 1966; Shepard, 1984, 1994). The structure of the social environment should also be reflected in the nature of cognitive processing, a theme emphasized by evolutionary psychologists (cf. Barkow, Cosmides, & Tooby, 1992). Just as general process learning theory has dominated research on the animal mind, they argue, a model of human cognition as a single, general-purpose mechanism, the Standard Social Science Model (Cosmides & Tooby, 1992), has unduly dominated research on the human mind.

The idea that there may be a number of different, adaptively specialized, kinds of learning or cognition is related to two other ideas in the study of human cognition: intelligence is modular (Fodor, 1983), and memory consists of more than one system (Sherry & Schacter, 1987; Tulving, 1985). A module, in Fodor's sense, is an informationally encapsulated perceptual system. This means that it acts on a restricted kind of input unconsciously but in an apparently intelligent way. For example, visual perception includes a module that makes inferences about relative sizes and distances of objects. It is encapsulated because its operation is impervious to all but a specific kind of information. For example, measuring the lines in the Muller-Lyer illusion (figure 3.1) and discovering that they are equal does not prevent one's perceiving them as different lengths. The module that unconsciously perceives relative size is impervious to the "higher level" information obtained from measurement. The "intelligent" inference implicit in operation of a particular module can be applied only to that module's own constrained kind of information.

Striking examples of cognitive modularity abound in animal behavior. For instance, Cheng (1986) trained rats to find food buried in a rectangular box (figure 3.2). At the start of each trial the rat was exposed to the location of the food for that trial by being allowed to eat some of it. The rat was then removed and placed in an identical box with food hidden in the same relative

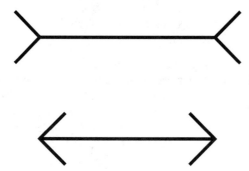

Figure 3.1. The Muller-Lyer illusion. The horizontal lines are the same length.

location. Rats found the food in the test box at well above the levels expected by chance, but many of their errors consisted of searching in the diagonally opposite side of the box from the goal. Even prominent visual, auditory, and olfactory cues, which rats could learn about under other circumstances, did not prevent this kind of error. These data seem to mean that under these conditions behavior reflects the output of a place-determining module that uses only geometric information, even when reinforcement contingencies favor overriding it (Cheng, 1986; Margules & Gallistel, 1988; see also chapter 7).

3.2 A Framework for Thinking about Learning

3.2.1 What Is Learning?

Learning, or equivalently memory, is a change in state resulting from experience. Obviously, this definition includes too much. For instance, 24 hours without food changes a rat's state so it is more likely to eat when given food again, but this change in state is commonly called hunger, not learning. Running 10 kilometers a day improves a person's endurance, but although a person may learn something from it, physical training is not normally called learning, either. The changes in state referred to as learning seem to involve a change in cognitive state, not just behavioral capacity, but this is helpful only if it is possible to distinguish cognitive from other kinds of changes.

So why start with such a broad definition? In the past learning has often been defined too restrictively, in a way that automatically rules out consideration of diverse and novel forms of behavioral plasticity (Rescorla & Holland, 1976). For example, saying that learning is the result of reinforced practice equates learning with instrumental conditioning. Specifying that learning must last for at least 24 hours implies that a small effect of experience lasting, say, 20 hours is qualitatively different from one lasting two days. Saying that motivational changes such as increases in hunger can be reversed easily while developmental changes like learning cannot (Hogan, 1994b) is not helpful

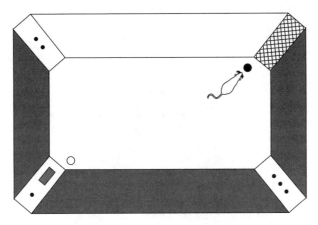

Figure 3.2. Overhead view of the apparatus used in demonstrations of the geometric module in the rat. Adapted from Cheng (1986) with permission: Black dot indicates the location of food; many errors were directed at the location marked by the white dot.

because it does not specify where to draw the line between "easy to reverse" and "hard to reverse." It is important to begin without such constraining definitions in order to consider the broadest possible range of experience-induced cognitive changes.

The changes in state commonly referred to as *learning* or *memory* have the potential to be read out in behavior. But by itself a change in behavior with experience is not diagnostic of learning. To decide whether or not any sort of learning has occurred, it is always necessary to compare two groups of individuals. One has the experience of interest at an initial time, T1. The other, control, group does not have that experience. In effect, therefore, the control has a different experience, and thoughtfully defining that experience is essential to understanding the nature of learning. In any case, the two groups given different experiences at T1 must be compared *on a standard test* at some later time, *T*2 (Rescorla, 1988b; Rescorla & Holland, 1976). This simple but important notion is diagrammed in figure 3.3a. To give it some more realism, consider a simple demonstration (figure 3.3b). Suppose we want to know whether male canaries learn how to sing from other canaries. A first step would be to raise some male canaries in isolation and others in normal social groups, with adult males and females. This rearing period, during which the birds are treated differently, is T1. We might well observe that males kept in groups begin to sing more or in a different way than isolated males, but we would not know whether this difference in behavior at T1 reflects learning. For instance, maybe being with other birds, in itself, causes young males to sing more or in a different way. This is why the standard test at T2 is necessary. In our example, this test might consist of placing each male with a female and recording his vocalizations. We would almost certainly observe that the socially raised males sang more complex and varied songs than those raised in isolation. We could safely conclude that some learning had occurred,

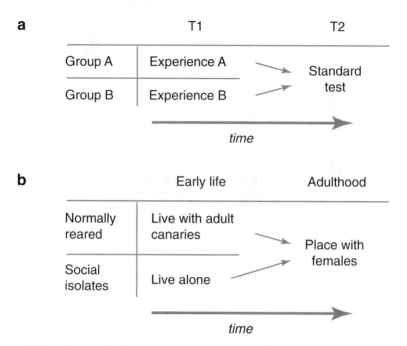

Figure 3.3. a. Essentials of any experiment designed to demonstrate learning. b. The abstract design illustrated by a test of the contribution of early experience to adult behavior in canaries.

but we could not conclude that the *form* of the songs was learned. Maybe, for instance, the males raised in isolation are frightened of the females and therefore behave differently from males that are familiar with females. Further comparisons would be necessary to isolate such factors. For instance, in many studies of song learning the possibility that differences in social experience contribute to the results has been ruled out by raising both "experienced" and inexperienced birds in isolation and playing them tape-recorded songs of their own or another species (see chapter 10).

3.2.2 Three Dimensions of Learning

Three basic questions can be asked about any learning phenomenon (Rescorla, 1988a, 1988b): What are the conditions that bring learning about? What is learned? How does learning affect behavior? Of course one can ask other questions about learning, too. How widespread among species is it? What function does it serve? How did it evolve? How does it develop within the individual's lifetime? What brain processes underlie it? However, most experimental analyses of learning at the behavioral level have been directed toward understanding the conditions for learning, the contents of learning, or its effects on behavior.

Conditions for Learning   The first step in understanding any instance of learning is to analyze the conditions that bring it about. What kind of experience is responsible for the behavioral change are we interested in? Does the age, the sex, the species, or the past experience of the subject matter? In our example of song learning in canaries, studying the conditions for learning might involve exposing different groups of birds to different amounts and kinds of auditory input and doing so when they are at different ages. In general, when relevant experience is repeated more often, lasts longer, and/or is more intense, more learning occurs, as measured in some way, such as how many subjects show the behavioral change of interest, how much of it they show, or how long it lasts. Qualitative features of the experience matter, too. For instance, while canaries may learn the song of another canary, they will probably show less evidence of learning if they have listened to the song of a sparrow for the same amount of time.

Deciding which of the many possible conditions for learning to investigate requires a preexisting idea about what kinds of events might be important. For example, our experiments on bird song are unlikely to include tests of the effects of barometric pressure, but they are likely to include comparisons of the effects of conspecific songs vs. the songs of other species. Choice of what to look at is often based on the assumption that, in general, the function of learning is to allow an animal to fine-tune its behavior to the specific environmental conditions that it encounters during its lifetime. If the male canary learns his song at all, he is likely to learn in such a way as to make him better at singing canary song, not sparrow song. Therefore, experience with canaries, not sparrows, is likely to influence his singing. However, sometimes experiences seemingly having little to do with the function of a behavior play an important role in its development. For example, if ducklings do not hear their own vocalizations while they are still in the egg, they do not prefer calls from adults of their species after they hatch (Gottlieb, 1978). A strictly functional approach can mislead investigators into overlooking such events of developmental importance. Indeed, such developmental effects are not usually classified as "learning" (Hogan, 1994a), although the underlying neural and other conditions producing them may not differ in any way from those underlying "learning."

Some conditions for learning reflect general facts about the world. For instance, the more something has occurred in the past, the more likely it is to occur in the future. Thus behavior should be better adjusted to frequently recurring events than to rare ones. An event of great biological importance, like arrival of a fierce predator or a large meal, requires more or faster changes in behavior than a small and insignificant one, and learning is accordingly faster and more complete the larger the reinforcer. Such properties of learning seem so obvious and reasonable that it is easy to forget they are not necessary features of the way behavior or the nervous system changes with experience. Rather, they should remind us that evolution has produced nervous systems that respond adaptively to experience.

Contents of Learning   If learning is thought of, as it is by radical behaviorists, as a change only in behavior, questions about the contents of learning and the effects of learning on behavior do not even exist. They arise only if one thinks that observable behavioral changes are the potentially flexible readout of some underlying cognitive change. That is, these questions assume a distinction between learning and *performance* based on that learning, between what the animal knows and what it does. For instance, a young male white-crowned sparrow is normally exposed to the songs of adults during his first summer, but he will not begin to sing himself until the next spring. The learned information is stored for months, until singing is stimulated by hormonal changes (Marler & Peters, 1981). We can find out what the animal knows only by observing what it does (though techniques for imaging brain activity may be changing that). Nevertheless, the knowledge exists even when it is behaviorally silent.

There are two general classes of answer to the question "what is learned?" The associationist's answer is that experience changes the strength of excitatory and/or inhibitory connections among nodes corresponding to stimulus and response elements. The cognitivist's answer (Gallistel, 1990) is that experience changes a structured representation of some aspect of the world. Depending on the type of learning being considered, this representation might be referred to as a cognitive map, a neuronal model, or a template, among other things. For instance, the now-classic model of song learning depicts the effects of experience with song as being stored in an auditory template against which the bird matches its own vocal output (see chapter 10). Connectionist modeling (McClelland, Rumelhart, & the PDP Research Group, 1987) assumes that such representations can usefully be reduced to systems of connections among elements and proceeds to work out how.

Effects of Learning on Behavior   If learning is simply a change in strength of a connection between a stimulus processing center and a response generating center, as in Pavlov's (1927) model of classical conditioning, learning automatically changes the strength or probability of a response to a stimulus. The response must follow processing of the stimulus. However, if learning is seen as changing a representation of some aspect of the world, then a mechanism for generating behavior based on that learning is required. Such a mechanism should specify what behavior will occur as a result of learning and when it will occur. For instance, in terms of the model of behavior discussed in chapter 1, one might ask whether a particular kind of experience changes a single motor pattern or a whole behavior system.

Changes in a central cognitive representation are generally expected to be reflected in behavior in a flexible way. For instance, when marsh tits (*Parus palustris*) have stored food in sites in the laboratory, they show that they remember the locations of those sites in two different ways. When they are hungry and presumably searching for food, they return directly to the sites holding hoarded food. In contrast, when they are given more food to store, they go to new, empty, sites (Shettleworth & Krebs, 1982). Thus the birds are not merely returning automatically to the sites with food. They seem to have a representation of food in the site that they can act on in a flexible functionally appropriate way.

3.2.3 Implications

Understanding learning in terms of questions about the conditions for learning, its contents, and its effects on behavior makes clear that learning mechanisms can differ from one another, or be specialized, in many different ways. Just as birds' beaks have evolved adaptive differences in length, thickness, sharpness, size, and so on (figure 1.15), learning phenomena can differ from one another in any of a number of features. For instance, conditioned taste aversion (see box 3.1), the prototypical example of a "constraint" or adaptive specialization of learning, seems to be affected by all the usual conditions for Pavlovian conditioning discussed in upcoming sections. It is exceptional mainly in the long intervals between CS (flavor) and US (illness) over which conditioning is possible. Thus we might want to say that what defines a learning phenomenon as specialized is some special values of one or more conditions affecting it, or perhaps special contents or effects on behavior. But since no two examples of learning are exactly alike, we might want to conclude that every learning phenomenon is specialized in its own way.

Whether learning is *adaptively specialized* is another question. Typically, psychologists have used this term to describe examples of learning whose properties seem to be well suited to do a particular job (Rozin & Kalat, 1971; Sherry & Schacter, 1987). Conditioned taste aversion is a good example: if the effects of ingesting something with a certain flavor can be felt only hours later, the learning mechanism for avoiding illness-producing foods should be capable of bridging this temporal gap. Strictly speaking, however, conclusions about adaptation can be reached only by showing that animals with the supposed adaptation have greater fitness than animals lacking it or by taking a comparative approach. In the case of the ability to learn flavor aversions over a long delay, this might mean comparing a specialist feeding species with a closely related generalist species, as was attempted by Daly, Rauschenberger, and Behrends (1982). Specialists would be expected to have less need to learn flavor aversions because they are less likely to be sampling a variety of foods. Therefore, if the ability to learn flavor aversions is adaptive, members of the generalist species should perform better than specialists.

So when do we start to talk about specialized *kinds* of learning or separate learning modules? The view developed in this section implies that this decision is based largely on which similarities or differences among learning phenomena are seen as most important. For instance, some, like the late Robert Bolles (1985), scorn the view that flavor aversion learning is "just another example of Pavlovian conditioning" with very extreme parameter values, whereas others might see it as illustrating how the general mechanism for causality detection can be tweaked by evolution for a specific job. In general, the more distinctive features a learning phenomenon has, the more likely people are to conclude it is a "special kind of learning," different from Pavlovian or instrumental conditioning (Shettleworth, 1993a). The issue of when and how to distinguish among kinds of learning or cognitive modules arises in many of the other chapters. Chapter 13 draws some conclusions about it.

3.3 When Will Learning Evolve?

Learning allows individuals to adjust their behavior to the local state of the world—for example, to local spatial, temporal, social, and causal relationships. Animals need to know such things as what locally available food is good to eat, where and when to find it, whom to avoid and whom to approach. A capacity for learning will evolve whenever specific events of importance for each individual differ across generations but remain the same within generations (Johnston, 1982; Stephens, 1991). The general nature of the events to be learned about must be the same in every generation, otherwise no single learning ability could cope with between-generation variation. For instance, as the local structure of the habitat changes, members of each new generation may find food in different places, but there may always be some advantage in being able to learn where food is. The conditions that bring learning about should be reliable correlates of the state of the world that the animal needs to adjust to. This correlation is encoded in learning mechanisms, cognitive modules, so that particular sorts of experiences bring about particular changes in cognitive state. The effects of learning on behavior must also be intimately related to its function. It would be no good to a blue jay to associate the orange and black pattern of a Monarch butterfly with the emetic effects of ingesting it if this association caused the blue jay to attack Monarchs more avidly rather than rejecting them (see box 5.1).

The view of learning just stated is radically different from that which drove research on learning in animals throughout most of its first century. That rather abiological view was based on two anthropocentric assumptions. First, the ability to learn is an unadulterated good and, second, animal learning abilities are like human intellectual abilities, which most of us experience as being of completely general and unlimited applicability. On the contrary, learning has a cost and learning abilities are adaptively specialized. A major cost of learning is less than optimal behavior during acquisition (Johnston, 1982). For instance, many songbirds experience very high mortality during their first summer, and this may be due to their not yet having learned to forage efficiently on locally available prey. Figure 3.4 shows an example of dramatic age differences in the time free-ranging yellow-eyed juncos (*Junco phaeonotus*) took to consume experimentally provided mealworms. Recently independent juveniles spent most of the daylight hours foraging, yet 3.85% of them died every day (Sullivan, 1988). Species that must learn to exploit essential resources therefore may experience other costs of learning (Johnston, 1982). For instance, the more young animals need to learn before they can feed themselves, the longer they will remain dependent on parental feeding and the longer they will have to delay reproduction. Adults should not pro-

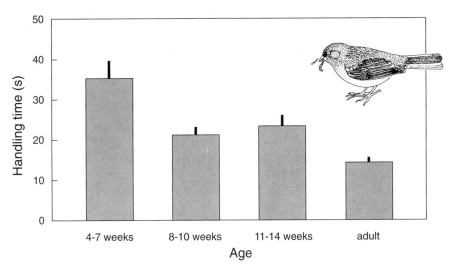

Figure 3.4. Development of foraging efficiency in yellow-eyed juncos, as indicated by reductions in the time taken to ingest a mealworm. Data from Sullivan (1988)

duce more young than they can feed to the age of independence, or their reproductive effort will be wasted. As these notions suggest, long-lived animals with complex foraging skills, like chimpanzees and albatrosses, tend to have small families and long periods of association between parent and young (Johnston, 1982). Of course, animals with short life spans such as bees learn, too (see box 3.2). Patchiness of resources favors learning (Krakauer & Rodriguez-Girones, 1995), and this may account for bees having evolved such good learning abilities.

When learning is a matter of life or death, there is not time to try out all possible solutions to a problem while learning the best one. Animals including human beings (Cosmides & Tooby, 1992) must be preprogrammed to take in only the most relevant information and use it in relevant ways. Lorenz (1965) called this tendency "the innate schoolmarm," a phrase that emphasizes that learning is not possible without an underlying predisposition to learn. This same kind of idea leads to the prediction that animals will evolve multiple kinds of learning or memory systems when they face functionally incompatible requirements for processing different kinds of information (Sherry & Schacter, 1987). This idea has already been discussed in chapter 1, and chapter 2 provided examples in the form of specialized perceptual abilities. Future chapters provide more examples.

3.4 Pavlovian Conditioning

In the prototypical example of Pavlovian conditioning, a dog stands on a platform with a fistula extending from its cheek, allowing its saliva to be measured drop by drop (figure 3.5). A bell sounds and shortly afterward the dog gets a

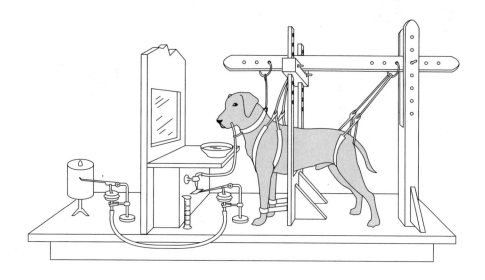

Figure 3.5. Two preparations for studying Pavlovian conditioning. Upper panel, salivary conditioning in a dog, after Yerkes and Morgulis (1909). Lower panel, autoshaping in a pigeon, after Colwill (1996) with permission. In autoshaping, lighting of the pecking key (the disk on the wall) precedes delivery of food in the opening below it. The pigeon begins to peck the key even though food is given regardless of whether it pecks or not.

morsel of food. The food itself evokes copious salivation, but after several pairings the dog begins to salivate when it hears the bell. The dog has undoubtedly learned something, but what has it learned, and what are the essential features of the experience that brings this learning about?

Historically, the ability of the bell to evoke salivation would have been attributed to the transfer of control of a reflex (the *unconditioned response* or *UR* of salivation) from the innate eliciting stimulus of food (the *unconditioned stimulus* or *US*) to the initially neutral stimulus of the bell (the *conditioned stimulus* or *CS*). Now, however, learning theorists would be more likely to say that the dog has learned the predictive relation between the bell and the food (Rescorla, 1988a). Its salivation is merely conveniently measured evidence of that knowledge. If the dog were free to move about it might instead approach the feeder or beg and wag its tail at the sound of the bell (Jenkins, Barrera, Ireland, & Woodside, 1978). Indeed, in most of the currently popular preparations, such as autoshaping (figure 3.5), conditioning is measured by changes in skeletal behavior of the whole animal. On either interpretation, however, Pavlovian conditioning is a case of *associative learning*, the formation of some sort of mental connection between representations of two stimuli. The rest of this chapter is a bare-bones review of the properties of associative learning, as exemplified by Pavlovian conditioning. It is organized in terms of the three aspects of learning introduced in section 3.2: the conditions for learning, the contents of learning, and the effects of learning on behavior. Section 3.5.1 sketches the distinguishing features of instrumental conditioning and compares them to those of Pavlovian conditioning.

There are at least four reasons for discussing Pavlovian (or classical) conditioning before any other examples of learning. First, in recent years it has been the most thoroughly studied form of learning. The experimental and theoretical analysis of Pavlovian conditioning illustrates how to answer the three central questions about learning outlined in the preceding section and thereby provides a model for how other learning phenomena can be studied (Rescorla, 1988a). Second, although studying Pavlovian conditioning has been thought of as measuring mere "spit and twitches," some examples of conditioning turn out to have complex and interesting cognitive content (Rescorla, 1988a). Thus Pavlovian conditioning belongs in any account of animal cognition. Third, most analyses of apparently different forms of learning have been organized around the question, "Can this be explained as associative learning?" To evaluate such analyses, we need to be familiar with the properties of associative learning. In the context of this book, it is particularly important to appreciate the subtlety and complexity of what apparently simple animals can learn from apparently simple experiences. Finally, the basic phenomena of conditioning are phylogenetically very widespread, perhaps more so than any learning phenomenon other than habituation (Macphail, 1996). The ability to acquire simple Pavlovian associations allows animals to adjust their foraging, predator avoidance, social behavior, and other aspects of their existence to their individual circumstances. Humans' contingency judgments may be accounted for by simple associative learning, too (Allan,

1993; Shanks, 1994). Some knowledge of basic conditioning principles is therefore useful for understanding the mechanisms behind some important phenomena in behavioral ecology. For instance, the ability to learn from punishing experiences may play a role in organizing animal society (Clutton-Brock & Parker, 1995).

3.4.1 The Conditions for Learning

Associative learning can be described as the process by which animals learn about causal relationships between events and behave appropriately as a result (Dickinson, 1980; Mackintosh, 1983; Macphail, 1996; Rescorla, 1988b). Associations are hypothetical connections within the animal that represent causal connections between events in the animal's environment. This functional description makes almost perfect sense of the conditions for associative learning. It also reflects the philosophical basis of the study of conditioning in associationism, which suggested that effects should be associated with their causes (Hall, 1994; Young, 1995). Associations have traditionally been thought of as the building blocks of all cognition, but seeing them as allowing animals to represent distinctively causal relationships makes associative learning just as adaptively specialized as, for example, learning about spatial or temporal relationships (Gallistel, 1992). In chapter 11 we consider whether different mechanisms are needed for processing information about distinctively social causation, as opposed to the physical causation being discussed here.

Contingency   As we will see, the presence of an association can be evidenced in a variety of ways. However, to be sure that one is studying behavior reflecting the animal's knowledge of a predictive relationship, it is necessary to be able to discriminate this behavior from similar behavior brought about for other reasons. In the terminology of section 3.2, animals that have experienced a predictive relationship between CS and US at T1 must behave differently at T2 from control animals that experienced some other relationship between CS and US. The best way to isolate the effects of a predictive CS-US relationship is to expose the control group to the CS and US occurring randomly with respect to each other. The behavior of these latter, random control animals is a baseline that takes into account possible effects of exposure to CS and US individually in the experimental context (Rescorla, 1967). Against this baseline, the effects of both positive contingency (CS predicts US) and negative contingency (CS predicts absence of US) can be assessed (figure 3.6).

The importance of the random control group has been appreciated only relatively recently. Traditionally, temporal contiguity, or pairing, between two events was thought to be the necessary and sufficient condition for associative learning. The most popular control conditions eliminated contiguity by presenting just the CS or just the US or by presenting them systematically separated in time. But this condition has associative effects of its own. For in-

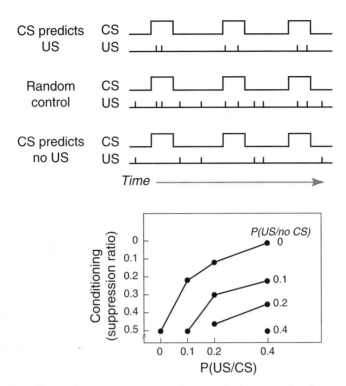

Figure 3.6. Effects of contingency on conditioning. In this example, illustrating the methods and results of Rescorla (1967), shock USs occurred with a constant probability per unit of time in the random control condition. Positive and negative contingencies were created by removing the USs between or during CSs, respectively. The effects of US rates on fear conditioning are plotted as a function of the probability of shock during the CS, with a separate function for each likelihood of shock in the absence of the CS. Rats were bar-pressing for food and fear conditioning was indexed by comparing bar-pressing rate during the CS to ongoing response rate. Zero indicates maximal conditioning; a suppression ratio of 0.5 indicates no conditioning. Redrawn from Rescorla (1988a).

stance, it can teach the animal that the US never follows the CS, thereby establishing a *conditioned inhibitor*. The truly random control condition is not without critics, however (Papini & Bitterman, 1990). An alternative approach often used with invertebrates to establish that they can learn at all is differential conditioning with two CSs. When a US is paired with one CS and concurrently not paired with another, associative learning should lead to differential responding to the two CSs. However, as a test of CS-US associations, this design is subject to a subtle confounding from possible differential habituation, since habituation may be selectively prevented to a CS that is always quickly followed by a US (Colwill, 1996). Colwill argues that the most convincing tests of associative learning make use of the fact that, as reviewed in section 3.4.2, a genuine CR reflects the quality and value of its associated US.

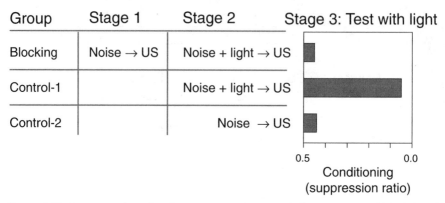

Group	Stage 1	Stage 2	Stage 3: Test with light
Blocking	Noise → US	Noise + light → US	
Control-1		Noise + light → US	
Control-2		Noise → US	

0.5   0.0
Conditioning
(suppression ratio)

Figure 3.7. Design and results of Kamin's (1969) original demonstration of blocking of fear conditioning in rats. As in figure 3.6, conditioning was measured by suppression of bar pressing: lower suppression ratios correspond to greater conditioned fear.

Even the relatively simple stimuli used in most laboratory experiments on Pavlovian conditioning have many features. For instance, a tone comes from a particular location and has a particular loudness and duration. A visual stimulus has brightness, size, shape, and perhaps other features. How are multifeatured events processed—as a unit or as a sum of features? What about features that are added after initial learning? These questions are not settled yet even for simple associative learning (Fetterman, 1996; Hall, 1994). To see how they have been addressed, we start with a very influential model of Pavlovian conditioning based on the notion that animals learn separately about the features of events. The total *associative strength* of (or amount learned about) a compound stimulus, such as a light plus a tone, is the sum of the strengths of its separate elements. However, if an animal has learned that, say, a light causes food, and a new stimulus, say a tone, now accompanies the light so that the compound light + tone predicts food, learning about the tone, the new element, is blocked (Kamin, 1969; figure 3.7). Like the contingency effects in figure 3.6, *blocking* means that mere temporal contiguity between two events is not sufficient for associative learning. The CS must also convey new information about the US. In the case of blocking, the added CS conveys no new information about the occurrence of the US. When it does, as when the US is now larger or smaller than it was when predicted by the first CS, animals do learn (Mackintosh, 1978). This *unblocking* shows that blocking is not merely due to a failure of attention to the added element. It suggests that animals associate two events only when the second one, the US, is somehow surprising or unexpected.

The notion that surprisingness is essential for conditioning is captured in the influential formal model proposed by Rescorla and Wagner (1972). It generates the properties of associative learning reviewed so far, and many others besides. In that model, the amount of associative strength that a given CS accrues on a trial with a given US is proportional to the difference between the

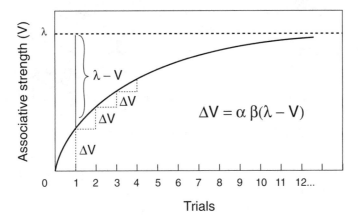

Figure 3.8. How the Rescorla-Wagner model generates a negatively accelerated learning curve.

maximum associative strength that the US can support (λ) and the current associative strength of all CSs currently present (V). The current associative strength of all CSs represents the degree to which the animal expects the US in the presence of those CSs, or the discrepancy between what the animal needs to learn and what it already knows (see figure 3.8). The parameters α and β in the equation are constants related to the particular CS and US being used. They reflect the fact that performance changes faster with salient or strong stimuli than with inconspicuous or weak ones.

The Rescorla-Wagner model readily accounts for blocking. When a novel stimulus, B, is added to an already-conditioned stimulus, A, the total associative strength of the compound is close to the maximum, thanks to the contribution of element A. If we assume that the environment in which an explicit CS occurs itself functions as a CS, the model also accounts for the effects of contingency as due to contiguity between CS and US. An explicit CS can be viewed as a compound of CS and context. When the predictive value of the CS is degraded by extra USs, as in figure 3.6, what really happens is that the context becomes associated with the extra USs and blocks conditioning to the CS. In this view, an animal exposed to random occurrences of CS and US is not an animal that has learned nothing; it may have associated the US with the environment or learned that the CS and US are unrelated.

The Rescorla-Wagner model has had a tremendous influence on the study of associative learning (Miller, Barnet, & Grahame, 1995; Siegel & Allan, 1996). Within the more than 25 years since it first appeared, most other proposals have been elaborations or variants on it. Two recent proposals have some essential differences from the Rescorla-Wagner model. In Pearce's (1994a) configural model animals process compound stimuli as unitary configurations rather than as the sum of elements. This model makes different predictions from the Rescorla-Wagner model for the results of some experiments on discrimination learning reviewed in sections 5.4 and 5.5. It is dis-

	Stage 1	Stage 2	Test
Sensory Preconditioning	A → B	B → US	A
Second Order Conditioning	B → US	A → B	A

Figure 3.9. Procedures for sensory preconditioning and second-order conditioning.

cussed further there. The other alternative model (Gallistel, 1990, 1992) proposes that rather than simply storing the effects of durations, times, and numbers of events as the strength of an association, animals represent durations, times, and numbers explicitly. Both the Rescorla-Wagner model and its alternatives are largely based on data from vertebrates, mostly rats and pigeons. Invertebrates also show the basic phenomena of conditioning (Macphail, 1996). Indeed, this observation is the basis for an important body of research that uses the simple nervous systems of species like the sea slug *Aplysia* to investigate the neural mechanisms of learning (Macphail, 1993). Another invertebrate whose simple learning has been studied extensively is the honeybee. The learning phenomena demonstrable in bees are similar to those in vertebrates, though the processes may not all be (box 3.2).

The Events to be Associated: Biological Significance   In the most familiar examples of associative learning, the US is food, a painful stimulus, or some other event with preexperimental significance for the animal. In these cases learning is usually easy to measure because the animal clearly behaves as if it expects the US when the CS occurs. Animals run about, salivate, peck, or gnaw in the presence of signals associated with food; they become immobile ("freeze"), squeak, or try to escape in the presence of danger signals. But preexisting biological significance is not an essential feature of the events that enter into associations. In *sensory preconditioning*, two relatively neutral stimuli are associated by being presented under the same kinds of conditions necessary for conditioning with food, shock, and the like. After such experience, the animal's knowledge about their relationship can be revealed by making one of the events behaviorally significant and observing behavior toward the other. For instance, if the animal first learns "tone causes light" and then "light causes food," it behaves as if making the inference, "tone causes food." *Second-order conditioning* is similar to sensory preconditioning in that initially neutral stimuli are associated with each other, but here one of them is given biological significance beforehand. That is, the animal first learns "light causes food" and then "tone causes light." When tested appropriately, it behaves as if inferring that "tone causes food." Figure 3.9 depicts the experimental arrangements in these two kinds of paradigms. Experimental arrangements for studying simple associative learning in humans resemble those for sensory preconditioning in that the stimuli being learned about have little or

Box 3.2. Do Bees Learn Like Rats and Pigeons?

How and what bees learn about nectar-producing flowers has been studied experimentally since days of Karl von Frisch (1953), using methods outlined in chapter 7. These ethological studies of learning, many of them done in the field, have revealed some remarkable abilities seemingly closely matched to the bees' natural requirements for learning. Although closer analysis has sometimes revealed that bees learn no differently from other animals, the work with bees nevertheless provides some excellent illustrations of the fit between learning and ecological requirements.

When leaving a recently discovered nectar source, bees fly in increasingly wide loops above it, facing their point of departure all the while (figure B3.2a; Collett & Zeil, 1996; Lehrer, 1993). If the bees were using this "turn back and look" behavior to learn the features of flowers, they would have to be learning via backward conditioning. Indeed, some researchers have suggested that some features of nectar sources are learned only after nectar has been sampled and not before (Couvillon, Leiato, & Bitterman, 1991). However, experiments in which bees are exposed to different cues before and after contact with nectar and then allowed to choose between them clearly show that although backward conditioning does occur when bees "turn back and look," the cues present during approach are generally more powerful (figure B3.2a). Nevertheless, the "turn back and look behavior" is a good example of a special behavior that brings animals into contact with events to be learned about.

⟱

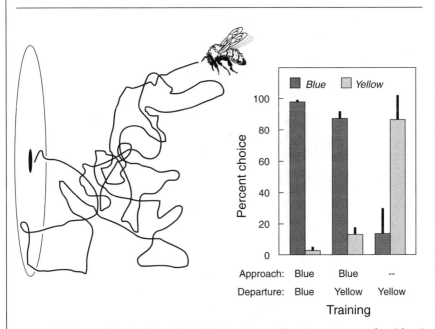

Figure B 3.2. a. "Turn back and look" behavior in a bee leaving an artificial food source it has just visited for the first time and results of an experiment in which the target changed color between approach and departure for some bees. The bees were given a choice between blue and yellow in the test. Redrawn from Lehrer (1991).

Box 3.2. Do Bees Learn Like Rats and Pigeons? (*continued*)

In recent years, M. E. Bitterman and his associates have carried out detailed analyses of honeybees' performance in the whole range of standard Pavlovian and instrumental conditioning paradigms (Bitterman, 1996; Menzel & Muller, 1996). Not surprisingly, bees develop stronger preferences for artificial flowers with bigger, better, or more frequent rewards. When it comes to more subtle aspects of conditioning, however, an interesting difference from vertebrates is the apparent absence of blocking: learning about one feature such as color, odor, or shape does not interfere with learning about another feature added later on (Funayama, Couvillon, & Bitterman, 1995). Thus, the best formal model of conditioning here is not the Rescorla-Wagner model but one in which cues gain strength independently. This finding fits with Gould's (1996)

➡

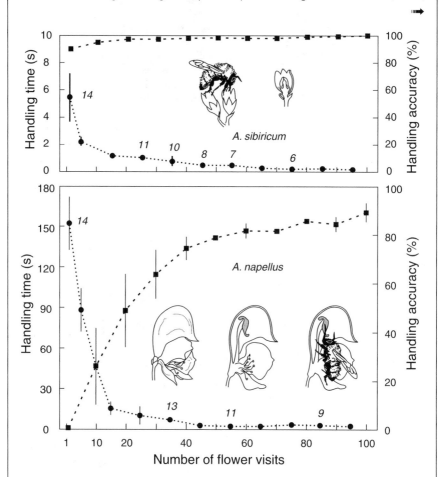

Figure B 3.2.   b. Comparison of the rates at which bumblebees learn to locate and extract nectar from a simple cup-shaped flower and a more complex one, measured as increasing handling accuracy (squares) and decreasing handling time (dots). Numbers are bees tested. After Laverty (1994) with permission.

no preexisting biological significance for the subject. This insight may be the key to understanding why some phenomena seen in first-order conditioning with animals fail to appear in humans (Denniston, Miller, & Matute, 1996).

The Rescorla-Wagner model does not allow for any preexperimental relationship between events to influence their associability. The salience of the particular CS or US determines the speed of learning, through the parameters α and β respectively. But, contrary to the model, it may also matter how particular events are paired up. The best-known example is conditioned taste aversion or poison-avoidance learning, discussed in box 3.1. In general, if associative learning is a mechanism for learning true causal relations in the environment, then if one event is a priori likely to cause another, it should take less evidence to convince the animal of its true causal relationship than if it is a priori an unlikely cause. As this notion suggests, the importance of what has been called relevance (Dickinson, 1980), belongingness (Thorndike, 1911/1970), preparedness (Seligman, 1970), or intrinsic relations between events (Rescorla & Holland, 1976) has been demonstrated in a number of situations other than conditioned taste aversion (Domjan, 1983). Far from being the evidence for special laws of learning it was once supposed to be, relevance or belongingness of stimuli is now recognized as being generally important in conditioning. For instance, pigeons more readily use visual than auditory stimuli as signals for food, but sounds are better than lights as danger signals. In both food getting and shock avoidance with pigeons, the "relevant" stimulus has a privileged status in that it cannot be blocked (LoLordo, Jacobs, & Foree, 1982). Pigeons trained to press a treadle for grain in the presence of a tone still learned about an added light, whereas prior learning about the light did block the tone. Temporal cues and spatial context appear to have similarly privileged access to associative mechanisms in rat fear conditioning in that they cannot be blocked by other cues (Williams & LoLordo, 1995). In chapter 10, we will see that monkeys selectively develop fear to things like snakes that might be important to fear in the wild. A much-discussed suggestion (Davey, 1995) is that human phobias are underlain by an evolved predisposition to fear objects that were dangerous to our ancestors. For instance, people appear more likely to develop phobias toward things like snakes, spiders, mushrooms, or high places than flowers, electric outlets, soft beds, or fast cars.

Belongingness could reflect a preexisting connection that gives a head start to learning (Davey, 1995; LoLordo, 1979). Some accounts of the neural basis of learning have suggested that all associative learning is built on such preexisting connections. Alternatively, experience of a given US may direct attention to certain kinds of stimuli. For instance, a rat that has recently been sick may pay particular attention to flavors. This possibility can be ruled out by exposing all animals to both USs of interest or by giving only a single training trial. The possibility that prior learning plays a role can be addressed by using very young animals or animals with controlled past history. Finally, apparent belongingness may not represent different degrees of learning but differential readiness to exhibit that learning in performance. Evidence of learning might be seen especially readily, for example, if the response evoked by expectation of the US is similar to the response which the CS tends to evoke on its own (Holland, 1984; Rescorla, 1988a). Each of these and possibly other mechanisms may play a role in some situations. They also suggest various possible bases for the apparent selectivity that is common in other kinds of learning.

The Events to be Associated: Similarity and Spatial Contiguity   Classical associationism did recognize one kind of "belongingness." Namely, similarity and spatial contiguity of the events to be associated were thought to favor learning. Of course, similarity and spatial contiguity can both be seen as reasonable prior predictors of causal relationships. However, it is not necessarily easy to disentangle them from other factors that may influence learning or performance. For instance, a CS that is similar to a given US may evoke responding via stimulus generalization. An elegant experiment with pigeons by Rescorla and Furrow (1977) has shown that, over and above any such effect, similarity can enhance associability. As indicated in figure 3.10, all their birds were exposed to all the stimuli used in the experiment; they differed only in whether similar or dissimilar stimuli were paired in the critical second-order conditioning phase. Similarly designed experiments have shown that spatial contiguity or a part-whole relation between CS and US can also facilitate second-order conditioning (Rescorla & Cunningham, 1979). Although it is difficult to vary the spatial contiguity of CS to US without also affecting tem-

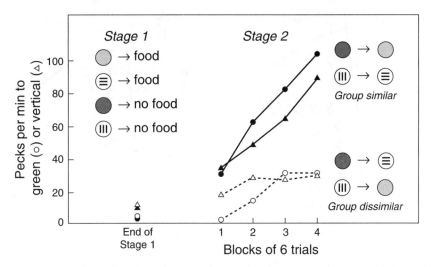

Figure 3.10. Effects of similarity between the stimuli to be associated on speed of second-order autoshaping in pigeons. Data for the end of Stage 1 are each group's rates of pecking the two stimuli that became CSs in second-order conditioning but that predicted no food during Stage 1. The unpatterned stimuli were green and blue, shown here by dark and light shading respectively. After Rescorla and Furrow (1977) with permission.

poral contiguity, spatial contiguity by itself does appear to influence learning (Christie, 1996).

Temporal Relationships   Within limits, conditioning is more rapid the more closely in time the US follows the CS. The exact parameters of this relationship depend on the events involved. With eyelid conditioning, the CS must precede the US by no more than a second or so, while in conditioned taste aversion, flavor can precede illness by twelve hours or more. In general, conditioning improves at first as the temporal separation of CS and US increases, then declines (figure 3.11). A functional reason is easy to see: causes often precede their effects closely in time and seldom follow them. However, it is easy to imagine cases in which a cause follows its effect from the animal's point of view. A stealthy predator might not be noticed until after it has attacked, but this does not mean that the victim (if it's still alive to benefit from its experience) should not learn about its enemy's features. This argument has been advanced to account for the relatively few cases of successful *backward conditioning* (Keith-Lucas & Guttman, 1975; Spetch, Wilkie, & Pinel, 1981).

The data presented in figure 3.11 seem to suggest that simultaneous events are not associated. However, simultaneous conditioning can be quite robust in second-order conditioning or sensory preconditioning, as when a pigeon associates patterns on two halves of a pecking key (Rescorla, 1988a). This paradigm may capture how animals learn about the individual features of events. It is discussed further in this chapter's section on within-event learning and in chapter 4.

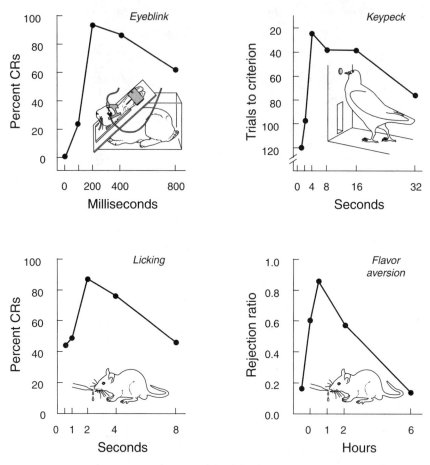

Figure 3.11. Conditioning as a function of the delay between CS and US in different conditioning preparations. Eyeblink conditioning in rabbits, redrawn from from Smith et al. (1969) with permission; rabbit redrawn from Domjan and Burkhard (1986) with permission; autoshaping in pigeons, data from Gibbon et al. (1977); conditioned licking with water reinforcement in rats redrawn from Boice and Denny (1965) with permission; flavor aversion in rats from Barker and Smith (1974). After Rescorla (1988b) with permission.

Prior Learning   In blocking, previous learning about one element of a compound stimulus reduces learning about the other. But the effects of past experience on present learning are more widespread. For example, exposure to a CS by itself, before pairing with a US, leads to *latent inhibition,* retarded conditioning to that CS. It is as if, having learned that the CS signals nothing of importance, the animal ceases to pay attention to it. Latent inhibition is similar to habituation, in that mere exposure to an event results in learning, but, as discussed in chapter 4, it is not clear whether the two phenomena reflect the same mechanism. Exposure to the US alone in the conditioning context also reduces its effectiveness when a CS is later introduced. This can be explained as blocking of the CS by the context: the animal already expects the US, so the CS adds little new information. Conditioning to the context itself is readily observed; animals obviously learn what to expect in particular places, be they conditioning chambers or parts of the natural environment. For example, a pigeon that has received food in a distinctively wallpapered Skinner box becomes more active when placed in that environment than in an environment where it has never been fed.

If exposure to either the CS or the US alone reduces conditioning, one would expect that prior exposure to random presentations of both CS and US would have an even more detrimental effect. Of course, this is the random control condition. The nature of its effects is captured very well by the name *learned irrelevance* or, in the case of instrumental conditioning, *learned helplessness*. However, it is debatable whether animals actually learn that CS and US have a random relationship. An alternative possibility is that their behavior can be accounted for by the sum of effects of CS and US preexposure (Bonardi & Hall, 1996). Learned irrelevance is specific to the particular CS and US the animal has experienced. For example, random presentations of tone and water retard tone-water but not tone-food associations in rats (Mackintosh, 1973). Effects of past history like these could underlie some belongingness effects. That is, if an "unnatural" CS-US relationship is learned only with difficulty, this could be because the animal has already learned that stimuli like the CS and US are usually unrelated to each other.

Extinction   If conditioning represents learning a causal relation between two events, then conditioning should be abolished if the animal has opportunity to learn that the relation no longer holds. Traditionally it was given this opportunity by removing the US and observing how the CR waned. However, the logic behind the random control condition for original learning implies that the proper way to teach an animal that CS and US are now unrelated, and thereby produce *extinction* of responding, is to present CS and US in a noncontingent relation to each other. In one dramatic demonstration of the effectiveness of this procedure, Gamzu and Williams (1971) extinguished pigeons' autoshaped key pecking by adding extra food presentations between keylight-food pairings, preserving contiguity between the keylight and food but degrading the predictive relationship between the key and food.

Extinction may appear to involve loss of a learned association, unlearning. However, considerable evidence indicates that—contrary to the depiction in the Rescorla-Wagner model—associations are not really lost during extinction (Miller, Barnet, & Grahame, 1995). *Savings* after extinction, speeding up of relearning compared to initial learning, is one such piece of evidence. Further evidence that the original association is retained comes from examples of *reinstatement*: simply presenting the US alone in the experimental context after extinction can get responding going again. These and considerable other data indicate that rather than losing its original association during extinction, the animal acquires a new association, an inhibitory association specific to the temporal and spatial context in which extinction occurs (Bouton, 1993). In this view, extinction is like loss of memory, a loss which can be restored by the appropriate retrieval cues (see chapter 6).

3.4.2 Contents of Learning

S-S or S-R Associations?   Historically, the question "What is learned in conditioning?" was posed as "Are associations formed between CS and US (stimulus-stimulus, S-S, associations) or between CS and UR (stimulus-response, S-R, associations)?" The 1940s and '50s saw a number of attempts to determine whether learning consisted of S-S or S-R connections, mainly using instrumental learning paradigms. In experiments with mazes, this amounted to the question of whether animals learned a rigid response, such as turning right, or whether they acquired knowledge about the location of the goal, a cognitive map (see chapter 7) that they could use to reach the goal in different ways as circumstances required. As usual in controversies of this kind, the answer seemed to be "it depends," in this case on factors such as the amount and conditions of training. In recent years, the S-S versus S-R distinction has been rephrased for Pavlovian conditioning as a distinction between *procedural* and *declarative* learning. Does the animal merely learn what to do in the presence of the CS (procedural learning) or does it form a representation that could be expressed as a proposition, "A causes B," and base action on this knowledge in a flexible way (declarative learning)? Experiments to be reviewed in which the value of the CS or the US is changed after training have shown that either may occur. Such studies indicate that animals encode a number of features of the individual events that enter into associations.

Connection or Contingency Representation?   A more fundamental question than whether associations are S-S or S-R is whether the contents of associative learning are best conceptualized as connections at all. An important condition for learning is contingency between events, so why not conclude that the animal learns the contingent relationship itself? Gallistel (1990, 1992) has developed a model of conditioning that makes this assumption. The animal records the times of onset and offset of potential CSs and USs and computes whether the statistical likelihood of the US increases during the CS. Responding is determined not by associative strength but by the statistical uncertainty about whether the US will follow the CS. This analysis is useful because it formalizes the notion of contingency. However, the fact that a theorist can compute contingency in this way does not mean that animals must do the same computations in order for their behavior to reflect the contingencies they experience. Sensitivity to the sorts of experiences afforded by conditioning experiments has likely evolved to enable animals to track causal, or contingent, relations among events in the environment. Describing the functions and conditions for learning as contingencies does not mean that they constitute the contents of learning. We have already seen that an animal that blindly forms associations by contiguity in the way described by the Rescorla-Wagner model may track causality very well without having any representation of causality as such.

Nevertheless, Gallistel (1990) and others (Miller & Barnet, 1993) have correctly pointed to one serious problem with an associative model of the contents of learning: an association as traditionally conceived has only one dimension, strength. Such an association cannot encode, for example, the temporal relationship between CS and US, even though it has become clear that animals learn this. Traditionally, the temporal aspects of conditioning were explained with the concept of the stimulus trace. For instance, the silence five seconds after a tone goes off is a different stimulus from the same silence ten seconds later because the aftereffect or trace of the tone changes systematically with time. Similarly, different times within an extended CS can be thought of as different stimuli. This reasoning may possibly be used, if somewhat strained, to account for the effects to be discussed in a moment. However, the evidence, to be reviewed in chapter 8, showing that animals accurately time short intervals makes an account in terms of direct sensitivity to the durations of CSs, USs, CS-US intervals, and the like seem more natural. For instance, blocking is maximized when the CS-US interval is the same for both the pretrained and the to-be-blocked CS (Barnet, Grahame, & Miller, 1993). It seems more plausible that the CS-US interval itself is appreciated than that the traces of two qualitatively different CSs, with which the US is associated, are most similar after identical intervals.

The notion that the temporal relationship between CS and US is itself learned, rather than simply being one of the conditions affecting learning, suggests a novel way of viewing what goes on in simultaneous and backward conditioning. Perhaps animals learn that CS and US are in fact simultaneous or in a backward temporal relationship, but responding is not the same as in forward conditioning because the behavior appropriate to anticipation of an event may not be the same as that appropriate to its presence or its recent occurrence. As this notion suggests, rats given first-order conditioning in which a tone occurred at the same time as a shock showed little conditioned suppression of drinking in the presence of the tone CS, but nevertheless they acquired second-order conditioned suppression when a second-order click CS preceded the tone (figure 3.12; Barnet, Arnold, & Miller, 1991; Cole, Barnet, & Miller, 1995).

In unidimensional associative strength models, associations of the same strength acquired in different ways are equivalent. This assumption of *path independence* is clearly not always correct (Miller, Barnet, & Grahame, 1995). For instance, an equally weak CS-US association could be present early in training or after extinction, but further training would proceed faster after extinction than it did originally, indicating that the animal has retained some effect of the original training that is not evident in performance of the CR. It remains to be seen whether simple associative models can be rescued from such difficulties or whether some sort of hybrid model will eventually be more accepted.

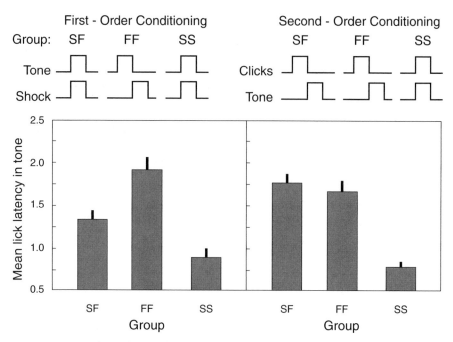

Figure 3.12. Evidence that rats learn the temporal relationship between CS and US. Three groups of rats receiving first-order and then second-order conditioning differed in whether the stimuli to be associated were simultaneous (S) or in a forward temporal relationship (F)—i.e., with CS preceding US. A long latency to drink in the presence of the signal is indicative of conditioned fear. Data from Barnet at el. (1991) redrawn with permission.

Learning about the CS   Any CS has a variety of sensory features. It has a certain duration and intensity; it may have shape, brightness, size, loudness, taste, odor, or texture; and it occurs in a certain context. Which of these are included in the animal's representation of the CS? One popular way to answer this question is to change features of the CS after conditioning and observe the effect on responding. With simple CSs that can be varied along a physical continuum like wavelength or auditory frequency, variations away from the training value often lead to orderly variations in responding as in the generalization gradients in figure 2.9. Obviously, some specificity in responding is a prerequisite for concluding that conditioning has occurred at all. For example, if a rat responds in the same way to any and all sounds after tone-shock pairings, one would probably conclude that the animal was *sensitized* rather than conditioned to the tone (see chapter 4).

The Rescorla-Wagner model treats separable features of a CS as if they gain associative strength independently. This makes some sense for compounds of discrete CSs from different modalities like the proverbial light + tone. But what about a compound of features from the same modality, say a red cross on a blue pecking key? Why should we think that a pigeon represents this as blue field with a red cross superimposed on it? Maybe instead it encodes a configuration. If the key with the red cross is paired with food, the bird will come to peck it, and it will probably peck white keys with red crosses or plain blue keys, too. But maybe this is not because the bird has acquired a red cross association and a separate blue key association. Maybe instead the bird pecks at the red cross or the blue key alone because they are similar to the original training stimulus — that is, through generalizing from the configuration. A formal *configural model* of learning based on this intuition has recently been quite successful in accounting for a large body of data, including some that the elemental Rescorla-Wagner model cannot deal with (Pearce, 1994b).

Learning about the US   When Pavlov's dog salivated to a CS for food, what had it actually learned? Did the CS evoke a complete representation of the food's taste, texture, and the like, thereby causing the dog to salivate? Or did the CS evoke salivation directly? If the dog could talk, would it say "I'm salivating because I'm thinking of food" or would it say "This tone makes me salivate, but I don't know why?" A classic demonstration that animals encode the features of reward comes from a delayed-response experiment by Tinklepaugh (1928). Monkeys saw a piece of their favorite banana or less-preferred lettuce being hidden. After a retention interval, the animals were allowed to uncover the reward and eat it. When lettuce was substituted for banana on occasional test trials, the monkeys showed signs of surprise and anger, indicating that they knew not simply where the reward was but what kind it was (figure 3.13). Watanabe (1996) repeated such observations using an operant task and recorded distinct patterns of cortical activity corresponding to the monkeys' expectations of raisin, apple, cabbage, water, grape juice, and other rewards.

Questions about how the US is represented can be addressed in conventional Pavlovian preparations by changing the value of the US after conditioning has taken place. If responding is unaffected, the conclusion is that the animal has merely associated the CS with the response or response system elicited by the original US. Often, however, responding changes with post-conditioning changes in the value of the US in a way that indicates the animal has associated the CS with a detailed representation of the US. For instance, the value of a food to a rat may be decreased by pairing it with poison. The rat then shows less conditioned responding to a CS previously paired with that food (Holland & Straub, 1979). This technique can be used to discover which sensory features of the US are encoded. For instance, rats can be trained with two different CSs, each paired with a distinctive type of food — say, food pellets and sucrose. If the rat represents both USs merely as "food," "something tasty," or the like, then it should not matter which of them is later paired with poison: conditioned responding should decrease to both CSs. However, responding decreases selectively to the CS whose US was devalued and not to other CSs (Colwill, 1996; Colwill & Motzkin, 1994). Selective satiation or deprivation also change US value. For instance, pigeons that are hungry but satiated with water reduce pecking at a CS signaling water but not at one sig-

Figure 3.13. Tinklepaugh's monkey Psyche looking for banana when lettuce had been secretly substituted. After a photograph in Tinklepaugh (1928)

naling food (Stanhope, 1989). Analogous experiments have established that features of the reinforcer are encoded in instrumental learning as well (Colwill, 1993; Dickinson & Balleine, 1994). However, responding may sometimes continue at a high rate even though the reinforcer has been devalued. Animals apparently learn about both the sensory and the affective or response-eliciting features of USs, perhaps to different degrees in different circumstances (Dickinson, 1980).

Images of the US   So far, this section on the contents of learning indicates that a CS evokes a representation of a particular US arriving at a particular time, an image of the US in some sense. As this idea suggests, associatively evoked stimulus representations can substitute for the stimuli themselves in new learning (Hall, 1996; Holland, 1990). In one demonstration (Holland, 1990), rats were exposed to pairings of a tone with food until they showed clear evidence of anticipating food in the presence of the tone. The tone was then paired with injections of a mild toxin adequate to condition aversion to any distinctive flavor paired with it though not to the tone itself (see box 3.1). As a result of the tone-toxin pairings, the rats developed an aversion to the food previously paired with the tone. It was as if during these pairings the tone evoked an image of the food and that image was associated with toxin.

Further evidence that an association between two stimuli allows one to evoke an image of the other comes from the establishment of backward sensory preconditioning (Ward-Robinson & Hall, 1996). Conventional forward sensory preconditioning (see figure 3.9) consists of A-B pairings, where A precedes B, followed by B-US pairings. The fact that A then evokes a CR can be accounted for by an associative chain: A calls up a representation of B, which in turn calls up a representation of the US. But the chaining explanation does not fare so well when the first stage of the experiment consists of presentations of B followed by A. Stimulus A does evoke a CR following such backward sensory preconditioning, and the reason may be that the B-A pairings allow B to activate an image of A, which is then associated with the US. Such findings and their interpretation in terms of imagery are particularly interesting because they suggest that conditioning allows animals to bring absent events to mind and acquire new information about them, a primitive form of thought (Hall, 1996; Holland, 1990).

3.4.3 Effects of Learning on Behavior

Learning and Performance   In the view that Pavlovian conditioning is merely transfer of control of a reflex, S-R learning, behavior automatically results from learning so there is no distinction to be made between learning and performance. However, numerous examples of "behaviorally silent learning" (Dickinson, 1980) bring home the point that learning and performance must be distinguished. In one of the most important examples, inhibitory learning —that is, below-zero associative strength in Rescorla-Wagner terms—normally becomes evident only when the conditioned inhibitor is presented in combination with an excitor and suppresses conditioned responding (Rescorla, 1969). As another example, Holland and Rescorla (1975) trained rats to expect food following either a tone or a light. Increased activity was soon evident during the tone, but activity changed little or not at all during the light. That is to say, at this stage of the experiment the rats' behavior indicated that they had learned only about the tone. Nevertheless, when rats trained with the light had second-order conditioning consisting of presentations of the tone followed by the light, they became more active to the tone—that is, the light to which there was apparently little first-order conditioning did support second-order conditioning. The light could also block first-order conditioning to the tone, indicating that some conditioning had occurred to it. Later, more detailed, observations (Holland, 1977) revealed that the rats' behavior did change during the light, but not in a way that influenced motion of the jiggle cage that Holland and Rescorla (1975) had used to record general activity. In fear conditioning, too, rats show different CRs to tones and lights that support the same underlying learning (Kim, Rivers, Bevins, & Ayres, 1996).

If learning is separate from performance, then *performance rules* are needed to describe how learning is translated into behavior. The traditional Pavlovian performance rule was *stimulus substitution*: the CS becomes a substitute for the US. A dog salivates when fed, so it salivates to a signal for food. Pigeons made both hungry and thirsty peck a lighted key signaling food in the same way as they peck at food, whereas they "drink" a key signaling water (Jenkins & Moore, 1973). But much of the behavior resulting from Pavlovian conditioning is not exactly stimulus subsitution. For example, if rats see another rat passing by on a trolley just before they are fed, they don't try to eat the signal rat but direct social behaviors toward it (Timberlake & Grant, 1975). Hamsters, animals that would not normally interact socially over food, do not develop any social or feeding behavior in such a situation (Timberlake, 1983). One way of describing results of this kind is to say that species-specific behavior appropriate to the US occurs during the CS if there is stimulus support for it. Thus, diffuse visual stimuli paired with food cause pigeons to become active rather than to peck. Shock generally causes rats to jump and squeak, but shock from a small prod causes rats to throw sawdust over the prod and bury it, whereas they freeze in the presence of diffuse signals for shock to the feet (Pinel & Treit, 1978). In such cases behavior is determined by the nature of the CS itself, not merely by what stimuli happen to be present when it appears. This is shown very clearly by observations of rats' behavior to a compound of a diffuse light and a tone CS for food (Holland, 1977). Rats pretrained to the light (i.e., rats for which conditioning to the tone was blocked) behaved in a way appropriate to the light when the light and tone were presented together, whereas rats pretained to the tone behaved in the way normally seen with the tone alone. In part, differences in CR form can be accounted for as enhanced orienting responses to the CS (Holland, 1984). For instance, animals approach and direct responses to a localized CS even if the US is delivered elsewhere (Jenkins et al., 1978).

Behavior Systems   Can all the different kinds of CRs animals display be described in a unified way that allows unambiguous predictions for new species and situations? Two kinds of approaches to this problem have been explored, a causal one based on the ethological notion of behavior systems introduced in chapter 1 and a functional one. The behavior systems approach says that the CS brings into play the behavior system relevant to the US (Hogan, 1994b; Holland, 1984; Suboski, 1990; Timberlake, 1990, 1994). Because behavior systems can be assessed outside of conditioning situations, this approach offers a powerful causal analysis of conditioned behavior (Shettleworth, 1994a). In terms of the model of a behavior system in figure 1.10, Pavlovian conditioning could result in modification of either perceptual-motor or perceptual-central connections. Perceptual-motor conections correspond to S-R learning: recognition of the CS triggers a particular movement. However, many of the results discussed earlier in this section suggest that conditioning often results in new perceptual (CS) - central connections that facilitate the whole system of behaviors relevant to the US (Hogan, 1994b). This model captures very well the notion that behaviors shown after conditioning have a preexisting organization that influences their performance as CRs. For example, pigeons normally peck only stimuli much smaller than the usual 2.5 cm diameter pecking key. If a 6-mm dot, smaller than the pigeon's gape, is put onto the key in an autoshaping experiment, pecking develops much more quickly than with a normal blank key (Jenkins, Barnes, & Barrera, 1981). In the behavior system view, this illustrates the joint control of a CR by its normal causal factors (the size of spots) and associative ones. The behavior systems account also readily explains why CRs are not necessarily the same as URs. For instance, when young chicks are placed in a cool environment and exposed to pairings of a lighted pecking key and a heat lamp, they come to peck the key even though they never peck the heat lamp (Wasserman, 1973). If the lamp is seen as a surrogate mother hen, the

CR of pecking can readily be understood: chicks peck at the mother's feathers and snuggle underneath her when she sits down to brood them (Hogan, 1974).

Fear in rats (Fanselow, 1994), feeding in rats (Timberlake, 1994), and sexual behavior in quail (Domjan, 1994) have been successfully analyzed using the behavior system approach. In all three systems, conditioning occurs even with quite long intervals between CS and US, but what CR is seen depends on the CS-US interval. The influence of CS-US interval on CR form has long been recognized—for instance, in Konorski's (1967) distinction between preparatory and consummatory CRs. In these terms, preparatory behaviors tend to be shown with long CS-US intervals and consummatory behaviors with short ones. In the behavior system account, the behaviors within appetitive behavior systems such as feeding can be classified functionally as general search (e.g., general activity in search of food), focal search (e.g., striking and pouncing on prey), and consummatory behaviors (e.g., tearing and chewing prey) (Timberlake, 1994; figure 3.14). Similarly, the perceived imminence of attack determines which defensive behaviors are activated (Fanselow & Lester, 1988). Preencounter behaviors such as reorganization of feeding occur in places where predators have been encountered before; an animal actually meeting a predator engages in postencounter behaviors like freezing or fleeing, but if the predator attacks it shows rather different, circa-strike behaviors—perhaps vocalizing and striking back at its attacker. These ideas have proved useful in accounting for the CRs shown with CSs of different durations, in conditioning with sexual (Domjan, 1994) as well as food and shock USs. The behavior system view also has comparative implications—for instance, how seven species of rodents treat a moving ball bearing that signaled food can be accounted for by the nature of their predatory behavior (Timberlake & Washburne, 1989). Another example is the difference between hamsters and rats in CRs to a social CS for food mentioned above. Species and sex differences in the tendency to show conditioning of sexual and aggressive behaviors and in the CSs to which they are shown might also be predicted by thinking of how conditioning taps into the preorganized behaviors of the species and—as discussed in a moment—what its function would be (Domjan & Hollis, 1988; Hollis, 1990).

The Function of Conditioned Responding   If the function of conditioning is to allow animals to learn cause-effect relationships, then the response to a known cause (a CS) should reflect anticipation of its effects (the US)—that is, the CR should be such as to optimize the animal's interaction with the US (Hollis, 1982). This hypothesis does not mean that CRs are instrumental responses learned through reward and punishment. It is not an answer to Tinbergen's mechanism or development why question but to the current function question. Indeed, *omission training* experiments show that CRs may be largely involuntary and occur despite adverse experimental consequences. For instance, in an autoshaping experiment, where lighting of a pecking key is followed by food, pigeons go on pecking even if pecking cancels food (see

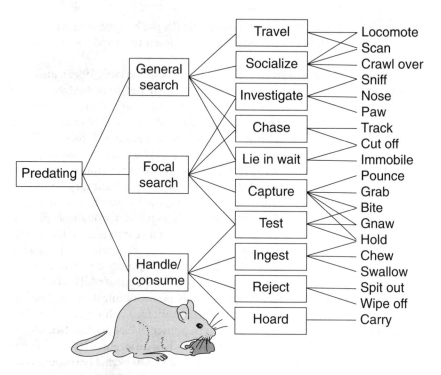

Figure 3.14. The rat's feeding system, redrawn from Timberlake (1994) with permission.

chapter 11). Evidence from conditioning with USs from drugs to shock to sexual behavior show that this functional approach makes sense of the variety of CRs that animals display (Hollis, 1982). In stimulus substitition the CR is very similar to the UR, but with some drugs as USs the CR is opposite to the UR. Vasodilation may occur instead of vasoconstriction, body warming instead of cooling, and so on. Such CRs help to maintain homeostasis by counteracting the drugs' tendency to push important physiological variables outside of normal ranges (Siegel & Allan, 1996). These compensatory CRs makes sense in the same framework as stimulus substitution: both function to optimize interaction with USs.

The notion that the tendency to display particular CRs must have evolved because they gave a selective advantage to the individuals displaying them would be difficult to test directly, but it suggests testable predictions about the present-day function of conditioning. In the best-studied example, Hollis has shown that sexual and aggressive CRs do in fact give some fish an advantage that is very likely to translate into reproductive success, and in one case she and her colleagues have measured reproductive success directly. Male blue gourami fish (*Tricogaster tricopterous*) were trained to expect an encounter with a territorial rival following lighting of a red panel on the side of their tank. The fish evidenced knowledge of the predictive relationship between the panel and

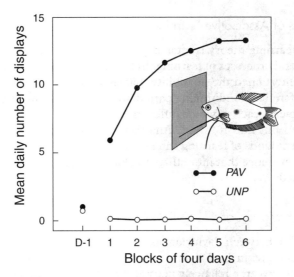

Figure 3.15. Male blue gouramis' aggressive display toward a light paired with a rival (Pav group) and in an unpaired (UNP) control group. D-1 is the level of display before training. Redrawn from Hollis (1984) with permission.

the rival's arrival by beginning to display aggressively during the CS (figure 3.15). Control males were given either unpaired exposure to rivals and the red panel or exposure to rivals alone. When pairs of conditioned and control males were shown the CS at the same time and then allowed to fight each other, the conditioned males showed more bites and tailbeating responses than their rivals, and they nearly always won the fights (Hollis, 1984; Hollis, Dumas, Singh, & Fackelman, 1995).

In many species, breeding males holding territories behave aggressively toward any animal approaching their territory, even females. Mating might be facilitated if the male could anticipate the approach of a female and inhibit undue aggression. Indeed this has proved to be the case in blue gouramis. Male blue gouramis' sexual behavior can be conditioned with a female as a US using methods otherwise like those for conditioning aggressive behavior (Hollis, 1990; Hollis, Cadieux, & Colbert, 1989). After presentations of the CS, conditioned males direct fewer bites and more courtship movements at a test female than do controls. Moreover, this behavior translates into spectacularly enhanced reproduction in the ensuing mating. When conditioned and control males remained with females after a single presentation of the CS, the conditioned males spawned sooner and fathered on average over a thousand young, compared to a mean of less than 100 fathered by controls for which the CS had been explicitly unpaired with a female (Hollis, Pharr, Dumas, Britton, & Field, 1997). Gutiérrez and Domjan (1996) have also demonstrated that the ability to anticipate the arrival of a female endows conditioned male Japanese quail (*Coturnix japonica*) with a mating advantage.

3.5 Varieties of Associative Learning

Associative learning theory is often depicted as a monolithic account of supposedly general processes of learning. In fact, however, learning theorists have frequently entertained the possibility that more than one kind of learning is going on in familiar conditioning paradigms. In this section we consider four such phenomena, each of which differs from ordinary Pavlovian conditioning in some ways but not in others. Analyses of them illustrate how questions about different kinds of learning can be addressed by a well-developed theory and provide evidence that more than one kind of relationship between events can be learned.

3.5.1 Pavlovian and Instrumental Learning

The distinction between Pavlovian and instrumental conditioning is perfectly clear operationally: in Pavlovian conditioning, the experimenter arranges a contingency between a relatively neutral stimulus and a reinforcer; in instrumental conditioning, the contingency is between some aspect of the animal's behavior and a reinforcer. The evidence that instrumental learning has occurred is usually some change in the frequency of the response. However, this operational difference is not enough to infer that the underlying learning processes differ, and in fact historically they were not always considered separately (see Rescorla & Solomon, 1967). Any instrumental conditioning setup inevitably includes external stimuli, and it could be their relationship with the reinforcer that the animal learns about. A rat reinforced with food for pressing a lever, for example, receives the food after close contact with stimuli from the lever. This Pavlovian, lever-food, contingency could be what actually controls the rat's behavior. Such an account is particularly plausible in the light of our knowledge of autoshaping and related phenomena.

Pavlovian conditioning does contribute to many instances of successful instrumental training, but it is far from being the whole story. For example, when hamsters expect food or electrical brain stimulation, they rear and perform certain other activities whereas grooming and scent-marking on the walls of the cage are suppressed (see figure 8.2). If food or brain stimulation is made contingent on one of these activities, any activity that is not inhibited can be instrumentally trained, while the inhibited activities are difficult or impossible to train (Shettleworth, 1975; Shettleworth & Juergensen, 1980). The animal's Pavlovian expectation of the reinforcer in the experimental context facilitates a whole behavior system. The instrumental contingency can selectively strengthen any activity within it. This kind of result, among others, points to a role for response-reinforcer contingencies as well as stimulus-reinforcer contingencies in instrumental performance. It also indicates how Pavlovian conditioning may explain some constraints on instrumental action, such as the hamsters' failure to groom at a high rate when rewarded with food.

The traditional account of instrumental performance was that it reflected

S-R learning: the response became connected to situational stimuli through the stamping in action of reinforcement. This account provides no role for a representation of the reinforcer in instrumental performance. Watching an animal perform an instrumentally trained activity, one would imagine it "knows what it is doing," but the S-R account does not indicate how this could be. Performance of an instrumental action is, in fact, controlled by the current information about the reinforcer (Colwill, 1994; Dickinson, 1994). For example, a rat trained to press a lever for sucrose and pull a chain for food pellets will stop lever pressing but not chain pulling after it has learned that sucrose is followed by poison. Animals learn response-reinforcer associations through the same laws of learning as in Pavlovian conditioning (Dickinson, 1994; Mackintosh, 1983) as one would expect if associative learning is a general mechanism for learning causal relationships between events regardless of their nature.

But how is performance generated from the animal's knowledge of the causal link between response and reinforcer? One possiblity is that instrumental performance can best be understood as an inference from the information contained in the response-reinforcer association, together with motivational information (Dickinson & Balleine, 1994). The animal puts together the information "bar pressing produces food" with the information "I need food" and infers the instruction "press the bar." A related view is suggested by the notion that learning acts within preexisting behavior systems (section 3.4.3). In this view, experience of a response-reinforcer association in some way connects the response to the behavior system relevant to the reinforcer (hunger in the case of food reinforcement, sex in the case of sexual reinforcement, etc.). The response is then automatically influenced by the factors like food deprivation or hormones that influence the behavior system as a whole, as well as by its own original causal factors (see Dickinson & Balleine, 1994, for a model and data consistent with this interpretation).

Neither of these views is without problems. The behavior system view appears to imply that although the animal is exposed to conditions designed to teach it a response-reinforcer association, in fact it has acquired a connection that works in exactly the opposite direction: the drive state or behavior system excites the response. The alternative view sounds like a reinterpretation of the observed behavior in terms of implicit inferences by the animal, a possibility discussed further in chapter 11. Neither model allows an obvious role for the stimuli that come to control instrumental responding. For example, a rat can learn to press a lever for food when a tone is on and refrain from pressing when the tone is off. The tone here is referred to as a *discriminative stimulus*. In Skinner's terms, it "sets the occasion" when bar pressing will be reinforced. The discriminative stimulus is not itself an excitor of bar pressing but rather a modulator of the association, telling the animal when the information it contains is valid. In behavior system terms it is not simply another causal factor for the response, any more than it is the first term in an excitatory association. As we see below, this kind of stimulus function is not unique to instrumental learning.

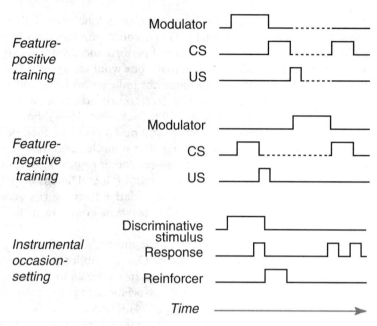

Figure 3.16. Procedures for training Pavlovian modulators and instrumental occasion setters.

3.5.2 Conditional Control of Behavior: Occasion Setting and Modulation

Consider the following problem, known as a *feature positive discrimination*: In the presence of a stimulus, A, nothing happens, but when A is preceded by another stimulus, X, reinforcement is delivered (figure 3.16). The Rescorla-Wagner model predicts that conditioning here will accrue only to X because it is the only reliable predictor of reinforcement. Stimulus A should gain no strength because the US occurs whether or not A is presented. This is indeed what happens if X and A are simultaneous. However, if X and A are presented serially, so that X precedes reinforced occurrences of A while A alone is not reinforced, X does not become an excitor. Rather, it acquires the ability to modulate excitation to A. The serial feature positive discrimination appears to support a different, higher level kind of learning from the simple excitatory or inhibitory connections between event representations discussed so far. This kind of learning has been called, alternatively, *facilitation*, by analogy with inhibition, whose conceptual opposite it appears to be (Rescorla, 1987), and *occasion setting*, by analogy with the occasion-setting function of discriminative stimuli in instrumental learning (Holland, 1992), or simply *modulation*. (Swartzentruber, 1995). A stimulus can be simultaneously an excitor and a modulator, and these functions can be manipulated independently.

Two kinds of evidence show that modulation is functionally independent from simple Pavlovian or instrumental excitation. These are, first, different conditions for acquisition and extinction and, second, failure of excitors and occasion setters to block each other, indicating that the contents of learning are different. For instance, the necessary condition for extinction of facilitation is that X no longer predict that A will be reinforced. Simply presenting the facilitator, X, alone, with no reinforcement and no occurrences of A, is inadequate to extinguish its facilitatory function (Rescorla, 1986). One of the two traditional paradigms for demonstrating Pavlovian conditioned inhibition (Rescorla, 1969) parallels that for training a positive modulator: a CS is reinforced when presented alone but nonreinforced when preceded by another stimulus, the conditioned inhibitor. It now appears that conditioned inhibitors trained in this way (as opposed to those trained with simultaneous presentations with the nonreinforced CS) are best viewed as modulators with properties analogous to those of positive modulators (Swartzentruber, 1995; Williams, Overmier, & LoLordo, 1992).

Modulation has only begun to be investigated relatively recently, and the conditions governing its acquisition are not yet fully understood (see Swartzentruber, 1995). It has been investigated in several different preparations, sometimes with different results. What is clear so far is that facilitation differs from simple conditioning in a number of ways. It seems to develop in parallel with excitation and to serve a kind of higher level modulatory function that is not readily captured by simple connectionist models of conditioning. Moreover, although it has been useful to study modulation using discrete stimuli as modulators, it is clear that environmental contexts are important modulators of associative information (Bouton, 1993; Swartzentruber, 1995). For example, a response learned in one context and extinguished in another is still performed in the first context, apparently because the new context modulates the original association (Bouton, 1993). In general, the ability to learn about modulators allows animals to use associative information in a flexible and appropriate way rather than mindlessly performing a CR whenever the CS appears.

3.5.3 Within Event Learning

We have already encountered the question of whether animals treat a single stimulus as a sum of elements or as an unanalyzed configuration. One way to study this issue is to create events with separable elements, expose animals to their union, then give one element a new significance and measure behavior to the other, as in sensory preconditioning. If the animal views the elements as aspects of the same event, then its behavior to the unconditioned element should be affected by conditioning with the other (Rescorla & Durlach, 1981). For example, suppose rats are allowed to drink two compound flavors such as sweet-sour and salty-bitter. Then a member of one compound is paired with poison and as a control the rats are exposed to a member of the other compound alone. When the rats choose between the two elements they had not encountered in the second phase of the experiment, they preferred to drink the flavor not paired with the poisoned one. Parallel results have been obtained using lights and tones for rats and visual stimuli for pigeons (Rescorla & Durlach, 1981). They suggest that the elements making up each compound are associated with each other. Such *within event learning* increases rapidly and monotonically with number of exposures to the compound. Learning about simultaneous events can even be superior to learning about successive events. And, as one would expect, within-event learning can be extinguished by presenting one or other element of the event by itself. However, although retraining after extinction is normally quicker than original acquisition with Pavlovian or instrumental conditioning (the phenomenon of savings), retraining of within-event learning is difficult or impossible after extinction. This finding is consistent with the view that animals originally treat the compound stimulus as a single unanalyzed unit or configuration. In this view (Pearce, 1994b), the acquired value of one element transfers to the other through generalization because each element is treated as similar to the compound. However, exposure to the elements in isolation sets up representations of these as separate events and associative changes involving them are no longer related back to the compound. In this view, therefore, learning about single events is not a matter of associating simultaneously presented events but rather a kind of perceptual learning. Indeed, if associative learning is fundamentally a process of learning cause-effect relationships, one may question whether the idea of associating simultaneous events, where there is no separable cause and effect, even makes sense. Perceptual learning is discussed further in chapter 4.

3.5.4 Overshadowing and Potentiation

If a rat learns to expect shock after a light and a noise come on together and is tested with the light and the noise alone, the rat will show less conditioning to either the light or the noise than if this had been the only signal (Kamin, 1969). This phenomenon of mutual *overshadowing* is embodied in the Rescorla-Wagner model in the assumption that the gain in associative strength of each element of a compound is determined by the total associative strength of all stimuli present at the time. However, if instead of exposing rats to lights and noises paired with shock, one exposes them to odors and flavors paired with poison, the results are different. Conditioning is much better to the odor when it is presented in compound with a flavor than when it is trained alone (Domjan, 1983). It is as if association of the odor with poison is potentiated by the presence of a flavor. This makes functional sense in that the flavor can be seen as directing attention to odors, and perhaps visual features of food as properties worth learning about (Galef & Osborne, 1978).

When it was first discovered in taste aversion learning, such *potentiation* was interpreted as a specific adaptation for learning about the properties of foods. There are two kinds of evidence that this is not so. First, potentiation has been observed with stimuli other than odors and in other conditioning situations such as eyelid conditioning in rabbits (Domjan, 1983). This does not mean the phenomenon is not a true potentiation of association, but the determinants are more complex than originally thought. Second, at least some instances of potentiation are attributable to within-event learning. Rather than being directly associated with poison by virtue of accompanying a flavor, odors could be associated with the accompanying flavors and rejected because the flavors are aversive. This kind of evidence suggests that the original claims that potentiation was a special kind of learning, a violation of the Rescorla-Wagner model, may not have been justified. However, the determinants of potentiation have not been thoroughly analyzed in all the preparations where it has been demonstrated (Domjan, 1983). It therefore remains possible that it sometimes results from special mechanisms whereby one element of a compound enhances learning to another, perhaps by enhancing attention to it (LoLordo & Droungas, 1989).

3.6 Summary

In recent years, the assumption that the human or animal mind is a single general-purpose learner or information processor has been challenged by the notion that cognition is modular. The modules are adaptive specializations that process restricted kinds of information in ecologically appropriate ways. In the study of learning, modularity is equivalent to the assumption that there is a variety of different kinds of learning. A general framework for analyzing and comparing learning phenomena is outlined in section 3.2. The conditions for learning, the contents of learning, and the effects of learning on behavior are central to a behavioral analysis. Learning phenomena can differ from one another along any of these dimensions. The decision as to how many or what sort of differences make a different kind is a theoretical one.

Associative learning is an adaptation for learning about causal relationships in the environment. As this idea suggests, sensitivity to associative relationships is phylogenetically very widespread, although the events that enter into associations vary in a species- and situation-specific way. The review of associative learning, principally Pavlovian conditioning, in sections 3.4 and 3.5 shows how the three basic questions about learning have been answered in one very well-studied case. The study of Pavlovian conditioning thus provides a model for analyzing other forms of learning that we will encounter in future chapters. But even in this apparently simple form of learning, animals show evidence of subtle and interesting cognitive processing. For instance, rats or pigeons learn about multiple features of the CS and the US, the context in which they occur, and the temporal relationship between them. Access to some of this information is later conditionally controlled by the context, so that only the information most relevant in the current situation controls behavior. Thus associative learning is not a stupid, low-level process to be contrasted with more "cognitive" mechanisms. In future chapters, it will be important to keep in mind the power of conditioning processes to produce subtle and sophisticated adjustments to the local environment in order to evaluate claims that some examples of adaptive behavior require other cognitive mechanisms for their explanation.

Further Reading

The notion of adaptive specialization in learning was introduced to contemporary learning theory by Rozin and Kalat (1971). This article is still well worth reading, even though some of the phenomena Rozin and Kalat discuss, such as conditioned taste aversion, are now interpreted differently (Domjan, 1983). Rozin and Schull (1988) brought some of the ideas in it up to date and analyzed them more thoroughly. Sherry and Schacter (1987) further developed the idea of adaptive specialization and related specializations in animals to memory systems in people. The article by Shettleworth (1993a) discusses in more detail the ideas in section 3.2 about the dimensions of learning, which were originally laid out by Rescorla and Holland (1976). Johnston's (1982) review is a thorough and stimulating discussion of the costs and benefits of learning. A number of stimulating discussions about evolution and learning can be found in Bolles and Beecher's (1988) edited volume of that name.

An up-to-date introduction to Pavlovian and instrumental conditioning can be found in the text by Domjan (1998). A brief review of the modern cognitive view of conditioning is Rescorla's (1988a) article entitled, "Pavlovian conditioning: It's not what you think it is." A more advanced but eminently readable and scholarly treatment of associative learning is the book by Mackintosh (1983). Recent reviews of selected problems are the chapters by Hall on associative learning and by Dickinson on instrumental learning in the book edited by Mackintosh (1994b). Gallistel's (1992) approach is presented in an article entitled "Classical conditioning as an adaptive specialization: A computational model." His book (Gallistel, 1990) contains a further critique of the Rescorla-Wagner model.

The role of behavior systems in learning is discussed in a collection of five articles in the December 1994 issue of *The Psychonomic Bulletin and Review* (Domjan, 1994; Fanselow, 1994; Hogan, 1994b; Shettleworth, 1994a; Timberlake, 1994). A related approach is Suboski's (1990) "Releaser-induced recognition learning."

4

Simple Recognition Learning

To recognize literally means "to know again, to perceive to be identical with something previously known" (*Oxford English Dictionary, 3rd edition*). Therefore, in a sense all learning involves recognition. This chapter focuses on how animals come to recognize events they are simply exposed to, in the absence of obvious relationships with other events. Such learning seems to reflect what people usually mean by *recognition*. If I ask, "Do you recognize that woman?" what I want to know is "Have you seen her before?" Psychological experiments on recognition capture this meaning (see chapter 6). In behavioral ecology, by contrast, *recognition* can refer to classifying objects or other animals appropriately on first encounter. For instance, *kin recognition* refers to a tendency to treat relatives differently from other conspecifics, regardless of whether they have ever been encountered before. This corresponds to a second definition, "to know by means of some distinctive feature."

Kin recognition is discussed at the end of this chapter. First, however, we consider three ways in which animals appear to acquire detailed representations of single events simply by being exposed to them. These are habituation, perceptual learning, and imprinting. In each case we will ask two questions: What is the nature of that representation (i.e., what is the content of learning?) and how does experience change the representation (i.e., what are the conditions for learning?). The section on perceptual learning describes a general model of how such representations are formed and what they consist of.

4.1 Habituation

4.1.1 Response Habituation

When a frog's back is tickled, the frog reflexively wipes the spot that was tickled. If the same place is touched repeatedly, the wiping reflex becomes less and less vigorous. When a male white-throated sparrow hears the song of a neighbor on the edge of his territory, he approaches and flies back and forth, finally perching on a branch to sing a territorial song. Over the breeding season this aggressive behavior wanes toward familiar neighbors, but it is still shown toward strangers and toward familiar neighbors in new places (box 4.1). The waning of the frog's wiping reflex and the waning of the sparrow's

---

Box 4.1. Habituation and Individual Recognition

Males in many species of songbirds hold territories in the breeding season and exclude other males of their species from them. Singing and aggressive interactions are prominent near territory boundaries, especially early in the breeding season. Birds that can learn who their neighbors are and spend time and energy only on repelling new arrivals will have more time for other activities such as attracting females. As this functional notion suggests birds do in fact respond less and less to familiar neighbors as the season goes on. The learning responsible for this individual recognition has been studied in a large number of bird species (reviews in Catchpole & Slater, 1995; Falls, 1982; see also box 6.1). White-crowned sparrows habituate to the same song played repeatedly from the same location (Petrinovich & Patterson, 1979). However, many birds not only recognize specific familiar songs, as evidenced in habituation but they also seem to associate the songs of a particular singer with the place where he usually sings. For instance, in playback experiments in the field, white-throated sparrows behaved just as aggressively toward a neighbor's song played from a new location as toward a stranger's song played from that location (figure B4.1; Falls & Brooks, 1975).

Males of some species have repertoires of up to hundreds of different songs. One theory is that large repertoires function to prevent habituation in potential rivals or mates (see Catchpole & Slater, 1995). If neighbor-stranger discrimination depends on associating the neighbor's songs with the direction from which they are usually heard, neighbor-stranger discrimination might be less sharp in species with large repertoires. This is not always true, however. Songs within an individual's repertoire may have some shared characteristics, permitting generalization among them. Such individual differences have been documented in great tits the field. Furthermore, male great tits trained to respond differently to songs from two individuals in the laboratory generalize from the training songs to unfamiliar songs of the same individuals (Weary & Krebs, 1992). However, red-winged blackbirds do not generalize habituation across different songs of an unfamiliar individual (Searcy, Coffman, & Raikow, 1994). Perhaps great tits have the equivalent of distinctive tones of voice and red-winged blackbirds do not.

Responding acquired to one feature of a familiar individual would transfer to his other features if his various features had become associated, in much the same way

◼➡

Box 4.1. *(continued)*

as in other examples of perceptual learning. Hamsters show evidence for this sort of learning (Johnston & Jernigan, 1994; see figure 2.4). A male hamster habituated to the vaginal scent of a familiar female proves to be habituated to her flank gland scent as well. That this is not merely due to generalization from one scent to the other is proved by testing males that have never met the stimulus female: they do not transfer habituation between scents. Social interactions with a female would allow plenty of opportunity to associate her various scents, in much the same way as small birds are suggested to associate the various features of their mothers during filial imprinting (see section 4.3.3). In chapters 11 and 12 we will consider the possibility that social primates acquire elaborate networks of associations among the characteristics of social companions, but clearly this sort of recognition learning is not exclusive to them.

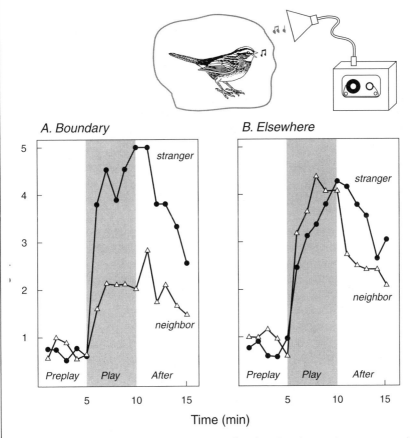

Figure B4.1. Response (songs per minute) of male white-throated sparrows to the recorded songs of neighbors or strangers presented either at the territorial boundary shared with the neighbor or elsewhere in the subject bird's territory. Data from Falls and Brooks (1975), redrawn with permission.

aggressive display have both been studied as examples of habituation even though the behaviors differ considerably in complexity and wane over different time courses. In both cases behavior changes in such a way that time and energy are not wasted in unnecessary, inappropriate, or ineffective behaviors. However, the habituated animal does not necessarily do nothing or become entirely indifferent to the habituating stimulus. When the single response measured in a typical habituation experiment is considered in the context of the animal's whole behavior, habituation may be more a matter of one response being replaced by another that experience shows is more appropriate.

Habituation is perhaps the most widespread form of behavioral plasticity, found in many behavior systems and in species including one-celled organisms and humans (Thorpe, 1956; Macphail, 1993). It also appears to be the simplest: exposure to a single event is certainly the most elementary experience an animal can have. However, this apparently elementary experience can have a number of effects, some of them quite complex. Repeated presentation of a single event can have both long-term and short-term effects. Responses may either increase or decrease in intensity when they are repeatedly elicited. Sometimes a single response does both. In addition, exposure to a single event can produce perceptual learning, latent inhibition, and/or imprinting. Until relatively recently psychologists barely regarded habituation as genuine learning at all (Harris, 1943). However, in the past 25 years or so habituation has become an important part of the "simple systems" approach to learning because it may be more amenable to physiological analysis than is associative learning (Groves & Thompson, 1970; Macphail, 1993; Thompson & Spencer, 1966). This section is organized around the topics outlined in chapter 3. We look first at the conditions for habituation, its contents, and the effects of learning on behavior. After reviewing the basic facts, we consider three theories about the content of learning in habituation.

4.1.2 Conditions for Learning

Habituation may be identified operationally as a decrease in responding resulting from repeated stimulation. The responses considered can be anything from simple reflexes to complex activities of whole animals. However, changes in behavior owing to fatigue of receptors or effectors are not accepted as habituation even though they do result from repeated stimulation. Receptor and effector fatigue can be eliminated as explanations for decreased responding by a demonstration of *dishabituation*: a novel stimulus restores responding to the habituating stimulus (figure 4.1).

Experience with a single event is completely described by the answers to a few simple questions: What is it? How long and intense is it? How often does it occur? How many times has it occurred? What was the animal's age and motivational state during exposure? These same questions apply to any form of simple recognition learning and define the important parameters that determine the speed and durability of the response decrement in habituation.

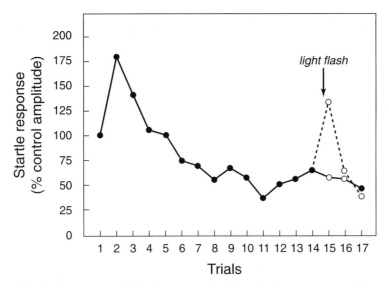

Figure 4.1. Habituation and dishabituation of rats' startle response to a sudden sound. Rats whose data are represented by the dotted line received a flash of light just before the 15th sound. Redrawn from Groves and Thompson (1970) with permission.

Stimulus Quality   Specificity is one of the defining features of habituation. Completely generalized response decrement would be attributed to receptor adaptation or response fatigue. However, habituation does generalize to stimuli physically similar to the habituating stimulus. Taking the stimulus-specificity of habituation as a given implies that in dishabituation the animal is classifying the new, dishabituating stimulus as different from the old one. Because the behaviors observed in tests of habituation do not have to be trained initially, the habituation-dishabituation paradigm is therefore a powerful tool for studying basic memory and classification processes in nonverbal organisms, including human infants. The data on hamsters' odor discrimination in figure 2.4 is one example. A large body of literature on infant perception and cognition rests on the fact that babies orient toward novel visual and auditory stimuli. Orienting (looking and/or modifying sucking rate) habituates to repeated stimuli and is restored when a novel stimulus appears. Thus, for example, a baby hears "ba . . . ba . . . ba . . ." and then "pa . . . pa . . ." to see if she notices a difference. More complex kinds of categorization can be tested, too, such as sound sequences that do and do not have the same statistical regularities (Saffran, Aslin, & Newport, 1996). Similar tests of looking time have also been used with free-ranging monkeys (see chapters 11 and 12). As another example, Heinrich (1995) used the fact that young ravens peck at novel objects to demonstrate that the birds very quickly acquire amazingly detailed knowledge about their local environments.

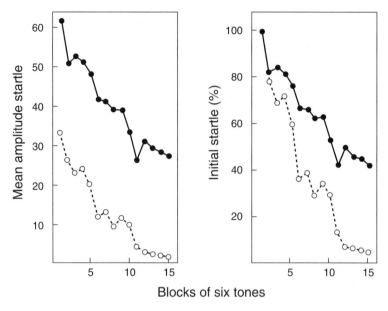

Figure 4.2. How choice of an absolute or relative response measure can influence the pattern of data, illustrated with results of an experiment on the effects of amphetamine on habituation of startle in rats. The panel on the left suggests that the drug (filled circles) raises the level of responsiveness without affecting the rate of habituation, whereas that on the right suggests that the drug slows the rate of habituation. Redrawn from Davis and File (1984) with permission.

Number of Stimulations   It almost goes without saying that the more the eliciting stimulus is presented, the more the response decreases. In an influential article, Thompson and Spencer (1966) claimed that responding was a negative exponential function of number of stimulations. This suggests that habituation is like associative learning in reducing the discrepancy between "expected" and actual sequels to an event in a manner proportional to the discrepancy. However, the exact form of habituation curves depends on how responding is measured (Hinde, 1970b; figure 4.2). In associative learning theory, the Rescorla-Wagner model does not claim to describe changes in performance but rather changes in underlying associative strength (V). Performance need only be some monotonic function of associative strength. Theories of habituation have not always differentiated the underlying learning, the theoretical habituation process, from performance of the habituated response. However, the phenomenon of *habituation below zero* (Hinde, 1970b; Thompson & Spencer, 1966) suggests that a learning-performance distinction may be needed for habituation, too. Continuing stimulation after the measured response can no longer be observed results in slower recovery than simply habituating to zero, suggesting that learning continues in the absence of measurable responding.

Increasing numbers of presentations not only decrease responding to the

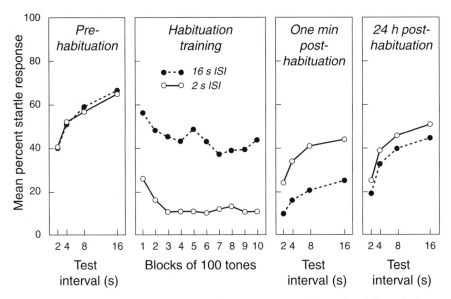

Figure 4.3. Illustration of the importance of giving a standard test after different habituation experiences. Two groups of rats were habituated to tones presented with an interstimulus interval (ISI) of either 2 or 16 seconds and tested 1 minute or 24 hours later at a variety of ISIs. Redrawn from Davis (1970) with permission.

eliciting stimulus but also reduce generalization of habituation. For example, Gillette and Bellingham (1982, cited in Hall, 1991) habituated rats to drinking a novel fluid flavored with salt (NA) and sucrose (S). The rats drank little of these novel fluids at first but gradually increased their consumption. Generalization was measured by the rats' willingness to drink NA or S alone. Relative to consumption of the compound flavor, the rats drank *less* NA or S the more they had been habituated. That is, the more they had been exposed to NA+S, the better they discriminated this compound from its elements. This is just the opposite of what would be expected if the compound was simply the sum of elements that were habituating. Such findings indicate that exposure results in learning about the stimulus, not just reducing responding to it (Hall, 1991).

Timing and Intensity   Responding typically declines faster during *massed* than during *spaced* presentations of the eliciting stimulus. But since differences in learning at T1 (i.e., during the train of stimuli) must be assessed by a common test at T2, this observation is not enough to infer that learning depends on rate of presentation. What is needed is a standard test at T2. When this methodology has been applied, the more profound decline has been found after spaced training (figure 4.3; Davis, 1970). The same idea applies to the effects of stimulus intensity (Davis & Wagner, 1969). Thompson and Spencer (1966) stated that habituation is "more rapid and/or pronounced" with weaker stimuli. But when responding is measured in a standard test after ex-

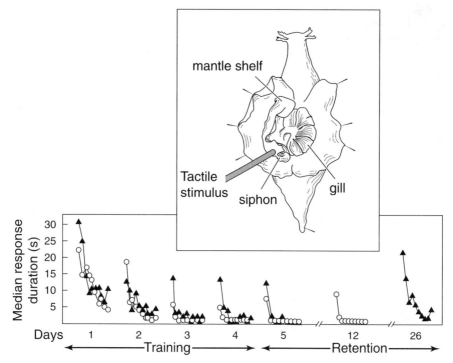

Figure 4.4. Long-term and short-term habituation of *Aplysia*'s siphon withdrawal to a jet of water applied to the siphon (tactile stimulus). No trials were administered between the last training day and the tests on day 5 and day 12 (group represented by open circles) or day 26, yet habituation was retained. At the same time, habituation developed within each day. Redrawn from Carew, Pinsker and Kandel (1972) with permission.

posure to different schedules and intensities of stimulation at T1, the results can be surprising. For instance, a relatively loud tone evokes a smaller startle response in rats habituated with a series of tones of gradually increasing loudness than in rats exposed to an equal number of tones of the same loudness as the test tone (Davis & Wagner, 1969).

The Interval between T1 and T2   Thorpe (1956) stipulated that a response decrement should be "relatively permanent" to count as habituation. In fact, however, repeated stimulation can have two distinct effects, one short term one long term, lasting for days or weeks (Staddon & Higa, 1996). Even very simple response systems such as gill withdrawal in *Aplysia* show long-term retention of habituation (figure 4.4). However, long-term habituation is also gradually forgotten, and generalization gradients broaden as time passes, as if the animal forgets the precise features of the habituating stimulus (Hall, 1991).

State Variables: Sensitization   Repeated stimulation can increase responding as well as decrease it. This is particularly likely to be true if the stimulus is moderately aversive. In the experiment on the rat's startle response to loud sounds shown in figure 4.1, the rats were actually more startled by the second and third tones than by the first one, although startle later declined. This biphasic curve is typical of the results of many experiments on habituation. The initial increase seems to reflect an independent process of *sensitization*, a general enhancement of responsiveness to a whole class of stimuli, not just the one being habituated. In many cases, sensitization has a shorter time course than habituation, as in figure 4.1.

The sensitizing effect of moderately strong stimuli may be responsible for some instances of "dishabituation." Functionally, it seems as if a sign of potential danger alerts the animal, making it more responsive to whatever comes next. Associative potentiation of the rat's startle response (Davis, Falls, Campeau, & Kim, 1993) fits this description: rats react more strongly to a sudden loud tone if they are in the presence of a signal previously associated with shock. However, dishabituation can also reflect a separate process from sensitization. Siphon withdrawal in the sea slug *Aplysia* wanes when the siphon is repeatedly squirted with a jet of water (figure 4.4). If the animal's tail is touched or shocked, siphon withdrawal is enhanced in both habituated and untrained animals. In an elegant series of experiments, Marcus, Nolen, Rankin, and Carew (1988) showed that sensitization and dishabituation can be dissociated in *Aplysia* in three independent ways. For instance, the best dishabituating stimulus is a touch to the tail or a relatively weak shock whereas strong shocks or many shocks to the tail are the best sensitizing stimuli. Dishabituation also appears earlier in development than does sensitization. Such dissociations lend support to a two-process theory of habituation (Groves & Thompson, 1970).

4.1.3 Diversity of Effects on Behavior

In examples of habituation like startle in the rat or the wiping reflex in frogs, learning seems to be little more than a change in a specific S-R relation, perhaps reflecting a decrease in synaptic transmission. However, as we have seen already, complex and variable behaviors of whole animals also habituate. The territorial behavior of birds described in box 4.1 is an example. Hamsters released into an open field repeatedly approach and sniff any new objects in it, exploring them. Exploration wanes over time, but if some of the objects are moved to new places, the hamsters start sniffing them again. Because the hamsters selectively investigate the objects that have been moved, renewed exploration is evidence for a map of the locations of objects rather than general dishabituation. It can be used to assess hamsters' sensitivity to spatial relations (Thinus-Blanc et al., 1987). As another example, when wild vervet monkeys hear the alarm call of a member of their troop broadcast from a loudspeaker, they gradually stop looking toward the hidden speaker (Cheney & Seyfarth, 1988; see also chapter 12). Habituation transfers to acoustically dissimilar calls by the same individual if the calls have the same referent (e.g., both are leopard alarms) but not if they have different referents (e.g., eagle and leopard alarms). It seems the animal is not habituating to the physical stimulus so much as to a class of signals from a specific signaler with a certain meaning. The monkey seems to learn "don't pay any attention when Joe says there's a leopard because Joe is unreliable when it comes to leopards." Tests of the generalization of habituation have been used in a similar way to inquire into what children understand about causation (e.g., Dasser, Ulbaek, & Premack, 1989; see also box 11.1).

4.1.4 Contents of Learning: Three Models

Over 50 years ago, one of the first reviewers of habituation concluded, "It will be obvious . . . that no 'mechanism' of habituation will be found. There are quite probably several mechanisms. . . . [A]ny single explanatory principle would have to be too general to be satisfactory" (Harris, 1943, p. 388). This conclusion is just as apt today. In this section we consider three models of habituation. The two classic ones differ in a familiar way: one is a simple model of changes in S-R connections, and the other assumes a more complex kind of representation. The third, more recent model depicts habituation as a form of associative learning (see Hall, 1991; Macphail, 1993, for further discussion).

Sherrington's Reflex Model   The simplest model of habituation dates from the work of Sir Charles Sherrington, who studied how reflexes habituate in animals with severed spinal cords. Because the surgery removes influences from the brain, habituation in spinal animals necessarily reflects decreased efficacy of specific reflex pathways, S-R connections. As in S-R accounts of associative learning, this model does not distinguish between learning and performance: learning, the decrement in connection strength, is directly reflected in decreased responding. As a general account of habituation, this is simply a restatement of behavioral observations in neural terms and as such is relatively impoverished. It does not predict any new phenomena or specify the precise form of the decrement in connection strength. However, this model can be elaborated in a number of ways to account for phenomena such as dishabituation and sensitization (e.g., Davis & File, 1984; Horn, 1967). It is a reasonable account of some examples of habituation such as startle in the rat or siphon withdrawal in *Aplysia*. Nevertheless, a simple S-R model is not very useful for understanding habituation of more complex behaviors or behavior systems. Moreover, a simple S-R model does not allow for changes in the representation of stimuli that may go on during habituation.

Sokolov's Neuronal Model   A more complex model that is also couched in neural terms in Sokolov's (1963) comparator model. In this system, learning consists of building up a representation of the features of a stimulus—visual, auditory, temporal, spatial—the *neuronal model*. The details of how this takes place are not specified, but it could involve the kind of within-event learning to be discussed in section 4.2. Incoming stimuli are compared to existing neuronal models before being acted on. To the extent there is a match, the initial response to the stimulus is inhibited—that is, behavioral habituation is observed. If the incoming stimulus is discrepant from the neuronal model, an *orienting response* (OR) occurs and the neuronal model is modified so as to reduce its discrepancy from the incoming stimulus. Therefore, this scheme distinguishes between learning (modification of the neuronal model) and performance (the OR based on detection of a discrepancy).

Some examples of habituation seem to require such a comparator account. One is the *missing stimulus effect* (Sokolov, 1963). If an animal is habituated to stimuli coming at regular intervals and then one stimulus is omitted, the habituated response reappears at the time the omitted stimulus was due. This is hard for the simple reflex model to account for because the absence of a stimulus has significance only by comparison to expected input. However, evidence for this phenomenon is actually rather weak, and, in any case, the effect can be generated by other models (Hall, 1991). Some phenomena are problematical for the comparator model, too. In particular, an increasing series of stimulus intensities should not result in greater response decrement than a series of presentations of the same, intense, stimulus (Davis & Wagner, 1969; Groves & Thompson, 1970; see also section 4.1.2). The neuronal model should match the test stimulus better when that stimulus has been presented all along than when different stimuli have been presented.

Sokolov proposed a specific neural embodiment of his model: the neuronal model is built up in the cortex, and it inhibits activity in the reticular formation, but this system cannot apply to habituation in spinal animals or in *Aplysia*. There are probably many specific neural mechanisms for behavioral habituation. As far as potential generality there is a lot to be said for more abstract "black box" models like the one discussed next (Davis & File, 1984; Whitlow & Wagner, 1984).

Wagner's SOP Model   Accounting for an apparently simple kind of learning in terms of a more complex one may seem unappealing, a violation of Lloyd Morgan's Canon. Yet one influential model of habituation does just that: in this model, habituation results from associating the habituating stimulus with the context in which it appears (Wagner, 1978, 1981). This account integrates habituation with associative learning and with standard features of short-term memory. (Hence its acronym, *SOP*, for *standard operating procedure* of memory.) In the SOP model (figure 4.5), incoming stimuli are compared to the contents of active or *working memory*. Working memory has two levels or states. The highest level of activation, A1, corresponds to the focus of attention or "rehearsal." In animals, the contents of A1 are directly read out in behavior appropriate to the stimulus being processed. If food stimuli are in A1, the animal will be engaged in food-related activities; if a sudden loud noise is being processed, the animal will startle. Behavior appropriate to incoming stimuli will be observed whenever the incoming stimulus is not already represented in one of the levels of active memory (A1 or A2).

Representations (nodes) in A1 fade into the A2 state, corresponding to

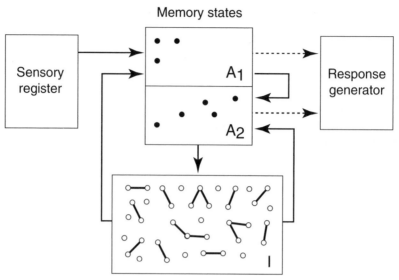

Figure 4.5. Wagner's SOP model of habituation as depicted by Roitblat (1987), indicating memory nodes (circles). Redrawn with permission.

representation in working memory just outside the immediate focus of attention, and thence into long-term or inactive memory (I). The behavioral readout of A2 is, therefore, behavior appropriate to the memory of a very recent event. This is not necessarily the same as a weak form of the direct (A1) response to the event. Representations can also be activated into A2 associatively—that is, the animal can be reminded of them. The distinction between the two states of active memory captures the notion that remembering something and experiencing it directly are not the same and may evoke correspondingly different behaviors. If an event is already represented in A2 this will interfere with its ability to be evoked into A1. In this way, expected events (associatively activated into A2) evoke a smaller response than unexpected ones. Short-term memory has limited capacity so that new, unexpected stimuli displace stimuli currently being processed in A1 (or *rehearsed*; see chapter 6). Associative learning will occur only when the stimuli to be associated are processed simultaneously in A1. On this view associatively activated representations (represented only in A2) should not be able to function as USs, although evidence in section 3.4.2 indicates that they can.

Unlike the other two models, this one distinguishes between short-term and long-term habituation. Short-term habituation occurs because the more recently a stimulus has been primed into A1, the more it will occupy A1 and/or A2. This will limit the ability of new occurrences of that stimulus to command processing in A1 and evoke a new behavioral response. Long-term habituation reflects association of the habituating stimulus with its context. The SOP model generates a number of novel predictions that have inspired clever experimental tests. For example, habituation should be retarded by presenting "distractors" between occurrences of the target stimulus in a sort of dishabituation paradigm. Whitlow (1975) tested this prediction by presenting tones to rabbits and measuring evoked vasoconstriction in the ear. He tested the prediction that responding is evoked if incoming stimulation does not correspond to the stimulus representation currently active in short-term memory by presenting series of tones at various intervals. When the same tone was presented twice in succession, the response to the second tone was reduced up to inter-tone intervals of 150 seconds. However, if two successive tones differed, the response to them was the same, even when the inter-tone interval was as little as 30 seconds. The stimulus-specific response decrement could be eliminated by presenting a distractor consisting of a flashing light and a tactile stimulus between successive presentations of the target stimulus (see chapter 6, figure 6.9).

In this model, the animal becomes less responsive to the target stimulus because it learns to expect it in the experimental context (i.e., the representation is associatively evoked into A2 by the context). This means that habituation should be context-specific. Furthermore, it should be possible to "extinguish" habituation by exposing the animal to the context in the absence of the habituating stimulus. Latent inhibition reflects the same mechanism as habituation in this model. If the stimulus is less well represented in A1, then it is less available to be associated with some other stimulus. Tests of the prediction that both latent inhibition and habituation should be specific to their original training context have had mixed results (Hall, 1991; Mackintosh, 1983). As discussed in the next part of the chapter, latent inhibition generally fails to transfer to new but familiar contexts whereas habituation does transfer. Functionally, however, whether or not habituation transfers should perhaps depend on the animal and the context. For instance, contact with the body of another animal is innocuous as long as you are in a herd or a communal burrow, but it's potentially dangerous when you are alone.

In conclusion, although its unique predictions are not always fulfilled, the SOP model is appealing because it applies to a broader range of phenomena than either of the other models discussed in this section. It allows for complex behavior and for short-term as well as long-term habituation, and it has links with standard memory models and associative learning theory. It also provides a mechanism for the effects of surprise or discrepancy in the Rescorla-Wagner model. Although it does not allow for changing the representation of the habituating stimulus with experience, it might be made to incorporate something like the model of stimulus representation discussed in the next section.

4.2 Perceptual Learning

4.2.1 Data

Perceptual learning refers to learning the characteristics of stimuli, as opposed to learning their relationship to other stimuli. The classic demonstration of

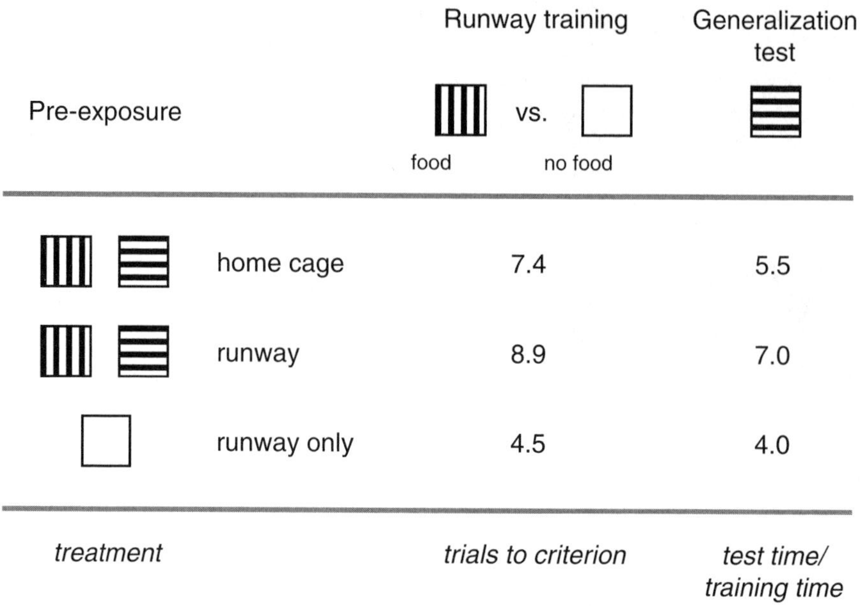

Pre-exposure		Runway training ▦ vs. ▢ (food / no food)	Generalization test ☰
▦ ☰	home cage	7.4	5.5
▦ ☰	runway	8.9	7.0
▢	runway only	4.5	4.0
treatment		*trials to criterion*	*test time/ training time*

Figure 4.6. Procedure and results of Hall and Honey's (1989) demonstration of how pre-exposure both reduces associability and enhances discriminability. Faster discrimination learning is indicated by fewer trials to criterion. In the generalization test, the striped plaque not used for training was presented in extinction and its effects measured as the ratio of running times to running time at the end of training; hence, the higher the ratio the less the generalization—i.e., the rats ran more slowly than to the reinforced plaque.

perceptual learning is an experiment by Gibson and Walk (1956). Young rats were exposed to large cut-out triangles and circles on the walls of their home cages until they were 90 days old. Then they were trained to approach one of these patterns and avoid the other. Rats that were familiar with the stimuli learned the discrimination much faster than those for which the stimuli were novel. This result is directly opposite to what would be expected if exposure to the shapes produced latent inhibition. A way to understand it is to realize that learning depends on both *discriminability* and *associability* of the stimuli involved. Exposure to stimuli to be discriminated may enhance discriminability and reduce associability at the same time, as suggested by the following experiment (Hall & Honey, 1989).

⌐ Rats were exposed to a horizontally and a vertically striped plaque in either a runway or their home cages. Then they had a go/no go discrimination in the runway with one of the plaques as the reinforced stimulus (i.e., they were rewarded for running when the designated plaque was at the end of the runway but not otherwise). The preexposed rats learned the discrimination more slowly than a control group that had been preexposed to the runway alone (figure 4.6). This illustrates latent inhibition: preexposure slowed associating the familiar plaque with reward. After learning the presence-absence discrimination with one of the striped plaques, the rats were tested in the runway with the other one. The control rats generalized their relatively fast running to the second plaque, which they had not seen before. The preexposed groups generalized less—that is, they discriminated better between the patterns. Some of the more recent research on perceptual learning in rats has preexposed them to liquids made up of different components and followed this with a test of flavor aversion learning. For instance, two flavored solutions such as saline and sucrose may be made more similar to one another by adding a third flavor such as lemon to both of them (see also Kiernan & Westbrook, 1993; Mackintosh, 1995; Mackintosh, Kaye, & Bennett, 1991).

4.2.2 A Model of Stimulus Representation

Over a century ago, William James (1890, p. 511) described what seems to go on during perceptual learning as follows.

> [H]ow does one learn to distinguish claret from burgundy? . . . When we first drank claret we heard it called by that name, we were eating such and such a dinner, etc. Next time we drink it, a dim reminder of all those things chimes through us as we get the taste of the wine. When we try burgundy our first impression is that it is a kind of claret; but something falls short of full identification, and presently we hear it called burgundy. During the next few experiences, the discrimination may still be uncertain—"which," we ask ourselves, "of the two wines is this present specimen?" But at last the claret-flavor recalls pretty distinctly its own name, "claret," "that wine I drank at So-and-so's table" etc.; and the name burgundy recalls the name burgundy and someone else's table. . . . after a while . . . the adhesion of each wine with its own *name* becomes . . . inveterate, and . . . each flavor suggests instantly and certainly its own name and nothing else. The names differ far more than the flavors, and help to stretch the latter further apart.

James's idea—that things initially difficult to discriminate become more discriminable by means of associations among their unique features—is captured in a general model of stimulus representation proposed by McLaren, Kaye and Mackintosh (1989). The model starts from the assumption (Estes, 1950) that stimuli are composed of a number of discrete elements. In James's example, the stimulus elements of each wine included its name, its flavor, the occasions on which it had been drunk, perhaps its color, odor, and so on. Elements are assumed to be sampled randomly each time the stimulus is encountered (figure 4.7a). To take another example, each time it is lit, the pecking key in an operant chamber has a color, brightness, a pattern perhaps, shape, size, location, duration, and so on. Stimulus sampling theory assumes only some random subset of these elements affects the animal on each trial. What the elements are is usually unspecified, though there may be many more than in this example. In previous versions of stimulus sampling theory (e.g., Estes, 1950; Pearce, 1987) each stimulus element is a little CS independently associated with the US as in the Rescorla-Wagner model. But this approach becomes much more interesting and powerful if we imagine that elements are

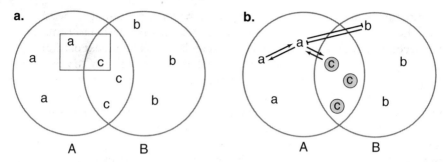

Figure 4.7. The model of perceptual learning proposed by McLaren, Kaye, and Mackintosh (1989). a. Circles represent two stimuli, A and B, that have some common elements (c's) as well as unique ones (a's and b's). A subset of elements (inside the rectangle) is sampled when A appears. b. The situation that develops after exposure to A and B, with reference to representative elements. Each a element develops excitatory associative links with other a elements and with the common elements, c's. Inhibitory links develop between a and b elements. Meanwhile, the most frequently encountered elements, the c's, acquire most latent inhibition (gray circles). After McLaren, Kaye, and Mackintosh (1989) with permission.

also associated with each other, as suggested by James. Each stimulus element activates a node or unit in a network of interconnected nodes. When a stimulus is presented the nodes corresponding to stimulus elements being sampled are activated both externally, by the sampled element itself, and internally, through associatively modifiable links with other nodes. Learning reduces the discrepancy between internal and external inputs to a node by strengthening connections among the nodes most often activated together—that is, those corresponding to features of the same stimulus. This is how stimuli become "unitized": nodes corresponding to the "central tendency" of the set of stimulus elements, the nodes most frequently activated simultaneously, will eventually be activated together. As a result, a subset of elements will tend to activate nodes corresponding to the whole set (figure 4.7b). The taste of claret will immediately remind one of the name, the occasions on which it was drunk, and so on. In effect, the associated nodes are a neuronal model of the stimulus.

This much will lead to stimuli with common elements becoming "unitized" and more discriminable from one another with experience. This Jamesian account indicates why clarets are more easily discriminated from burgundies, but does not explain why at the same time different clarets might become more discriminable from one another. McLaren et al.'s explanation calls upon latent inhibition, a phenomenon unknown to James (see also Mackintosh, 1995). Exposure to stimuli with common as well as unique elements will give most latent inhibition to their common elements, since by definition they appear most often. Thus when one of these familiar stimuli is to be associated with a US, strongest associations will develop to the unique elements. In other words, experience will make stimuli that are initially confused more discriminable. In addition, sets of nodes corresponding to elements unique to the different stimuli will develop inhibitory connections with each other, as indicated in figure 4.7b. In James's example, burgundy reminds the inexperienced taster of claret—that is, claret elements are activated internally. Inhibition develops between elements unique to burgundy and those unique to claret because the expectation of "claret" is not activated externally when burgundy is presented. One prediction of these ideas is that perceptual learning will be more evident relative to latent inhibition with stimuli that are initially less discriminable—that is, have more common elements. The relevant data are consistent with this prediction (Hall, 1991, 1996; McLaren, 1994; McLaren, Kaye, & Mackintosh, 1989).

This model takes latent inhibition for granted by assuming that the system of associatively interconnected nodes has a modulator that discriminates novel from familiar stimuli and increases the associability of the novel stimuli. It does this by detecting the discrepancy between internal and external inputs to nodes and boosting the activation of nodes for which the discrepancy is high. Increased activation is reflected in increased associability of that node with other CS and US nodes. This is the same as saying that unexpected stimuli or stimulus elements are more associable. Since the context is treated as a stimulus like any other, latent inhibition will be context-specific, just as in Wagner's model.

This model is an effective account of how animals form representations of the events to which they are exposed (see Hall, 1996; Schmajuk, Lam, & Gray, 1996, for further discussion). In chapter 5, we will see how it applies to category learning. The experiments on within event learning discussed in chapter 3 can be seen as studying associations between stimulus elements. Just as in the experiments described there, the present model assumes that these associations are being formed at the same time as the individual stimulus elements are being associated with any US that may be present. Presumably the same perceptual learning process is going on during habituation, too, as well as during imprinting, which is discussed next.

4.3 Imprinting

Young *precocial* birds like chickens, ducks, and geese are covered with down when they hatch, and they can run around within a few hours. In natural conditions they are kept from running away from their mother at this time, when they still need her for food and warmth, by rapidly developing a preference for following her rather than other large moving objects. In experimental conditions, they can become attached to moving balls, dangling sponges, flashing lights, stuffed ferrets, and a variety of other objects instead, through the learning process known as *imprinting*. Although imprinting had been described earlier, Konrad Lorenz's (1935/1970) discussion of it was responsible for an outpouring of experiments in the 1950s and '60s (see Bateson, 1966). Lorenz described how birds that had been removed from others of their own kind early in life would court and try to mate with members of the species that had raised them, including Lorenz himself. Lorenz claimed that the process responsible for acquisition of such social preferences was a kind of learning distinct from "ordinary learning," by which he meant Pavlovian or operant conditioning (Lorenz, 1970, p. 377). He based this claim on four apparently special characteristics: (1) Imprinting could occur only during a *critical period*, early in life; (2) after this, it was irreversible; (3) imprinting influences behavior that is not, and often cannot be, shown at the time of learning—that is, adult sexual behavior; and (4) from experience with a particular individual, normally the mother, the animal learns characteristics of its species.

It soon became apparent (cf. Bateson, 1966; Bolhuis, 1991) that Lorenz's description of a gosling instantaneously and irreversibly imprinted with a life-long preference for people after one brief glimpse is far too simple to apply to most cases. The phrase *critical period* was replaced by *sensitive period* or *sensitive phase*, implying that the onset and offset of sensitivity were gradual. And, as Lorenz (1935/1970) had acknowledged, the nature of the imprinting stimulus was important. Rather than being irreversible, early preference for an inadequate stimulus could sometimes be replaced by preference for another, more nearly adequate object. And the differences between imprinting and "ordinary learning" turned out to be not so great after all.

Imprinting is usually depicted as a "special," "preprogrammed" kind of learning because it is shown only by certain species at certain times in their lives (e.g., Staddon, 1983). But it is actually no more "preprogrammed" than any other kind of learning, and the same questions can be asked about it, even though the answers to some of them may be different (Shettleworth, 1994b). Most of this section is about *filial imprinting*, acquisition of social preferences in young birds, because most work has been done in this area. Formation of sexual preferences may involve some different processes, as discussed in section 4.3.4.

4.3.1 Conditions for Learning

Laboratory Tests of Imprinting   When a young chick or duckling is exposed to an effective imprinting object, it spends more and more time close to it, twittering softly and snuggling up to it. It spends less and less time shrilly peeping ("distress calling") and trying to escape. But young animals' sensory and motivational systems can change very quickly, and two stimuli that evoke the same reaction on one day can evoke quite different ones the next day even without special intervening experiences. A standard design for laboratory studies of imprinting therefore employs two potential imprinting stimuli, A and B. Some animals are exposed to A in the imprinting situation and some to B. Then all animals are given a choice between A and B. For example, in one now-popular method, Bateson and Jaekel (1976) placed chicks in a running wheel facing a red or a yellow flashing light. The chicks could run toward the light but they did not get any closer to it. After varying amounts of experience with one light or the other, the chicks were tested in another running wheel mounted on a track with the red light at one end and the yellow light at the other (figure 4.8). When the chick ran toward one light it was trans-

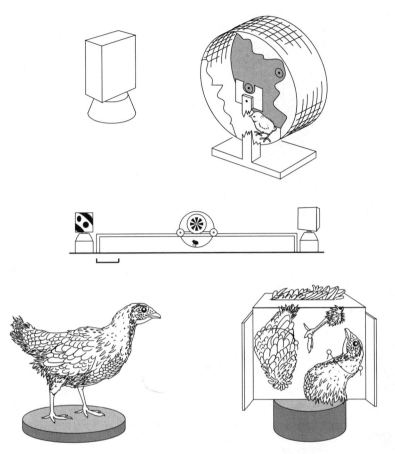

Figure 4.8. Running wheels for imprinting chicks (*top row*) and testing their preferences (*middle*), and some of the stimuli used by Bateson, Horn, and their colleagues. Redrawn from Horn (1985) with permission.

ported toward the other, but if it strongly preferred one it might continue to run toward it even when carried to the opposite end of the track by its efforts. Preference was measured as proportion of all wheel revolutions in a particular direction. Other tests of imprinting take advantage of the fact that a bird will learn an instrumental response in order to see an object on which it has been imprinted (e.g., Hoffman, 1978; figure 4.9). Such an object also suppresses distress calling when it appears. Whatever behavior is measured, it is essential to show that the effectiveness of one of two objects depends on which one the bird was exposed to in the imprinting situation.

Length of Exposure   The early picture of imprinting was of an instant all-or-nothing acquisition process, but just as with taste aversion (chapter 3) and song learning (chapter 10), this has given way to one of gradual incremental learning. Notice that when birds are trained in a running wheel, running is

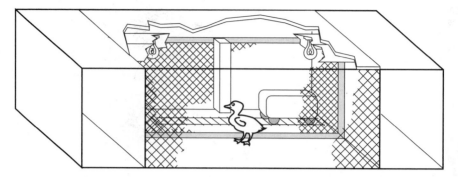

Figure 4.9. Apparatus used for imprinting ducklings and for testing instrumental respond-ing reinforced by presentation of the imprinting stimulus. The duckling pecks the pole in the middle of his compartment to illuminate the compartment in which the imprinting ob-ject moves back and forth. Redrawn from Eiserer and Hoffman (1973) with permission.

not instrumentally reinforced because they never get any closer to the im-printing object. Thus, sheer exposure to an object is sufficient for imprinting. In fact, if exposed to them for long enough, chicks prefer objects patterned like the walls of their rearing pens over other objects (see Bateson, 1966). Just as with any other learning phenomenon, length of exposure, type of stimulus, and the state of the animal must all be considered together. A few minutes' exposure to a conspicuous moving object during the first day or two after hatching may have effects matched only by many days' exposure to an in-conspicuous stationary object (ten Cate, 1989). The effects of length of ex-posure may depend on the species being tested. Lorenz (1935/1970) de-scribed two extremes of imprintability. A greylag gosling that had once seen people would never afterward associate with geese, but curlews would always flee from people no matter how much they had been exposed to them. Yet Lorenz's assertion that imprinting is instantaneous and irreversible has nearly always been tested on species other than greylag geese, such as do-mestic chicks and ducklings.

Type of Stimulus: Hens, Boxes, and Ferrets   Artificial imprinting objects vary greatly in effectiveness. Lorenz (1935/1970) claimed that adults of the bird's own species were more adequate imprinting objects than artificial stimuli. Species-specific stimuli do seem to be special for both domestic chicks and ducklings, but not exactly in the way one might expect. Domestic chicks pre-fer stuffed hens of the junglefowl (their wild ancestors; see figure 4.8) to ar-tificial objects, but this preference develops in the first two to three days of life as a result of certain nonspecific experiences. The fowl does not seem to be a uniquely effective stimulus for learning. Instead, a preference for fowl like ob-jects sums with learned preferences. What makes the fowl effective is its head and neck: cut up stuffed fowl are approached as much as the whole fowl as long as they include a head and neck. Stuffed ducks or even ferrets are approached as much as the junglefowl (Johnson & Horn, 1988). Eyes may be the important common feature of all these objects (Bolhuis, 1996). These findings suggest that in natural conditions imprinting to the mother may be supported, or canalized by preferences for species-specific stimuli that ensure that the young bird is attracted to the mother rather than to other moving objects in the first place (see ten Cate, 1994, for further discussion of perceptual predispositions). The role of filial imprinting may be to establish not species identification, as suggested by Lorenz, but identification of a particular individual—the mother—within that species (Bateson, 1979).

Since mother birds sometimes make special calls, species-specific auditory stimuli have also been assumed to be important in imprinting. Henlike sounds have often been played while chicks are being imprinted, and the mother duck's calls do seem to play a role in imprinting ducklings on her visual characteristics (Johnston & Gottlieb, 1981). However, calls may not work by supporting imprinting themselves but rather by increasing arousal, drawing attention to the mother, or becoming associated with visual imprinting stimuli. On the whole, sounds appear to be rather weak imprinting stimuli for chickens, and if they do influence filial behavior it is through other mechanisms (Bolhuis & van Kampen, 1992; van Kampen, 1996).

Is Imprinting a Kind of Conditioning?   The observation that conspicuous moving or flashing objects lead to faster imprinting than stationary ones has resulted in suggestions that imprinting is a form of Pavlovian conditioning in which the static features of the object function as the CS and visual motion as the US (Bolhuis, de Vos, & Kruijt, 1990; Hoffman, 1978; Hoffman & Ratner, 1973; Rajecki, 1973; van Kampen, 1996; Zolman, 1982). The suggestion that imprinting consists of associating some innately reinforcing features of the object such as motion or flicker with its less conspicuous features leads to a number of testable predictions that can be contrasted with those of the most explicit alternative theory—namely, that imprinting is a form of perceptual learning in which the animal simply becomes familiar with, or learns the features of, the imprinting object and approaches it because it is familiar (Green, 1982; Sluckin, 1962; Sluckin & Salzen, 1961; review in van Kampen, 1996). On the perceptual learning view, moving objects are effective because they are more conspicuous than stationary objects. When this view was first put forth, there was no well-developed theory of perceptual learning. As a result, most evidence for the perceptual learning theory consisted of failed predictions of the conditioning theory. But in section 4.2 we have seen that perceptual learning about an object can be going on while the animal is learning associative relationships involving that object. This suggests that the conditioning theory and the perceptual learning theory could both be correct, and, as we will see, both are incorporated in recent models of imprinting (Bateson & Horn, 1994; van Kampen, 1996). To appreciate the contributions of such an integrative approach, we first need to look further at the conditions for learning and the effects of imprinting on behavior.

The conditioning analysis of imprinting is supported by evidence that

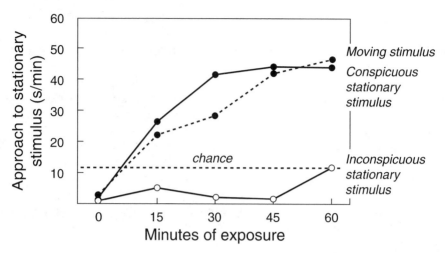

Figure 4.10. Mean time (in seconds per minute of test) ducklings spent approaching a stationary imprinting stimulus after three kinds of experience with it. Redrawn from Eiserer (1980) with permission.

some aspect of stimuli supporting imprinting functions as a US, or is innately reinforcing. Chicks and ducklings will perform an instrumental response to get a view of an imprinting object (Bateson & Reese, 1969; Hoffman & Ratner, 1973). They will do so even when the imprinting object is completely unfamiliar—that is, before imprinting can have taken place (see van Kampen, 1996, for discussion). Since most commonly used reinforcers like food, water, and shock can also be used as Pavlovian USs, it seems reasonable to conclude that some feature of the imprinting object, such as motion, functions as a US in imprinting.

Also consistent with the Pavlovian conditioning view is evidence that an object that does not initially evoke any filial behavior comes to do so when the bird has seen it moving but not stationary (Hoffman, 1978). This is equivalent to comparing a CS-alone group with one that experiences pairings of CS and US. Contrary to the conditioning model, however, filial behavior does eventually develop to a sufficiently conspicuous stationary object (Eiserer, 1980; figure 4.10). The conditioning model also predicts that imprinting to an object in motion will extinguish if the object is kept stationary. This does not happen, and on the perceptual learning view it should not. Furthermore, if imprinting is a matter of associating the static features of the object with some feature of the object in motion, then presenting the object stationary before presenting it in motion should slow down imprinting. On the perceptual learning theory, however, such a latent inhibition procedure should speed up imprinting (see Eiserer, 1978).

If imprinting involves associative learning, imprinting to some features of an object should block learning about features added to it later. Overshadowing and/or potentiation should also be found under appropriate conditions. Such ideas have generally been tested using artificial imprinting objects with discrete features that can be manipulated independently of each other. For instance, de Vos and Bolhuis (1990) looked for blocking by imprinting chicks to two red or two yellow cylinders and then replacing the original imprinting stimulus with one consisting of a blue and a yellow cylinder. Imprinting to the added blue cylinder should have been blocked in the group already imprinted on yellow cylinders. As predicted, the chicks exposed to red cylinders in the first phase showed more evidence of imprinting to blue in the second phase than those imprinted on yellow. Because the stimulus elements in this experiment were actually two separate objects, the chicks imprinted to yellow cylinders might not have learned about the added "stimulus element" of the blue cylinder if they spent most of their time close to the familiar yellow one. However, further studies without this problem have produced similar results (van Kampen & de Vos, 1995). On the whole, the results of experiments of this sort are consistent with the view that the features of objects are associated with one another and with the "US" (whatever it is) in imprinting as described by the principles of associative learning outlined in chapter 3 (review in van Kampen, 1996).

The Animal's State: The Sensitive Period   In chicks and ducklings, filial imprinting takes place most readily between a few hours and a few days after hatching. If the immediate function of filial imprinting is to keep the young bird with its mother for food and warmth and away from unrelated adults who might attack it, the process underlying it only needs to be available at the beginning of life. In contrast, conditioning or recognition learning are clearly necessary throughout life: any animal may well need to learn about many signals for food, many danger signals, and the characteristics of many other features of its environment. By itself, however, the sensitive period does not make imprinting qualitatively different from associative learning. How learning depends on the animal's state, in this case its age, is a different question from what kind of experience is responsible for learning in the first place. However, one account of the end of the sensitive period does assume that imprinting is fundamentally different from most cases of associative learning because once an animal is fully imprinted to one object it cannot become imprinted to any other object. This model—the *competitive exclusion model* (Bateson, 1981, 1987), *the capacity model* (Boakes & Panter, 1985), or the *self-termination model* (ten Cate, 1989)—can be contrasted with the intuitively simpler *clock model* (ten Cate, 1989). In the clock model, imprintability is a matter of the animal's stage of development: it becomes possible at a certain point in motor and sensory maturation, and maturational processes later bring it to an end. The clock model is roughly correct for the onset of the sensitive period, but it does not explain the end of the sensitive period.

The competitive exclusion model assumes that imprinting is intrinsically self-terminating (Bateson, 1981, 1990), as if there were a fixed number of neural connections that it could occupy. Once these have been used up, the animal may still learn to recognize other stimuli in its environment such as food or siblings, but these do not, in Bateson's terms, "gain access to the executive system" for filial behavior. This model thus distinguishes between S-S learning (learning the characteristics of the imprinting object) and S-R learning (connecting the features of the object to the filial behavior system). Only a certain amount of the latter is possible; the S-R connections are taken over quickly with some stimuli like conspicuous moving objects making the sounds of mother hens, and slowly with others like inconspicuous, static, silent objects. If only a little imprinting has occurred, a second object can also gain control of filial behavior, but if the animal is strongly imprinted to the first stimulus no more "connections to the executive system" are available.

Past History: Reversibility and "Resurfacing"   Most of the evidence for irreversibility of imprinting consists of cases in which birds raised by a species other than their own retain a sexual preference for that species even when they have mated and raised offspring with conspecifics (Immelmann, 1972; Lorenz, 1935/1970). However, if a bird is exposed successively to two potential imprinting objects within the sensitive period, the evidence supports Lorenz's statement that the effects of early exposure to a relatively inadequate imprinting object can sometimes be reversed. With two artificial objects like balls and boxes (Bolhuis & Bateson, 1990) or two natural objects like hens (Kent, 1987), the initial filial preference can be reversed. An initial preference for a hen is not reversed by later exposure to an artificial object (Boakes & Panter, 1985), but preference for an artificial object can be reversed by exposure to a hen (Bolhuis & Trooster, 1988). The initial preference is not necessarily forgotten. If chicks live with both A and B in their cages between exposure to B and the final test, preference for A "resurfaces" under some conditions (Bolhuis & Bateson, 1990).

Conditions for Learning: Summary and Conclusions   Imprinting is influenced by the same kinds of conditions that influence other learning about single events: the quantity and quality of stimulation to which the animal is exposed, its duration, the animal's state (i.e., its age and past experience), the interval between experience at T1 and the test of its effects at T2, and what happens during that interval. Exactly how these factors matter is specific to imprinting and probably differs among imprintable species. The discussion of whether imprinting is an example of classical conditioning (i.e., whether the conditions of learning include a positive contingency between neutral and US-like features) reduces to two questions. Does the experience at T1 that is necessary for the acquisition of filial behavior include a specifiable US? If so, do manipulations of the CS-US relationship influence imprinting as predicted by conditioning theory? Clearly we cannot specify a single US such as motion, since young birds deprived of exposure to a conspicuous moving object will imprint to almost anything else eventually. One solution is to conclude that the "real" US is some feature shared by all effective imprinting objects such as arousing a particular affective state (Bolhuis, de Vos, & Kruijt, 1990). This doesn't say much except that objects that support imprinting support imprinting. However, there are other cases of simultaneous conditioning in which an initially neutral object seems to acquire affective value. For example, if rats that have been exposed to a salty solution mixed with an initially neutral flavor are made salt-deficient, they will drink the neutral flavor alone (Berridge & Schulkin, 1989; Boakes & Panter, 1985). CSs that have acquired positive value in this way tend to support responding even after their reinforcer has been devalued, suggesting that they have acquired their own independent affective value. This is one way to describe the apparent failure of imprinting to extinguish. Similarly, ducklings imprinted to an object at one to two days of age will learn to peck a pole to see it when they are ten days old, although they will no longer imprint at this age nor learn the pole pecking response without prior imprinting (Hoffman, Searle, Toffey, & Kozma, 1966).

4.3.2 Effects of Learning on Behavior

In the laboratory, the effects of experience with an imprinting object are usually measured as time spent following or choice in a preference test. But, like Pavlovian conditioning, imprinting endows a stimulus with control over a whole behavior system (van Kampen, 1996). The behavior system is filial or attachment behavior, behavior that functions to keep the young bird close to its mother and the mother close to it. It includes pecking at the hen, nestling against her, and vocalizing quietly (see Hogan, 1974). Once a chick or duckling has been imprinted, it peeps loudly, "distress calling," in the absence of the imprinting object and flees from novel objects (Hoffman, 1978).

One of Lorenz's claims for the uniqueness of imprinting was that it influences behaviors that have not yet appeared at the time of learning—namely, sexual behaviors. In nature, filial imprinting must play at least an indirect role in establishing sexual preferences because the animals with which the young bird associates will necessarily be the ones giving it the experiences relevant for mate choice. However, this does not mean that the same experience directly determines both filial and sexual preferences. Indeed, sexual preferences seem to be influenced by processes separate from filial imprinting (section 4.3.4).

4.3.3 What Is Learned in Filial Imprinting? A Hybrid Model

What is learned in imprinting has been described as a neuronal model or representation of the features of the imprinting object, an association of the neutral features of the imprinting object with its US-like features, and a combination of both. Each of the first two accounts is incomplete in important ways. The neuronal model or perceptual learning account does not distinguish recognizing the imprinting object from recognizing anything else familiar. The conditioning model does not account for possible later effects of the imprinting experience like gradual learning of the imprinting object's features. This aspect of imprinting is addressed by the competitive exclusion

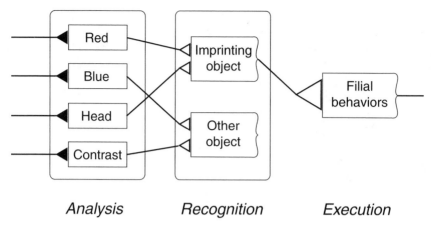

Analysis   Recognition   Execution

Figure 4.11. The "ARE" (Analysis, Recognition, Execution) model of imprinting. The four features are examples of the kinds of features into which an imprinting object might be analyzed. After Bateson (1990) with permission.

model (Bateson & Horn, 1994; Bateson, 1981, 1990; Hollis, ten Cate, & Bateson, 1991; van Kampen, 1996; figure 4.11), according to which imprinting results in two kinds of learning: recognition of the individual imprinting object (perceptual learning) and connections of its representation to "the executive system" for filial behavior (S-R learning). It consists of three systems: *analysis* of incoming stimuli into features; *recognition* of familiar features; and *execution* of behavior patterns, corresponding to the perceptual, central, and motor aspects of any behavior system (van Kampen, 1996; see figure 1.10).

The function of filial imprinting, as distinct from the function of sexual imprinting, must be to allow the young animal to recognize a particular individual, its mother, not, as Lorenz suggested, its species. In fact, we have seen that ducklings and chicks may respond to species-characteristic calls or appearance without any specific experience. Initially, imprinting may be to the most salient features of the mother. Later the mother's distinguishing characteristics, such as details of her plumage and voice, may gradually be combined into a unitary representation. If the young animal gradually builds up a more and more detailed picture of the parent, relatively inconspicuous elements should only slowly come to affect filial behavior. Inconspicuous details of the imprinting object need not be directly associated with the US-like feature but can be associated with the conspicuous features. Once the conspicuous features have acquired value through exposure in the sensitive period, the inconspicuous features can go on being learned about. As this discussion suggests, the phenomena of perceptual learning reviewed earlier in the chapter may be found using imprinting objects as the stimuli. For instance, chicks imprinted to a visual pattern and later trained on a heat-reinforced discrimination between two patterns learned faster if the imprinting stimulus was one of the to-be-discriminated patterns (Honey, Horn, & Bateson, 1993).

Imprinting to a live hen requires a sort of perceptual constancy: a side view of the hen brooding must be reacted to in the same way as a front view of the hen standing and pecking, a back view of her running and flapping her wings, and so on. This constancy might be acquired by associating, or "classifying together" two views of an object (or views of two different objects) that are seen sufficiently close together in time (Chantrey, 1972, 1974). In Chantrey's experiments young chicks saw two objects pass by their cages periodically. Then they were trained on a food-rewarded discrimination between two objects in a runway. If they had seen the test objects in quick succession, thus having opportunity to "classify them together," they learned much more slowly than controls that had seen other objects; but if the objects had been separated by five minutes or more, they learned more quickly than controls. However, if the objects are very similar to each other, the opposite results are obtained: a shorter interval between exposures facilitates discrimination learning rather than retarding it (Honey, Bateson, & Horn, 1994), as if opportunity to compare two similar stimuli is important.

Birds raised in a family group may imprint on their siblings (Lorenz, 1935/1970). But a young bird's appearance is constantly changing (figure 4.12). This observation suggests that the original representation of "sibling" must be gradually updated. Ryan and Lea (1990) modeled gradual change in a chick's appearance using a string of four Ping-Pong balls with a bell at the end. Chicks in their main experimental group started life with one of these objects in their cages, an artificial sibling, that was either all brown or all white. Every four days one ball was replaced with a ball of the other color, so eventually the object was entirely the opposite color from the original. When tested with an all-brown versus and all-white string of balls, these birds showed no significant preference, suggesting that they had formed a series of equally attractive representations of different objects. These and other results of this clever experiment are most consistent with the notion that the chick enlarges its category of preferred objects as its siblings develop. Like the experiments on overshadowing and blocking (section 4.3.1), Ryan and Lea's work illustrates how imprinting objects can be dissected into manipulable elements in order to test specific hypotheses about what is learned in imprinting.

4.3.4 Sexual Imprinting

Hand-reared birds may prefer to court humans even after months or years of social experience with their own kind (Immelmann, 1972; Lorenz, 1935/1970). But is filial imprinting directly responsible for such sexual preferences? We have already seen some functional reasons to think not: in filial imprinting the young bird needs to learn the characteristics of a particular individual, normally its mother; in sexual imprinting, species characteristics are what matter. However, early learning about the mother could produce a generalized preference for individuals of the same species later on. If the mother is not present when the young are seeking mates, as in species where the young disperse from the natal area, the bird may simply choose the closest match it can find. In addition, fine details of the mother's appearance may be forgot-

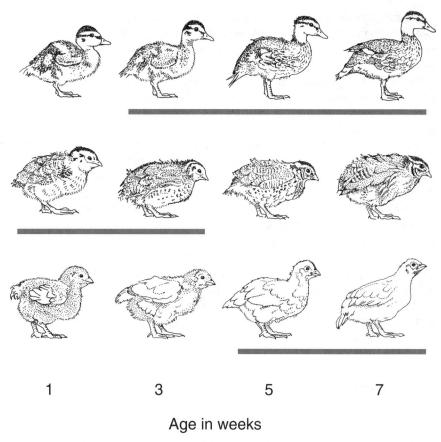

1   **3**   **5**   **7**

Age in weeks

Figure 4.12. Changes in appearance of developing ducks, quail, and chickens. The dark bar indicates the age at which experiences relevant to later sexual preferences are thought to be taking place in each species. After Bateson (1979) with permission.

ten between infancy and maturity while salient features, characteristic of species members generally, are not (Zolman, 1982). Moreover, the preference for the mother developed early in life need not be specifically sexual. The adolescent male bird may simply approach females of his species because they resemble his mother and thereby find out that they can provide sexual interactions (Bischof, 1994).

Attempts to distinguish sexual and filial imprinting experimentally have chiefly asked two questions: Do they occur at the same time (i.e., are the conditions of learning the same)? And they the same learning (i.e., are the contents of learning the same)? Finally, the optimal discrepancy hypothesis (Bateson, 1979) suggests that not only the behavior systems affected but also the principle of choice might differ between filial and sexual imprinting: the bird should direct filial behavior to something as similar as possible to its learned representation but direct sexual behavior toward something slightly different.

Timing of Sexual Imprinting and Effects on Behavior: The Optimal Discrepancy
Model   Filial and sexual imprinting can be dissociated. Vidal (1980) exposed
domestic cockerels of three different ages to a cleverly constructed imprinting
object that could support both filial and sexual behavior (figure 4.13). When
tested at sexual maturity, the birds that had been exposed to the model at the
youngest age and had shown most filial behavior showed the least sexual behavior. Those exposed latest, the group that had shown least filial behavior toward the model, showed most sexual behavior toward it. In quail and ducks, as
well, sexual imprinting occurs after filial imprinting, while birds are still in the
family group but beginning to develop adult plumage (Bateson, 1979; see also
figure 4.12). In natural conditions, these species learn the characteristics of
siblings, not exclusively those of the mother. Having learned the characteristics
of its close relatives, the young bird then chooses a mate slightly different, but
not too different from them. The function of this combination of mechanisms
of learning and choice is to promote an optimal degree of outbreeding. Animals, the notion goes, should be selected to avoid the deleterious effects of
breeding with very close relations but not outbreed so much as to dilute adaptations to local conditions. If this is the function of sexual imprinting, the representation of "close relative" should be based on siblings rather than mother
alone because the siblings provide a larger sample of close relatives, and one
which includes characteristics of the father's family.

Evidence consistent with the optimal outbreeding hypothesis comes from
studies in which quail raised in family groups were later exposed to siblings,
cousins, and nonkin in the multiple-choice apparatus shown in figure 4.14.
Birds of both sexes spent most time near first cousins (Bateson, 1982). When
quail of different degrees of relatedness were housed together after being
raised in families, those housed with cousins layed fertile eggs sooner than
those housed with siblings or more distant relatives (Bateson, 1988), showing
that preferences evident in the choice apparatus could have a real impact on
reproduction. Other species that prefer mates slightly different from those
they were raised with include mice and great tits (Barnard & Aldhous, 1991;
Boyse, Beauchamp, Yamazaki, & Bard, 1991).

It is not clear how widely the optimal outbreeding hypothesis applies (Burley, Minor, & Strachan, 1990). Snow geese choose mates of the same color as
their parents, blue or white, but more subtle diferences seem to be unimportant
(Cooke & Davies, 1983). Mating within the immediate family simply does
not occur in this species because males and females disperse to different areas.
The deleterious effects of too much inbreeding are well established and are assumed to have been an important factor in the evolution of mating patterns, but
there is little evidence that too much outbreeding is a bad thing as long as matings between species are avoided. If this is so, preferences for close but not-too-
close relatives may function only to avoid too much inbreeding.

Contents of Learning: Combining Standards   The optimal discrepancy model
raises the question of how information about different family members is represented: does the bird form a representation of a prototypical family mem-

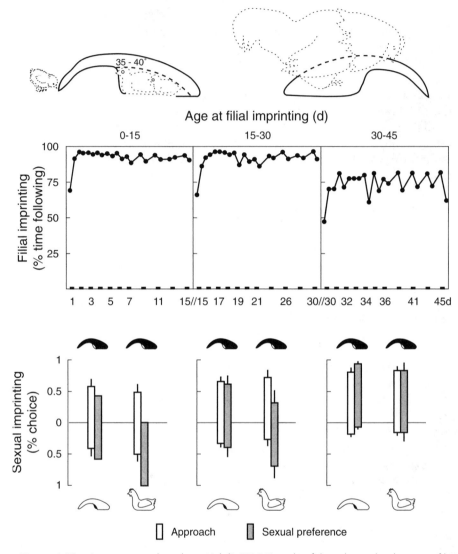

Figure 4.13. Apparatus and results in Vidal's (1980) study of the relationship between filial and sexual imprinting in domestic cockerels. Filial imprinting is shown in the top panels. Between 150 and 165 days of age, all the birds had two kinds of choice tests, one between the training model and a model of the same shape but different colors and one between the training model and a stuffed conspecific (*bottom row of panels*). Both approach and sexual behavior were measured. Redrawn from Vidal (1980) with permission.

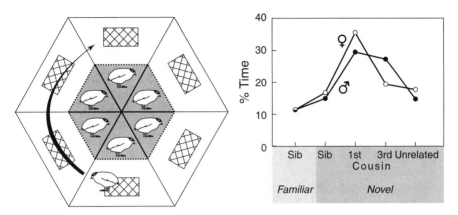

Figure 4.14. Overhead view of apparatus for testing sexual preference in quail. A pedal in front of each window records how long the subject spends there, presumably viewing the stimulus bird inside. Redrawn from Bateson (1982) with permission.

ber or does it store information about each individual separately? This is a general question about category learning which we will meet again in chapter 5. Prototype theory predicts that after training with a number of specific instances of a category, the *prototype*, or central tendency, will be better identified than any other instance, even if it is novel. Ten Cate (1987) tested this notion for "double imprinting" in zebra finches. If male zebra finches are raised by their own parents for about the first thirty days and then housed with Bengalese finches, some of them become "ditherers" in later sexual preference tests (ten Cate, 1986). They direct sexual behavior about equally to both zebra finches and Bengalese finches, although they prefer either to a novel species (figure 4.15). Have such birds formed two separate representations of acceptable sexual partners or a single composite representation? Ten Cate (1987) tried to find out by offering them a choice between a zebra finch–Bengalese finch hybrid and a zebra finch or a Bengalese finch. If we assume that the hybrid combines features of both species, the prototype or "single standard" theory predicts that ditherers should prefer it to either a zebra finch or a Bengalese finch. This is not a prediction unique to the prototype theory, however. The same outcome is predicted by the "double standard" or exemplar-learning model if generalization gradients from the two separate standards overlap enough. Ditherers did prefer the hybrid, and the results of the tests of birds imprinted on just one species indicated that such a preference could not result from summation of two separate generalization gradients (see figure 4.15). Thus the birds did seem to acquire a representation of a prototype. While this research is a good example of how a framework for thinking about the development of representations may be transferred from one context (conditioning theory) to another (imprinting), the conclusions from this particular study may not apply when zebra finches are raised by zebra finch parents of two different colors (Vos, Prijs, & ten Cate, 1993).

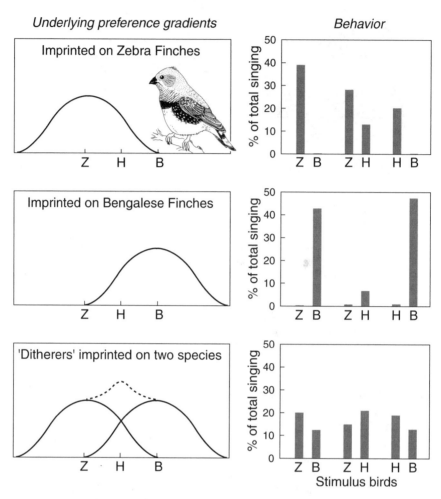

Figure 4.15. Panels on the left show hypothetical generalization of sexual preference in male zebra finches imprinted to zebra finches (Z), Bengalese finches (B), or on both species. In the latter case, the sum of the two preference gradients (dotted line) is maximal for a bird resembling a zebra finch–Bengalese finch hybrid (H). Panels on the right show sexual preference in pairwise tests with a zebra finch, a Bengalese finch, and a hybrid, measured as proportion of songs directed to each stimulus bird. Redrawn from ten Cate (1987) with permission.

Conditions for Learning: Predispositions to Learn Specific Stimuli?   **Many birds** more readily develop sexual preferences for their own species than for another species (Immelmann, 1972). For example, zebra finches raised by a mixed pair consisting of a zebra finch and a Bengalese finch are more likely to court zebra finches than Bengalese finches later on. In zebra finches, the species-specific advantage appears to result from how the potential imprinting object interacts with the young bird, not—as in filial imprinting—what it looks like. In a mixed pair of "parents" consisting of a zebra finch and a Bengalese finch, the zebra finch parent directs more feeding and aggressive behavior toward the young zebra finches than does the Bengalese finch parent. The zebra finch parent can be replaced with another zebra finch that does not participate in parental care, for example because it is in the wrong hormonal condition. Then sexual preference shifts toward Bengalese finches. When mixed species pairs raise a mixed species brood of young, the same-species young and adults interact most with each other (ten Cate, 1989, 1994). How far these findings can be generalized to other species is unclear. Social interactions may be important in chickens, too (Kruijt, 1985), but other species could be predisposed to prefer individuals with species-specific visual or vocal characteristics. Other species, too, may be even more malleable. Cowbirds, for instance, seem to change their sexual preferences back and forth with adult experience (Freeberg, King, & West, 1995).

Consolidation of Sexual Preferences: Two Stages of Sexual Imprinting   So far we have ignored the fact that zebra finches are not precocial like chickens, ducks, and quail but altricial. They don't need to have the same kind of filial behavior system as those species since they sit helplessly in the nest for the first two or three weeks while their parents bring them food. Yet, as we have seen, experience during this stage of life still influences zebra finches' mating preferences. Recent data indicate, however, that preferences developed during early life need to be consolidated through sexual contact in order to be long-lasting (Bischof, 1994). The first evidence of this appeared in two parallel experiments (Immelmann, Prove, Lassek, & Bischof, 1991; Kruijt & Meeuwissen, 1991) in which zebra finch males were raised by Bengalese finches for the first month or so, a period encompassing the sensitive phase for sexual preference. After a period of isolation the subjects were placed with zebra finch females, and since they had no choice at this stage, they bred with these females. "Classical" sexual imprinting theory predicts that when now given a choice between zebra finch and Bengalese finch females, the males should still prefer the Bengalese finches, the species that raised them. It turned out, however, that the results of this test depended on whether or not the subjects had had an earlier test of sexual preference. Even a single short exposure to Bengalese finch females during such a test consolidated the preference for this species built up in the nestling phase so that it survived the whole experience of breeding with a female zebra finch (figure 4.16). Details of the male's interactions with his foster parents and with his first potential sexual partner appear to predict individual differences in the strength of the initial preference and its susceptibility to being replaced by preference for another species (Bischof, 1994; Oetting, Pröve, & Bischof, 1995).

Sexual Imprinting?   Acquisition of sexual preferences would be a better term than sexual imprinting to summarize the findings described in this section. Acquisition of sexual preferences is not a unitary learning phenomenon. In some cases (e.g., Gallagher, 1977; ten Cate, Los, & Schilperood, 1984; Vidal, 1980), mere exposure to animals with certain characteristics influences later

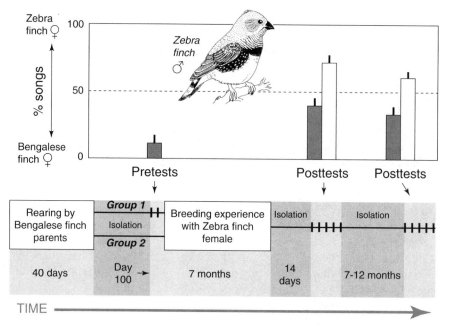

Figure 4.16. Effects of a brief preference test at 100 days of age on later sexual preferences in male zebra finches reared by Bengalese finches. Group 1 (dark bars) had the preference pretest. Sexual preference was measured as proportion of songs directed to the zebra finch. After Immelmann et al. (1991) with permission.

choice. It is not always clear, however, whether these preferences are strictly sexual, as opposed to general preferences for affiliating with the familiar regardless of its sex or the subject's motivational state. In cases where interaction with other animals influences later sexual preferences, it is not yet entirely clear how these interactions exert their effects. The recent research with zebra finches just reviewed indicates that sexual imprinting in these birds is a two-stage process, in which forming a representation of the familiar object and attaching it to a behavior system are separable aspects of sexual imprinting, as well as of filial imprinting and some other forms of learning (Bischof, 1994; Hogan, 1994b; van Kampen, 1996).

4.3.5 Conclusions

Imprinting can be defined functionally as the process by which animals acquire social preferences. But it is not just one process. Defining any type of behavioral change in terms of its outcome (i.e., functionally) is no guarantee that it takes place by means of a single mechanism. An enormous amount of effort has gone into examining evidence for Lorenz's (1935/1970) assertions about the special nature of filial imprinting: that it must occur in a critical period, after which it is irreversible, and that it includes learning supra-individual, species-identifying charateristics that guide mate choice later on. Every one of these claims needs at least some qualification. Some of these qualifications are ones Lorenz himself recognized (Lorenz, 1935/1970). The critical period, better described as a sensitive period, is not absolute. Its offset can depend on what the animal has experienced. One of the few unique features of filial imprinting may be its preemptive character: the imprinting experience itself may reduce susceptibility to further such experiences. However, under some circumstances early preferences may be replaced by preferences for objects encountered later on (Bischof, 1994; Bolhuis & Bateson, 1990). In other cases, early and later experiences combine in their effects (Ryan & Lea, 1990; ten Cate, 1987). These apparently conflicting conclusions (early experience is preemptive; its effects are reversible; it combines with later experience) come from different species and different experimental paradigms, and species differences are another factor complicating any attempts to arrive at a general account of imprinting.

Filial imprinting does not necessarily determine sexual preferences. The critical experiences for mate choice may occur later and be different in character from those involved in filial imprinting. Again, however, this conclusion is based on research with only a few species. Some of the species with which Lorenz was most familiar may be different from those which have been the most popular subjects since. The results of research with chickens, ducks, quail, zebra finches, and a few other sorts of birds can serve as a guide to what factors are likely to be important in the acquisition of sexual preferences, but the exact ways in which they work are likely to differ across species. Comparative research could be used to test functional speculations about details of the imprinting process, including imprinting in precocial mammals like sheep and guinea pigs.

4.4 Recognition and Altruism

4.4.1 The Puzzle of Altruism

As a technical term in behavioral ecology *altruism* refers to behaving so as to increase the reproductive success of another individual at a cost to one's own reproductive success. But if genes are selfish, why do animals ever help each other? Altruistic behavior can evolve under two sorts of conditions. Behavior that benefits close relatives is subject to *kin selection* (Hamilton, 1963). Kin selection arises because what really counts in evolution is the *inclusive fitness* of an act, its effects on the actor's individual fitness plus its effects on the fitness of the actor's relatives in proportion to their relatedness (see box 1.2). For example, since siblings share half their genes with each other, behavior that increases two siblings' reproductive success more than it reduces the reproductive success of the altruist will increase the altruist's inclusive fitness and hence be selected. Florida scrub jays and some other birds show helping at the nest that can be accounted for in this way (Woolfenden & Fitzpatrick, 1984). Rather than leaving their parents' territory and starting their own families, some young scrub jays remain at home and help to feed their younger siblings. Helping at the nest tends to occur when the availability of good territories is so low that young, inexperienced birds are unlikely to be able to breed successfully on their own. But for kin selection to work animals must have some means of favoring their kin—that is, *kin recognition*.

Reciprocal altruism, the second set of circumstances permitting the evolution of altruistic behavior, also depends on altruists being able to recognize others. Individuals will be selected who help those unrelated to themselves if they are later repaid by those same individuals (Trivers, 1971). Good examples of reciprocal altruism are rare. It implies a stable social system in which individuals are somehow able to recognize each other and remember past social encounters. In such a situation individuals can also shape one another's behavior through mutual punishments (Clutton-Brock & Parker, 1995), but the better-studied case of positive interactions is more often emphasized. What is known about the mechanisms involved in recognizing kin or partners in an altruistic relationship, and how do they compare to the mechanisms considered earlier in the chapter?

4.4.2 Kin Recognition

A system in which behavior is biased toward kin has four components (Waldman, Frumhoff, & Sherman, 1988; figure 4.17). We encountered similar distinctions in section 2.5.2 when discussing Beecher's work on parent-offspring recognition in swallows. First, relatives must be labeled in some way—that is, they must emit a distinctive signal reliably correlated with their genetic identity. Second and third, the altruist must be able to perceive this signal and to recognize it—that is, relate it to some internal representation that corresponds to "relative" (but this does not mean animals are aware in any sense that those recognized are relatives). Finally, the perceiver must direct some behavior discriminatively to those recognized. The behavior shown and the threshold for showing it may depend on the social context (Reeve, 1989).

As theorists have pointed out (Barnard, 1990; Blaustein & Porter, 1995; Hepper, 1986; Waldman, Frumhoff, & Sherman, 1988), what is selected is *kin discrimination*—that is, behavior that favors kin. This must be based on some sort of *kin recognition*, but recognizing kin is not necessarily accompanied by behavior discriminating in their favor. (The familiar distinction between cognition and performance again!) Kin recognition may be direct, in that individuals may respond to some signal directly linked to genes similar to their own. However, this sort of system is unlikely because it suggests that a single gene controls production of signal, recognition, and discriminative behavior (Grafen, 1990). Most often, kin recognition is indirect: the altruist responds to a contextual stimulus normally correlated with kinship. For instance, parents of *altricial* young—that is, those born naked and helpless like many songbirds or small rodents—are usually safe in responding to anything they find in their nest as if it is their offspring, for example by feeding it. Cuckoos, cowbirds, and other nest parasites exploit this rule by laying their eggs in other

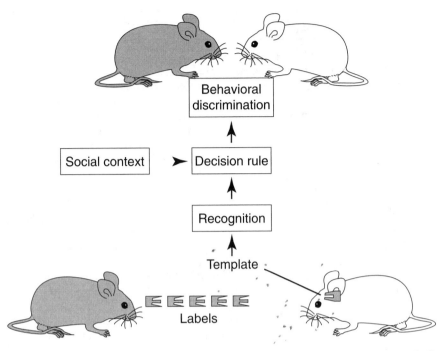

Figure 4.17. The elements of a recognition system. Adapted from Waldman, Frumhoff, and Sherman (1988) with permission.

birds' nests. When the young cuckoo hatches, it pushes its foster siblings out of the nest, so the host birds put all their reproductive effort into feeding the young cuckoo (box 4.2).

Following a simple rule like "treat everything in the nest as your offspring" does not require kin recognition nor learning the features of the offspring as such. Recognition might be completely tied to location, so that a relative encountered elsewhere is treated as a stranger. However, in many species family members are together in the same nest or territory at a predictable time in the life cycle, and this sets the stage for learning that permits recognition later on outside that spatial context. We have already seen examples of this in imprinting. For instance, newly hatched chicks and ducklings behave as if following the rule: "The first large moving object you see is your mother." This rule works because the mother is virtually certain to be near the nest when the babies hatch. The same kind of principle also allows young animals to learn characteristics of their siblings and later behave altruistically toward them.

In Belding's ground squirrels (*Spermophilus beldingi*), males disperse from the area where they were born, but adult females establish burrows close to their natal area (Holmes & Sherman, 1982). Females are completely responsible for parental care because the male leaves the female's territory soon after mating. Therefore, females often interact with relatives—their own offspring, their sisters, and the sisters' offspring—while males do not. As kin selection

Box 4.2. A Cost of Recognition

The European cuckoo (*Cuculus canorus*) lays its eggs in other birds' nests. When the young cuckoo hatches, it pushes the eggs or young of its host out of the nest, thereby monopolizing all the host's parental effort while reducing the host's reproductive success to zero (Davies & Brooke, 1988). It would seem that the small songbirds parasitized by cuckoos should be able to recognize their own eggs and/or offspring so they can discriminate against cuckoos. Some such birds do learn what their own eggs look like and reject eggs that are too different (Davies & Brooke, 1988; Lotem, Nakamura, & Zahavi, 1995). However, cuckoos' eggs are very good mimics of their hosts' eggs; different races (*gentes*) of cuckoos specialize on different host species and lay eggs that closely resemble the eggs of those hosts. Thus the potential host faces a difficult signal detection problem, and its behavior can be understood in terms of the costs of and benefits of accepting vs. rejecting unusual eggs in the nest (Davies, Brooke, & Kacelnik, 1996; figure B4.2a). When the small bird ejects one egg from its nest it may break some other eggs in the process, and in any case rejecting an egg entails some risk of rejecting one's own egg. When the probability of parasitism is low, the host's expected reproductive success will be highest if it has a relatively lax criterion for rejecting eggs. But when the probability of parasitism is high, the benefit of rejection outweighs the cost, and potential hosts should discriminate more strongly against deviant eggs. Some birds adjust their criterion on a short-term basis: seeing a stuffed cuckoo on the edge of the nest increases reed warblers' tendency to reject a model cuckoo egg (Davies, Brooke, & Kacelnik, 1996).

   Why doesn't this reasoning also apply to offspring recognition? One possibility is that any mechanism for rejecting parasites like cuckoos would require that the hosts learn what their own offspring look like in the first place. If this learning depended on

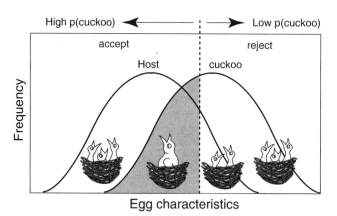

Figure B4.2a. The decision whether to accept or reject eggs with different characteristics as a signal detection problem (see section 2.4). Payoffs are represented as raising a full brood of one's own (three small nestlings), a reduced brood, or a cuckoo (single big nestling). The optimal placement of the decision criterion depends on the probability of cuckoos in the environment as indicated. After Davies, Brooke, and Kacelnik (1996) with permission.

Box 4.2. (*continued*)

a process like imprinting on the first brood of offspring raised, it would go wrong whenever the first clutch was parasitized: the parent would learn to accept cuckoos and reject all future offspring of its own. The formal argument depicted in figure B4.2b shows that on average birds that always accept any offspring in the nest win more reproductive success than birds that learn what their offspring look like on the basis of their first brood and reject any future offspring that look different (Lotem, 1993). Here is a case where learning is more costly than not learning.

Learning to recognize eggs and offspring has been studied comparatively in colonial- and solitary-nesting gulls and swallows (Beecher, 1990; Storey, Anderson, Porter, & Maccharles, 1992). Species in which individuals nest close together and in which the young may wander should have mechanism for parent-offspring recognition. However, as discussed in chapter 2, the same end could be accomplished by differences in discriminability of cues to identity of the eggs or young and/or by differences in the adults' ability to discriminate those differences as well as by specializations in recognition learning ability. In the case of swallows, at least, colonial and solitary species differ in the signals given off by the young rather than in adult perception or learning (see section 2.5.2).

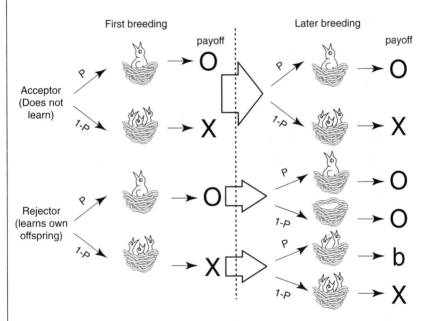

Figure B4.2b. Reproductive success of cuckoo hosts that accept any baby in their nest (acceptors) compared to that of birds that learn the appearance of their own offspring based on their first breeding experience and reject different-appearing offspring thereafter. P = probability of being parasitized; X = average number of offspring of a nonparasitized host; O = zero, the reproductive success from a parasitized nest; b = reproductive success of a parasitized host that rejects a cuckoo egg—i.e., the benefit of rejection. Redrawn from Lotem (1993) with permission.

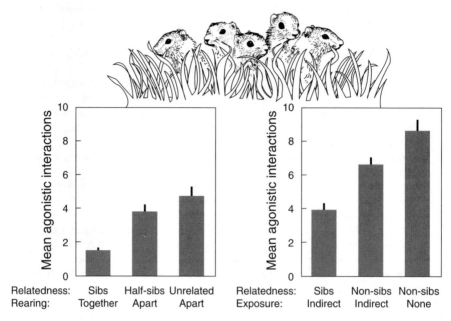

Figure 4.18. Aggressive responses of female Belding's ground squirrels to test females of different degrees of relatedness and familiarity. "Indirect exposure" means that the subject had previously encountered a sibling of the test animal but not the test animal herself. Data from Holmes (1986a, 1986b), redrawn with permission; drawing after a photograph in Krebs and Davies (1993), with permission.

predicts, closely related females behave altruistically toward each other in defense against predators and territorial disputes. In the presence of sisters and offspring, females are more likely to alarm-call, a behavior that may increase their own risk of being caught by the predator. Sisters are also more likely to collaborate in chasing territorial intruders than are unrelated individuals.

The role of experience in kin recognition in this species has been investigated in laboratory and field *cross-fostering experiments*. In such experiments, babies from one nest are placed into the nest of another mother, to be raised with babies to which they are unrelated. (Until the time when the young are ready to start leaving the nest, mothers accept foster babies and rear them as their own—that is, they use a location rule, a good guide to kinship at this stage.) Kin recognition can be tested in the laboratory by allowing two animals to meet in a neutral arena and recording the incidence of aggressive and other behavior patterns. Such studies show that Belding's ground squirrels treat the animals they were raised with as kin. However, this does not necessarily mean that they treat as kin only the individuals in their natal nest. Unrelated females raised with each others' siblings are less aggressive toward each other as adults than are pairs of unfamiliar animals not raised with each others' relatives (Holmes, 1986a; figure 4.18). In effect, this is an example of generalization between genetically similar individuals whose characteristics

were learned in the natal nest. This generalization is likely based on genetically similar individuals having similar odors (see box 4.3).

Female Belding's ground squirrels also respond altruistically to those genetically similar to themselves even if they have never encountered each other
or each other's siblings before (Holmes, 1986a). For instance, figure 4.18 reveals an effect of relatedness on agonistic behavior over and above the effect
of exposure to the opponent or her relatives. Adults recognize not only full
siblings but siblings with whom they share only one parent (*half sibling*). Because the males of this species mate with many different females, adults may
encounter half siblings who share the same father but grew up in another lit-
ter. Females, but not males, behave less aggressively to unfamiliar paternal
half siblings than to unfamiliar unrelated individuals (figure 4.18). Again, this
behavior could reflect generalization from the odors of familiar full siblings.
However, some behavioral ecologists have suggested what initially sounds like
a more complex mechanism, *phenotype matching*. Through exposure to its own
odors and those of its littermates, the individual is assumed to build up a representation or template of the characteristics of close kin. Novel individuals
are compared to this template and responded to accordingly—that is, an animal is treated in a more friendly manner the more nearly its features match
those in the stored standard (Holmes & Sherman, 1982). The proposed phenotype matching mechanism is no different from other recognition learning
mechanisms we have considered: it consists of a stored representation and an
appropriate response rule.

An interesting proposal is that the phenotype matched can be the individual's own, in particular its odor. (Note that an individual can smell itself much
as others do, though it cannot see or hear itself in the same way.) Evidence for
this hypothesis comes again from studies of Belding's ground squirrels. Because females in this species may mate with more than one male, litters may
contain both full siblings (same father and mother) and half siblings (same
mother, different father). Who is who can be determined by DNA finger-
printing. Females raised with full and half sisters behave most altruistically toward their full sisters, both in the field and in laboratory tests (Holmes &
Sherman, 1982). Only something like phenotype matching could account for
apparent recognition of completely unfamiliar kin. The notion that genetically
similar individuals share distinctive odors is strongly supported by research
on mate choice in inbred mice. Different strains of inbred mice differ genetically primarily in a group of genes called the *Major Histocompatibility Complex
(MHC)*. These genes are responsible for the recognition of tissue as "self" or
"not self" in all kinds of organisms. The MHC differs in different strains of
otherwise genetically identical mice. Male mice prefer to mate with females of
a different MHC from themselves, and this preference is based on the ability
to discriminate female odors (Boyse, Beauchamp, Yamazaki, & Bard, 1991).

In the examples of experience-based kin recognition discussed so far, the
requisite experience may be quite long-lasting. For example, baby Belding's
ground squirrels stay in their family group for several weeks before dispersing. The learning that takes place during this time has to last a lifetime. There

is plenty of time for it, although researchers have apparently not tried to narrow down the time when it occurs. Thus we know little about the conditions for learning other than that they include exposure in the family group. In other situations, however, it is essential to learn other individuals' odors very quickly. This happens in the phenomenon known as *the Bruce effect*, learning the characteristics of a mate during a brief mating encounter (box 4.3). Although this is not kin recognition, it is an example of olfactory learning the conditions and neural basis of which have been studied in some detail. It also shows how experience can change behavior simply by changing stimulus processing at a low level rather than by influencing some higher level template or decision mechanism.

4.4.3 Reciprocal Altruism

The notion that reciprocal altruism depends on individuals recognizing each other and remembering each other's altruistic acts suggests that reciprocal altruists must keep sophisticated mental balance sheets. Indeed, one hypothesis about human intelligence is that it was selected for keeping track of social relationships and obligations in early hominid groups (Cosmides, 1989; Humphrey, 1976; see also chapter 11). Nevertheless, reciprocal altruism may occur in much simpler systems. Such a system of altruism among fish and their cleaners was described by Trivers (1971) in his initial theorizing about reciprocal altruism.

Like nearly all animals, fish can be subject to the destructive effects of ectoparasites. Gills, mouths, scales, and fins may all become infested. Although a nuisance to their host, parasitic organisms are meals for other fish, and some such species subsist on the parasites they clean from the surfaces and even the gills and mouths of other fish. Cleaners are allowed to approach hosts, which are often larger predatory species, very closely, even swimming in and out of their mouths and gills, but the cleaners are seldom eaten. Cleaners may have specialized coloration and behaviors that signal their approach; in fact, some species have evolved as "cleaner mimics," looking and behaving like a cleaner and then rushing in to take a bite of a host's fin or flesh. Hosts likewise have special behaviors of resting in a trancelike state while being cleaned and then appearing to signal to the cleaner when they are about to depart. The host

---

Box 4.3. Olfactory Recognition in Mating and Mothering

When a female mouse that has recently mated encounters the odor of a strange male, pregnancy is blocked. This phenomenon, originally known as the Bruce effect, means that the female has learned in some way to recognize the mate who mated with her and can discriminate novel males from him. The dynamics of this memory and its neural basis have been studied by using as novel animals males of a different strain

⟶

Box 4.3. (continued)

from the familiar, stud, male (Brennan, Kaba, & Keverne, 1990). Acquisition of stable recognition depends on four to six hours of exposure to the stud male after mating. If he is removed immediately after mating, then presentation of a novel male the next day does not block pregnancy. Once acquired, recognition lasts about 50 days, as shown by the experiments diagrammed in figure B4.3. In these experiments (Kaba, Rosser, & Keverne, 1988), the original pregnancy was blocked by presenting a novel male 24 hours after initial mating. Then, after a retention interval of up to 50 days, this novel male mated with the female. If she still recognized her original mate, then his odor did not block this second pregnancy.

Mate recognition in mice is mediated not by the primary olfactory system but by an accessory olfactory system served by the vomeronasal organ. Learning is triggered by the vaginal and cervical stimulation that normally accompany mating and takes the form of changes in the first synapses in this sensory pathway. A remarkably similar system, both behaviorally and neurally, is evident in mother-offspring recognition in sheep (Kendrick, Levy, & Keverne, 1992; review in Levy, Porter, Kendrick, Keverne, & Romeyer, 1996). Ewes that have never given birth are not attracted to the odors of lambs, but as soon as they have given birth they start to be attracted to lamb odors in general, and their own lamb's odor in particular. As in mice, the underlying neural changes are triggered for a sensitive period of a few hours after vaginal and cervical stimulation, and they are long-lasting. An experienced ewe responds more readily to subsequent lambs and is less likely to reject them than is a first-time mother. Olfactory mother-offspring recognition has been studied most extensively in rats (Fleming, Morgan, & Walsh, 1996). Here, as in sheep, the simple olfactory recognition triggered by events during parturition is the basis for the development of more elaborate interactions between mother and young based on a variety of sensory modalities.

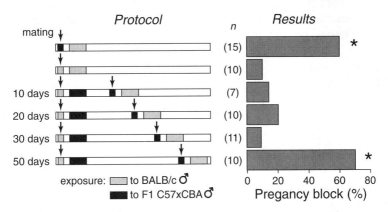

Figure B4.3. Design and results of an experiment testing the duration of recognition memory for a mate in female mice. The higher the proportion of pregancies blocked by exposure to a male of a different strain, the stronger memory for the first mate is inferred to be (BALB/c, C57 and CBA are strains of mice). Redrawn from Brennan, Kaba, and Keverne (1990) with permission.

benefits by being cleaned, and the cleaner gets a meal. However, it is not clear whether the participants in this relationship suffer any cost; if they do not it would more appropriately be described as a symbiosis than as reciprocal altruism.

Individual hosts and cleaners can have long-lasting relationships. Some of the mechanisms by which hosts and cleaners recognize each other have been studied by Losey (1979) in Hawaiian reef fish. Cleaners have fixed "stations" on the reef, which parasitized individuals visit regularly. Contact with cleaners is reinforcing for host species. Hosts seem to be learning not the identity of their cleaners as such but the locations where they can be cleaned. In the laboratory, hosts will learn to enter an area where they are contacted by a cleaner model (Losey, 1979).

When members of the same species are involved, reciprocal altruism can be difficult to distinguish from kin selected behavior. For instance, apparent reciprocal altruism has been described in vampire bats (*Desmodus rotundus*) (Wilkinson, 1984), which fly out each evening from communal roosts in hollow trees to seek a meal of blood. A substantial blood meal allows a bat to survive another 50–60 hours before feeding again, but not every bat succeeds in getting a meal every night. Unfed bats may starve within 24 hours, but a starving bat can be rescued if a recently fed bat regurgitates blood for it. Some regurgitations take place between relatives, particularly mothers and babies, but others appear to involve nonrelatives, and feeding is most probable between bats that likely know each other as individuals. To test whether feedings were truly reciprocal, groups of bats were kept in the laboratory and each night one was kept without food while the others fed. When the hungry bat was returned to the group, in 12 of 13 cases it was fed by another bat from the group it had come from in the wild. Moreover, the recipients of regurgitations tended to reciprocate the donation on a later night.

These observations suggest that vampire bats recognize unrelated individuals and retain some memory of past interactions with them. However, the relatedness of the bats involved was not always known, so the possibility remains open that the behavior was kin selected. Among primates, many species have much more subtle and sustained social interactions—both positive and negative (see Clutton-Brock & Parker, 1995)—than the vampire bats do. For a few species, experiments have revealed something of what individuals know about each other, although not much about how they come to know it. Some of this research is discussed in later chapters.

4.5 Summary and Conclusions

Animals learn the features of events they are exposed to, even in the absence of specific contingencies with other events. The three examples of simple recognition learning that have been analyzed most extensively are habituation, perceptual learning, and imprinting. The same sorts of conditions for learning are important in each case, but their details and the resulting behavioral changes are qualitatively different. In habituation, a preexisting response decreases in probability or intensity. In imprinting, sexual or filial preferences develop. Perceptual learning can be assessed by testing whether an arbitrary relationship is learned more readily with a familiar than with a novel stimulus. Despite these differences in the effects of learning on behavior, what is learned about a single stimulus can be thought of in a similar way in each case: its elements or features become associated with each other so that exposure to one feature recalls other features. Comparator models have been prominent in accounts of recognition learning: present input is compared to a stored representation and responding is based on the discrepancy between them. The models of recognition in habituation, imprinting, and kin discrimination are essentially the same, as can be seen by comparing figures 4.5, 4.11, and 4.17. In general, however, it is difficult or impossible to distinguish the predictions of such a model from those of a model of changes in the threshold of activation for acquired or prefunctionally existing S-S and/or S-R connections.

The section of the chapter on kin recognition and reciprocal altruism describes a number of natural situations in which individuals appear to recognize each other. In a few of these cases, something is known about what cues are used and how they acquire their significance. In most of these cases, too little is known about the conditions and contents of recognition learning to compare it in detail to the examples described earlier in the chapter. However, there seems to be no reason to question that the same sorts of learning are involved. For instance, in Belding's ground squirrels, "phenotype matching" of the individual's odor might be involved in initial recognition of kin, but other individually distinctive features such as appearance and voice may later be associated with this feature to permit kin to be recognized at a distance. The results of the many studies of how animals learn subtle features of the objects to which they are exposed in the laboratory make it plausible that similar learning goes on in natural situations in the field.

Further Reading

The book by Hall (1991) is a thorough review of habituation and perceptual learning as studied by learning theorists and develops an argument for an integrated model of habituation, latent inhibition, and perceptual learning. Hall (1996) is a brief update. Macphail (1993) thoroughly reviews habituation in invertebrates as well as vertebrates, with particular attention to implications for the neurobiology of learning. Ethological observations of habituation in a wider variety of species and response systems are reviewed by Hinde (1970a, chap. 13). The book edited by Hogan and Bolhuis (1994) contains several insightful chapters on imprinting, perceptual learning, and the relationship between developmental phenomena and conditioning.

The most comprehensive recent review of imprinting is that by Bolhuis (1991), following the review of earlier work by Bateson (1966). Van Kampen (1996) is an excellent recent review in which filial imprinting is analyzed much as it is here. Horn's (1985) book is a readable and well-illustrated account of early studies on the neural basis of imprinting; Bolhuis (1994) brings this work more up to date.

In spite of all the recent work on imprinting, it is still very worthwhile to read Lorenz's (1935/1970) own account of his work.

Chapter 11 of Krebs and Davies (1993) is a good introduction to theory and data on altruism and kin recognition, as are the articles by Hepper (1986) and Waldman et al. (1988). The book edited by Hepper (1991) includes chapters on kin recognition in species from insects to primates, a much wider variety of examples than is covered in this chapter. The chapter by Sherman, Reeve, and Pfennig (1997) is a general review of recognition mechanisms organized similarly to parts of this chapter.

5

Discrimination and Classification

5.1 Three Examples

A male stickleback with a bright red belly, ready to mate, swims about in a tank. A grayish model fish with a swollen "belly" appears, and our subject begins to display courtship movements. Their vigor increases when the model assumes a diagonal posture with its head up. A short time later, another model, with a red, unswollen, belly, is introduced. The male darts toward it, ready for a fight (figure 5.1).

A hungry budgerigar perches in a small chamber, pecking at a lighted key. As it pecks it hears brief, regular, pulses of sound, the recorded contact calls of other budgies: "chirp . . . chirp . . . chirp." Suddenly the sound changes to one with canary calls alternated: "chirp . . . cheep . . . chirp . . . cheep." The bird begins pecking a second key and is promptly rewarded with a few seeds.

A pigeon pecks rapidly at a small photograph of Harvard Yard containing trees, buildings, people, sky. After a few seconds, a hopper of grain appears and the pigeon eats. Now the scene changes to a treeless Manhattan street. The bird emits a few desultory pecks, then turns away and paces about. After a minute or so, a picture of a leafy suburban garden appears and the bird begins pecking again.

Behaviorally, all three animals are *discriminating* among model fish, recorded sounds, or pictures. In operational terms, they are exhibiting *stimulus control*. At the same time they are *classifying* or *categorizing* complex stimuli, in

185

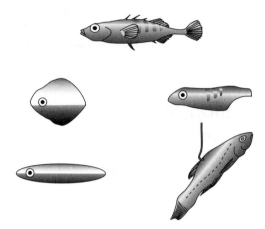

Figure 5.1. Model fish used to discover what stimuli control sexual and aggressive behaviors of male sticklebacks. *Top:* a normal male stickleback. Models on the left have red undersides, like normal males. On the right is a model with the swollen belly characteristic of egg-laden females and a dead tench presented in the upright posture of a courting female stickleback. Redrawn from Tinbergen (1951) with permission.

that they give one response to one set of stimuli and different responses to others. This chapter asks what mechanisms underlie such behavior. When animals behave in the ways described above, do they necessarily have an underlying *concept*—that is, a single representation to which each instance is compared? Does the stickleback, for example, have a concept of "mate" or "rival male"? Or can their behavior be explained as responses to a few simple stimuli? What do these apparently different explanations mean? And how does discriminative behavior develop?

Clearly, the issues here are not unrelated to those in the chapters on perception, learning, and recognition. In general, in this chapter animals are discriminating among stimuli that they readily perceive as different. How they classify such stimuli depends on the consequences associated with them, during evolution or during current training. In chapter 4 we were concerned with how discriminative behavior is acquired through simple exposure. Here we will be concerned with processes of explicit *discrimination training*, in which some stimuli are paired with one consequence and others, with another. Nevertheless, the same ideas about stimulus representation from chapters 3 and 4 will be useful in understanding the phenomena discussed here.

We start, however, in section 5.2, with some ideas about responses to natural stimuli—that is, discriminations that are not explicitly trained. Experience may contribute to what animals do in these situations, but the focus is on what aspects of natural objects control discriminative responding and how they do so, not on how it develops. In section 5.3 we look at the results of experiments in which animals are trained to perform arbitrary responses to naturalistic stimuli, as in the second example above. What can such experiments tell us about how animals classify signals in the wild? Traditional studies of discrimination learning have used simple stimuli like tones and lights. Section 5.4 reviews the principles of discrimination learning revealed by these sorts of experiments and illustrates the roles these principles play in the arms race between predators and prey. The final section of the chapter returns to classification of complex stimuli, this time in the context of experiments on category discrimination as in the third example. In such experiments, differential responding to complex stimuli has been explicitly trained. Is the animals' behavior in such experiments evidence that they have a concept or are they just clever memorizers? What kinds of concepts might animals have?

5.2 Untrained Responses to Natural Stimuli

5.2.1 Sign Stimuli

One of the key observations of classical ethologists was that, like the stickleback in our first example of discrimination, animals respond selectively to objects in their environment. Among the wide range of stimuli that an animal's sense organs can detect, some elicit one behavior, some another. Other features of natural objects are apparently ignored in certain contexts. For example, male sticklebacks in breeding condition attack very crude models with red bellies even if they lack most other fishlike characteristics. The red belly is referred to as a *sign stimulus*. Subtle features of sign stimuli can be important, however, particularly their configuration. For instance, the red on the model is more effective if it is on the "belly" region, not the "back." To take another example, baby thrushes show begging behavior to crude model "parents," a black disk "body" with a smaller "head" disk, held above the nest. If such a model has two "heads" of different sizes, the nestlings beg most toward the one that has the more nearly natural size in relation to the model's "body" (Tinbergen & Kuenen, 1939/1957).

Apparent demonstrations of the importance of configural cues have not always controlled for nonrelational properties. For example, Tinbergen (1951) concluded that pecking of young herring gull chicks was influenced by the position of a red spot near the end of the parent's lower mandible (see figure 5.3). Chicks pecked less at spots on the forehead area of models. However, the models with spots on the forehead were held at the same height above the nest and swung to and fro at the same rate as models with spots on the bill. This meant that the forehead spots were higher above the ground and, because the axis of rotation was near the model's "neck," they moved more slowly than spots on the beak. When these two factors were equated between spots in different positions, black-headed gull chicks pecked equally at spots in both configurations (Hailman, 1967).

5.2.2 Heterogeneous Summation and Supernormality

It often turns out that more than one feature of a natural stimulus influences responding. For example, a model's "posture" and its way of moving as well

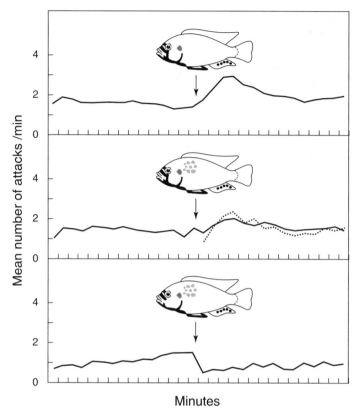

Figure 5.2. Summation of the inhibitory effect of orange spots (bottom panel) and the excitatory effect of a black eye bar (top panel) on attack rate of male cichlids, *Haplochromis burtoni*. Dotted line in the central panel is the sum of the curves in the two other panels; the solid line represents the data. Redrawn from Heiligenberg (1974) with permission.

as its color determine how vigorously a male stickleback attacks it. When more than one feature contributes, their configuration may be important, as in the examples above. In some cases, separable cues have a precisely additive effect, a phenomenon known as *heterogeneous summation* (see Margolis, Mariscal, Gordon, Dollinger, & Gould, 1987, for discussion). Heiligenberg (1974) provided an elegant example. He measured aggression in the cichlid fish, *Haplochromis burtoni*, by observing how much one fish attacked smaller fish of another species living in its tank. The modest baseline level of attack could be temporarily raised or lowered by presenting a model conspecific outside the tank. A model with a black eye bar raised the level of attack; a similar model with orange spots but no eye bar reduced attack (figure 5.2). These effects summed algebraically: a model with both a black eye bar and orange spots caused little change in the attack rate. Sometimes stimuli with more extreme values than those found in nature are most effective. For instance, incubating herring gulls retrieving eggs placed just outside the nest prefer eggs that are larger or more speckled than normal. By combining such extra-attractive characteristics in a single model, it is possible to create a *supernormal stimulus* (or *supernormal releaser*) (Baerends, 1982; Tinbergen, 1951; see also section 5.4.2).

Classic cases of heterogeneous summation are consistent with an additive model of the actions of different sign stimuli, analogous to the additivity of CSs in the Rescorla-Wagner model of conditioning (see chapter 3). However, as in conditioning, the notion that physically separable cues act independently and additively is too simple to be completely general. For instance, in conditioning, modulators have conditional control, telling the animal when a CS-US relationship exists. An analogous unconditioned stimulus would be one that does not elicit responding itself but in the presence of which the animal responds to a sign stimulus. Separable features may form a configuration, psychologically different from the sum of its parts, a possibility discussed by Tinbergen (1951). In some cases, the relative rather than absolute values of cues may be important (Fetterman, 1996; see also chapters 7 and 8). The way in which multiple cues are used is also an issue in behavioral ecology (Johnstone, 1997). For instance, males in many species of birds have multiple sexual ornaments as well as other signals: why do males invest in bright colors plus long tails plus costly displays (Moller & Pomiankowski, 1993b)? Does each feature signal something different or are multiple signals redundant? How do females combine information from diffent signals (Dale & Slagsvold, 1996)?

5.2.3 "Perceptual Sharpening"

Sign stimuli may have their effects on very young animals the first time they are presented. In other cases, a sign stimulus is effective as soon as the animal performs the appropriate responses—for example, when it is hormonally ready to breed for the first time. Many of the stimulus- response connections appropriate for species-specific feeding, breeding, and other behaviors exist prefunctionally (Hogan, 1994b; see also chapter 1), but this need not mean that learning cannot occur later on. Such learning may result in control by subtle features of an object that are not effective originally. One well-analyzed example involves pecking at the parent's bill by gull chicks.

The chicks of many species of gulls are fed regurgitated fish by their parents. Adult laughing gulls have a red spot near the end of the lower mandible, and the chicks' pecking at this spot stimulates the adult to regurgitate food. The red color of the spot is a sign stimulus. A red knitting needle held in a beaklike way is a supernormal releaser of pecking (Hailman, 1967). Newly hatched laughing gulls seem to ignore features of model gull heads like shape and color and respond only to the presence of a red bill-like area (figure 5.3). However, older chicks are also influenced by more subtle features like the shape of the head. They peck more at more realistic models. Laughing gull chicks fed in the presence of one model and not in the presence of another soon learn to discriminate between them, reflecting a process Hailman called

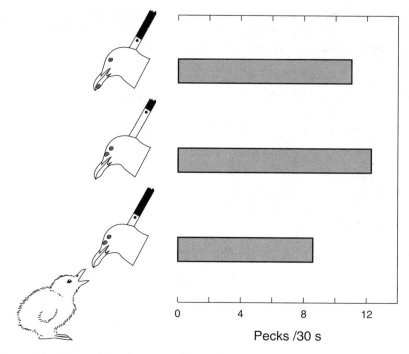

Figure 5.3. Effects of the placement of the red spot normally at the end of the parent's bill as in the top model and the point at which the model pivots (black dots) on pecking by herring gull chicks. Redrawn from Hailman (1967) with permission.

perceptual sharpening. There seems no reason to think this is not the same as the perceptual learning process discussed in chapter 4: with experience, initially ineffective features of an object become associated with an effective feature so that objects originally treated as similar are differentiated. Indeed, more recent work has demonstrated that the young gulls learn to recognize their parents by associating visual and auditory features of the model with the food reinforcement they provide (Margolis, Mariscal, Gordon, Dollinger, & Gould, 1987; Griswold, Harrer, Sladkin, Alessandro, & Gould, 1995).

5.2.4 Discussion and Conclusions

Ethological terms like *sign stimulus* and *releaser* summarize important facts about animal behavior. However, few researchers today, if they study such phenomena at all, would refer to their work in the terms used by classical ethologists. One reason for this is that the analysis of sign stimuli was intimately related to the Lorenzian model of motivation, now considered by many to be oversimplified and unrealistic (but see Hogan, 1994a). Sign stimuli were assumed to release accumulated *action-specific energy* via a species-specific decision mechanism, the *innate releasing mechanism,* or *IRM.* One objectionable feature of this scheme was the term *innate.* As discussed in chapter

1, this term fell out of use as all involved in debating it accepted that both environmental and genetic factors contribute to all behavior. The developmental history of behavior is a separate question from how it is controlled at any moment in development. It is instructive to compare how untrained or prefunctional responses are controlled by sign stimuli to how explicitly trained responses are controlled by discriminative stimuli. The characteristics of untrained discriminative behavior that are shared with explicitly trained discriminations can be summarized as follows.

1. Not all features of a relevant situation or object control behavior equally, even though all might be discriminable by the animals involved.
2. Features that do influence behavior have additive effects. The Rescorla-Wagner model (see chapter 3) says the same thing about explicitly trained discriminations. However, it is important to keep in mind that independence/additivity is not the only possible model for combining the effects of signals (Fetterman, 1996). Conditional control and control by configurations or relationships are among other possibilities.
3. Stimuli other than the ones that occur in nature may be most effective and/or be preferred to natural objects. This statement describes both supernormality and peak shift in trained discriminations, as discussed in section 5.4.2.
4. Discriminative behavior may be specific to certain motivational states. For example, a male stickleback behaves most differently toward males and females when he is in reproductive condition. The herring gull chick's level of hunger affects how much it pecks at the parent's bill. In explicitly trained behavior, as well, we have already seen that at least some learned responses appear only in the presence of the relevant motivational state. For instance stimuli associated with food may no longer evoke CRs in sated animals (see section 3.4.2).

5.3 Classifying Complex Natural Stimuli

5.3.1 Classifying Multidimensional Signals in the Field

In classic research on sign stimuli, models were compared in as natural a situation as possible. Features to be varied were selected on the basis of observations in the field and initially tested one at a time. For example, two of the fish models in figure 5.1 have more or less the same red belly but differ in shape. Recent years have seen the development of a mathematically more sophisticated approach in which stimuli are represented as points in a multidimensional stimulus space. This approach has benefited from the availability of statistical techniques for analyzing multidimensional stimuli and computers for processing large data sets.

The best-developed example of this approach is research on how birds discriminate the vocalizations of their own species from those of other species (Dooling, Brown, Park, & Okanoya, 1990; Nelson & Marler, 1990). How, for example, does a robin classify songs as "robin"? Nelson and Marler tested the hypothesis that birds rely on the features that best distinguish their songs from the songs of other species found in the same habitat, the local *sound environ-*

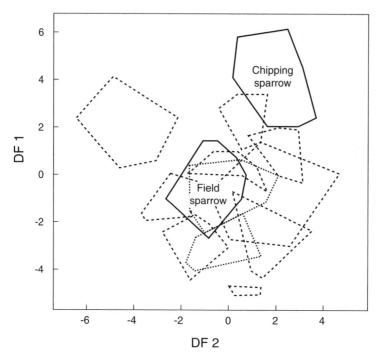

Figure 5.4. Two-dimensional space of song characteristics showing the extent to which chipping sparrow and field sparrow songs are similar to those of 11 other species found in the same habitat. Polygons enclose all songs sampled for each species. DF1 is positively correlated with song duration and number of notes; DF2 is correlated positively with minimum frequency and negatively with internote interval and note duration. Redrawn from Nelson and Marler (1990) with permission.

ment. They studied two North American songbirds, the field sparrow (*Spizella pusilla*) and the chipping sparrow (*S. passerina*). To discover how these birds' songs differed from the other songs they hear in the wild, Nelson and Marler analyzed a number of parameters of the songs of these and 11 other species commonly singing in the same habitat in upstate New York. Many examplars of each species' song were described along a number of dimensions such as maximum and minimum sound frequency, number of notes, note duration, and song duration to discover which feature or combination of features discriminated best among species. When the average song of each species and its range of variation were placed in the multidimensional *signal space* so defined, three variables were sufficient to differentiate chipping sparrow song from those of the other species, while four additional variables were needed for field sparrow song—that is, this song overlapped with more of the other songs in the signal space (figure 5.4). For both species, however, maximum frequency was sufficient to classify over 90% of the samples correctly.

To discover whether field sparrows actually use the features that best define their species-typical song in signal space, Nelson and Marler observed the birds' aggressive responses to songs played in the middle of their territories (see box 4.1). Each experiment consisted of playing two synthetic songs, a standard species-typical song with median values of all features, and one differing in just one feature. The two test songs were alternated between two speakers to see if birds attacked one more than the other regardless of its location in their territory. The feature being tested—note duration, for example—was altered until the test signal reliably elicited less territorial threat than the normal song. The difference from normal defined the *just meaningful difference* (*JMD*) for that feature. In general, birds did not respond differentially to altered and normal songs as long as the value of the altered feature was within the range of variation found in species-typical songs in the field, but they did respond less when features took on values more than about 2.5 standard deviations away from the average value for the species. Notice that the just meaningful difference is most likely larger than the psychophysical just noticeable difference (JND; see also chapter 2); the birds could probably be trained to make much finer discriminations than they do in the field.

To find out how features were weighted in the birds' decisions to attack or not, Nelson and Marler conducted a new series of choice experiments, this time using two altered songs in each test. For example, a song with its maximum frequency altered by one JMD was pitted against one with its duration altered by one JMD. If the bird directed more aggressive behavior toward the song with altered duration than toward the song with altered frequencies, it could be concluded that duration was less important than frequency in the classification of song as "field sparrow" vs. "other species." For field sparrows, sound frequency was the most important feature, consistent with the hypothesis that birds should be most responsive to features that best differentiate their song from others in the same sound environment. However, other features were ranked in a way consistent with the hypothesis that species recognition is based on the least variable features of species-specific signals.

Combining analysis of the features that animals would be expected to respond to with testing whether they do respond to these features in natural situations has comparative potential that could be more throroughly exploited. For example, the features of a species-typical signal that vary most across individuals should be the ones which species uses for individual recognition. Some studies with great tits (*Parus major*) have produced results consistent with this hypothesis (Weary & Krebs, 1992).

5.3.2 Classifying Signals in the Laboratory

A thorough multidimensional analysis requires large amounts of data from standardized tests, and these may be difficult to obtain in the field. Therefore, some investigators have turned to operant tests in the laboratory. The second example at the beginning of this chapter illustrates this sort of experimental procedure. The animal performs one response to present a steady background stimulus. From time to time a second stimulus appears against this background. The animal is reinforced for performing a second response when the "different" stimulus appears, and its speed of reporting "different" is taken as evidence of the ease with which it perceives the difference. A relatively large set of stimuli is used, maybe a dozen or more, and each appears sometimes as background and sometimes as the alternated stimulus, so data are obtained on all possible pairs. The data are converted into a representation of psychological distances among the stimuli in a multidimensional space: pairs of stimuli for which "different" is reported quickly are far apart, while pairs for which the latency is long are close together—that is, they are perceived as similar. Each cluster of stimuli in such a space defines a psychological category.

This method does not impose a classification scheme on the animal. Rather, the animal's behavior shows how it classifies the stimuli on its own. This contrasts with the method of category discrimination training that we will meet in section 5.5. There the experimenter imposes a classification scheme—for example, by designating some stimuli to be paired with reinforcement and others not—and asks whether or how quickly animals learn the discrimination. In principle, these two approaches might lead to the same conclusions.

Dooling and his collaborators have extensively exploited the technique of the second example to study how birds classify vocalizations of their own and other species (Dooling, Brown, Manabe, & Powell, 1996; Dooling, Brown, Park, & Okanoya, 1990). For example, Dooling, Brown, Klump, and Okanoya (1992) tested canaries, zebra finches, budgerigars, and starlings with the contact calls of canaries, zebra finches, and budgerigars. For each species of subjects, the sounds formed three clusters in multidimensional stimulus space corresponding to the three species' calls (figure 5.5). When it came to detecting differences within species, the canaries, zebra finches, and budgerigars were each quickest at detecting differences between individuals of their own species. Psychophysical studies on these species indicate that this species-specific advantage is unlikely to reflect basic differences in auditory perception. It may therefore reflect more central processing, perhaps related to the auditory template hypothesized to guide song learning (see chapter 10).

Canaries, zebra finches, and budgerigars do not share the same sound environment in the wild, so these results cannot be related to the birds' task in nature as easily as Nelson and Marler's. However, a similar study with primates (Brown, Sinnott, & Kressley, 1994) showed that two species of primates, humans and Sykes's monkeys (*Circopithecus albogularis*), classify monkey and bird alarm calls as predicted on functional grounds. In the wild, the monkeys should respond similarly to all monkey species' alarm chirps because any of them could signal a predator threatening to all. They should ignore the chirping of forest birds, even though it is acoustically similar to monkey calls. As this notion predicts, Sykes's monkeys classified alarm chirps of their own and another sympatric monkey species as more similar to each other than either was to a sample of bird calls. People tested in the same way classified the bird calls as more similar to those of monkeys and the monkey calls as more different from one another than the monkeys did.

In all these cases, comparative data on classification raise almost more questions than they answer. For example, how do difference thresholds com-

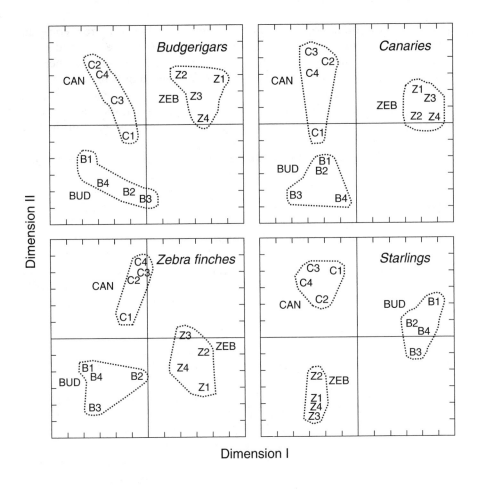

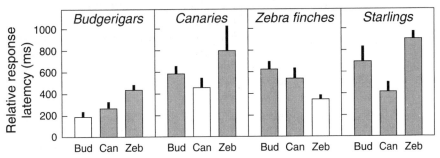

Figure 5.5. *Top*: Plots similar to that in figure 5.4 showing how budgerigars, canaries, zebra finches, and starlings classified the songs of four canaries (C1–C4), four budgerigars (B1–B4), and four zebra finches (Z1–Z4). *Lower panels*: Latency with which birds of the four species tested responded when the test stimulus changed from one song to the song of another individual of the same species. Response to vocalizations of the subject's own species shown in white. Redrawn from Dooling et al. (1992) with permission.

pare for Sykes's monkeys and humans over the range of sound frequencies in the calls? Would monkeys raised in the laboratory classify the bird and monkey calls in the same way as monkeys that had lived in the wild? Another important question is whether the animals are treating sounds broadcast in an operant chamber as species-specific signals. How can we tell whether they are or not? With sounds, we can at least be reasonably sure that the physical stimuli being classified are the same in the laboratory as in the field. But the fact that sounds of the same species are classified together may reflect physical similarity rather than a common representation or template of species-specific sounds. There is some evidence that birds performing arbitrary food-reinforced responses in the laboratory do treat recorded species-specific vocalizations as vocalizations. Cynx and Nottebohm (1992) trained zebra finches to perform a different response to each of two zebra finch songs. Birds trained when they were in reproductive condition—that is, when they would be especially responsive to zebra finch songs—learned the task faster than birds not in reproductive condition. If this does not represent a hormonal effect on learning or sound perception in general (which remains to be determined), it suggests that the birds were processing the sounds in the operant experiment as zebra finch vocalizations.

A few experiments have used methods similar to those of Dooling et al. (1992) to study how birds classify visual signals. As discussed in box 5.2, it can be more difficult with visual stimuli than with sounds to be sure that what is presented in the laboratory is the same stimulus from the animal's point of view as that stimulus in the field. Nevertheless, Brown and Dooling (1992, 1993) have made some progress in analyzing how budgerigars classify the faces of budgerigars and other birds. Their testing procedure paralleled that used in Dooling's lab for classification of auditory stimuli as in the second example at the beginning of the chapter. The birds classified slides of natural budgerigar faces using features that would be socially significant in the wild. They did not seem to be influenced by purely pictorial features like the proportion of the slide occupied by the image, suggesting that they really were processing the slides as bird faces. Moreover, just as with vocalizations, there was a species-specific advantage: budgerigars detected a difference between budgerigar faces quicker than one between zebra finch faces, in spite of the fact that people judged zebra finches to differ more.

By themselves none of these findings necessarily means that the stimuli were processed in some special way as faces, although there is good evidence that monkeys and sheep, like people, do have a special face-processing module (Kendrick et al., 1995; Phelps & Roberts, 1994). Sheer perceptual similarity could as well account for the way the birds grouped the faces. However, studies of scrambled bugerigar faces indicated that the configuration of features into a face made an image more discriminable for the birds. Budgerigars were asked to report "different" with a set of four stimuli, two normal faces and two faces with the features moved around (figure 5.6). Latencies were longer with scrambled than with normal faces. This result would not be expected if the birds were merely responding to individual features, since the

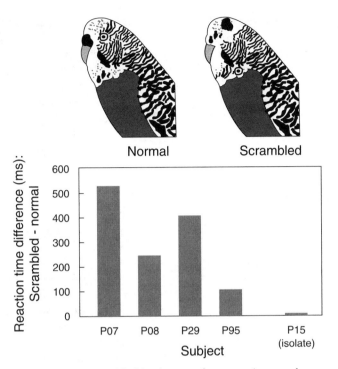

Figure 5.6. Normal and scrambled budgerigar faces used to test face perception in budgerigars. Data are the increase in latency when individual budgerigars were required to discriminate between scrambled faces compared to their latency to discriminate between two normal faces. The isolate was raised apart from other budgerigars. Redrawn from Brown and Dooling (1993) with permission.

same individual features were present in both normal and scrambled faces. However, this experiment is not conclusive because the birds had extensive experience in the task with normal faces before testing with scrambled faces and the single isolate bird (figure 5.6) did not. Poorer performance with scrambled faces could reflect lack of familiarity with them. The experiment needs to be repeated with animals equally experienced with scrambled and normal faces in the experiment.

5.3.3 Conclusions

The research discussed in this section is a continuation of classic research on sign stimuli. However, in addition to looking at natural responses to signals, some researchers have also asked how natural stimuli are classified by using arbitrary responses to such stimuli in the laboratory. Some of the research has also analyzed the discriminations that must be made in the field and used the results to predict what features animals should use in individual or species recognition.

Suppose we carry out the kind of program envisioned by Nelson and Marler (1990) and find species differences in how natural stimuli are classified. For example, suppose we have tested classification of visual images of species A and B by individuals of species A and B. Further, suppose the predominant color of species A is green-blue and that of species B is red-orange and that each species discriminates better among images of conspecifics than images of heterospecifics. Do the results reflect differences in general perceptual mechanisms or special processing (Dooling et al., 1992) of species-specific stimulus configurations? "Special processing" here means comparing each instance to a representation of species-specific signals so as to allow rapid classification of stimuli as "signal" or "nonsignal." In the current example, an obvious alternative possibility is that each species is especially sensitive to wavelength in the range within which its species-typical colors vary. That is, individuals in each species classify images of conspecifics easily because the colors in those images are especially salient for them. It would not matter if the images were of upside down or scrambled conspecifics or some other objects entirely: the species difference would be the same. Ruling out this possibility would require testing the two species' color vision in ways discussed in chapter 2. If color vision and perception of the other features involved were the same between species, and classification depended on the integrity of the stimuli as images of conspecifics, we might conclude that instances were being classified by reference to a stored representation of conspecific.

5.4 Discrimination Learning

The preceding three chapters are all about discrimination. Sensory systems (chapter 2) have evolved to permit different behaviors to things in the world that have different significance such as mates, food, and predators. The capacity to learn (chapter 3) allows discriminative behavior to be based on individual experience, and recognition (chapter 4) is but a label for some sorts of discriminative behavior. In psychology, however, *discrimination training* traditionally refers to procedures in which animals are differentially reinforced for performing a different, arbitrary, response to each of two or more stimuli. Training with a single stimulus is discrimination training of a sort, too, since the animal has to discriminate the experimental context or background alone from the context plus the reinforced stimulus. Methods of training with two or more explicit stimuli have led to a distinctive body of data and theory. The results have considerable usefuless in the study of animal perception (chapter 2), as well as theoretical implications for the nature of animal concept learning, discussed later in this chapter. In the wild, animals must be learning simple discriminations all the time. Information about how they do so has implications for how the minds of predators have influenced the evolution of their prey (box 5.1).

Box 5.1. Evolution and Discrimination Learning in the Wild: Models and Mimics

Brightly colored or patterned, noisy, or otherwise conspicuous prey tend to be bad tasting or illness producing, suggesting that their conspicuous features are warning predators to leave them alone. Although warning (*aposematic*) colors or other signals may be avoided when novel, potential predators usually must learn to avoid them. Many aposematic species have *mimics*—palatable species that acquire protection from their resemblance to the unprofitable *model* species. For instance, some flies look like bees (figure B5.1), some harmless snakes look like poisonous coral snakes, and orange and black Viceroy butterflies have wing patterns remarkably close to those of poisonous Monarch butterflies. These are examples of *Batesian mimicry*; cases in

⟶

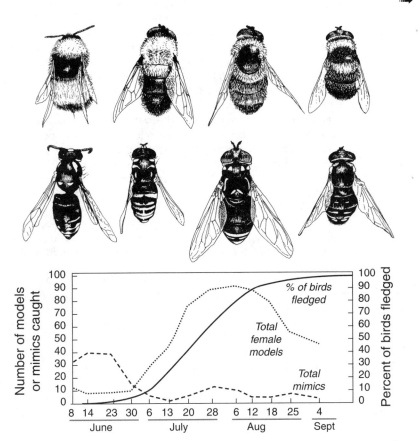

Figure B5.1. Top: Examples of Batesian mimicry complexes in which species of syrphid flies have evolved the appearance of stinging wasps and bees (Hymenoptera). In each row the insect on the left is the model; all the rest are different species of mimics. After a photograph in Waldbauer (1988) with permission. Bottom: Seasonal asynchrony of stinging Hymenoptera and their mimics in northern Michigan and the relationship of model and mimic abundance to the presence of naive predators, fledgling insectivorous birds. Redrawn from Waldbauer and LaBerge (1985) with permission.

Box 5.1. Evolution and Discrimination Learning in the Wild: Models and Mimics
(*continued*)

---

which two or more unpalatable species resemble one another have traditionally been referred to as *Mullerian mimicry*.

The influence of predators' perception, learning, and memory on the evolution of mimicry and on relationships among populations of models and mimics has been widely discussed and investigated (see Brower, 1988; Guilford, 1989). For instance, because a stronger punishment should be retained over more trials of extinction, relatively aversive models should confer protection on relatively large numbers of mimics. Because a stronger aversion should generalize more widely, more aversive or more numerous models will support cruder mimicry. If predators can remember for a reasonably long time, mimics need not even be present at the same time and place as models. For instance, a bird that has learned to avoid one species of insect in the fall may avoid a species that resembles it the next spring. The life histories of some mimics fit well with this scenario: they appear in the spring when they are avoided by experienced birds, but disappear by the time young, inexperienced birds have begun to forage on their own, which is when models appear (figure B5.1; Waldbauer, 1988).

Cryptic prey may benefit from being dispersed because this reduces the likelihood that predators will develop a search image for them (chapter 2), but aposematic species might be expected to be aggregated. The possible association of aposematism and aggregation has been much debated from the viewpoints of both evolutionary and psychological mechanisms. Warning coloration may evolve through kin selection: the conspicuous bad-tasting individual that is killed cannot pass on its characteristics to its offspring, but if similar related individuals are nearby, the predator may retain a memory of its bad experience long enough to give them a selective advantage. Psychologically, aggregation should hasten initial learning and later avoidance because a group presents a stronger signal than does a single individual. A number of laboratory experiments have addressed the question of whether or why noxious prey are actually better avoided when aggregated (Alatalo & Mappes, 1996; Gamberale & Tullberg, 1996; Guilford, 1988; Hauser, 1996). Whatever the resolution of this question, such research illustrates the intimate relationship between evolutionary and psychological issues that exists in this area. Further illustrations are attempts to build quantitative models of learning that account for the properties of model-mimic complexes (e.g., Huheey, 1988), and the application of signal detection theory to the question of how close mimicry needs to be to be advantageous (Getty, Kamil, & Real, 1987). Clearly, too, as chapter 2 suggests, conspicuousness, distastefulness, and resemblance are all functions of the perceptual systems of the predators involved, and explanations of particular examples of mimicry need to take this into account (Cuthill & Bennett, 1993).

5.4.1 Methods

Discrimination training may involve simultaneous or successive presentation of the stimuli to be discriminated. For example, training a rat on a simultaneous black-white discrimination in a T-maze means having one black and one white arm with black sometimes on the left, sometimes on the right. The rat might receive food in the white arm, no food in the black arm. Gradually, it will learn to enter the white arm, regardless of which side white is on. Performance is measured as proportion of choices of white in successive blocks of trials. In contrast, in a comparable successive black-white discrimination the rat finds food at the end of a white alley but not at the end of a black one. In this *go/no go* discrimination, performance is assessed by comparing running speeds or latencies to reach the end of the white vs. black alleys.

A frightened rat runs into a dark, black compartment rather than into a white one even in a novel environment. What rats learn in the examples above is not to tell black from white but what to do in the presence of each brightness in the training situation. This is not as easy as it sounds, however, because the rat may initially learn about completely irrelevant aspects of the situation, such as the position of the arms. In the successive procedure, at first it may learn simply that food is at the end of the alley and run equally fast all the time, particularly if errors are not costly. In the conditions typically used in the laboratory, reinforcement from chance correct responses eventually outweighs the effects of unreinforced trials. However, *correction procedures* can be helpful in exposing the animal to the to-be-learned associations: in such procedures, if the animal makes an unrewarded choice at the beginning of the trial, it may be "corrected" by removing opportunity for all but the rewarded response. In simultaneous discriminations, there is always a correct, rewarded response, and this may make these procedures more sensitive for detecting the early stages of learning or acquisition of difficult discriminations because the animal never has to withold responding, just direct it in a certain way.

Much of the traditional literature on discrimination training (see Mackintosh, 1974, for a review) used rats in alleys and mazes, as described above. Nowadays, operant methods are widely used because they allow automated testing of large numbers of animals for large numbers of trials. Pigeons have become popular subjects because their acute vision means they can be trained on many complex discriminations at once. Operant procedures may have *discrete trials* as in the T-maze and runway, but *free operant* procedures are also used. In these procedures, one or another of the stimuli to be discriminated is always available and response rates are compared in the different stimulus-reward conditions. A successive free-operant discrimination procedure is also referred to as a *multiple schedule*. Simultaneous free-operant discriminations are *concurrent schedules*, of which we will see more in chapter 9. *Intermittent reinforcement* may be scheduled with a different frequency or pattern in the presence of each of the stimuli to be discriminated and response rates compared. It is not necessary that one of the stimuli be completely unrewarded; with sufficient exposure animals can learn quite subtle differences between reinforcement contingencies paired with different stimuli. They sometimes learn all sorts of other things the experimenter may not intend, too, and it is especially important to control for these when trying to establish control by a particular feature of a training situation. For instance, in a successive free-operant discrimination with intermittent reinforcement in the presence of one stimulus and no reinforcement (extinction) in the presence of the other, animals can learn to use the presence or absence of reinforcement in the first few seconds of each stimulus presentation as a cue to whether to keep responding while that stimulus is on.

These descriptions of discrimination procedures suggest that they all involve instrumental learning. However, nowadays it is clear that procedures the experimenter views as instrumental may be effective because of the Pavlovian contingencies embedded in them. As we have seen in chapter 3, approaching a stimulus paired with food and retreating from one not paired with expected food are natural outcomes of Pavlovian conditioning procedures. Contemporary theoretical discussions of the discrimination learning process generally do not specify whether it is instrumental or Pavlovian, or else they assume it is Pavlovian.

5.4.2 Results

The Course of Acquisition   Even in simple black-white discriminations, many trials may elapse before experimentally naive animals perform differently from chance. This is not surprising if we consider that on the first trial the situation is completely novel for the animal. If a food-reinforced discrimination is being trained, the first thing to be learned is that food is available somewhere in the situation. But before the animal can become interested in eating, its fear of the novel situation has to habituate. In operant experiments, this learning occupies a separate phase of pretraining, or feeder training (often called *magazine training* in operant experiments) in which the animal may also be taught to press the lever or peck the key so that it responds readily when stimuli to be discriminated are introduced. Even without such initial nondifferential reinforcement, from the animal's point of view the most salient aspect of the training situation may be the presence of the reinforcer, so that initially it presses the lever or runs down the alley whatever stimuli are present. Even once it begins to show some differential behavior, this may be controlled by irrelevant stimuli. In two-choice situations, animals commonly adopt *position habits* during the acquisition phase, or *presolution period*. For instance, a rat being trained on a simultaneous black-white discrimination may always choose the stimulus on the left whatever its brightness. Historically, this kind of consistent response to incorrect features was called *hypothesis testing*, as if the animal was acting on the hypothesis "left is correct." Considerable debate was devoted to the question of whether animals learn anything about the correct features during this phase. This debate is associated with *continuity* vs. *noncontinuity* theories of discrimination, referring to their proponents' positions on the question whether or not animals learned continuously about the reinforcement contingencies even while apparently testing incorrect hypotheses (see Mackintosh, 1974).

In nature, it must be pretty rare for an animal to find itself in an entirely novel situation, with little similarity to situations it has encountered in the past. Perhaps a bird on its first migration, arriving in a wholly new habitat, is faced with the same problem as a naive rat in a maze, but even here the bird may be able to generalize from its natal habitat. Things shaped like worms and insects are still likely to be food, even if it is necessary to learn which are the best ones in the new environment. More commonly, though, animals may need to learn the characteristics of a new food object, predator, or conspecific appearing in a familiar habitat. This corresponds to training a discrimination in a familiar or latently inhibited context (see chapter 4).

Not surprisingly, similarity between the stimuli to be discriminated plays a role in the speed of discrimination learning. A discrimination between two shades of gray or two widths of stripes is learned more slowly than one between black and white. If the stimuli to be discriminated differ in several features, providing redundant cues, acquisition is faster than if they differ in only one feature (Mackintosh, 1974). Learning a difficult discrimination may be facilitated by starting training on an easy but related one.

Generalization and Peak Shift   No stimulus is ever perceived in exactly the same way twice. If nothing else, the internal state of the perceiver or the orientation of the receptors may change. *Generalization* from one episode to others that are merely similar to it, therefore, makes it possible to benefit from experience at all. The experience of eating a particular seed or butterfly is a good indication of what will follow from eating other seeds or butterflies of the same kind, so there is a sense in which the universal tendency to generalize expresses a creature's estimate that a new thing is the same kind as a thing previously encountered (Shepard, 1987, 1994). In nature, there is a tradeoff between generalizing and discriminating (McLaren, 1994). For instance, generalizing fear responses will be favored if the cost of ignoring the slightest sign of a predator is greater than the cost of making a startle response to a falling leaf. When the animal is not very hungry or other food is nearby, sharp discrimination among potential cues to food may be favored. Reflecting the effects of such functional tradeoffs, the extent of generalization may depend on the behavior system and the strength of motivation underlying responding (see figure 5.10).

Generalization may be tested along a stimulus continuum orthogonal to that on which a discrimination has been trained, or there may have been no explicit discrimination training. For example, suppose a pigeon is reinforced intermittently for pecking the key in an operant chamber when the key is lighted with green light but not when the key is dark. All it has to learn here is a discrimination between light on and light off. If it receives food intermittently, perhaps on a *variable interval (VI) schedule*, it will peck steadily whenever the light is on. (On a VI schedule, food is programmed with a specified average frequency but at intervals varying from very short to very long.) When

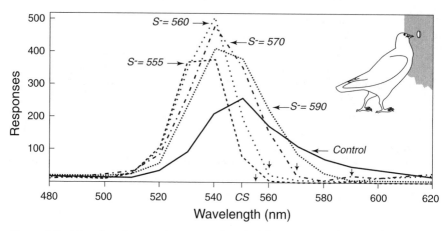

Figure 5.7. Wavelength generalization and peak shift in pigeons. The control group was simply reinforced for pecking at a key illuminated by 550 nm. The other four groups were also extinguished at one other, S-, wavelength. Redrawn from Hanson (1959) with permission.

the wavelength of the light is now varied, the pigeon's rate of pecking varies in an orderly way with wavelength, as shown in figure 5.7.

Generalization may be tested after discrimination training by varying stimuli along a dimension shared by the positive and negative stimuli. For instance, in the example above, suppose the pigeon is reinforced for pecking when the key is illuminated with one wavelength and not reinforced, or reinforced less often, for pecking at another wavelength. Now generalization testing along the dimension of wavelength will reveal the highest rates of pecking not to the reinforced wavelength but to one displaced away from the unreinforced wavelength (figure 5.7). This is the phenomenon of *peak shift*, found with many species and stimulus dimensions (see Cheng, Spetch, & Johnston, 1997). Peak shift is more marked the closer together are the positive and negative stimuli (*S+ and S-*). Notice that in figure 5.7, training an explicit wavelength discrimination also increased the rate of pecking to the reinforced stimulus compared to what it was in the simple discrimination between light on and light off. This increase in rate is related to the phenomenon of *behavioral contrast*: behavior in the presence of a stimulus correlated with an unchanging schedule of reinforcement depends on the reinforcement rate during other stimuli that may be present. If less frequent reinforcement is sometimes available, responding in the constant schedule will be higher than when that schedule is contrasted with lower reinforcement rates, as if an unchanging schedule is evaluated relative to other current options.

In generalization testing, the experimenter has to decide whether or not to reinforce responses to the novel generalization test stimuli. If only pecking at green has been reinforced, for example, should pecks to yellow or blue be reinforced during tests of generalization to those colors? Experimenters face this kind of dilemma in almost any situation in which behavior to novel stim-

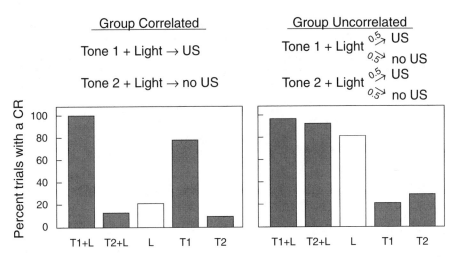

Figure 5.8. Method and results of the "stimulus validity" experiment of Wagner et al. (1968).

uli is tested after a training procedure: the animal doesn't stop learning just because the experimenter is giving a test. Reinforcing the animal for any response it makes in the test may teach it to respond indiscriminately, but never reinforcing it for responding to the test stimuli is no better. A common solution to this dilemma is to reinforce responding intermittently during the training phase. This increases *resistance to extinction*—that is, the animal will keep responding longer during unreinforced test trials. It is now possible to sneak in brief occasional presentations of unreinforced test stimuli without the reinforcement contingencies being very noticeable to the animal, again increasing the number of tests that can be given.

5.4.3 Models and Mechanisms

Conditions for Learning   So far, the conditions for discrimination learning have been described somewhat informally as differential reinforcement in the presence of two or more stimuli. To see that matters are more complicated, consider the following experiment on eyelid conditioning in rabbits (Wagner, Logan, Haberlandt, & Price, 1968; figure 5.8). (In eyelid conditioning, a CS signals a puff of air or a mild shock to the eyelid; the rabbit closes the nictitating membrane over its eye in anticipation of the US.) Two groups of rabbits were each exposed to two tone CSs, T_1 and T_2. Both tones were always presented in compound with a light, L. In the *uncorrelated group*, $T_1 + L$ and $T_2 + L$ were each followed by the US on 50% of trials. In the *correlated group*, $T_1 + L$ was always reinforced and $T_2 + L$ was never reinforced. Notice that the light was followed by the US half the time for both groups. If the number of pairings of light with the US is all that matters in learning to discriminate the light from the context, all the rabbits should respond similarly on test trials with the light alone. In fact, however, only the animals in the uncorrelated group showed substantial numbers of CRs to the light alone. This group responded rather little to either of the tones alone (see figure 5.8). In contrast, rabbits in the correlated group responded to T_1 and not to T_2 or L alone. This pattern of results, and others like it in instrumental paradigms (Mackintosh, 1983), is accounted for by the notion that the predictive value of a CS relative to that of other potential CSs in the situation is what matters (see chapter 3). Here the light always predicts the US for the uncorrelated group, regardless of which tone is present. For the correlated group, T_1 predicts the US perfectly but the light is irrelevant.

The tendency to learn most about the best predictors can have ecological implications. Dukas and Waser (1994) exposed bumblebees (*Bombus flavifros*) to patches of artificial flowers, each decorated with two colors. For example, a bee might find yellow + blue, yellow + purple, white + blue, and white + purple flowers. Bees for which a single color reliably predicted nectar (e.g., only white + blue and white + purple rewarded) gradually increased the proportion of visits they made to rewarded flowers, but those for which no single color was a reliable predictor (e.g., only white + blue and yellow + purple rewarded) did not improve their foraging efficiency in over 300 visits. This finding also suggests that bumblebees may not readily learn about configurations of colors when unique configurations rather than single cues predict reward (see box 3.3).

Contents of Learning   From the time of Pavlov, theories of discrimination learning have been based on the notion that discrimination training results in the acquisition of connections between central representations of stimuli and a representation of the reinforcer or response (Pearce, 1994b). Reinforcement results in excitatory connections; nonreinforcement, in inhibitory ones. This simple notion accounts very well for many effects of discrimination training. Peak shift can be accounted for on the assumption that behavior toward a stimulus reflects its net excitation (i.e., excitation minus inhibition), as shown in figure 5.9 (but see Thomas, Mood, Morrison, & Wiertelak, 1991).

In both peak shift and supernormality in untrained discriminations, stimuli other than those normally present evoke the most responding, suggesting that the two phenomena reflect similar mechanisms (Hogan, Kruijt, & Frijlink, 1975; Staddon, 1975; Weary, Guilford, & Weisman, 1993). However, the shifted preference in peak shift experiments is not open-ended (see figure 5.7), whereas in supernormality it may be—that is, a wide range of stimuli with characteristics more extreme than normal may evoke greater than normal responding. This difference may reflect mechanistic and functional differences between the two phenomena. Whereas peak shift results from the interaction of excitatory and inhibitory training at particular values along a continuum, supernormality might be the outcome of natural selection against responding only to values below some criterion, for instance, any objects that are not big enough to be eggs (Baerends, 1982; Staddon, 1975). Mechanistically, too, it is not clear that supernormal responding need result from an in-

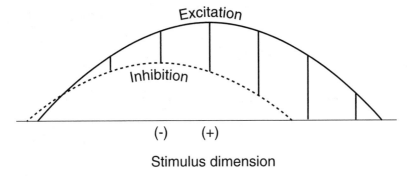

Figure 5.9. How additive gradients of excitation and inhibition can generate peak shift. The net excitation from reinforcement at S+ minus inhibition from extinction at S- is represented by the length of the vertical lines. The longest such line is not at S+ but to its right. Redrawn from Spence (1937) with permission.

teraction between excitation and inibition. Some examples of supernormality seem more like the examples of sensory bias discussed in chapter 2. For instance, the male grayling butterfly is most attracted to much higher rates of flicker than would be produced by a female butterfly fluttering her wings (see Baerends, 1982).

The Hull-Spence model in figure 5.9 takes generalization for granted rather than trying to explain it from first principles. A recent alternative (D. S. Blough, 1975) is similar to the model of perceptual learning discussed in chapter 4. This predicts generalization by viewing the S+ and S- as each consisting of a number of elements separately associated with the US. If elements acquire associative strength as described by the Rescorla-Wagner model, it follows that discriminations should be learned more slowly between similar than between dissimilar stimuli (but see Pearce, 1994b). Common elements will alternately gain and lose associative strength, retarding the emergence of a difference in net associative strength, the more so the more common elements there are. Table 5.1 shows how this approach accounts for peak shift.

Pavlov, with his background in physiology, as well as Hull and Spence, ac-

Table 5.1. An elemental analysis of peak shift

Stimuli 1–4 are composed of various proportions of elements 1–5, as indicated. If 3 is the positive stimulus in discrimination training and 4 is the negative stimulus, stimulus 2 will acquire greater net positive strength than stimulus 3.

Stimuli	1	2	3 (S+)	4 (S-)
Elements	0 1 1 2	1 2 2 3	2 3 3 4	3 4 4 5
+		+	+ + +	+ + + +	+ + +
−			−	− − −	− − − −
Net =/−	+1	+2	+1	−1

After Mackintosh (1995) reproduced with permission.

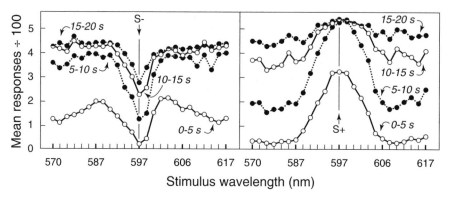

Figure 5.10. One pigeon's excitatory and inhibitory wavelength generalization gradients in Blough's (1975) experiment. Separate gradients are shown for each 5-second period of the 20-second stimulus, timed up from zero. Redrawn from D. S. Blough (1975) with permission.

cepted that inhibition plays a role in behavior. However, in the 1950s and '60s Skinnerian radical behaviorism made inhibition disreputable because it is so difficult to measure directly. Since *inhibition* implies suppression below a "zero" level, it cannot be distinguished from absence of excitation without a moderate baseline level of behavior. There are several ways around this problem (Mackintosh, 1983). One is to compound the putative inhibitory stimulus with an excitor and test whether it reduces responding more than does an untrained stimulus (Rescorla, 1969). Another is to test whether excitation is acquired more slowly to the supposed excitor than to a neutral stimulus (the *retardation test*). D. S. Blough (1975) conducted what is essentially a summation test in which a whole range of stimuli were reinforced at a low level to generate a stable baseline of behavior across the wavelength continuum. Selected values were then reinforced more or less than this baseline to generate excitators and inhibitors. Pigeons pecked a key with a single colored line on it which could be illuminated by any of 25 wavelengths (figure 5.10). Each time the key lit up, pecking produced food on a fixed-interval (FI) 20-second schedule—that is, when 20 seconds elapsed since the beginning of the trial, the next peck would be reinforced. In general, food was only given on about 10% of the trials, but pecking was maintained by presenting a gray square sometimes paired with food (*a secondary reinforcer*) at the end of every trial. This procedure resulted in an increasing rate of pecking with the time a stimulus was on and similar average rates to all 25 stimuli. Generalization of excitation was studied on this baseline by giving extra reinforced presentations of a selected wavelength. Similarly, inhibitory generalization gradients resulted from extra nonreinforced presentations of a selected wavelength. Because intermittent reinforcement was continued at the other wavelengths, this procedure permitted prolonged assessment of generalization under unchanging conditions.

The sharpness of the gradient obtained in this procedure (figure 5.10) depends on when it is measured during the 20-second fixed interval. Early in the interval, the birds respond rather little, and responding is at its most selective. The pecking rates to all wavelengths increase throughout the interval so the excitatory gradient is nearly flat near the time of reinforcement. No other evidence is needed that generalization does not reflect merely lack of ability to discriminate. Here one might say that when there is little cost to responding and much to gain, as at the end of the FI, animals generalize more. An interesting feature of the gradients in figure 5.10 is the "shoulders" in the inhibitory gradients on either side of the nonreinforced value. They can be generated by the elemental model in a similar way to the enhanced responding that accompanies peak shift.

Compounds as Configurations   Consider the following discrimination learning problem, the "exclusive or" problem in logic or computer programming. Stimulus A is reinforced; stimulus B is reinforced; but their compound, stimulus AB, is not reinforced. According to the Rescorla-Wagner model, it is impossible for animals to learn to respond to A and to B but not to AB in this situation because there is no way for both A and B to be excitatory while their compound is neutral or inhibitory. In fact, AB should be even more excitatory than A or B alone. Nevertheless, rats or pigeons can learn this kind of configural discrimination. To explain how they do, elemental theories have to assume that the compound, AB, contains an extra, configural element. In a sense, this corresponds to the animal's knowledge that A and B are occurring in a compound, that AB is a distinct entity more than the sum of its parts. While the separately reinforced A and B are still excitatory when they appear in compound, the configural element can gain enough inhibitory strength to cancel out their effects.

In contrast to this approach, Pearce's (1994a, 1994b) configural theory (see chapter 3) suggests that a compound is treated as a unique stimulus, albeit one with some similarity to A and to B. Thus generalization between the compound and its elements makes the configural discrimination difficult, but not impossible. To account for behavior in this particular discrimination problem, there is not much to choose between the configural and the elemental models. Pearce's theory provides a better account of performance in some more complex discriminations involving three or four elements in different combinations, but on the other hand, there are some situations for which the Rescorla-Wagner elemental approach is the better account (Miller, Barnet, & Grahame, 1995; Pearce, 1994b). The configural approach will not be developed further here, mainly because the elemental one provides a reasonable account of the examples of the "concept discriminations" to be discussed in section 5.5. At present, however, both the elemental and the configural approach suffer from vagueness in the specification of similarity. How do we identify the "elements" that two stimuli may or may not have in common or quantify the similarity between two compounds with common features (see Fetterman, 1996, for further discussion)?

5.4.4 Other Processes in Discrimination Learning

In the wild, animals must be learning new discriminations all the time. For instance, some small passerine birds eat mainly insects during the breeding season and seeds during the winter. As each new type of prey becomes available, the bird may need to learn such things as how to discriminate it from the substrate, where it is most abundant, and how to handle it. Birds that migrate have to learn quickly about new food items at stopovers along the way and in their final wintering grounds (see Greenberg, 1984). Long-lived territorial animals may have to learn the characteristics of new neighbors and territories in each new breeding season. Thus animals in the wild are likely to have ample experience in learning to discriminate one thing in the environment from another, and one might wonder whether there is any evidence that discrimination learning becomes easier as more discriminations are learned. That is, is there any evidence that animals "learn to learn"? This question also has theoretical relevance because it amounts to asking whether animals acquire anything during discrimination training besides excitatory and inhibitory connections to specific positive and negative stimuli. This general issue has been investigated in a number of ways (see Mackintosh, 1974), but here we focus on evidence from discrimination reversal learning and learning sets. Studies of these phenomena have also yielded some interesting comparative data.

Serial Reversal Learning   *Discrimination reversal learning* is just what it says: after being exposed to a given S+ and S- for a certain number of trials, or until performance reaches a criterion, an animal is now exposed to the same stimuli with their significance reversed. So, in a black-white discrimination, if black was initially the positive stimulus, black becomes negative. In *serial reversals*, from which the most interesting data come, the animal is exposed to a long series of reversals. Often, the significance of the stimuli changes at the beginning of each experimental session. Rats, which have been studied more than any other species in this paradigm, typically perform worse in the first few reversals of a given problem, but they eventually perform better than they did on the first discrimination (figure 5.11). The optimal performance is one error per reversal. This can be attained by adopting a *win stay–lose shift* strategy: always try the response that was last rewarded, and if that is no longer rewarded, shift to the other response, otherwise stay. Monkeys seem to learn this strategy, but rats do not. Instead, two other things seem to happen. First, a long series of daily reversals causes *proactive interference* (*PI*; see chapter 6) in memory. The rat has had so many reversals that it cannot remember at the beginning of one day which response was rewarded yesterday, so it performs at chance. (At the beginning of each early reversal performance is below chance; at this stage the rat evidently does remember the last problem.) Second, performance increases from 50% correct, or chance, more quickly in late than early reversals, suggesting that rats gradually learn what stimuli to pay attention to in the experimental situation. The notion that successful dis-

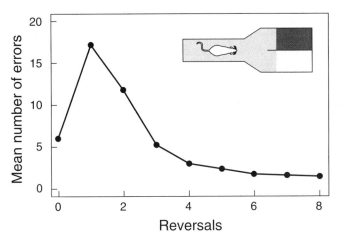

Figure 5.11. Mean total errors before making 18 correct choices out of 20 for rats trained on serial reversal of a black-white discrimination in a choice apparatus like that shown. After Mackintosh et al. (1968) with permission.

criminative performance depends on two kinds of learning: learning what stimuli to attend to and learning what response to attach to each one applies in other situations, too (Sutherland & Mackintosh, 1971). In terms of the Rescorla-Wagner model, it means that α as well as V changes during training.

Rumbaugh and his colleagues (Rumbaugh & Pate, 1984; Rumbaugh, Savage-Rumbaugh, & Washburn, 1996) have compared primates on a variant of reversal learning in which the animal is first trained to a fixed criterion, either 67 or 84% correct, with a given pair of objects and then given ten trials with the significance of the objects reversed. This procedure is repeated with a series of new pairs of objects. An animal that behaves only on the basis of past reinforcement with given objects should reverse more slowly the higher the original criterion, whereas one that has learned the principle of reversal should do just the opposite. In a comparison of 13 primate species, most of the prosimians tested showed the former pattern, the apes showed the latter, and the monkeys were intermediate. Because the species compared are relatively closely related, with similar sensory and motor abilities, these differences may well reflect genuine differences in cognition and associated brain areas (Rumbaugh et al., 1996).

Learning Set   Tests for the acquisition of a *learning set* are like discrimination reversals in that the animal is trained on many discrimination problems in succession, but in learning set experiments the stimuli are different in each problem. As in reversal learning, there are doubtless general factors like latent inhibition of irrelevant cues that improve performance with increasing numbers of problems. For instance, in a simultaneous black-white discrimination, if black is rewarded regardless of its location, left will be rewarded half the time and nonrewarded half the time. Thus left and right will acquire learned irrelevance. Contextual cues that are always present, like the odor or illumination of the experimental chamber, will be latently inhibited. These processes should facilitate further learning in the same context with the same relevant and irrelevant cues and retard learning if cues that were once irrelevant become relevant.

The optimal strategy in a test of learning set is win stay–lose shift, just as in reversal learning. Here, an animal can do no better than choose randomly on the first trial of each problem. Then it should stay with the alternative chosen first if it was rewarded, otherwise shift. Proportion of correct choices on the second trial is a good measure of the extent to which the animal has acquired this strategy. The ability to acquire a learning set has been used to compare animals in "intelligence." This is an appealing kind of test because "learning to learn" does seem intelligent from an anthropocentric point of view. In addition, the shape of the curve representing number of errors as a function of successive problems seems to be a meaningful measure of learning regardless of its absolute level. That is, whether individuals of a particular species learn the first problems slowly or quickly, one can still ask whether they improve over problems and whether they eventually attain the optimum of perfect performance on the second trial of each new discrimination.

The view that learning set is a good test of animal intelligence was encouraged by early data from mammals (figure 5.12). The ordering of species, with rhesus monkeys performing better than New World squirrel monkeys, which performed better than cats, and rats and squirrels doing worst, is consistent with the assumption that animals can be ordered on a single ladder of intellectual improvement. However, not only is this notion erroneous (see chapter 1), it is not even supported by further data on learning set. Data of other mammals do not fall where they would be expected to in figure 5.12 (Macphail, 1982), and extensive studies with bluejays have shown that these birds perform in a qualitatively similar way to rhesus monkeys (review in Kamil, 1985). Like rhesus monkeys, blue jays acquire a win stay–lose shift strategy. In both these species, staying or shifting depends—as it would be expected to—on memory for the first trial of a problem. Accuracy on the second trial of a new discrimination falls as the intertrial interval lengthens so that the outcome of the first trial is forgotten.

The results of learning set experiments with rats deal a further blow to the idea that learning set performance is a unitary reflection of a species' "intelligence" because the sensory modality of the stimuli to be discriminated has an overwhelming effect on rats' learning set performance. The rat data in figure 5.12 come from an experiment with visual stimuli: in over 1,000 problems, the rats' accuracy on their second choices hardly rose above chance. But with spatial cues rats acquire a learning set within fewer than 50 problems (Zeldin & Olton, 1986), and with olfactory cues they do so even faster (Eichenbaum, Fagan, & Cohen, 1986). These results might mean that rats process olfactory and spatial cues differently from visual cues, or the difference may be a one of stimulus salience. Many procedural details differed

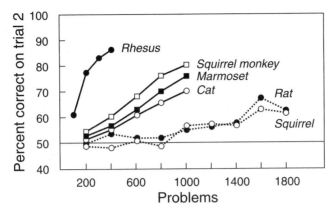

Figure 5.12. Visual discrimination learning set performance of six mammalian species, redrawn from Warren (1965) with permission.

among experiments with visual, spatial, and olfactory cues and these contextual variables could also have contributed to the differences in results.

Attention   In the Rescorla-Wagner model (see chapter 3), the learning rate parameter α is related to the salience of the stimulus being learned about. Salience is assumed to be determined by the physical features of the CS—for instance, a dim light has lower salience than a bright light—as well as by the animal's species-specific sensory abilities. For instance, odors might be more salient than colors for rats, while the reverse is likely true for most birds. The associability or salience of stimuli can also change with experience. In some such cases, experience appears to change not just excitatory and inhibitory strengths of particular stimuli but attention to whole stimulus dimensions. For example, D. S. Blough (1969) reinforced pigeons intermittently for pecking in the presence of a single combination of tone frequency and wavelength out of 49 such compounds made up of 7 tones and 7 wavelengths. The birds could perform well only by paying attention to both tone and light. That they did so was shown by steep generalization gradients along both tone frequency and wavelength dimensions (figure 5.13). But when one feature of the reinforced stimulus was made irrelevant by keeping it constant for several sessions, the gradient along that dimension flattened out dramatically, indicating that the birds were paying less attention to that feature. What was going on here is clearly similar to the procedure in Wagner et al.'s experiment on predictive value (figure 5.8). The difference is that Blough's pigeons were very well trained (i.e., associative strength was asymptotic) before the predictive value of the the stimulus elements was varied.

Several other sorts of data have also been thought to point to changes in attention during discrimination training (Mackintosh, 1974, 1983). For instance, performance on a color discrimination is better following previous training on another color discrimination than following training on, say, an

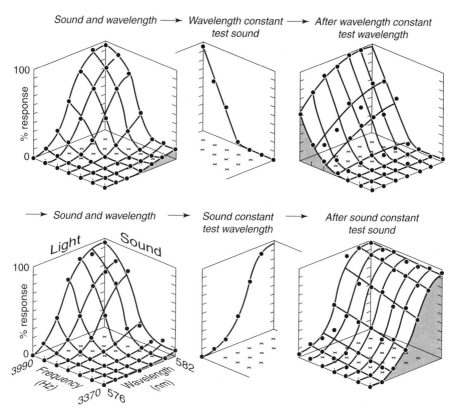

Figure 5.13. Generalization along the dimensions of wavelength and sound frequency following reinforcement at a single combination of wavelength and frequency. A single pigeons' rate of pecking is shown as proportion of rate to the reinforced wavelength and tone frequency. After Blough (1969) with permission.

orientation discrimination. In such experiments, possible effects of simple stimulus generalization from one discrimination to the next need to be ruled out by varying the positive and negative stimuli for different animals and by making them as dissimilar as possible from one discrimination to the next. If an animal trained with red positive and green negative showed positive transfer to a discrimination with orange positive and blue negative, an appeal to stimulus generalization would be more appropriate than an appeal to increased attention to wavelength. Despite the intuitive appeal of the notion that animals learn what to pay attention to, it has proved remarkably difficult to obtain unambiguous evidence for changes in attention in conventional discrimination learning because of the difficulty of ruling out such specific transfer effects (Mackintosh, 1983). Procedures like Blough's together with tests of short-term memory have turned out to be more illuminating (Riley & Leith, 1976; see also chapter 6). Nevertheless, this does not mean that animals do not learn what to attend to as well as learning what responses to make in discrimination learning experiments. The ability to acquire new discriminations does improve with experience, most likely for a variety of reasons. The processes involved are likely to be important in variable environments in nature.

5.5 Category Discrimination and Concepts

5.5.1 Category Discrimination

The third example of discrimination at the beginning of this chapter depicts a now-famous series of experiments (Herrnstein, 1979; Herrnstein, Loveland, & Cable, 1976) in which pigeons were trained to classify photographic slides according to their membership in experimenter-defined categories such as "tree" and "nontree." Typically, birds were trained with about 40 S+ slides, all having *examplars* of the category, and 40 S- slides without exemplars. The slides were presented in random order on a multiple schedule, so that each one was on for a minute or so. A bird was reinforced intermittently for pecking at S+ slides and not reinforced for pecking at S- slides. A correction procedure might be used in which each negative slide remained on until a certain number of seconds had elapsed without pecks. The data consisted of response rates before the first reinforcer in positive slides and during a comparable period for negative slides. In general, pigeons learn remarkably quickly with such a procedure to classify photographs representing a large number of human-defined natural categories including water, fish, and people, as well as trees (review in Watanabe, Lea, & Dittrich, 1993). Most important, they generalize to new instances. For example, birds that respond at a higher rate to trees than to nontrees continue to do so when shown slides they have never seen before (Herrnstein, 1979).

This research has attracted attention because the results seem to suggest that the birds "have a concept" in the same way humans do. Most readers of this book will have a notion, based on introspection, of what it means to have a concept, but students of human cognition are far from agreeing on what this phrase means. Some claim that because concepts can be defined only with reference to language, nonhuman species cannot have them (Chater & Heyes, 1994). Others (e.g., Wasserman & Astley, 1994) take an operational approach, seeing the behavior in "concept learning" experiments as no more than performance of a discrimination with unusually complex stimuli. On this view, analyzing the determinants of animals' behavior in such experiments may help us to understand what people are doing in comparable situations (Mackintosh, 1995; Shanks, 1994).

The results of "concept learning" experiments are also of interest from an ecological point of view because objects to be discriminated in nature are, like the slides in Herrnstein's experiments, more complex and variable than the tones and pure wavelengths typically used in the laboratory. Do any special processes govern the learning of such discriminations? We will see that the results can largely be accounted for by principles of discrimination learning and stimulus generalization. In order to see why this is true, we need to be clear on a few points. First, animals do not have to see slides as representations of objects in order to classify them correctly. It is questionable whether the pigeons do see the photographs used in most such experiments as anything other than arrays of colored blobs (box 5.2). Monkeys trained to discriminate slides with people from those without people proved to be responding partly to red patches: slides showing a slice of watermelon or a hyena carrying a dead flamingo were treated like slides of people (D'Amato & Van Sant, 1988). Second, most progress in understanding what is going on in so-called concept learning experiments can be made by focusing on the animals' behavior and not by assuming that it reflects some hypothetical special conceptual process. Thus what the animals are doing in such experiments is best referred to operationally, as *category discrimination*. This description leaves open whether or not behaving differently to items in different experimenter-defined categories means the animals have learned a concept in any sense. The pigeons in experiments like Herrnstein's are discriminating on the basis of membership in a *perceptual category*, as distinct from a *functional* category. Members of the former have some perceptual features in common, whereas members of the latter do not need to. For example, screwdrivers belong to a perceptual category of *long thin objects* along with pencils and carrots, but they could be placed in the functional category *tools* along with hammers and saws.

5.5.2 Memorizing and Generalizing

Because memorizing 80 or more individual slides seems quite a feat, the possibility that pigeons solved category discriminations by doing so was initially discounted. However, it turns out that pigeons can memorize many more than 80 slides. Vaughan & Greene (1984) trained birds with a total of 160 S+ and 160 S− slides. This was not a category discrimination: slides were assigned to the positive and negative sets regardless of perceptual similarity or natural category membership. Nevertheless, within a few sessions with each new set of 40 positive and 40 negative slides, each appearing twice per session, the birds were pecking more to most positives than to most negatives. Moreover, they still performed the final discrimination with 320 slides well above chance after a rest of more than two years.

Pigeons are also sensitive to fine details like those differentiating one photograph of a scene from another taken a few minutes later (Greene, 1983). But memorization is not the whole story. Pigeons generally learn faster and perform better with categorical groupings than with arbitrary groupings of slides, sometimes called *pseudocategories* (Watanabe, Lea, & Dittrich, 1993). But superior acquisition with categories need not mean the birds have learned anything different than with pseudocategories. Slides of members of a perceptual category like "tree" or "fish" will have more in common as visual stimuli (e.g., patches of green, certain kinds of contours) than members of a random collection of slides. Thus simple stimulus generalization among category members will tend to improve performance with categories while, if anything, the same process will impede learning of pseudocategories.

Box 5.2. How Do Animals See Pictures?

Following Herrnstein's (1979) demonstration that pigeons could acquire and generalize a discrimination between pictures with trees and pictures without trees, Herrnstein
and de Villiers (1980) asked how pigeons peform when slides of fish—a natural category irrelevant to present-day pigeons—are used instead. Their experiment is interesting only on the assumption that pigeons recognize objects and scenes in back-
projected colored slides just as people do. If all the pigeon sees is an array of colored
blobs, the ease of discrimination learning should not be affected by whether the slides
depict objects natural or unnatural to pigeons' environment, as indeed it was not.
Clearly, how animals see the pictures in colored slides, movies, or video images has
to be tested experimentally. One reason other species might not perceive them as we
do is that such images are designed to capture colors as perceived by humans. For
instance, because some birds are sensitive to ultraviolet wavelengths that are invisible to us (see chapter 2), whether or not UV wavelengths are preserved may influence
the discriminability or recognizability of pictures for them. If a species' flicker fusion frequency is higher than that in humans, the number of frames per second that produces
a sensation of smooth motion in people would be perceived as a jerky succession of
individual frames (see Adret, 1997).

In fact, the best answer to the question asked by this box is, "It depends"—on the
species of animal and the kind of discrimination being tested. Jumping spiders court
conspecifics and attack prey that they see on TV, apparently not discriminating a
video image from the real thing (Clark & Uetz, 1990). When shown videotapes of
conspecifics or predators, chickens behave as if seeing the real things, apparently
reacting to simple sign stimuli such as shape or motion (see sections 10.2 and 12.2).
But slides or video images do not capture the fine details that chickens use to recognize other chickens individually (review in Patterson-Kane, Nicol, Foster, & Temple,
1997). Monkeys, though, do recognize familiar group members in slides (Dasser,
1987; section 5.5.5). Transfer between arbitrary objects or scenes and images of
them has been tested fairly extensively in pigeons, with somewhat mixed results (Fetterman, 1996; Watanabe, 1997; Watanabe, Lea, & Dittrich, 1993). Pigeons trained
to find food in a distinctive part of a large room seemed to transfer this discrimination
to slides of different parts of the room (Cole & Honig, 1994). In contrast, exposure
to a particular outdoor location did not speed learning of a discrimination between
slides of it and a second outdoor location (Dawkins, Guilford, Braithwaite, & Krebs,
1996; but see Wilkie, Willson, & Kardal, 1989). As in tests with simple objects and
slides of those objects (see Watanabe, Lea, & Dittrich, 1993), transfer may be possible if positive and negative stimulus classes are distinguished by global features such
as color but not otherwise (but see Watanabe, 1997). Moreover, tests of transfer between places and pictures of them fail to take into account that animals moving
around in a place can use many cues to depth and distance unavailable in pictures
(see Dawkins, Guilford, Braithwaite, & Krebs, 1996, for further discussion). Also, photographs or video images to be discriminated in the laboratory are sometimes presented at viewing distances that would be unnatural for the real objects they depict
(Dawkins & Woodington, 1997).

In retrospect, the notion that slides of objects and scenes are more naturalistic or
ecologically valid stimuli than simple patterns and colors because animals see them

➠

Box 5.2. How Do Animals See Pictures? (*continued*)

as depicting places and things in the real world appears naive and misguided (Fetterman, 1996). Nevertheless, when used with appropriate caution, slides and video images of real-world things and events can be extremely useful for answering certain questions about how animals discriminate and classify events of importance in nature. The work of Dooling, Brown, and their colleagues on face recognition in budgerigars described earlier in this chapter is one example; another is the research on vocal communication in chickens discussed in chapter 12.

The earliest experiments on category discrimination consisted largely of demonstrations that pigeons and a few other species could learn most—though apparently not all—category discriminations (Watanabe et al., 1993). However, to understand what such performance is based on, a more analytical approach was needed. Such an approach has been pursued in most depth by Wasserman and his colleagues (review in Wasserman & Astley, 1994). Their training procedure essentially consists of asking pigeons, "What category does this slide belong to?" and giving them four possible answers. This is like the "name game," in which an adult shows pictures to a young child and asks, "What is it?" The pigeon views a central slide representing a member of one of four categories—for example, cats, flowers, cars, and chairs (figure 5.14). After being required to peck at the slide a number of times, ensuring that it is processed, the bird chooses among four keys, one at each corner of the viewing screen. A peck at the upper right, red key might be reinforced if the slide shows a cat, a peck at the lower left, green key, reinforced if the slide shows a car, and so on. With 10 instances of each category, pigeons choose correctly about 80% of the time within 10 days of training, seeing each slide just once a day (note that chance performance is 25% correct here).

This procedure has been used in a whole series of experiments that document how category discrimination is based on a combination of memorizing exemplars and generalizing from them. For instance, when the number of training slides per category is varied from 1 (i.e., a discrimination among only four slides) to 12, pigeons learn more slowly the more slides per category, consistent with a role for memorizing individual slides. On the other hand, when tested with new slides after reaching 70% correct on training slides, they perform better the more exemplars of each category they have been trained with. This result should not be surprising. The more, say, cat slides the bird has been exposed to, the more likely a new cat slide will be similar to one seen before. Perhaps the best evidence for the joint contribution of memory and stimulus generalization is an experiment in which pigeons were able to learn a category discrimination even though each slide was shown only once (figure 5.14). The birds evidently learned enough from a single trial with each slide to allow them to generalize to new slides of the same category. This result could mean that what was learned was just the common features of each category, since these would be repeated from examplar to examplar. However,

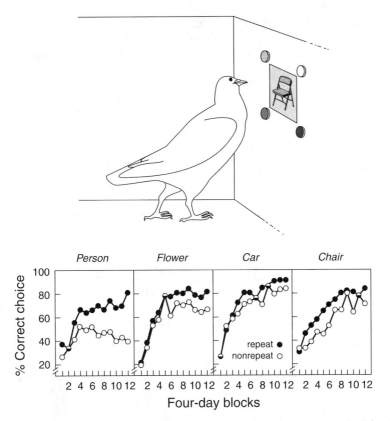

Figure 5.14. Apparatus for training four-way categorization in pigeons and performance on slides never seen before compared to performance on slides repeated from session to session. Data redrawn from Bhatt et al. (1988) with permission.

when novel slides were intermixed with slides being shown for the second time, performance was worse on novel than on familiar slides. Thus, the birds apparently memorized features or combinations of features unique to single slides as well as features common to many slides.

5.5.3 The Contents of Learning: Exemplars, Features, or Prototypes?

The experiments by Wasserman and his colleagues have provided much new information about the conditions for category discrimination learning, but what has an animal learned when it can accurately classify stimuli into perceptual categories? There are essentially three answers to this question (Pearce, 1994b), although it is not always clear how to distinguish among them experimentally, with either animal or human subjects.

One answer was hinted at in the preceding section: the animal simply learns the characteristics of every slide as a whole. Associative strength is acquired to each individual stimulus, as in the Rescorla-Wagner model, and, by definition, there is more stimulus generalization within than between perceptual categories. A model based on this idea accounts well for most data on category discrimination (Wasserman & Astley, 1994). However, the data are about as consistent with an elemental analysis as with a holistic or configural one. The elemental approach suggests that category membership is defined by the possession of certain features. For example, trees are likely to be green, have leaves and/or branches, dark vertical trunks, be outdoors, and so on. Obviously, many nontrees—for instance, celery stalks—have one or more of these characteristics, too. Furthermore, category membership is *polymorphous*—that is, not all category members have all the same features, although each has at least a subset of them. For instance, birch trees have trunks and leafy branches but white bark, pine trees have trunks with dark-colored bark but needles in place of leaves. A featural analysis of categories nevertheless assumes that a set of features can be found such that the conjunction of some number of them separates category members from other things. The number and identity of conjoined features may vary from instance to instance, as in our example of trees.

The features that control successful discrimination of categories of photographs can be mysterious (Herrnstein, 1979). For instance, in the experiment with monkeys in which nonpeople slides with red patches were treated as people (D'Amato & Van Sant, 1988), red was not the only feature defining people slides for the monkeys. Many slides lacking red were correctly classified as showing people. A more analytical approach is to create categories of artificial stimuli (figure 5.15). Reinforcement for responding to each feature can be made to depend on the other features with which it appears, much as with objects forming natural categories (e.g., in a tree–no tree discrimination, a leafy oak tree is positive, but a leafy celery stalk is negative). Pigeons can learn category discriminations with stimuli like those depicted in figure 5.15 (Huber & Lenz, 1993, 1996; Lea, Lohmann, & Ryan, 1993), but they do not always respond as predicted by feature theory (Watanabe, Lea, & Dittrich, 1993), nor do they always learn as quickly as they learn to categorize colored slides of natural scenes. One reason may be that, unlike the case with natural categories, the artificial categories have been designed so that no one feature or cluster of features is more predictive of category membership than others. For instance, each artificial seed in figure 5.15 is described by values of each of five features (spotted/plain, fat/thin, stripe curved/straight, horizontal/vertical, rounded/pointed). Because category membership depends on any three or more features being shared with the perfect exemplar, each feature is equally important. This situation is very different from that in the natural categorization problem depicted in figure 5.4, in which some dimensions of birds' songs predict species membership better than others.

Both exemplar-learning and feature-learning accounts of category discrimination are fundamentally associative: exposure to each instance increases associative strength of a representation of the whole exemplar or of its features, and performance to other exemplars and nonexemplars is based on stimulus generalization. A somewhat different account, popular in discussions

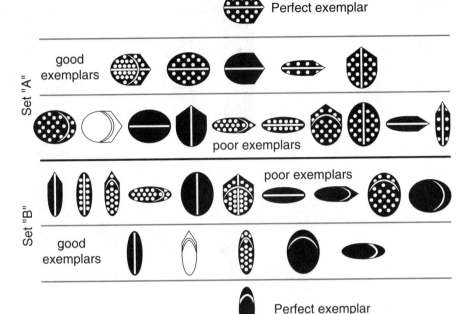

Figure 5.15. "Artificial seeds" for category discrimination experiments. The perfect ex-amplar of Set A is fat, dotted, horizontal, irregular, with a straight stripe present and a curved stripe absent. The perfect examplar of Set B has the opposite value of each feature. "Good" and "poor" exemplars have only 4 or 3 features, respectively, in common with the perfect exemplar of their category. Redrawn from Lea et al. (1993) with permission.

of concept learning by humans (see Shanks, 1994), is that exposure to indi-vidual exemplars results in the formation of a representation of a category *pro-totype*, a sort of ideal exemplar or central tendency of all exemplars. The pro-totypical bird, for instance, is more like a robin or a sparrow than a penguin or an ostrich. Categorization of new exemplars is then based on comparing them to the prototype. There is some evidence that pigeons do perform bet-ter with slides closer to what humans would see as the prototypical member of categories like "tree" or "fish" than with aberrant examplars (Herrnstein, 1979; Herrnstein, Loveland, & Cable, 1976), and similar results have been found with artificial categories (Jitsumori, 1996).

Prototype theory makes two predictions that at first appear to be unique, but on closer inspection it is evident that they can equally well be generated by associative theories. One prediction is that categorization of the prototype stimulus itself should be more accurate than categorization of any exemplars, even if the prototype has never been seen before. Pearce (1988, 1989) tested this prediction using artificial categories consisting of patterns of three col-ored bars (figure 5.16). Individual bars varied in height from 1 to 7 units, and

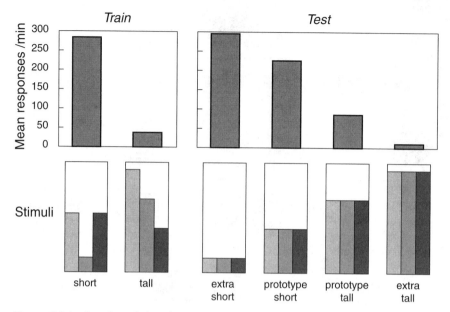

Figure 5.16. Stimuli and data from Pearce's (1989) experiments on artificial category learning by pigeons. After Pearce (1989) with permission.

patterns were classified in terms of the total height of the three parallel bars making them up. Patterns with total height of 9 units were positive; a total height of 15 units defined a negative pattern. Within each category, the individual bars could be 1–5 units high in the positive patterns and 3–7 units high in the negative patterns. Thus, as in other experiments with artificial categories, some individual stimulus elements (here, bars 3, 4, or 5 units high) could appear in a pattern belonging to either category. One would suppose that the prototypical positive pattern would be one composed of three 3-unit bars; similarly, the negative prototype is three 5-unit bars. Pearce's pigeons saw neither of these patterns in training, but they were tested with the prototypes and other novel patterns after learning the category discrimination (figure 5.16). Response rates were not highest to the prototype "short" pattern and lowest to the "tall" one, as predicted by prototype theory. Instead, the birds showed the most extreme response rates to extra-short and extra-tall patterns. This result can best be described as peak shift. One way to account for it is to assume that the birds treated the individual bars as the stimulus elements or features, and these each gained excitatory or inhibitory strength as they were paired with reinforcement or nonreinforcement, respectively. Because bars 1 unit high could occur in positive but not negative patterns, they would be more strongly associated with reinforcement than bars of length 3, which could occur in both positive and negative patterns. A parallel argument applies to the acquisition of inhibition by bars of length 7.

The associative, feature-based account of prototypes suggested by this ex-

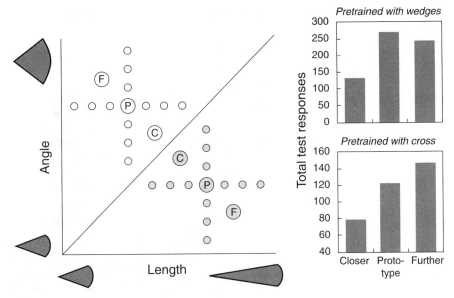

Figure 5.17. Two-dimensional space defining the stimuli used by Mackintosh (1995). Pigeons were trained in two different ways to discriminate stimuli above the diagonal line from stimuli below it. Small disks represent the stimuli used in training; larger disks, the stimuli used in testing, i.e. the category prototype (P) and stimuli closer to (C) and farther from (F) the category boundary than the prototype. After Mackintosh (1995) with permission.

planation of Pearce's results implies that a *prototype effect* (best discrimination between the central tendencies or prototypes of the categories) might still be found with certain categories and training procedures. Mackintosh (1995) has reported just such an effect (figure 5.17). As in Pearce's experiment, pigeons were trained to discriminate two artificial categories without being exposed to the prototypes of those categories during training. Later they were tested with the prototypes or central tendencies of the training categories and with novel stimuli that were either closer to or further from the category boundary than the prototype. Depending on how the birds had been trained, the results could be described either as a prototype effect or as peak shift. The prototype effect was obtained if the birds had been trained initially simply to peck at all 12 stimuli that defined the positive stimulus class. By itself, this training results in greatest associative strength to the stimuli with the central values of the set—that is, the prototype. In Mackintosh's experiment, this superiority evidently survived subsequent discrimination training in which stimuli near the boundary with the negative category would have acquired some generalized negative associative strength. The peak shift effect was obtained when instead the birds had only pecked at a black cross before category discrimination training began.

None of the foregoing results indicates that animals (mostly pigeons) trained on a category discrimination acquire a representation of a prototypical category member to which they compare new instances. Another approach to testing prototype theory has fared equally poorly. This approach is based on the notion (Lea & Dow, 1984) that if what is learned is the significance of the prototype or concept—for example, "fish are positive"—then performance toward all category members should be affected by changing the significance of one of them. This sounds a lot like stimulus generalization, but there is one difference: if category members form an *equivalence class* (see Hall, 1996, for review) then all should change significance together regardless of their perceptual similarity to the prototype. The best way to test this notion is with categories of perceptually dissimilar stimuli—that is, pseudocategories. Vaughan (1988) did this by training pigeons with 40 unrelated positive slides and 40 unrelated negative slides. When the birds were reliably pecking more to most of the positive than to most of the negative slides, Vaughan reversed their significance. The birds were then reinforced for pecking the originally negative slides and not for pecking the original positives. This treatment continued until the birds were once more responding appropriately. Then the significance of the two categories was reversed again, and so on. Finally, after 20 or more reversals, the birds showed some evidence of treating the slides as two classes. Experiencing a reversed contingency with a few slides was enough to cause them to show appropriate response rates to the remaining slides. Wasserman, DeVolder, and Coppage (1992) obtained quicker results with a somewhat different procedure in which members of each category of perceptually dissimilar stimuli were associated with a single distinctive response key. No special conceptual process is needed to explain them. Rather, they may be seen as an instance of *mediated* or *secondary generalization* in which stimuli are treated as similar not because they share perceptual elements but because they are associated with the same thing. The common associate of all category members serves as a common element, mediating generalization among them.

Section 5.2 showed how members of some ecologically important functional categories like "mate" or "parent" are identified by sign stimuli. Other functional categories that animals might be expected to have, like "food" or "enemy," could be learned by mediated generalization. For example, foods can be chewed and swallowed while rocks and twigs generally cannot. The visual characteristics of foods could all be associated with the common consequences of ingesting them. Watanabe (1993) attempted to study whether pigeons treat foods as such a category. He conducted a category discrimination experiment using various grains and nonfood objects like twigs and screws. Some of the birds were trained with the real objects, viewed through a transparent pecking key. Groups trained with true categories of foods vs. nonfoods learned more than twice as fast as those trained with pseudocategories, and they generalized well to new exemplars. Although Watanabe does not say whether his pigeons had ever been fed all the kinds of grain used as stimuli, these results are consistent with the birds coming into the experiment with a preexisting "food" category. However, because all the foods were grains it seems likely that they were perceptually more similar to one another—for example, in shape or color—than to the nonfoods. Thus primary stimulus generalization rather than mediated generalization may account for Watanabe's results. Nevertheless, this approach could be pursued to investigate one natural functional concept some animals might be expected to have.

5.5.4 Abstract or Relational Concepts

So far we have primarily considered categories defined by simple physical attributes, but humans, at least, classify things according to more abstract properties, properties that emerge out of relationships among things. Do any animals use such apparently higher level abstract categories (Herrnstein, 1990)? One of the candidates most discussed in a comparative context is same/different or matching. For instance, do animals trained to match to sample (see figure 6.4) have a generalized ability to match? Pigeons trained in the standard way, with just a few stimuli, do not match novel samples but apparently memorize conditional rules ("If the sample was red, choose red; if green, choose green."). In contrast, various corvids such as rooks acquire a matching concept after similar treatment (Mackintosh, 1988; Wilson, Mackintosh, & Boakes, 1985). Monkeys and chimpanzees, too, match novel stimuli after exposure to just one matching problem, though the monkeys' transfer is not complete (D'Amato, Salmon, & Colombo, 1985; Oden, Thompson, & Premack, 1988). Pigeons do eventually acquire generalized matching if they are trained for thousands of trials with a large set of stimuli (Wright, Cook, & Rivera, 1988). However, it can be argued that the matching to sample paradigm, in which the animal responds first to the sample and then to the comparison stimulus, is a test of relative familiarity rather than identity, "Which did I just respond to?" rather than "Are these two things the same?" Indeed, pigeons perform quite well in a paradigm in which they are reinforced for responding to a novel slide the second time it appears in a session but not the first (but see Macphail, Good, Honey, & Willis, 1995; Macphail & Reilly, 1989).

Premack (1983) has argued that only language-trained chimpanzees are capable of discriminating same/different relations among simultaneously presented stimuli, a problem that cannot be solved using conditional discriminations or relative novelty. Young chimpanzees that have not had language training like that described in chapter 12 cannot, in fact, be trained to match displays of two identical items to one another. However, chimpanzees trained to use numerical symbols (see chapter 8) match "same" and "different" displays spontaneously (Thompson, Oden, & Boysen, 1997). Thus, not language training per se but perhaps some aspect of training with abstract symbols fosters this sort of performance. If that is the case, though, what are we to make of the results of recent research on the same/different concept that used stimuli like those in figure 5.18 (Wasserman, Hugart, & Kirkpatrick-Steger, 1995)? Pigeons were exposed to a category discrimination training procedure similar to that depicted in figure 5.14. Pecks to one side key were reinforced in the presence of a display of 16 identical elements; pecks to a second side key were reinforced in the presence of a display of 16 elements, each differ-

"Same"

 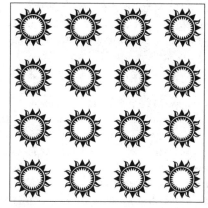

"Different"

Figure 5.18. Examples of the kinds of stimuli used to train pigeons in same/different discriminations. After Wasserman et al. (1995) with permission.

ent from the others. After being trained to 83% correct with 16 arrays of each kind, pigeons averaged 71% correct on arrays composed of novel symbols. Similarly, transfer was also found in pigeons trained with stimuli like those in figure 2.15 to discriminate large homogenous arrays of tiny elements from arrays containing a rectangular area of elements different in color and/or shape from the surroundings (Cook, Cavoto, & Cavoto, 1995).

Are these new findings with pigeons evidence of a low-level perceptual mechanism or a true same/different concept? The authors of both reports (Cook et al., 1995; Wasserman, Hugart, & Kirkpatrick-Steger, 1995) argue that their birds must have been doing more than responding to the overall texture of the displays because transfer was not perfect. Rather, the pigeons must have been processing the individual elements and then extracting a same/different judgment at a higher, conceptual, level (Cook & Wixted, 1997;

Young & Wasserman, 1997). Nevertheless, consideration of this line of research suggests that the line between abstract concepts and direct perception
of relationships may not be easy to draw. Implicit knowledge of some abstract
relationship may be embedded in a highly specific perceptual module without
the animal being able to access it to control explicit, arbitrary, discriminative
responses. For instance, biological motion (Thompson, 1995) and connect-
edness (Hauser, 1996) have been suggested as abstract concepts that some
animals may have, but they could just as well be described as higher-order
properties that are perceived directly.

Same/different is not the only relational concept that has been investigated
comparatively (Fetterman, 1996). Starlings have been trained on abstract auditory concepts such as rising vs. falling series of tones. (Starlings are a good
species of bird to use in such studies because they mimic a wide variety of natural and man-made sounds in the wild, which implies that they perceive them
very accurately.) Just as in the studies with visual arrays, the birds respond to
both the absolute values of the training stimuli and to their relationships
(MacDougall-Shackleton & Hulse, 1996). Future chapters discuss research
on some other abstract concepts that animals might have, including number
(chapter 8), self-concept (chapter 11), and serial order (chapter 12). The example in box 5.3 illustrates an issue that will arise in considering all these
other cases: can the behavior taken as evidence of an abstract concept be described more simply as resulting from associations formed to specific stimuli
during training or during previous tests?

5.5.5 Concepts in the Wild?

In most studies of categorization discussed in the last section, pigeons discriminated visual categories for food reward. Many of the experiments in this
area have presented animals with colored slides of real objects, but the learning process involved may have little to do with the ecological significance, if
any, of those objects. However, in a handful of experiments the methods of
category learning experiments have been used to investigate the acquisition of
category discriminations that might be ecologically relevant for the species involved. Among other things, this research expands the range of species and
functional contexts in which category discrimination has been documented.

Birds that feed on caterpillars or other insects can locate their prey directly,
but they might also make use of other signs of the prey's presence. Cryptic
palatable caterpillars tend to be neat eaters, leaving the leaves they have bit-
ten with smooth contours like the contours of undamaged leaves. Unpalatable species are more likely to be messy eaters, turning leaves into conspicuous ragged tatters. Captive black-capped chickadees can learn to search for
insects on trees, or on particular species of trees, with damaged leaves (Heinrich & Collins, 1983). This suggests that palatable caterpillars have enhanced
their crypticity by evolving neat feeding behavior under pressure from the
learning abilities of bird predators, another sort of mimicry to add to those
mentioned in box 5.1. Real, Iannazzi, Kamil, and Heinrich (1984) demon-

Box 5.3. Transitive Inference and Value Transfer

Transitive inference problems are familiar to every schoolchild. "If Susan is taller than Polly and Polly is taller than Carol, then who is the tallest—Susan, Polly, or Carol?" Similarly in animal social life, if A dominates B, and B dominates C, then A most likely dominates C. It has been suggested (see Wynne, 1995) that transitive inference in a species with such a linear dominance hierarchy might convey the ability to learn one's place without having to fight with everyone in the social group. So are any animals capable of transitive inference?

Recent research on how pigeons solve an operant analogue of transitive inference suggests that it may be unnecessary anthropomorphizing to suppose that transitive inference-like behavior is always evidence of logical reasoning. Following on from reports that monkeys (McGonigle & Chalmers, 1977) and chimpanzees (Gillan, 1981) perform transitive inference, von Fersen, Wynne, and Delius (1991) trained pigeons on the nonverbal transitive inference task depicted on the left of figure B5.3. The animal learns four simultaneous discriminations that can be construed as forming a series, A>B, B>C, C>D, and D>E, where $X>Y$ means X is reinforced and Y is not. The

➡

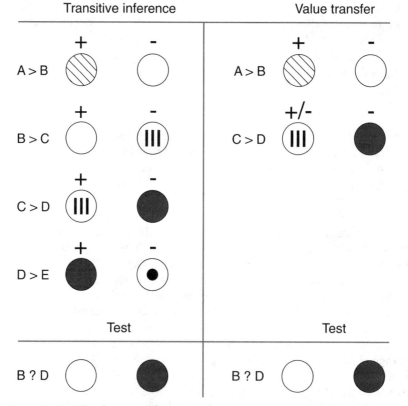

Figure B5.3. Procedures used for training and testing pigeons or monkeys in experiments on transitive inference (left side of the figure) or value transfer.

Box 5.3. (continued)

animal is then given a choice between the novel pair B and D, each of which has been both reinforced and nonreinforced during training. Lo and behold, pigeons reliably peck more at B than D, but why?

An explanation is evident if we consider that although B and D have similar histories of primary reinforcement, they have appeared in the company of other stimuli with different histories. In particular, B appears not only with C but also with A, which should be very highly valued thanks to never being a negative stimulus in any discrimination in the series. Moreover, D appears sometimes in the company of E, which should be the least-valued stimulus in the series. Thus, if B and D gain value by association with the other positive or negative stimuli with which they simultaneously appear, B should be preferred over D. This sort of indirect acquisition of associative strength is referred to as *value transfer* (von Fersen, Wynne, Delius, & Staddon, 1991). Value transfer has been demonstrated directly using the procedure shown on the right of figure B5.3 (Zentall & Sherburne, 1994; Zentall, Sherburne, Roper, & Kraemer, 1996). Of interest was what pigeons would do when confronted with negative stimuli, B and D, from two independent simultaneous discriminations, in one of which (A vs. B) the positive stimulus had been reinforced 100% and in the other of which (C vs. D) it had been only partially reinforced. Although both procedures lead to similarly high rates of responding to the reinforced alternative, pigeons reliably pecked more at B than D in the test. The role of value transfer in transitive inference performance was tested directly by, in effect, bending the linear series in on the left of figure B5.3 around on itself by adding to it E>A so E and A, together with their associates B and D, no longer had differential value. As value transfer predicts, pigeons did not choose B over D in this "circular" series (von Fersen, Wynne, Delius, & Staddon, 1991). In later chapters, we will see numerous other examples of how apparently "clever" or "thoughtful" behavior can be accounted for by simple associative mechanisms, at least in some species.

However, while the research on pigeons provides a good example of how simple associative mechanisms may explain apparently "clever" or "thoughtful" behavior, value transfer does not suffice to account for the performance of macaque monkeys (*Macaca mulatta*) in transitive inference tasks (Treichler & van Tilburg, 1996). Rather, monkeys seem to acquire a representation of the series as a whole. Monkeys were trained on two separate series of pairwise associations like that depicted in figure B5.3. Then the series were linked by training a discrimination between the last item of one series and the first item on the next. When then confronted with one item from each series, the monkeys chose between them as if they had mentally combined all the items into a single ordered set. A similar species difference in ability to represent items in a series as such is reflected in performance on serial order tasks, as discussed in Box 8.1. Interestingly, under some conditions rats also appear to acquire a unified representation of a series of items (Phelps & Roberts, 1994; see Roberts, 1998, for further discussion). At present one can only speculate on what differences in ecology, social organization, or brain structure might be related to these apparent differences in abstract conceptual ability.

"Neat"

"Messy"

Probe

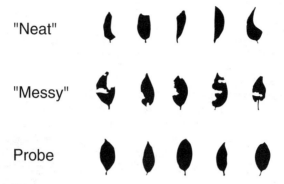

Figure 5.19. Stimuli used by Real et al. (1984). The left-most "neat" and and "messy" leaves were used in training; other stimuli in those rows are examples of leaf patterns used in generalization testing. The bottom row shows probes representing undamaged leaves. Redrawn from Real et al. (1984) with permission.

strated that some birds can easily learn and generalize the required discrimination. They trained bluejays to respond differently to a slide silhouette of a cherry leaf damaged by a "neat" caterpillar than to one damaged by a "messy" caterpillar (figure 5.19). After training on one exemplar of each type, the birds generalized the appropriate response patterns to new exemplars. Furthermore, responding like that associated with the "neat" leaves generalized to silhouettes of undamaged leaves. Compared to colored slides of scenes, the silhouettes used in this experiment and a related one with pigeons (Cerella, 1979) are very simple. This may be one reason why the shape or outline of such a silhouette seems to be so salient, at least for bluejays and pigeons.

The experiment by Real et al. shows that a typical laboratory category discrimination training procedure can be used to investigate learning of an ecologically relevant category. Similarly, Dasser (1988a, 1988b) used a standard category discrimination procedure to ask whether Java monkeys (*Macaca fascicularis*) could discriminate pairs of other monkeys on the basis of whether they were mother and offspring. One of the subjects was trained in a discrimination task in which positive slides showed a mother-daughter pair from the subject's social group and negative slides showed a pair of unrelated monkeys. After training with five slides of a single mother-offspring pair and five different unrelated pairs, the subject monkey responded correctly to 14 out of 14 sets of slides showing new pairs of monkeys. Another monkey performed comparably on a matching to sample procedure. It is not clear from these results whether the perceptual similarity between mothers and offspring played any role here or whether performance entirely reflected knowledge of relationships gained in the subjects' social group, a kind of functional category. One way to test this would be to compare performance with familiar vs. unfamiliar mother-offspring pairs. The extent to which performance was above chance levels with unfamiliar pairs would be a measure of the role of perceptual similarity between mother and offspring. Of course, if monkeys do prove to have a functional category, "mother-offspring pair"—and there is evidence from the field suggesting that some species do (Seyfarth & Cheney, 1994)—this does not mean they understand relatedness as such, nor does it tell us how a monkey learns about this or any other social relationship among group members.

Our final example of ecologically relevant categorization also comes from the behavior of monkeys. Free-ranging vervet monkeys (*Cercopithecus aethiops*) give and respond to three different types of alarm calls, each for a different type of predator and antipredator response (Seyfarth, Cheney, & Marler, 1980a, 1980b). Eagle alarms are given to aerial predators and cause their hearers to look up. Snake alarms are given to pythons and other potentially harmful snakes and cause other monkeys to look down in the grass. Leopard alarms cause vervets hearing them to run into the trees. Formally, this is exactly the sort of situation modeled by Wasserman's four-way classification procedure. Because one animal is giving a vocal signal to conspecifics it also shares a property of human language. The vervets' system of signals also appears to be learned, although observations in the wild have not separated effects of experience from simple maturation. Young vervets generalize the calls very broadly—for example, giving eagle alarms to a variety of harmless birds. Classification improves with age and experience. These observations, discussed again in chapter 12, have featured prominently in discussions of whether animals exhibit intentionality or a simple form of language. Regardless of one's views on this complex issue, behaviorally the vervets are doing no more than dividing the other animals in their environment into functional and/or perceptual categories. Some, if not all, of the processes involved are likely the same as those used by pigeons when responding differently to each of four categories of visual images.

5.6 Summary and Conclusions

Any animal must respond differently to different things in its world, food and nonfood, mate and enemy. This chapter started by discussing discriminative behavior that is not obviously trained, as studied in classical ethology. Behavior toward complex natural objects generally turns out to be controlled by one or a few simple features, the ethologists' sign stimuli. The effective features have additive effects (heterogenous summation) and this may mean that objects never found in nature are more effective than natural objects (supernormality). Recently, multidimensional scaling has been used to analyze what features animals use to classify complex species-specific signals, both in the field and in laboratory tests. Again, some features or combinations of features are more important than others. Animals may discriminate among signals of their own species more accurately than among similar signals of other species. How this species-specific advantage develops has not generally been studied. In a noteworthy integration of psychological and evolutionary thinking, Nelson and Marler (1990) suggest that classifying signals on the basis of a species-specific prototype may be less useful than classification based on similarity to memorized exemplars because the latter will be fine-tuned to the local environment.

The discussion of how discriminations are learned in the laboratory, in sections 5.4 and 5.5, parallels that of how natural discriminations are controlled, starting with classical studies of simple discrimination training and concluding with discrimination among categories of complex stimuli. The Rescorla-Wagner model, introduced in chapter 3, provides a good account of how the features that best predict reward or nonreward gain most control over discriminative behavior. However, discrimination training has some effects that cannot readily be explained as changes in excitatory or inhibitory strength. These include the acquisition of learning sets by some species and possible changes in attention to the relevant dimension in successive reversal training. Discrimination among complex polymorphous categories like photographic slides of natural scenes does not seem to involve any special processes such as "concept learning." Changes in associative strength of common and shared elements of category members may account for prototype effects in animals trained to discriminate between categories.

In summary, similar principles apply to most, if not all, discriminative behavior, whether explicitly trained or not. Only some features of objects control behavior, although this control may be modulated by attention or motivation. In individual experience the features most predictive of biologically important consequences come to have most influence over behavior. An analogous process has likely acted in evolution to determine what aspects of the world are responded to or learned about.

Further Reading

Tinbergen's (1951) *The Study of Instinct* is highly recommended as an introduction to ethology. Hinde's (1982) *Ethology* is a more recent, personal, account of the development of the field and its relationship to other areas of behavioral science. Dooling et al. (1990) provide a good introduction to the use of multidimensional scaling to study natural perceptual categories, as does the chapter by Nelson and Marler (1990).

For studies of discrimination learning, Mackintosh (1974) provides a thorough review of traditional work, while Mackintosh (1983) brings the material more up to date in a concise manner. The chapter by Pearce (1994b) relates the most recent developments to research on category discrimination. Fetterman (1996) thoughtfully discusses the issue of "what is a stimulus," especially as it applies to recent psychological research on category learning. Both Herrnstein (1990) and Watanabe et al. (1993) summarize, in contrasting ways, the literature on category discrimination by pigeons. Wasserman and Astley (1994) summarize the research from Wasserman's laboratory, and Thompson (1995) reviews laboratory studies on a wider range of species, including some studies of abstract and relational categories discussed in later chapters.

6

Memory

Forming a search image, acquiring a conditioned response, recognizing one's mother—all are examples of learning. But they are also examples of memory. In order for learning to occur, information must be retained from one occasion to the next—that is, it must be remembered. In psychology, however, *learning* and *memory* define separate bodies of research, even though this separation is difficult to justify theoretically. Research on learning has traditionally dealt with how information about relationships between events is acquired. Learning is generally measured by fairly long-lasting changes in behavior. Research on memory, in contrast, deals with how information is stored, retained, and retrieved. The cognitive changes of interest often take place rapidly, may not be very long lasting, and may be read out in a variety of behaviors. But parts of this description apply to examples of "learning." For instance, flavor aversions can form in one trial, and Pavlovian conditioning may influence a whole behavior system, not just a single response (see chapter 3). As another example, habituation appears at first glance to be a simple straightforward example of nonverbal memory, but we have seen that some fairly elaborate associative learning may underlie it (see chapter 4). The contemporary emphasis on a variety of distinct cognitive modules or memory systems gradually may—and perhaps should—cause the simple traditional dichotomy between *learning* and *memory* to be abandoned.

From early in the century until the 1960s, most research on memory was done on humans, even though much of the theorizing that drove it came from

associative models based on research with other species. The "cognitive revolution" of the '60s turned the tables. Research on human memory began to
focus on the nature of information processing and representation. About 10
years later, research on animals followed, with the development of the subfield
of animal cognition (Hulse, 1993; Wasserman, 1993). At least initially, research on animal memory was an exceptionally clear example of the anthropocentric program. Often, the point of experiments on animal memory was
simply to discover whether or not representatives of some convenient species
like Norway rats or pigeons behaved like people when they were tested in a
parallel way. Some of this research took on a life of its own, with questions
directed more at the nature of particular species' performance in particular
paradigms than at the nature of memory generally. Moreover, although the
findings and techniques from research on animal memory have become
widely used in research on the neural basis of memory, many students of
human cognition feel that the results of research on other species are of little
relevance to important issues in their own field (Baddeley, 1995; Schacter &
Tulving, 1994; Wright & Watkins, 1987).

This chapter starts with a brief look at some attempts to predict the properties of memory from considering what memory is used for. Section 6.1 also
outlines a framework for asking questions about memory like that for studying learning in chapter 3 and discusses the notion that animals might have a
number of different memory systems. Studying memory in animals poses the
same kinds of problems as studying perception: whereas human subjects can
be asked "What do you perceive?" or "What do you remember?" subjects of
other species have to be asked in other ways. Section 6.2 outlines methods for
studying memory in nonverbal species. Section 6.3 summarizes the main conditions that affect memory. Section 6.4 discusses the notion that species differ adaptively in how much or how long they can remember and reviews several research programs that have tested this notion. Theories about the
contents of memory are reviewed in section 6.5.

6.1 The Issues

6.1.1 Functions of Memory

What determines what information is retained, how long it is retained, and how
it is expressed in behavior? These questions about the mechanisms of memory
map into a set of functional questions: what information is useful? how long is
it useful? and what is is useful for? Behavioral ecologists have considered these
questions primarily as they apply to foraging: given that the distribution and

type of food in the environment changes and that animals cannot have perfect
knowledge of its current state, how should they use experience to estimate environmental quality (Mangel, 1990)? Predictions about the properties of memory help to answer this question because the rate of forgetting should track the
rate at which the environment changes. The more quickly old information becomes useless, the more quickly it should be forgotten.

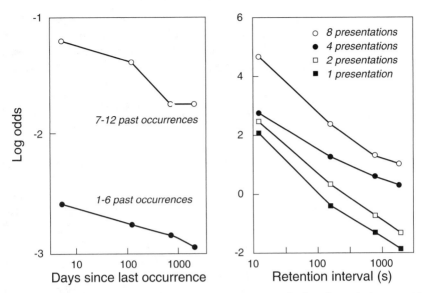

Figure 6.1. Left panel: The odds of a word appearing in the headline of *The New York Times* related to the days since it last occurred and the number of times it occurred in the past. (Odds is defined as follows: if *p* is the probability of an event, $q = p/(1 - p)$ is the odds of that event.) Right panel: Forgetting curves from a study of human memory that have an analogous pattern. Redrawn from Anderson and Schooler (1991) with permission.

A related functional approach to memory is based on the notion that the probability of retrieving a particular memory should track the probability that it is needed (Anderson & Schooler, 1991). Two variables predicting the likelihood that information will be needed now are how often it was needed in the past and how long ago it was last needed. These correspond to *practice* and *retention interval*, respectively, in tests of memory. To discover whether the effects of practice and retention interval do match the properties of the environment, Anderson & Schooler (1991) looked at three sources of data on the temporal distribution of information. One was words in the headlines of the *New York Times*. These reflect demands on memory use because when a word like *Persian Gulf* or *Gingerich* appears, the reader has to retrieve a memory of its significance in order to interpret the headline. As might be expected, a given word was less likely to appear the longer since it last appeared and the less often it had appeared in the past (figure 6.1). Data from experiments on memory retrieval as a function of time and number of past exposures in humans and other species have the same form as these functions (figure 6.1; Wixted & Ebbesen, 1991).

With some success, Anderson and his colleagues (Anderson, 1991; Anderson & Milson, 1989) have explored a number of other ways in which the properties of cognition in humans can be related to the requirements for information-retrieval systems. But this approach is not very biological. Our ancestors were not reading the *New York Times*, so to consider Anderson and

Schooler's results relevant to pressures that have caused memory to evolve, one has to assume that headlines in a late 20th-century newspaper reflect a general and enduring property of events in the world. There have been few, if any, comparable attempts to describe formally the environmental characteristics that members of any other species must remember in order to see how well the properties of memory match the properties of their environment. But there is no shortage of informal arguments. For example, different kinds of information might need to be remembered differently. A mother hen doesn't change her appearance very fast and she is very important for her chicks to know about, so information about her should be retained for a long time even after a single experience. In contrast, where a particular grain was eaten at 10 A.M. on Monday may not have much lasting significance, although the general characteristics of grains and where to find them may well be worth remembering. A system for retaining large amounts of detail about single experiences may not be good for generalizing on the basis of common elements in repeated experiences. Such considerations suggest that memory is not unitary but consists of a number of distinct modules or *memory systems*. Processing one kind of information well may be *functionally incompatible* with processing another kind of information well (Sherry & Schacter, 1987; see also chapters 1 and 13). When functional incompatibilities have an impact on fitness, separate memory systems will evolve, each of which processes, stores, and retrieves different information in different, functionally appropriate ways. We consider this idea in more depth in chapter 13, after we have looked at some of the properties of memory for different kinds of events.

6.1.2 Questions about Memory

The same three questions can be asked about memory as were asked about learning in chapter 3: (1) What are the conditions under which information is retained (the conditions for memory)? (2) What are the contents of memory, the *memory code*? This question, about the nature of representation in memory, can be answered at differing levels of detail. For example, we might infer that information about the location of food is remembered by observing that a hungry animal goes back to where it last found food. But what the animal had actually remembered might be the position of the food relative to nearby landmarks, the path it took to get to the food, or a variety of other kinds of information. Experimental analysis is generally required to define the contents of memory. (3) What are the effects of memory on behavior? Traditionally, this last question has been of little interest, as it is assumed that a memory can be accessed in a variety of ways. For example, a subject shown a list of words can later be asked to recognize them in a larger list or to write them down or call them out. A rat can indicate which arms of a maze it remembers entering last by selectively returning to those arms or by avoiding them. However, recently it has become apparent that some kinds of memory can be accessed only in highly specific ways—for example, through certain

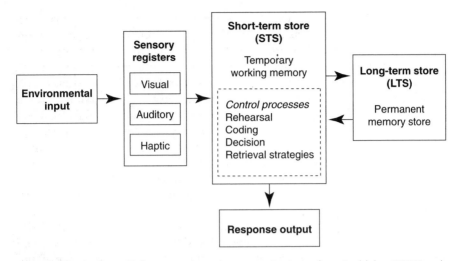

Figure 6.2. The flow of information through memory. Redrawn from Baddeley (1995) with permission.

kinds of behavior but not verbally. This difference between *implicit* and *explicit* memory is discussed in section 6.5.4.

6.2 Methods for Studying Memory in Animals

6.2.1 Some Distinctions

Figure 6.2 depicts a standard conception of the structure of memory. Environmental input is first processed in sensory registers and stored temporarily in a *short-term store* (or *short-term memory, STM*), where it is accessible to decision processes. The short-term store also includes information called up from the *long-term store* (or *long-term memory, LTM*). Current input and stored information about its significance, together with motivation, control response output. Some of the contents of the short-term store are lost after a brief time, while others become part of long-term memory. An important focus of research on human memory has been the nature of these memory stores and their relationship. The most closely parallel work with nonhuman species is that of Wagner and his associates using habituation, discussed in chapter 4. In place of the distinction between short-term and long-term memory, those who work with animals distinguish between *working memory* and *reference memory*. Working memory in this context does not necessarily mean the same thing as working memory in humans (Baddeley, 1995). Working memory in experiments with animals is defined operationally as memory for events on a specific trial whereas reference memory is memory for the unchanging characteristics of a task (Honig, 1978). For example, a test of memory might require the animal to learn "food can be obtained from that hole in the wall" or "always choose the color you saw most recently." This information about what happens on every trial is part of reference memory. Information like "no food this time" or "the most recent stimulus was a red square" is part of working memory. As we will see, the time scale over which working memory in this sense is measured depends greatly on the task. Reference memory in animals is actually little studied as such, possibly because laboratory animals have so little to do between experimental trials that they don't forget very much. Obviously, however, the experiments on "learning" reviewed in previous chapters are about information storage in long-term memory. Some paradigms used in the study of conditioning parallel standard tests of reference memory (Bouton, 1993; see also section 6.3.3).

Related to the distinction between working and reference memory is that between *episodic* and *semantic* memory in humans (e.g., Tulving, 1985). Episodic memory is memory for events in one's own personal past, as distinguished from memory for facts and ideas. The difference between episodic and semantic memory is the difference between memory for the experience of dinner at Luigi's Restaurant last Saturday night and knowledge about what is involved in having dinner at a restaurant in general. Supported by evidence that episodic and semantic memory are dissociated in some amnesic patients, the definition of episodic memory has evolved to include conscious recollection of personal experience (e.g., Schacter & Tulving, 1994). This makes it almost impossible to test for in nonverbal subjects (see chapter 1 and section 6.5.4). Another distinction bearing on the contents of memory is that between *procedural* and *declarative* memory—that is, memory for what to do vs. memory for facts or states of affairs. As we have seen in chapter 3, these two kinds of contents are reflected in different behaviors in some tests of conditioning.

With humans, either *recognition* or *recall* of past input can be tested. That is, a person can be presented with a stimulus and asked "Have you experienced this before?" (recognition) or simply instructed to "Tell me what you remember" (recall). Performance on recognition tasks is typically better than on comparable recall tasks, possibly because there are more *retrieval cues* in the test of recognition (see section 6.3.3). Most tests of animal memory are tests of recognition. Often the same items are used over and over again, so the animal is really being trained in a *recency discrimination* (Staddon, 1983). That is, rather than discriminating something familiar from something novel, it has to discriminate the stimulus presented most recently from other familiar stimuli that may have been presented just a few seconds or minutes ago. Still, the situation is no different in traditional tests of human memory with lists of words. Subjects are being asked whether familiar words were presented in the experiment, not whether they have ever seen them before. *Recognition memory* in animals is often distinguished from *associative memory*, memory for whether reward or nonreward accompanied the event in the past. When the same items are used repeatedly, it may be difficult to disentangle recognition from effects of past reinforcements and nonreinforcements (Macphail, Good, & Honey, 1995).

6.2.2 Habituation

Most contemporary research and theorizing about memory in nonhuman species is based on data from the performance of rats and pigeons in three kinds of tests of memory. We have already encountered one of these in chapter 4, where we saw how the habituation of untrained responses provides evidence for both short-term and long-term memory. The logic of these experiments is simple: if behavior toward an eliciting stimulus changes from one occasion to the next, and if motivational and peripheral causes of the change in responding can be ruled out, information about the earlier presentation must have been stored in memory. Unlike the other two popular methods to be described, the habituation method does not require training the subjects beforehand. This is both a strength and a weakness. The strength is that it can be used with species and stimulus-response systems where training is difficult or impractical; the weakness is that its use is limited to memory for events that initially evoke a well-defined response.

6.2.3 Delayed Response Tasks

Hunter (1913) was one of the first to use the type of delayed response procedure now widely employed to test memory in animals (see Boakes, 1984). Rats, raccoons, and dogs were trained in appropriately sized versions of the apparatus shown in figure 6.3 to approach the door under the light to obtain food. The light was over a different door on each trial so that the animal had to learn to approach the light regardless of its location. Then the animal was tested by restraining it in the start area while the light was turned on briefly. If it could still choose the correct door when it was released after the light went out, it must have retained information about the location of the light during the delay, the *retention interval*. Hunter's purpose was to discover whether animals had "ideas," representations of objects or events that were not present at the time of responding. But some animals performed well by standing facing the correct door during the delay. Disrupting this orientation—for example, by removing the animal from the start area during the delay—could reduce accuracy to chance levels. The necessity for eliminating orienting during the retention interval in order to study the mental rather than motoric traces of events may explain why until recently tests of short-term spatial memory have been less popular than tests of memory for nonspatial stimuli.

Figure 6.4 depicts one of the currently most popular tests of animal short-term or working memory, the *delayed matching to sample* procedure, as it might be used for pigeons in an operant chamber. A trial begins with display of a *sample*, the to-be-remembered stimulus, on a center key. The bird is generally required to peck the sample a number of times in order to extinguish it and advance to the next stage of the trial. This ensures that the animal has actually seen the sample and gives the experimenter some control over the duration of

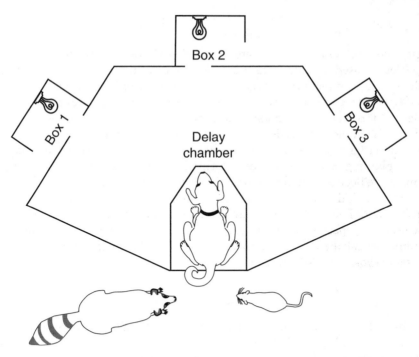

Figure 6.3. Schematic view of Hunter's apparatus for studying delayed response. The size was adjusted for the different species. After Maier and Schneirla (1935/1964) with permission.

exposure to it. Primary reinforcement such as food is usually not given for responding to the sample, so if the animal chooses a stimulus like the sample in the test phase of the trial, it is doing do despite earlier nonreward. The sample is separated from the test phase of the trial by a retention interval (*RI*). At the end of the RI the animal is presented with a choice between the stimulus it saw before, say red on the key, and a *comparison stimulus*, say green. Because these stimuli are on two side keys whereas the sample was on the center key, memory for the sample's location cannot influence choice in the test. If the bird chooses correctly in the test phase, it will be reinforced, typically with food; if it chooses incorrectly, it may proceed directly to the intertrial interval or it may be punished or corrected in some way. For example, the lights in the testing chamber may go out for a few seconds, or the trial may be repeated until the bird makes the correct choice. In any case, an intertrial interval (*ITI*) ensues and then a new trial begins. The identity of the sample and the location of the choices on the side keys change randomly from trial to trial. A typical daily session might include from 50 to 100 or more trials, and the same small set of stimuli (often just two) is used over and over. What the animal is exposed to, then, is a rapid-fire series of events: "Red" . . . "Was it red or green?" . . . "Green" . . . "Was it red or green?" . . . "Green" . . . "Was it red or green?" Small wonder that pigeons' performance in this type of task

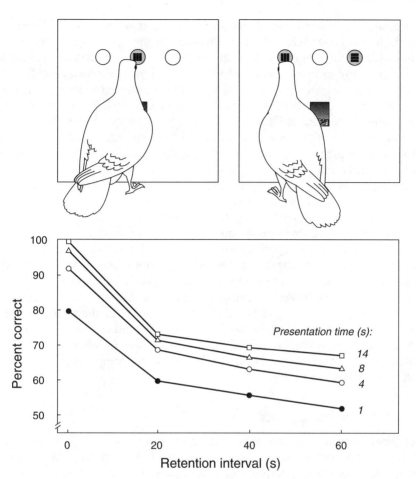

Figure 6.4. *Top:* Typical delayed matching to sample procedure for pigeons. Here the pigeon is reinforced (by grain appearing in the opening below the keys) for pecking the pattern that matches the pattern pecked in the first part of the trial. Redrawn from Wright (1991) with permission. *Bottom:* Effects of retention interval and duration of sample exposure on pigeons' matching to sample performance. Redrawn from Grant (1976) with permission.

is typically quite poor in absolute terms, even after thousands of trials of training. Figure 6.4 shows an example. Of course, the precise slope and height of forgetting curves like that in the figure depend on details of the testing procedure like those discussed in section 6.3 (van Hest & Steckler, 1996; White, Ruske, & Colombo, 1996).

Memory for a sample can also be tested by reinforcing choice of the comparison stimulus that differs from it—that is, *delayed nonmatching to sample* or *oddity*. Despite its name, pigeons generally do not acquire a concept amounting to "choose the comparison stimulus that matches (or doesn't match) the sample" in these procedures, although some animals do. Indeed, pigeons do just as well at *symbolic matching* as at literal matching (Zentall, Urcuioli, Jagielo, & Jackson-Smith, 1989, contains some examples). In symbolic matching, each sample stimulus is associated with one or more arbitrary comparison stimuli. For example, choice of a horizontal line might be correct following a red sample, whereas a vertical line might be correct following a green. There are many other variants on the basic delayed matching test of memory. For example, in *successive matching*, the sample is followed by a single comparison stimulus. The animal is reinforced for responding only if the comparison matches the sample. Latencies, probabilities, or rates of responding to matching and nonmatching comparisons are compared. In *delayed alternation*, an animal is reinforced for responding to the stimulus it didn't just respond to. For instance, a rat may be allowed to visit one arm of a T-maze, replaced in the start box and required to visit the opposite arm. After doing so, it must visit the first arm again, and so on. The memory of small birds (Brodbeck, Burack, & Shettleworth, 1992) and primates (Platt, Brannon, Briese, & French, 1996) has been tested in a three-dimensional spatial matching task. In the first, sample phase of each trial, the animal is allowed to find a bait such as a peanut in one of several distinctive sites in a large room (strictly speaking, this reward makes it a test of associative memory). When the animal returns after a retention interval, all possible locations for food are covered. When it relocates the baited site, the animal can finish the food. In this and other tests, memory can be compared for different features of the sample such as its color and location (see chapter 7).

6.2.4 The Radial Maze

In typical delayed matching tasks, memory of a single sample is not retained for more than a few seconds or minutes. Imagine, then, the sensation created by an article entitled "Memory for places passed: Spatial memory in rats" (Olton & Samuelson, 1976), which described how rats could apparently retain information about all the arms they had visited in an 8-arm *radial maze* for at least several minutes. As devised by Olton and Samuelson, a radial maze (figure 6.5) consists of eight flat, unwalled arms, elevated (so rats don't climb off), each about a meter long, radiating out from a central platform. The maze is placed in a normal, lighted, laboratory room, with pieces of furniture, windows, doors, posters on the walls—in short, numerous objects to provide the rat with cues about where it is on the maze. At the start of a trial, a small piece of food is concealed at the end of each arm. The rat is placed on the central platform and allowed to remain on the maze until it has collected all the food. Once rats have been accustomed to being on the maze and finding food there, they collect all the bait very quickly and seldom revisit already emptied arms while doing so. Thus, they seem to exhibit working memory for the locations already visited on the current trial.

The first thing that will occur to anyone skeptical of this conclusion is that rats use olfaction in some way to detect unvisited arms, or that each rat memorizes a particular successful pattern of visits, or that they use an *algorithm*, a

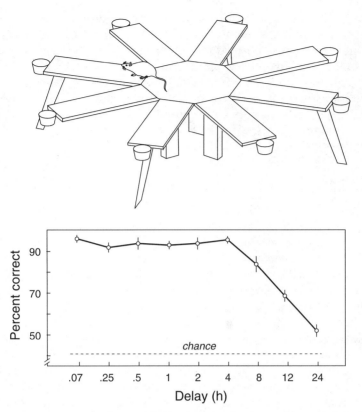

Figure 6.5. A rat on an eight-arm radial maze with a food cup at the end of each arm, re-drawn from Roitblat (1987) with permission. Data are mean (± SE) proportion correct choices out of the first four choices following a retention interval during which rats were removed from the maze, having already visited four arms. The calculation of chance performance assumes the first choice is random, but then the rat never revisits the arm most recently chosen. Redrawn from Beatty and Shavalia (1980) with permission.

rule like "always go into the next arm to the left." All these possibilities have been ruled out by straightforward control procedures. Confining the rat in the middle of the maze and cleaning or moving the arms between visits does not eliminate accurate performance, nor does introducing a strong smell like aftershave lotion that might be thought to mask odors of food or odor left by the rats themselves. Individual rats generally do not repeat the same pattern of visits from one trial to the next, nor do they follow an obvious rule in choosing successive arms (Olton & Samuelson, 1976; W. A. Roberts, 1984).

In delayed matching to sample, as in most tests of memory in humans, the experimenter chooses the items to be remembered, but in the radial maze as first described, the animal chooses them because it controls the order of arms it visits. The to-be-remembered items can be controlled in the radial maze, however, by placing doors around the center platform and opening only one or a few at a time. This simple modification also allows control over the interval over which the experimenter-selected "items" must be remembered. In a typical procedure that does this, a rat is placed on the maze with four doors open. Once the rat has collected food from these arms, a retention interval ensues, which the rat may spend off the maze. Then all eight doors are opened and only the arms not visited in the first phase of the trial are baited. With this procedure, rats perform better than chance at retention intervals up to 24 hours (figure 6.5). Radial mazes and equivalent arrangements have now been used to test many other species, including hummingbirds collecting nectar from artificial flowers in the field (Healy & Hurly, 1995).

6.2.5 Delayed Matching, the Radial Maze and Foraging

In figure 6.4, one item is completely forgotten in a few seconds. In figure 6.5, four items are retained for hours. Why do pigeons perform so much worse on operant delayed color matching than rats do on the radial maze? A number of possible reasons immediately suggest themselves: rats vs. pigeons, "natural" vs. "unnatural" tasks, spatial vs. nonspatial tasks, rich multiple cues vs. impoverished single cues. Less obviously, the typical testing regimes differ drastically. Rats are generally given just one trial of eight choices a day on a radial maze, whereas a daily session of operant delayed matching consists of many trials. No wonder the animal performing the operant task is sometimes more confused about which stimulus it saw last! The two tasks typically differ enormously in difficulty as *relative recency discriminations* (Staddon, 1983), in terms of the potential for *interference* between one trial and the next (section 6.4). This is because, although the animal has to base its choices in either task on a discrimination between a stimulus experienced on the current trial (the sample, or the arms already visited) and stimuli experienced only on earlier trials, trials in the radial maze are separated by hours or days, whereas trials of delayed matching are separated by only seconds or minutes. Moreover, in delayed matching of colors the stimuli to be discriminated differ in only one respect whereas the cues differentiating the arms of a radial maze typically differ in many respects. The richness of cues also help to make the spatial task easier. This point is brought home by some operant analogs of radial maze tasks.

Wilkie and Summers (1982) trained pigeons on delayed matching to sample with spatial cues, using as samples nine white pecking keys in a square array. It is not surprising that performance fell to chance at a retention interval of eight seconds in this test of spatial working memory if we consider that the to-be-remembered items were visually identical and just a few centimeters apart. Making the keys different colors in a similar task and arranging them in a matrix—that is, two-dimensionally—rather than in a row improved performance to the point where birds could remember their first few choices for up to an hour (Zentall, Steirn, & Jackson-Smith, 1990). Nevertheless, pigeons still may not perform as well as rats on spatial working memory tasks where they move about in a large space (see Spetch & Honig, 1988).

The variety of cues available and the fact that the animal travels from place to place rather than being passively exposed to the to-be-remembered items makes the radial maze seem more "natural" than operant tasks. Indeed, the radial maze does have natural analogs in the problems encountered by a number of species while foraging. Not all of them solve these problems using spatial working memory, however. In the original radial maze test, once-depleted feeding sites are not replenished immediately. Animals like bees and hummingbirds that feed on nectar encounter the same situation while foraging. Some apparently deal with it by remembering when particular sites have been visited and avoiding them for a while afterwards, but others accomplish the same end by adopting a systematic pattern of visits, following a "trapline" (Gill, 1988). It may be profitable for animals that exploit food sources with a predictable cycle of depletion and repletion to hold territories so they can control and remember the pattern of depletion. For instance, territory-holding Hawaiian honeycreepers, *Loxops viren,* were most likely to visit specific flowers at 1–2 hour intervals, when nectar had had time to regenerate. Intruders visited at random times, thereby showing that a flower's fullness could not be detected directly (Kamil, 1978).

Bumblebees (e.g., Hartling & Plowright, 1979) and pied wagtails, *Motacilla alba* (Davies & Houston, 1981) also avoid revisiting recently depleted feeding sites by adopting a systematic pattern of travel. Bees collect nectar from closely spaced blossoms by following a fixed movement rule: "start at the bottom and always move to the next higher inflorescence" (Pyke, 1979). Some wagtails hold winter territories along riverbanks where they feed on dead insects washed up on the shore. A bird makes repeated circuits of its territory, walking up on one side of the river, then flying across and walking down the other. By the time it gets back to where it started, a fresh supply of food has washed up. Wagtails apparently do not remember where they are in a circuit. If one is interrupted—say, by flying off to chase an intruder—it does not always resume its circuit where it left off.

Because different kinds of flowers refill at different rates, nectar feeders might be expected to be able to adjust their intervisit intervals on the basis of experience. Hermit hummingbirds do seem to do this (Gill, 1988). Interestingly, after finding a flower empty, these birds return sooner next time, not later. Since the flower may have been emptied by an intruder, returning sooner reduces the chance that the intruder has come back again to that flower and may discourage it from remaining on the territory. However, quicker return by the territory holder is not the result of a conscious calculation, nor even a specific adaptation to the characteristics of its food sources. A similar behavioral mechanism may be reflected in the *omission effect* on schedules of reinforcement (Staddon, 1983): when schedules provide food at regular times, rats and pigeons begin responding sooner after an occasional omitted reinforcement.

Scatter hoarding animals retrieving their stores also face the problem of remembering where they have collected food and not going back there. Marsh tits, *Parus palustris,* showed evidence of remembering as many as 35 previously visited sites for at least a few minutes (Shettleworth & Krebs, 1982).

Sherry (1984) tested black-capped chickadees' ability to remember what storage sites they had already depleted by allowing them to retrieve part of a batch of stored food one day and the rest the next day. On the second test, the birds visited storage sites still holding food rather than those they had already visited. One interesting thing about this behavior, like that of rats in radial mazes (Maki, 1987) and hummingbirds and honeycreepers collecting nectar, is that the animal is responding to food as information, not reinforcement (Maki, 1987). Reinforcement would seem to dictate that an animal should return to a place where it got food, not go somewhere else. The propensity to display a win-shift rather than a win-stay strategy might be an adaptation to foraging on food sources that can be depleted in one visit. As this notion predicts, hummingbirds tested in an aviary learn a win-shift task faster than a win-stay task (i.e., a task in which the last rewarded site is rewarded again, or matching to sample) (Cole, Hainsworth, Kamil, Mercier, & Wolf, 1982). They start out by shifting away from the most recently rewarded site, and their performance improves faster on the shift than on the stay task. In rats, however, whether or not all the food in a place depletes in one visit influences the tendency to shift or stay (Gaffan, Hansel, & Smith, 1983).

In summary, the radial maze test clearly captures a kind of behavior and a need for spatial working memory shared by many species. The situation presented by operant matching and nonmatching tasks is more impoverished and artificial, even when used to test memory for stimuli in different locations. It has been argued (Zentall, Steirn, & Jackson-Smith, 1990) that operant tasks are a good test of memory precisely because they do not tap a specialized adaptation. In chapters 7 and 13 we will again take up the question of whether spatial working memory is part of a different memory system than, say, memory for visual or auditory patterns or whether spatial tasks are simply on the easy end of a continuum of difficulty determined by variations in the conditions for memory.

6.3 Conditions for Memory

Not surprisingly, the conditions that influence memory are similar to those that influence association formation (see chapter 3) and simple recognition learning (see chapter 4). The more salient, long-lasting, or frequent an event, the better it is remembered. In the study of memory, attention has been directed not only at the conditions present at T1 (the time of input or *encoding*) but also at the conditions between T1 and T2—that is, during the retention interval—and at how the conditions at T2, the time of test, influence the *retrieval* of memories. Of course the primary measure of memory is the influence of information present at T1 on behavior at T2. However, showing that two treatments at T1 lead to different behavior in a standard test at T2 does not allow one to distinguish effects on encoding—that is, on how well the information was stored in the first place—from effects on retention. This theoretical distinction explains why many investigations of the conditions for memory include tests at a variety of retention intervals. Two of the possible

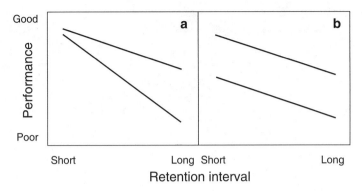

Figure 6.6. Hypothetical forgetting curves showing different possible effects of two treatments on performance after various retention intervals.

patterns of data are shown in figure 6.6. In figure 6.6a, two treatments at T1 have resulted in the same performance in immediate tests but performance later declines at different rates. In figure 6.6b, immediate performance differs, but it declines in a parallel way in the two hypothetical groups. The first pattern indicates that initial encoding or storage of information is unaffected but retention is; the second, the reverse.

6.3.1 Conditions at T1

Amount and Distribution of Experience   Grant (1976) trained pigeons to match samples of colors at retention intervals up to 60 seconds long. The birds' exposure to the samples was varied from 1 second up to 14 seconds. The results (figure 6.4) were as in figure 6.6b: longer exposure, which presumably produces more complete encoding, led to an equal increment in performance at all retention intervals. Presenting the same sample twice before a single test improves performance, too, the more so the longer the sample is presented the first time and the shorter the time between the two presentations of the sample (Roberts & Grant, 1974). An analogous effect is seen in habituation: when the same habituating stimulus occurs twice in quick succession, a smaller response is elicited on the second presentation than on the first (Wagner, 1978). The time between entire trials—that is, episodes in which information is presented and then tested—is also important. *Spacing* of trials in which different information is presented—lengthening the *intertrial interval* or *ITI*—improves performance. For instance, in delayed matching to sample with colors, pigeons averaged 90% correct with an ITI of 20 seconds but only 73% correct with an ITI of 2 seconds (Maki, Moe, & Bierley, 1977). Figure 6.7 shows an example in which rats had eight successive trials on a radial maze in one day. This is an example of *proactive interference*, discussed in section 6.3.2.

Surprise and Distinctiveness   Intuitively, sample duration and intertrial interval could be described as contributing to the salience of to-be-remembered

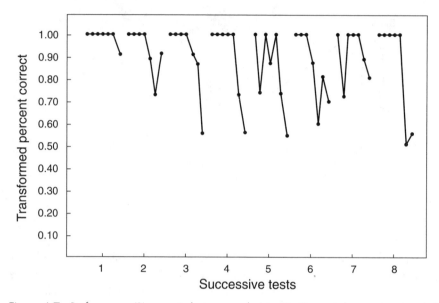

Figure 6.7. Performance (% correct choices on choices 2–8) on eight successive radial maze trials within the same day, an example of proactive interference. The data are transformed so that zero is chance. Redrawn from Olton (1978) with permission.

events: if an event lasts a long time or if nothing like it has occurred for awhile, it is more memorable. The similarity of the current event to other to-be-remembered events also contributes to memorability. In studies of human memory, a distinctive item such as a flower name in a list of vehicles is remembered especially well, a phenomenon known as the *von Restorff effect*. The isolated item need not be suprising, however (Hunt, 1995). The same kind of effect has been investigated with nonverbal species. W. A. Roberts (1980) trained pigeons to match either colors or lines and then exposed them to sessions in which a single trial with lines followed every three trials with colors. The birds matched samples of lines more accurately than under control conditions in which line trials were less distinctive. An event can also be surprising and hence memorable because of previous conditioning; for instance, food is surprising after a CS that has always predicted no food (Grant, Brewster, & Stierhoff, 1983; Wagner, 1978).

Increasing the number of discriminable features of to-be-remembered events improves performance: pigeons match more accurately with samples consisting of a distinctive color plus a location than with key locations alone (Zentall, Steirn, & Jackson-Smith, 1990). Similarly, rats perform less well on a "radial maze" with the arms folded together so they all point in the same direction than on a truly radial maze (Staddon, 1983). In these experiments, the distinctiveness of both the to-be-remembered stimuli (the five keys or the eight maze arms) and the test items is varied, so it is not clear whether distinctiveness increases memorability per se. Whatever the mechanism, the effect of added features might help to account for the fact that warningly col-ored prey often have several distinctive features (Guilford & Dawkins, 1991; see also box 5.1). For example, bees are bright yellow and have conspicuous black stripes and they buzz. The flip side of this issue is what happens to the memorability of a single feature when it is accompanied by other memorable features. Is the memorability of a bee's yellow color, for instance, affected by the presence of black stripes or buzzing? Research on *divided attention* in matching to sample addresses this question. Most experiments on this topic with animals have used pigeons as subjects and color and shape or orientation as the to-be-remembered features. An example is shown in figure 6.8. The essence of such experiments is to ask the pigeon "what color was it" or "what shape was it" and compare accuracy on element sample trials, when only color or only shape have to be processed, to accuracy on compound trials in which both color and shape are to be remembered. With two visual features, pigeons typically match an element more poorly on compound than on element trials, as if any one element is processed less well when the animal divides attention between it and another element (figure 6.8). Interestingly, however, the supe-riority of matching after element samples persists even when the sample is dis-played for a relatively long time, a finding not entirely consistent with the no-tion that the results simply reflect lack of time to process both features.

The kind of result displayed in figure 6.8 is not found with all combina-tions of features or all species. One feature may completely preempt process-ing: pigeons can symbolically match samples of sound, but performance falls to chance when a sample of sound is accompanied by a to-be-remembered vi-sual signal (Kraemer & Roberts, 1985). On the other extreme, no interference may accompany processing of multiple features. Pigeons match visual and spatial stimuli as well when they have appeared in a compound as when they have appeared separately—that is, they seem to be able to process both at the same time (Kraemer, Mazmanian, & Roberts, 1987). Species may differ in how they allocate processing among different kinds of features. Food-storing species of birds process spatial cues in preference to other cues to an object's identity whereas nonstoring species allocate processing more evenly (Brod-beck & Shettleworth, 1995).

Most experiments on the effects of divided attention on memory employ a relatively small set of stimuli, often two colors and two shapes, and the fea-tures are not combined in a consistent way—for example, the shape of the sample does not predict its color. Therefore the animal has to process and re-member features independently. This seems a very unnatural state of affairs. In the real world, the various features of objects are associated in a consistent way so that perceptual learning can assist retrieval of memories. One experi-mental example is provided by a series of studies of pigeons' ability to recog-nize travel slides seen just once before in a session. Pigeons can perform this task with fair accuracy when new slides are used in every session, but they do better when the same set of slides is used repeatedly. Perceptual learning en-hances performance with the repeatedly used slides (Macphail, Good, & Honey, 1995).

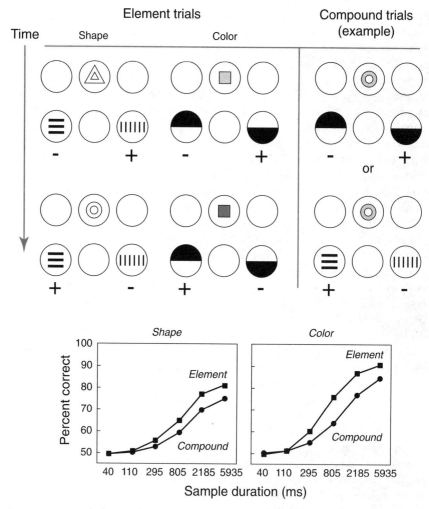

Figure 6.8. Symbolic matching to sample procedure used by Langley and Riley (1993) to test for divided attention in pigeons, together with their results. Two examples of compound trials are shown in which the sample is the same colored shape but memory for the color (*top*) or shape (*bottom*) is tested, unpredictably to the pigeon. Data redrawn from Langley and Riley (1993) with permission.

Chunking We have already seen that when several events have to be remembered at once, as in the radial maze, they are better remembered if they are more distinguishable from one another. At the same time, however, items are better remembered if they fall into subsets, or *chunks* of similar items. For example, people recall more of a long list of words if the words can be grouped into categories such as names of cars, flowers, and animals than if they are all unrelated. Pigeons learning to peck several displays in a fixed sequence do so more quickly if the displays are chunked by the experimenter—

for example, with three colors to be pecked first followed by two patterns (Terrace, 1991). Perhaps more interesting, rats behave as if they spontaneously chunk information on a radial maze. Macuda and Roberts (1995) exposed rats to a 12-arm radial maze with three different kinds of food: cheese, chocolate cereal, and pellets of rat chow. Each kind of food could be found on four different arms of the maze. Rats acquired accurate performance on the maze more quickly when the same food was assigned to each arm on every trial than when the locations of the different food types were not predictable from trial to trial. The rats in the former condition tended to visit the arms with cheese first, then those with cereal, then those with the least preferred pellets. Thus their visits were chunked by food type. This behavior might have reflected simply the predictability of the positions of the different food types and the rats' preferences, not anything special about their working memories. To check on this possibility, the rats that had learned the maze with fixed food types were tested next by selecting four arms for them to visit at the start of each trial, then allowing a free choice among all 12 arms of the maze. In the whole chunk condition, the four arms selected in the first part of the trial all had the same type of food; in the broken chunk condition, they included arms with all three of the foods. Arguably, rats in the whole chunk condition had to remember only one item of information whereas in the broken chunk condition they had to remember all four individual visited arms. As this notion predicts, rats in the whole chunk condition performed more accurately.

6.3.2 Events during the Retention Interval: Interference

Performance at T2 may fall if the interval between T1 and T2 contains events similar to the to-be-remembered target event, an effect called *retroactive interference* (*RI*). An example from habituation is shown in figure 6.9. The measured response was vasoconstriction in rabbits' ears; behaviorally, this would be evident in the rabbits' pricking up their ears to a novel sound. Memory for the habituating sound was evidenced in the fact that the rabbits responded less to the second sound in a trial if it was the same as the first sound than if it was different. Interference with memory for the habituating sound was produced by presenting a *distractor* stimulus such as a brief flash of light shortly after the habituating stimulus. In this case, response to the second tone of the series was undiminished whether or not it was the same as the first, habituating, tone. The rabbits apparently forgot the first tone. Comparable effects have been demonstrated in pigeons and monkeys performing delayed matching to sample (Jarvik, Goldfarb, & Carley, 1969; Roberts & Grant, 1978). For example, if the lights in the testing chamber are usually off, turning them on during the retention interval disrupts pigeons' matching performance (Maki, Moe, & Bierley, 1977). In contrast, similar manipulations during the retention interval between the first and last four choices in a radial maze have no effect on performance (W. A. Roberts, 1981). This result does not reflect a species difference: pigeons performing delayed alternation in a T-maze are also resistant to retroactive interference (Olson & Maki, 1983). Similarly, if

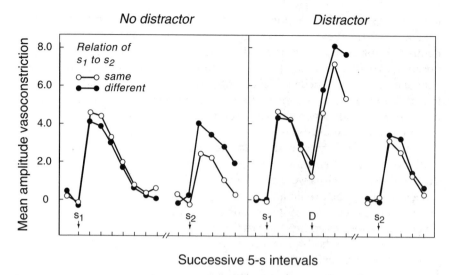

Figure 6.9. Demonstration of retroactive interference produced by a distractor stimulus (D) between successive presentations (S1 and S2) of a tone to which rabbits are being habituated. Reaction to the tone is measured as the temporal pattern of vasoconstriction in the ear. Redrawn from Whitlow (1975) with permission.

marsh tits (*Parus palustris*) store two batches of seeds in a laboratory aviary, memory for the second batch stored interferes little if at all with memory for earlier stores (see also Crystal & Shettleworth, 1994; Shettleworth & Krebs, 1982). These findings suggest the possibility that different kinds of memories differ in susceptibility to RI (box 6.1).

In *proactive interference* (*PI*), memory for later events is degraded by memory for earlier ones. There is an example of PI in figure 6.7: rats' accuracy on a radial maze is worse on later trials of a single day than on the first. PI can also be produced by events within a trial, as when the sample in a delayed matching trial is immediately preceded by a different sample. Delayed matching to sample experiments with pigeons have provided the most data on what influences interference (Edhouse & White, 1988). Interference effects can build up over a long time. For example, monkeys' accuracy at matching to sample with the same set of stimuli in every session fell over many sessions, but it shot up when a new set of stimuli was introduced (Wright, 1989; Wright, Urcuioli, & Sands, 1986). This may be another example of the more general beneficial effect of novelty on processing. When lists of items have to be remembered, the interplay of RI and PI produces the *serial position curves* discussed in section 6.4.4

6.3.3 Conditions at T2: The Importance of Context

Memory for the significance of certain cues should be independent of the current temporal and spatial context. Mother, a dangerous predator, or a tasty bit

---

Box 6.1. Birds' Memory for Songs

Many birds learn the songs they sing (see section 10.3). In some species, songs heard in the first summer are not sung until the next spring. Thus these song memories must be retained for eight months or more (Marler & Peters, 1981). Studies of birds that learn a variety of different songs, like nightingales (Hultsch, 1993) and some wrens (Kroodsma & Pickert, 1980), have shown that some of the conditions affecting memory for other sorts of material also affect memory for songs. Nightingales exposed to numerous strings of training songs later produce the learned songs in "packages" of songs that occurred close together in a string, a phenomenon similar to chunking (Hultsch & Todt, 1989). Speeding or slowing the pace of training songs showed that the songs forming a package need to be heard within a certain time window. Massing songs too much in time does not increase the number per package, suggesting a limit on short-term memory capacity during package formation (Hultsch, 1992; but see Podos, 1996)

Birds also use song memory to recognize their neighbors (see box 4.1), and this memory, too, can be very long-lasting. Individual males of some territorial species occupy the same territory year after year. Male hooded warblers returning in the spring recognize the songs of old neighbors they have not heard singing for 8 to 10 months (Godard, 1991). In a field study of great tits, long-term retention of memories for former neighbors appeared to create proactive interference, reducing the ease of learning songs of new neighbors (McGregor & Avery, 1986). The idea that the capacity for acquiring new song memories might be limited was examined in the laboratory by training male song sparrows to discriminate among 32 different pairs of songs (Stoddard, Beecher, Loesche, & Campbell, 1992). Later discriminations were learned just as fast as early ones, providing no suggestion of proactive interference or limited long-term memory capacity in this species. Memories for neighbors' songs that a bird acquires as an adult may have different properties from early song memories acquired for use in song production. A large number of them may be acquired at any time of life, even in a species that normally learns only a few songs for singing in just its first year (McGregor & Avery, 1986). Study of the neural basis of song learning (e.g., de Voogl, 1994) may well provide further evidence for the possibility of two song memory systems.

---

of food should be recognized wherever and whenever they are encountered. On the other hand, the temporal and spatial context may predict what memories are most likely to be useful and therefore ought to be retrieved (Anderson & Schooler, 1991). In general, evidence of memory for an event is more likely to be found the more similar the current context to the event's original context. For example, a predator may be more strongly responded to in the environment where predators have been seen before than in a new environment. A well-studied laboratory example of such an effect is the enhancement of startle responses in the presence of cues associated with shock (review in Davis, Falls, Campeau, & Kim, 1993). Time of day can also be a powerful contextual cue for memory retrieval. Effects of time of day on memory retrieval exemplify the more general phenomenon of *state-dependent learning*, also seen when learning acquired under the influence of a drug is less evident in the drug-free state or the reverse (review in Gordon & Klein, 1994).

The importance of context in guiding memory retrieval is well established (Gordon & Klein, 1994). The similar effects of context on memory in non-humans are summarized in four principles (Bouton, 1993, pp. 90–91): (1) "Contextual stimuli guide retrieval." (2) "Time is a context." This principle amounts to a theoretical assertion that the ability to retrieve memories declines with time because the present temporal context becomes increasingly different from the original one. (3) "Different memories depend differently on context." As suggested above, events of great significance for survival seem to be remembered better than less important events. As one might expect from this adaptationist prediction, the effects of fear conditioning are especially well retained and transferred to new contexts. (4). "Interference occurs at output." That is to say, failure to show evidence of retention reflects not the absence of memory but the lack of appropriate context. Several standard paradigms in which animals learn first one thing then another, competing, thing can be seen as studies of interference (Bouton, 1993). For example, when conditioning is followed by extinction, animals may not have lost the memory of conditioning. Rather, they have two competing memories and will evidence one or the other, according to the current context. Memory of conditioning may be reinstated by noncontingent presentations of the original reinforcer, part of the original training context (see chapter 3).

Behavior in experiments on memory may change when the context changes for reasons unrelated to changes in the memories being tested. For example, animals placed in a new environment may explore it before performing the previously reinforced response, and the resulting delay in responding may wrongly be interpreted as evidence of forgetting (Devenport, 1989). The typical experimental procedure of removing an animal from a radial maze or other apparatus as soon as it has collected any programmed reinforcement means that it must confine its exploration of the apparatus to the time before it collects the reward. Entries to unrewarded arms of a radial maze ("errors") following a change of experimental context might be evidence of the rats exploring their new context rather than indicative of forgetting. To test this notion, Devenport (1989) trained rats on a reference memory task in which a single arm of the maze, marked with a carpeted floor, was rewarded on each trial. The rat was placed at the far end of another, randomly chosen arm and had to walk to the central platform and enter the baited arm. Rats in one group were removed from the maze as soon as they ate the food, as in conventional procedures. Rats in the other group were given extra time to explore the maze *after* they consumed the reward. The rats given extra time reduced their errors per trial more quickly during acquisition than the rats without extra time. As a result, they had no more total time on the maze than the rats without extra time. When the maze was moved to a different room to test the effects of context change, accuracy stayed high in the extra time group while accuracy fell in the group forced to confine their exploration to the period before finding the reward. These results are consistent with the hypothesis that neither group had forgotten the location of the food and the "errors" of the group without extra time resulted from exploring their new surroundings.

6.4 Species Differences in Memory?

"Elephants never forget." The notion that some animals might be especially good at remembering is a pervasive one. From the days of Hunter's (1913; see also section 6.2.3) research on delayed reactions, psychologists have regarded the ability to remember something for a long time as evidence of great intelligence. Biologists struck by some species' apparent reliance on long-lasting or capacious memories have also accepted that some animals can remember more things or remember them for longer than other animals. In operational terms, this means that some species should perform better on a given test of memory than others. Given some of the material in chapters 1 and 5, readers of this book should be suspicious of this notion. However, from the early days of research on animal cognition, there has been a whole series of research programs designed to test it. These illustrate very well the difficulty in getting hard evidence for what may seem an obvious conclusion, as well as some problems that afflict comparative research on any aspect of cognition. This section of the chapter reviews four sorts of tests of the notion that some animals remember things differently from other animals. They are discussed in order of increasing sophistication so that at the end of the section we can better assess in what ways, if any, memory in different species can meaningfully be compared.

6.4.1 Memory Duration and Capacity

In chapter 3 of *The Descent of Man and Selection in Relation to Sex*, Darwin (1871) adduced evidence for evolutionary continuity between humans and other species from all the "mental powers" that other species share with humans. One of these is memory. One example of memory was provided by the behavior of Darwin's own dog when Darwin returned from his voyage on the *Beagle* after an absence of five years and two days. Although normally unfriendly to strangers, the dog ran out of the barn when Darwin called and greeted his master as if he had never been away. This and Darwin's other anecdotes suggesting that animals can sometimes remember for a very long time are among the first contributions to a still-growing body of research on the persistence and capacity of memory in different species.

There is much evidence that the results of simple instrumental training procedures are retained even when animals are removed from the experiment for months or years (see Vaughan & Greene, 1984). It does not seem very remarkable that well-learned habits are well retained, especially when the subjects typically do not have much else to learn during the retention interval. In recent years, interest has been directed more at two examples in which large numbers of discriminations between complex visual stimuli can be remembered for long periods. One of these is Vaughan and Greene's (1984) study of pigeons' discriminations between large numbers of photographic slides, reviewed in chapter 5. In one of their experiments, accurate performance with 320 slides (160 positive, 160 negative, divided into four sets of each) was retained for over two years. Initial performance after a similar retention interval was somewhat worse if the birds had originally learned a series of different discriminations involving the same slides in different orientations. This could be interpreted as resulting from interfering memories. Even here, however, performance improved quickly after the retention interval—that is, the birds showed substantial *savings*.

Another example of persistent, large-capacity memory in birds that has sometimes been compared with Vaughan and Greene's (e.g., Vaughan & Greene, 1984) is Clark's nutcrackers' memories for the locations of their buried caches. In the field, these birds bury several thousand caches of pine seeds in the late summer and retrieve them up to six months or more later (see box 1.4 and section 6.4.3). Nutcrackers performed above chance levels in the laboratory when retrieving 18–25 caches 285 days (9–10 months) after making them. Performance was worse at this retention interval than at 183 days (6 months), a more realistic interval from the point of view of what happens in the field (Balda & Kamil, 1992).

Remembering 25 locations for 9 months is not as impressive as remembering 320 slides for 2 years. Does this mean that the excellent memory of food-storing birds is a myth, that they are outclassed by ordinary laboratory pigeons? Clearly not. Absolute memory duration is not a meaningful measure when comparing species tested in two such different tasks as those experienced by the pigeons and the nutcrackers. For instance, one involves spatial information, the other two-dimensional visual patterns. Perhaps most important, the food-caching bird has just a brief encounter with each to-be-remembered site, as it pokes its beak into a hole to bury the pine seeds, whereas Vaughan and Greene's pigeons were trained extensively. The pigeons had the first set of slides for a total of 52 sessions, in each of which every slide was shown twice for a minimum of 10 seconds each time. Clearly, the conditions for memory differed considerably from those experienced by the nutcrackers. While both sets of data can be taken, along with the story of Darwin's dog, as evidence that animals may have remarkably durable memories, they tell us nothing about whether one animal remembers more or for longer than another.

Even testing animals in the field is no guarantee that experimental details do not influence the results. In the first experiments designed to test memory of food-storing birds in the field, marsh tits (*Parus palustris*) in Britain stored sunflower seeds collected from a feeder (Cowie, Krebs, & Sherry, 1981; Stevens & Krebs, 1986). Items were retrieved by the individuals that stored them, but all retrieval was recorded within 2–3 days and only about 30% of the items stored were retrieved by the bird that stored them (Stevens & Krebs, 1986). This is not exactly long-term memory for large numbers of items. However, it now appears that birds treat spatially concentrated sources of large food items differently from natural food items. Small seeds and bits of insect matter stored naturally by willow tits (*P. montanus*) in Sweden disappeared gradually over a period of 2–3 months (figure 6.10). Predation on these items was low, and it took about six weeks after storage for the rate of

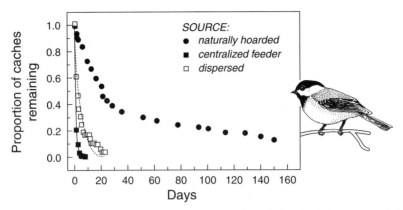

Figure 6.10. Willow tits' rate of retrieving food items hoarded in the field varies with the original source of these items. Redrawn from Brodin (1994) with permission.

disappearance of the stored items to fall as low as the experimentally determined background pilfering rate, indicating that memory was being used for at least six weeks (Brodin, 1994).

6.4.2 Comparative Tests of Delayed Response

The first major research program designed to compare memory in different species was begun by Hunter (1913), using the delayed response task described in section 6.2.3. Its purpose was to compare species in "intelligence" by measuring the maximum delay at which they could still perform above chance levels on this task. As readers may already suspect, this enterprise was beset by the same problems as the comparative studies of successive reversal and learning set reviewed in chapter 5. The results of much of the early research were summarized by Maier and Schneirla (1935/1964, table 30, p. 449). Rats, cats, dogs, raccoons, and five species of primates could all perform correctly without observable orienting responses during the delay. However, the maximum delay possible varied drastically among studies. For example, for chimpanzees it ranged between 2 minutes and 48 hours, but rats were hardly worse, with a range between 11 seconds and 24 hours in different studies. Obvious differences among the procedures did not seem to account for the pattern of results within a given species. Maier and Schneirla therefore concluded "differences in results obtained in the various experiments on delayed reaction are artifacts and not measures of a special ability to delay a reaction. As a result, the delayed reaction cannot be regarded as a measure of some higher process, or a demonstration of ideational behavior" (p. 453). More recent research has not altered this conclusion (Macphail, 1982). Comparing species on the shape of an entire forgetting curve, as in figure 6.11, does not eliminate the problem, either. Making the task easier or harder for a particular species simply raises or lowers its curve relative to those of other species. The influence of such contextual variables serves to underline

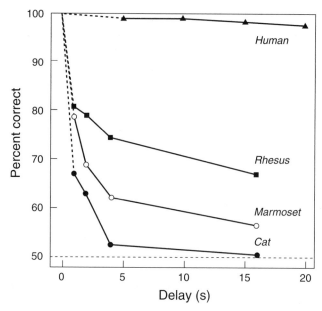

Figure 6.11. Forgetting curves for four mammalian species on a spatial delayed response test. Chance performance is 50% correct. Redrawn from Miles (1971) with permission.

Macphail's (1982, p. 275) conclusion that "delayed response tasks will not provide unique rankings of species and cannot be used as a measure of general intelligence." Nor, we may add, of general ability to remember.

6.4.3 Spatial Memory in Food-storing Birds

The comparative study of memory in food-storing and nonstoring species of birds, introduced in chapter 1 (box 1.4), as an example of the ecological or synthetic approach to comparative cognition, also involves comparing forgetting curves of different species in similar testing situations. So isn't this program subject to the same kinds of problems with contextual variables as the anthropocentric comparative study of delayed response?

In the ecological or synthetic approach to animal intelligence (Kamil, 1988) species differences are predicted from ecological considerations and tested for in more than one way. If several tests of the same cognitive process reveal the same ranking of species, this indicates that they do not differ merely in response to some contextual variable peculiar to one or two of the tests. Confidence in this conclusion can be increased by comparing the species of interest on tests in which they are predicted to differ in different ways. If species A is predicted to do better than species B on tests of spatial memory, and the species are never compared on anything other than tests of spatial memory, it is impossible to know whether A outperforms B because it has a specifically better spatial memory, because it has better memory in general,

Table 6.1. Rankings of four food-storing corvids on food-storing, hippocampus, and four tests of memory.

	Clark's Nutcracker	Pinyon Jay	Mexican Jay	Scrub Jay
Reliance on storing	1	2	3	4
Relative hippocampal volume	1	2	3	2
Cache retrieval accuracy	1	2?		3
Radial maze performance	1	1	2	2
Spatial DNMTS	1	2	2	2
Color DNMTS	2	1	1	2

Note: Same rank indicates no significant difference between the given species on that test. References are as mentioned in the text. DNMTS = Delayed nonmatching to sample. Blank = not tested.

because it adapts better to the laboratory, or for some other reason (see also Shettleworth & Hampton, 1998; Lefebvre & Giraldeau, 1996).

One of the most thorough and successful applications of this approach is the body of research testing the hypothesis that food-storing corvids (jays, crows, and nutcrackers) that store more food in the wild have better spatial memory (table 6.1; see also box 1.4 in this book and Shettleworth, 1995). The star of this show is Clark's nutcracker (*Nucifraga columbiana*), which makes a few thousand pine seed caches every fall and retrieves them throughout the winter and following spring. The dunce is the scrub jay (*Aphelacoma coerulescens*), a bird much less dependent on stored food. In between are the pinyon jay (*Gymnorhynus cyanocephalus*) and the Mexican or gray-breasted jay (*A. ultramarina*). Pinyon jays are intense food-storers but are thought to be less dependent on stored food than Clark's nutcrackers; Mexican jays are thought to store more than scrub jays because they live at higher elevations (Kamil, Balda, & Olson, 1994). These birds' hippocampal volume correlates pretty well, though not perfectly, with dependence on stored food, as shown in table 6.1, second row.

Clark's nutcrackers, pinyon jays, and scrub jays have been given a series of tests of spatial memory ranging from retrieving stored food in the laboratory to delayed spatial nonmatching to sample in an operant chamber. One might expect that species differences in memory related to ecology are most likely to be found in situations most like the natural situation in which the memory supposedly functions. However, the ranking of species is fairly consistent across all the tests that have been employed (table 6.1). All four species were tested on a radial mazelike task in which the birds had to remember sites in a large room like that used for the caching experiment for up to 24 hours (figure 6.12). Nutcrackers and pinyon jays consistently performed better than birds of the other two species. However, their advantage was greatest at the shortest retention intervals. This is surprising because the species are assumed to differ in the wild in their ability to retain information for a very long time. This might mean that the species differ in initial processing of spatial information rather than ability to retain it (Kamil, Balda, & Olson, 1994). How-

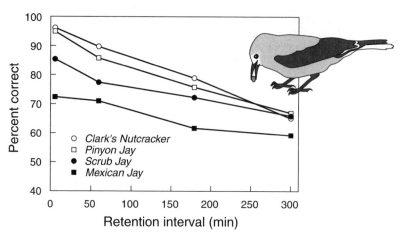

Figure 6.12. Performance of four species of corvids on a radial-maze–like task as a function of retention interval between the first and last four choices. Retention intervals were randomly intermixed, unpredictably to the birds. Percent correct is based on the last four choices. Redrawn from Kamil et al. (1994) with permission.

ever, differences in initial processing alone should be reflected in forgetting curves that are parallel rather than converging, as in figure 6.5.

The third test in this series was even more remote from food storing in setting, type of information, and retention intervals than the radial maze. This was a test of spatial delayed nonmatching to sample in a two-key operant chamber (Olson, Kamil, Balda, & Nims, 1995). After the birds were trained with minimal retention intervals, the retention interval was increased gradually for each individual as long as it was performing above a standard criterion level. Thus, each bird had the opportunity to show the best it could do: birds with good memory would have the retention interval increased faster than birds with poor memory. The nutcrackers performed vastly better than any of the other three species, which performed similarly to each other (figure 6.13). Food-storing birds need to remember an extraordinarily large number of items of spatial information, as well as to remember locations for a long time. Accordingly, when Clark's nutcrackers and scrub jays were compared in memory capacity in operant spatial nonmatching, nutcrackers again outshone the birds that store less food in the wild (Olson, 1991).

The results decribed so far are consistent with at least three hypotheses: nutcrackers have better spatial memory in some way than the other three species, they have better memory in general, or some contextual variable common to all three sorts of experiments favors the nutcrackers. Here is where it is necessary to test some ability on which the species are predicted *not* to differ. The same birds whose data are shown in figure 6.13 were tested on delayed nonmatching with samples of color (Olson, Kamil, Balda, & Nims, 1995). Pinyon jays and Mexican jays learned this task fastest and achieved the longest retention intervals (figure 6.13), indicating that the su-

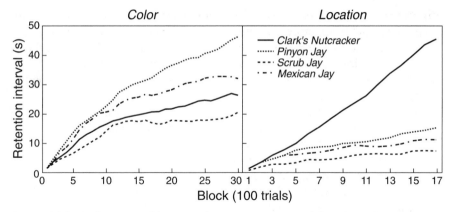

Figure 6.13. Performance of four corvid species on operant delayed matching with samples of color or location. Performance is retention interval attained as a function of trials when the retention interval was increased for each bird whenever it performed above a criterion level. Redrawn from Olson et al. (1995) with permission.

perior performance of nutcrackers is not general but may be confined to spatial tasks.

Table 6.1 reveals that the four species are not always ranked in precisely the same way. A possible explanation for reversals of rank is that the different tasks actually emphasize slightly different cognitive abilities. For instance, some tasks may emphasize rapid encoding and others good retention, while yet other tasks may require superior resistance to interference in memory. This suggestion raises a problem for the ecological program, however, since that program hinges on being able to test the same ecologically relevant cognitive ability in a variety of different ways. If food-storing birds were to display unusually capacious and persistent memory only for locations where they had stored food, the program outlined by Kamil (1988) would not work. It tells us something important about the organization of memory that species differences consistent with the requirements for spatial memory in the wild appear in situations other than food storing. For instance, the fact that nutcrackers excel in spatial delayed matching to sample in an operant chamber might mean that they differ from the other corvids tested in the early stages of spatial memory encoding or storage.

It is important here to keep in mind the distinction between performance in a task and the cognitive mechanisms that underlie that performance. There may be more than one way to retrieve a lot of caches. Encoding spatial information more accurately, retaining it longer, or being able to keep more items of spatial information in memory could all, singly or together, be selected because they enhance the ability to retrieve stored food. Noncognitive modifications could play a role, too. More efficient food-storing behavior could evolve, or ways of storing that make cache sites more memorable. The cognitive and neural mechanisms that underlie the ability to retrieve stored caches might differ in different groups of species. There are many examples in which the same function is served by different modifications in different kinds of animals. Fur and feathers help maintain body temperature in mammals and birds, but reptiles and amphibians have evolved sophisticated behavioral thermoregulation instead. Mammals that do not sweat cool themselves off in other ways, as by panting (dogs) or spreading saliva on their tails and bodies (rats).

Any adaptationist hypothesis demands testing on more than one group of four species (see chapter 1). The prediction that food-storing species have better spatial memory than other species has also been tested with birds of the family Paridae, the chickadees and titmice, but the pattern of results has not been so obviously consistent with the hypothesis that spatial memory varies with dependence on stored food (Shettleworth, 1995). The more general notion that greater use of spatial information in the wild should be correlated with enhanced spatial ability (and a larger hippocampus) has also been tested by examining possible sex differences, as discussed in chapter 1. Sex differences in spatial behavior are also associated with nest parasitism in birds (Sherry, Jacobs, & Gaulin, 1992). Female Eastern cowbirds (*Molothrus ater*) lay their eggs in other birds' nests. They have an elaborate sequence of behavior that involves "prospecting" extensively for possible host nests and apparently memorizing their locations for later use. Since male cowbirds do not need to use spatial memory in this important way, they should have smaller hippocampi and less well-developed spatial memory than females. The first part of this prediction appears to be correct, for Eastern cowbirds (Sherry, Forbes, Khurgel, & Ivy, 1993) and for some Argentinian species (Reboreda, Clayton, & Kacelnik, 1996), but behavioral tests of possible sex differences in memory in these animals have yet to be reported.

6.4.4 List Learning in Pigeons, Rats, Monkeys, and People

A classic observation in studies of human memory is the *serial position effect*: memory for items at the beginning and end of a list is typically better than for items in the middle. The typical U-shaped curve describing accuracy as a function of position in the list thus contains both *primacy* (better performance with items at the beginning) and *recency* effects (better performance for items at the end). Since the serial position effect is well established in humans, any attempt to test for it in other species is frank anthropocentrism. Nevertheless, a recent body of comparative work on list learning illustrates how asking a rather nonecological question about more or less arbitrarily chosen, unrelated species can lead to important insights into general mechanisms of memory. This is the research of Wright and his colleagues on *serial probe recognition* of visual stimuli in pigeons, monkeys, and people (Wright, 1989; Wright & Rivera, 1997, report similar results for sounds). In the serial probe recognition procedure they used, the subject sees a series of visual images, the to-be-remembered list, followed after a retention interval by a single probe image. If the probe is the same as an item in the list, the subject is reinforced for mak-

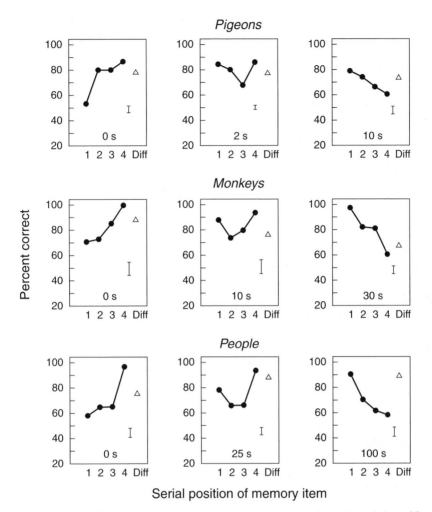

Figure 6.14. Serial probe recognition in pigeons, monkeys, and people with lists of four items as a function of the position of the tested item in the list and the retention interval between the last item and the test (times indicated in each panel). Triangles are accuracy of indicating "different" on trials in which the probe was an item that had not appeared in the just-presented list. Redrawn from Wright et al. (1985) with permission.

ing one response—say, pecking the right key; if it is different from any item in the list, an alternative response is reinforced. Typically, only one item is probed after each list so that memory for the first, second, and so on list position is tested in a standard way. (Methodological issues in this area are discussed by Gaffan, 1992, and Wright, 1994.)

In pigeons, monkeys, and people, recency is evident at the shortest retention interval tested, and recency gradually gives way to primacy as the retention interval lengthens (figure 6.14). The classic U-shaped serial position curve therefore appears only at intermediate retention intervals. The three species differ, however, in the range of retention intervals over which this dynamic pattern appears. "Long" for pigeons is 10 seconds; for the monkeys, 30 seconds; and for the humans, it takes 100 seconds for recency to be replaced completely by primacy. The time scale may also depend on the task. Rats tested on the radial maze by requiring them to discriminate between one of four arms already entered and an unentered arm show the same sort of dynamic serial position curves displayed in figure 6.14, but they change shape over 16 minutes (Bolhuis & van Kampen, 1988; see also Harper, McLean, & Dalrymple-Alford, 1993).

A striking feature of the data in figure 6.14 is that as time passes the items from the beginning of the list are responded to more accurately. For instance, on the first item pigeons are at chance on an immediate test but about 80% correct after 10 seconds. One way to understand this effect, as well as the whole pattern of dynamic change in the serial position curve, is to suggest that at short retention intervals the early items suffer from retroactive interference from the last items, which are still held in primary or short-term memory at that time. Such retroactive interference must dissipate rapidly, perhaps as items move from short-term to long-term memory. Storage in long-term memory has been thought to be accomplished by *rehearsal*. In humans, rehearsal may be just what the word implies: the person silently repeats the item, thereby giving it longer exposure. The importance of rehearsal for long-term storage can be demonstrated by inserting *distractors* between items, curtailing rehearsal by making the subject process new, irrelevant material. However, the effect of a distractor on habituation shown in figure 6.9 obviously cannot reflect disruption of verbal rehearsal because the subjects were rabbits.

There are two problems with using the straightforward notion of rehearsal to explain the emergence of a primacy effect in the experiment of Wright et al. (1985). The first was already mentioned: performance on the early items improves in absolute terms as time passes. If the items were available to be rehearsed at the shortest retention intervals, shouldn't they have been recognized at this retention interval, too? The second problem is that all three species were tested with complex meaningless patterns. For the monkeys and pigeons, these were travel slides; for the humans, photographs of kaleidoscope patterns were used, presumably putting them in the same position as the nonhumans as far as being able readily to name and verbally rehearse the to-be-remembered items. Thus the data in figure 16.14 indicate that the primacy effect can be obtained without items being verbally rehearsed.

To show more directly that the serial position effect in humans can be dissociated from effects of rehearsal, Wright and his colleagues (Wright, 1989; Wright, et al., 1990) turned to testing the effects of the interval between successive items in the list, *the interstimulus interval* or *ISI*. People perform better with verbal material as the interstimulus interval is lengthened, presumably because there is greater opportunity to rehearse each item as it comes along. On this reasoning, interstimulus interval should have no effect if the items cannot be given verbal labels and thereby rehearsed. To test this prediction, one group of subjects was trained to recognize and name a group of kaleidoscope patterns. A control group was preexposed to the same patterns for an equal amount of time but merely required to identify their colors. The group that had learned names for the patterns later performed better on list learning with those patterns and showed a prominent interstimulus interval effect, lacking in the control group. Nevertheless, both groups had similar serial position functions, with sharp primacy effects. These results, together with those of the pigeons and monkeys, indicate that rehearsal in the sense of verbally repeating the name of an item cannot be the general cause for the primacy effect. As an example of the comparative study of cognition, this research is unusual because it started from an anthropocentric question (do other species show serial position effects like people?) but wound up answering a general question about memory mechanisms in a situation in which people are made to behave like nonverbal animals.

6.4.5 Summary and Conclusions

The discussion of comparative studies of list learning has anticipated the next major section of the chapter, on theories of memory. First, however, we can briefly summarize the results of comparative studies of memory. The section has discussed some of the methodological problems involved in comparing different species' memory and reviewed in most detail one example of the ecological approach to species comparison and one example of the anthropocentric approach. Neither reveals any qualitative differences between species but rather quantitative adjustments in mechanisms common to all species being tested. Analogously, the food-storing species being studied by Kamil, Balda, and their colleagues differ quantitatively in a number of morphological and behavioral characteristics relevant to food storing. For instance, the Clark's nutcracker breeds exceptionally early, feeding its young on food stored the previous autumn. It has a sublingual pouch, a unique structure that allows it to carry large numbers of pine seeds to suitable storage sites. It also has an exceptionally long, sharp beak used for prying seeds out of unripe pine cones (VanderWall & Balda, 1981) Quantitative, adaptive, species differences in aspects of memory are to be expected on functional grounds, just as in other characters.

6.5 Contents of Memory

6.5.1 Issues

Does memory consist simply of the persistence of neural activity set up when a remembered event is first perceived—that is, a *stimulus trace*, or is the direct effect of a stimulus transformed in some way for storage in memory? This is one of the most investigated theoretical questions about memory. A related question is whether forgetting is the result of the passive fading of a trace or of some more active process. The answer to this question almost certainly depends on the species and type of event. In some species and systems, memory may well be no more than the passive decay of neural activity. In other cases, as we will see, it may reflect the active maintenance of a highly derived, situation-dependent representation of the to-be-remembered event. How events are represented in memory and what causes them to be forgotten have been most thoroughly investigated in nonhuman species in pigeons performing delayed matching to sample tasks. The earliest data seemed to show that traces of samples decayed passively and independently within a relatively short time (Grant, 1981). However, with the accumulation of data from more and more elaborate tests, this notion has evolved into one in which information about the identity of the sample is transformed and actively maintained in short-term memory.

6.5.2 How Are Events Represented in Memory?

Retrospective. vs. Prospective Coding   A stimulus trace is a *retrospective code*. Intuitively, performance based on stimulus traces results from mentally "looking back" (retrospecting) at recent traces. In a *prospective code,* in contrast, information is transformed at the time of input into some representation of what is to be done at the time of test—that is, the code looks forward or prospects. In simple red/green matching to sample, for instance, retrospective coding of the red sample is a trace corresponding to the experience of red, whereas prospective coding of the same sample amounts to an instruction, "peck red on the test." Notice that it is impossible to form a prospective code without information about what the memory will be used for. The most primitive and general kind of memory code therefore must be retrospective. Only when the same items are tested over and over in the same kind of way, either during an individual's lifetime or during evolution, is prospective coding possible.

The most extensive investigations of the conditions favoring one form of code or the other have been done with pigeons performing various forms of symbolic matching to sample. In *many-to-one* matching, each of several different samples is associated with the same comparison stimulus. For example, Grant (1982) trained pigeons to choose a red comparison stimulus after samples of red, 20 pecks, or a brief presentation of food and to choose green following a sample of green, 1 peck, or no food. One might imagine that in such a case there would be some advantage to recoding all the samples associated with a single comparison in a common way—for example, "peck red." To test this idea, Grant presented one, two, or three samples in succession before the retention interval. Consistent with the idea that samples associated with a common comparison are coded in the same way, birds performed more accurately with multiple samples regardless of whether or not they were the same sample (e.g., two food presentations) or just samples associated with the same comparison (e.g., one food presentation and one presentation of the red key).

Although pigeons seem to have coded samples prospectively in Grant's situation, this does not mean they always code information prospectively in matching to sample, let alone in general. For one thing, initial learning of any kind would be impossible without retrospective coding. As with many issues in psychology, one should be asking not the yes/no question," Is coding retrospective *or* prospective?" but rather "*Under what conditions* is coding retrospective and under what conditions prospective?" One condition favoring retrospective coding is the use of highly discriminable samples. For pigeons, colors on the pecking key are much more salient than lines of different orientations. Colors seem to be coded retrospectively even under conditions favoring prospective coding of less discriminable stimuli such as lines (Zentall, Urcuioli, Jagielo, & Jackson-Smith, 1989).

Under some conditions, the type of code used appears to switch within a trial. Near the beginning of each trial, a rat on a radial maze has to keep in working memory only a few items of information, corresponding to the arms already visited on that trial. As the trial progresses, the rat has more and more arms to remember. Thus, it ought to do worse and worse in successive choices. In fact, however, rats tested repeatedly on a 12-arm radial maze are least accurate on their middle choices (Cook, Brown, & Riley, 1985). Increasing accuracy in the last few choices may reflect a switch from retrospective coding to prospective coding. If the arms are coded in terms of whether they are still unentered, there is less information to keep in memory as the end of the trial approaches. Interestingly, an analogous phenomenon has been found in people performing a radial-maze-like task (Kesner & DeSpain, 1988) and in pigeons in the operant radial maze analogue (Zentall, Steirn, & Jackson-Smith, 1990). An alternative interpretation of it, based on a signal detection analysis like that outlined in box 6.2, suggests that the animal's choice criterion changes as the trial progresses (Brown, Wheeler, & Riley, 1989).

A good deal of research has been done on the type of code used in common laboratory tests of animal memory (Grant & Spetch, 1994; Urcuioli & Zentall, 1992). Clearly, the answer depends not only on the structure of the situation, such as whether it is one-to-many or many-to-one matching, but also on the type of events to be remembered. In tests of memory using the radial maze, for example, an important issue is how spatial information is coded in the first place: as a map of the maze, a list of locations, or in some other way (see chapter 7). In general, however, it is difficult to think of many, even any, natural situations in which an animal would repeatedly encounter exactly the same bits of information and have exactly the same later choices dependent on what had happened earlier. It is not clear what prospective coding of short-term memories would be good for in the world outside the laboratory. Nevertheless, the distinction between prospective and retrospective processes has wider applicability to cognitive processes (Wasserman, 1986). For instance, prospection can be seen as the general ability to use information in memory to anticipate and make plans, an issue discussed in chapter 11.

Box 6.2. Memory as Signal Detection

Just as in studies of perception, in studies of memory the behavior taken as evidence of the underlying cognitive process being studied can also occur for other reasons. For instance, the pigeon in a delayed matching experiment might prefer to peck a red key rather than a green one, regardless of which had just been presented as a sample, or a rat might prefer to visit some arms of a radial maze rather than others. Signal detection analysis (see chapter 2) again provides a way to distinguish such response biases from effects on memory. By analogy with perception, in the simple case of two possible sample stimuli the animal's job can be seen as to distinguish which has the larger value along some continuum of trace strength. With the passage of time, the distribution of trace strengths from the most recent stimulus moves toward that for past stimuli (figure B6.2a).

➡

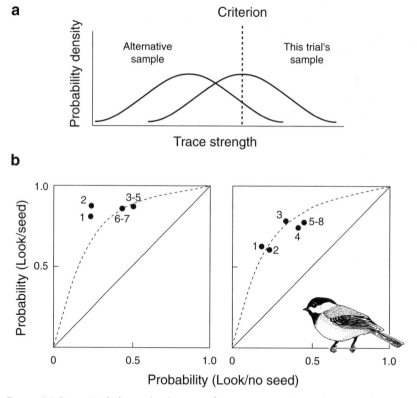

Figure B6.2. a. Underlying distributions of memory trace strength assumed in analyzing performance in a test of memory as signal detection. As time passes, the distributions will overlap more and more. b. An example in which two individual marsh tits' performance in a test of memory (looking into sites where seeds could be stored in artificial trees) is converted into ROC curves. The numbers beside the data points indicate the number of times that individual had used the storage sites in a series of 12 trials—i.e., higher numbers correspond to a greater bias toward visiting the site. Redrawn from Shettleworth and Krebs (1982) with permission.

Box 6.2. (*continued*)

Plotting results of manipulations thought to affect memory as ROC curves allows effects on response bias, like those created by stimulus preferences or changes in reinforcer value, to be distinguished from genuine effects on memory. Figure B6.2b shows an example from a study in which marsh tits' memory for the locations of stored seeds was tested in the laboratory (Shettleworth & Krebs, 1982). Each bird was tested 12 times by allowing it to store 10 seeds in any of about 100 holes drilled in artificial trees and retrieve them two hours later. Most of the birds used certain sites for storage quite often and others relatively seldom. To distinguish these site preferences from effects of memory, we looked at each bird's probability of visiting a site while retrieving seeds on trials when a seed had been stored there (hits) and on trials when it had not (false alarms), yielding the ROC curves in the figure. Over and above the birds' preferences for visiting some sites more than others, there was a clear effect of memory (i.e., d' was positive): a site of any preference value was more likely to be visited when a seed had been stored there two hours earlier than when it was empty.

Signal detection theory has many uses in the analysis of animal as well as human memory (Marston, 1996). A particularly clever and revealing example is the work of Wixted (1993) on pigeons' delayed matching with samples of food and no food. Also worthy of attention is Blough's (1996) analysis of the sources of errors in delayed matching tasks.

6.5.3 Directed Forgetting

One way to test whether forgetting is merely a matter of passive trace decay or a more active process is to see whether it can be brought under stimulus control. People can be told to remember some things and forget others, and such instructions do influence later recall (Roper & Zentall, 1993). In similar *directed forgetting* experiments with nonverbal species, the role of instructions to forget or remember is played by distinctive stimuli inserted into the retention interval (figure 6.15). Presenting the cues to remember or forget after the to-be-remembered or to-be-forgotten sample stimulus means that when the sample is presented the animal does not know whether or not memory of that sample will be tested. This ensures that any effects of the cues cannot be attributed to effects on processing the sample. But there are a lot of differences between "forget" and "remember" trials. After a forget cue, the animal is never reinforced; it does not have to do anything but wait for the next trial. This might teach it to turn away from the pecking keys and walk around the testing chamber as soon as it sees a "forget" cue. No wonder, then, that performance may be poor on occasional test trials. In addition, the unusualness of these tests alone could be enough to degrade performance below that seen with remember cues, through generalization decrement.

In general, pigeons do perform worse on tests of memory following cues to forget than following cues to remember (Roper & Zentall, 1993). But it has proved difficult to get solid evidence that this effect represents differences in memory processing following the two types of cues. For example, pigeons

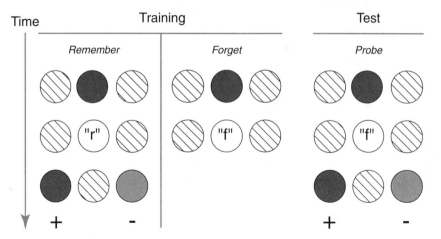

Figure 6.15. Conventional procedure for testing directed-forgetting in pigeons using delayed matching to sample; "r" and "f" represent distinctive stimuli after which the bird is reinforced for pecking the most recent sample or after memory is not tested, respectively. Redrawn from Roper and Zentall (1993) with permission.

have been trained in a procedure in which an unrelated discrimination rather than just an intertrial interval follows the forget cue. This should ensure that after forget cues, just as after remember cues, they continue to attend to the keys. In such procedures, probes of memory following forget cues may lead to performance as good as that following remember cues (Roper & Zentall, 1993, but see Grant & Soldat, 1995). Such results seem to suggest that, at least in pigeons, forgetting is not an active process that can be brought under stimulus control. With human subjects, however, typical directed forgetting procedures are rather different from that depicted in figure 6.15. People are given several items of information and told which to remember; implicitly, this means forget the others. A way of giving pigeons these instructions is diagrammed in figure 6.16 (Roper, Kaiser, & Zentall, 1995). The bird's memory is always tested; what varies from trial to trial is whether the test is of memory for the first of two stimuli presented (a color sample stimulus) or the second (a sample for a symbolic matching test). The appearance of one of the symbolic matching samples, the dot or circle in the example, in effect tells the bird it can forget whether red or green was presented just beforehand. Pigeons do show evidence of directed forgetting in this procedure (figure 6.16). Therefore, it may finally allow detailed comparisons of controlled memory processing across species. The notion that memory processing is active also raises the question of whether animals can detect the strength of their memories, as discussed in box 6.3.

6.5.4 Implicit and Explicit Memory

In delayed matching to sample or serial probe recognition, an animal is exposed to a sample and then asked, "Is this test stimulus the same as a recent

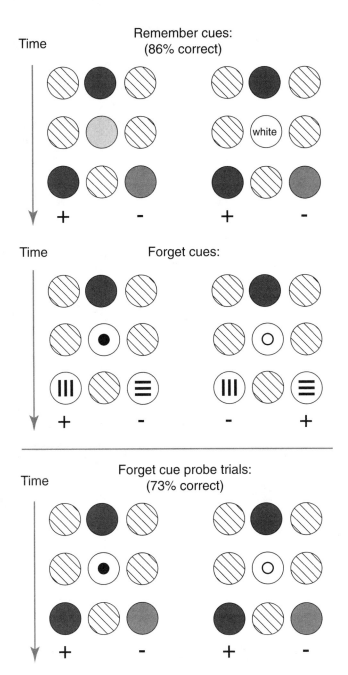

Figure 6.16. Examples of trials with remember cues, forget cues, and probes in the directed-forgetting procedure devised by Roper, Kaiser, and Zentall (1995). The "forget" cues (small white and black disks) are themselves samples for a subsequent symbolic matching test. Redrawn from Roper et al. (1995) with permission.

Box 6.3. Metamemory in Animals?

Do animals "know what they know"—that is, do they exhibit metamemory? An example in humans is the "tip of the tongue phenomenon," when people say, "I'm sure I know the answer, I just can't bring it to mind right now." Figure B6.3 depicts a

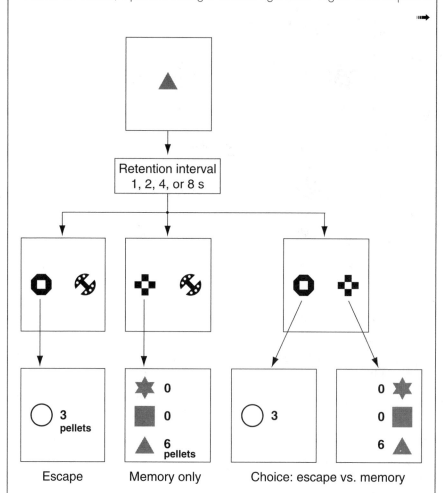

Escape   Memory only   Choice: escape vs. memory

Figure B6.3. Procedure used by Inman and Shettleworth (1996) to test pigeons for metamemory. The bird has to remember one of three samples, each a different color and shape. At the end of the retention interval, it is confronted with choices involving three symbols. One leads to a test of memory (i.e., choice among the three possible samples) with six pellets reward for correct choices; one escapes the memory test and gives opportunity to peck a white key for three pellets' reward (i.e., more than the bird will get from chance performance on a test of memory), and the third ends the trial. On trials when its memory is poor, such as after a long retention interval, an animal with metamemory should choose the escape option if offered a choice between that and a test of memory.

Box 6.3. (continued)

---

procedure designed to test for metamemory in pigeons (Inman & Shettleworth, 1996). If a bird could use the strength of its memory as a discriminative stimulus, it should chose a test of memory when its memory for the sample was strong and the alternative, safe, stimulus when the sample was forgotten. However, the data did not provide clear evidence that the birds could use the strength of their own memories as a cue. They did not chose the safe option more at long than at short retention intervals, and they performed no better on the test of memory when they chose it than when there was no choice. Notice that in this study matching accuracy was compared on trials with and without the escape option within the same stage of the experiment, and the animals could gain more food if they could predict from trial to trial whether they were going to match accurately or not.

Metamemory might be a useful faculty for animals to have. For example, it would allow selection of areas for foraging on the basis of whether or not the patches and items in them were already known. However, the same function might be served by the ability to recognize novelty vs. familiarity and/or by sheer memory for past reinforcements. Since both of these abilities are well established in animals, metamemory may be unnecessary. Still, a negative result in one experiment is no reason not to try testing for metamemory in other species and/or other ways. Related experiments have asked whether humans and monkeys selectively escape from difficult trials in psychophysical tasks (Smith, Shields, Schull, & Washburn, 1997). Here a possible response to perceptual uncertainty has not always been carefully distinguished from the effects of differential reinforcement for escaping specific stimulus values. However, there may be a real difference between monkeys and pigeons here. Since metacognition seems to be one aspect of consciousness, we may expect more comparative research on it in the future.

---

sample?" Repeated trials of the same type reinforce the animal for processing the sample. Experiments on directed forgetting indicate that such "instructions" are successful in instigating a kind of processing that seems to correspond to an intention to remember. Most traditional tests of memory in people were tests of *explicit memory*. Subjects were told to study material for a later test, and at the time of test they were asked to recall or recognize that same material. Recently, however, considerable attention has focused on tests of *implicit memory* (Schacter, 1995b). In such tests, subjects are generally not told that previously studied material is being tested, and the effect of recent experience of the material is assessed otherwise than through recall or recognition. Surprisingly, recent experience can affect various measures of performance with studied items even when subjects do not report recalling or recognizing them. That is, implicit memory appears to be unconscious whereas explicit memory is conscious. The two forms of memory are at least somewhat independent in their neural bases and in how they are affected by some experimental manipulations.

Some of the now-classic examples of implicit memory come from studies of word fragment completion (e.g., Schacter, 1995b; Tulving, 1985; Tulving,

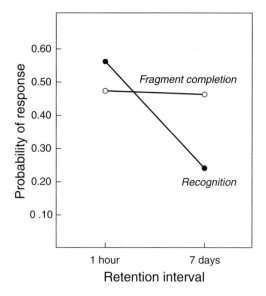

Figure 6.17. Dissociation of word fragment completion (implicit memory) and explicit recognition of words presented under the same conditions. Redrawn from Tulving et al. (1982) with permission.

Schacter, & Stark, 1982). In word fragment completion, people are shown just a few letters of a word and asked to fill in the blanks. Items might include _ _s_s_in or _l_p_an_ (for *assassin* and *elephant*). Subjects are more successful with fragments of words they have recently studied for a test of recall or recognition, even if they do not recognize the completed items as the same ones they just studied. That is to say, conscious recognition of the items appears to be dissociated from another form of memory, referred to as *priming*, which is implicit and nonconscious. Implicit memory can be dissociated from explicit memory in at least three ways (Tulving, 1985). First, in individual subjects, the items explicitly remembered are not necessarily the same ones showing priming. Second, priming and explicit memory may decay over different time courses (figure 6.17). Third, some brain-damaged patients with little or no ability to remember new experiences explicitly nevertheless show normal priming effects. The three kinds of evidence for a dissociation between implicit and explicit memory encourage the conclusion that they represent separate memory systems (e.g., Tulving, 1985, 1995). Effects like those on word fragment completion are also seen with other kinds of material such as line drawings of objects. Such data indicate that priming with verbal material is but one manifestation of a more general *perceptual recognition system*, or *PRS* (Tulving & Schacter, 1990). Because the perceptual recognition system appears to operate nonconsciously on all sorts of input, it may be an evolutionarily primitive memory system (Tulving, 1995). Does this mean that all tests of memory in nonhuman species are necessarily tests of implicit memory? If explicit memory is defined as being accessible to conscious verbal report, doesn't this make it impossible to distinguish between explicit and implicit memory in nonverbal subjects (see box 1.1 and Roberts, 1998, for further discussion)?

One way to approach this issue is to focus on the distinctive ways in which the two proposed memory systems are affected by experimental procedures and attempt to reproduce these in nonverbal tests of memory. For instance, in tests of implicit memory, memory for material studied for one kind of test (e.g., a test of recognition) is evidenced in another, unrelated, test (e.g., fragment completion). Brodbeck (1997) captured this feature of tests of implicit memory in an experiment with pigeons. The birds were trained to discriminate slides of cars and cats in a procedure resembling category learning (see chapter 5). On each trial, a cat and a car slide appeared, one on each side of the central panel in the pigeon chamber, and the bird was reinforced for pecking the one from its positive category. Each trial was preceded by a warning stimulus on the central panel that the bird had to peck 20 times to present the to-be-discriminated stimuli. In general the warning stimulus was not a cat or a car, but in the tests for priming it was one of the to-be-discriminated cats or cars. In addition, in these tests the side screens were covered by masks that blacked out a random 25% of each cat or car, making them harder to recognize. Would recent exposure to a slide as a warning stimulus enhance performance when it appeared in degraded (masked) form as S+ or S− in the next few trials? The answer is displayed in figure 6.18: clearly, the birds did show an effect analogous to priming. It lasted considerably longer than the perceptual priming effects in pigeons reviewed in chapter 2—minutes rather than seconds. More could be done to test how the process revealed by this experiment is related to attentional priming, on the one hand, and perceptual learning and the PRS revealed in studies of human priming, on the other.

Data and theory about implicit memory have been developing rapidly in the last 10 to 15 years (Schacter, 1995b). Initially, interest focused on the nature of the memory process evidenced by priming. However, as the study of consciousness became respectable in the 1990s (see chapter 1), the absence of conscious recollection became one of the defining features of implicit memory (cf. Schacter, 1987; Tulving, 1995). If the quality of verbally reported private experience is essential to distinguishing implicit from explicit memory, then it is meaningless even to ask whether or not these two forms of memory can be distinguished in nonhuman species: they cannot be (see chapter 1). Brodbeck's research is an example of an attempt to focus on distinctions among procedures and patterns of data rather than on questions about consciousness to make a comparative question experimentally tractable (see Roberts, 1998, for further discussion).

A contrasting approach to trying to distinguish between explicit and implicit memory in nonhuman subjects has been based on the behavioral neuroscience of human amnesia. In Pavlovian eyelid conditioning, some patients with hippocampal damage do not learn in a trace conditioning procedure (i.e., when there is a temporal gap between the end of the CS and the onset of

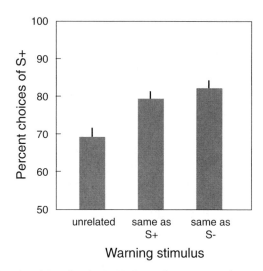

Figure 6.18. Results of Brodbeck's (1997) test for priming of memory in pigeons. Regardless of its identity, the warning stimulus had only to be pecked to start a delayed matching to sample trial; when the sample photograph was partially obscured by a mask, matching was influenced by the relationship between the warning stimulus and stimuli in the subsequent matching test.

the US, see chapter 3) whereas they do acquire an eyeblink CR in delay conditioning (i.e., when a temporally extended CS ends in the US). Moreover, in normal people exposed to these same procedures learning in trace conditioning is always associated with awareness of the temporal relationship between CS and US, whereas learning in delay conditioning seems to be unconscious. That is to say, at least in human eyeblink conditioning, the trace and delay procedures seem to be accessing two different forms of memory, explicit and implicit memory respectively, and to depend on different areas of the brain (Clark & Squire, 1998; Schacter, 1998). Since these discoveries are based on a form of simple nonverbal memory, it has been suggested that trace and delay conditioning also access different levels of awareness in animals. However, just as in the example discussed in box 1.1, the problem with making such an inference is that we have no independent access to the animal's mental state while it is performing in these tasks.

6.6 Summary and Conclusions

Memory is the most general term for the process that allows animals to base their behavior on information from individual past experience. Within psychology, *memory* and *learning* have typically been treated as separate topics, with *learning* referring to associative processes and long-term storage of the effects of experience. This chapter focuses largely on short-term memory. Subjects are exposed to an event and later reinforced for responding differentially depending on what that event was. Most of the common tests of memory in animals are tests of recognition in that the same stimulus that was studied in the first phase of a trial is presented after the retention interval. Tests of symbolic matching are more like tests of recall because the animal is not asked to respond to the remembered stimulus itself but to an associate of it. The questions we can ask about memory parallel those asked about learning in chapters 3 and 4: what are the conditions under which memories are acquired, the contents of memory, and the effects of memory on behavior? The last of these questions has received little attention here because memory is typically assumed to be accessible to an unlimited variety of behaviors. An exception is implicit memory. In people, implicit memory is memory that can be detected in certain kinds of behavioral changes but not in verbal reports of conscious recollection.

Many of the conditions affecting memory parallel those affecting the learning phenomena reviewed in previous chapters. These include frequency, duration, and number of exposures to the to-be-remembered events—factors that have also been identified as important in functional models of memory. Other conditions include proactive and retroactive interference from previous, similar experiences, and the similarity between the current context and that in which the memory was acquired. These factors are also important in associative learning and much may be learned by bringing ideas about memory to bear on understanding the effects of certain associative learning paradigms (Bouton, 1993). Notice that they are thought to be important regardless of what is to be remembered, suggesting that even if it is possible to identify different memory systems in some sense, they will have a number of common properties.

Since before the beginning of experimental studies of animal cognition, people have wondered whether some animals have better memories than others. Section 6.4 examined several research programs inspired by this question, including early comparative studies of delayed response, recent ecologically based comparisons of closely related species that rely on spatial memory to differing extents in the wild, and comparisons of serial position effects in widely divergent species. Any attempt to collect meaningful comparative data on memory in different species faces a number of difficult problems, such as how to deal with possible contextual variables. The research reviewed in this chapter has revealed, at most, quantitative differences among species in capacity and durability of memory. Box 6.1 looked at a highly species-specific memory system having similar general properties. In the next few chapters, we will consider memory for space and time, among other things. Then, in chapter 13, we will be in a better position to evaluate the notion that animals exhibit a variety of different memory systems, either within a species or from one species to another.

Further Reading

The development of contemporary research on animal memory and cognition can be traced in a series of edited books: Hulse, Fowler, and Honig (1978); Roitblat, Bever, and Terrace (1984); and Honig and Fetterman (1992) are among the landmarks. W. A. Roberts (1998) can be consulted for a comprehensive recent review of data and theories on animal memory. Kamil (1988) is a readable and wide-ranging discussion of the ecological approach to animal cognition. Bouton's (1993) integration of research on conditioning and memory is highly recommended.

7

Getting Around

Limpets are small molluscs that live on coastal rocks where they are exposed to the air at low tide. As it grows, each limpet erodes a scar on the rock that perfectly matches the irregular outline of its shell. By clinging tightly to this spot during low tide, the limpet can protect itself from dehydration (and from predators, as anyone who has tried to pry one loose can testify), but to find food it must forage over the rock face while the water is high (Cook, Bamford, Freeman, & Teideman, 1969; Cook, 1969).

Many mobile animals face the same problem as the limpet: food and other resources are separated from places of refuge, and the animal has to be able to travel between them without getting lost. There is a premium on making this trip efficiently rather than wandering at random until the goal is found, which in the limpet's case might be too late to prevent drying out. The limpet's problem is a miniature one in space and time compared to the orientation problems solved by other species (figure 7.1), but they all have certain features in common. Each individual, or group of individuals, is locating its own home, hoards, or other resources. Therefore, some sort of acquired representation of the goal's location, or how to get to it, is required. Some animals, like the limpet, create such a representation in the external world in the form of a chemical trail (Chelazzi, 1992). However, we will be most concerned with cases in which animals acquire an internal representation of the location of the goal or how to reach it—that is, they show some form of spatial learning.

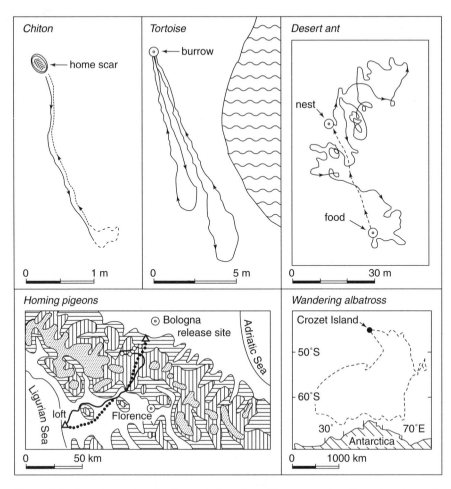

Figure 7.1. Homing paths of individuals from five different species, illustrating the wide range of spatial scales over which journeys out from a central place and back may take place. After Papi (1992b). Tortoise from Chelazzi and Francisci (1979); albatross from Jouventin and Weimerskirch (1990). Redrawn with permission.

Of our three questions about learning—the conditions for learning, the contents of learning, and its effects on behavior—in the area of spatial behavior the most attention has been devoted to the contents of learning. In practical terms, asking about the contents of spatial learning means discovering what features of the goal control behavior. The effects of learning on behavior are generally taken for granted: the animal reaches the goal in the presence of the appropriate cues. The most controversial question about the content of spatial learning is "Do animals have cognitive maps?" That is, is accurate spatial orientation controlled by a representation of distances and directions that allows the animal to select an efficient route when displaced to a new location? This question turns out to be difficult to answer, for two reasons. First, although a map is a powerful metaphor for spatial knowledge, sometimes different investigators mean different things by *cognitive maps*. Second, there is a large number of mechanisms for reaching a goal like a nest or a cache of food. Therefore, before we can consider whether any animal might have a cognitive map in any sense, we need to consider all the simpler mechanisms animals can use to find their ways to goals. These are the subject of section 7.1. In section 7.2, we consider how some of these mechanisms function together. Then we will be in a position to look at evidence for cognitive maps in section 7.3. Section 7.4 discusses how animals acquire spatial knowledge and asks whether any unique processes are involved. Is spatial information processed in a specialized cognitive module?

7.1 Mechanisms for Spatial Orientation

7.1.1 Dead Reckoning

A foraging desert ant (*Cataglyphis fortis*) wanders here and there, taking a long and tortuous path in its search for food, but as soon as it finds a prey item, it heads straight back to its nest, over a hundred meters away (figure 7.1). These ants return to the vicinity of the nest using *dead reckoning*, an internal sense of the direction and distance of the nest from their current position. If the ant is picked up and moved several hundred meters just before it starts the homeward journey, it does not head for the nest but takes a path parallel to that which it would have taken in its original location. For instance, if the nest was originally to its south, the ant will still head south even if the nest is now to the east (Wehner, 1992). Moreover, when it has gone about the right distance for finding the nest from its original starting point, the ant abandons its straight path and begins to circle around as if looking for the nest in the place where it should be (figure 7.2). Like the straight return from the food to the nest, this searching behavior suggests that the ant is performing *path integration*. That is, it appears to be continuously integrating (in the mathematical sense) information about its changes in distance and direction to keep track of its location with respect to the predicted location of the nest. The computations it implicitly performs while searching for the nest in displacement experiments are just as remarkable as those performed on the outward journey from nest to food. Although they take a roughly spiral path, the ants continually break it off and return to the point where they began searching. This behavior shows that the ant is keeping track of its position with respect to the most likely nest position, and it ensures that this area is crisscrossed most often (Wehner & Srinivasan, 1981). The search for the nest entrance can go on for an hour or more, with the ant traveling many meters before it dies from the desert heat or is rescued by an experimenter.

Dead reckoning is one of the most basic and ubiquitous ways in which animals keep track of their location with respect to a known postion. (*Dead reckoning* is a navigator's term; it is often used interchangeably with *path integration*, although the latter term implies a particular mechanism.) How dead

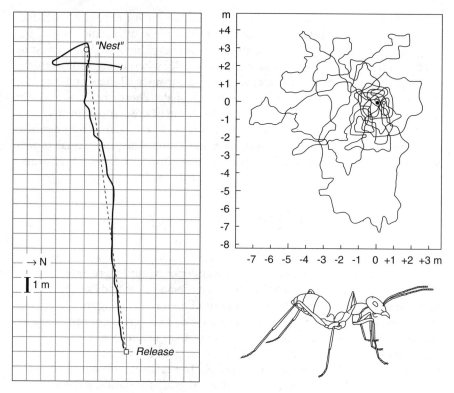

Figure 7.2. Homing in desert ants (*Cataglyphis albicans*). Left: Path of an individual displaced to unknown territory for the first 70 seconds after release. The open circle shows where the nest would have been relative to the release site if the ant had been in its home territory. Right: The spiraling path taken by the ant once it arrives in the vicinity where the nest should be, recorded over one hour. Data redrawn from Wehner and Srinivasan (1981) with permission; ant from Wehner (1992) with permission.

reckoning works has been studied most in insects such as ants, bees, and spiders (Dyer, 1994; Wehner, 1992). An example from small mammals comes from the maternal behavior of gerbils (*Meriones unguiculatus*) (Mittelstaedt & Mittelstaedt, 1982). Mother gerbils and their pups are given a nest at the edge of a large circular arena. If the pups are taken from the nest and placed in a cup somewhere in the arena, the mother soon begins to search for them. When she finds the pups, she picks one up in her mouth and runs almost straight back to the nest, even in total darkness and even if her outward path had zigzags and detours. If the nest is moved by rotating the edge of the arena while the mother is at the cup, she returns to the starting point of her journey like the desert ant, ignoring any cues emanating from the nest in its new location. In contrast, if the cup is rotated briskly while the mother gerbil is in it, she compensates for the rotation and heads straight back to the nest as before. But if the cup is rotated slowly or slowly moved sideways, the gerbil does not compensate and is misoriented. In mammals, information about changes in angular orientation is processed by the animal's vestibular system, which senses accelerations and decelerations.

More extensive studies like the Mittelstaedts' with gerbils have been done by Etienne and her colleagues (e.g., Etienne, Maurer, Saucy, & Teroni, 1986) with golden hamsters (*Mesocricetus auratus*) hoarding food from the center of an arena back to their nest (see section 7.2). Geese carried in a cart up to a kilometer or so from their home also appear to home by dead reckoning (Saint Paul, 1982). They obtain information about displacement from the patterns of visual flow. If they cannot see out of the cart for parts of the outward journey, they act as if discounting this part of the trip. Some wasps also use flow of the visual field as a source of information about the direction of displacement (Ugolini, 1987). Unlike this mechanism, the vestibular system can compensate for active or passive displacement in the dark as long as the motion is rapid enough. This makes dead reckoning particularly useful for nocturnal animals like hamsters.

Dead reckoning allows *egocentric* spatial localization—that is, the animal using it is localizing things in the environment with respect to itself. *Allocentric* or *geocentric* mechanisms locate the animal with respect to some external frame of reference such as landmarks, the sun, or the earth's magnetic field. We have already seen one of the major disadvantages of egocentric mechanisms: if the animal is slowly "blown off course," as by the experimenter moving it, path integration does not necessarily compensate. A second limitation of path integration is that it accumulates error. For instance, the more the hamsters have been turned around or have turned themselves around while collecting food from the center of the hoarding arena, the less accurately they return to the nest (Etienne, Maurer, & Saucy, 1988).

Errors in angular orientation can be measured by forcing an animal to take a two-legged outward journey with a controlled turn between the two legs and relating the direction of homeward orientation to the angle of turn (review in Maurer & Seguinot, 1995; Muller & Wehner, 1988; Seguinot, Maurer, & Etienne, 1993). When desert ants are exposed to this treatment, the error in their homeward heading is systematically related to the angle through which they are forced to turn, as shown in figure 7.3. The greater the turn, the greater the error. These systematic errors indicate that the ants are not continuously integrating perceived distance and direction from home but using a simpler approximate solution in which each direction taken, as perceived by the ant's solar compass (see section 7.1.1) is weighted by the distance for which it maintained (Muller & Wehner, 1988). The ants' localized search for the nest at the end of their straight run seems to be programmed to overcome the inherent errors of path integration. The farther an ant has traveled from the nest, the wider its spiraling loops when it returns to the nest's vicinity (Wehner & Srinivasan, 1981). Moreover, the ant turns left and right about equally often, so errors tend to cancel out, and it seldom takes the widest turns, at which error is greatest. Dead reckoning is suitable for brief, round-trip excusions, since it behaves as if reset at the start of each new journey. As we will see, it is often combined with orientation based on other cues.

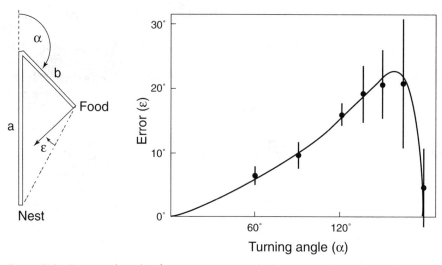

Figure 7.3. Setup and results of an experiment in which ants were forced to make a two-legged journey from the nest to food, along a and b, and then headed home. Redrawn from Muller and Wehner (1988) with permission.

7.1.2 Beacons

We might have expected odors or sounds from the nest itself to act as a *beacon* for the mother gerbil returning with a wandering pup. Beacons are sometimes referred to in the psychological literature as *proximal cues*—that is, cues close to the goal, as distinct from *distal cues*, the landmarks to be discussed in the next section. Often animals can use either proximal or distal cues, depending on which are available. A now-classic laboratory example was devised by Morris (1981; figure 7.4). A rat is placed in a circular pool of water in which it must swim until it finds a single, small dry platform, a Plexiglas cylinder standing somewhere in the pool. For some rats, the cylinder is black and visible above the water. Thus the platform can function as a beacon, and since rats would rather be dry than swim, they soon learn to approach it wherever it is in the pool. For other rats, the water is made opaque by the addition of milk, and the platform is transparent and slightly below the water surface. These rats must use distal cues, objects in the room surrounding the pool, to localize the platform, and they also learn quickly to approach it, provided it stays in the same place from trial to trial. When the platform is removed on test trials, these rats still swim directly to the correct location. Like a desert ant searching for its nest, they crisscross the correct location, as if searching for the platform (figure 7.4).

Intuitively, using a goal as a beacon is computationally less demanding than using distal cues. Cues from a desired object, almost by definition, draw the animal to them. A classic area in animal behavior was the analysis of the mechanisms that bring this about (Fraenkel & Gunn, 1961). Learned as well as unlearned features attract the animal to the goal: one of the most basic effects of conditioning (see chapter 3) is that animals approach CSs associated

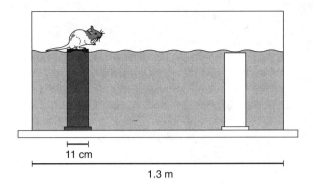

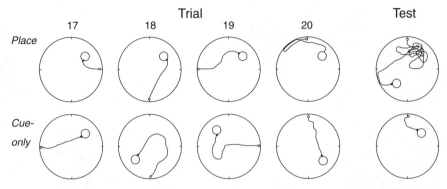

Figure 7.4. The Morris water escape task ("water maze"). At top, a cross section of the pool with a black visible platform and a white plaform designed to be invisible to a swimming rat. Bottom: performance on trials 17–20 and a single test trial of one rat trained with the invisible platform always in the same place until the test ("place" condition) and one rat trained with the visible platform in a new place on each trial ("cue only" condition). After Morris (1981) with permission.

with positive USs. For mammals, the intuition that beacons and landmarks demand different kinds of cognitive processing is supported by evidence from behavioral neuroscience. Rats with hippocampal lesions can still learn to approach a beacon like the dry platform, but they cannot learn tasks in which a goal is identified only by its spatial relationship to distal cues (Leonard & McNaughton, 1990). But while finding a goal by approaching cues attached to it may be computationally simple, it has a major practical drawback: the animal must stay within range of those cues. In most natural environments, an animal that had to be able to see, smell, or hear its nest at all times would have its travels severely limited.

7.1.3 Landmarks

When features of a goal are not immediately perceptible from a distance, other objects in fixed locations—that is, landmarks—can guide the animal to

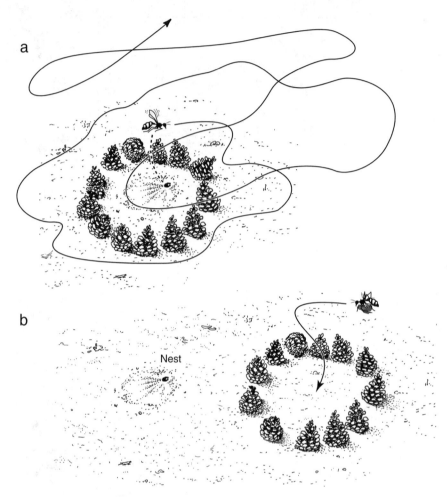

Figure 7.5. Control of orientation in the digger wasp (*Philanthus triangulum*) by nearby landmarks, a circle of pine cones. After Tinbergen (1951) with permission.

it. A classic demonstration of the use of landmarks is Tinbergen and Kruyt's (1938/1952) study of homing in the digger wasp (*Philanthus triangulum*). These wasps lay their eggs in a number of separate burrows, which they provision with bees. Each bee that a wasp collects requires a separate foraging trip from the burrow, which means the female wasp has to learn the location of each of her burrows. This learning takes place during a brief orientation flight. When leaving the nest for the first time, the wasp turns and faces the nest entrance and flies around in ever-increasing loops, apparently inspecting the nest entrance and the objects around it (figure 7.5a). If the objects surrounding an established nest are altered while the wasp is inside, a new orientation flight will be elicited the next time she departs (Collett & Lehrer, 1993; Lehrer, 1993; see also box 3.3).

To discover whether digger wasps were locating their nests using nearby landmarks, Tinbergen and Kruyt made a circle of pine cones around a nest while the wasp was inside and allowed it a number of trips in which to learn about them. Then they moved the pine cone circle to one side of the nest while the wasp was out foraging and observed where it landed first when it returned (figure 7.5b). Even though the disturbed sand indicating the nest entrance was still visible, wasps nearly always landed in the pine cone circle and searched for the nest entrance there. Only when the experimenters chased the wasp off and moved the pine cones back did she reenter the nest.

Which Landmarks Are Used?   To discover which nearby landmarks the wasps learned about, Tinbergen and Kruyt (1938, in Tinbergen, 1972) made landmark circles from two kinds of objects and then tested wasps with a circle of each type, both circles being equidistant from the nest. Wasps preferentially used as landmarks objects that were large, nearby, and three-dimensional. Such a preference makes considerable functional sense. Large three-dimensional objects are more likely to be visible from a distance than small flat ones, and if perception of distances and directions obeys Weber's law (see chapter 2), objects close to a goal can be used to localize it more accurately than objects farther away. Thus, it is not surprising that similar preferences have been found in other animals that have been tested appropriately. For instance, food-storing European jays (*Garrulus glandularius*) trained to find buried food in a laboratory room use the nearest tallest landmarks in an array surrounding the goal (Bennett, 1993). Honeybees also are most influenced by the landmarks nearest a goal (Cheng, Collett, Pickhard, & Wehner, 1987). Other attributes of landmarks determining how heavily they are weighted are discussed in section 7.4.

How Are Landmarks Used? The Vector Sum Model   To use a landmark, an animal has to perceive the distance and direction from itself to the landmark, remember the distance and direction between the landmark and the goal, and use this information in an implicit computation of the distance and direction between itself and the goal. Vectors are quantities that have both distance and direction, and accordingly, the mental computations implicit in animals' behavior toward landmarks can usefully be discussed in terms of the mathematics of vectors, as shown in figure 7.6.

While a single beacon is sufficient to indicate the location of a goal, a single symmetrical landmark is not. Such a landmark indicates only the distance to the goal, so unless the animal can obtain directional information from another source, it can do no better than search in a ring around the landmark. Two discriminably different landmarks unambiguously specify a single position, and an array of three of more landmarks provides redundant information. How is information from two or more landmarks combined? In general there are two sorts of answers to this kind of question: either the two sources of information compete for control, with the winner taking all, or the information they convey is averaged in some way. In a sense, these two alternatives

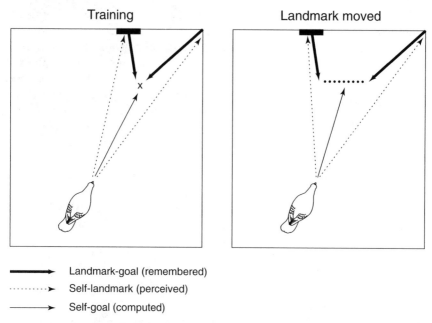

Training   Landmark moved

━━━━━━━►   Landmark-goal (remembered)

·········►   Self-landmark (perceived)

────────►   Self-goal (computed)

Figure 7.6. Hypothetical vectors involved in computation of the distance and direction to a goal (x) during training with a conspicuous landmark (black bar). The corner of the search space is treated as a second landmark. The self to landmark and landmark to goal vectors sum to produce the self to goal vector (the distance and direction resulting from summing two vectors is found by placing them head to tail). When the landmark is moved the animal will search somewhere along the dotted line, searching further toward the left the more heavily the black bar landmark is weighted relative to other objects in the box.

are on a continuum. "Winner take all" is the extreme of a weighted average in which all the weight goes to one competitor.

To discover how information from different landmarks is combined, animals can be trained to find a goal with two or more landmarks present, and then one or more of the landmarks is moved. Such tests have produced evidence of both averaging and competition. When gerbils were trained to search between two landmarks that were then moved farther apart, the gerbils concentrated their searching in two spots, each at the correct distance and direction from one of the landmarks (Collett, Cartwright, & Smith, 1986). In contrast, pigeons trained to search in a constant location, in front of a wide stripe on the wall of a large rectangular box, behaved as if averaging information from the conspicuous stripe and other features of the box (Cheng, 1989). After the birds were well trained, they were given occasional test trials in which no food was present and the stripe was moved. When the single landmark was shifted along the wall of the box, the position where the birds pecked most shifted along with it, but typically not as much—that is, the birds averaged information from the landmark with some other feature, possibly the corners or visible features of the room outside the box (figure 7.6).

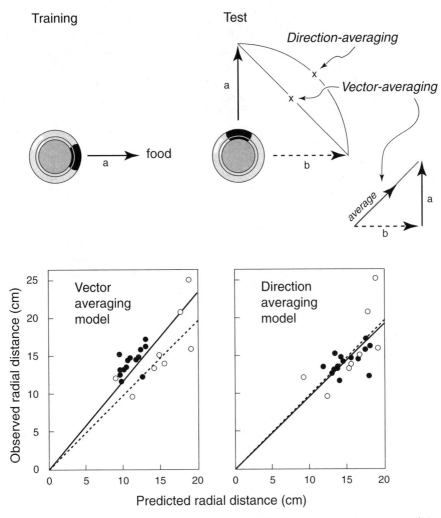

Figure 7.7. Overhead view of the setup Cheng (1994) used to test predictions of the distance-averaging vs. the direction-averaging models of landmark use. In the test with the striped bottle twisted 90° direction-averaging predicts searching along the arc whereas vector averaging predicts searching along the straight line indicated. The best fit to the data (solid line) is compared to the predictions of each model (dotted lines). After Cheng (1994) with permission.

If the landmark is moved perpendicular to the wall of the box, searching also shifts toward or away from the wall, but not as much as when the landmark is moved the same distance sideways. The nearby wall of the box seems to be weighted relatively heavily in the bird's determination of how close to the wall to search. And as this model would predict, if the landmark is moved diagonally from its usual position, the birds' peak search position also moves diagonally, more so in one direction than in the other.

So far, these findings from pigeons, and similar ones with black-capped chickadees (Cheng & Sherry, 1992) and Clark's nutcrackers (Gould-Beierle & Kamil, 1996) can be accommodated by a vector-averaging model, as shown in figure 7.6. But what exactly is being averaged? Are whole vectors averaged or are distances and directions computed separately? In certain situations, these two possibilities make different predictions, as shown in figure 7.7. Pigeons are tested in a circular arena with a single cylindrical landmark decorated with a conspicuous vertical stripe. When the cylinder is rotated, searching should rotate along with it. If the birds are averaging the self-to-goal vector indicated by the stripe with that indicated by other (unspecified) cues, they should search at the same distance from the center of the arena as before. If they are averaging distances and directions separately, they should search closer to the center, and this is what they do (figure 7.7). These results indicate that, in pigeons at least, separate sources of information about a goal's location are not combined initially and then averaged. Rather, the animal behaves as if computing on distance and direction information in separate modules and then combining the outputs of these modules (Cheng, 1995). However, if the conflict between the different sources of information is too great, one of them may be overruled. For instance, a landmark is ignored if it is moved too far from its usual location. This kind of result underlines the problem of how currently perceived landmarks are matched with remembered landmarks. Functionally, if an animal encounters similar landmarks in different parts of its territory, it has to know which one is which to behave appropriately. Honeybees seem to use distant landmarks or memory of the recent route to recognize ambiguous nearby landmarks. Bees were trained to find artificial nectar in each of two small featureless huts. Within each hut, the position of the food was specified by an identical array of four landmarks, but it was on the left of the landmarks in one hut and on the right in the other. Nevertheless, the bees learned to search in the appropriate position, controlled by the remembered global spatial context (see also Chittka, Geiger, & Kunze, 1995; Collett & Kelber, 1988).

How Are Landmarks Used? Template Matching   So far we have taken for granted that animals perceive distances and directions fairly directly and are able to move appropriately to decrease their distance from a desired goal. One way to compute the correct way to move is for the animal to compare its current view of the surroundings with a stored template, a "snapshot" stored in memory, of how the surroundings look from the goal. Experiments with bees trained to search in a featureless room and tested with familiar landmark arrays expanded or contracted show how plausible this notion is, at least for bees. When a single landmark defining the goal's location was doubled in size, bees searched twice as far away from it as usual; conversely, when landmark size was halved, bees halved the distance at which they searched (Cartwright & Collett, 1983). The bees behave as if moving to reduce the discrepancy between the current retinal image and the stored snapshot. This can be done by comparing individual areas of light and dark, as shown in figure 7.8. In effect,

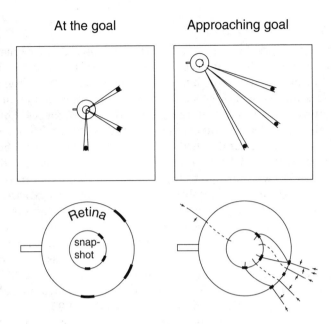

Figure 7.8. Cartwright and Collett's (1987) "snapshot" or template matching model for bees. The bee acquires a memory of the pattern of retinal stimulation from the three landmarks (black dots) when she is at the goal. When approaching the goal later, she moves as indicated by the little arrows in the lower right panel, so as to match the current with the remembered pattern of stimulation. After Cartwright and Collett (1987) with permission.

the two-dimensional retinal image is broken down into elements, and the direction in which the bee should move is computed as the average of the vectors dictated by discrepancies between individual elements of the retinal image and corresponding elements in the snapshot. The bee makes the matching task easier for itself by facing important landmarks in a standard compass direction, which it gets from its magnetic sense (Collett & Baron, 1994). Thus the animal apparently does not need to memorize how the goal looks from all directions.

One way in which the bee could get close enough to a goal to make use of nearby landmarks would be to have an "album of snapshots" (Cartwright & Collett, 1987) from different locations within familiar terrain. Each one would be associated with a vector from that location to the hive. As we will see in section 7.3, a set of vectors linking the hive with known feeding sites may suffice to allow bees to behave as if they have cognitive maps. In rodents, this kind of mechanism is known as the *local view hypothesis* (Leonard & McNaughton, 1990). In any case, a way of locating a goal from close by is no good without a way to get close to the goal in the first place and a way to match currently perceived with remembered landmarks.

7.1.4 Routes

"The animal got home because it had learned a route." As an explanation of accurate orientation, this statement is not very useful because "learning a route" can mean two different things. On the one hand, "learning a route" can refer to a mechanism of egocentric orientation in which an animal records the movements it makes in traveling between two places. This is usually referred to as *response learning* in psychology, to distinguish it from *place learning*. For instance, a rat that had learned to go to the left goal box in a T maze might have learned "run straight for a certain distance and then turn left," as opposed to learning "go to the goal box" regardless of the responses required. In the 1950s, considerable effort was devoted to experiments designed to discover whether rats learned mazes primarily as chains of responses or whether they learned about the relationships between places in the maze. Clark Hull is usually identified with the first view, and E. C. Tolman with the second. Like many controversies in psychology, this one was resolved—insofar as it ever was—by accepting that the answer to the question, "What does a rat learn in a maze?" is "It depends." Some conditions favor place learning and others, response learning (Gallistel, 1990; Nadel, 1995).

A classic example of response learning comes from Konrad Lorenz's (1952, p. 109) depiction of how his pet water shrews followed their "path-habits,"

> as strictly bound to them as a railway engine to its tracks and as unable to deviate from them by even a few centimetres. . . . The shrews, running along the wall, were accustomed to jump on and off the stones which lay right in their path. If I moved the stones out of the runway. . . . the shrews would jump right up into the air in the place where the stone should have been; they came down with a jarring bump, were obviously disconcerted and started whiskering cautiously left and right, just as they behaved in an unknown environment.

Gallistel (1990, pp. 96–98) reviews analogous examples from the behavior of rats in mazes. As he points out, the animal must be keeping track of its distance and direction from the starting point (otherwise, it would not know when to jump), and it must use other cues to orient itself at the start. For the nearly blind water shrew, these are tactile and perhaps olfactory cues, gained by "whiskering." The disadvantage of sacrificing continuous monitoring of the environment for speed is that changes in the environment are not detected immediately. However, as Lorenz (1952, p. 111) pointed out, the shrew's brand of route learning has some advantages. It

> compensates the shrew for being nearly blind and enables it to run exceedingly fast without wasting a minute on orientation. On the other hand, it may, under unusual circumstances, lead the shrew to destruction. . . . [W]ater shrews have broken their necks by jumping into a pond which had been recently drained. In spite of the possibility of such mishaps, it would be short-sighted if one were to stigmatize the water shrew as stupid because it solves the spatial problems of its daily life in quite a different way from man . . . by learning by heart every possible spatial contingency that may arise in a given territory.

We will see this theme echoed in the discussion of whether bees use cognitive maps in section 7.3.

In discussions of orientation in natural environments, route learning often refers to reaching a goal using a series of landmarks. This kind of orientation can be illustrated with examples of guides for hikers (O'Keefe & Nadel, 1978). A person may be instructed "after crossing the bridge, turn left and proceed along the bank of the stream until you reach a hedge. Turn right and climb the hill." Similarly, an animal may learn its way around familiar territory in terms of distances and directions of travel with respect to landmarks. This kind of orientation has been demonstrated in honeybees by training bees to find food in a fixed position relative to a conspicuous feature of the landscape, like a line of trees. When the bees' hive is moved to another location with a similar feature and the bees are released under a cloudy sky, they orient themselves with respect to the line of trees as before, even if it points in a new compass direction (Dyer, 1994; see also section 7.3). Desert ants use landmarks on the route between the food and the nest in addition to path integration when they repeatedly visit the same foraging site. But they learn which side of the landmark to walk on, not its spatial location (Collett, Dillmann, Giger, & Wehner, 1992). One way in which insects could store information about specific routes is described by the "snapshot" hypothesis discussed in section 7.1.3.

If an animal has learned a route among known landmarks, altering features along the route should misorient it. In our example of the hiking guide, if the hedge is cut down after the book is published, users of the guide will not know when to head up the hill. In contrast, the hiker equipped with a good map showing the trail will still be able to turn away from the stream at the right place. Route learning in either of its senses does not allow this. Neither a chain of actions nor a chain of reactions to landmarks necessarily encodes the relationships among points along the route in a way that permits shortcuts or accurate orientation when the environment changes.

7.1.5 Environmental Shape

In 1986, Ken Cheng published a remarkable discovery. He had devised a simple test of spatial working memory in which rats found food in a large rectangular box placed within a dark room, were removed from the box for about a minute, and then replaced in an identical box to dig for the now-buried food. In test trials, no food was present and digging was recorded. The rats showed good memory for locations of food that they had experienced just once, in that they dug in the correct place at above chance levels. But, amazingly, they dug nearly as often in the diagonally opposite point in the box (see figure 3.2). Notice that in diagonally opposite locations the animal's relationship to the box's geometry is the same. For example, a short wall may be on the left, a long wall on the right. And geometry, the box's shape, seems to be what the rats are paying most attention to (Cheng, 1986; Gallistel, 1990, chapter 6). For if geometrically identical locations are made more discriminable—for instance, by coloring one long wall white and the others black—the rats still make diagonal errors. Similarly, placing distinctive panels with different patterns and odors in the corners still does not reduce diagonal errors to chance levels. Yet rats can learn a reference memory task in which food is in the same place on every trial relative to such panels.

Cheng took pains to force his rats to rely on spatial cues within the boxes. They were in a dark and relatively featureless room. Testing the rat in a different box in a different part of the room from that in which it was exposed to the food meant it could not rely on dead reckoning to return it to the same location in space after it had been removed from the first box. These conditions are important for revealing the importance of geometric cues. When Cheng's experiments are repeated but with the room visible outside the box and the test and exposure boxes in the same location within the room, rats search almost exclusively in the correct location and make no more diagonal errors than other kinds. When they are disoriented by making the room dark, not always having the exposure and test boxes in the same place, and being gently rotated between exposure and test, the same rats make as many diagonal errors as correct responses (Margules & Gallistel, 1988, experiment 3). Disorientation resulting from being in the dark and/or being rotated between trials impairs rats' performance in other food-rewarded spatial tasks as well. However, it seems to have less effect on performance in aversively motivated tasks like the Morris water-escape task (Martin, Harley, Smith, Hoyles, & Hynes, 1997; Dudchenko, Goodridge, Seiterle, & Taube, 1997).

The fact that shape of the environment seems to take priority over features of the very surfaces that define that shape can be interpreted as meaning that environmental geometry is processed in a dedicated cognitive module, impervious to other kinds of spatial information. But rats are not usually in the kind of impoverished situation they encountered in Cheng's experiments, so one might wonder whether the results have any generality (Nadel, 1995). However, the same kind of results are found when young children are tested in a similar way. Hermer and Spelke (1994, 1996) showed college students and 20-month-old toddlers the location of an object in a room and then asked them to find it after they had shut their eyes and turned themselves around about 10 times. If the room was white and featureless, the students and the toddlers behaved just like Cheng's rats—not surprisingly, since they had no cues to disambiguate the correct corner from its diagonal. When the room was given one blue wall, the students searched mostly in the correct place, but the babies were just as confused as before (figure 7.9). Like Cheng's rats, they could be provided with salient features in the room (a teddy bear, a toy truck) that they could use for orientation, but when they were disoriented by being rotated before searching, they still fell back on purely geometric information. Thus, like rats, people seem to possess a cognitive module for processing environmental shape, but in humans the limitations of exclusive reliance on environmental shape are overcome during development. This appears to be a case of what Rozin (1976) calls increasing *accessibility* of modular processing, in this case occurring during development (Hermer & Spelke, 1994, 1996).

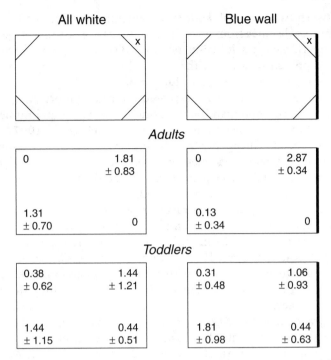

Figure 7.9. Experimental setup and results from tests of the geometric module in toddlers and adults. X marks the location of the goal. Data are mean number of trials out of 3 or 4 (+ standard deviation) that each subject searched in the locations indicated. After Hermer and Spelke (1994) with permission.

Young chickens also respond to environmental shape, though it does not appear to be as important relative to landmarks as it is for rats (Vallortigara, Zanforlin, & Pasti, 1990). In any case, birds likely rely on vision to detect the shape of the environment, whereas rats may encode their distances from nearby surfaces by dead reckoning from when they last bumped into them (McNaughton et al., 1996).

Not only surfaces but also configurations of landmarks have geometric properties, but the importance of landmark geometry as such varies considerably across species. This is well illustrated by the simple case in which an animal is trained to search in a spot equidistant from two landmarks and a little way from the imaginary line that joins them. Bees appear to learn "search in the middle," because when the landmark array is either expanded or compressed, they do search in the middle, and at a distance proportional to the change in landmark size (Cartwright & Collett, 1983). But, as already mentioned, such behavior is accounted for by the snapshot model of landmark use. Similarly, an animal behaving as depicted in the vector sum model would continue to search in the middle of a compressed or expanded array if it weighted the landmarks equally. But this does not always happen, even with two identical landmarks. Gerbils trained to find buried sunflower seeds halfway between two identical landmarks evidently encoded the location in terms of absolute distance from one of the landmarks: when they were moved twice as far apart, the animals maintained their distance from one of the landmarks while apparently ignoring the other (Collett, Cartwright, & Smith, 1986; see Cheng & Spetch, 1998, for further discussion).

Spetch and her colleagues have explored the role of more complex geometric relationships among landmarks using both pigeon and human subjects. Tests in both naturalistic environments (Spetch et al., 1997) and on touch screens (Spetch, Cheng, & MacDonald, 1996) gave similar results. Figure 7.10 shows what happened when subjects searched in an open field for a goal located in the middle of a square array of four identical landmarks. People encoded the landmark location as "middle," whereas pigeons encoded a distance and direction from an arbitrary one or two of the landmarks. When Clark's nutcrackers were trained to find a seed at the midpoint of two landmarks, they went to the middle in tests with novel interlandmark distances, like the people (Kamil & Jones, 1997). Unlike the subjects in the other "middle" experiments, they were trained with a variety of interlandmark distances to begin with, so it remains to be seen whether they differed from the pigeons because of their species or their experience. It is of interest to consider when and why abstract encoding of geometric relationships develops, but it is also worth bearing in mind that absolute distances among landmarks are likely to remain constant in most natural situations. Real landmarks seldom move around in such a way as to maintain only their geometric relationship to a goal. Nevertheless, the more general issue of how and why (in both mechanistic and functional senses) animals respond to configurations of landmarks as such is one that requires further study (see Cheng & Spetch, 1998, for discussion).

7.1.6 The Sun Compass

Animals active during the day can use the sun or the pattern of light it creates in the sky to indicate direction relative to the earth's surface—that is, in geocentric coordinates. The sun is useless as a landmark because it moves continuously relative to the earth, but many animals use it for directional information—that is, they have a *sun compass*. For example, the desert ants described in section 7.1.1 use the sun and patterns of polarized light in the sky for directional information when computing their path from the nest to food. If an ant is trained to find a food source on a featureless patch of desert at one time of day and then kept in the dark for a few hours, it heads roughly homeward when released even though the direction it travels relative to the sun's position is different from what it was during training. Wehner and Lanfranconi (1981) showed that ants can get their direction from the sun alone by releasing them for their return journey in a featureless patch of desert some way from the nest. The ants were accompanied from the release site by a small cart under which they walked. The cart blocked off sight of landmarks and could optically shield or change the position of the sun or the patterns of polarized

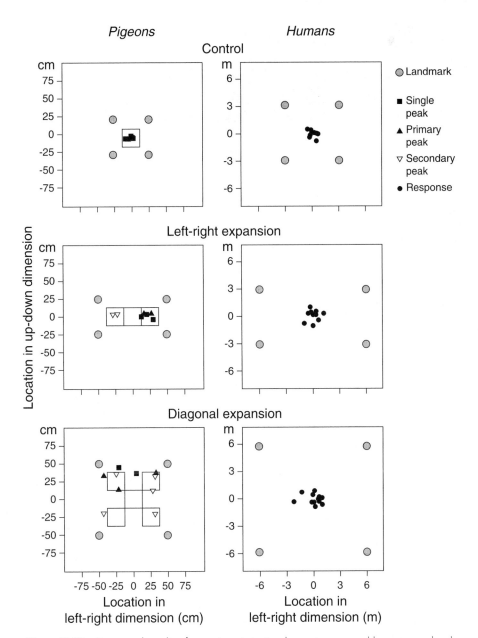

Figure 7.10. Setup and results of experiments testing how pigeons and humans use landmarks when trained to find the middle of a square array of landmarks in an open field. Data for the pigeons represent the center (peak) of the locations of the first 50 pecks in unrewarded test trials. Redrawn from Spetch et al. (1997) with permission.

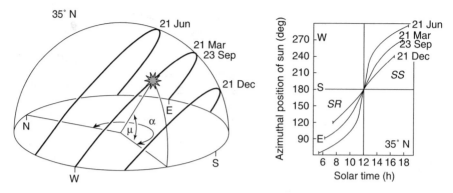

Figure 7.11. How the apparent path of the sun across the sky (arcs) varies with time of year at a particular latitude, 35° North. Angle α on the surface of the earth is the sun's azimuth; μ is the sun's elevation. Ephemeris functions (right) give the sun's azimuth as a function of time of day and time of year at a particular latitude, here 35° North. SR = sunrise; SS = sunset. After Wehner (1992) with permission.

light from the sky. When they could not see the sun, ants headed off in random directions, but when they could see the sun in its correct position for the time of day, they headed in the compass direction of home.

Reading direction from the sun regardless of the time of day requires two things: a stored representation of how the sun, or some correlate of it, moves across the sky at the current location and season (an *ephemeris function*), and an internal time sense or clock. Figure 7.11 illustrates how the sun's apparent path across the sky changes with the season in a temperate latitude. The sun's position overhead is converted to a compass direction (i.e., direction relative to North) by computing the sun's *azimuth*. As shown in figure 7.11, this means taking the imaginary arc that connects the sun with the closest point on the horizon and measuring the angle on the surface of the earth between that point and North. This kind of computation is implied by statements like "The sun is in the South" at noon in the Northern Hemisphere. But while the sun *is* in the South at noon for most of the year, the sun's elevation at a given time of day—that is, its height above the horizon—changes with the time of year. This means that the sun's azimuth moves at different rates at different times of year and at different times of day.

Sun compass orientation is widespread, but it has probably been studied the most in homing pigeons and bees. To show definitively that an animal is using a sun compass it is necessary to shift its internal clock and test whether orientation shifts accordingly. The logic of such experiments is depicted in figure 7.12 with a hypothetical example using bees. As another example, pigeons can be trained to home—that is, to fly back to their loft when released a few kilometers away—at one time of day, say noon. Having shown that they can home successfully, some birds now have their biological clocks advanced by 3 hours by being kept indoors for a week or so with lights coming on and going off 3 hours earlier than local sunrise and sunset. Others can have their clocks

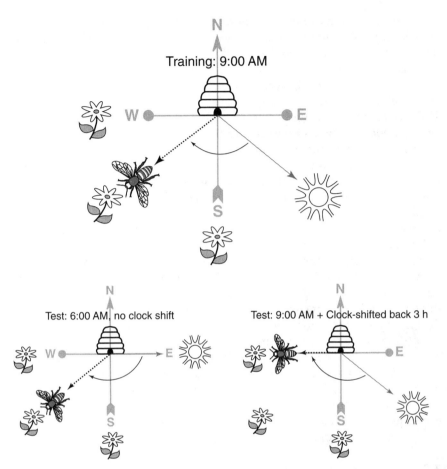

Figure 7.12. The logic of clock shift experiments, showing how to tell which way a clock-shifted animal will head. In this example, a bee trained to find food in the position indicated has its clock shifted back 3 hours. At 9 A.M. it experiences the time as 6 A.M. When it flies from the hive it will maintain the same angle to the sun as when heading to the goal at 6 A.M. before clock shifting.

delayed by having "day" and "night" start 3 hours later than outside. Now, when these birds are released at noon, the advanced group should experience the current time as corresponding to 3 P.M., while the delayed group will experience it as 9 A.M. If they are using the sun as a compass, both groups will be misoriented by approximately 45°, but in opposite directions. This is generally what homing pigeons do in such experiments (Papi & Wallraff, 1992). However, in a short-distance homing experiment like that described here, most of the birds do get home eventually, apparently by using landmarks or other cues.

In laboratory experiments on small-scale spatial learning, animals cannot use a sun compass since the sun is not visible. However, several species of birds have proved to use the sun compass in learning simple spatial discriminations trained outdoors under sunny skies. For example, Bingman and Jones (1994; see also Chappell & Guilford, 1995) trained homing pigeons in an octagonal outdoor arena to find food in the same compass direction at any time of day. Food-storing scrub jays (*Aphelocoma coerulescens*) and black-capped chickadees use a sun compass to retrieve seeds stored in an outdoor arena (Sherry & Duff, 1996; Wiltschko & Balda, 1989). When scrub jays were clock-shifted by 6 hours between storing and retrieving, the segment of the arena in which they searched shifted accordingly. The birds relied on their sun compass in spite of the fact that distant landmarks were visible outside the arena. The chickadees used the sun compass only when the arena was in a familiar location relative to distant landmarks; otherwise they searched randomly. These results raise something of a paradox: the birds rely on the sun compass in preference to landmarks, yet they apparently do not use it at all unless familiar landmarks are visible (Sherry & Duff, 1996)

To use the sun for directional information, animals must acquire some representation of the local ephemeris function and continually update it. Experiments with bees have provided the most extensive information about how this happens. As explained in box 7.1, some of this research has capitalized on the fact that returning honeybee foragers perform a dance in the hive that represents the distance they have traveled and the direction to the food source. The results seem to show that bees have a detailed representation of the local ephemeris function that they acquire by experiencing the position of the sun relative to prominent landmarks. Desert ants use a similar mechanism (Wehner & Lanfranconi, 1981). Birds that migrate at night get similar information from star patterns (see box 7.2).

7.2 How Is Spatial Information Integrated? Modularity and Averaging

7.2.1 Spatial Processing Modules?

Diurnal animals with good vision, like many birds, insects, and primates, have a wealth of cues for orientation available at once—the sun, far and near landmarks, cues emanating from important goals (beacons), features defining environmental shape, path integration, memory for the chain of responses that got them from one place to another. These different kinds of cues constitute different kinds of input demanding different implicit computations. For instance, dead reckoning takes as input some correlate of distances and directions traveled and outputs an approximation of the distance and direction to the starting place. The sun compass takes as input some correlate of the sun's azimuth, processes this with reference to a representation of the ephemeris function, and returns a direction relative to geocentric coordinates. Orienting by landmarks takes as input the currently perceived array or elements of it and returns a distance and direction from the current position to a desired position.

7.1. Updating the Ephemeris Function

Dyer (1987) trained bees to find food by flying out from the hive along a line of trees. When the bees were well trained, the hive was moved to another site, again facing along a line of trees, but the line of trees in the new site was approximately perpendicular to the compass direction of the old line of trees. Test feeders were placed both in the new position indicated by this landmark and in a position in the same compass direction and distance from the hive as the old feeder. When bees were released from the hive under thick clouds, most of them flew to the feeder along the line of trees, presumably finding it using landmarks alone. But when these same bees returned to the hive and danced on the comb, their dances indicated the compass direction of the old feeder, not the new one (for an explanation of bees' dances see chapter 12). Thus, they had referred the location of the new feeder, recognized by landmarks, to their memory of the landmarks' compass direction. The angle of their dances from vertical changed with the sun's azimuth even when the day remained cloudy—that is, the bees updated their representation of the sun's position based on memory of its movements on previous days. When the sun became visible, many bees immediately changed their dance angles to reflect the new compass direction of the feeder.

The solar ephemeris varies with the time of year and the location on the earth (figure 7.11), so bees must have to learn the local ephemeris. To find out how they do it, Dyer and Dickinson (1994) worked with newly hatched forager bees before they had ever left the hive. These bees' first experiences outside were restricted to the late afternoon. Then they were released in the morning under dense clouds so they could not learn anything about the morning sun, and their dances were observed. Although they had never seen the sun in the morning, these bees behaved as if they thought it was roughly opposite to where it had been in the afternoon sky. Unlike experienced bees, however, as long as the morning remained cloudy they did not alter their estimate of the sun's position until noon, at which time they abruptly switched their dance directions by 180° (figure B7.1). In a kind of process that is general to many kinds of learning, bees apparently begin life with a crude default ephemeris function, a best guess about the conditions they are likely to meet, and this is fine-tuned with experience (Dyer & Dickinson, 1996).

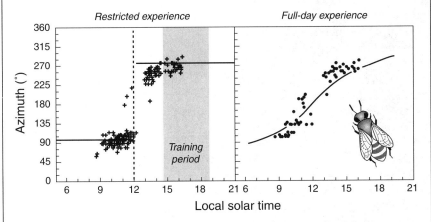

Figure B7.1. The solar azimuth indicated by the dances of bees that had seen the sun only in the afternoon compared to data from bees with normal experience. Redrawn from Dyer and Dickinson (1994) with permission.

What has led some people (Cheng, 1986; Gallistel, 1990) to emphasize the modularity of spatial processing is not so much differences in implicit computations as striking observations of apparently stupid behavior in which one kind of spatial information is used to the exclusion of others that the animal is manifestly sensitive to. The displaced dead reckoning desert ant runs right past its nest, the mother gerbil searches a blank wall even though within range of the smells and cries of her babies, the water shrew jumps over a nonexistant stone, the rat turns its back on a conspicuous landmark that defines the correct corner and digs on the opposite side of the box. In natural environments, redundant cues are normally not dissociated, so relying on just one at a time is likely to work and may be more efficient than processing lots of cues at once. If all possible cues are going to point to the goal, why not just pick one and use it? Reliance on one cue at a time may also reflect the path of evolution. More sophisticated and flexible orientation may have evolved by the addition of new modules rather than the modification of old ones. However, relying on just one source of information at a time is at the extreme of a continuum of rules for combining information from different sources.

7.2.2 Combining Outputs of Different Modules

To discover how different spatial cues are weighted, they can be placed in conflict, with one indicating one goal location and one, another. Does the animal search at one place, at the other, or somewhere in between? The relative weightings of different sources of information may change with the conditions. If the conflict between them is too great, animals appear to fall back on one and disregard the other. Thus, an additive model of cue use may be inappropriate when it comes to combining information from different spatial modules (see Biegler & Morris, 1996b, for an extensive discussion). Rather, some cues may be primary, providing a context in which other kinds of cues are used. In this section we consider how cues are combined after an animal has had opportunity to learn about them. Then in section 7.4 we consider the principles by which spatial cues acquire control in the first place.

In the vector sum model discussed in section 7.1.3, information from two or more landmarks—that is, from within one module—is averaged. Nearby landmarks are weighted more heavily. An especially elegant illustration of this principle comes from a study of how food-storing Clark's nutcrackers relocate their caches (Vander Wall, 1982). Birds buried pine seeds within a 1.5-meter-long oval that had several prominent landmarks at each end. The arena was then expanded by shifting all the landmarks at the right hand end 20 centimeters to the right (figure 7.13). Thus, caches nearer the right end of the arena were nearer to shifted landmarks than were caches on the left end. Birds probed farther from the stationary position of their caches and closer to a position shifted 20 centimeters the closer those caches were to the shifted landmarks. The continuously graded effect shown in figure 7.13, with searches in the middle of the arena shifted an intermediate distance, indicates that the

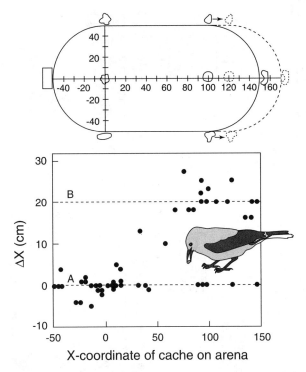

Figure 7.13. Setup and results of experiment to investigate response of Clark's nutcrackers to moved landmarks. Scale on diagram of the arena is in cm. Data are the distance between the location of the nutcrackers' probes for hidden seeds and the left-right location of the caches, as indicated on the map of the arena. Lines A and B represent, respectively, the loci of probes if the birds ignored the moved landmarks or followed them entirely. Redrawn from Vander Wall (1982) with permission.

moved landmarks were averaged with stationary features surrounding the arena.

Although information from landmarks relatively close to a goal may be averaged as described by the vector sum model, very distant landmarks sometimes completely override ones nearby. For example, Collett and Kelber (1988) trained bees to enter little huts to search for artificial nectar. When one of two otherwise fairly featureless huts had an array of yellow cylinders and the other had an array of blue triangles, trained bees searched in the position defined by the particular landmark array even if it was moved to the other hut. However, when the arrays of triangles and cylinders were on two outdoor feeding platforms, the bees disregarded changes in shape and color of the landmarks and searched in the correct position for the given platform—for example, to the left of the landmarks on the east platform. Here, distant visible landmarks were more important in defining location than shape and color of nearby objects.

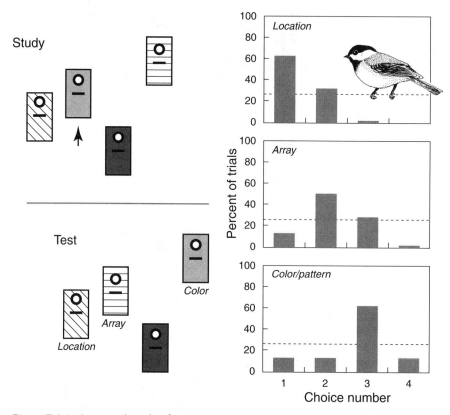

Figure 7.14. Setup and results of experiment investigating which cues to the location of reward are used by black-capped chickadees. On test trials the arrangement of feeders and their location in the room was changed as indicated between the study phase, in which the birds ate part of a peanut in one feeder (arrow), and the unrewarded test phase. Data are the proportion of trials in which the birds looked first, second, etc., into the feeder in the formerly rewarded location in the room, in the same position in the array of feeders, or into the feeder of the rewarded color. Redrawn from Brodbeck (1994) with permission.

The primacy of global spatial position is also illustrated by experiments with food-storing black-capped chickadees. The birds were shown a peanut in one of four distinctively colored feeders in an aviary and returned after a short retention interval to retrieve it (Brodbeck, 1994; figure 7.14). When the array of feeders was moved a relatively short distance along the aviary wall, the birds searched first in the feeder closest in the aviary to the position of the originally baited feeder, even though that might be in a new position relative to the array of feeders. The chickadees tended to search next in the feeder in the correct position in the array, suggesting that they were using spatial cues in a hierarchical manner. However, when the array was moved too far along the wall, performance fell to chance, as if the birds did not recognize the feeders out of their global spatial context. In other animals, too, features near a goal are not reacted to as such unless distant cues or dead reckoning tell the animal it is in fact near the goal (Cheng, 1995; Ellard & Bigel, 1996).

In Brodbeck's task, the baited feeder itself, as defined by distinctive colors and pattern, could function as a beacon. To discover the importance of color and pattern, these cues were placed in conflict with spatial cues by swapping the formerly baited feeder with another feeder in the array on occasional unrewarded test trials (figure 7.14). Chickadees went first to the feeder in the formerly baited location, even though it now looked different. Finding no peanut there, they tended to search next in the feeder with the correct color and pattern. Much of the time, these birds used the redundant cues in the sequence, global spatial, local array, and color/pattern. In contrast, dark-eyed juncos, which do not store food in the wild, weight color and pattern cues about equally with spatial cues. The same pattern of species difference is found in an analogous operant task (Brodbeck & Shettleworth, 1995) and in two other pairs of food-storing vs. nonstoring birds (Clayton & Krebs, 1994). The food-storers' greater reliance on spatial cues in the laboratory may be related to their need for good spatial memory in the wild (see chapter 6).

There are some striking examples of how dead reckoning and landmarks may be used successively, as when the desert ant runs past its nest. However, information from different spatial modules may sometimes be averaged instead, as in the homeward orientation of hamsters carrying hoarded food (Etienne, 1992). When features of the room outside the testing arena provide landmarks that the animals can learn about during the laboratory "day," these landmarks predominate over dead reckoning when the hamsters are tested in the light. For example, if the nest is moved 90° around the edge of the arena before the hamster leaves in search of food, the hamster returns to the usual location of the nest as indicated by landmarks. However, if hamsters are tested in the dark under otherwise identical conditions so they must rely exclusively on dead reckoning, they return to the shifted nest. The continued influence of dead reckoning during testing in the light is evident in a slight shift of the homeward orientation in the direction of the shifted nest (Etienne, 1992). If the hamsters are provided with a single light cue in the dark, they use it as a landmark, too. However, if it is shifted too much relative to the nest before the hamsters depart for the hoarding site, they tend to ignore the light, and some fall back on dead reckoning entirely (Etienne, Teroni, Hurni, & Portenier, 1990). It is as if dead reckoning leads the hamster to expect the light in a certain position and it is disregarded if it is too far from that position. Dead reckoning seems to provide part of the context in which landmarks are recognized. Interestingly, if hamsters are repeatedly tested in the light after the nest has been moved, so they are led astray by the landmarks, they learn to rely more on dead reckoning and less on landmarks, as if they recalibrate their relative weighings (Etienne, 1992).

When animals are navigating in natural landscapes, information from the sun compass may interact with that from landmarks in a way analogous to the interaction of dead reckoning and landmark use in hamsters. Such interactions have been studied most in insects and homing pigeons. One problem in

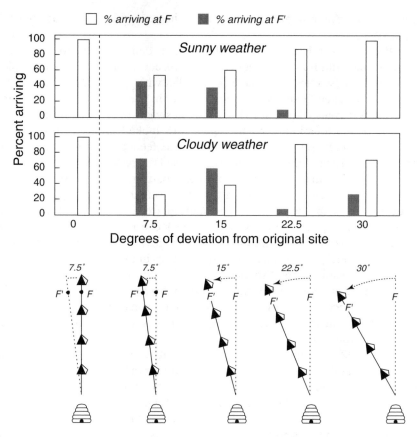

Figure 7.15. Setup and results of an experiment with bees pitting information from landmarks against information from the sun. Redrawn from Chittka and Geiger (1995a).

such work is how to control the kinds of landmarks that might be meaningful in a natural landscape. Chittka and Geiger (1995a) overcame this problem by placing a hive of experimental bees in the middle of a flat 2-kilometer-square meadow surrounded by a nearly uniform line of forest. The bees could find food at the end of a line of yellow tents. When they were well trained, the line of tents was moved up to 30° to one side of the training site. The number of bees arriving at the position now indicated by the landmarks was compared to the number arriving at the original site, its direction now indicated only by the sun compass. The landmarks had more influence under cloudy than sunny skies, but in either case, the more they were shifted, the more bees seemed to ignore them and arrive at the original training location (figure 7.15). The results of this and other experiments with competing cues in natural environments lead Geiger, Kratzsch, and Menzel (1995, p. 344) to conclude that "honeybee orientation appears to result from a set of context-specific interdependent and hierarchically organized mechanisms.

7.2.3 Rules for Combining Cues: Summary

Separate modules for processing different kinds of spatial information combine to determine the animal's decision about what distance and direction to go. Various combination rules may be used. Modules may be employed one at a time, in a hierarchical manner. This hierarchy may reflect the hierarchical structure of the environment. For instance, nearby landmarks or beacons are simply not evident at all distances from the goal. Distant landmarks, dead reckoning, or random search *must* be used to get the animal to the vicinity of the goal before it can use nearby landmarks. Alternatively, rather than being used one at a time the outputs of different modules or information from different cues processed in the same module may be averaged. The weights given to each sort of input may depend on species and individual experience (Cheng, 1995). However, even if averaging is the rule with moderate conflicts between cues, one cue may predominate when the conflict is extreme. The rules for relative weightings may have evolved so that cues that are likely to be more reliable, perhaps because they change less over an individual's lifetime, are weighted more heavily. For instance, because snow and leaves may come and go between the time food is cached and when it is retrieved, relatively large-scale spatial cues are more reliable indicators to its location than the local appearance of the storage site, and this may be the evolutionary reason for chickadees and nutcrackers' reliance on global spatial cues in preference to more local ones.

So far this discussion has focused on how already-acquired information from different sources interacts. But different kinds of information may also interact in various ways when an animal is learning how to find its way in a new environment. This issue is discussed in section 7.4.

7.3 Do Animals Have Cognitive Maps?

7.3.1 What Is a Cognitive Map?

Representations have three essential parts: a represented system, a representing system, and rules for correspondance between them. In the case of spatial knowledge, distances and directions in the world are the represented system and animals' nervous systems are the representing systems. When we encountered representations of CSs and USs in chapter 3, "How does the animal represent the CS" meant simply "What features of the CS are encoded or remembered?" The animal's representation of the CS stood for the CS in the external world, a rather minimal kind of representation. In contrast, the representation embodied in a cognitive map is typically assumed to encode distances and directions and to enable mental operations on them. To take an example we will shortly consider in more detail, an animal that can encode the distance and direction of two feeding sites from a home base and whose nervous system is capable of implicit computations analogous to the operations

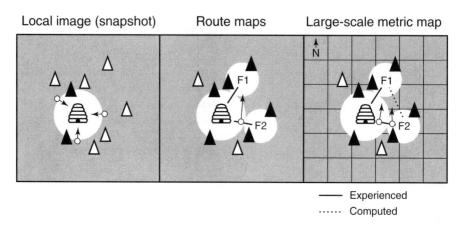

Local image (snapshot)   Route maps   Large-scale metric map

—— Experienced
······ Computed

Figure 7.16. Three ways in which an animal may encode spatial information about the area around its home (the hive). F1 and F2 are two feeding sites, the black triangles are known landmarks, and the white triangles are unknown. The grid in the large-scale map represents the idea that only in this kind of representation is information about different locations related to a common coordinate system. After Dyer (1996) with permission.

of vector algebra can move directly between the two feeding sites without going home in between (figure 7.16). Such a mental representation embodies a *functioning isomorphism* between events in the world and cognitive processes (see Gallistel, 1990, for an extensive discussion).

Distances and directions are the *metric properties* of space. Blueprints, city plans, road maps, atlases, and globes are useful because they represent distances and directions accurately. But plenty of useful maps do not preserve distance and direction. A familiar example is a subway route map. Such a map is useful for planning a trip on the subway because it shows which station is on which route and what order they can be reached in. It can be used without knowing the actual distances between the stations or the metric relationship of the routes to each other. Indeed, because these may not be represented accurately, a tourist wanting to explore the city on foot would be foolish to use it as a guide. In contrast to the subway route map, a map that preserves distance and direction information allows the planning of novel routes to unseen goals. This property of real maps has traditionally distinguished a cognitive map from "mere" reliance on one or more kinds of spatial cues. As we have seen, however, single cues or combinations of them can guide animals very effectively to goals. And desert ants and other animals routinely generate novel routes back to unseen nests by dead reckoning. Therefore, it is not ever easy to be sure that an animal is using a cognitive map. We need to consider the possibility that this is because what a cognitive map is is not as well specified as first appears.

Tolman   E. C. Tolman (1948) introduced the term *cognitive map* into psychologists' debate about place vs. response learning. Rather than simply learning chains of stimulus-response connections, Tolman claimed, rats in mazes learn about places. They acquire "something like a field map of the environment" (p. 192). Stimuli influence behavior not directly, through S-R connections, but through the mediation of the cognitive map. Cognitive maps could be broad and comprehensive or "narrow strip maps," confined to knowledge of specific routes. The most compelling data Tolman cited in support of his hypothesis were from tests of *latent learning* and ability to take novel shortcuts in mazes. In a typical latent learning experiment, a rat was allowed to explore a maze without receiving any reward. For instance, food might always be present in one location but the rat would be satiated. If the rat ran straight to the food when it was made hungry later on, its behavior could not have resulted from the reinforcement of S-R connections because it had not been getting any reinforcement. Therefore, it must have learned the location of the food and generated appropriate behavior on the basis of this knowledge. Similarly, an animal that took an efficient novel shortcut when displaced to a new location or when its usual path to a goal was blocked must have acquired knowledge about the goal as a place.

O'Keefe and Nadel   Although Tolman's views are important in the history of psychology, he actually said rather little about the properties of cognitive maps and how they might be acquired. After a lapse of 30 years, this gap began to be filled by O'Keefe and Nadel (1978) in their influential book *The Hippocampus as a Cognitive Map*. They developed the view that some organisms, including humans, rats, and migratory birds, possess cognitive maps, in the sense of an allocentric, connected, unitary spatial representational framework in which experience locates objects and events. Acquisition and use of the cognitive map is supported by the *locale system*, a cognitive module located in the hippocampus of vertebrates. The locale system contrasts with the *taxon system*, which supports route learning and other relatively inflexible S-R learning and is located elsewhere in the vertebrate brain. Table 7.1 lists the major contrasts between routes and maps, as described by O'Keefe and Nadel. The differential behavioral implications of maps vs. routes are the same as those proposed by Tolman: maps are acquired through exploration (latent learning) and they allow more flexible behavior than route learning. As we will see, one problem with translating these differences into telling behavioral tests is that, on some interpretations, route learning also allows flexible behavior.

Gallistel   Between 1978 and 1990, the cognitive revolution in psychology made the notion of cognitive mapping more acceptable. This period also witnessed an explosion of relevant research, especially with insects and homing pigeons and with rats in situations like the Morris swim task. Thus Gallistel's (1990) review of spatial behavior in animals has a very different flavor from O'Keefe and Nadel's. His overriding theme is the same—animals use cognitive maps—but his definition of *cognitive map* is considerably looser than O'Keefe and Nadel's. In Gallistel's terms (e.g., chap. 6, p. 121), any orientation based on implicitly computing distances and directions rather than re-

Table 7.1. Properties of routes and maps

	Route	Map
Motivation	The final stimulus is the goal; the route is built with this in mind	No object or place on the map is a goal; the map is usually built out of curiosity
Flexibility	Routes are rather rigid; they are rendered useless by any damage, or by the loss of a guidance, or direction	Maps are extremely flexible, and relatively invulnerable to noise and damage
Speed	Very fast	Relatively slow
Information content	Relatively little; each route contains only a small amount of data	Maps are one of the most efficient information storage devices known, with very large capacity
Access	No specialized knowledge is required for access; no coding strategies	Special knowledge of coding strategies required
Manipulation	None	Maps can be compared; places on maps can be compared

Reproduced from O'Keefe & Nadel (1978) with permission.

sponding to a beacon is evidence of a cognitive map. Dead reckoning, matching "snapshots," or responding to landmarks is ipso facto evidence of a cognitive map, albeit perhaps a small-scale and limited one. Species may differ in the richness and detail of their cognitive maps, but evidence for them is ubiquitous. Cognitive maps are constructed by a combination of dead reckoning and direct perception of environmental geometry. "Combining geocentric representations of vantage points and angles of view with egocentric representations of the segment of the world perceived from each vantage point yields a representation of the shape of the behaviorally relevant environment in a system of coordinates anchored to the earth, a geocentric cognitive map" (p. 106).

Alternatives: The Local View Hypothesis   In the opinion of neurobiologist Bruce McNaughton and his colleagues (Leonard & McNaughton, 1990; McNaughton, Knierim, & Wilson, 1995), there is no need to suppose that animals form cognitive maps. Instead, they acquire a set of memories of local views of the environment associatively linked by memories of the movements that take them from one to another. "A location is nothing more than a set or constellation of sensory/perceptual experiences, joined to others by specific movements" (Leonard & McNaughton, 1990, p. 366). This view has been supported by neural net models and studies of the functions of various populations of cells involved in spatial learning. Since it allows for some generalization from previously experienced to related views of the environment, its behavioral implications are difficult if not impossible to distinguish from those of a cognitive mapping hypothesis, as we will shortly see.

Bennett   The map as a metaphor for spatial knowledge has been captivating researchers for at least the past half-century. But this brief review suggests that (1) people haven't always meant the same thing by the term *cognitive map*, and (2) the only generally agreed on behavioral assay of cognitive mapping is the ability to take a novel route without using dead reckoning or simple generalization from familiar local views. This is the conclusion reached recently by Bennett (1996). In his view, there is no solid evidence for cognitive mapping in any species. Discussion of cognitive mapping should be abandoned in favor of more operational discussion of how animals get from place to place. In the next few pages we will review some of the most often-cited evidence for cognitive maps in bees, rats, and other species in the light of this recommendation.

7.3.2 Do Bees Have Cognitive Maps?

Honeybees are ideal subjects for studies of spatial orientation in natural landscapes because foragers routinely make many round-trips each day between the hive and feeding sites hundreds of meters away. Using methods pioneered by Karl von Frisch, marked individuals can be trained to artificial feeding sites selected by the experimenter. Bees captured and released at new sites can be assumed to be heading either home or to a familiar source of food. We have already seen how these methods have revealed how bees use memories of the views near a feeding site to locate it (section 7.1.3). Landmark memory also plays a role in bees' long-distance orientation. Newly emerged foragers gradually become familiar with the area around the hive, as shown, for example, by the observation that when bees are released some distance from the hive, the experienced individuals are more likely to find their way back (review in Dyer, 1994). All of this information suggests that extensive and detailed spatial knowledge exists in bees' tiny brains, but can this knowledge be described as a cognitive map?

Discussion about the answer to this question has centered around a classic detour experiment originally reported by Gould (1986) and since repeated by others, sometimes with different results (Dyer, 1991, 1994; Wehner & Menzel, 1990; review in Gallistel, 1994). Bees were trained to one of two feeders, A and B, equidistant from the hive but out of direct sight of each other. The lines connecting A, B, and the hive formed an approximately equilateral triangle, as in the arrangements depicted in figure 7.16. The test of whether the bees knew the relationship of a feeding site to the landscape as a whole—that is, whether they had placed the familiar feeding site on a cognitive map—consisted of capturing marked individuals as they left the hive for one site and releasing them at the other. A bee released at a novel location flies up maybe 9 or 10 meters, circling around as if getting its bearings, and then heads off in a definite direction. Data consist of the compass bearing recorded when the bee vanishes from view. Evidence of cognitive mapping would consist of average vanishing bearings pointed toward the familiar feeding site. The arrangement of the hive and the feeding sites in Gould's design guaranteed that either of these alternatives could be distinguished from heading in a fixed compass direction from the hive or heading back to the hive.

Gould's bees tended to head toward the familiar feeding site when released at either new site. Therefore, Gould concluded that the bees had a "maplike representation" of their local environment. However, there are two problems with this interpretation. First, if the bees had ever flown the route between A and B before, taking it during the experiment would be evidence of route memory rather than cognitive mapping, and the experience of Gould's foragers was not controlled. Second, even if the bees had not been at the novel release sites before, when they flew up to get their bearings they could have gotten a view of the landscape sufficiently similar to that near the familiar feeding site to allow them to orient. This explanation assumes they could use snapshot memory for orienting over relatively long distances by matching currently perceived features with features in the stored image of the environmental panorama. This requirement of snapshot memory was exploited in a test of Gould's hypothesis done in a landscape with one very interesting feature: one of the two critical feeding sites, B, was down in a quarry whereas A was up at the same elevation as the hive (Dyer, 1991, 1994). Thus when bees trained to B and released at A flew up and viewed the landscape, they obtained a fairly similar view to that which they saw when leaving the hive for B. These bees behaved like Gould's bees and headed off from the novel release site, A, to the feeding site B. But bees trained to feed at A and released at B, in the quarry, could not easily get a view similar to that which they saw when leaving the hive for A. Experienced bees possessing a cognitive map that (by definition) integrates information local to different sites and routes into a single overall representation of distances and directions might be expected to depart from B for either A or the hive. But, in contrast to this prediction, Dyer's bees departed from B in the same compass direction they had been taking when they left the hive. To show that this did not reflect some peculiarity of site B in the quarry, Dyer then trained some bees to fly directly between A and B by gradually moving the target feeder between them. These bees were able to orient accurately.

These results and others like them (Dyer, 1994) seem to reveal that bees are not using a cognitive map to orient effectively from unfamiliar locations. But this interpretation is not universally accepted (e.g., Gallistel, 1994; Gould & Gould, 1994). On Dyer's interpretation, the results of the detour experiments show the impressive flexibility afforded by memory for specific routes and views of the environment. Configural or conditional use of the bees' multiple memories may play a role in this flexibility (Menzel et al., 1996). Once such flexibility is granted, however, is this mechanism behaviorally distinguishable from an integrated representation of distances and directions — that is, a cognitive map? It is hard to see how it is. Recognizing a landscape panorama and moving to reduce the discrepancy between the current and the desired view of it is a mechanism for implementing mapping-like behavior. No map, however rich and accurate, is useful unless its possessor can recognize the current location so as to tell in what direction to head. This recognition can be provided by dead reckoning or in other ways, but for bees traveling hundreds of meters around the hive, it seems to be provided by views of landmarks combined with a sun compass for direction finding.

7.3.3 Do Rats Have Cognitive Maps?

Much of the early work on cognitive mapping in rats inspired by Tolman investigated whether they select efficient detours in mazes (Gallistel, 1990; Leonard & McNaughton, 1990). More recent work has used the Morris swim task (see section 7.1.2). Rats trained to find the hidden platform are clearly using landmarks outside the tank, and there have been numerous tests of whether this memory is based entirely on local views and associated swimming experience in the tank or whether the rat has a map of the environment in some other sense.

Rats experienced in the swimming task rapidly approach the hidden platform no matter where they are released in the tank (Morris, 1981). However, this does not necessarily mean they are generating efficient routes from novel locations because rats typically swim all over the tank early in training. Most likely no location or local view in the tank is completely novel to an experienced rat. (Notice that we met this same argument in the discussion of whether Gould's bees were computing a novel path to a known feeder.) When the rats' experience of different routes has been restricted during training in the radial maze or water tank, they are sometimes unable to navigate successfully when released for the first time in the novel locations. However, limited experience of different routes to the platform need not impair navigation. Keith and McVety (1988) allowed a group of rats to learn the general procedural requirements of the swimming task by training them to approach the platform in one tank from all directions. Control groups either just swam around in the tank or were placed on the platform. Then the rats were placed on the platform of a second water tank, in a novel environment, for 2 minutes, before being required to swim to that platform. The rats that had previously learned the task in a different room located the platform in the new room at least twice as quickly as the rats with other sorts of prior experience. Familiarity with the requirements of the task somehow allowed them to base an efficient trajectory to the platform on the view of the environment they received from it. This result seems to depend on the rats being allowed to swim very soon after placement on the platform; unlike the information acquired when a rat finds the platform by itself, the information acquired from placement is not very long-lasting (R. J. McDonald, personal communication, October 1995). Such results (see also Sutherland & Linggard, 1982) mean that under some conditions rats do not need experience of specific routes or specific views of the environment from their starting place in the water. Passive placement at the goal might allow rats to form a cognitive map of its location. One might equally well conclude that past experience of how its own movements transform its view of the environment allow a rat to move toward a goal at which it has previously been passively placed (Leonard & McNaughton, 1990).

A different approach to distinguishing maps from routes and local views is to ask whether information about distances and directions obtained in different ways, say by dead reckoning and by memorizing landmarks, can be put together into a unitary spatial representation. If an animal's travels are controlled by reference to a single overall allocentric representation of space, it should not matter if information about different parts of a journey is obtained in different ways. One way to test this is to train rats in the swim task or in a large circular arena with a single escape hole or feeding site, with large-scale visual landmarks visible in only part of the space (Arolfo, Nerad, Schenk, & Bures, 1994; Benhamou, 1996; Brown & Bing, 1997; Schenk, Grobety, Lavenex, & Lipp, 1995). The rat's view of the wider environment may be limited by curtains and walls surrounding the goal or by turning off the lights when the rat nears the goal. Although such modifications do interfere with performance, they do not make it impossible for rats to learn to locate the goal. For example, when rats trained to swim to a hidden plaform with the lights on are switched to a condition in which darkness descends as they draw near the platform, they do not approach as rapidly as before (Arolfo et al., 1994). It might be expected that they would be unaffected if they continuously integrated visual information and dead reckoning into a unified representation of their location. Thus these results complement those of Keith and McVety in indicating that the view of the environment from the goal plays an important role in orientation.

Unlike research on spatial cognition in bees, that with rats has been done almost entirely in the laboratory and makes little or no reference to what the animals might be doing in nature. Indeed, since wild rats are nocturnal and tend to travel along established routes and paths (Chitty & Southern, 1954), it is not clear what role the kind of visual orientation just discussed might normally have. Blind rats (Zoladek & Roberts, 1978) perform well on a radial maze, and rats placed in a complex network of enclosed tunnels explore them efficiently, even without food reward (FitzGerald, Isler, Rosenberg, Oettinger, & Battig, 1985). All these animals must be keeping track of where they are by some combination of dead reckoning and senses other than vision. Data showing how voles, chipmunks, and other rodents use space in their natural environments (e.g., Bovet, 1992; Ostfeld, 1990; Ostfeld, Pugh, Seamon, & Tamarin, 1988) might profitably be better integrated with what is known about mechanisms of orientation in the laboratory. Research on spatial cognition in rats differs from that on bees in another important respect: in recent years it has been accompanied by attempts to understand its neural basis. Although whether or not the hippocampus *is* a cognitive map (if any animals have one in any meaningful sense) is still debated, some of the relevant research has led to important discoveries about how space is represented in a mammalian brain (e.g., McNaughton, Knierim, & Wilson, 1995; Nadel, 1995).

7.3.4 Do Any Other Animals Have Cognitive Maps?

A different approach to testing spatial knowledge is to observe how animals travel among multiple goals. Emil Menzel (1978) tested chimpanzees in this way by showing one individual the locations of up to 18 pieces of food, hidden in a large outdoor enclosure. The chimpanzee to be tested on a particular trial was carried around the enclosure by one experimenter while the other deposited the food. Other members of the social group, serving as controls for possible influences of olfactory cues or general knowledge of the experimental space, watched from a nearby cage. When all the animals were released into the enclosure shortly afterwards, the one that had observed the food being hidden went around collecting it. What was striking was that these animals did not necessarily follow the same path they had been carried along while the food was being hidden, though there does seem to have been more than chance similarity between them. Animals did not move at random among the food sites, either, but took a fairly efficient route, tending to minimize the total distance traveled. Such a tendency is difficult to quantify with as many as 18 food sites, so it was also tested with just 4 or 5 sites, 2 or 3 being on one side of the enclosure and the remainder relatively far away on the other. Here, animals visited the side with most food first in 13 out of 16 cases (figure 7.17a). However, 13/16 does not differ significantly from the 9.6/16 expected from random choice with 60% of the food on one side. Notice, too, that many of the paths in figure 7.17a cross the field before all the items on the first side are collected.

Clearly, the chimpanzees in these experiments were able to acquire some representation of multiple locations in a familiar space with only brief experience and then approach those locations from a distance. Food-storing birds behave similarly. For instance, marsh tits (*Parus palustris*) do not retrieve seeds stored in an aviary in the order in which they stored them, nor do they retrace the path that they took while storing (Shettleworth & Krebs, 1982). While storing, they take seeds from a central place one at a time, but while retrieving they travel directly from one storage site to another. Like the chimpanzees, black-capped chickadees remember not only where items are hidden but also something about their relative value (Sherry, 1984). In all of these laboratory tests, the animal is never very far from at least some of the multiple goals. As long as features defining some of the different goals are within sight of each other, the animal will likely approach the nearest or most valuable. That is, a relatively efficient overall route need not mean the animal has a representation of the environment as a whole and plans its entire trip within it. Rather, it may make local choices, one at a time, based on currently perceptible cues.

Experiments with vervet monkeys modeled on Menzel's have recently been reported by Gallistel and Cramer (1996; Cramer & Gallistel, 1997), who propose that cognitive mapping (or at least planning a route beyond the next move) can be distinguished from wholly local choices by using certain kinds of arrangements of food sites. For instance, the optimal path for col-

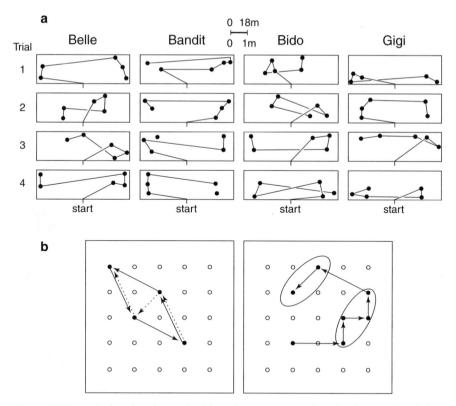

Figure 7.17. a. Paths taken by each of four chimpanzees in their first four trials with five hidden food items. Redrawn from Menzel (1978) with permission. The marker indicates the scale in both a (above) and b (below). b. "Diamond" and "unequal sides" configurations used for testing vervet monkeys. In the diamond configuration, the shortest path among all four corners is the dotted one if the animal is not planning to return to the start (lower right vertex) but the black route if it is. Redrawn from Gallistel and Cramer (1996) with permission.

lecting food from the diamond-shaped arrangement shown in figure 7.17b depends on whether or not the animal is going to return to the starting point. The animal can make the optimal choice after the second food item only by planning beyond the next two choices. Similarly, when four food items are on one side of an arena and two on the other, the animal must mentally look beyond the first two items to be collected in order to move optimally. Cramer and Gallistel (1997; Gallistel & Cramer, 1996) report that their vervets behaved as if planning routes in both of these tests. However, without knowing the animals' reinforcement histories in the testing situation, which are not reported, it is difficult to know how to evaluate these data. As in tests of other kinds of abstract representational abilities, it is important to know how the animals behaved the first time they were tested and what experiences led up to the tests. Moreover, in the four vs. two item test, the monkeys might simply have remembered the area with four items better if they spent more time there while the sites were being baited. Nevertheless, this is a clever proposal, one especially worth pursuing in comparative tests with other primates. Field workers have produced an abundance of information about the spatial and temporal distributions of food eaten by different species of primates. Indeed, differences in relative brain size among primates have been correlated with fruit vs. leaf-eating, with the larger-brained fruit-eaters supposedly experiencing greater cognitive demands associated with tracking temporary and spatially dispersed resources (Clutton-Brock & Harvey, 1977, but see also section 11.5). Field data also indicate that some primates routinely plan efficient foraging routes covering long distances (Byrne, 1995). Such data suggest a wealth of possibilities for comparative tests of the kinds of spatial representations animals might have (see Platt, Brannon, Briese, & French, 1996, for one example). Apes and monkeys may be better candidates for possessors of large-scale integrated representations of space than rats and bees.

7.3.5 Conclusions

Deciding whether any animal is using a cognitive map raises issues similar to those involved in testing whether animals have a concept (see chapter 5), can count (see chapter 8), have a theory of mind (see chapter 11), or are conscious (see chapter 1). Translating an intuitively appealing explanation of apparently intelligent behavior into testable implications in a way that researchers agree on is seldom easy. When the results of behavioral tests cause theorists to revise ambiguous and slippery concepts, agreement can become almost impossible. In the case of cognitive mapping, there is little if any unambiguous evidence that any animal is capable of representing the position of a distant goal and planning how to get there. Bennett (1996; see also section 7.3.1) has a point: most tests of this idea boil down to tests of whether animals can select novel shortcuts to known goals. Rather than asking "Does this animal have a cognitive map or not?" we might more profitably ask, "How does this animal represent space" or "How does it get around?" Since workers in this area (e.g. Menzel et al., 1996; Thinus-Blanc, 1995) are increasingly coming to the same sort of conclusion, research may open up in new directions in the next few years.

7.4 Acquiring Spatial Knowledge: The Conditions for Learning

Up to now, we have focused on the content of spatial learning without saying much about the conditions necessary for acquiring it. This emphasis reflects the current state of research. The conditions for spatial learning are not nearly so well studied as those for simple associative learning (see Cheng & Spetch, 1998; A. R. L. Roberts & Pearce, 1998). Up to now, studies of the acquisition of spatial knowledge have focused on three issues: the role of exploration, whether redundant spatial cues are learned about in the same way as redundant cues in conditioning, and whether one kind of spatial information is calibrated against another in some way. Underlying all these issues is the question of whether there is, as O'Keefe and Nadel (1978) suggested, a special spatial (locale) learning system, distinct from associative learning (the taxon system).

7.4.1 Exploration

From Tolman onward, it has been claimed that animals acquire spatial information by exploring the environment. Exploration was a problem for S-R learning theory because it apparently resulted in learning without reinforcement, but in the 1960s the idea that behavior could be spontaneous and continue without reinforcement became more acceptable (Berlyne, 1960; Hinde, 1970a). The fact that animals tend to explore novel objects and environments is one of the best examples of how the equipment for learning includes special behaviors that expose animals to the conditions for learning. The rat sniffing a novel object, the young pigeon flying in circles over its loft, or the wasp performing an orientation flight are actively exposing themselves to objects and spatial relationships that they need to learn about.

For many birds and mammals, spatial learning begins in the area around the natal nest or burrow. A typical altricial rodent like a ground squirrel ventures out of its burrow a few weeks after birth but stays close to the entrance, maybe just rearing up and looking around from the mouth of the burrow. As the days pass, it makes longer and longer excursions around its mother's territory. Why don't the young range as widely as adults as soon as their eyes and ears are open and they are able to move about? Quite likely one function of the gradual increase in mobility is to allow the young animal to learn gradually about its territory. Knowledge of the whole territory may be built up by connecting a series of "local charts," detailed knowledge about areas around important sites for food or refuge (Poucet, 1993; see also figure 7.16). Indeed, one of the functions of territoriality may be to permit animals to acquire information allowing them to get around more safely and efficiently than they could in unfamiliar areas (Stamps, 1995). For terrestrial animals, information from dead reckoning may be primary here, telling the animal where it is relative to its starting place at the nest or burrow. By integrating the earth-based dead-reckoned coordinates with the perceived egocentric coordinates of prominent landmarks in some way, perhaps associatively, an animal could learn the position of nearby landmarks relative to its burrow (figure 7.18; McNaughton et al., 1996).

The acquisition of spatial knowledge in the wild has been studied most in bees and homing pigeons. Pigeon racers have accumulated a vast fund of lore about what is necessary for the birds to learn the location of the loft (Berthold, 1993; Keeton, 1974). Training racing pigeons typically begins with letting young birds fly around close to the loft and then releasing them increasing distances away. In contrast, laboratory studies of exploration and spatial learning typically begin by dumping an animal into a completely novel environment. Even here the tendency gradually to venture farther and farther

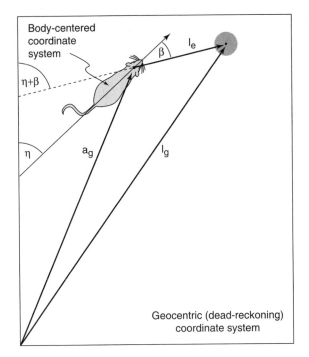

Figure 7.18. How geocentric position can be computed from dead reckoned vectors (thick lines) and egocentric vectors (thin lines). The animal's starting place, the origin for computations by dead reckoning, is the lower left corner. The gray disk is a landmark. Once it has learned the landmark's position in geocentric coordinates, the animal can combine information from the perceived self-to-landmark vector l_e and the remembered landmark to goal vector l_g with currently sensed body-centered coordinates to head home from anywhere within range of the landmark. Redrawn from Gallistel and Cramer (1996) with permission.

from a central place, presumably building up spatial knowledge, can be observed. For instance, rats placed in a large room to live travel over more and more of it in successive nights and gradually organize the initially homogeneous space into nesting sites, food stores, runways, and latrines (Leonard & McNaughton, 1990).

The two paradigms that have been used most extensively to study learning through exploration are habituation and tests of latent learning in mazes. In chapter 4 we saw that habituation is a useful way of studying perceptual learning, and it is equally useful for studying animals' knowledge about what's where. Moving objects around, removing them, or introducing new ones generally elicits investigation of the altered object or location, evidence that the animals knew the features of the environment before it changed (Menzel, 1978; Poucet, Chapuis, Durup, & Thinus-Blanc, 1986; Thinus-Blanc et al., 1987). This method can be used to find out what free-ranging animals know about their environment. For instance, wild rats eat less than usual from a familiar feeder displaced as little as a foot, showing they had learned its location

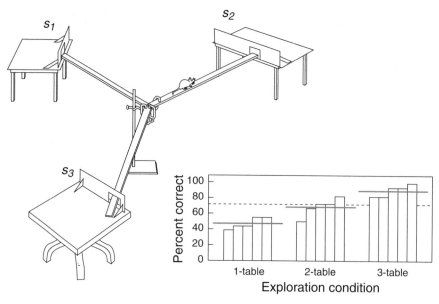

Figure 7.19. Setup for the Maier three-table task, redrawn from Maier (1932b) with permission. Screens are are placed so that rats cannot see from the runways whether or not food is on any of the tables. Data redrawn with permission from the experiment of Ellen et al. (1984) in which rats explored the maze piecemeal, one, two, or three tables at a time before being tested. Results are shown from five rats in each group; solid lines are group means; dotted line is performance level that could occur by chance only 5% of the time or less.

quite precisely (Shorten, 1954; see Shillito, 1963, for similar observations on voles). And, to take a rare example of spatial memory not involving food, free-ranging male thirteen-lined ground squirrels return to locations in their large (average 4.7 hectare) home ranges where they have previously encountered females. If the female has been removed, they spend longer searching for her if she had been about to go into heat the day before. The males also visit a female's territory earlier in the day when she is potentially receptive than otherwise, as if planning their route based on memory of the female's state (Schwagmeyer, 1995).

What aspects of exploration are important? Does the animal have to experience different routes through the environment, different views of it, or what? Some of the best examples of attempts to answer such questions come from studies of restricted exploration in the Maier three-table task (Maier, 1932a; figure 7.19). Three tables in a large well-decorated room are connected by a Y-shaped runway with a central platform from which arms project at 120° angles from one another, each leading to one of the tables. At the beginning of a conventional trial on this maze, a rat is allowed to explore the whole apparatus, which is empty of food. It is then placed on the day's goal table with a large pile of food. After the rat has eaten for a few minutes, but before it has depleted the food, it is removed and placed on one of the other two tables, from which it may return and finish its meal. Trials are typically run only once a day, with the goal table changed from trial to trial. Thus, just as in food storing or the food-retrieval tasks described in the last section, the animal has to rapidly encode a new location for food in a familiar space.

The three-table task was originally devised as a test of "reasoning" or delayed response in rats (Maier & Schneirla, 1935/1964). Experienced rats typically do quite well in it, even with delays of hours between feeding on a table and testing, but accurate choice of the goal table does depend on prior opportunity to explore the maze (Maier, 1932a; Stahl & Ellen, 1974). To discover whether rats can link together two parts of space that have never been experienced close together in time, Ellen, Sotere, and Wages (1984) restricted rats' experience in the exploration phase. Three groups of rats all had 15 minutes a day to explore the maze, but one group was confined to a different single runway and table each day; a second group explored a different pair of connected runways and tables on each day of a three-day cycle; the third group explored all three runways every day. After every three-day cycle of exploration, the rats were given the standard test of working memory for the location of food. The rats that explored only one runway at a time never performed above chance in 18 repetitions of the procedure, whereas most of the rats given full exploration performed above chance from the outset. Rats allowed to explore two tables at a time were intermediate. Thus, in this situation the information gained from piecemeal exploration does not seem to be knitted together into a unitary representation. A similar conclusion can be drawn from earlier work by Maier (1932a; also see Maier & Schneirla, 1935/1964) and from research on the effects of partial exploration of swimming pools and radial mazes (e.g., Sutherland, Chew, Baker, & Linggard, 1987) or limited visual or locomotor access to an arena with objects in it (Save, Granon, Buhot, & Thinus-Blanc, 1996). All these findings seem to indicate that in order to treat different parts of space as connected, a rat has to actually travel between them. Seeing that they are connected is not enough. Perhaps this finding should not be surprising for an animal that normally does most of its traveling in the dark.

7.4.2 Latent Inhibition, Perceptual Learning, and Cognitive Mapping

According to O'Keefe and Nadel (1978), place learning is subserved by a special learning and memory system, the locale system, whereas response learning, route learning, and classical conditioning are part of the taxon system. Some of the ways in which these systems were supposed to differ are listed in table 7.2. Notice that most of these differences are quantitative and do not hold up to close scrutiny in the light of contemporary thinking about associative learning (i.e., the taxon system). Related distinctions have been observed in more recent classifications of mammalian memory systems (e.g., Squire, 1992). Currently some of the best evidence for different systems

Table 7.2. Properties of the taxon and locale systems

	Taxon	Locale
Motivation for learning	Biological need: to obtain reward or avoid punishment	Cognitive curiosity: to construct and update a map of the environment
Learning change	Incremental or decremental	All-or-none
Persistence	High esp. orientation hypotheses	Low
Temporal changes after activation	Marked changes in threshold and strength as a function of time after activation: sensitive to intertrial interval	Minimal changes with time after activation; insensitive to intertrial interval
Interference between similar items	High	Low

Reproduced from O'Keefe & Nadel (1978) with permission.

comes from manipulations of the brain showing that place learning, cue (beacon) learning, and response (route) learning can each be selectively eliminated by a different kind of lesion (McDonald & White, 1993). For instance, a rat in a radial maze may learn to approach a certain light regardless of the location of the light or its own starting position (stimulus-response learning), it may learn a Pavlovian place preference by being placed in an arm which always has food (cue learning), or it may perform the usual radial maze working memory task, collecting one piece of food from each arm of the maze (place learning). A different kind of lesion impairs performance in each of these tasks. But anatomical separability does not have to mean that place, cue, and response information are acquired in fundamentally different ways. Since O'Keefe and Nadel first wrote, the properties of associative learning have been characterized more fully (see chapter 3), but there have been surprisingly few incisive experiments designed to ask whether spatial cues function as CSs and USs. In this and the next two sections we consider the relationship between latent inhibition and spatial learning and how redundant or competing sources of spatial information are learned about.

In associative learning, exposure to a situation may retard acquisition—that is, it can lead to latent inhibition (see chapters 3 and 4). In contrast, exploring novel items in a familiar space is assumed to allow an animal to update its cognitive map in the same way as a cartographer adds a new farmhouse or removes a hedge from a printed map (O'Keefe & Nadel, 1978). Updating can be very rapid, as witnessed by the examples of one-trial learning about the position of food in familiar spaces by chimpanzees, rats, and food-storing birds. Latent inhibition seems to be at odds with cognitive mapping theory, so it is of interest that exposure to a particular spatial context does sometimes retard later learning about locations in it. Just as in associative learning, preexposure enhances discrimination (i.e., perceptual learning occurs) when the locations to be learned about are similar, while latent inhibition occurs when they are very different (Rodrigo, Chamizo, McLaren, & Mackintosh, 1994).

7.4.3 Learning about Redundant Cues: Competition or Parallel Processing?

Another way to ask whether spatial learning is like association formation is to ask whether different spatial cues combine in the same way as different CSs do. Do overshadowing and blocking occur in spatial learning? The Rescorla-Wagner model (see chapter 3) describes a tradeoff among potential cues, but redundancy makes more sense for important tasks like getting home. If simultaneously available sources of information were learned about independently and without mutual interference, then redundant cues could be used as backups if the primary cues were unavailable. The principle of backup mechanisms is well established in studies of orientation in free-ranging animals. For example, experienced homing pigeons tested on sunny days use a sun compass, but birds tested under thick cloud cover can home just as well, relying on landmark memory, olfaction, magnetic information, and/or infrasound (Keeton, 1974). Overshadowing and blocking seem to occur *within* spatial modules (e.g., between different landmarks), permitting the most informative cues of a given type to take control, but other principles may sometimes apply *between* modules (e.g., between dead reckoning and landmarks), permitting different orientation mechanisms to back each other up. And sometimes the outputs of certain modules take priority, setting the conditions under which outputs of other modules are used.

In relatively short-distance spatial orientation by bees, rats, and pigeons in the laboratory, cues of the same type seem to trade off as they do in associative learning. For example, in tests with bees (Cheng, Collett, Pickhard, & Wehner, 1987) and pigeons (Spetch, 1995), landmarks closest to a goal overshadow more distant landmarks. Learning to use a set of three landmarks to locate the hidden platform in a swimming pool blocks rats' learning about a fourth landmark added later on (Rodrigo, Chamizo, McLaren, & Mackintosh, 1997). Blocking and overshadowing have also been found between intramaze cues (floor texture) and extramaze cues in the radial maze (Diez-Chamizo, Sterio, & Mackintosh, 1985; March, Chamizo, & Mackintosh, 1992). For instance, rats that had learned to choose a rubber-covered arm regardless of its location were retarded in learning about the added cue of a fixed location in the room. Studies with the swimming pool task also indicate mutual overshadowing between landmarks and cues close to a goal (Morris, 1981; Redhead, Roberts, Good, & Pearce, 1997). In Morris's study, different groups of rats could learn about either just the location of the invisible escape platform (i.e., it was in a constant location), just the cues associated with the platform (i.e., the platform was visible and moved around from trial to trial) or both the cues and the place (i.e., a visible platform was always in the same place). The rats trained with place alone learned more slowly than those in the other two groups, suggesting that the platform as a beacon was more salient than place cues (see also McDonald & White, 1994). Consistent with this suggestion, when rats were tested with the platform absent, those trained with a visible, unmoving, platform (i.e., place + beacon) spent less time in the part of the tank that had previously contained the platform than those trained with the invisible platform (i.e., place alone). However, the place-alone group had spent longer in the tank on acquisition trials, so they had more opportunity to learn about spatial cues. Moreover, the effects of brain lesions referred to earlier are thought to indicate that although the outputs of the place, cue, and response learning systems may conflict and produce an effect like overshadowing, this reflects competition at output rather than during learning (McDonald & White, 1994).

Another approach to comparing spatial and associative learning is to vary the relative predictiveness of different sources of information present at a single stage of training, as was done by Wagner, Logan, Haberlandt, and Price (1968) with conventional CSs (see chapter 5). As in the tests of overshadowing and blocking, when landmarks are manipulated in a way analogous to CSs, analogous results are obtained. For instance, when one landmark was in a fixed position relative to food and a second landmark moved around and hence was an unreliable cue, gerbils ignored the unreliable landmark (Collett, Cartwright, & Smith, 1986). However, a different picture emerges from some experiments manipulating the relative predictiveness of information thought to be processed by different spatial modules. In a series of experiments, Biegler and Morris (1993, 1996a, 1996b) exposed rats to landmarks that were unstable with respect to the larger space in which the animals searched for food. For instance (Biegler & Morris, 1996b, experiment 2), food was buried in a fixed position 50 centimeters away from one object placed in the central part of 3.3 × 3.3 meter room (figure 7.20). The otherwise homogeneous room was structured by covering three walls with black curtains and the fourth wall with a white one and placing a loudspeaker behind this wall. These polarizing cues remained in a fixed position and the rats were not systematically disoriented between trials, so they could also have used dead reckoning to keep track of their global position. The relative predictiveness of the global cues vs. the landmark was varied for two groups of rats. For the fixed-landmark group, the landmark always stayed in the same position in the room and the polarizing cues were removed every fourth trial, which was unrewarded. Thus, for these rats the global cues predicted reward better than did the landmark. The varied-landmark group was trained similarly except that the landmark together with the food moved from trial to trial within the central part of the arena. This instability meant that the landmark better predicted the food's location than did the global cues. After being trained to find the food accurately, the rats were tested with the landmark in new positions.

Rats in the fixed group should have learned faster than rats in the varied group to find the food since its location was predicted by both global position

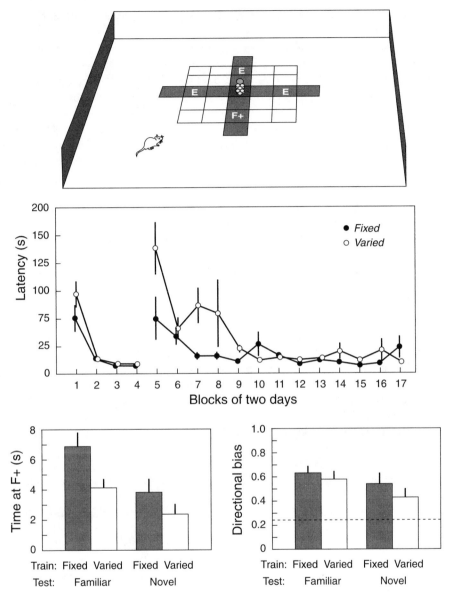

Figure 7.20. Experimental setup and results of experiments testing the effects of environmental stability on landmark use. Food was at F+; during training three of the walls of the room were black and one, the polarizing cue, was white. Data are the mean (+ standard error) latency to find food at F+ during training. The feeder was visible during the first four 2-day blocks. Bottom panels show results of unrewarded tests at the end of training with the landmark in either a familiar or a novel location and polarizing cues present. Data are time spent in F+, both in total seconds and relative to total time in the control areas labeled E in the figure. Redrawn from Biegler and Morris (1996b) with permission.

and landmarks, but by analogy with Wagner, Logan, Haberlandt, and Price's (1968) results, they should have searched less accurately in the tests. The first prediction was borne out, but the second was not (figure 7.20). Both in this and another experiment, increasing the predictiveness of landmarks while decreasing their stability relative to global cues reduced their control in tests rather than increasing it. Yet global context cues alone did not control searching very well in these experiments. Biegler and Morris (1996a) explain this finding by suggesting that the global stability of objects determines the degree to which they will be treated as landmarks. Objects that move around in space may acquire associative strength and hence be approached if associated with, say, food, but they are not used to orient search elsewhere—that is, in distinctively spatial processing (see also Biegler & Morris, 1993).

The generality of Biegler and Morris's findings remains to be determined. Contrary to their results but consistent with associative learning theory, rats in a swimming pool performed better if the landmark defining the location of the dry platform moved around with respect to the space around the pool than if it was stable (A. D. L. Roberts & Pearce, 1998). However, in this study not only was the task different from that used by Biegler and Morris, but also the larger space was rich in cues and the rats were not disoriented before each trial. Few, if any, other studies have systematically compared control by moving and stationary landmarks. However, in other experiments animals of a variety of other species have been trained—apparently without difficulty—to locate a goal defined by the position of landmarks that move around. The experiments by Bennett (1993) with European jays and by Collett and his group with bees (e.g., Cartwright & Collett, 1983; Cheng, Collett, Pickhard, & Wehner, 1987) are examples. Moreover, as with Roberts and Pearce's rats, manipulating the stability of landmarks relative to a larger space can produce results consistent with associative learning theory. Gould-Beierle and Kamil (1996, experiment 3) trained Clark's nutcrackers to find a buried pine nut a fixed distance and direction from a single landmark that moved around within a room, and the birds' search was controlled perfectly by the landmark's position. Global cues that influenced search when they provided redundant information early in training lost control when they became irrelevant. Again, this experiment differed from those of Biegler and Morris not only in the species used but also in procedural details. Regardless of what factors turn out to be involved, varying the relative predictiveness of different kinds of information seems likely to be a productive approach for further tests of possibly unique forms of spatial learning.

7.4.4 Calibration

Calibrating a physical measuring instrument means comparing its readings to those of an independent standard and adjusting it so its readings match the standard's. An electronic thermometer might be calibrated against a mercury thermometer, for example. Analogously, one orientation mechanism may be changed by experience so that its outputs more closely match those of a sec-

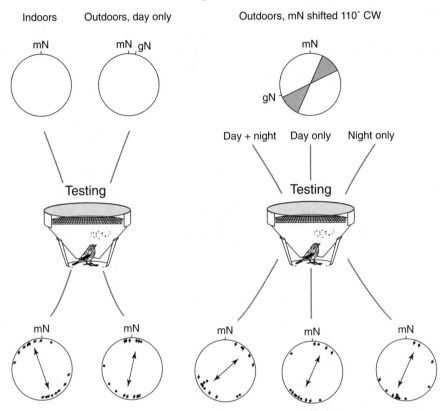

Figure 7.21. Magnetic orientation of groups of savannah sparrows raised and tested under five different conditions. mN = magnetic North; gN = geographic North; cw = clockwise. Arrows show average orientation of groups of birds (dots) tested indoors in funnel cages. Redrawn from Able and Able (1990) with permission.

ond, independent mechanism. Calibrational learning differs from imprinting or associative learning because both the calibrated and the calibrating mechanism support more or less appropriate behavior by themselves in advance of the experience that calibrates one against the other.

The prime example of calibration involves magnetic orientation and the celestial compass in migratory birds (Able, 1991; Able & Able, 1990; box 7.2). Like other species of migratory birds, young savannah sparrows (*Passerculus sandwichensis*) have a magnetic compass. In their first autumn, birds reared and tested indoors exhibit migratory restlessness and orient along the magnetic north-northwest to south-southeast axis, showing that the magnetic compass alone is sufficient for inexperienced birds to orient appropriately. To see how sight of the sky and associated cues to geographic north might alter the magnetic compass, Able and Able (1990, 1996) exposed young sparrows

Box 7.2. Celestial Cues and Long-Distance Migration

Even though they are normally active only during the day, many species of small birds migrate at night. The primary directional cues available then are the earth's magnetic field and, on clear nights, the stars. But the pattern of stars varies with geographic location, time of night, and season, and it changes over geologic time. Some insight into how birds nevertheless use the stars to tell direction comes from some now-classic experiments by Steve Emlen (1970) on indigo buntings (*Passerina cyanea*). He raised three groups of birds indoors, out of sight of the sky, except that late in their first summer he gave two of those groups 22 nights' exposure to the "sky" in a planetarium. For one of those groups, the star patterns moved around the North Star, as they would normally; the other group also saw a slowly rotating star pattern, but the center of rotation was the bright star Betelgeuse in the constellation Orion. Then, in October and November, all the birds spent some nights in the planetarium under star patterns typical for the time of year, but those patterns were stationary. The birds with no experience of the sky were not well oriented (but see Emlen, Wiltschko, Demong, Wiltschko, & Bergman, 1976), whereas the birds exposed to the normal sky oriented southward, away from the Pole Star, indicating that they had somehow learned to use the stationary star patterns during earlier exposure to the normal night sky. How they learned is revealed by the behavior of the third group. They treated Betelgeuse as the North Star, flying "south" with respect to it, indicating that the star or stars near the

➠

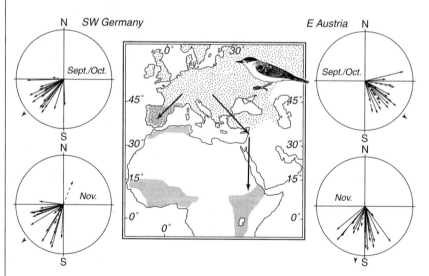

Figure B7.2. Breeding (dotted) and wintering (gray) areas of two populations of European blackcaps with their major migration routes. Arrows inside the circles represent orientation of hand-raised birds from the two populations tested in funnel cages during the period when they would normally be migrating. Each vector is the mean orientation of a single bird; the longer the arrow the stronger the directional tendency. Redrawn from Helbig (1994) with permission.

Box 7.2. (*continued*)

center of rotation of the night sky is used to give direction. Magnetic information interacts with this information during normal development (see Weindler, Wiltschko, & Wiltschko, 1996).

Emlen's experiments made use of two aspects of behavior that have provided much data in experiments on bird migration. One is that even captive, hand-reared birds exhibit nocturnal activity, so-called migratory restlessness, at the time of year when they would normally migrate (see Gwinner, 1996). The other is that this activity is oriented: even birds in indoor cages tend to hop toward the compass direction in which their conspecifics are flying at that time of year. Which way birds hop is cleverly recorded in the funnel-shaped cages depicted in figure 7.21: the bottom of the funnel is covered with an inked pad, and the sides of the funnel, with white paper that absorbs ink. The density of inky footprints around the cage wall is a record of the relative frequency of different headings.

Whereas Emlen's birds simply headed south when it was time to migrate, some species change direction in mid-journey, following routes that take them around inhospitable places like the Alps and the Sahara. Young birds raised in captivity show evidence of population-specific genetic programs that specify direction and duration of migratory restlessness with respect to the magnetic field (Helbig, 1994, 1996). Figure B7.2 shows an example in which two European populations of a single species, the blackcap (*Sylvia atricapilla*), migrate in different directions, and one changes course partway while the other does not.

---

in their first summer to various kinds of experience of the sky in the presence of a magnetic field. In the autumn, they tested the birds indoors in the natural magnetic field (figure 7.21). Experience of the daytime sky in the normal magnetic field had only a small effect on the birds' orientation, consistent with the fact that geographic north is almost the same as magnetic north near Albany, New York, where the experiments took place. Three groups of birds had experience outdoors in view of the sky with magnetic north shifted 110° counterclockwise. For them, geographic north, indicated by the stars or patterns of light in the daytime sky, was shifted relative to magnetic north. This discrepancy resulted in recalibration of the magnetic compass: when the birds were tested indoors in the autumn (i.e., with magnetic cues alone), their orientation was shifted an average of 108° compared to the orientation of the control groups (figure 7.21).

Some birds acquire a star compass through early experience seeing the slow rotation of the night sky (box 7.2). And as we have just seen, the magnetic compass can also be used independently, when star or sun compass information is not available. The fact that celestial information about the direction of north takes precedence over, or calibrates, magnetic information may reflect the fact that celestial information—for example, the center of rotation of star patterns—is a reliable cue to geographic north whereas magnetic information may vary in strength from place to place (Able & Bingman, 1987).

7.5 Summary and Conclusions

This chapter began by describing a wide range of mechanisms animals use for getting around. By itself, each of them has advantages and disadvantages. Dead reckoning tends to accumulate error and does not always compensate for passive displacements, making it most useful for short journeys back and forth to a central place. Dead reckoning is especially useful in an environment with relatively few landmarks, as in the dark or in the desert. Other ways of getting back and forth to a starting place include route learning both in the sense of a memorized sequence of motor patterns (response learning) and in the sense of a sequence of responses to landmarks. Dead reckoning and route learning in either sense leave the animal lost if it is displaced too far off its usual route. However, stimulus generalization between familiar and unfamiliar views of the environment might give route learning some flexibility. During evolution, both diurnal and nocturnal species have been able to rely on celestial cues for direction relative to the earth's surface. However, the sun compass or star compass gives only directional information. Additional information is required for the animal to know *where* it is on the earth's surface and therefore which way to head to reach a given goal. Landmarks can provide this information.

The varieties of spatial information—from landmarks, beacons, the sun, the stars, magnetism, dead reckoning, environmental shape, and so on—are processed in different cognitive modules. These modules take different kinds of input and output decisions about what distance and/or direction to move relative to different kinds of cues. All but the simplest of animals in the simplest of situations have many spatial cues available simultaneously. A great deal of attention has been devoted to the question of whether any animal integrates different sources of spatial information into a unified allocentric representation of distances and directions, a cognitive map. This question turns out to be difficult to answer, partly because cognitive maps can mean different things to different people. Furthermore, the kind of flexible behavior predicted by cognitive mapping can be generated by simple stimulus generalization from familiar views of the environment. This does not necessarily mean that discussion of cognitive mapping should be abandoned, but that what a cognitive map uniquely implies for behavior needs to be made more precise.

Most analysis of spatial orientation has been done with three very different groups of animals: small nocturnal rodents (rats and hamsters); diurnal, central-place foraging insects (bees, wasps, and ants); and birds that orient over tens to hundreds of kilometers (homing pigeons and migratory species). The ways in which these animals perceive the world (consider, for instance, the very different visual systems of rats, pigeons, and bees) and the cues relevant for orientation in their natural environments differ enormously. Nevertheless, it is still possible to consider some orientation mechanisms such as landmark learning in a way that cuts across phyla. Mechanisms of orientation in bees, homing pigeons, and migratory birds have been analyzed in the animals' natural environments, and people studying these species have acquired a very detailed understanding of how their subjects get around. In contrast, rats may have been the subjects of more research, but too little of it has taken into account what rats do in the wild, and until recently, at least, orientation by visual cues seems to have been overemphasized. Fortunately, theorizing now seems to be moving in a less anthromorphic direction (e.g., McNaughton et al., 1996) and recognizing the possible primacy of dead reckoning and other nonvisual information such as tactile input from the rats' whiskers.

Some of the most interesting questions about the acquisition and use of spatial information concern how the outputs of different spatial modules are combined. Are different kinds of information processed in parallel during acquisition, is redundant information ignored, or is the output of one module calibrated against that of another? When are modules used in a hierarchical manner, and why? When spatial cues have acquired their significance, do they compete for control or are their outputs averaged? When does each kind of combination rule operate? For instance, does the system that has been more reliable during evolution or individual experience or that evolved earlier take precedence? The study of spatial orientation is a very active area using a wide variety of species and approaches from field work to neuroscience. Therefore, we may hope for new insights into these and other issues in the not too distant future.

Further Reading

The January 1996 special issue of *The Journal of Experimental Biology* is a collection of up-to-date and authoritative discussions of nearly every issue, species, and research program discussed in this chapter, with substantial sections devoted to homing, migration, and short-distance orientation. The book edited by Healy (1998) provides introductory overviews of most of these areas by some of the major players in the field. A number of other recent books can be consulted for longer reviews of homing and migration. *Animal Homing* (Papi, 1992a) discusses orientation in each animal group separately. Wehner's chapter on arthropods is especially useful. Schöne (1984) is a comprehensive catalogue of spatial orientation mechanisms. Gould and Gould (1994) contains an extensively illustrated discussion of bee behavior. Dyer (1994) is recommended for a thoughtful analysis of insect orientation and a contrary point of view. Berthold (1993) is a useful introductory survey of bird migration and homing, while Dingle's (1996) *Migration* covers all species.

The chapter by Thinus-Blanc (1995) is an insightful discussion of how animals (mostly mammals) acquire spatial knowledge, like this one emphasizing what can be accomplished with combinations of simple mechanisms. The first six chapters of Gallistel (1990) discuss all aspects of animal spatial cognition and place it in the context of human navigation. Cheng (1995) is a recent theoretical overview. The article by Biegler and Morris (1996a) contains a thorough and insightful review of the ways in which different spatial modules may interact. For a discussion of exploration, Berlyne (1960) is recommended. The theoretical context may be dated, but it contains a lot of wisdom and a summary of much of the psychological and ethological literature. The first two chapters of O'Keefe & Nadel's (1978) book are an excellent introduction to philosophical and psychological notions about space. Many of the recent theories of the role of the hippocampus in spatial and other behavior are discussed in *Memory Systems 1994* (Schacter & Tulving, 1994).

8

Timing and Counting

Just as sunset gives way to dusk, the dark silhouettes of bats and nighthawks appear, swooping and gliding over city rooftops or close to the surfaces of lakes, catching insects. Like most other living things, these animals have an internal rhythm, a biological clock with a period of about 24 hours that allows them to become active at the same time each day. Some of the most impressive evidence for such a clock is the nightly appearance of thousands of South American oilbirds, pouring out from their roosts deep in caves where no sunlight reaches.

Clocks that time intervals much less than 24 hours are evident in classical and instrumental conditioning. Pavlov (1927) described the first examples. For instance, a dog trained with a three-minute whistle predicting weak acid to its mouth salivated most during the last minute of the whistle. This phenomenon, called *inhibition of delay* by Pavlov, suggests that the dog was timing the signal in some way. Contemporary research on how animals time intervals seconds to minutes long includes some of the most elegant experiments and quantitative models in the study of animal cognition. It is worth knowing about for that reason alone.

Timing is also worth knowing about for functional reasons. Information about how animals time events will come in handy in the chapter on foraging that follows this one. Models of foraging suggest that animals need to be sensitive to rates of occurrence. Mathematically, rate is number divided by time, so this idea implies that we need to know how animals both count and time to understand foraging behavior. Another reason for discussing counting as well as timing in this chapter is that one theory of animal counting suggests that it reflects the same mechanism as timing. Neither counting nor timing, however, reflects the same clock that underlies the bats' nightly appearances. Timing short intervals and adjusting the daily activity cycle to local light and darkness are the outputs of two different information-processing modules with different properties.

8.1 Circadian Rhythms

The regular alternation of day and night is perhaps the most predictable event on earth. Therefore it is not surprising that nearly every organism that has been studied, including plants, bacteria, and human beings, has an internal model of this daily rhythm. This internal model is evident in a daily cycle of activity and/or physiological state that persists even when organisms are kept in unchanging light or darkness. Endogenous circadian rhythms are not usually regarded as part of cognition, but they appear in this book for three reasons. First, the way in which circadian rhythms are synchronized with (or *entrained to*) local day and night is an instructive example of behavioral plasticity in response to experience. Biological rhythms illustrate beautifully the general principle that animals have evolved implicit internal representations of important aspects of the world, representations programmed to be modified in adaptive ways by the sorts of experiences that are functionally relevant in nature (Shepard, 1984, 1994). Second, animals learn about events that recur on a daily basis, linking them to the state of their circadian clock. Such learning is likely important in the wild for many species. Finally, by understanding something about timing daily events, we will be able to see why timing intervals in the seconds to minutes range requires a different mechanism.

8.1.1 Entrainment: Synchronizing Endogenous Cycles with Environmental Cycles

Some animals, like most of us, get up in the morning and sleep at night. Others, like bats and moths, do the reverse. Still other species are most active at dawn and dusk. Casual observation in nature suggests that animals' and plants' daily rhythm of activity is driven by cues from the environment. However, in general, daily behavioral rhythms are controlled by an underlying pacemaker that runs independently of the environment but that needs continual environmental input if behavior is to remain synchronized with day and night. The very earliest studies of biological rhythms revealed that daily rhythms of activity and other physiological variables persist, often indefinitely, when animals are isolated from the influence of local day and night. The persistent rhythm cannot be produced by some unknown signals from the earth's rotation reaching into laboratory rooms because these *free-running* rhythms are generally slightly more or less than 24 hours long. This means that after awhile animals kept in the laboratory will be active when their conspecifics outdoors are asleep, and the reverse. Because the *endogenous* (i.e., self-generated) daily rhythm is not exactly 24 hours in length, researchers refer to *circadian* rhythms—rhythms of approximately (*circa*) a day. An example is shown in figure 8.1.

The process by which the underlying rhythm-generator or *pacemaker* is synchronized with environmental signals is referred to as *entrainment*. The signal that entrains the rhythm is referred to as an *entraining agent* or *zeitgeber* (literally "time-giver" in German). The most-studied zeitgeber is light, but other stimuli can also function as entraining agents (Mrosovsky, Reebs, Honrado, & Salmon, 1989). Our examples are almost all of activity rhythms because these are easily measured in the laboratory and have featured in large numbers of studies, but most physiological variables exhibit a daily cycle; it is difficult to find one that does not. The propensity to be entrained is an adaptive feature of the circadian system that adjusts behavior to the local environment. However, the behavioral and physiological variables controlled by the underlying circadian pacemaker can also be influenced in other ways, and it is important to distinguish these from the effects of entrainment. For example, during a total eclipse of the sun, birds stop singing and sit still, as if dusk were falling. Conversely, a diurnal rodent asleep in its burrow can be stimulated to activity if a predator breaks in on it. Such transient changes are not symptoms of the underlying rhythm; they simply *mask* it.

Several well-defined criteria distinguish entrainment from other forms of plasticity (Moore-Ede, Sulzman, & Fuller, 1982):

1. The putative entraining agent must act in the absence of other cues.
2. It must act to adjust the period of the animal's free running rhythm to the period of the signal. The unlikely hypothetical case in which a signal repeated every 19 hours caused an animal to become active every 24 hours would not be a case of entrainment because the periodicity of the behavior would not match the periodicity of the signal.
3. The entrained rhythm must adopt a stable phase relationship with the imposed cue. For example, if a group of animals is isolated in constant light or constant darkness, the free-running rhythms of different individuals will eventually be out of phase with one another, reflecting individual differences in free-running period. On any given day, one animal may become active at 10 A.M., another at noon, and so on. Yet if all the animals are now exposed to the same light-dark cycle, before very long their activity rhythms will be synchronized with the environment and, incidentally, with one another. The original phase relationship of the pacemaker with the entraining agent does not influence the final, species-specific relationship.
4. Entrainment can be distinguished from direct driving of the rhythm (i.e., masking) by putting the animals back into constant conditions and observing the relationship between the phase of the free-running rhythm and the phase of the just-removed environmental cycle (figure 8.2). If the animals in our example are truly entrained, then their activity rhythms will all start their free-running drift in the same place. For example, if laboratory "dawn" and the onset of activity had been at 10 A.M., the animals will still become active about 10 A.M. on the first day with constant lighting conditions. However, if

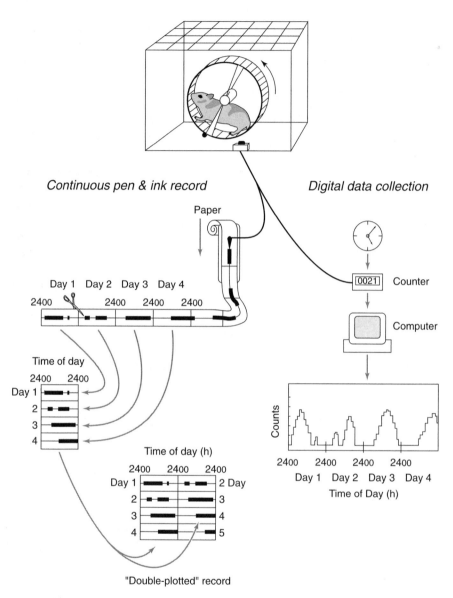

Figure 8.1. Setup for recording rhythms of locomotor activity in hamsters and typical data. (Golden hamsters are used in much contemporary research on mammalian rhythms because of their very clear and reliable rhythms of running wheel activity.) In the traditional method (left), each revolution of the running wheel results in a pen mark on a continuously running roll of paper. When the records of successive days are mounted one under the other, as at the lower left, regularities in the daily pattern of activity can easily be picked out by eye. This is even easier when each day is "double plotted," as at the bottom. Using a computer to record the activity counts, as is often done nowadays, may facilitate detailed quantitative analyses. Redrawn from Moore-Ede et al. (1982) with permission.

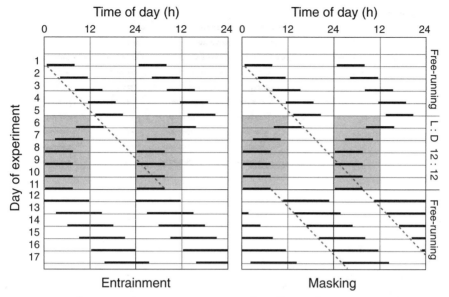

Figure 8.2. The contrast between entrainment and masking. A free-running activity rhythm (in this case, one with a period slightly greater than 24 hours, as indicated by its drift to the right) is synchronized by imposition of a 12-hour light–12-hour dark schedule (L:D 12:12; gray rectangles represent the dark period). When the synchronizing cue is removed, the animal on the left shows that it has been entrained; the other's activity returns to where it would have been without the cue, indicating that the underlying rhythm had simply been masked by the L:D cycle.

the laboratory light cycle is simply masking the effects of the circadian pacemaker, each animal may become active at a different time when constant conditions are instituted. In masking, the time of activity is predicted by extrapolating from the drift in the free-running rhythm before the environmental cue was imposed (figure 8.2).

Entrainment is a kind of behavioral plasticity in which the animal's internal model of the cycle of day and night is brought into register with true day and night. It is analogous to the calibration of the magnetic compass discussed in chapter 7, in that experience brings a preexisting adaptive response into better agreement with the environment. Like many other kinds of preprogrammed, adaptive, behavioral plasticity, entrainment of the 24-hour rhythm is most sensitive to modification by conditions close to those found in nature. Circadian rhythms can be entrained only to periods of about 24 hours. "About 24 hours" means different things for different species and situations, but a range of three or four hours around 24 hours is typical. Thus, it might be possible to entrain activity to 22- or 26-hour days (i.e., a period of light plus a period of darkness every 22 or 26 hours), but unlikely that the rhythm could be entrained to 19- or 29-hour days.

The fact that a free-running rhythm can be brought into a predictable re-

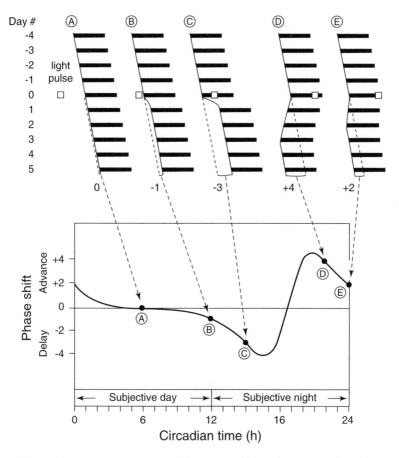

Figure 8.3. A phase-response curve and how it was derived. Data are from five experiments with a nocturnal species. In each, a brief pulse of light is presented at a different phase of the free-running rhythm and the effect on activity is measured as number of hours' advance or delay. Redrawn from Moore-Ede et al. (1982) with permission.

lationship with a zeitgeber means that a cycle of changing sensitivity to the zeitgeber underlies the measured behavioral or physiological rhythm. This sensitivity can be revealed by experiments in which a single pulse of light 10 or 15 minutes long is presented to animals free running in constant conditions. The effects of a few minutes of light on one occasion are evident in the ensuing few days, in which the activity rhythm first shifts and then runs freely again. Figure 8.3 shows an example for a nocturnal animal like a golden hamster. In a regular 24-hour cycle of light and dark, the animal would become active at the onset of darkness. When the rhythm is free running, the period of activity reveals this nocturnal animal's *subjective night*; *subjective day* is the period of prolonged inactivity. (For a diurnal animal the terms are reversed: subjective day is the active period.) In this typical example, a pulse of light early in the subjective night causes the animal to become active later the next day—that is, the phase of the rhythm has been delayed relative to the external 24-hour cycle. Conversely, a pulse of light toward the end of the subjective night advances the rhythm—the animal becomes active earlier the next day. Somewhere toward the middle of subjective night, the effect of a light pulse switches from delaying to advancing. Light has little or no effect in the middle of subjective day. Hamsters' activity rhythms can also be entrained by social stimulation like the regular arrival of a mate or rival or by activity in a novel environment. Such zeitgebers have a characteristic pattern of effects different from those of light (Mrosovsky et al., 1989). In contrast, nonphotic stimuli associated with light through Pavlovian conditioning may affect rhythms in rats in the same way as light does (Amir & Stewart, 1996).

The fact that the circadian rhythm is most sensitive to light near the beginning and end of subjective night means that, in nature, dawn and dusk are constantly pushing and pulling animals' endogenous circadian rhythm into synchrony with day and night. In the laboratory, synchrony can be produced by exposing animals to *skeleton photoperiods*—that is, a pulse of light at the beginning of laboratory "day" and another one at the end. This mimics the regime that a nocturnal cave- or burrow-dweller might expose itself to naturally. If it ventures out too early in the evening, its activity will begin later the next day (i.e., its rhythm will be delayed), whereas if it stays active too long, the pulse of light at dawn will advance its activity, causing it to rise earlier the next night. This suggests that an animal that stays in its den for many days on end may become desynchronized with the external day and night (i.e., its rhythm free runs). This is exactly what happens to beavers that stay in their lodges and under the snow-covered ice throughout the Canadian winter (Bovet & Oertli, 1974).

The direction and amount of shift in the free-running rhythm produced by a single pulse of light are summarized in a *phase response curve*, a plot of the response of the rhythm to a constant signal as a function of the rhythm's phase when the signal was applied. Figure 8.3 shows an example and how it was derived. A phase response curve (PRC) is analogous to the function relating learning to the CS-US interval or the number of conditioning trials (see chapter 3) in that both describe the effect of an environmental event as a function of systematic variation in its features. Learning is usually thought of as generating new knowledge and behavior, whereas entrainment brings a preexisiting cycle into register with a cycle in the environment. However, as we have seen in chapter 3, conditioning can be seen as bringing a preorganized sequence of behavior, or a behavior system, under the control of certain kinds of environmental events (Timberlake, 1994). This provocative analogy summarizes the notion that conditioning does not create the behavior expressive of conditioning any more than entrainment creates the behaviors that change on a circadian cycle. But it is no more than an analogy: entrainment and associative learning otherwise have very different properties, as the next section emphasizes.

8.1.2 The Effect of Regular Meal Times: Learning or Entrainment?

The 24-hour cycle of day and night is ubiquitous on earth, but in an individual's own environment, other events may also have a daily periodicity. Hummingbirds or bees may find their favorite flowers open only in the morning; kestrels find the rodents they prey upon out of their burrows at some times and not others (Rijnsdorp, Daan, & Dijkstra, 1981). A major function of the circadian system is to allow each behavior to be performed at the most appropriate times of day. The most-studied example is feeding. Many animals can adjust their activities to periodic feeding opportunities, but how do they do it? There are three possibilities. One is that the circadian oscillator that can be entrained by light is also entrained by regular feeding. A second possibility is that activity in anticipation of regular feedings represents the output of a second endogenous oscillator that is entrained by food (i.e., a food-entrainable, as distinct from a light-entrainable, oscillator). Third, the animal may simply learn at what time of day—at what phase of its circadian clock—to expect food.

A landmark in research in this area was a study in which rats in running wheels were fed two one-hour meals a day, at 10 A.M. and 4 P.M. (Bolles & Moot, 1973). The rats soon began to show a pattern of anticipatory running beginning in the hour or so before each feeding and increasing up to the time when food was given (figure 8.4). Because hunger was presumably greater near 10 A.M., after 17 hours of deprivation, than near 4 P.M., the rats were not simply running more as they became hungrier. They must have been using time of day as a conditional cue. Moreover, when food was omitted on test days, running peaked around the usual time of feeding, then declined and increased again before the next usual mealtime. Thus, the rats were apparently learning when their mealtimes were. It could be suggested instead that the two periods of running represent the output of two separate food-entrainable oscillators. However, this kind of interpretation becomes less and less plausible as there are more and more separate mealtimes to learn. As we will see shortly, some birds can learn about four separate daily feeding times, and bees can apparently learn nine (Gallistel, 1990; Mistlberger, 1993).

The data for days when food was omitted in figure 8.4 resemble data for timing shorter intervals to be discussed in section 8.2. However, when events are just seconds or minutes apart, the exact interval doesn't matter: animals can learn to time any arbitrary short interval. But events that occur just once or twice a day do not affect behavior unless they have roughly 24-hour periodicity. If food is given just once a day in experiments like those of Bolles and Moot, rats develop anticipatory running only with interfood intervals around 22 to 26 hours. They do not show any sign of learning about feedings 19 or 29 hours apart (review in Mistlberger, 1993). However, food anticipatory activity does not seem to be characterized by a phase response curve: it appears to be acquired equally well with feedings at any time of day (Honrado & Mrosovsky, 1991).

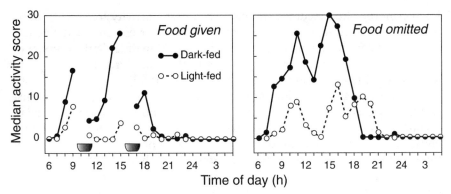

Figure 8.4. Running activity (wheel revolutions per hour) of rats fed twice a day, during the dark or the light phase of the light-dark cycle, and activity in a test with no food given. Redrawn from Bolles and Moot (1973) with permission.

When rats whose circadian clocks are free running in constant darkness are fed regularly once every 24 hours, they do tend to be most active just before the feedings. Thus their activity records resemble those of rats entrained to a daily light cycle, suggesting that the main light-entrainable oscillator was entrained by feeding. But when regular feedings are discontinued, the rats' free-running activity rhythm resumes as predicted from before the spell of regular feedings rather than as predicted by entrainment. Interestingly, when food restriction is reinstated after a period of ad lib food, the activity reappears at the old phase of daily cycle, as if reflecting a persistent memory of when feedings occurred under restriction (Gallistel, 1990). However, such data have also been interpreted as indicating that an oscillator entrained by periodic feedings ran free in their absence and is expressed again when food is restricted (Mistlberger, 1993). The notion that feeding entrains a separate circadian oscillator rather than conditioning anticipation to a particular phase of the rhythm entrained by light is also supported by evidence that it is easier to anticipate feedings separated by 25 or 26 hours than by 22 or 23 hours (Mistlberger & Marchant, 1995). This asymmetry is difficult for a learning model to account for. The conclusion that rats, which have been studied most, seem to have separate food-entrainable and light-entrainable oscillators is also supported by neurobiological studies. Rats with lesions to the suprachiasmatic nucleus of the hypothalamus, which abolish circadian rhythms, still show activity that anticipates daily feedings (review in Mistlberger, 1993).

The relative contributions of entrainment and learning about circadian phase to the effects of periodic feedings vary across species (Mistlberger, 1993). In contrast with rats, bees appear to have just one circadian oscillator, which can be entrained by food as well as light. Bees kept in constant light and offered sugar water once a day had their free-running activity rhythm entrained to the time of feeding (Frisch & Aschoff, 1987). Each experimental nest's daily bout of activity shifted progressively until it began around mealtime; the phase of the rhythm and the zietgeber had a predictable relationship.

Furthermore, when feedings stopped, each nest's activity free-ran from its new position in time, satisfying another criterion for entrainment. The few species that have been studied in depth also appear to differ in the number of different daily feeding times they can learn. Bees and birds may be able to learn more different times than rats (Mistlberger, 1993).

The preceding brief review indicates that in some species and situations, regular feedings at one or more times of day may entrain a distinct circadian oscillator while in others they are linked by learning to the circadian rhythm entrained by light. Currently, there are two ways of describing learning about time of day. In one interpretation, the internal 24-hour rhythm provides a contextual stimulus with which other events like feeding or the arrival of a mate or predator can be associated. In this view, learning that food occurs at noon is no different from learning that food occurs in a striped chamber or when a tone is on rather than off. However, learning about time of day has also been discussed in terms of a computational model that is seen as rather different from this simple associative account (Gallistel, 1990; Mistlberger, 1993). The computational model emphasizes that animals should always encode the time of day at which important events occur. On subsequent days the animal consults its circadian clock to see whether the current time matches the remembered time of feeding or some other event (i.e., it generalizes along the dimension of circadian time). Several days of regular feeding are generally needed before activity anticipates the next feeding. In terms of the computational-representation model, this reflects the animal's need to accumulate enough observations to raise its estimate of the likelihood that food will be forthcoming at the given time. In associative terms, it reflects the gradual buildup of associative strength to a level above the threshold for behavior. There is no practical difference between these two proposals. The computational model is a way of describing the conditions for learning a time of day in terms that make functional sense of them. However, just as we have seen in chapter 3, this does not have to mean that the mechanism for learning is anything other than mindless, mechanical association-formation.

8.1.3 Time and Place Learning

A rat in a cage becoming active before the time of feeding is showing that it knows when food is coming. But in nature, food doesn't just drop into a rat's burrow. The animal has to know where to get food as well as when. In nature, anticipatory activity like that shown by rats given regular feedings may function to get animals to the right place on time. Indeed, one of the first examples of circadian rhythms ever studied was the predictable arrival of bees at the jam pots on a family's outdoor breakfast table (see Gallistel, 1990; Moore-Ede, Sulzman, & Fuller, 1982). Since many flowers are open and producing nectar only at certain times of day, the ability to learn time and place is important to bees, hummingbirds, and other nectar feeders (see section 6.2.5). However, when social insects like honeybees are observed in nature, it is difficult to be sure what any individual is learning. Different bees may have their feeding rhythms entrained by different food sources and then re-cruit others to them by dancing in the hive (see chapter 12). This would result in many bees behaving appropriately, but it would not necessarily mean that each individual had learned where to forage at each time of day.

This problem has been solved in laboratory experiments with birds (review in Wilkie, 1995). In the prototypical experiment of this sort (Biebach, Gordijn, & Krebs, 1989), individual garden warblers (*Sylvia borin*) lived in a large cage that had a central area with four feeding compartments ("rooms") opening off it (figure 8.5). During each three hours of the daily 12-hour pe-riod of light, food was available in a different room. Each bird found food in the same place at the same time each day. In order to feed, the bird had to start in the central chamber and move into one of the rooms. If it chose the correct room for the current time, it would find the door over the food bowl unlocked and be allowed to feed for a few seconds before the door locked. The bird could then return to the central area and make a new choice. With a stable light-dark cycle and a stable association of feeding place and time of day, the birds apportioned over 70% of their visits appropriately within about 10 days. Then they had tests with food available in all four places throughout the day. The pattern of visits persisted, indicating that the warblers were not simply going back to the room where they had most recently been fed (figure 8.5). A further test of whether the pattern of visits was associated with the cir-cadian clock consisted of preventing birds from visiting any of the feeding rooms for one three-hour period. When visits were permitted again, the birds went to the correct room for the time of day, not the room that would nor-mally follow the one they had been visiting before the block (Krebs & Biebach, 1989). Furthermore, when garden warblers or starlings that had learned a time-place pattern were placed in constant dim light with food al-ways available in all four rooms, the pattern persisted for several days but with a shorter, free-running phase (Biebach, Falk, & Krebs, 1991; Wenger, Bie-bach, & Krebs, 1991).

Observations of behavior in the wild suggest that animals commonly de-velop daily routines based on time-place associations. The ability of bees to learn to visit different food sources at different times of day has already been mentioned. Rijnsdorp et al. (1981) documented how the daily hunting rou-tines of kestrels (*Falco tinnunculus*) were adjusted to the emergences of the voles they preyed on. To bolster their claim that the kestrels learned to hunt when and where prey were most abundant, they regularly released mice in a field at a time when kestrels were not often seen there and observed that for-aging visits to that field became more regular around the release time. Be-havior suggestive of time-place learning has now been demonstrated in the laboratory in pigeons (Wilkie, 1995), ants (Schatz, Beugnon, & Lachaud, 1994), rats (see Mistlberger & Marchant, 1995), and fish (Reebs, 1996), al-though not all examples have been analyzed as thoroughly as that of the war-blers (review in Carr & Wilkie, 1997b). Since the studies with rats reviewed earlier indicate that a single feeding at the same time and place each day en-trains a special oscillator rather then being associated with the rat's light-

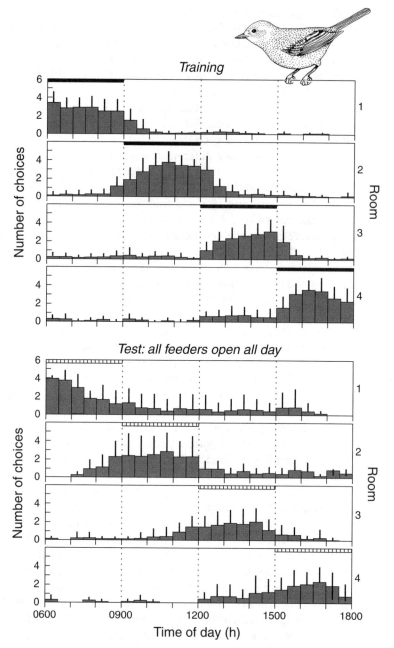

Figure 8.5. Time and place learning in garden warblers, illustrated by the number of entries to each room per half hour throughout the day. During training, food was available for three hours in each of rooms 1 to 4, in that order (dark bars). After Biebach et al. (1989) with permission.

entrainable oscillator, the question arises which of these oscillators participates in time and place learning (Mistlberger & Marchant, 1995).

The ability to learn the time and place of feeding might be expected to be especially well developed in species whose food varies predictably with time and place. As already mentioned, this applies to nectar feeders. Some insects are most active at predictable times and places, so insectivorous species might also be predicted to be good at time and place learning. In contrast, seeds sit where they fall, so granivores might not have much need for time-place associations in their foraging. Falk, Biebach, and Krebs (1992) made a start at testing the comparative hypothesis this notion suggests. They compared learning in their four-compartment feeding task in an insectivorous and a granivorous species of weaver bird. The granivores learned the task faster, but the insectivores' pattern of visits was the more stable when one room was blocked or when their circadian rhythm was phase shifted. These tantalizing observations suggest that a more thorough comparison of insectivores' vs. granivores' time-place learning would be rewarding.

Learning about time of day not only allows predators to adjust their activities to the availability of prey; it may also allow family members to coordinate their activities with one another. Ring dove (*Streptopelia risoria*) parents share incubation: the male sits on the nest most of the day and the female the rest of the time (Silver, 1990). Each member of the pair leaves the foraging area and approaches the nest at a distinctive time of day. Young rabbits and hares meet their mother for nursing just once or twice a day (Gonzalez-Mariscal & Rosenblatt, 1996). Time-place learning may also play a role in other situations where conspecifics need to meet periodically.

Although there has clearly been considerable interest in establishing that animals can learn to visit a certain place at a certain time, so far not much attention has been paid to how time-place learning might work. There are several possibilities. Gallistel (1990) suggested that linked records of what, where, and when are formed automatically, all the time, in parallel. Memory for an event thus inevitably includes information about its time and place of occurrence. Circadian information could act as an occasion setter, much like a physical context. So just as a rat can learn "bar pressing is reinforced during the tone but chain pulling is reinforced during the light," it can learn "pressing the lever at A is reinforced from 9 to 10 o'clock, but pressing the lever at B is reinforced from 2 to 3 o'clock." In such a situation, time of day might also act as an associative excitor or inhibitor. It might be possible to distinguish these possibilities with experiments analogous to those discussed in section 3.5.2. Finally, Carr and Wilkie (1997b) have suggested that a daily routine of visiting a series of foraging sites reflects what they term *ordinal timing*. They (Carr & Wilkie, 1997a, 1998) trained rats to press one lever for an hour in the morning and a second lever for an hour in the afternoon and found evidence that the second lever was encoded in terms of its order in the day. In fact, a variety of species can learn about sequences of responses or stimuli (box 8.1), though they differ in the degree to which they appear able to acquire an overall representation of the sequence as opposed to a chain of associative con-

Box 8.1. Learning Serial Order

The question of whether and how animals learn arbitrary sequences of responses or stimuli is closely related to some of the issues in this chapter. In principle, such a sequence can be represented either as a series of associatively linked events or as an overall structure. Pigeons appear to use the first mechanism and monkeys, the second. This conclusion comes from experiments with sequence production tasks, in which the animal is confronted with an array of, say, five simultaneously presented visual stimuli, A–E, such as slides or colored pecking keys. The animal's task is to touch or peck them in the sequence A-B-C-D-E. The stimulus array does not change as the animal responds, so it has only internal cues to its position in the sequence. The spatial arrangement of the stimuli changes from trial to trial so that the animal cannot memorize a sequence of motor acts.

Both pigeons and monkeys can learn such tasks, but tests with subsequences of items such as AB, AC, CD reveal apparent qualitative differences in the mechanisms underlying their performance (D'Amato & Columbo, 1988; Terrace, 1993; Terrace, Chen, & Newman, 1995). Monkeys apparently acquire a linear representation of the sequence as a whole, in effect five ordered mental slots occupied by specific items. When presented with subsets of items, they appear to mentally scan this sequence from beginning to end for matches, as indicated by the data in figure B8.1 (see also Swartz, Chen, & Terrace, 1991). The latency to respond correctly to the first item increases with its position in the sequence, and the latency to respond correctly to the second item increases with its distance from the first item (e.g., D is responded to more quickly in CD than in AD tests). Pigeons, in contrast, respond equally quickly to the first and to the second items of all subsets. Trained on a sequence of similar items, they respond at chance to subsequences like BC that contain only interior items. Various aspects of their performance (review in Terrace, 1993) suggest that they learn a rule

⟶

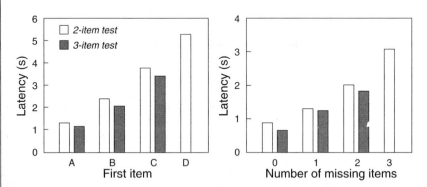

Figure B8.1. Performance of cebus monkeys trained to respond to five simultaneously presented items, ABCDE, in a fixed sequence in a test with only two or three of the items. *Left:* Latency of correct responses to the first item as a function of its position in the list. *Right:* Latency of correct responses to the second (2-item tests) or second and third items (3-item tests) as a function of the number of missing items between it and the previous items. Comparable data for pigeons are flat. Redrawn from D'Amato and Columbo (1988) with permission.

Box 8.1. *(continued)*

---

something like "respond first to A, if present, then respond to any other item; if E is present, respond to any other item and then to E." Results like these suggest that there may be genuine qualitative differences among species here. The difference between cognitive structures in monkeys and pigeons that is tapped by sequence production tasks seems very similar to—perhaps the same as—that tapped by the transitive inference tasks discussed in Box 5.3.

---

nections. Typically, the stimuli or responses in such experiments follow each other immediately, though there is no reason to think that they would have to. But it is debatable whether serial order learning should be treated as a third kind of timing mechanism, as Carr & Wilkie (1997a, 1997b) suggest.

8.1.4 Summary

Circadian rhythms of activity and rest run freely in constant conditions. They are adjusted to the local environment by the process of entrainment, which has several distinct properties. The evolutionarily primary entraining agent is probably the daily cycle of light and darkness, but other events can also influence animals' daily pattern of activity. There are three ways in which they can do so. Social stimuli and other sources of arousal may entrain the light-entrainable circadian oscillator through a separate mechanism with a phase response curve different from that of light (Mrosovsky et al., 1989). Regular daily feedings may also entrain a circadian oscillator; in rats, the food-entrainable oscillator appears to be separate from the main light-entrainable oscillator (Mistlberger, 1993). Under other conditions, such as when an animal is exposed to a 24-hour light-dark cycle and has several regular feedings a day, the time and place of feeding is linked through learning to the circadian rhythm entrained by light. This learning has been described theoretically either associatively or in terms of a computational-representational model. However, there may not be any practical difference between the mechanisms implied by these descriptions.

To decide whether activity that anticipates a regular environmental event reflects entrainment or learning of circadian phase, several questions need to be asked (Aschoff, 1986). Is the effect described by a phase response curve—that is, does the possible entraining agent pull the free-running rhythm into a predictable relationship with itself? Does the rhythm free-run from its new phase when the entraining agent is removed? Does the effect of the possible entraining agent depend on its original relationship to the free-running rhythm? For example, the effects of social stimuli on hamsters' subsequent activity depend on when in the circadian activity cycle they occur, indicating that they entrain the rhythm. In contrast, birds exposed to four times and places of feeding seem to apportion their feeding to all four times equally readily, indicating that they associate each feeding place with the appropriate time of day (Honrado & Mrosovsky, 1991). Learning about the times and places of food availability and encounters with predators, prey, or conspecifics are likely all important in allowing animals to organize efficient daily routines.

8.2 Characteristics of Interval Timing

In circadian timing, an endogenous oscillator that runs freely in a predictable, species-specific way is entrained to periods not too different from 24 hours by light and a few other kinds of stimuli. In interval timing, in contrast, behavior is controlled by events of arbitrary periodicities considerably shorter than a day, signaled in arbitrary ways. Interval timing has been studied most with operant conditioning procedures in the laboratory. This research has led to an extensive body of data and three contemporary theories. We first review some widely used procedures for studying timing and some of the results they have produced and then discuss models of interval timing.

8.2.1 The Peak Procedure, Temporal Generalization, and Weber's Law

Pavlov's demonstrations of inhibition of delay in classical conditioning, referred to at the beginning of the chapter, indicate that animals are sensitive to the time that has elapsed since a signal came on. Operant studies using the peak procedure (S. Roberts, 1981) tap into the same interval timing mechanism. In the peak procedure, animals (typically rats or pigeons) are exposed to many daily trials in which food can be earned a fixed time after the onset of a signal. For instance, in a widely used procedure for pigeons, a pecking key lights up and the first peck 20 seconds later is reinforced with food. The key then goes dark for an intertrial interval and lights up again some variable number of seconds later to begin another trial with the same sequence of events. An omniscient pigeon need only peck once per trial, at the end of the programmed interval, but as pigeons are not omniscient and as they are typically fairly hungry in these sorts of experiments, they peck many times per trial and do so at a faster average rate as the time for food approaches.

To discover how precisely the animal knows the time of feeding, so-called *empty trials* are added to this basic procedure. These are occasional trials, maybe 20% of them, in which no food occurs and the signal stays on much past the usual time of feeding. Animals accustomed to this procedure respond most just around the scheduled feeding time, as shown in figure 8.6. Average response rates describe a nearly symmetrical normal distribution with its peak close to the interval being timed. When the interval to be timed is varied across animals or across blocks of sessions, a set of identically shaped curves results. The longer the interval being timed, the greater the spread of the distribution. If the X-axis of these plots is rescaled as proportion of the programmed interval, the stretched or compressed response rate graphs can be superimposed on one another (figure 8.6). This means that, for given species and testing conditions, a predictable proportion of the maximum response

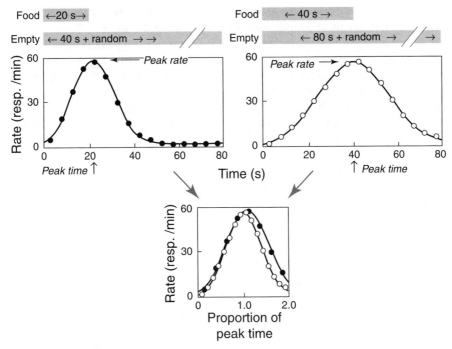

Figure 8.6. Examples of data from rats trained in the peak procedure with reinforcement 20 or 40 seconds after the beginning of the interval on food trials; no food was given on empty trials. The lower part of the figure shows how such data can be superimposed by rescaling the *x*-axis. The *y*-axis is sometimes scaled as proportion of peak rate. Redrawn from S. Roberts (1981) with permission.

rate is reached a c　tain proportion of the way though the interval regardless of how long the interval is. If we quite reasonably interpret an animal's rate of instrumental responding for food as an indication of how near in time it perceives the food to be, this result can be seen as an instance of Weber's law (see chapter 2). Just as in other perceptual tasks, small amounts are judged more accurately than large ones.

One beauty of research on interval timing is that a variety of different procedures can be used to tap into sensitivity to time, and they all converge on the same conclusions about the underlying mechanism. Temporal generalization, for example, produces the same pattern of data as the peak procedure. In a test of temporal generalization, an animal is reinforced for responding after a signal of one duration but not after other durations. In a procedure for rats (Church & Gibbon, 1982), the light in the operant chamber was turned off for a few seconds and then a lever slid into the chamber for five seconds. The rat was reinforced with food for pressing the lever if the period of darkness had been, say, four seconds, and not otherwise. This procedure yields a typical generalization gradient (see chapter 5) with its peak centered at the reinforced duration. Longer reinforced durations give broader gradients and, as in the peak procedure, these gradients can be superimposed when the X-axis is rescaled in terms of proportion of the reinforced duration.

An animal tested with temporal generalization or the peak procedure can be seen as comparing a current interval with a memory of reinforced intervals in past trials. The pattern of data in figure 8.7 indicates that this comparison is based on the ratio of current elapsed time or signal duration to the re-membered interval. Equal ratios (i.e., equal proportions of the reinforced in-terval) lead to equal response rates or probabilities. If instead responding in the peak procedure were based on the difference between the current elapsed time and the remembered duration of the trial, responding would always begin the same time away from food or from the start of the trial, whether the interval was long or short. Other possibilities can be imagined, but none fits the data as well as a ratio comparator.

8.2.2 Bisecting Time Intervals

Consider the following discrimination training procedure for rats. A tone comes on for either two or eight seconds. Then two levers slide into the op-erant chamber. The rats are reinforced for pressing the left lever if the tone lasted two seconds and for pressing the right lever if it lasted eight seconds. In effect, the rats are reporting their judgment of whether the tone is relatively short or long. When they are choosing correctly on a high proportion of trials, they can be tested with tones of intermediate durations. They then divide their choices between the two levers in a predictable way, pressing the "long" lever on a higher proportion of trials the longer the tone is (Church & Deluty, 1977). What is especially interesting is the duration at which they choose each lever 50% of the time, interpreted as the duration they perceive as halfway be-tween long and short. Arthmetically, 7.5 is half way between 3 and 12, but if animals compare time intervals by implicitly computing their ratios, the half way or bisection point from the rats' point of view will be not 7.5 seconds but 6. (The ratio of 12 to 6 is the same as the ratio of 6 to 3.) This is, in fact, the bisection point in such an experiment (figure 8.7). Equivalent results are found with different pairs of long and short intervals (Church & Deluty, 1977). Another way to describe this result is to say that the animals bisect the temporal interval not at its arithmetic mean but at its geometric mean. (The geometric mean of two numbers is the square root of their product—for ex-ample, $6 = \sqrt{(3 \times 12)}$).

8.2.3 Measuring the Time Left to Reward

So far, we have assumed that a given interval of real time is subjectively the same whether it is at the beginning or at the end of a longer interval being timed—that is, subjective time measures real time linearly. When we found that time intervals are not psychologically bisected at their arithmetic middle, for instance, we looked for an explanation in the nature of the animal's deci-sion process, not in its perception of time. But there are other possibilities.

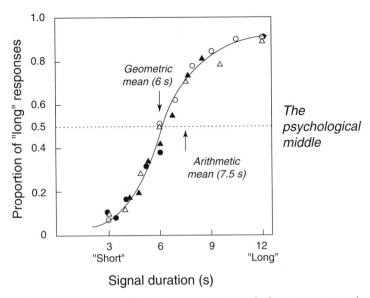

Figure 8.7. Results of a temporal bisection experiment in which rats were trained to press one lever after a 3-second signal ("short") and another after a 12-second signal ("long") and then were tested with intermediate durations. Different symbols represent different sets of test trials. Redrawn from Church and Deluty (1977) with permission.

The one that has been taken most seriously is that elapsed time might be perceived logarithmically with real time. If subjective time measures real time logarithmically, each successsive segment of an interval will seem shorter than the one before (figure 8.8).

On a logarithmic scale, equal ratios are converted to equal intervals. Thus one possible account of why animals bisect intervals at the geometric mean is that the durations are perceived logarithmically but compared arithmetically. Some of the most direct evidence against logarithmic timing comes from a clever test for asking animals at any point at an elapsing interval whether they think the time left in that interval is more or less than a standard interval. The rationale for this so-called *time-left procedure* (Gibbon & Church, 1981) is explained graphically in figure 8.8. If elapsing time is assessed logarithmically, a fixed duration, say 10 seconds, late in an interval will seem shorter than 10 seconds early in the interval, whereas if time is assessed linearly, 10 seconds will seem the same anywhere.

In the time-left procedure, a rat or a pigeon is trained that one signal means food for a given response after one interval and a second signal means food for a second response after an interval half as long. Having learned to time these two signals, the animals are queried while they are working during the long signal, "Would you rather have food after the short signal than after the time left in this signal?" Suppose the long interval is 60 seconds and the short one 30 seconds. Clearly, the way to get food quickest when confronted with this choice is to select the short signal when it is presented less

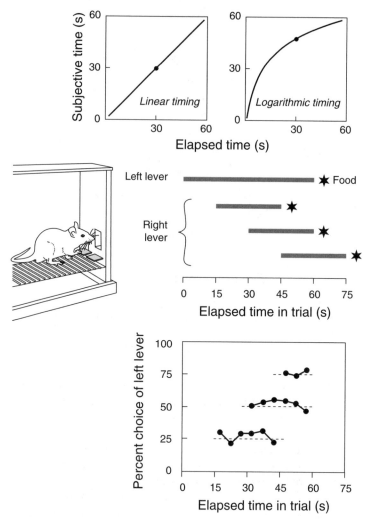

Figure 8.8. Top: How subjective time grows as a function of real time if timing is linear or logarithmic. Middle: Time left procedure for rats. Dark bars represent availability of the designated lever; stars are reinforcement. Bottom. Choice of the left, "time left," lever when the right lever enters 15 (bottom line), 30, or 45 seconds after the trial begins. Data redrawn from Gibbon and Church (1981) with permission.

than 30 seconds into the 60-second interval and choose what's left of the long signal after the half way point of the interval. Around 30 seconds into the interval, animals should be indifferent to the two alternatives. But if time is measured logarithmically, the last 30 seconds of the elapsing 60-second interval will be subjectively less than the new 30-second alternative and the animal will opt for the time left before the middle of the longer interval.

Both rats and pigeons choose as predicted by linear timing (Gibbon & Church, 1981; figure 8.8). These data are fairly conclusive support for the assumption that animals measure time linearly. If subjective time were not linear, animals would sometimes make less than optimal choices in the time-left procedure, opting for food later rather than sooner. Relating mechanisms of timing and choice to optimality is the subject of the next chapter, but it is encouraging to see that animals apparently start with an approximately veridical assessment of time.

8.2.4 Stopping and Starting the Clock

Sensitivity to the duration of a signal implies that the onset of the signal starts a clock or timer of some sort (S. Roberts, 1981). Laboratory experiments with many identical trials suggest that this timer resets before the start of each new trial. If the timer were not reset or were only partially reset, successive presentations of the same signal could not be timed equally accurately. Thus the interval timing mechanism may be like a stopwatch that starts running at the start of a new and interesting event and resets at the event's end. The analogy to a stopwatch suggests other questions. For example, can the timer be stopped and restarted without resetting? The answer to this question has been sought by seeing what animals do when a familiar signal of fixed duration is interrupted earlier than usual and then started again a few seconds later (figure 8.9). For instance, suppose a rat is pressing a lever for food during a 30-second tone and the tone is interrupted briefly 10 seconds after its onset. When the tone comes on again, will the rat respond at the rate characteristic of 10 seconds into the interval with a peak 20 seconds later, or will it start again from zero with a peak 30 seconds after the interruption? The former would indicate that the rat's interval timer had been stopped and restarted, the latter that it had been reset at the interruption.

At one time it appeared that the results of such interruption experiments depended on the species being tested. Rats resumed timing after an interruption (S. Roberts, 1981) whereas pigeons reset (Roberts, Cheng, & Cohen, 1989). However, not surprisingly, it turns out that procedural variations can produce these different outcomes within a species (Cabeza de Vaca, Brown, & Hemmes, 1994). It is not hard to understand why if we notice that in order to time an interrupted signal accurately, it is necessary to retain an accurate memory of the time that elapsed before the interruption and add the time after the interruption to it. Forgetting the time before the interruption leads to the same result as resetting: the animal appears to time only the part of the signal after the interruption. This insight predicts that the results should depend in a continuous way on the size of the break. The longer the break, the more the first part of the signal is forgotten and the later in the resumed signal is the peak time of responding. This prediction has been confirmed in an elegant series of experiments with pigeons (Cabeza de Vaca et al., 1994; figure 8.9).

The metaphor of a clock that times events like those in the peak procedure also raises the question of what kind of events stop and start the clock. Both rats and pigeons have been trained to time both lights and tones, so it is clear

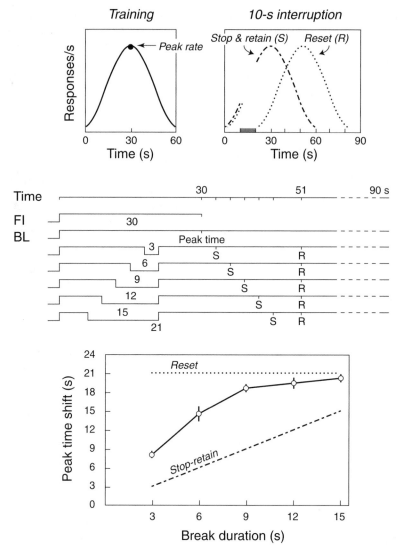

Figure 8.9. Top: Two hypothetical results of training on a 30-second peak procedure and then interrupting the 30-second signal for 10 seconds. Middle: Peak times, in seconds from the start of the interval, predicted by the two models for an experiment with interruptions of different lengths programmed to end at the same point in the interval. FI fixed interval after which food was delivered; BL blank trial, no food. Bottom: Predictions and results for an experiment with pigeons following the design above. Redrawn from Cabeza de Vaca et al. (1994) with permission.

that different modalities have access to the interval clock. Moreover, animals show transfer from timing one signal to timing another, novel signal in a different modality (Roberts et al., 1989). These findings suggest that a single timer tracks events within a trial. But animals are also capable of timing two or more events simultaneously, suggesting that several timers can run at once. For instance, pigeons can learn that each of two or more key colors predicts a different time to food (Cheng, Westwood, & Crystal, 1993; Fetterman & Killeen, 1995). Pigeons in laboratory studies of foraging decisions time the length of foraging bouts while keeping track of the durations of several events within them (Plowright, 1996). Such findings mean that different cues can access different interval timers.

8.2.5 Summary

The two most important properties of interval timing are (1) subjective time grows linearly with real time and (2) timing obeys Weber's law. Longer times are perceived and/or remembered with greater variance than shorter times, and that variance is proportional to the duration being timed. This latter property is referred to in discussions of timing as *the scalar property* (Gibbon, 1991). Timing shares both linearity and conformity to Weber's law with perception of other features of the world such as space. Interval timing also shares with spatial cognition its sensitivity to multiple sources of information (Cheng, 1992).

As this section reflects, the most analytical experiments on interval timing have been done with rats and pigeons. Humans have also been tested extensively in a variety of timing tasks like temporal generalization and discrimination, with results generally similar to those from other species (Church, 1993; but see Fetterman, Dreyfus, & Stubbs, 1996; Gibbon & Allan, 1984). Comparable data from a rodent, a bird, and a primate are suggestive of pretty wide phylogenetic generality among vertebrates. Although other species have not been tested so extensively as these three, what data there are indicate that a variety of other species time events similarly (Lejeune & Wearden, 1991). These data consist mainly of patterns of responding on *fixed interval (FI) schedules*, which are essentially the same as the peak procedure but without the empty trials. All species tested show an increase in response rate up to the time of food, and this pattern has the scalar property when different intervals are tested. What does appear to vary across species is the sharpness of the increases in response rate: turtles, for instance, have a much shallower slope than monkeys or rats, suggesting that they do not perceive interval duration as accurately. (Recall that an animal able to perceive and remember the exact length of an interval without any error would respond just once, at the end of the interval.) However, the apparent precision of interval timing can also vary within a species with the response used to index timing. For instance, pigeons appear to time more accurately when they have to hop on a perch for food than when they have to peck (Jasselette, Lejeune, & Wearden, 1990). It may be that more effortful, costly responses lead to apparent increased accuracy.

Attempting to capture species differences in a model including both response mechanisms and sensitivity to time leads to the conclusion that species differ in both (Lejeune & Wearden, 1991). Experiments using temporal discrimination or bisection procedures are needed to test this conclusion by assessing temporal discrimination independently of response rate. Lejeune and Wearden (1991) suggest that precision of temporal discrimination increases roughly along the conventional phylogentic scale. Ecological hypotheses about species differences in interval timing accuracy have apparently not been tested. For example, one might predict that hummingbirds would be very sensitive to intervals in the minutes range because they need this ability for tracking the availability of nectar in depleting and repleting flowers (cf. Gill, 1988).

8.3 Models of Interval Timing

8.3.1 The Information Processing Model

Figure 8.10 depicts the dominant model of the processes underlying interval timing. It has three major components: a clock that measures current time in linear fashion, a memory for storing information about past times, and a comparator for comparing current time to remembered time. The clock in this model rests on a pacemaker that is assumed to generate pulses at a fairly high rate. The onset of a signal to be timed switches these pulses into an accumulator, a working memory that tracks the duration of the signal. The comparator computes the ratio of the value in the accumulator to a value of reinforced time stored in reference memory and outputs a decision about whether the current time is closer than a threshold amount to the remembered time. Behavior is generated in an all-or-nothing way depending on whether or not the ratio exceeds the threshold. This conclusion is based on the fact that on single trials of the peak procedure rats and pigeons do not increase responding gradually as the time for reinforcement approaches. Rather, responding has a *break-run-break* pattern—that is, at a certain point in the trial the animal switches suddenly from a very low rate of responding to a high steady rate. In empty trials, it maintains this rate until after the time of reinforcement, and then there is another break in responding. The time at which the run of responding begins shows when the ratio of current time to remembered time of reinforcement exceeds the threshold, and the break in responding at the end of the run shows when the ratio falls below the threshold again (Cheng & Westwood, 1993; Church, Meck, & Gibbon, 1994).

This model is also known as *Scalar Expectancy Theory*, or *SET* (Gibbon, 1991). The model's general structure has much in common with the structure of the memory model of habituation presented in chapter 4 and with models of information processing in other realms of cognition (Church & Broadbent, 1990). In all of them, a current event is perceived and encoded and then compared to a stored representation of similar events. Behavior reflects the outcome of the comparison. For nearly 15 years, the information-processing

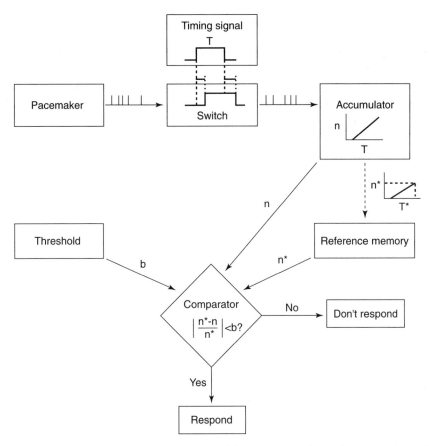

Figure 8.10. The information-processing model of timing. Redrawn from Church et al. (1994) with permission.

model of timing depicted in figure 8.10 has been guiding study of interval timing. One of the central questions is why timing is scalar—that is, why the variance in temporal generalization, the peak procedure, and the like increases with the length of the interval being timed. What is the source of this variance? It cannot, for example, be in the operation of the switch that causes an event to be timed. The switch is assumed to close just once, at the start of the timed event, and open again at the event's end. Any variability in the latency of the switch's operation would be constant regardless of the length of the interval to be timed. Variability in the speed of the pacemaker, on the other hand, could produce scalar variance because it would influence the total number of pulses in working memory more in long intervals than in short ones. There are clearly other possibilities as well, not all of which are easy to disentangle from one another experimentally.

Analysis of the pattern of data on single trials has given considerable insights into the moment-by-moment dynamics of animals' decision processes

(Cheng & Westwood, 1993; Church, Meck, & Gibbon, 1994). For instance, different, possibly variable, thresholds may be used to decide when to start responding and when to stop. These analyses also indicate that the animal can be seen as taking a single sample from the memories of times to reinforcement stored in its reference memory and comparing this continuously to the time in the accumulator. The notion that a distribution of experienced times to reinforcement is stored in reference memory and that this distribution is sampled on each trial can be distinguished from the possibility that what is represented is an average time to reward, a single quantity that may be updated with each new experience. Storing a continually updated average seems cognitively less demanding than storing a distribution. Nevertheless, as we will see in chapter 9, a model based on memory for the distribution of individual intervals accounts very well for a number of different kinds of foraging decisions.

8.3.2 Reading the Status of Oscillators

The model of timing in figure 8.10 is the most longstanding and influential model of interval timing. Recently, Gallistel (1990; see also Gallistel, 1994) has suggested a variation of it that replaces the pacemaker plus accumulator with a system of oscillators and status indicators. Rather than counting pulses, this model times by recording the state of each of a set of oscillators of different periodicities, as shown in figure 8.11. We have already seen that animals appear to record the phase of a circadian oscillator when learning the time and place of feedings. The appeal of an oscillator model of interval timing is that it unifies timing at all scales in terms of a single set of oscillators. One or more of these may have a period longer than a day, perhaps one of months, years or the animal's lifetime.

Figure 8.11 indicates why more than a single circadian oscillator is needed to do the job of timing all lengths of intervals. The sorts of intervals we have just been talking about, of the order of seconds or a few minutes, are just a tiny fraction of a day. For instance, 10 seconds is 1/8640 or less than two hundredths of 1% of 24 hours. To time 10-second intervals accurately using its circadian oscillator, an animal would have to discriminate very tiny changes in the phase of that oscillator. It is much more reasonable to assume that it possesses an oscillator with a phase around, but somewhat longer than, 10 seconds. It cannot be shorter than 10 seconds because reading off its phases at 10 second intervals would not uniquely indicate how much time had passed between readings. A good solution to this problem is to record the state of a number of oscillators, each of which oscillates about twice as fast as the next slower one. According to this model, interval timing is not counting pulses but recording the times of a signal's onset and offset in terms of oscillator status indicators and computing its duration from this information.

Although the oscillator model appears merely to replace the pacemaker and accumulator with oscillators and status indicators, there are some reasons to favor it over the information-processing model. Oscillators are biologically

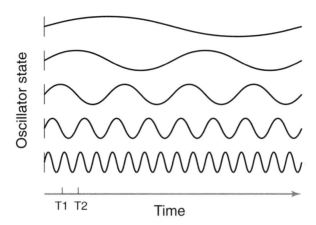

Figure 8.11. Timing with a set of oscillators. Each oscillator has a period half that of the next slower. Unambiguously distinguishing T1 from T2 here requires reading the status of all the oscillators at both times.

realistic. The physiology and behavior of most organisms provide evidence of numerous biological oscillators driving repetitive motor patterns like flapping, walking, or licking, and rhythmic functions like heart beat and breathing. On the other hand, though, linking shorter-term oscillators to circadian and possibly longer-term oscillators is unrealistic because interval and circadian timing are dissociable by brain lesions. In mammals, removing the suprachiasmatic nucleus abolishes daily rhythmicity but leaves intact the ability to time intervals of seconds or minutes (Mistlberger, 1993). In addition, some of the different components of the information-processing model, such as clock speed and memory, can be dissociated pharmacologically (Meck, 1996). Furthermore, learning about short intervals is not the same as entrainment of circadian rhythms. For instance, there is no evidence for a free-running short-interval timer nor for an ability to learn only a restricted range of periodicities.

On the more positive side, the oscillator model readily translates into a neural net model in which times of occurrence are stored in a matrix representing the status of each oscillator (Church & Broadbent, 1990). On the whole, the predictions of this model do not differ from those of the information-processing model. For instance, it effectively simulates data from the peak procedure and fixed interval schedules (Wearden & Doherty, 1995). However, it does predict that with particular periods of the underlying oscillators, some longish intervals may be more discriminable than shorter intervals. Crystal, Church, and Broadbent (1997) have reported data from rats that are consistent with this idea. And Broadbent (1994) attempted to detect the "oscillator signatures" by looking for periodicities in the bar pressing rates of rats responding for food on a random interval schedule. In fact, rats trained on such a schedule, where food is completely unpredictable in time, do show a tendency to respond in bursts separated by 20 to 50 seconds. It is interesting to note that, as we will see in the next chapter, optimal foraging models have shown that when food occurs randomly in time the optimal strategy is to search at regular intervals, which Broadbent's rats were in effect doing.

8.3.3 The Behavioral Theory of Timing

The third important model of interval timing is more fundamentally different from the information-processing model. The behavioral theory of timing (Killeen & Fetterman, 1988) does not assume that animals count pulses or record states of oscillators, much less that they perform implicit computations on such hypothetical entities. Rather, it is almost an exercise in seeing how far a purely behaviorist approach can go in accounting for behavior that has seemed to others to demand a cognitive explanation.

The inspiration for the behavioral theory of timing comes from observations of *adjunctive behaviors* that animals show when they are exposed to food deliveries spaced regularly in time regardless of their behavior (*fixed-time schedules*). Immediately after each food delivery, animals tend to engage in behaviors not related to food, such as grooming and walking about. As the interfood interval elapses, food-related behaviors such as gnawing or pecking in the vicinity of the feeder come to predominate (figure 8.12). This predictable temporal organization can be understood as reflecting the underlying organization of feeding and other behavior systems, discussed in chapters 1 and 3. In the language of chapter 3, we might say that the association of a certain elapsed time with food is evidenced by the animal performing activities in its feeding system and that behaviors from other systems, like grooming or exploration, are performed at other times. In contrast, in the language of the behavioral theory of timing, the succession of adjunctive behaviors reveals the succession of a series of underlying states. When food is more frequent, animals generally appear more excited. This observation can be interpreted as meaning that the states succeed each other more rapidly the higher the rate of food presentation.

The behavioral theory of timing proposes that accurate choice or anticipation of food in operant experiments like the peak procedure or temporal discrimination arises because operant responding becomes conditioned to the interfood state present when food is delivered. For example, imagine a rat in a temporal discrimination procedure in which it is reinforced for pressing the left lever when 4 seconds have elapsed after the last reinforcement and the right lever when 12 seconds have elapsed. Because a certain overall rate of food presentation engenders a reliable sequence of postfood behaviors (and states), we can imagine that the rat will be reliably, say, sniffing the corner of its operant chamber 4 seconds after food is delivered and rearing near the feeder 12 seconds after food delivery. This rat's left-lever responses are reinforced when it has just been sniffing the corner (i.e., in the presence of the 4-second state) and right-lever responses when it has just been rearing near the feeder (i.e., in the presence of the 12-second state).

Described in this way, the behavioral theory of timing appears to have dis-

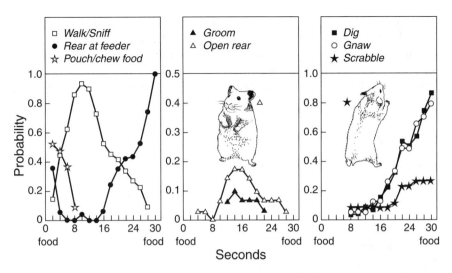

Figure 8.12. Typical behavior of golden hamsters given food every 30 seconds in an open field. Some activities appear reliably just before or after feeding whereas others (the adjunctive behaviors) are performed most in the middle of the interfood interval. Data from one animal, redrawn from Anderson and Shettleworth (1977) with permission; hamsters from Shettleworth (1975) with permission.

pensed with internal clocks, comparators, and decision processes. However, it is a little more elaborate than it appears in our example of the rat discriminating between two times (see Machado, 1997, for further development). First, behavior organized in time is conditioned to an interfood *state*; it is not necessarily merely part of a chain of behavior like "eat the food, groom, sniff the corner, press the left lever." The succession of states is controlled in a probabilistic way by a pacemaker that generates pulses more slowly than the pacemaker in the information-processing model. The speed of this pacemaker increases with the overall rate of food presentation. This means that short intervals are timed more accurately than long ones—that is, timing is scalar, just as it should be. However, this is only true if the short intervals are generated in a way that increases the average rate of feeding in the experimental context, as when the interval between trial onsets in the peak procedure remains constant while the interval to be timed is shortened.

The prediction that pacemaker rate should vary with overall reinforcement rate is unique to the behavioral theory of timing. It has received some experimental support (cf. Bizo & White, 1994; Fetterman & Killeen, 1995), but there is contradictory evidence, too. For example, if a single interval is timed while the overall reinforcement rate is varied by requiring the animal to time a second, longer or shorter, interval on some of the trials, the length of the second interval should affect how accurately the standard interval is timed. Having to time a shorter interval to food will raise the overall reinforcement rate and the accuracy of timing; timing a longer one will lower it. According to scalar expectancy theory, however, the presence and length of the second interval should make no difference, and it does not (see also Bizo & White, 1995; Leak & Gibbon, 1995; Machado, 1997). Furthermore, details of the timing of the breaks and runs in responding on individual trials of the peak procedure also cannot (as yet) be accounted for by the behavioral theory, whereas they have a natural interpretation in terms of the processes assumed by SET (Church, Meck, & Gibbon, 1994).

8.3.4 Models and Modules for Timing: Conclusions

The circadian timing system, discussed in the first part of this chapter, consists of an endogenous oscillator with a period of about a day that is normally entrained by light or any of a few other biologically important events. The circadian oscillator runs freely in the absence of effective entraining agents, and it can be located in the suprachiasmatic nucleus of mammals. A primary function of the circadian system is to adjust the animal's behavior to local day and night. Among other things, it allows animals to learn when and where food is regularly available. The function of interval timing, in contrast, is to adjust behavior to important events with durations much shorter than a day. Unlike day and night, the duration and time of occurrence of these events are not predictable in advance of individual experience, and they can take on any value. Accurate timing can be demonstrated with intervals too short to reasonably discriminate in terms of phase of the 24-hour cycle. Furthermore, acquiring a regular sequence of behavior after experiencing a sequence of events that is predictable on the scale of seconds to minutes does not occur through entrainment. In entrainment, the underlying rhythm free-runs and is brought into register with the environmental rhythm as described by a phase response curve. It has a restricted range of entrainable phases. Neither of these characteristics applies to learning of short intervals. There is a single, generally agreed on model of circadian timing, but there are three such models of interval timing. One of these, the oscillator model and its realization as a neural net, links circadian and interval timing as different expressions of a single set of oscillators with phases ranging from fractions of seconds to multiples of days. However, it does not appear to account for the unique characteristics of the circadian oscillator just reviewed. Although the behavioral theory of timing is likely to go on generating challenging data, scalar expectancy theory still appears to provide the most powerful account of all aspects of interval timing. SET reappears in chapter 9, where we will see that it provides a useful account of how animals assess and compare rates while foraging.

As this summary indicates, circadian and interval timing represent the outcome of two functionally and causally distinct information-processing systems or modules. Learning serial order is a third mechanism for organizing behavior in time, as in adopting a daily foraging routine, but, unlike circadian and interval timing, ordinal timing (Carr & Wilkie, 1997b) does not involve response to time per se. In section 8.1 we considered how information about circadian time is combined with other kinds of information. The same issue can be considered with respect to the output of the interval timing module, regardless of how this module is supposed to operate. Here again, temporal information may be processed in parallel with associative information provided by explicit external CSs. Recall from section 3.4.2 that temporal information such as when the US occurs during the CS is part of what is learned in conditioning. Furthermore, temporal information appears to be especially powerful when used as an explicit associative cue (Williams & LoLordo, 1995). In rats, learning to expect shock at a fixed time after arriving in a particular context blocked later learning about a brief CS that predicted the same shock, but the brief CS did not block the temporal cue, suggesting that time has privileged access to associative mechanisms.

The integration of interval timing with other information has been explored in a different way by Cheng, Spetch, and Miceli (1996), who taught both pigeons and people to respond when a moving shape on a video monitor reached a certain position on the screen. During training, the shape always moved at the same speed, so subjects could respond to its position, the time since it started to move, or both. When the stimulus moved faster or slower than usual, both the pigeons and the people appeared to respond to both temporal and spatial information and average them when they conflicted (figure 8.13). When marsh tits, a food-storing species, and blue tits, nonstorers, were trained in a similar procedure (H. Broadbent, personal communication, September 1996), marsh tits relied more strongly on the spatial cues than blue tits did, just as when spatial and color information conflict (see section 7.2.2). In circadian time-place learning, by contrast, animals clearly know both the time and the place of important events, but it is not clear what averaging this information could mean. The discussion of conditioning in chapter 3 provides an example of well-developed models of how different sources of information—CSs, occasion setters, and the like—combine. Studies of spatial (see chapter 7) and temporal (this chapter) information processing suggest other possibilities, possibilities that need to be more fully elucidated and tested.

8.4 Do Animals Count?

Readers who know the story of Clever Hans will realize that the question of whether animals count is one of the oldest in the experimental study of animal cognition. Clever Hans was a horse in the early 1900s who appeared to be able to count and do arithmetic (Candland, 1993; Pfungst, 1965). He answered questions about numbers by tapping with his hoof. Although a committee of 13 eminent men was satisfied that Hans really could count, investigations by the young experimental psychologist Otto Pfungst revealed otherwise. Hans *was* clever, but not in the way he originally appeared to be. He proved to be responding to slight, unconscious movements of questioners who knew the correct answers.

The story of Clever Hans may have cast a pall over research on animal counting, but it did not put a stop to it (Rilling, 1993). In recent years, research on animal counting has shown a resurgence, along with research on other questions about animal cognition. Discussion of research on counting

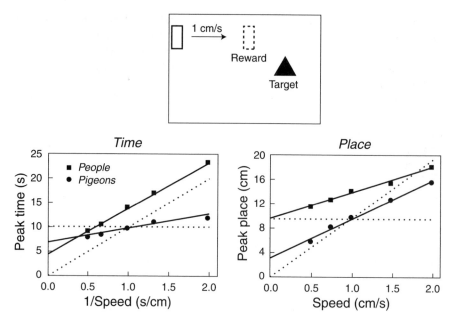

Figure 8.13. Top: Procedure for testing how pigeons and people combine temporal and spatial information. Subjects were reinforced for pecking or touching the target when the moving rectangle reached the dotted position on the video monitor (in the experiment this position was indistinguishable from the rest of the screen). Bottom: Data from test trials in which the rectangle moved faster or slower than usual. Horizontal dotted lines are predicted results if subjects relied only on time (left panel) or place (right panel); slanted dotted lines are predictions if only the other feature was used. Redrawn from Cheng et al. (1996) with permission.

encapsulates contrasts that pervade the area of comparative cognition: the ecological approach vs. anthropocentrism, behaviorism vs. cognitivism, and skepticism vs. credulity about animals' abilities. Underlying the whole area is the matter of definition: what are we going to mean by counting anyway, and how can we tell if a nonverbal creature is doing it?

Much of the controversy is summed up by quotations from two of the researchers whose work is central in the current study of animals' numerical abilities. In 1982, Davis and Memmott concluded from a review of research up to that time that "Counting behavior appears to be a relatively unnatural response in infrahumans, and its acquisition may reflect the boundaries of the animal's associative abilities" (p. 547). But, about a decade later, Gallistel (1993) concluded that, on the contrary, "the common laboratory animals order, add, subtract, multiply, and divide representatives of numerosity. . . . Their ability to do so is not surprising if number is taken as a mental primitive . . . rather than something abstracted by the brain from sense data only with difficulty and long experience" (p. 222).

What explains the difference between these two conclusions? Of course, Gallistel had available data from several research programs that were just getting off the ground when Davis and Memmott wrote, but he also differed from Davis and Memmott on what was acceptable evidence of numerical abilities. Whereas Davis and Memmott had focused on explicit countinglike behavior, Gallistel was impressed by behavior that implied internal mathematical operations like the sensitivity to ratios of time intervals discussed earlier in this chapter. Clearly, then, we need to begin our discussion of animal counting with some definitions.

8.4.1 Degrees of Numerical Competence

Counting is near the top end of a continuum of abilities collectively termed *numerical competence*, or sensitivity to numbers of things (Davis & Perusse, 1988; Gallistel, 1993). Near the bottom end in terms of apparent cognitive complexity and resemblance to what people do when they count is *numerosity discrimination*, or discrimination among sets of things according to how many items they contain. The simplest case and the one most often tested with animals is a many-few discrimination: a set with a relatively large number of responses or stimuli is the discriminative stimulus for one response and a set with a relatively small number is the discriminative stimulus for another response. As we have seen in chapter 2, one of the fundamental adaptive properties of perceptual systems is to give a bigger response to things that are more numerous, bigger, or more intense. These are likely to be indicative of more food, a more dangerous enemy, a hungrier baby, or a more enthusiastic mate. Discriminating between relative numerosities or amounts in this way does not necessarily mean that an animal can be trained to make one arbitrary response to a small set of items and another to a large set. However, members of common laboratory species have been trained to do just that, as we will shortly see. But numerosity discrimination is not the same as having *a concept of number*. To have a concept of the number 8, for instance, is to understand that eightness is a property of all sets with eight items. Thus number (or absolute, as opposed to relative, numerosity) is an abstract category: once learned with one class of exemplars it transfers to other examplars. However, the concept of 8 goes beyond the ability to categorize sets as having eight members or not. It includes understanding the mathematical properties of the number 8—for instance, that it is the product of 2 and 4 or the sum of 7 and 1 (Gallistel, 1993). *Counting* does not necessarily require this kind of understanding. In counting, each member of a set to be counted is tagged ("one," "two," "three"). These numerical tags are referred to as *numerons* (Gallistel, 1990). The tags are applied in a fixed order, but the order in which the items in the set are counted doesn't matter as long as each item gets one and only one tag. The final tag is the *cardinal number* of the set, the number of items in it. Thus a creature that can count can, among other accomplishments, apply the same numeron to sets of all sorts of things in all sorts of arrangements. Numerons need not be words in any human language. Animals' number tags can be "unnamed numbers" (Koehler, 1951).

Beyond counting in the hierarchy of numerical competence is the ability to do arithmetic—that is, to apply the operations of addition, subtraction, multiplication, and division to numerons, an ability that depends on having a concept of number. Since the days of Clever Hans, only primates have been asked to perform explicit arithmetical tasks, and a few of them have seemed able to do so (section 8.4.4). Such performance should be distinguished from the arithmetic ability of the nervous system that is implicit in animals' sensitivity to ratios of time intervals or rates of reinforcement. Such abilities, which we will examine more closely in the next chapter, likely represent the operation of encapsulated, domain specific information-processing abilities. These may be no more accessible to explicit tests of mathematical ability than the triangulation skills implicit in landmark use are accessible to explicit tests of geometrical knowledge.

8.4.2 Numerosity Discrimination

Although researchers may differ on where particular species' performance lies along the continuum of numerical competence, there is no disagreement that many animals can discriminate numerosity. Indeed, relative numerosity discrimination may be the only numerical ability most animals have because it is all they need in the wild (Davis, 1993). Nevertheless, in the laboratory it is not easy to disentangle control by numbers of things from control by all the other dimensions of stimuli that vary with number. More objects occupy more space or take longer to present. If more numerous objects are squeezed together in time or space so their total extent is the same as that of less numerous objects, the intervals between objects are smaller for the more numerous ones. An elegant way to deal with this sort of problem is to acknowledge that number is inevitably confounded with other features and to test for control by number along with control by the other features. Such an approach has been used to test whether animals are sensitive to numbers of stimuli and numbers of responses. The training procedure is essentially the same as that used to test temporal discrimination: a stimulus is presented (in this case a certain number of pulses of light or sound) and then the animal has opportunity to choose between two responses. One is correct after the larger number, the other after the smaller.

Meck & Church (1983) used this sort of procedure to test numerosity discrimination in rats. Responses on one lever were reinforced following two 1-second pulses of tone; responses on a second lever were reinforced after eight such pulses (figure 8.14). Thus, in this stage of training the total duration of the pulse train was perfectly correlated with number of pulses it contained. Once the rats were performing accurately, two types of unreinforced test trials occurred. In tests for control by number, the total duration of the stimulus was constant at 4 seconds and the number of tone pulses varied between two and eight. In tests for control by duration, there were always four tone pulses but the duration of the four tone on/tone off cycles varied between 2 and 8 seconds. The rats' discrimination proved to be controlled by both time and number: their tendency to choose the "long/many" lever (i.e., the

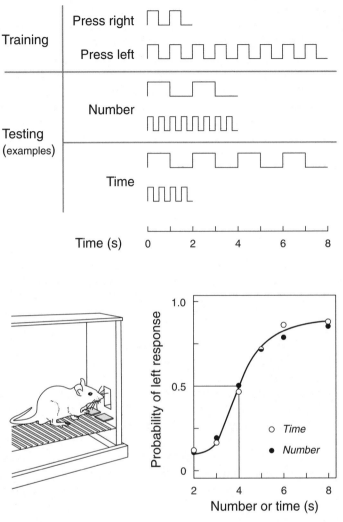

Figure 8.14. Procedure and results demonstrating joint control of rats' choices by duration and number of tone pulses. Data from Meck and Church (1983) with permission.

one that was correct after 8 pulses/8 seconds) increased with either the duration or the number of tone pulses, as shown in figure 8.14. Notice that the number at which "two" and "eight" are chosen equally often—that is, the number perceived as halfway between two and eight, is not five but four. That is, the numerosity continuum, like the temporal continuum, is bisected at the geometric rather than the arithmetic mean (but see Fetterman, 1993). This finding suggests that successive events are counted using a mechanism similar or even identical to the timing mechanism described in section 8.3 (Church & Meck, 1984).

Although time and number controlled the rats' responding about equally, pigeons trained with flashes of the light illuminating the operant chamber as the stimuli to be counted were more influenced by time than by number (Roberts & Mitchell, 1994; see Breukelaar & Dalrymple-Alford, 1998 for a similar study on rats). Control by number increased relative to control by time when the birds were trained for several sessions with number relevant and time irrelevant. The results from both rats and pigeons suggest that time and number are processed simultaneously, in parallel. Roberts and Mitchell (1994) performed a clever experiment to test this conclusion. They first trained their pigeons to use the colors of the response keys as instructions whether to report the time or number information in the just-presented signal. If the response keys were green, the birds were to report the number of flashes: left meant "2 flashes," and right meant "8 flashes." If the response keys were red, birds were reinforced for reporting "2 seconds" on the left key and "8 seconds" on the right key regardless of the number of flashes. After 44 sessions of 64 trials each, the birds chose correctly on more than 80% of trials even when time and number trials were mixed randomly. Because the response keys were never lit until after the stimulus to be timed and counted had been presented, it might seem that the birds had to be timing and counting every stimulus in order to perform so well. However, they could instead have memorized a set of conditional responses based on interflash intervals and key colors. For instance, after a long interflash interval (2 flashes/8 seconds), left was correct if the keys were green, whereas right was correct if the keys were red. To show that this was not what going on, Roberts and Mitchell went back to test trials lasting 4 seconds with two or eight flashes or containing only four flashes but lasting 2 or 8 seconds. Consider, for example, a 4-second test trial with two flashes. If the birds were using the key colors as instructions as to whether to report time or number, they should choose the left key when the keys are green ("Was it two or eight flashes?") but choose left and right about equally if the keys are red ("Was it 2 or 8 seconds long?"). This is exactly what the birds did (figure 8.15), showing convincingly that, at least after their lengthy and specialized training history, they were processing both time and number on every trial. This does not necessarily mean that the pigeons were processing these two sorts of information in parallel without competition, let alone that they were doing so from the outset. Recall that in Langley and Riley's (1993; see also chapter 6, figure 6.8) demonstration that pigeons divide attention between shape and color of a visual stimulus, performance on each feature was compared on trials with each feature alone and with the two features presumably competing for attention. The same kind of comparison has not been done with time and number. However, one model of counting for this situation consists of the information-processing model of timing depicted in figure 8.10 with a channel added for accumulating counts and comparing them with the contents of a reference memory for counts (Roberts & Mitchell, 1994). Notice that if animals respond to rates of events by in some sense mentally dividing numbers by times, a possibility discussed in the next chapter, they would have to track time and number in parallel and not in competition as this model suggests.

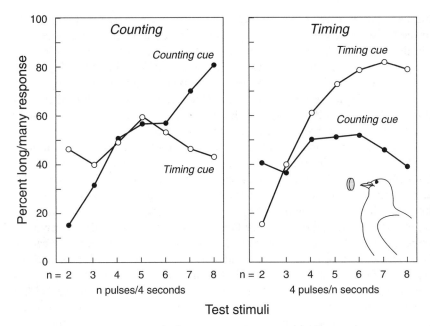

Figure 8.15. Conditional control of timing vs. counting in pigeons. Trials accompanied with a cue to time or to count either lasted 4 seconds with 2 to 8 tone pulses (counting test) or contained 4 pulses but lasted between 2 and 8 seconds (timing test). Redrawn from Roberts and Mitchell (1994) with permission.

Animals also count their own responses: a certain number of responses on a central key or lever presents two side keys or levers, and the animal is reinforced for choosing one after one number of responses and the other after a different number of responses. Just as when stimuli are counted, both time and number matter in discriminations of response numerosity (Fetterman, 1993). Discrimination of response number obeys Weber's law. For example, if data from discriminations of 5 vs. 10, 10 vs. 20, and 20 vs. 40 responses are rescaled in terms of the probability of choosing "many" as a function of the ratio between the small and the large response number, the curves can be superimposed (Fetterman, 1993).

8.4.3 Number Concepts?

Discriminating numbers of stimuli or responses does not require a concept of number. A number concept can be applied to anything—pulses of sound, pieces of food, remembered summer days—and such generality was simply not tested in the experiments reviewed so far. However, some limited generality has been demonstrated in operant numerosity discriminations. For instance, rats trained to discriminate two from four sound pulses in a procedure like that depicted in figure 8.14 continued to perform better than chance when tested with two vs. four light pulses (Church & Meck, 1984). More remarkably, they added tones and light together. The rats treated two tones followed by two lights like "four" in spite of the fact that this stimulus was a double dose of stimuli in the presence of which they had been reinforced for pressing the "two" lever. If a train of two tones or a train of two lights were simply an excitatory stimulus, there should be a greater than usual probability of a "two" response in the presence of a compound of both of these stimuli. This result therefore suggests that events to be counted are processed in a different module from conditioned excitors and inhibitors.

Rats also count small numbers of feedings and transfer this count across food types. Capaldi and his colleagues (Capaldi, 1993; Capaldi & Miller, 1988) have studied this ability by training rats to expect several pellets of food at the end of a runway on two or three trials in a row and then no food on a final trial. The rats show that they are counting the number of rewarded trials by running fast on the rewarded trials and very slowly on the terminal, unrewarded trial. So that the rats have to count feedings and not trials, each rat is typically exposed to two trial sequences in random order during each session. For instance, the sequences NRRN and RRN would be used in "counting to two," where N stands for nonreward and R stands for reward. With intertrial intervals of less than a minute, rats show evidence of counting two or three rewarded trials within 10 days of training with three daily exposures to each sequence (figure 8.16). The type of behavior shown in figure 8.16 transfers immediately to new foods—for example, from rat pellets to Cocoa Puffs cereal. As well, rats exposed to sequences like RR'R'N, where R and R' represent different foods, show evidence of counting both all the rewards and the rewards of each type. Capaldi (e.g., 1993) concludes from the ease with which rats learn and transfer such discriminations that counting (or at least, counting small numbers of rewards) is completely natural and automatic for animals, not the highly trained strategy of last resort that Davis and Memmott (1982) claimed.

Sensitivity to amounts of food in different places or different circumstances is a fundamental part of foraging, so it should not be surprising if animals show it. It may not be irrelevant that Capaldi's procedure for demonstrating counting mimics a situation in which a patch (here, the goal box in the runway) has a fixed amount of food that is predictably depleted. Chapter 9 contains more direct evidence that animals can use the number of rewards gained as a cue for patch depletion. As another example of possible counting in foraging, some birds calibrate amounts of food in numbers of items pecked. A large amount of food divided into several small pieces is preferred over the same amount of food in a single piece (Shettleworth, 1985). Sensitivity to number of items eaten was exploited by Koehler (1951), who trained parrots, jackdaws, and other birds to eat only a certain number of items from a pile before stopping by shooing them away when they reached the criterion. Davis and Bradford (1986) performed similar demonstrations with rats. Davis (1984) also trained a raccoon to select the one box out of five that had three items of food or three other objects in it, thus indicating that this animal, like Capaldi's rats, had at least a limited number concept.

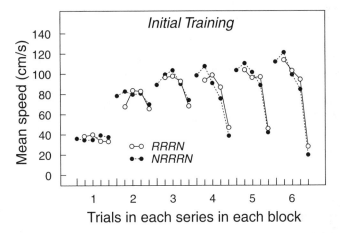

Figure 8.16. Rats learn to count rewards. Each rat received both trial sequences depicted. Counting rewards is indicated by development of a slow speed on the last, unrewarded, trial of each sequence. Redrawn from Capaldi and Miller (1988) with permission.

As a final example of automatic counting of ecologically relevant objects, Chittka and Geiger (1995b) trained honeybees to a feeder about 250 meters from their hive, placed between the third and fourth in a line of four equally spaced yellow tents. The tents were then squeezed together or spread out so that the bees passed more or fewer tents before arriving at the training location. Many bees disregarded the displacement of the landmarks and returned to the original feeder, but a substantial number behaved as if they were counting the landmarks between the hive and the feeder. These bees searched at test feeders placed after the third landmark rather than in the original feeder location. Bees may need to keep track of landmarks in this way so as to relocate profitable food sources when they have been blown off course or experience unusually strong head- or tailwinds. Box 8.2 describes a few other tantalizing but less well-analyzed cases of apparent counting by animals in the wild.

8.4.4 Parrots, Chimpanzees, Babies, and Monkeys Count and Do Arithmetic

The modern-day counterparts of Clever Hans are Alex the parrot and a few highly trained monkeys and chimpanzees. They are Hans's counterparts not because their behavior is controlled by unintended extraneous stimuli—these have generally been eliminated—but because they have received specialized training designed to probe their potential for humanlike mathematical achievements. But precisely because this training is lengthy and specialized and because it includes many different kinds of tasks, it is difficult to conclude more from the results than that animals as diverse as parrots and primates *can* sometimes, under complex and difficult-to-specify circumstances, apply number tags to arbitrary novel arrays and/or add them.

Box 8.2. Do Wild Animals Count?

By definition, true counting can be applied to anything. There is no evidence for such generalized abstract counting ability in any wild animals, but there are many provocative examples of animals apparently responding to specific numbers of things, as if they are counting eggs, young, vocalizations, or companions. European cuckoos, (*Cuculus canorus*) generally remove one or two eggs from a host's nest before depositing an egg of their own. Since cuckoos need to lay quickly, this time-consuming behavior must have some selective advantage. Is it that hosts can count and would notice the extra egg? Apparently not, at least if the host is a reed warbler. In fact, a reed warbler is most likely to desert if the clutch is reduced to one, so there is pressure against the parasitic cuckoo eating too many of its host's eggs (Davies & Brooke, 1988). More generally, the ease with which researchers can experimentally enlarge and reduce clutches of eggs, broods of nestlings, and litters of rodent pups without disrupting parental behavior suggests that mother birds and rodents, at least, do not routinely count their offspring.

Counting has also been suggested to play a role in responses to species-typical vocalizations and visual displays. Crows identify other individuals by the number of their caws (Thompson, 1969). The distinctive patterns in bird song consist, among other things, of specific numbers of repetitions of notes or phrases. The individuals that respond selectively to these must be counting song elements, in some sense. To take a visual example, when a peacock spreads his tail in full sexual display, 150 or more eye-shaped spots may be revealed. On average, males with more of these eyespots copulate with more females, a mating advantage that appears to result from females responding to the number of eyespots, in some sense counting them. Males with 20 eyespots removed at the end of one season lost matings in the next season, whereas control males that had been handled in a similar way did not (Petrie & Halliday, 1994).

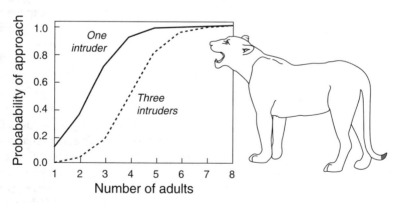

Figure B8.2. Proportion of lionesses approaching a speaker playing recorded roars from another lion pride (simulated intruders) as a function of the number of lions heard roaring and the number in the subjects' pride. Redrawn from McComb et al. (1994) with permission.

Box 8.2. (*continued*)

McComb, Packer, and Pusey (1994) have suggested than when lions hear another pride roaring, they decide whether to respond aggressively or to retreat from the perceived threat by counting both the number of individuals roaring and the number in their own group. McComb and her collaborators played recorded roars from one or three lions to 21 different lion groups. The bigger the group and the smaller the number of individuals heard roaring, the more likely the subjects were to approach the speaker (figure B8.2). McComb et al. (1994) suggest that numerical abilities might be common among social animals precisely because responses to rival groups should depend on the number of companions and rivals present. Davis and Memmot (1982) and Rilling (1993) provide other suggestive, though generally inconclusive examples of possible counting in the wild.

Alex the African grey parrot has been trained for over a decade to describe aspects of his surroundings with English words (Pepperberg, 1987, 1994). His vocabulary was designed to reveal his ability to categorize objects in terms of features like color, shape, material, and number. After being trained to report the number of items in collections of up to six objects, Alex correctly labeled novel collections and arrays of objects on about 80% of test trials. He could also tell how many objects of a certain type were contained in a larger array of objects—for example, "How many keys?" in an array of two keys and four rocks. Like young children, his errors consisted mostly of responding with the total number of objects in the array—"six" rather than "two."

Discriminating numbers of items in very small arrays has sometimes been attributed to *subitizing*, an assumed ability to apprehend small numbers immediately, without counting, perhaps by recognizing the distinctive patterns formed by 1, 2, 3, etc. objects (e.g., Davis & Perusse, 1988). That is, subitizing is supposed to be a perceptual process that occurs preattentively, in contrast to the more laborious, attention-demanding counting process. Not everyone agrees that there is a subitizing process separate from counting (Gallistel, 1990; Miller, 1993), but if there is it would most likely be used on simultaneously presented arrays of small numbers of items, like those being labeled by Alex and the chimpanzees in some of the experiments described below. By definition, subitizing cannot be used if the objects to be counted are defined by a conjunction of two or more features, each of which they share with other members of a larger set. This is because, as we have seen in chapter 2, identifying objects defined by a conjunction of features requires attentive, serial processing. This line of reasoning suggests that Alex might have been subitizing when he indicated that there were two keys among four rocks, but that he would not be able to do so when asked the number of yellow keys in a display containing yellow keys, green keys, yellow rocks, and green rocks. Nevertheless, Alex did respond correctly to more than 80% of questions of this kind (Pepperberg, 1994).

The research by Boysen and her colleagues with chimpanzees is similar in some ways to the work with Alex. Three chimps were trained to label small collections of objects with Arabic numerals (review in Boysen, 1993). Their education began with training on one-to-one correspondance, matching numbers of gumdrops to numbers of tokens stuck on cards. Then cardinal numbers replaced the tokens. Eventually the animals could make appropriate choices of arrays when shown Arabic numerals and *vice versa*. They could use numbers up to 6 or 8 as well as zero. Finally, one chimp, Sheba, who had the free run of a laboratory room, was allowed to find up to four oranges in any of three places in the room. She reported what she saw by searching the hiding places and then returning to the experimenter and choosing the correspond-ing numeral. The cards with numerals were placed so that Sheba could not see the experimenter while making her choice (figure 8.17). When oranges were in more than one place, Sheba correctly reported the total number of or-anges, apparently adding the numbers found in different locations. To probe further the extent to which numerals represent numbers of things for the an-imal, Boysen and Berntson (1989) then hid cards with numerals. For in-stance, a 1 might be hidden in one place and a 3 in another. Having seen two numerals, Sheba correctly reported their total. Most remarkably, Sheba's per-formance was better than chance from the very first encounter with this task.

Rumbaugh and his colleagues have also probed chimpanzees' ability to add numbers of food items, though without the mediation of number tags (Rumbaugh, Savage-Rumbaugh, & Hegel, 1987; Rumbaugh, Savage-Rumbaugh, & Pate, 1988). Their subjects were Sherman and Austin, two an-imals with extensive language training. They confronted an animal with two trays, each with a pair of food wells. (To reduce the likelihood that the per-son presenting the trays influenced the animal's choice, the trays slid out from beneath a blind.) Each tray held a different total number of chocolate bits. For instance, in the left-hand tray one well might have one bit and the other three, while the right-hand tray might hold wells with two and four bits. The chimp was allowed to choose one tray and eat the contents of both wells. In preliminary trials with only one baited well on each tray, the animals sponta-neously chose the tray with more chocolate bits. In the "summation" condi-tion, they initially chose the greater sum only about 50% of the time, but eventually they almost always chose it, especially when the ratio of larger to smaller amounts was relatively high. Having done this when the individual wells contained zero to four items, they immediately transferred to choices with five items in one or more wells. Control tests showed that the chimps were not basing their choices on the contents of just one well, for example avoiding the tray with the smallest single quantity (Rumbaugh et al., 1988).

Boysen & Berntson (1995) gave two number-trained chimpanzees a choice between two quantities of food as Rumbaugh et al. did, but in their experi-ments the quantity the subject selected was given to another chimpanzee in a cage facing the subject, while the subject was allowed to have what re-mained. In nearly 100 trials' exposure to this contingency, their first two sub-jects, our old acquaintances Sheba and Sarah, persistently pointed to the larger quantity more than 50% of the time. Moreover, their tendency to do so was greater the greater the disparity between the two quantities—that is, the

Figure 8.17. Sheba reports the total number of oranges she found distributed among three hiding places (gray circles). After Boysen and Berntsen (1989) with permission.

more they had to lose. However, when Sheba had numerals substituted for numbers of treats, she immediately began to indicate the smaller amount at greater than chance levels. Five more animals tested similarly peformed in the same way (Boysen, Berntson, Hannan, & Cacioppo, 1996). When sessions with real objects alternated with sessions using numerals, all the animals performed so as to maximize their rewards when numbers were used, but reverted to suboptimal choice with confronted with the actual treats, even after hundreds of trials. Thus even though numerals represent numbers of objects for the animals, the candies themselves arouse an irrepressible "greedy response" that the numerals do not, despite many experiences during which numerals were associated with numbers of rewards. Recall from chapter 3 that ordinary CSs seem to represent multiple aspects of USs, including quality and amount. If numerals functioned as CSs for these chimpanzees, one would expect them to be treated just like the objects themselves. But apparently they symbolize number in the abstract (see Boysen et al., 1996), perhaps because their significance has been acquired through pairings with many different kinds of objects that have only their numerosity in common.

The chimpanzees in the research just described were all trained extensively. So were two squirrel monkeys that learned to associate Arabic numerals up to 9 with numbers of peanut pieces and add them (Olthof, Iden, &

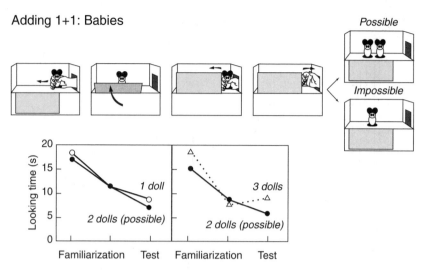

Figure 8.18. Counting in infants. Babies sat in an infant seat watching the "puppet show"; in the familiarization phase they were exposed to the individual events later presented in the test. Redrawn from Wynn (1992, 1995) with permission.

Roberts, 1997). But without any training at all, 5 to 6-month-old human infants (Wynn, 1995) and wild rhesus monkeys (Hauser, MacNeilage, & Ware, 1996) show behavior that has been interpreted as due to adding and subtracting very small quantities. They look longer at a numerically impossible display—for instance, one corresponding to "1 + 1 = 1"—than to a possible one such as "1 + 1 = 2" (figures 8.18 and 8.19). In both species, a small number of habituation trials with possible displays or with displays involving no changes in numbers of objects (see figure 8.19) is followed by a test trial in which response to possible and impossible displays can be compared in different groups. Looking time on various sorts of control trials is measured to control for the possibility that subjects simply look longer at certain static displays—for instance, those containing more objects. Discrimination between possible and impossible displays has been claimed to rest on ability to add and subtract (Wynn, 1992). But rather than being a primitive ability onto which infants later built explicit counting and arithmetical skills, it can be seen as evidence for perceptual tracking of object tokens (see chapter 2). The fact that the changes in the displays must take place rather quickly, as if tracking a temporary perceptual representation, argues in favor or this interpretation (Hauser & Carey, in press; Hauser, MacNeilage, & Ware, 1996).

We seem to be ending our discussion of animal counting where we began, by contrasting the view that counting is natural and automatic with the view that genuine counting appears only, if at all, after extensive training. So, if animals do count, how do they do it? Several models have been alluded to here, and each one seems to be appropriate for different situations. When rats and pigeons respond to the numerosity of successive responses or stimuli in op-

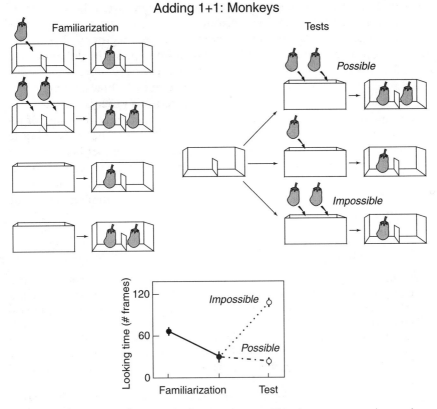

Figure 8.19. Counting in free-ranging rhesus macaques. The objects were purple eggplants. Familiarization involved exposure to two of the four sequences on the left. As in figure 8.18, looking times (measured here in film frames) were scored by observers unaware of which condition the subject was viewing. Redrawn from Hauser et al. (1996) with permission.

erant tests, both the training paradigms and the results fit comfortably into an accumulator model parallel to the information-processing model of timing depicted in figure 8.10. At the same time, the idea that humans and other animals immediately apprehend (subitize) the number of objects in arrays of simultaneously presented items seems to describe data from other kinds of situations. And the experiments on looking time just reviewed may be tapping into a simple short-term perceptual process very different from the human-like symbolic use of numerals seen in highly trained chimpanzees. This possibility is probably best assessed with developmental studies in humans and with further comparative work (see Hauser & Carey, in press).

8.5 Summary

This chapter juxtaposes biological rhythms, timing of short intervals, numerosity discrimination, and use of human language to label small numbers of things. If there is any general conclusion to be drawn from this diversity of problems, it is that animals have distinct mechanisms for solving each of them. Endogenous circadian rhythms are brought into register with local day and night through entrainment, a kind of behavioral plasticity different from associative learning. Timing of intervals in the seconds to minutes range occurs through a different mechanism. There are currently three contenders for the best theoretical account of it. Finally, members of a variety of species have learned quickly and well to discriminate between different numbers of responses, reinforcers, or signals and have been shown to be responding to number per se, perhaps along with some correlate of number like spatial or temporal extent. Once again, there are currently several possible mechanisms to underlie such behavior, and each one may contribute in some situations. In the next chapter we consider how sensitivity to time and number contribute to foraging behavior.

Further Reading

An authoritative as well as amusing brief introduction to circadian timing is the article by Aschoff (1989), one of the founders of the field. A more extensive review is the text by Moore-Ede et al. (1982). Chapters 7–9 of Gallistel (1990) discuss both circadian and interval timing from the author's "computational representational" point of view; the computational model of food anticipation is presented here. A more thorough review of food anticipation is Mistlberger (1993). Wilkie (1995) or W. A. Roberts (1998) may be consulted for a brief review of time and place learning.

A good elementary introduction to interval timing can be found in the first part of chapter 6 in Roitblat's (1987) text. The book edited by Gibbon and Allan (1984) reveals the whole scope of the field of interval timing; more recent reviews of many topics can be found in a 1991 special issue of *Learning and Motivation*. A lucid account of the oscillator vs. information processing models is the article by Church & Broadbent (1990).

For greater depth on animal counting three books are recommended. The one edited by Boysen and Capaldi (1993) contains reviews of all the currently important research programs and ideas as well as a very useful historical introduction by Rilling. Pfungst's account of Clever Hans has been reprinted in English with an introduction by Robert Rosenthal discussing the general problem of inadvertent cueing and other experimenter influences in psychology (Pfungst, 1965). Candland (1993) has written an entertaining and thoughtful book for the general reader that puts Clever Hans and the contemporary work with chimpanzees in the context of a long history of attempts to probe the "silent minds" of animals and feral children by teaching them to use language.

Foraging and
Measuring Rate

A starling walks slowly across a pasture, stopping frequently to poke its beak into the grass and pull out an insect larva. When it has three larvae lined up in its beak, it flies off, carrying the load of prey to its nestlings. A crab crawling over a bed of mussels picks up a small mussel in its claws, handles it for a few seconds, then drops it. The next mussel encountered is bigger; this one the crab crushes and eats. A female apple maggot fly lands on a hawthorn tree and flies from one fruit to another till she locates a good place to lay her eggs. A rat in an operant chamber presses one lever for a few seconds, then switches to a second lever and is rewarded with a pellet of rat food.

All these animals are foraging, gathering some resource that is distributed unevenly in space or time. Their behavior has been analyzed from two distinct points of view: as data to be compared with the predictions of optimality models, and as evidence of memory, information processing, and choice. From the first point of view, that of a behavioral ecologist, the question is, What *should* animals do, and do they do it? From the psychologist's point of view, the question is, *How* do animals do whatever they do? In discussing the "how they do it" of foraging, we will meet some familiar mechanisms like spatial memory and interval timing. But we will also need to consider some new ones, most importantly those for assessing rates of occurrence and choosing between alternatives. The study of foraging is one of the best examples of how functional and mechanistic approaches to behavior can interact (Dukas, 1998; Kamil & Yoerg, 1982; Real, 1991; Shettleworth, 1989). It also exemplifies what a thoroughgoing cognitive ecology might look like, in that questions about how animals process and use information have been formulated and tested with close reference to theory about what information animals need to use (see Dyer, 1998).

We begin with a brief overview of optimal foraging theory and how it is related to the study of cognition. Then we consider some classic foraging problems, how animals should solve them, and how they actually do so. In fact, any foraging animal—a bat catching a moth, a sheep taking a bite of grass, or a female ruff mating with one male rather than another—has implicitly made a nested hierarchy of foraging decisions. Whether or not to forage as opposed to doing other things such as grooming, resting, exploring, or singing must be decided first. Given that it's time to forage, where will the animal forage? A starling living near the coast, for instance, might visit fields at one time of day and tidal marshes at another. Once in an area where prey may be found, the animal consumes some prey and passes over other, similar items. Finally it leaves, perhaps to forage elsewhere or to resume other activities. Not all of these foraging decisions are considered in detail here, partly because the aspects of cognition that some of them entail have been treated in depth in other chapters. For instance, knowing where and when to search is the subject of chapters 7 and 8. This chapter focuses especially on aspects of foraging that illustrate interactions between tests of optimality models and studies of information processing and decision making. Many of the studies we will consider had birds as subjects, reflecting the fact that the most detailed analyses in this area have been done using birds. There is no reason to think that the principles this research has uncovered would not apply to other sorts of animals. Indeed, similar issues even arise in the study of human decision making, touched on briefly in box 9.4.

9.1 Optimality Modeling

The starting point for optimality models in behavioral ecology is to assume that behavior has been selected that maximizes fitness (Parker & Maynard Smith, 1990; Stephens & Krebs, 1986). Because fitness (see box 1.2) is often difficult to measure directly, modelers usually deal in a more easily measured *currency* that is assumed to contribute to fitness. The currency serves as a surrogate for fitness in quantitative models. Rate of energy intake is frequently used in this way. An animal with a relatively high rate of energy intake will quickly get the energy it needs to survive the day or produce a clutch of eggs and may spend less time exposed to predators and have more time to do other things, like defend its territory or search for mates. Therefore it may have higher fitness than a conspecific that has to spend more time foraging. In an experimental demonstration of this, zebra finches were fed on seeds mixed with different proportions of gravel. Although all birds got the same amount of food, groups that had to spend longer searching for it reproduced more slowly (Lemon, 1991). Net rate of energy intake is frequently used as a currency in models of optimal foraging, reflecting the fact that the energy con-

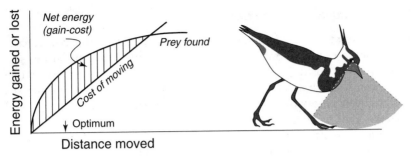

Figure 9.1. Graphical calculation of the optimal size of move for a foraging lapwing. The optimum is the point where the distance between energy intake and energetic cost of moving is maximal. After Parker and Maynard Smith (1990) with permission.

sumed in getting a prey item has to be taken into account along with the energy that the prey item yields. Sometimes other currencies are more obviously related to fitness. For a chickadee in winter the most important determinant of whether it can survive to breed next spring may be whether it can store enough fat by dusk each day to get through the next long night. For a male dungfly searching for mates, a good measure of fitness might be the total number of females he inseminates in his short lifetime.

The second ingredient of an optimality model is a formal characterization of the situation of interest. This includes the *constraints* on the forager. Consider a visual forager like a lapwing walking across a meadow scanning the ground for insects (figure 9.1). How far should the bird move between scans? Walking consumes energy, so the cost of moving increases linearly with the number of steps the bird takes. However, the chance of spotting a new prey item increases as the bird moves away from the area it has just scanned. If the bird can scan a circular area, it should move just the diameter of one scan before stopping to scan again (O'Brien, Browman, & Evans, 1990; Parker & Maynard Smith, 1990). As illustrated in figure 9.1, the tradeoff between the cost of moving and the benefit of scanning a new patch of meadow can be quantified to compute the course of action that maximizes the lapwing's net rate of energy intake. This model must take into account measurable constraints like the bird's field of view and its ability to detect prey as a function of their distance from its eyes. The bird's visual system imposes psychological constraints. At least two physiological constraints are also apparent: the bird cannot move and probe for insects at the same time, and moving consumes energy. A third category of constraint may be imposed by the structure of the environment. For example, when night falls, a diurnal animal like the lapwing will have to stop foraging. Thus it must gather its entire 24-hour energy requirement during the hours of daylight. Early studies of optimal foraging tended to pay most attention to physiological and environmental constraints on foragers, but, as we will see, more recent work has incorporated information about psychological constraints.

9.2 How Individuals Choose Patches

The omniscient theorist surveying the environment can see that resources are not distributed evenly. Flowers occur in clumps; berries are on bushes separated from other bushes; caterpillars infest some trees and not others. In these examples, areas with a particular type of prey are separated from other such areas by spaces empty of that type of prey—that is, prey occur in *patches*. In this section and those that follow, we consider a series of issues about cognition that arise in attempting to account for which patches a forager chooses, starting with the simple case of a single forager and two patches of unchanging average quality. We then consider in turn two kinds of complication to this simple picture: a group of foragers is exploiting the same environment (section 9.3) and a single animal depletes patches as it forages (section 9.4). A third kind of complication is considered in section 9.6: the patches differ in riskiness, or variance. Some of the mechanisms involved in choosing prey within patches are discussed in section 9.5.

9.2.1 Patches that Don't Deplete

Not only does food occur in *patches*, some patches of a given type have more prey than others. (*Prey* refers to both plant and animal food; for the moment we disregard the possibility that patches might differ in factors other than the food they offer such as how dangerous they are for the forager to visit.) If the currency to be maximized is energy intake per unit of foraging time, an animal choosing among nondepleting patches of more or less identical items should choose the patch with the greatest density of items. This is a trivially obvious prediction, but the problem is not trivial from a forager's perspective because solving it means gathering information about the available patches (*sampling* them) and deciding which is the best. Observations in the field indicate that predators do feed disproportionately in patches of highest prey density (see Smith & Dawkins, 1971), but the most detailed studies of how this comes about have been done in the laboratory. One of the first of these was a test of how individual great tits (*Parus major*) choose between two operant responses offering mealworm pieces with different probabilities, a problem referred to as a two-armed bandit, in reference to the Las Vegas "one-armed bandit" gambling machines that pay off unpredictably (Krebs, Kacelnik, & Taylor, 1978).

The birds in Krebs et al.'s study chose between two random ratio schedules that changed from day to day. (In a *random ratio schedule*, reinforcement is available for a specified proportion of responses. For instance, in random ratio 10 or RR 10, on average 1 response in 10, randomly chosen, is reinforced.) Intuitively, an animal in this situation should start by visiting both alternatives and use the information it obtains to decide which is the better, but formally predicting the behavior that maximizes reinforcement here is not simple. Krebs et al. (1978) assumed that behavior consists of a period of sampling, choosing both patches equally often, terminated by an abrupt switch to ex-

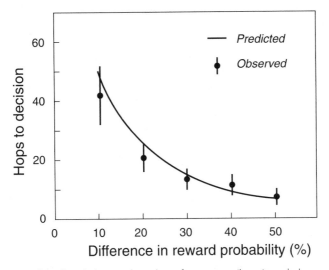

Figure 9.2. Predicted and observed number of responses (hops) made by great tits on two concurrent random ratio schedules before choosing one alternative on at least 90% of the remaining responses in a session. The difference in reward probability (x-axis) is that between the two alternatives—e.g., 50% reward on one schedule vs. 15% on the other is a 35% difference. Redrawn from Krebs et al. (1978) with permission.

ploitation, 100% choice of the patch which experience has indicated is the better. The best point to switch was found by working backwards, choice by choice, from the final choice in the session (a good example of how the theorist's computation of optimal behavior does not always reflect what animals do). It turned out to depend on the length of the session as well as the two patch densities. The longer the time available for foraging, the *time horizon,* the more the animal should sample; the greater the difference between the two reward rates, the less it needs to sample.

"Sampling" implies that food is used as information rather than simply strengthening or weakening preferences. During the sampling period, reinforcements and nonreinforcements are accumulated for both patches, but the patches are chosen equally often until the decision is made to exploit the one that has given the higher ratio of rewards to foraging attempts. Similarly, discussions of mate selection have suggested that animals should find out what options are available before choosing (box 9.1). A simple incremental model of learning, like the Rescorla-Wagner model (see chapter 3), predicts that preference should shift gradually toward the patch providing the higher reward rate. In Krebs et al.'s experiment, the point at which the birds switched from "sampling" to "exploiting" did change as predicted when reward rates were varied (figure 9.2). However, this fit to predictions was achieved at the expense of ignoring the possibility that behavior was changing gradually rather than abruptly; Krebs et al. simply defined the decision to exploit a patch as the point after which it was chosen on at least 90% of visits.

Further research on how animals learn which of two unknown random

Box 9.1. Foraging for Mates and Nests

Sexual selection theory (see section 2.5) implies that females actively choose mates rather than mating randomly. Currently there are two competing models of optimal mate choice (review in Gibson & Langen, 1996; Sherman, Reeve, & Pfennig, 1997). In the "best of n" model, the female inspects n males and then mates with the best (Janetos, 1980). The optimal number inspected, n, is determined by the time and energy costs of searching. For instance, if the female spends too long before mating, the breeding season may pass or the chances of raising offspring sucessfully before winter may decline. The best of n rule seems to require that females remember all the sequentially inspected males equally well—that is, without forgetting or primacy or recency effects. An alternative model apparently making less unrealistic assumptions about memory is that the female mates with the first male she encounters who surpasses some threshold value. The threshold should be determined by the average quality of males in the environment: a male of poor quality in absolute terms may be acceptable if most males are even poorer.

Females of many species that have been observed in the wild do have encounters with more than one male before mating (Gibson & Langen, 1996). One apparent difference in the predictions of the two models is that in the best of n model the first male encountered will seldom be accepted whereas in the threshold model he will be accepted if he is of high enough quality (Wiegmann, Real, Capone, & Ellner, 1996). Only the best of n model leads to the expectation that a male who has been inspected once and rejected will be reinspected and accepted later. Behavior fitting this description has been observed in a number of species in the wild (Gibson & Langen, 1996; Wiegmann, Real, Capone, & Ellner, 1996). If memory is imperfect or if several visits are necessary to assess a male's characteristics, the best of n model might even allow the same male to be inspected several times. However, the threshold model could also permit choosing a previously rejected male if the threshold is continuously adjusted on the basis of experience. Indeed, data from experiments with birds (e.g., Collins, 1995) and fish (e.g., Bakker & Milinski, 1991) reveal a kind of contrast effect in mate choice: a mate of a given quality is more likely to be preferred the lower the quality of previously encountered males. Another factor that may complicate the picture is that rather than sampling males for herself, a female may simply copy the mate choice of earlier-arriving females (Sherman, Reeve, & Pfennig, 1997; see box 10.2). Some species, too, may lack the memory and counting abilities presupposed by the original version of the best of n rule.

The recent flurry of research on sexual selection has clearly established that females of many species actively choose mates, but there is still need for better experiments to distinguish the possible mechanisms for search and decision making (Wiegmann, Real, Capone, & Ellner, 1996). Some other foraging problems present the same kinds of functional and mechanistic problems as mate choice. For instance, female brown-headed cowbirds prospect for nests in which to lay their eggs, spending much of each day searching for sites where potential hosts—generally small songbirds—are building or starting to lay. They apparently retain memories of the nests' locations and states and return later, in the early mornings, to lay. The demands on memory made by this important reproductive task have resulted in female brown-headed cowbirds having a relatively larger hippocampus than close relatives (Sherry, Forbes, Khurgel, & Ivy, 1993).

ratio alternatives is the better has focused on how changes in preference with experience on the schedules might be accounted for by various simple incremental learning rules (Kacelnik, Krebs, & Ens, 1987; Lea & Dow, 1984; Mazur, 1992, 1995; Plowright & Shettleworth, 1990). The simplest of these rules assumes that the value associated with an alternative on trial n, E_n, is given by the following equation.

$$E_n = wE_{n-1} + (1-w)\ C.$$

Here C expresses what happened on the most recent foraging attempt: if a prey item was captured $C = 1$; otherwise $C = 0$. Notice that the effect of most recent experience (i.e., $(1-w)C$) is added to the cumulated effects of past experiences (i.e., wE_{n-1}). The relative contributions of these two factors are weighted by w; the larger w, the more important the past (E_{n-1}) relative to the present. In effect, w is a measure of the *memory window*, the amount of the past that is taken account of. An animal with a long memory window will not be buffeted by short-term fluctuations in prey availability, but it will be slow to adjust to genuine change. In addition to a learning equation, applicable to each patch separately, any complete model of preference acquisition must include a rule for choosing between patches. If the rule is "choose the patch with the greater current value," abrupt all or nothing shifts in preference may result. Matching (see section 9.2.3) is one rule that can produce gradual shifts and partial preferences. In the field, animals that frequently have to learn about new patch densities might develop a learning set (see chapter 5), enabling them to acquire new preferences more quickly than inexperienced animals.

9.2.2 Sampling Patches that Change: Scalar Expectancy and Delayed Rewards

The two-armed bandit seems to capture a very basic foraging problem, and attempts to model it raise some general issues about how animals should and do gather information about prey densities. These issues have been more nearly resolved in studies of more complex foraging situations, like the one depicted in figure 9.3. Here, the animal chooses between a constant mediocre patch and a fluctuating patch where prey occasionally become very abundant. At other times, prey are scarce in the fluctuating patch, and the forager is better off in the mediocre patch. In some real-life situations of this kind, there might be reliable temporal or other cues to the state of the fluctuating patch, but if there are no cues to the state of the fluctuating patch, the animal can maximize its food intake by occasionally visiting the fluctuating patch to sample its state. When it is better than the constant patch, the animal can stay there until prey disappear again. The optimal behavior in this situation (Stephens, 1987) is to sample at fixed intervals—for instance, every tenth foraging trip—rather than at random. This makes sense because sampling too soon will not allow enough time for the patch to change state whereas waiting too long could result in missing some of the good state. Sampling should increase

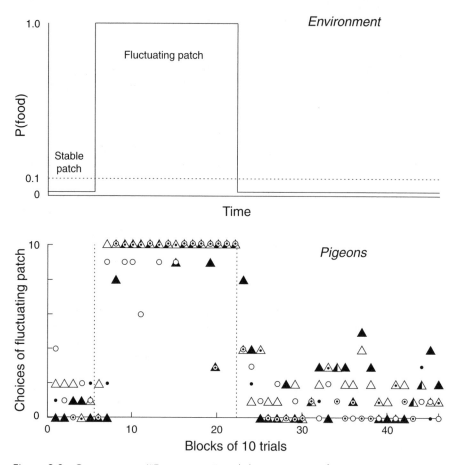

Figure 9.3. Contingencies ("Environment") and data ("Pigeons") from experiments on environmental tracking. The symbols in the lower part of the figure are data from four different birds in one session. Choices of the fluctuating patch while p(food) = 0 there are sampling responses. Redrawn from Shettleworth et al. (1988) with permission.

when the constant patch becomes worse or the fluctuating patch's good state becomes better: in both cases there is more to be gained by sampling.

In one laboratory test of these predictions (Shettleworth, Krebs, Stephens, & Gibbon, 1988; see also Krebs & Inman, 1994), pigeons were trained in a long operant chamber with a "patch" at each end. The "fluctuating patch" might change up to three times per session between a schedule delivering no food (extinction) and one delivering relatively frequent food on a random ratio schedule. Choosing the fluctuating patch gave immediate feedback about its state. When the fluctuating patch was bad, the pigeons generally chose the constant patch most of the time, only occasionally visiting the fluctuating patch (figure 9.3). When they found that patch in its good state, they continued to choose it until it became bad again. Furthermore, sampling increased as the reinforcement probability in the constant patch declined. However, behavior deviated from the predictions of the optimal sampling model in three ways: (1) sampling occurred at random, not at regular intervals; (2) sampling frequency did not change when the reinforcement probability in the good state varied; and (3) when the fluctuating patch was good, the birds occasionally visited the constant patch, a sort of "reverse sampling" that reduced their reward rate.

Just as with the two-armed bandit problem discussed in the last section, we can ask how a psychological model can be applied to this foraging problem. A model that works very well for the data collected by Shettleworth et al. (1988) was originally developed to account for choice between reinforcement schedules. It views choice between reward probabilities as choice between delays to food, a reasonable assumption if choices are made at a constant rate. So, for example, choosing once every 6 seconds to visit a patch that pays off on RR 10 means the average delay to food is 60 seconds. However, on a random ratio schedule the animal actually experiences a distribution of delays to food, and in the theory we are considering (Gibbon, Church, Fairhurst, & Kacelnik, 1988) each one is assumed to be remembered, with variance proportional to its mean (see chapter 8). Faced with a choice between two or more alternatives, an animal is assumed to sample from the distribution of remembered delays associated with each alternative and choose the alternative with the shortest sample on that trial (figure 9.4). In effect this is a model of maximizing rate under a psychological constraint.

This model, the scalar expectancy model of choice (Gibbon et al., 1988), also accounts for the results of other operant foraging experiments, as we will shortly see. Sampling the fluctuating patch occurs at random rather than at regular intervals because samples are taken from memory at random, and sampling behavior reflects the occasions when the shorter memory sample comes from the fluctuating patch. The bird keeps on choosing the fluctuating patch after finding it good because a different distribution of interreinforcement intervals is associated with the good state. "Reverse sampling" during the good state occurs because the memory sample from the constant patch occasionally corresponds to a shorter delay than that from the fluctuating patch. In an experiment similar to that of Shettleworth et al. (1988), starlings tended to sample at regular intervals rather than randomly (Krebs & Inman, 1994). This might reflect a species difference, but there were also procedural differences between the experiments. The starlings lived in the experimental chamber and got all their food there while the pigeons were tested once a day, when they were quite hungry. The former arrangement seems more natural, but it should not necessarily have affected the results (box 9.2).

9.2.3 Choice between Reward Rates

Concurrent Schedules   Discussing foraging in patches has led us into a consideration of how animals assess rates of prey capture and choose between alternatives. We have already met two general approaches to this issue. In the lin-

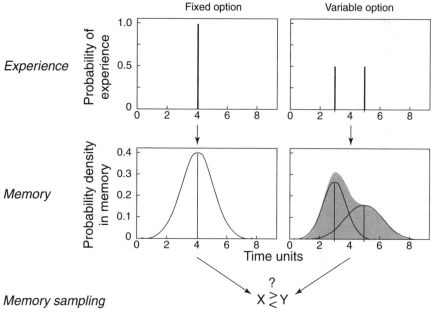

Figure 9.4. The scalar expectancy account of choice between a fixed interval schedule of reinforcement and a variable interval schedule with the same mean. In this example the variable schedule has two equiprobable intervals. The gray area is its memory distribution. After Bateson and Kacelnik (1995) with permission.

ear operator model of section 9.2.1, past history is stored as a single value, like excitatory strength in associative models, and this value is incremented or decremented on individual "trials" or choices. This rule amounts to a formalization of Thorndike's (1911/1970) Law of Effect: reinforcers strengthen (i.e., increase the probability, speed and/or vigor, of) responses they follow; punishers have the opposite effect. In the SET model, in contrast, experience is represented as a collection of memories of delays to food. But these summaries capture only half of how rates of occurrence affect behavior because an animal needs a rule for acting on information as well as one for acquiring it. The rule in the SET model is to maximize—that is, to choose the alternative with the currently shortest remembered delay to food. Maximizing might seem like the only adaptive response rule, but a popular alternative has been some form of *matching*. That is, options are chosen in proportion to past reinforcements associated with them. For example, if the better of two patches has yielded prey twice as often as the worse, it will be chosen twice as often under matching but all the time under maximizing.

Why might animals match rather than maximize? There are both functional and mechanistic answers to this question. Under some conditions, matching may be the outcome of a maximizing mechanism, as we will shortly

Box 9.2. Open or Closed Economy, Lab or Field: Does it Matter?

Throughout the book we have been applying conclusions based on studies in the laboratory to observations made in the field and vice versa. But some may object to using principles discovered in the lab to explain behavior observed in the field (see Kacelnik, 1993). Most of the issues involved have been considered in discussions of whether foraging can be studied using operant schedules in the laboratory. In most traditional studies of reinforcement schedules, very hungry animals work for small reinforcers in short daily sessions, and supplementary food is given in the home cages. Under such conditions, total responding per session increases as the amount of work required per reinforcer is increased, but responding eventually decreases at very high work requirements (high fixed ratio schedules; figure B9.2). For over 20 years, Collier and his colleagues (Collier, Hirsch, & Hamlin, 1972; Collier & Johnson, 1997; Collier, 1983) have been testing a variety of species in arguably more natural conditions. In their experiments, completing a schedule requirement is reinforced with a "meal": the animal can eat for as long as it wants. Subjects live in the experimental chambers and can work for food at any time. The absence of supplemental feeding makes this arrangement a *closed economy*, in contrast to the *open economy* of traditional experiments (Hursh, 1980). In a closed economy, total responding tends to decrease when response requirements increase (figure B9.2). Animals typically maintain their total daily intake by increasing the size of the meals they take at each opportunity. In the extreme, rats and other animals may press a bar thousands of times for a single daily meal.

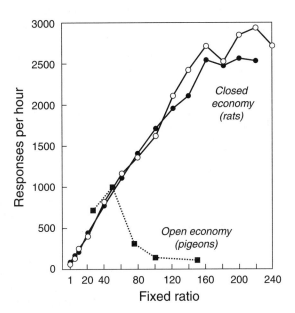

Figure B9.2. Mean responses per hour as a function of fixed ratio requirement in closed and open economies. After Hursh (1980) with permission. Rat data redrawn from Collier, Hirsch, and Hamlin (1972) with permission. Data for pigeons from Felton and Lyon (1966).

Box 9.2. Open or Closed Economy, Lab or Field: Does it Matter? (*continued*)

The differences in the two functions shown in figure B9.2 are striking, but they represent behavior under two very different sorts of conditions. It is more likely that parametric differences in reinforcer size, hunger, session length, and the like are responsible than that animals are affected differently by reward in "unnatural" open economies and "natural" closed ones. And in fact, under suitable conditions the rising-then-falling function typical of traditional experiments can be obtained in closed as well as open economies (e.g., Timberlake & Peden, 1987). Models of the functional and mechanistic factors involved have shown why this might be so (Houston & McNamara, 1989; Staddon & Reid, 1987).

Besides the parametric differences within experimental sessions, open and closed economies differ in whether or not the animal's daily intake depends on how hard it works, as it likely does in nature. Perhaps, it could be argued, animals in open economies respond less when the work requirement is high because they know the experimenter will feed them no matter what they do. In fact, however, rats respond just as much for food on ratio schedules whether they are fed immediately after the session or up to 20 hours later (Timberlake, 1984). And in general, as discussed later in this chapter, animals tend to respond so as to minimize the time to the next reward even when overall reward might be maximized by doing something else, such as waiting for a large reward.

Studying optimal foraging in the laboratory also raises the question whether it makes sense to apply adaptationist arguments to behavior in unnatural environments (cf. Houston & McNamara, 1989). Behavior selected in the natural environment is not necessarily adaptive in other environments, such as operant chambers. However, behavior mechanisms can be assumed to work the same way in any environment. We have already seen many experiments in which mechanisms underlying behavior are revealed by engineering unnatural conditions that make animals behave stupidly. Recall, for example, the digger wasp in chapter 7 flying around and around over solid sand just a few centimeters away from her nest or the rats and human babies looking for a goal precisely opposite from its true location. These animals are not adapted to a world in which whole landmark arrays move, yet by moving landmarks and enclosures we can reveal how creatures normally find their way around. Sometimes, of course, changing the environment does change the mechanisms brought into play. For instance, Nicol and Pope (1994; see chapter 10) found that one hen can learn what to do from watching through a screen while another hen performs a discrimination. Without the screen, however, the observing hen does not learn because she interferes with the trained hen, suggesting that such observational learning might have little or no importance in a normal flock. The work of Kacelnik and his colleagues on foraging in starlings discussed in this chapter is a rare example of a research program that combines observations and experiments in the field with analysis of the same phenomena in the laboratory (see Kacelnik & Cuthill, 1987). Ideally, too, analysis in the laboratory is followed by a stage of synthesis in which the original phenomenon is put back together again from the elements into which it has been dissected.

see. From a functional point of view, matching may result in maximizing in the long run. For instance, an animal that does not become fixated on one prey or patch type may be gaining information that it can use later or exposing itself to options that may suddenly change for the better (see Smith & Dawkins, 1971, for an example). These issues have been most thoroughly fought out in discussions of behavior on concurrent schedules of reinforcement. Therefore, before further discussion of the psychological mechanisms in foraging, we need to make a side trip into the literature of instrumental choice behavior to look more closely at rate assessment and choice.

The two-armed bandit is an example of a *concurrent schedule of reinforcement*. Just as its name says, on such a schedule, two or more separate reinforcement schedules run concurrently. At any moment, the animal can choose which one to respond on. Historically, students of behavior on concurrent schedules have been most interested in the *steady state*—that is, behavior after many sessions of exposure to the same conditions. As a result, concurrent ratios like the two-armed bandit have not received much attention because the steady state is the relatively uninteresting one of nearly exclusive choice of the more favorable ratio. Much more influential have been studies of behavior on concurrent variable-interval variable-interval (*conc VI VI*) schedules. On a VI schedule, as its name says, programmed interreinforcement intervals are chosen randomly from a large set of intervals with a mean specified by the VI value. Thus on VI 20 seconds reinforcement is available on average every 20 seconds, but with actual interreinforcement intervals typically ranging from effectively zero to much longer than 20 seconds. A VI schedule is like a patch that depletes when an item is found and repletes at unpredictable times afterwards. Once it becomes available, a reinforcer remains available until the animal responds, like a repleting patch for which there are no competitors. Such a situation is experienced by wagtails foraging along riverbanks in winter (Houston, 1986; see also chapter 6). These small birds feed on insect matter and seeds deposited at the water's edge. Each individual systematically patrols a territory along a stretch of riverbank. By keeping out competitors, it ensures that each segment of the bank yields prey on a VI schedule: after the bird has visited and collected any prey, the likelihood of prey being there again increases with the passage of time to a maximum when new items are deposited as fast as others are washed away.

The Matching Law   The way to maximize reinforcers on a conc VI VI schedule is to continually switch back and forth, checking each alternative in turn to see whether a reinforcer has become available there (Houston & McNamara, 1981). This is what animals do, even when direct reinforcement for switching has been reduced by imposing a cost of switching (a *changeover delay*), so reinforcers cannot be collected until a few seconds after switching. But more than just working on both options rather than fixating on one, animals match the proportion of time spent at an alternative, or the number of responses made there, to the proportion of reinforcers obtained there (Herrnstein, 1961). This result, illustrated in figure 9.5, has been found so consis-

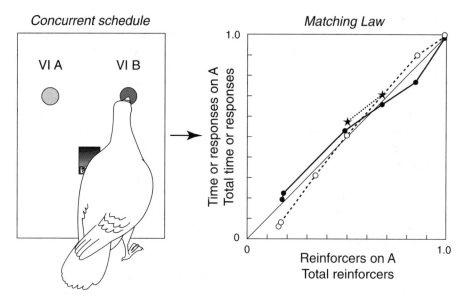

Figure 9.5. Typical experimental setup for studying behavior on concurrent schedules of reinforcement and data illustrating the matching law. Solid diagonal line is perfect matching. Each symbol represents data from a different pigeon. Data redrawn from Herrnstein (1961) with permission.

tently in so many species and situations that it is referred to as the *matching law* (review in Williams, 1988). Animals match behavior not only to numbers of reinforcers but also to reinforcement amounts or delays, in general to any measure of reinforcer value. Indeed, matching is so well established that it can be used to assess how animals value different alternatives (e.g., Hamm & Shettleworth, 1987; Shettleworth, 1985).

What psychological mechanism is responsible for matching? Much research has been devoted to this issue, but there is still no completely satisfactory answer (see Williams, 1988, 1994). Accounts of matching are of two general types: *molar*, or dealing with overall behavior in an experimental session; and *molecular*, or moment by moment. An appealing molar account is that animals match because matching actually maximizes reinforcers. This implies that responses would be allocated in some other way if maximizing required it. Concurrent schedules devised to test this prediction require the animal to respond on a seldom-reinforced alternative in order to advance the schedule on a more frequently reinforced one. Maximizing reinforcers requires responding more on the worse schedule than matching dictates. However, pigeons still match relative responding to relative reinforcers obtained on the two alternatives even though this means they earn fewer reinforcers than they could (Mazur, 1981; Williams, 1988). The mechanism that brings about matching on concurrent VI VI schedules may well have evolved because it results in maximizing fitness under natural conditions, but it does not consist of

comparing total intake after allocating choices in different ways and adopting the policy that gave the most food (Houston, 1987).

Most molecular theories of matching are also maximizing theories because
they assume that animals choose the option that gives the most reinforcement
at each moment. For instance, as time passes since switching onto one of two
concurrent VIs, the probability increases that a reinforcer will be available for
a response on the other VI, and choices might track that probability. Just like
molar maximizing, this sort of account suggests that matching reflects long
experience on a schedule. In fact, however, under some conditions animals
respond immediately to changes in the times between rewards. For example,
Mark and Gallistel (1994) exposed rats to concurrent VI VI schedules of positively reinforcing brain stimulation, with one schedule associated with each
of two levers. Once during each session, the levers were retracted briefly from
the operant chamber. When they were reinserted, the better schedule had
switched from one lever to the other. The rats switched their preferences almost immediately, within as little as one interreward interval (figure 9.6).
They also tracked random fluctuations in the times between rewards on each
schedule. These data suggest that rats assess rates of reinforcer delivery in
terms of the times between rewards, and that they may base their decisions on
just the last few such times. We will shortly see evidence for the overriding importance of very recent temporal information in other foraging situations.
However, longer term averages do seem to be used under some conditions.
Functionally, the degree to which animals track short-term changes might be
expected to depend on how stable the environment is in general: frequent
change should favor immediate tracking whereas stability should favor molar
averaging.

SET and Matching   The notion that animals allocate behavior using memories for the times between rewards on different alternatives is the basis of the
SET memory-sampling model of choice introduced in the last section. This
model does predict matching on concurrent VI VI schedules (Gibbon,
Church, Fairhurst, & Kacelnik, 1988). Importantly, it also predicts behavior
on concurrent schedules in which the alternatives are a VI schedule and a
fixed interval (FI) schedule with rewards available at regular intervals the
same length as the mean inter reinforcement interval in the VI. If choice is
governed by maximizing total rewards, animals should repond equally on two
such alternatives. In fact, however, the VI is strongly preferred (Herrnstein,
1964). This result suggests that animals are not responding to the total reinforcers a schedule yields over the time scale of a session or so. One possibility is that rather than doing something equivalent to counting reinforcers and
dividing by the total time over which they appeared, animals do someting
equivalent to computing a local reinforcement rate when each reinforcer is
obtained and average this rate — that is, they average local rates rather than
computing an overall rate. This approach is discussed further in section 9.6.
Another approach is based on the SET model's assumption that animals store
blurred memories of interreinforcement intervals (Gibbon et al., 1988). Re-

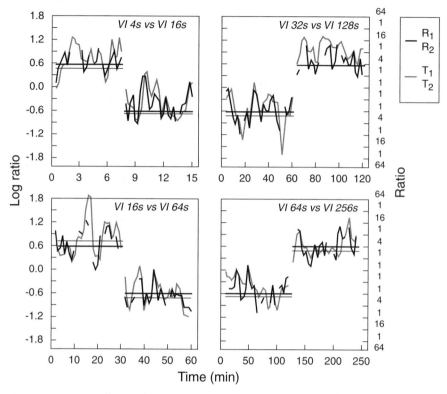

Figure 9.6. Ratios of rewards obtained (R) and time spent responding (T) on two levers that yielded brain stimulation reinforcement on the concurrent VI schedules indicated. Thick horizontal lines indicate the programmed ratio of 4:1 or 1:4; thinner horizontal lines are the ratio actually obtained over the whole trial. Breaks in the lines for obtained reward ratios occur when there were no rewards in that time bin. The time axis is scaled to the interreward interval. Each panel has data from one rat and one trial. Redrawn from Mark and Gallistel (1994) with permission.

call from chapter 8 that memory for time obeys Weber's law: a time interval is remembered with proportional variance. From this assumption, one can predict what any experienced distribution of delays to food should look like in memory. The memory distribution for a VI has an overrepresentation of short intervals, so a sample taken at random is more likely to represent a shorter interval than a random sample from the equivalent FI schedule (see figure 9.4). As this account suggests, pigeons do not prefer a VI schedule constructed so that its memory distribution more closely resembles that from a fixed schedule giving the same mean number of reinforcers per session (Gibbon et al., 1988).

Paradoxical Preferences   If the preference for VI over FI is unexpected, some relatively new findings of strong preferences where none should exist are even more suprising from a functional point of view. Belke (1992) trained pigeons

Training

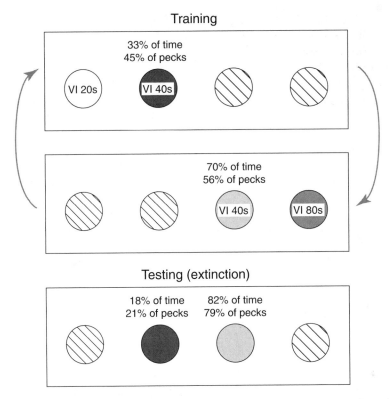

Testing (extinction)

Figure 9.7. Method and results of experiments demonstrating pigeons' paradoxical preferences for one of two keys that had previously been reinforced with identical schedules. Key colors as in the text. Slanted lines indicate darkened keys. Data from Belke (1992).

on two pairs of VI schedules concurrently, as shown in figure 9.7. One-minute periods in which a red key signaled VI 40 seconds and a white key signaled VI 20 seconds alternated with one-minute periods of VI 40 on a green key and VI 80 on a yellow key. As matching predicts, the VI 40 schedule was preferred when paired with VI 80, but the VI 20 was preferred to it in the other schedule pair. The interesting part of this experiment came on occasional unreinforced test minutes when the red key and the green key were presented together. Since they both signaled the same, VI 40, schedule, birds should have pecked about equally often at the red and green keys. Instead, the birds pecked the green key four times as much as the red one (figure 9.7).

This result was replicated and extended by Gibbon (1995) in a situation in which one key color and schedule appeared at a time and the birds had to peck a second key to change over to the second color in a pair. This arrangement generally produces similar results to the one in which both key colors are displayed continuously (Williams, 1988). Gibbon's tests included not only pairings of the colors associated with the two VI 40 second schedules but also pairings of the preferred alternatives from the two pairs—that is, VI 40 from the VI 40, VI 80 pair and VI 20 from the VI 20, VI 40 pair. In these tests, the birds delivered *more* pecks to the VI 40 key color, the one paired with *less* frequent reinforcement. Notice that this is the opposite of value transfer, discussed in box 5.3.

These findings appear to fly in the face of the SET model's assumptions that animals choose between alternatives by comparing their associated delays to reward. However, this is true only if memory is sampled at a constant rate regardless of what options are present. But suppose that memory is sampled more often the higher the overall rate of reinforcement (see section 8.3.3). For instance, when VI 40 has been paired with a better schedule, the memories of the interreinforcement intervals will be sampled more often than when it has been paired with a worse schedule, say VI 80. This idea leads to the prediction that animals will switch away from a given schedule more often the richer the overall reinforcement context in which it has appeared. However, having switched away from the VI 40 that was paired with VI 20 and onto VI 40 that was paired with VI 80, the animal will be slow to switch back because of this alternative's history in a poor context. Memory sampling rates may seem hypothetical, but they might reasonably be expected to be reflected in the frequency with which animals switch between alternatives. In fact, in Gibbon's experiment, as predicted, birds switched between alternatives more often the higher the overall reinforcement frequency. Most important, in the brief tests with novel pairings of schedules, the distributions of times between switches were the same as in training, leading to the paradoxical preferences he obtained. As summarized in the title of Gibbon's (1995) report of these results, "Arousal makes better seem worse."

Conclusions   Research on how animals match relative responding to relative reinforcement has been going on for over 30 years without yielding a consensus (Williams, 1994), so it is quite likely that the account that seems most satisfactory today will be challenged tomorrow. Although the SET model of Gibbon et al. (1988) should perhaps be treated as a heuristic more than a literal account of what underlies performance on schedules, it does have much to recommend it. It is based on data about timing gathered independently in the sorts of experiments reviewed in chapter 8. It accounts for a wide variety of data from conventional schedules of reinforcement, including the preference for variable over fixed interval schedules and the paradoxical preferences just discussed. Moreover, it can account for behavior in experiments designed to model a variety of foraging problems, like the patch sampling experiment in section 9.2.2 and others discussed below.

Perhaps because traditional research on reinforcement schedules emphasized behavior in the steady state, the SET model assumes the animal has an exhaustive memory of the delays to reward experienced on the alternatives before it (but see Brunner, Fairhurst, Stolovitzky, & Gibbon, 1997). Much of foraging theory, however, deals with an environment that is dynamic and ever-changing. Time runs out, competitors come and go, patches deplete and replete. The environment may change between one foraging bout and the next (box 9.3). Results discussed below indicate that, in accord with the need to track continual change, only one or the very few most recent delays may be remembered.

9.3 Choosing Patches in a Group

9.3.1 The Ideal Free Distribution

The foragers of the last section never have to compete with other animals for the same resources. But if animals forage in groups, the simple prescription "Find the best patch and stay there" may no longer lead to optimal behavior for every individual. It is easy to see why. Suppose there are two patches, one where 10 prey appear each minute and one where a single prey item appears each minute. The first foragers to arrive will do best by going to the 10 per minute patch, but when there are 10 foragers, the eleventh arrival will be better off in the worse patch, where it can get one item per minute rather than its 1/11th of 10 items per minute. If it does go to the already occupied patch, then one of the individuals there should leave. In general, as this example suggests, the only stable situation is that in which foragers are distributed so the proportion of foragers in each patch matches the proportion of prey available there. This is known as the *ideal free distribution* (see Milinski & Parker, 1991). It represents the way in which each individual can maximize its intake under the ideal conditions of perfect information about the alternatives and equal competitive abilities for all individuals. (For example, this means that the first arrival in a patch cannot keep later arrivals out.) The idealization also includes the assumption that individuals can move freely between patches. For example, the cost of traveling from one patch to another is negligible. In addition, only food intake is being maximized, so in the case above we ignored the possibility that the eleventh animal to arrive might be more at risk from predators if it chooses to feed alone.

At first glance, the ideal free distribution looks like the matching law on the level of populations, but the reason for introducing it at this point in the chapter is to contrast it with matching by individuals. The predicted distribution of the group under ideal free theory could as well arise from each individual staying in a single patch as from each individual matching. In the example above, either each individual could do 1/11th of its foraging in the worse patch, or 1/11th of all individuals could do all their foraging there. However, before we can consider individual behavior, we need to look at how well data about groups fit the matching prediction and how theory can deal with deviations from matching.

Early tests of ideal free theory appeared to support it quite well (see Milinski & Parker, 1991). Male dungflies searching for mates on a cowpat, ducks feeding on bread thrown into a pond, and other animals appeared to distribute themselves in proportion to the available resources. However, some of these studies can be criticized because they did not use a very wide range of ratios of prey availability in the two patches (Kennedy & Gray, 1993). When

Box 9.3. Forgetting, Spontaneous Recovery, and Environmental Tracking

When a resource frequently changes in value, as time passes since it was sampled last it begins to make sense to respond as if the resource has the average of its past values. For instance, if repeated encounters with two patches show that two-thirds of the time Patch A has food while B is empty and one-third of the time the reverse is true, and if the forager has not sampled either patch recently, its best bet is to visit A regardless of which patch was better on its last visit (J. Devenport & L. Devenport, 1993; Devenport, Hill, Wilson, & Ogden, 1997; L. Devenport & J. Devenport, 1994).

Behavior in accord with this informal prediction has been found in rats in runways (Devenport, Hill, Wilson, & Ogden, 1997), pigeons responding on conventional concurrent VI schedules (Mazur, 1996), dogs tested in their owners' backyards (J. Devenport & L. Devenport, 1993), and ground squirrels and chipmunks tested in the field (L. Devenport & J. Devenport, 1994). In the latter set of studies, two platforms that could be loaded with sunflower seeds were set up in an area that golden-mantled ground squirrels (*Spermophilus lateralis*) and least chipmunks (*Tamias minimus*) had been trained to visit. First one platform, A, was baited until the animals reliably chose it first. Then the second platform, B, was immediately baited instead until animals were visiting B first. Choice of A vs. B was tested either 1 hour or 24 hours later. Animals tested immediately always chose B first, but animals tested 24 hours later chose B only about 50% of the time. However, this finding is problematical since 50:50 choice of A and B could also result from complete forgetting. However, in a further experiment, three platforms—A, B, and C—were used. A was baited twice as often as B, and C was never baited. Here what Devenport and Devenport call the *temporal weighting rule* predicts that B will be chosen immediately after a trial in which it was baited, but A will be chosen after a delay. This pattern of choice was found in the field study with chipmunks and ground squirrels (figure B9.3), as well as in laboratory studies with pigeons (Mazur, 1996) and rats (Devenport, Hill, Wilson, & Ogden, 1997).

➠

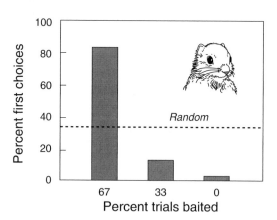

Figure B9.3. Percent of trials on which free-ranging ground squirrels chose each of three feeders first 24 hours after the last trial as a function of the percent of previous trials on which each one had been baited. Data from L. Devenport and J. Devenport (1994).

Box 9.3. (*continued*)

The procedure being used in these experiments is essentially successive reversal learning, where, as we have seen, extended training leads to random choice of two equally rewarded alternatives at the beginning of each new session. The discussion of successive reversals in chapter 5 suggested that interference in memory is responsible for this effect, but spontaneous recovery of the response not most recently reinforced may also play a role (Devenport, Hill, Wilson, & Ogden, 1997; Mazur, 1996; Rescorla, 1996). The ongoing research on this problem is a nice little example of how functional and mechanistic considerations, field and laboratory data can all converge to produce new insights into both foraging behavior and memory mechanisms.

the results of studies with a wider range of ratios are displayed in the way familiar to students of the matching law, with the log of the ratio of predators plotted against the log of the ratio of resources, systematic *undermatching* is apparent. That is, in the majority of cases, the slope of the best-fitting line through the data is not 1, or perfect matching, but less than 1, or closer to random than predicted, as in figure 9.8. One way to account for this pattern is to suppose that some individuals are unable to perceive the differences between patches and therefore behave randomly. It is also possible that the assumptions of the ideal free distribution have been violated. Travel between patches may be costly, or some individuals may be able to outcompete others for the same resources. In our original example, if one of the early arrivals

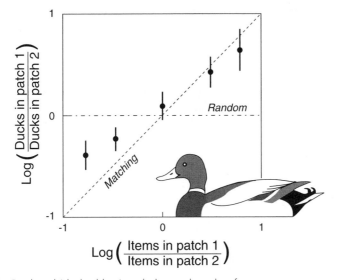

Figure 9.8. Predicted (dashed line) and obtained results of experiments testing the ideal free distribution with free-living mallard ducks. Redrawn from Kennedy and Gray (1993) with permission.

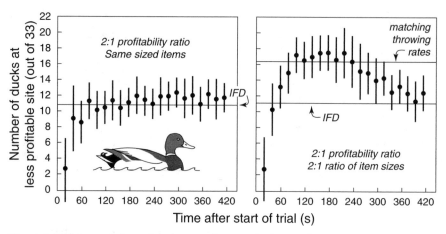

Figure 9.9. Mean number of ducks (out of 33) at the less profitable of two food patches as a function of seconds since experimenters began throwing bread in the two sites. IFD = ideal free distribution. Redrawn from Harper (1982) with permission.

is able to command 2/10ths rather than 1/10th of the resources in the richer patch, then fewer animals will be found in that patch than if all were equal competitors. These and other possibilities can be incorporated into a revised model (see Gray, 1994; Kacelnik, Krebs, & Bernstein, 1992; Kennedy & Gray, 1993; Milinski & Parker, 1991).

9.3.2 Individual Learning and Group Distributions

Even if the distributions of predators are not as extreme as predicted by the IFD, they are not completely random either, so the question arises what individual learning mechanisms lead to the observed allocations. Some research points to mechanisms that work very fast. For instance, Harper (1982) had two experimenters stand on the bank of a pond and throw equal-sized pieces of bread into the water at different rates. Ducks quickly collected in front of the two throwers, and the proportion of ducks in front of each one matched the proportion of bread being thrown there. What was remarkable about Harper's observations was that the distribution of ducks stabilized well before each individual had had time to visit the two patches and eat bread in each one (figure 9.9). Comparable results have been found with fish (Godin & Keenleyside, 1984). As Harper (1982) pointed out, the ducks must have been basing their behavior on observation of the experimenters' throwing rates. This conclusion is supported by an experiment in which the experimenters threw bread at the same rate in both patches, but the pieces of bread thrown in one patch were twice as big as those in the other, so the ratio of profitabilities was 2:1. In the first few minutes about equal numbers of ducks congregated in front of both throwers, consistent with their responding to the rates of throwing. Later, the ratio settled down nearer 2:1, as if the actual rates of bread intake were used too (figure 9.9).

Gallistel (1990, 1995) has pointed out that data like Harper's imply that animals can calculate rates of occurrence of observed events and compare them. The tendency to spend time in a patch does not need to be strengthened by primary reinforcement from food eaten in the patch. Moreover, decisions about time allocation can be made very quickly, on the basis of just one or a few observations. This does not mean, however, that the mechanism involved is fundamentally any different from that described by the SET model, just that the information going into it may be a small number of observed interfood intervals. The conclusions suggested by Harper's experiment should not be overgeneralized, however. Gotceitas and Colgan (1991) tested whether three-spined sticklebacks assess patch profitability by visual observation. They confined subject fish in the middle of a tank, from where they could see various numbers of fish feeding on food arriving at different rates in the two ends. The subjects spent most time near the patch with more fish, not necessarily the one with the more favorable ratio of food to fish. Similarly, starlings entering experimental patches in the field are attracted to starlings already feeding (Krebs & Inman, 1994). Starlings, and presumably other animals, can take advantage of companions' sampling and adjust their own feeding behavior after observing others' feeding success (Krebs & Inman, 1994; Templeton & Giraldeau, 1995). Thus animals foraging in groups may use multiple sources of information in deciding where to forage.

Adjustments to different patch densities are not always as complete as reported by Harper (1982). Gray and Kennedy (1994) repeated Harper's experiment but used a wider range of relative patch densities (Harper only reports 1:1 and 2:1). With payoff ratios of 3:1 and 6:1, the proportion of ducks in a patch was closer to 50% than the proportion of bread available there (i.e., the ducks undermatched, as in figure 9.8). A small flock of sparrows exposed to concurrent VI VI schedules of millet in an aviary also undermatched as a group (Gray, 1994). But some birds matched quite well, whereas others behaved almost randomly.

Clearly many factors will influence whether the simple predictions of the original IFD model are fulfilled. Like most in the first generation of foraging models, it sacrificed realism for simplicity and clarity, and later models have become both more realistic and more complex. As a contribution to ecology, the ideal free distribution is an attempt to predict how animals are distributed across the whole habitat, not just two neighboring patches. Bernstein, Kacelnik & Krebs (1991; see also Kacelnik, Krebs, & Bernstein, 1992) have attempted to model how individual predators' learning determines their distribution on a broad spatial scale when factors like the cost of traveling between patches, the rate of patch depletion, and the predators' learning rates are varied. They assumed that each forager learns according to the simple linear operator rule of section 9.2.1. A predator leaves a patch if it is experiencing a rate of food intake lower than its memory of the environmental average. If patches do not deplete and the cost of traveling between patches is not too high, predators with this learning rule will eventually reach an ideal free distribution. With a high cost of travel, animals will base their estimates of the environmental average on too small a sample of patches and thereby fail to achieve the IFD.

9.3.3 Conclusions

Research on the ideal free distribution is a good example of how a simple optimality model has been tested and refined. Some of these refinements have involved the model's assumptions about the nature of the environment (e.g., patches do not deplete, or are close enough together that travel costs can be neglected). Others have involved behavioral interactions among the foragers. For instance, within a stable group, certain individuals may prefer to associate with or to avoid each other (Moody & Houston, 1995). The model developed by Bernstein et al. (1991) shows how the variety of distribution patterns observed in the field can arise, at least in part, from predators' learning abilities. Predators seldom, if ever, have perfect information about the state of the environment, nor do they base their decisions only on their own feeding experiences. Species obviously differ in the kind and amount of information they are sensitive to, and attempts to understand the distributions of particular animals in particular environments need to take this into account (Kacelnik et al., 1992).

9.4 Leaving Depleting Patches

9.4.1 What Should Animals Do? The Marginal Value Theorem

In the last section, we added competing foragers to the simple environment of unchanging patches. In this section, we consider what happens when patches deplete—that is, each sucessive prey item takes longer to find than the one before. The forager's problem then is to decide when to leave the patch it is in and travel to the next one. The gain from a patch may decrease with time spent there even if the patch doesn't actually deplete. For example, starlings collect loads of leatherjackets (*Tipula* larvae) from fields to feed their young. To capture each leatherjacket the bird pokes its beak into the soil, opens it, and then closes it around the prey. The bird can line up several leatherjackets in its beak this way, but it takes longer and longer to collect each one the more it is holding already. Thus the rate of gain decreases the longer the starling stays in the field between trips back to the nest. Copulation can also function like foraging in a depleting patch: the longer a male dungfly remains coupled to a female, the more sperm he transfers. But there are diminishing returns in terms of the proportion of the female's eggs fertilized, so eventually the male should leave and search for another partner, even if this means his first mate will be taken over by another male (see Parker, 1978).

Intuitively, a forager should stay longer in one patch if the next patch is likely to be far away than if it is close by. For the starling collecting leatherjackets to feed its young, it makes sense to gather a large load when far from

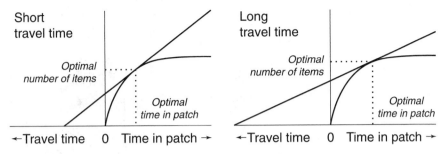

Figure 9.10. Graphical calculation of optimal patch residence time according to the marginal value theorem. Energy gain is in the vertical dimension. The slope of the diagonal line in each panel is the maximum net rate of energy intake in an environment with the given travel time and decreasing gain function (items vs. time in patch). The slope will necessarily be less if the animal stays a longer or shorter time.

the nest, but to start home with a small load when close to the nest. The solution to the problem of maximizing energy gain, shown in figure 9.10, is known as the *Marginal Value Theorem*, abbreviated MVT (Charnov, 1976). In general, to maximize its rate of energy intake, a forager should leave a patch when the rate of energy gain in that patch falls to the average rate in the habitat. Before this time, the forager is, by definition, doing better than it can do elsewhere. Afterwards, it could do better by leaving. In order to behave in this way, a forager has to keep track of its current rate of intake. If prey come in discrete similar-sized lumps, like leatherjackets in a field, this means accumulating information about times between prey captures. The forager must also know the average intake rate in the rest of the habitat. Among other things, this means storing information about travel times and intercapture intervals in other patches. Since the critical items of information are times, models of timing and averaging intervals are likely to be important in accounting for what animals do in the situation modeled in figure 9.10. However, in some cases simpler mechanisms can do the same job.

9.4.2 How Do They Do It? Rules for Leaving

One can imagine several simple rules that animals might use to determine when to leave a patch. They might spend a fixed time in each patch, stay until they have captured a fixed number of items, or stay until a fixed time has elapsed without any captures. This last rule, adopting a fixed *giving up time,* is consistent with leaving when the intake rate has fallen to a fixed value as the MVT says animals should, although in this case the estimate of rate is based on just the last item. According to the MVT, the giving up time should also depend on the overall quality of the environment; giving up time in a patch of a fixed type should be longer the poorer the overall environment. In one of the first experimental tests of the MVT, Krebs, Ryan & Charnov (1974) allowed black-capped chickadees to forage in an aviary furnished with artificial

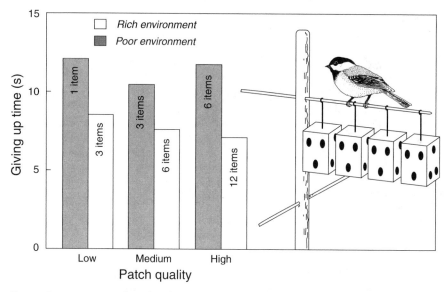

Figure 9.11. Setup and results of Krebs et al.'s (1974) test of the marginal value theorem. Numbers of items in the patches are indicated in the bars. After Krebs et al. (1974) with permission.

"trees" from which hung blocks of wood with holes that could contain pieces of mealworm. To search for these prey, the birds pulled off sticky tape covering the holes. Patches consisted of groups of four of these artificial pine cones hanging on one branch (figure 9.11). The birds were exposed to a poor environment, in which a group of "cones" could have 1, 3, or 6 larvae, and to a rich environment in which cone groups had 3, 6, or 12 larvae. The birds' responses to the patch types common to the two environments, those with 3 or 6 larvae, provided a test of the prediction that behavior to a patch of a given type depends on the quality of the environment in which it occurs.

This experiment had two major results. First, within each environment, the birds had a constant giving-up time—that is, whether a patch had a small, medium, or large number of prey for the particular environment, the chickadees tended to leave for a new patch the same length of time after finding an item (figure 9.11). Second, in accord with the MVT, this giving-up time was longer in the poorer environment—that is, the birds tended to stay longer in and to harvest more prey from, a 3-item or a 6-item patch when the other patch type had only 1 item than when it had 12 items. Thus, although using a giving-up time implies memory only for the time since capturing the most recent prey item, the birds also showed evidence of sensitivity to the current overall capture rate.

Nemeritis canescens is a parasitoid wasp that lays eggs in the larvae of flour moths. The female wasp searching for hosts in a granary walks about on the substrate. When she encounters a patch of chemicals secreted by the host, she stays in it by turning back whenever she comes to the edge of the patch. Lay-

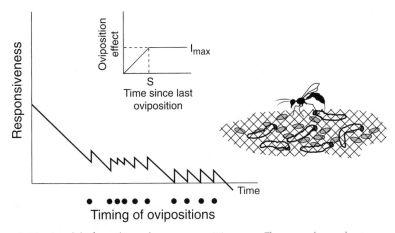

Figure 9.12. Model of patch residence time in *Nemeritis*. The inset shows the increase in responsiveness as a function of time since the last oviposition. When responsiveness to the current patch falls to zero, the wasp leaves. Redrawn from Waage (1979) with permission.

ing an egg also tends to increase her time in a patch. The wasp's behavior can be modeled by a very simple process in which responsiveness to the host chemical (reflected in the tendency to turn back into the patch upon reaching the edge) habituates with time in the patch but increases with each oviposition (Waage, 1979). A single oviposition has maximum effect; the effect of the next one depends how much later it occurs, as shown in figure 9.12. This simple mechanism keeps the wasp longer in a good patch because responsiveness keeps being pushed back up there but allows her to leave after long enough without encountering prey—that is, she has a giving-up time. The effect of overall environmental quality is not explicitly modeled here, but it could be reflected in the initial level of responsiveness. For example, initial responsiveness might be high if the wasp has encountered few hosts recently, resulting a longer stay in a given patch than after recent experience of more favorable conditions. In effect the wasp responds close to optimally to prey density without having any representation of prey number and interprey interval as such (further discussion in Dyer, 1994). A given level of responsiveness could equally well reflect initially high responsiveness lowered by a period in a poor patch or an initially low level that is being maintained by a high density of prey.

Figure 9.12 illustrates how a simple nonrepresentational process can generate an adaptive pattern of sensitivity to the environment. This particular mechanism, however, is adaptive only if prey occur in patches. The wasps studied by Waage do find their hosts in patches in granaries, but other populations of this species lay eggs in fallen figs and other mummified fruit. Here hosts tend to occur singly. Thus, rather than increasing responsiveness to the patch, oviposition should decrease it (Driessen, Bernstein, Van Alphen, & Kacelnik, 1995). This is, in fact, what happens when these wasps are studied in small patches with low host densities. This result raises the interesting question of whether and how the wasps change their way of responding to oviposition depending on the kind of prey distributions they encounter.

9.4.3 How Do They Do It? Remembering and Averaging Times

The MVT implies that animals need accurate representations of the time in the patch and the travel time between patches in order to behave optimally. Unlike theorists, however, animals do not measure time intervals with perfect accuracy. As we have seen, memory for times follows Weber's law so that longer intervals are remembered with greater variance. Moreover, we saw in the last section that the psychological average of a mixture of intervals is not the same as the arithmetic average, which means that expected values of environmental parameters may depend on how their experienced values are distributed. These features of timing act as psychological constraints on animals' ability to behave precisely optimally.

The most detailed investigations of the role of timing in patch departure decisions have been carried out by Kacelnik and his colleagues, primarily with starlings. In their earliest studies (Kacelnik & Cuthill, 1987), wild starlings feeding nestlings were trained to visit a small tent in which an experimenter sat dispensing mealworms down a pipe to the birds outside. Depletion of this patch was mimicked by increasing the time between successive prey deliveries. Travel time to the patch was varied by placing the tent at different distances from the bird's nest. The birds behaved roughly in accord with the MVT, collecting more worms per visit when the patch was farther from the nest (figure 9.13).

Breeding starlings are ideal subjects for foraging experiments because they spend nearly the whole day gathering food for their young, but they do so for only a few weeks each year. To collect more data, and under better controlled conditions, Kacelnik and his coworkers devised a test of patch choice in the laboratory in which the "patch" is a pecking key in the middle of one wall of a long cage, and the birds "travel" from one patch to another by flying between two perches a number of times (figure 9.14). Completing the travel requirement resets the patch to the shortest interprey interval, as if the bird has arrived in a new patch. If the "patch" delivers a varying number of prey (crumbs from a feeder) at equal intervals and then depletes entirely, the bird should depart as soon as the current interval exceeds the remembered standard interprey interval. However, since timing obeys Weber's law, a more realistic prediction is that there will be some variance in the time of leaving the patch, and this variance will be proportional to the interprey interval. This prediction was borne out when starlings were tested in this situation (Brunner, Kacelnik, & Gibbon, 1992, 1996). Pecking rate in the patch peaked at the value of the interprey interval, and the distribution of response rate vs. time broadened in proportion to the length of the interval, showing that the birds were timing the interprey interval using the same mechanism revealed in experiments with the peak procedure (see chapter 8). They were also timing the

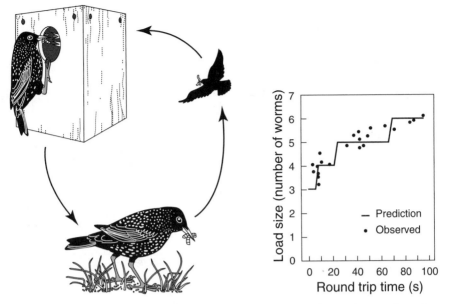

Figure 9.13. Predicted and observed numbers of mealworms that starlings collected as a function of the time required for a round trip between nest and patch. Predictions are derived from the marginal value theorem. Redrawn from Krebs and Davies (1993) and Kacelnik (1984) with permission.

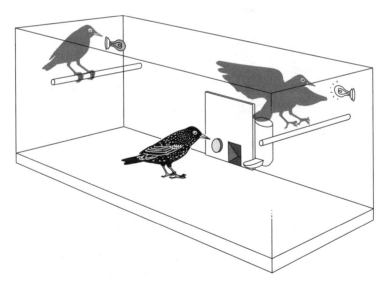

Figure 9.14. Setup used to study patch choice in captive starlings. To travel between patches, the starling hops from the perch with the light off to the one with the light on; the light at that perch then goes out and the opposite light goes on, and so on until the travel requirement is completed. Water is available from the device beside the feeder and pecking key. Redrawn from Brunner et al. (1992) with permission.

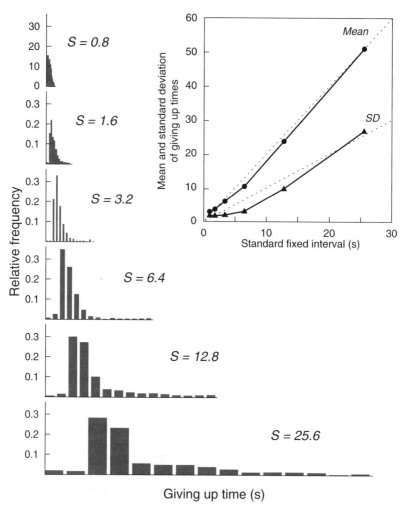

Figure 9.15. Relative frequency of giving up times of different lengths at six standard interprey intervals (S). The inset shows the means and standard deviations of the distributions. Dotted lines are regressions fit to the data. Redrawn from Gibbon and Church (1990) with permission.

decision to leave the patch after not receiving items for awhile. The last peck before traveling was a constant proportion of the interprey interval. Thus the birds waited longer after the expected time for an item before leaving a patch with a long interprey interval, as if their decision took into account the greater error in their ability to detect depletion of a less dense patch (figure 9.15).

The situation in the Brunner et al. (1992) experiment is not the same as the one addressed by the marginal value theorem because the experimental patch offered prey at fixed intervals throughout and because it depleted abruptly rather than gradually. Both of these features simplified the task of demonstrating that the birds were using timing to decide when to leave the patch. Moreover, although a patch that offers prey at fixed intervals until it depletes entirely may seem unrealistic, such a situation is experienced by animals that prey on swarms of insects. For example, spotted flycatchers (*Muscicapa striata*) hunt from fixed perches by flying out and catching insects in midair. A bird stays at a perch while a swarm is within range, capturing prey at roughly constant intervals. These birds tend to leave for another perch after a time without prey that is approximately 1.5 times the regular interprey interval (Davies, 1977; see also Kacelnik, Brunner, & Gibbon, 1990).

Do models of timing illuminate the way in which animals respond to variations in travel times between patches in tests of the MVT? Once again, psychological data on timing indicate that animals cannot behave precisely in accord with the prescriptions of the MVT. Consider the fact that the optimal moment to leave a patch depends in part on the average travel time in the environment. If animals remember distributions of travel times in the way described by scalar expectancy theory, the psychological average will depend on the experienced distribution of travel times and not just their arithmetic mean. In particular, a mixture of two travel times, one long and one short, will be treated as shorter than a single travel time equal to their mean. In accord with this prediction, both pigeons (Kacelnik & Todd, 1992; Todd & Kacelnik, 1993) and starlings (Rodriguez-Girones, 1995) stay longer and take more prey from a depleting operant patch in the context of a single travel time than in the context of two travel times with the same mean.

So far it may appear that the integration of foraging theory and psychological data is all one way, in that facts about timing are incorporated into foraging models as psychological constraints. However, optimality analysis of patch departure decisions also raises some new psychological questions. Most notably, how long a memory window do animals use to form their representation of the environmental average (Cowie, 1977)? For example, when travel times vary unpredictably but come from an unchanging distribution, the animal should take into account the average travel time. But how is it possible to do this and still respond to long-term changes in the average travel time? Evidently there must be a memory window that optimizes the tradeoff between averaging short-term variability and adjusting to long-term change. In the laboratory, at least, starlings and pigeons seem to solve this problem by responding to both the most recent travel and the long-term average. Starlings in a laboratory simulation with one depleting patch type and travel requirements of either five or 60 flights stayed longer in the patch after a long than after a short travel time (Cuthill, Kacelnik, Krebs, Haccou, & Iwasa, 1990). In this experiment, no evidence could be found for an effect of travel times before the most recent. For example, the birds stayed no longer after two short travels in a row than after a short travel preceded by a long one, suggesting that their memory window encompassed only one travel time. Contrary to the implications of this finding, however, when the travel time changed abruptly from long to short or the reverse, the birds took about six patch visits to complete their adjustment to the new travel time (Cuthill, Haccou, & Kacelnik, 1994).

The most elegant way to assess the relative contributions of very recent and longer term experience is to look at behavior after a travel requirement of constant length when that requirement occurs in different mixtures of other travels. In such experiments, pigeons and starlings are sensitive to both the most recent travel and the overall average (Kacelnik & Todd, 1992; Rodriguez-Girones, 1995). Scalar expectancy theory (SET) suggests that both the mixture's average and the intervals that make it up are important. Recall, however, that SET depicts animals as storing memories of all relevant intervals; the memory window over which this distribution of memories is accumulated is left an open question. The effects of the most recent travel time suggest, however, that very recent experience is weighted more heavily in this distribution. Todd and Kacelnik (1993) have used a linear operator model like that referred to earlier in the chapter to model the way in which the memory distribution might become more or less biased in the direction of the interval experienced most recently.

9.4.4 How Do They Do It? More Complex Decision Rules

So far our discussion of how animals decide when to leave one patch for another has focused on decisions based on time. But changes in the quality of a patch may be revealed by cues other than the time between successive prey captures. The animal may simply see, hear, or smell fewer prey. A lone forager can deplete a uniform patch by searching it systematically and then leaving. For instance, bumblebees tend to move from bottom to top of an inflorescence (Pyke, 1979). Here a simple spatial cue suffices to tell the animal when to leave. In other cases, more than one cue may be available and the by now familiar question arises of how disparate sources of information are combined. In one example, Kamil, Yeorg & Clements (1988) exposed bluejays to an operant schedule simulating one fixed, relatively poor patch and one suddenly depleting patch that started better than the poor patch. The birds could maximize their food intake by starting in the better patch and leaving as soon as they had collected the last item it offered. Unlike the case where depletion is detectable only as a long run of bad luck, here the birds could in principle have left immediately after collecting the last available item because the depleting patch always had the same number of items with variable interprey intervals. However, as in experiments described in chapter 8 (e.g., Roberts & Mitchell, 1994), the birds both timed and counted. They left the depleting patch after several trials without a prey item, but only if such a run of bad luck occurred after several items had already been found in the patch. This response to number of prey varied with the number of prey available: for instance, when the birds had learned to expect six or nine items, a run of bad luck after three items rarely caused them to depart, whereas in a patch with three items it did. Foraging behavior might be a good place to look for further examples of combining diverse sources of information in nonadditive ways (Fetterman, 1996).

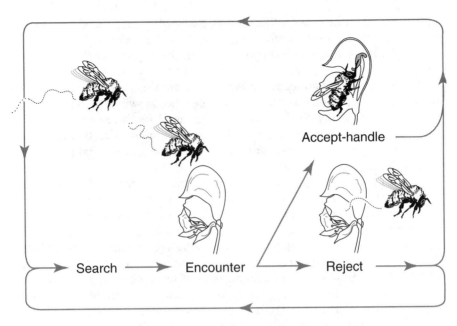

Figure 9.16. The cycle of events in prey choice.

9.5 Choosing Prey

9.5.1 How Should Animals Select Prey?

Unlike this chapter, many discussions of optimal foraging present prey choice before patch choice, as if prey choice is somehow more elementary. However, on the whole the cognitive mechanisms involved in prey choice either have been considered already in this book—for example, search image (chapter 2), or identification of suitable prey through conditioning and discrimination learning (e.g., box 5.1)—or they are the same as those evident in patch choice. Functionally, the principle of lost opportunity governs optimality models of both prey choice and patch choice (Stephens & Krebs, 1986): accept the current prey item unless by devoting time to it you lose the opportunity to find something better; leave this patch if by staying you lose the opportunity for a higher intake rate.

Choice of prey within a patch involves the cycle of events depicted in figure 9.16. In the simplest nontrivial case, prey items are encountered successively, and they are of two types. When the predator encounters an item, it can either accept that item or reject it and go on searching. Accepting an item entails devoting a *handling time* to it, time which cannot be devoted to searching. Pulling the stinger off a bee, shelling a nut, extracting nectar from a flower, tearing apart a carcass—all require handling time. The predator is assumed to recognize prey types immediately and to rank them in terms of the energy they yield per unit of handling time (E/H). Maximizing energy per unit of time foraging requires accepting all prey items when prey density is low but accepting only the better items (i.e., those with the higher E/H) when prey density is high. If there are just two item types, the predator's behavior toward the poorer items should reflect the density of better items: reject poor items when good items are abundant, otherwise accept them. There is a threshold of good item abundance at which the forager should switch from rejecting to accepting poor items. Such a policy makes good intuitive sense: when the world is a good place as regards food, mates, and homes, a creature can afford to be choosy, but when times are tough, it may be better to take what ever comes along.

The simple optimal prey selection model has received qualitative but not always precise quantitative support from a variety of kinds of data, including redshanks selecting worms in mudflats (Goss-Custard, 1977), great tits picking mealworms off a conveyor belt in the laboratory (Krebs, Erichsen, Webber, & Charnov, 1977), and pigeons pecking colors paired with different delays to reinforcement on a pecking key (Fantino & Abarca, 1985; Shettleworth, 1988). An almost universal deviation from optimality is that animals switch gradually rather than abruptly from accepting relatively poor items to rejecting them as the abundance of better items increases and that they almost never show perfectly optimal choice. Given all the evidence we have seen that perception and memory generally have some degree of error, these findings should not be surprising. Choice of suboptimal items has sometimes been attributed to deliberate sampling, but this suggestion is meaningful only if sampling can be distinguished from simply making mistakes. Signal detection theory (see chapter 2) specifies a precise quantitative relationship between correct choices and different kinds of errors. Animals could be said to sample when there are more acceptances of poor items (false alarms) than predicted by signal detection theory but not otherwise (Rechten, Avery, & Stevens, 1983).

9.5.2 Mechanisms for Prey Selection

Just as in patch departure, animals may use simple rules of thumb to select prey. Shrews take the largest items available (Barnard & Brown, 1981). Pigeons prefer many small pieces of food to one big one, even when the longer time taken to eat all the small ones reduces the rate of food intake (Shettleworth, 1985). In contrast, some animals learn about their own competence at handling particular item types. For example, Sullivan (1988; see Shettleworth, Reid, & Plowright, 1993, for further examples) offered mealworms of different sizes to free-ranging yellow-eyed juncos (*Junco phaeonotus*). Inexperienced juveniles took so long to handle and ingest large mealworms that smaller mealworms were almost twice as profitable for them as large ones. In contrast, small and large mealworms were about equally profitable for experienced juveniles and adults (see figure 3.4). The birds' prey choices reflected the developmental difference in handling competence, implying that individuals track their own handling times as they gain experience. In laboratory

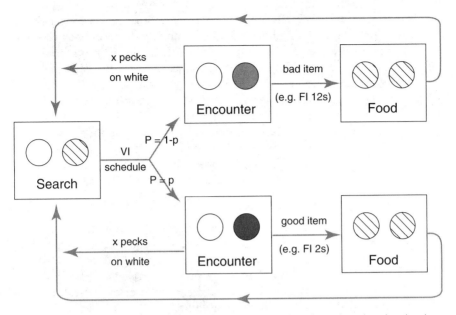

Figure 9.17. Operant schedule simulating prey choice. Pecking the white key leads to "encounters" with "items" in which the second key lights with one of two colors, each associated with a different delay to food ("handling time"). The bird can "accept" the item by pecking the second key or reject it by continuing to peck the white key. Redrawn from Shettleworth and Plowright (1992) with permission.

simulations of prey choice like those to be discussed shortly, handling time is nothing more than a delay to food associated with a particular signal, and animals clearly learn this.

Just as there is a range of mechanisms for assessing prey quality, there is a similar variety of mechanisms for assessing prey abundance. Prey catching is a reflex in the mantid *Hierodula crassa* (Charnov, 1976), but the animal's tendency to strike at flies is modulated by the fullness of its gut. With a full gut, only flies close by are attacked, but as the gut empties distant prey become more attractive. In a similar way, the shore crab's threshold for accepting relatively small mussels seems to fall with time since last encountering a large mussel (Elner & Hughes, 1978; see Shettleworth, 1984, figure 7.3). The apple maggot fly's acceptance of fruit in which to lay her eggs can also be modeled as reflecting a threshold that changes with recent ovipositions and host encounters (Mangel & Roitberg, 1989). As in the wasp's oviposition decision (see figure 9.12), this process results in adequately close to optimal behavior under normal conditions without any representation of prey density or profitability as such.

Accounts of behavior in operant analogues of prey choice like that diagrammed in figure 9.17 assume that animals acquire representations of the delays to food associated with the onset of the various item signals and the intervals between items. Animals trained on such schedules do accept nearly all the better "items" offered, and the effects of changing the frequency or profitability of items are seen in the choice of poor items. At the moment of encounter with a relatively poor item, the animal is choosing between the handling time (or delay to food) associated with that item and a second, variable delay to food composed of the average time befor encountering another item plus the expected time to handle that item. If the next item is equally likely to be a poor or a good item, for instance, the expected handling time is the mean of that for the two item types. Choosing the option that has been associated with the shorter delay to food is optimal here; it is also consistent with the scalar expectancy model of choice and an earlier, related account of behavior on reinforcement schedules known as the *delay reduction hypothesis* (Fantino & Abarca, 1985).

Just as when leaving patches, animals selecting prey may track changes over a short memory window. For instance, pigeons in an operant prey choice experiment encountering items at variable intervals accepted fewer relatively poor items the shorter the time since the most recent encounter (Shettleworth & Plowright, 1992). However, the tendency to track short-term variation was modulated by environmental variability. Birds that had experienced random interprey intervals were less influenced by the most recent experience than those exposed to predictable runs of interprey intervals. This result is consistent with the idea that the memory window may vary with the stability of the environment (Cowie, 1977).

One feature of optimal prey selection not anticipated by any model of behavior on conventional reinforcement schedules is that as the time available for foraging, the *time horizon*, grows short, animals should become less choosy, accepting more poor items even when better items are abundant (Lucas, 1983). It is easy to see why. If the time available for foraging is about to run out, there may not be enough time to encounter any more items, so more energy will be gained by taking the item at hand than by continuing to search. Several observations with natural prey items conform to this prediction. For instance, in 3-minute and 6-minute foraging bouts, shrews accepted both large and small mealworm pieces, whereas they rejected small pieces in 9-minute bouts (Barnard & Hurst, 1987).

In experiments with operant schedules, session lengths have traditionally been determined largely by factors of convenience, such as how many trials can be run before subjects show signs of satiation. Therefore, it has been of some interest to discover whether time horizon also has the predicted effects on choice on operant schedules. Plowright and Shettleworth (1991) studied pigeons on the operant prey selection schedule depicted in figure 9.17. Each bird had 10-minute sessions in one distinctively decorated operant chamber and 20-minute sessions in another. The birds accepted fewer poor items in the first 10 minutes of 20 minute sessions (i.e., when the time horizon was relatively long) than in the 10-minute sessions. A particularly elegant feature of this experiment was that it included a separate test of whether the birds had, in fact, learned to expect different session lengths in the two environments. At the end of each session, the key that the birds had to peck to "search" for items remained on for a few minutes but no more items were delivered. The birds' rate of pecking this search key revealed the extent to which they expected more items to appear. When this treatment was administered after 10 minutes in the chamber that usually had 20-minute sessions (i.e., sessions ended early), the birds pecked much more than they did after a 10-minute session in the 10-minute chamber.

9.6 Assessing Risk

9.6.1 When Variance Matters

The currency maximized in the classic optimal foraging models is net rate of energy intake—that is, total energy gained divided by total foraging time. Variance in travel times, item quality, or the like is not important in these models. But consider a small bird in winter nearing the end of the day and confronted with the choice between a predictable option that offers a known and steady rate of energy gain and a risky option. Sometimes the risky option is very good and sometimes it offers nothing, but in the long term it yields the same E/T. Does it matter which the bird chooses?

Our small bird in winter is exactly the sort of animal that should be sensitive to risk. As each long cold night draws near, it must have stored enough fat to stay alive till the next morning. Suppose it has had a bad day and its reserves are so low that it cannot survive on the certain option. If the risky option occasionally yields enough to get it through the night, the forager's only chance of surviving is by choosing it, even though over the long run both options yield the same energy. Formalizing this kind of argument leads to the *energy budget rule*: an animal below its energy budget should choose a risky option over a certain option with the same mean—that is, it should be *risk prone*. Otherwise, the certain option is the better choice—that is, the forager should be *risk averse* (McNamara & Houston, 1992; Stephens, 1981). The end of day is not the only time when variance matters. Risk sensitivity can also be expected in the context of other kinds of interruptions, like the end of the breeding season, the beginning of migration, or the arrival of predators (McNamara & Houston, 1992). Risk-sensitive foraging theory makes two important predictions of interest for a mechanistic theory of how animals evaluate foraging options and choose among them. First, variance should matter, not just the average value of an option. Second, in some circumstances changing the animal's energy budget should cause preference to shift between a fixed and a risky option.

Risk sensitivity has been sought in species that include bees, shrews, pigeons, starlings, and juncos (Bateson & Kacelnik, 1998; Kacelnik & Bateson, 1996). The procedure that has become standard in these sorts of experiments was introduced by Caraco, Martindale, and Whittam (1980). Generally there are two feeding locations or reinforced responses. The certain option offers delay or amount x every time it is chosen and the risky option offers $x - y$ half the time and $x + y$ the other half of the time, unpredictably. The animal first experiences a series of "forced" trials with each option, thereby presumably learning their characteristics. For example, the forager has opportunity to learn that there are always four items of food on the left and a 50:50 mix of 1 item and 7 items on the right. Then the animal is allowed to choose between the options, revealing whether it is risk prone (i.e., prefers the variable option), risk averse, or indifferent to risk. In such experiments animals generally prefer variable over fixed delays to food (i.e., they are risk prone in delay) but with variance in amount they are generally risk averse or indifferent to risk (reviews in Bateson & Kacelnik, 1998; Kacelnik & Bateson, 1996).

9.6.2 Explanations of Risk Sensitivity

Demonstrations of risk sensitivity rule out any mechanism of patch choice that computes feeding rates like classical foraging theory does, as long-term total energy gain divided by total time spent foraging. A risk-sensitive animal must store some details of the flow of items in time. Scalar expectancy theory (SET) describes one way of doing so. As we have seen, SET accounts for preferring variable delays to food over fixed delays with the same mean—that is, risk proneness in delay. SET depicts animals as constrained in their representation of rate. Although memories of all delays to food are stored, only one memory is sampled per choice. An alternative account proposes that rate of intake (energy/time) is computed for each item separately and this is averaged over items. This is referred to as the expectation of the ratios of E/T (EoR), in contrast to the standard approach of taking the ratio of the expectations of E and T (RoE). In effect, the EoR model suggests that animals perceive short-term rates directly. If there is no variance in times between items, these two ways of computing average rate are equivalent, but when there is variance, EoR is always greater (table 9.1). EoR and RoE represent two extremes in terms of the time frame over which the forager computes average rate (Bateson & Kacelnik, 1998; Real, 1991), but averaging short-term rates seems computationally simpler than computing $\Sigma E/\Sigma T$, and this may be the best animals can do.

The contrast among the three possible rate-computing mechanisms (EoR, RoE, and SET) was clearly drawn in a series of experiments with starlings (Bateson & Kacelnik, 1995, 1996, 1997). Bateson and Kacelnik's (1995) birds were trained in an operant key-pecking procedure. After a 40-second intertrial interval, a flashing light indicated the start of a trial. As soon as the starling pecked, this was replaced by a steady light signaling the programmed delay to food. The constant alternative was a 20-second delay to 5 units of food. In the variable amount condition, the risky alternative varied between 3 and 7 units of food with a 20-second delay; in the variable-delay condition, the risky option was 5 units of food with a 2.5- or 60.5-second delay. These values were chosen to make EoR equal on the two alternatives when the intertrial intervals were included in the computations of foraging time. The starlings preferred the variable delay and weakly avoided the variable amount (see

Table 9.1. Comparison of Ratio of Expectations (RoE) and Expectation of Ratios (EoR): An example

Suppose two prey items totalling 10 grams are found in 20 minutes. Net rate of energy intake in g/min is computed in the two ways for each of two cases: either a 5-g item is found at the end of each 10-min time unit or one is found after 5 min and the second after the next 15 min.

Amounts	Delays	Average gain: RoE	Average gain: EoR
Fixed: 5, 5	Fixed: 10, 10	(5+5) / (10+10) = .5g/min	((5/10) + (5/10))/2 = .5g/min
Fixed: 5, 5	Variable: 5,15	(5+5) / (5 + 15) = .5g/min	((5/5) + (5/15))/2 = .67g/min

also Reboreda & Kacelnik, 1991). This result is consistent with maximizing EoR if only the times during the trials are taken into account. The birds' patterns of pecking the keys, as well as their overall preferences, were also consistent with SET, in that the birds clearly knew all the individual intervals: in the "forced" trials, pecking rate rose smoothly to a peak on the color signaling the fixed 20-second delay, but in 60.5 second trials on the color signaling the unpredictable 2.5- or 60.5-second delay, pecking peaked first 2.5 seconds after the trial began, then fell, and rose again as 60.5 seconds approached.

Detailed evaluation of the different theories depends on knowing what fixed option a risky option is psychologically equivalent to. To find out, Bateson and Kacelnik (1996) turned to a *titration procedure*. Once again, starlings were exposed to a fixed option, a variable option, and choices between them, but this time the fixed option changed from one block of trials to the next. If the bird preferred the risky option in a block of free choices, then the fixed option would improve in the next block of forced trials—that is, the delay would get shorter or the amount would get bigger. If the bird preferred the fixed option in the next block of free choices, then it would be made a little worse, and so on. And if the bird chose the two alternatives about equally in a block of free choices, nothing would change in the next forced trials. The outcome of such a titration procedure is that the adjustable option (here the "fixed" option) oscillates around a stable value that can be taken as the psychological equivalent of the alternative to which the animal is comparing it, in this case the mixture of a large and a small amount or delay. The birds chose an adjusting delay or amount that equated EoR between the adjusting and the risky options, with rates computed over just the delay between choices and food—that is, without the intertrial intervals (figure 9.18).

For natural distributions of food items in the field, the difference between long-term and short-term rates can be substantial, as Bateson and Whitehead (1996) determined by recording the temporal distributions of items found by starlings foraging on natural pasture. If the birds had been allowed to choose between some of the patches they were exposed to, EoR would have led them to choose the lower overall average intake rate 25% of the time. It is a puzzle why animals might be selected to maximize average short-term rate of intake (EoR) rather than the long-term average (RoE). One possibility is that maximizing short-term rate is, in fact, optimal with respect to some currency that is not yet understood. Another is that animals are prevented by limited memory capabilities from averaging over more than a short memory window (Bateson & Kacelnik, 1998).

9.6.3 Variance or Uncertainty?

In the standard account of risk sensitivity sketched at the beginning of this section, the risky option is unpredictable, not just relatively high in variance. However, the experiments we have just reviewed do not test whether or not the unpredictability of the risky option influences animals' choices. And the EoR/SET account of risk sensitivity that seems to be supported by the data so

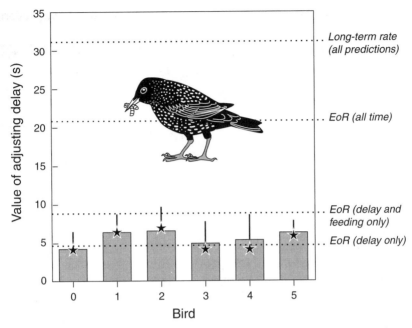

Figure 9.18. Mean and standard deviation of adjusting delays chosen by each of six star-lings as equivalent to a mixture of 60.5- and 2.5-second delays, compared to various ways of computing the average rate of food intake from the variable mixture. Stars are medians. EoR is computed including all time in the experiment, just delay to feeding plus the time taken to feed after choosing an alternative, and just the delays between choice and food. Redrawn from Bateson and Kacelnik (1996) with permission.

far does not assign any role to the unpredictability of the risky option. Bate-son and Kacelnik (1997) tested whether unpredictability was important by offering starlings two options with equal variance but different degrees of pre-dictability. As in standard tests of risk sensitivity, the birds had "forced" ex-posure to each of the options by itself followed by opportunity to choose be-tween them. Either option gave the starling a string of six rewards separated by 3-second or 18-second interreward intervals, and over the long run both gave an equal number of intervals of each length. On the predictable option the sequence of interreward intervals was always 3, 18, 3, 18, 3, 18, but on the unpredictable option it was random (figure 9.19). In accord with SET and EoR, the starlings preferred either one of these options to an option with a fixed interreward interval equal to their arithmetic mean of 10.5 seconds. In a titration procedure, the value of the equivalent fixed interreward interval was closest to that predicted by EoR. Most interesting, as long as the pre-dictable string always began with a 3-second delay, the birds preferred it to the unpredictable string of rewards.

The best account of the birds' choices was that they perceived each option as a collection of rewards, each delayed a certain time from the choice point. For instance, the predictable sequence was treated as one reward after 3 sec-

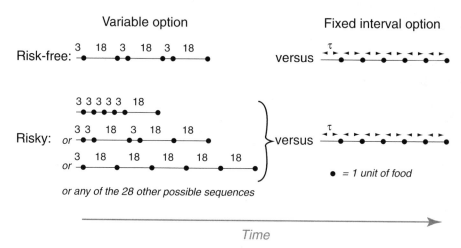

Figure 9.19. Test of the importance of variability vs. unpredictability in delays to reward in a "risky" option. τ = the value of the delays to food in the fixed interval option, which was adjusted so it was chosen as often as the variable option by the birds. Redrawn from Bateson and Kacelnik (1997) with permission.

onds plus another after 3+18 seconds, a third after 3+18+3 seconds, and so on. The unpredictable sequence was valued less than this one because about half the time its first reward was delayed for 18 seconds. Research on the value of rewards as a function of delay indicates that the psychological value of a delayed reward decreases proportionately with delay—that is, expected future rewards are discounted in value compared to immediate rewards. Food delayed by t seconds is only $1/t$ as valuable as if it occurred immediately. The starlings' choices suggest that they were discounting all six rewards in the string in parallel, in terms of each one's delay from the moment of choice. Brunner and Gibbon (1995) found analogous results with rats. These results, therefore, give no more reason than any of the others reviewed so far to conclude that animals confronted with risky options do anything other than behave as prescribed by general models of reinforcement (see also Montague, Dayan, Person, & Sejnowski, 1995, for bees). But considering questions about rate-assessing mechanisms within the functional framework of risk sensitive foraging theory has led to deeper understanding of these mechanisms.

9.6.4 The Energy Budget Rule

The energy budget rule means that deprivation and/or time horizon or body weight should influence whether a risky or a certain outcome is chosen. Mechanistically this must mean that the way in which the animal either values outcomes or compares them changes with energy budget. This is an interesting prediction because it is not clear how it could be made consistent with any exisiting mechanistic account of choice. In fact, however, the energy budget rule has not fared particularly well in experimental tests (review in

Kacelnik & Bateson, 1996). Regardless of energy budget, animals have always preferred variable delays to food over a fixed delay equal to their mean. This is just what would be expected if preference for variance in time is attributable to fundamental mechanisms of measuring, remembering, averaging, and/or comparing time intervals. Manipulations designed to influence energy budget have influenced animals' preferences in some experiments with fixed and variable amounts of food (e.g., Hamm & Shettleworth, 1987; see Houston & Mc-Namara, 1990). However, it turns out to be difficult to change correlates of energy budget such as the rate of food intake during an experiment without changing experimental parameters that might by themselves influence choice. For example, in the original test of the energy budget rule (Caraco, Martindale, & Whittam, 1980), birds on a negative energy budget were tested later in the day and with longer intertrial intervals than birds supposedly on a positive energy budget, and, in order to equalize overall rates of intake, larger amounts of food were followed with longer delays until the next trial, thereby confounding variability in amount with variability in delay.

One experiment has convincingly overcome such problems by testing birds at two temperatures (Caraco et al., 1990). Yellow-eyed juncos first lived at 1, 10, or 19° C to determine what rate of food intake they required to maintain their body weights at each one. Because small birds like juncos have a very high metabolic rate and relatively small fat stores, ambient temperature has a substantial effect on intake rate. In this case, the juncos ate about twice as much/day at the coldest as at the warmest temperature. Then birds were tested in the standard risk sensitivity paradigm at 1 and 19° C, but with reward sizes and intertrial intervals that gave the rate of food intake they needed at 10° C. Thus they got less than they needed (i.e., a negative energy budget) in the tests at 1°, but more than they needed (positive energy budget) at 19° C. Behavior switched accordingly: the birds tended to be risk averse at the higher temperature and risk prone at the lower. The birds' perception of the value of different amounts of food may change with temperature. What is needed now is some psychophysical comparisons of the psychological value of food to juncos at different temperatures. Whatever mechanism is found, theorists will have to come to grips with the fact that the effects of manipulating energy budget seem to depend on the size of the species being tested, with smaller species more affected (Kacelnik & Bateson, 1996). For instance, in Bateson and Kacelnik's (1997) test of predictability, starlings—bigger birds than juncos—were unaffected by changes in the overall rate at which they obtained food within experimental sessions. Such findings make functional sense in that a small animal is less likely to have the reserves to survive a temporary shortfall than is a large one, but they raise the interesting possibility of concomitant species differences in the mechanisms for evaluating rewards.

9.6.5 Concluding Remarks

Optimal foraging theory depicts animals as selected to behave as if they are looking ahead, evaluating options in terms of the principle of lost opportunity.

But general principles of reinforcement seem to account for how animals actually do behave in the situations of interest to foraging theorists. One way to look at what's going on in the standard sort of risk-sensitivity experiments, and indeed any similar choice experiments, is that associative strength develops to each of the options in the forced trials and the free trials reveal the relative values of those associative strengths. Looked at the other way around, tests of OFT have given some reason to see why the principles of reinforcement are as they are (Lea, 1981). If they had not been discovered already, they would have needed to be developed to account for how animals forage.

9.7 Summary

This chapter focuses on models and experiments dealing with foraging for food to illustrate the ways in which detailed optimality models can interact with models of learning and choice. The same sorts of issues arise in analyzing how animals search for other resources like mates or nest sites (see box 9.1). We considered a series of foraging problems starting with what an individual should do in a simple environment of unchanging patches, then what to do if those patches change, where to forage when in a group, what items to forage on, and how to respond to uncertainty. Each of these problems imposes distinctive cognitive demands, but there are many common themes:

1. Evolution sometimes produces simple ways of doing complex things. Animals may solve foraging problems using rules of thumb that do not parallel the theorist's computations and that do not entail explicit representations of the variables being optimized.
2. Because the environment varies from time to time and place to place, the best thing to do may depend not just on current options but also on those available elsewhere. Optimal decision making may therefore require information about the environment as a whole. Acquiring this information may involve sampling different options and remembering their characteristics.
3. Knowledge must continually be updated to track changes in the environment. A recurring question is, what is the best way to sample the environment and to combine old and new information?
4. The time available for foraging, the time horizon, is nearly always limited: night falls, predators arrive, the breeding season comes to an end. The best thing to do may change as time runs out.
5. Information about time intervals is of paramount importance in foraging. Some animals in some situations use simple mechanisms of threshold change to track rates of occurrence of important resources, but others represent and remember time intervals in ways described in chapter 8.

Classic optimality models were formulated from the point of view of an omniscient observer with unlimited computational capabilities. But real animals have a more limited view of the environment. They may not have experienced all relevant parts of the environment, and even if they have, they may not represent or retain information with perfect accuracy. Furthermore, the processes by which animals, including humans (box 9.4), act on experience

Box 9.4. Probabilistic Decision Making by Humans

With nonhuman subjects, "irrational," distinctly suboptimal behavior in the laboratory is generally taken as evidence for a mechanism that is adaptive in natural circumstances. Studies of how people reason about probabilistic information also provide many well-documented examples of irrationality (Kahneman, Slovic, & Tversky, 1982; Tversky & Kahneman, 1974), and recently some evolutionary psychologists have suggested that these "errors" in reasoning also have functional explanations.

One example of biased probabilistic reasoning is *base rate neglect*. People tend to make decisions based on information about a specific case in hand and do not take enough account of information about the overall probabilities of the events involved (review in Koehler, 1996). Consider the following problem (Tversky & Kahneman, 1982): "In a certain city, 85% of the taxis are green; the rest are blue. A witness to a hit-and-run accident says that the vehicle involved was a blue taxi. This witness correctly identifies the color of a taxi 80% of the time. What is the probability that the taxi actually was blue?" Most people give an answer closer to 80% than a statistician would, neglecting the information about the low overall probability of blue taxis. (The answer is 41% if Bayesian statistical reasoning is applied; see table B9.4.) Performance on such problems improves considerably when the same information is presented as frequencies (Gigerenzer & Hoffrage, 1995). But why should it matter if, instead of stating probabilities, the experimenter says something like, "There are 100 taxis in the city; 85 are green and 15 are blue"? The evolutionary psychologists' answer is that humans evolved to acquire information about probabilities by experiencing frequencies of events. Probability is not observed directly; the human mind has evolved to make inferences from experienced frequencies. Probabilistic information is represented as "I have hunted here ten times and seen impala only once," not "the probability of impala in this place is 0.1" (Cosmides & Tooby, 1996). This approach to decision making is controversial and may tend to oversimplify a large body of work (Kacelnik, 1997; Koehler, 1996), but it does represent a potentially fruitful attempt to provide a functional explanation for behavior that otherwise appears merely puzzling.

Table B9.4. Computation of conditional and unconditional probabilities in the taxicab problem

		Witness's Report*		
		green	blue	totals
	green	68	17	85
Correct Color	blue	3	12	15
	totals	71	29	100

* The witness would report 12 (80%) of the 15 blue taxis as blue and the rest as green, but she would also report 20% (17) of the green taxis as blue. Thus, given a report of a blue taxi, the chances that it really was blue are 12/29 or 41%.

do not always give the same output as the computational processes a theorist would use. In research on foraging behavior, detailed predictions about behavior derived from evolutionary first principles have confronted equally detailed and quantitative models of information processing and choice. Both have been refined and enriched as a result.

Further Reading

A useful introduction to optimal foraging theory is chapter 4 of Krebs and Davies's *An Introduction to Behavioural Ecology* (1993). Milinski and Parker (1991) discuss the ideal free distribution. The little book by Stephens and Krebs (1986) is an authoritative presentation of theory and a review of the data up to 1986. Foraging behavior has been the subject of three interdisciplinary conferences, which have resulted in the books edited by Kamil and Sargent (1981); Kamil, Krebs, and Pulliam (1987); and Commons, Kacelnik, and Shettleworth (1987). The chapter by Bateson and Kacelnik (1998) discusses risk-sensitive foraging theory with particular attention to psychological issues; Kacelnik and Bateson (1996) comprehensively review the data on risk-sensitive foraging. Williams (1988) thoroughly reviews behavior on operant schedules; his more recent chapter (Williams, 1994) is a shorter overview. Operant studies of issues in foraging theory are reviewed in the chapter by Shettleworth (1988) and briefly summarized in Shettleworth (1989).

10

Learning from Others

In the past 50 years or so, forests of Jerusalem pine have been planted in Israel. In these forests, black rats occupy the niche occupied by squirrels in other parts of the world, making their nests in the trees and eating pine seeds. Jerusalem pine seeds are protected by tough overlapping scales tightly wrapped around the central core of the pine cone. To obtain them efficiently, rats must strip the scales off the cones from bottom to top in a spiral pattern (figure 10.1). Black rats that have not previously encountered cones do not learn by themselves to extract the seeds in this way, nor do isolated young rats, but young rats growing up in the pine forests develop efficient stripping as they become independent (Terkel, 1995).

White-crowned sparrows (*Zonotrichia leucophrys*) are small songbirds, widely distributed in North America. Although they are a single species from Atlantic to Pacific, the songs that the males sing during the breeding season vary from one region to another. In California, for example, there is a recognizable Berkeley dialect and a Sunset Beach dialect sung by birds living less than 20 miles away (Marler & Tamura, 1964).

Populations of wild chimpanzees depend on different foods in different areas, and to get some of these foods they use tools (McGrew, 1992). The chimpanzees of Gombe, in Tanzania, gently poke grass stems into termite mounds to extract the insects. Chimpanzees in the Tai Forest of the Ivory Coast open rock-hard coula nuts by placing them on a stone "anvil" and striking them with a smaller stone, which they may carry around with them.

425

Figure 10.1. Mother black rat and her pup feeding on pine cones. After drawings and photographs in Terkel (1995) with permission.

Young chimpanzees accompany tool-using adults and appear to watch them intently.

In all of these examples, individuals seem to be learning from others in their social group. But if they are learning from one another, precisely what are they learning and how are they learning it? Are there are specialized mechanisms for social learning and, if so, are they better developed in species that live in groups? Should the localized groups of animals that share pine cone stripping, song dialects, or nut cracking be viewed as animal cultures?

Observations of animals apparently learning from one another raise both mechanistic and functional questions. Until recently, the answers to these questions have been pursued in two separate research traditions (Galef, 1988; Heyes, 1993a; Whiten & Ham, 1992). Since the days of Darwin and Romanes, psychologists interested in social learning have been obsessed with the question of whether animals can imitate—that is, whether they can come to perform an action as a result of seeing it done. In contrast, anthropologists and behavioral ecologists have been more interested in discovering the conditions under which behaviors spread through populations and are maintained from generation to generation. In this context, mechanisms are important only as they determine the conditions under which behavior is transmitted.

We start by surveying the behavioral ecology of social learning and then look more closely at how animals learn from one another. Song learning—learning by hearing—has typically been considered a special case. It is discussed in section 10.3. Tool use, especially by primates, has also been considered "special" because it appears to involve teaching of young animals by older ones and/or insightful, humanlike understanding how tools work. These issues are discussed in section 10.4. Theory and data about social learning have developed very rapidly of late (Heyes & Galef, 1996), but there are still a great many unresolved issues and areas ripe for future research. The chapter concludes with a summary of the current state of affairs.

10.1 The Behavioral Ecology of Social Learning

10.1.1 Why Live in Groups?

Two important determinants of species-typical group size are food and predators. For example, hamadryas baboons live in the North African semidesert. Food is sparse, and during the day the baboons forage in small bands. However, the safest way for a baboon to sleep is perched on the side of a cliff, and because suitable cliffs are few and far between, as many as 200 baboons gather at night on sleeping cliffs (Kummer, 1995). Many other animals congregate to nest or sleep and disperse to forage. In contrast, species dependent on a temporary resource that occurs in large patches, like the grasses of the African plains, forage in large herds or flocks. Still other species are solitary and territorial except for breeding. Other examples of comparative socioecology were touched on in chapter 1.

Group living has both costs and benefits (Krebs & Davies, 1993 chapter 6), and models of optimal group size must take into account the tradeoffs between them (Pulliam & Caraco, 1984). Among the costs, a group is more conspicuous to predators than a solitary individual, and animals foraging together may interfere with one another. On the benefit side, an individual foraging in a group can take advantage of others' vigilance and thereby devote more time to feeding (see section 2.7). When a predator does attack, the group may be able to confuse it (see section 2.7) or drive it off. In any case, the effect of the predator on any one individual will be diluted by the presence of other group members. Individuals foraging together may also help each other find food. They may be attracted to others of their species that are feeding, or they may follow each other, as ants follow each other along chemical trails. Colonies or roosting places may serve as information centers where individuals inform each other about good foraging opportunities in the neighborhood. At one time, information exchange was hypothesized to be a major factor in the evolution of sociality, but this *information center hypothesis* is now considered to be based on erroneous, group selectionist reasoning and without broad empirical support (Marzluff, Heinrich, & Marzluff, 1996; Richner & Heeb, 1995; but see Zahavi, 1996). Nevertheless, information exchange is a potential benefit of sociality, and there are some good examples of animals using information about food sources provided by others in their colonies. Rats communicate the flavors of edible foods (next section) and bees communicate the locations of nectar (chapter 12).

Whenever individuals are together they have an opportunity to learn from one another. Indeed, some developmental processes depend on social learning. Many species of birds need to hear their species-typical song while growing up in order to sing it when adults (section 10.3). Because the Israeli black rats depend on a complex feeding skill that they would be unlikely to acquire alone, social learning allows them to occupy a niche not otherwise open to them (Terkel, 1995). Social transmission of vocalizations, feeding skills, or other behaviors can lead to different populations of the same species showing markedly different behaviors, an analogue to human culture. Such *locale-specific behaviors* (Galef, 1996a) are shared by individuals in a particular area but are not shown by members of the same species living elsewhere even though all the physical conditions necessary for the behavior may be present there. For instance, chimpanzees in different parts of Africa use different tools and eat different foods, and to some extent these represent local traditions or cultures (McGrew, 1992; see also section 10.4). In the field it is usually impossible to see a tradition arise and analyze how it is transmitted (box 10.1), but there are now two well-studied examples of social transmission in the laboratory, as discussed in the next two sections.

10.1.2 Social Transmission of Food Preferences in Rats

Norway rats (*Rattus norvegicus*, the common laboratory rat) are colonial omnivores. They can and will eat almost anything that does not poison them. This means that young rats have a lot of potential foods to learn about, and they start learning before they are born. The flavors of foods eaten by a mother rat late in pregnancy influence the food preferences of her offspring when they begin to feed on solid food (review in Galef, 1996b). The pups continue to learn from their mother when they are suckling because the flavors of foods she ingests are present in her milk. Then when the weanling rats begin to leave the nest to forage, they prefer to forage where other rats are or recently have been feeding. These are three ways in which the young rat can become familiar with the flavors of foods being eaten safely by its mother and others in its colony. Combined with a preference for familiar flavors, these techniques all help to ensure that it eats things that are good for it, or at least not harmful. But the most thoroughly studied mechanism for the social transmission of food preferences in rats goes beyond simple preference for the familiar. It was discovered in experiments designed as depicted in figure 10.2 (Galef & Wigmore, 1983). In that design, pairs of rats lived together for a few days, feeding on normal laboratory rat chow. Then one rat in each pair, the *demonstrator*, was removed to another cage, deprived of food for 24 hours, and then fed cinnamon- or cocoa-flavored chow. Half the demonstrators got cinnamon and half got cocoa. Next, each demonstrator was returned to its previous companion, the *observer* rat, and demonstrators and observers interacted in the absence of food for 15 minutes. For the following 24 hours the observer, alone once again, had two bowls of food, one flavored with cinnamon and one with cocoa. As shown in figure 10.2, during this time observers whose demonstrators ate cinnamon consumed more cinnamon-flavored food relative to cocoa-flavored food than those whose demonstrators ate cocoa. A large number of related experiments has shown, among other things, that observers can be socially induced to choose a familiar food that a demonstrator has eaten recently and to seek out a place where that food is available (Galef, 1996b). These findings suggest that indeed a rat colony could function as a center in which rats, in effect, exchange information about what foods are currently available nearby (Galef, 1991).

Box 10.1. Sweet Potato Washing by Japanese Macaques

One of the most famous examples of apparent cultural transmission in free-ranging animals involves sweet potato washing by Japanese macaques. A colony on Koshima
Island was provisioned with sweet potatoes, and in 1953 a young female, Imo, was
first seen taking sand-covered pieces of potato to a stream and washing the sand off
before eating them (review in Nishida, 1987). Over the ensuing years, potato washing spread through the colony, first to animals closely affiliated with Imo (figure
B10.1). The way these observations were discussed in the secondary literature—as
an innovation invented by a young animal being imitated by social companions (e.g.,
Bonner, 1980; Gould & Gould, 1994)—shows how quickly people jump to conclusions when essentially unanalyzed observations coincide with anthropomorphic pre-
conceptions about "clever animals." However, the recent wave of critical thinking
about social learning documented later in this chapter has not left early conclusions
about potato washing unchallenged.

First, how consistent are the data in figure B10.1 with social transmission of potato
washing? Any behavior transmitted socially through a group should arise more or less
by chance, spread slowly at first and then more and more rapidly as more models are
available from which naive individuals may learn. In contrast, when individuals learn
entirely on their own, the number of individuals showing the behavior should rise at
a constant rate until all members of the group have learned. Clearly, the data shown
here are more consistent with the second of these scenarios than with the first. Notice,
too, that the time scale is years, suggesting that if social learning was occurring it
must have been very slow. The conclusion suggested by this analysis, due to Galef
(1996a), has been questioned by adding just one more data point, and, perhaps
more important, by analyzing 20 other cases in the literature on primates (Lefebvre,
1995b). The majority of these show an accelerating function, consistent with cultural
transmission.

Since the events involved in the spread of sweet potato washing took place nearly
half a century ago, we will never be certain exactly what went on. However, a variety of processes other than imitation could have been involved. There are suggestions

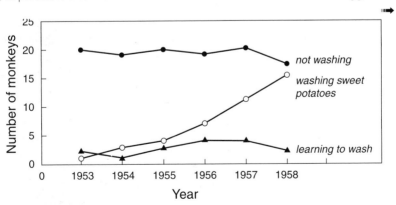

Figure B10.1. The incidence and spread of potato washing among Japanese
macaques on Koshima Island between 1953 and 1958. Redrawn from Galef (1996a)
with permission.

Box 10.1. Sweet Potato Washing by Japanese Macaques (*continued*)

in the literature that once washing had appeared in the colony, the keepers who provided the sweet potatoes encouraged the animals to wash them (see Galef, 1996a).
The activities of knowledgeable individuals with food near water could have provided
conditions under which their companions discovered food washing for themselves—
for instance, by picking scraps out of the water. And in any case, washing sandy food
is not as unlikely a behavior among monkey species as it might seem. A number of the
other examples of apparent cultural transmission analyzed by Lefebvre (1995b) involve washing food. For instance, macaques in the Kashima colony separated grains
of wheat from sand by dropping handfuls of sandy wheat in water, where the grains
floated to the top and could quickly be gathered up. When Visalberghi and Fragaszy
(1990b; see also Visalberghi, 1994), provided individual captive tufted capuchins
and crabeating macaques with sandy fruit and a tub of water, all five capuchins and
three of four macaques showed unambiguous food washing within a few hours. There
was less food-washing, and less interaction with the water altogether, in two larger
groups of capuchins. None of the animals appeared to be learning by imitation.
Rather, when food and water were close together and when animals were accustomed to play in the water and put objects in and out, contact of the sandy food with
water became likely, providing the conditions for individual learning.

How do demonstrators communicate about their experience? A rat that has
just been feeding might carry bits of food on its fur and whiskers, but that is
not all the observers detect. Observers need to smell the flavor in the context
of another rat's breath, more specifically in association with carbon disulfide, a
prominent component of rat breath (Galef, 1996b). Rats behave in a way that
facilitates this learning because when they encounter one another they engage
in mouth-to-mouth contact and sniffing. A further mechanism for social
transmission of food preferences in rats is described in section 10.2.2. To bor-
row a term from embryology (Waddington, 1966), development of food preferences in rats is *canalized*: in a kind of fail-safe system often found in development, several separate mechanisms independently and redundantly ensure
that young rats will eat what others in their colony are eating.

The social learning mechanisms available to adults are sufficient to transmit colony members' acquired food preferences to succeeding generations
(Galef & Allen, 1995). The most compelling evidence for this statement
comes from a study in which colonies of four rats were established in the laboratory and induced to prefer one of two experimental diets, flavored with
Japanese horseradish or cayenne pepper, by making them ill after they ate the
alternative diet. The rats in these "founder" colonies were gradually replaced
with naive rats until the colonies were made up entirely of rats that had never
been poisoned after eating either of the diets. Nevertheless, rats in each
colony were still preferring their colony's "traditional" diet, the one their pre-
decessors had preferred. In one experiment, the tradition was maintained
over four generations of replacement rats. Preference was still transmitted
even when the new colony members never actually fed in the presence of the

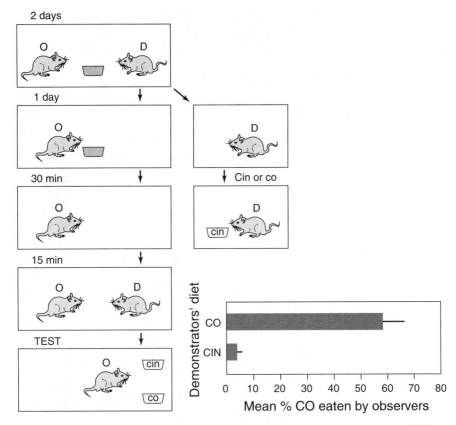

Figure 10.2. Design and results of experiments establishing social transmission of food preferences in Norway rats. D = demonstrator; O = observer; CO = cocoa-flavored food; CIN = cinnamon-flavored food. Data are grams of CO eaten as a proportion of total consumption in the first 12 hours of the test. After Galef and Wigmore (1983) with permission.

older members but just interacted with them in the hours between daily feedings. These findings clearly establish a simple animal culture, amenable to study in the laboratory. Even though cuisines are not perpetuated by people smelling each other's breath, some broad functional properties of traditional food preferences in rat colonies may be similar to those of human culture.

10.1.3 Social Transmission of Feeding Techniques in Pigeons

The rat colonies in Galef and Allen's (1995) experiments were relatively small, and all individuals adopted the colony traditions. Sometimes, however, populations are much larger and not all individuals learn the same thing. What determines the effectiveness of social transmission? For the past 10 years or so, Louis Lefebvre, Luc-Alain Giraldeau, and their colleagues have been attacking this question, using another common laboratory animal, the pigeon (*Columba livia*). Their research program combines experiments on single demonstrators and observers with tests on captive and free-ranging social groups. The results make clear that the skills birds will learn socially are not necessarily those they do learn when an alternative mode of food finding is available, as might be the case in the field.

Like rats, pigeons are highly social, opportunistic foragers that are widely associated with humans because of their ability to flourish in a variety of conditions. Pigeons in the laboratory learn some novel feeding techniques more readily if they have seen them used by another pigeon than otherwise. One such technique is pecking through a paper cover on a food dish. Pigeons that watch demonstrators both pierce the paper and eat grain perform the task themselves sooner than pigeons given partial demonstrations or no demonstrations (Palameta & Lefebvre, 1985). However, when a skilled paper piercer was placed in a laboratory flock of 10 birds, only 4 learned the skill. The others *scrounged* food produced by the birds that pierced (Lefebvre, 1986). In contrast, when a trained demonstrator was introduced into a free-flying flock in Montreal, 24 birds learned to pierce on their own and only 4 specialized on scrounging. The sample sizes here are just one captive and one free-living flock, but Lefebvre and Palameta (1988) suggest that one reason for the great difference in the proportion of learners is that, because individuals could come and go from the urban flock, scroungers sometimes found themselves without anyone to scrounge from and then learned to produce food from the apparatus for themselves. In free-ranging flocks, different individuals may specialize in different food-finding skills and change roles from producer to scrounger as the situation changes (Giraldeau & Lefebvre, 1986).

Scrounging interfered with social learning in a series of studies in which pigeons learned to remove a stopper from an inverted test tube, causing grain to fall out (figure 10.3; Giraldeau & Lefebvre, 1987). Eight out of eight observers that watched another pigeon remove the stopper and eat the grain did the same themselves when given the opportunity, but if the observers could scrounge some of the demonstrator's grain, only two out of eight birds learned in the same number of trials. Just as with paper piercing, when a trained observer was introduced into a laboratory flock, a few birds learned the tube-opening task and became consistent producers, while the majority scrounged as long as the producers were present. Similarly, naive zebra finches use a demonstrator as a cue to food rather than learning about other cues for themselves (Beauchamp & Kacelnik, 1991; but see Nicol & Pope, 1994).

Mathematical models of cultural diffusion generally predict that innovations will spread through a population slowly at first, when demonstrators are few. The rate of transmission rises as the proportion of demonstrators increases, increasing the chances that a naive individual will encounter one (see box 10.1). Studies in which pigeons viewed varying numbers of demonstrators and untrained "bystanders" have revealed that, at least in this species, the number of demonstrators or bystanders present at one time also affects the rate of learning. As the number of birds demonstrating tube opening to a sin-

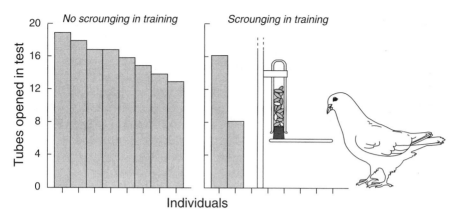

Figure 10.3. Apparatus and results of experiments demonstrating effect of the opportunity to scrounge from the demonstrator on social transmission of a food-finding skill. Data for eight individuals per group, each given 20 opportunities to open a test tube in the test phase. Data redrawn from Giraldeau and Lefebvre (1987) with permission.

gle caged observer was increased from one to nine, the observers' rate of learning increased. But in the same situation the rate of learning decreased when increasing numbers of bystanders surrounded a single tutor (Lefebvre & Giraldeau, 1994; Giraldeau, Caraco, & Valone, 1994).

10.1.4 Comparative Studies of Social Learning

There are at least three different hypotheses about the ecology of social learning, but only a small amount of systematic relevant data. Social learning might be the output of a separable learning module, an adaptive specialization for social living. In that case, it should be most evident in species that live in groups and perhaps even absent in solitary species (Klopfer, 1961; Lefebvre & Giraldeau, 1996). Alternatively, learning from others may reflect some more general learning ability. In this case, social learning would not show species differences independent of differences in other learning abilities. However, generally enhanced learning might itself be an adaptation for social learning, via the requirements for recognition and communication among group members. Consistent with this suggestion, social bees learn discriminations among flower colors faster than bees of a solitary species (Dukas & Real, 1991). Contrary to this idea, though, one might argue that social animals do not have to be such good learners because colony members all work together, whereas an animal that lives alone has to learn everything for herself.

A second kind of prediction about the ecology of social learning is that more opportunistic species — that is, animals like rats and pigeons that have fairly generalized food requirements and can take advantage of a wide range of niches — might be more prone to social influences than more conservative species (Klopfer, 1961). Again, though, opportunism might be expected to be correlated with generally enhanced learning ability, since by definition it consists of the ability to function effectively in many different circumstances. A third suggestion is that selection for social learning is especially strong in species where foraging is a matter of *scramble competition*, where many individuals feed at once on limited food sources, as opposed to *interference competition*, where foragers aggressively exclude competitors. Success in scramble competition is a matter of speed, so slow individuals can benefit by learning the techniques being used by their speedier competitors (Lefebvre & Giraldeau, 1996). If all these factors are important, then social, opportunistic animals that encounter scramble competitions for food will be the best social learners, whereas solitary species that compete with others by exclusion and have conservative food habits will be the poorest.

Like any predictions about learning based on ecology, predictions about the kinds of species that show social learning ultimately must be tested on a number of species representing phylogenetically independent comparisons (see chapter 1). So far, the most thorough program of this kind compares how a pigeon (*Columba livia*) and a close relative, the Zenaida dove (*Zenaida aurita*), learn various foraging tasks socially and individually. Pigeons are social and opportunistic and encounter scramble competitions while foraging, so they should excel at social learning. In Barbados, most Zenaida doves are territorial year-round. Each pair aggressively excludes other Zenaida doves from their territory, though they tolerate and even forage with birds of other species like grackles (*Quiscalus lugubris*). At first glance, Zenaida doves and pigeons differ in social learning just as the three ecological hypotheses predict. Naive pigeons and doves were equally unlikely to push the lid off a bowl of grain (figure 10.4, top row), but after watching a conspecific push off the lid and eat the grain underneath, more pigeons than doves pushed off the lid by themselves (Lefebvre, Palameta, & Hatch, 1996). However, the pigeons were also quicker to feed from an open bowl of food in the experimental situation, and pigeons pushed off the lid sooner than doves after simply eating from the bowl with no demonstrator present (figure 10.4, middle row).

The data in figure 10.4 suggest that pigeons and Zenaida doves differ not in social learning ability but in some more general learning ability or in how they respond to some contextual variable in the experimental situation (see section 1.4). However, the story is still more complicated: Zenaida doves' susceptibility to social influence depends on the species of tutor and on the social situation in which they have been living. Thirty territorial Zenaida doves were brought into the laboratory and allowed to view a grackle eating red rice and a dove eating green rice, or the reverse. When allowed to choose between red and green rice themselves, 21 of the birds copied the grackle on their first choice (Dolman, Templeton, & Lefebvre, 1996). More of these doves also copied a grackle rather than a dove when the task consisted of pushing a lid off a food container. In contrast, subjects from a gregarious population of Zenaida doves that feed socially around a Barbados granary learned more quickly from a dove than from a grackle. Gregarious doves could also be shaped more readily than territorial doves to perform a complex food-finding

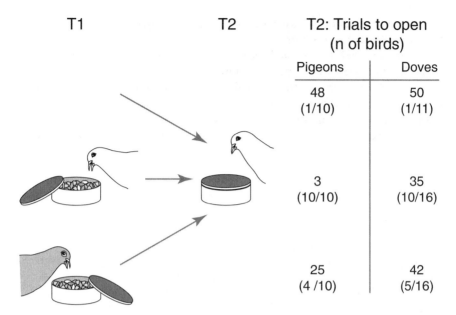

T1	T2	T2: Trials to open (n of birds)	
		Pigeons	Doves
		48 (1/10)	50 (1/11)
		3 (10/10)	35 (10/16)
		25 (4 /10)	42 (5/16)

Figure 10.4. Design and results of experiment by Lefebvre, Palameta, and Hatch (1996) comparing social and individual learning in feral pigeons and Zenaida doves. Each bird had 50 opportunities to open the lid in the test; birds that never opened it were given a score of 50. Numbers in parentheses are the number of birds ever opening the bowl as a fraction of the number of birds in the group.

task, suggesting they differ in some more general ability to learn (Carlier & Lefebvre, 1996; see also Carlier & Lefebvre, 1997).

These results establish adaptive population differences within a species, perhaps brought about by differences in experience. They imply that interpreting differences between species as evidence for genetically programmed adaptive specializations must done with caution. Unlike the case of spatial memory in food-storing birds (see chapters 1 and 6), the social learning studied in these experiments does not appear to represent an adaptive specialization, in that it does not vary independently of performance in nonsocial tasks. In the next part of the chapter, however, we will consider suggestions that the ability to imitate others' actions is a specialized cognitive ability, restricted to a few rather disparate species. This idea seems to be at odds with the tentative conclusion that social learning in Columbids and small passerine birds (see Lefebvre & Giraldeau, 1996) varies with some (generally unspecified) more general learning ability. Part of the problem is that so far we have used the term *social learning* as behavioral ecologists do, to refer to *any* learning from conspecifics. Social transmission of information is the *outcome* of social interactions—that is, it is defined functionally—but a variety of mechanisms play a role in it. For instance, the potential social learner has to attend to possible demonstrators and be able to perceive the information they have to offer. The events that play a role in episodes of social learning very often are ones that have species-specific relevance. For instance, smelling food together with carbon disulphide is of no more interest to a pigeon than seeing a pigeon pecking or hearing a white-crowned sparrow singing is to a rat. Part of what makes social learning possible is specializations of perception, attention, or motivation. Therefore, to get any further with understanding the evolution and function of social learning, we need to analyze in more detail how and what one animal may learn from another's behavior. In doing so, in the next sections, we will discover that there are a number of distinct mechanisms for social learning.

10.2 Mechanisms for Social Learning

10.2.1 Some History

Imitation was one of the mental faculties that Darwin (1871) claimed other species share with humans. Anecdotes about domesticated animals apparently imitating complex actions performed by humans featured prominently in the evidence for mental continuity that Romanes and others collected. Many of these anecdotes involved cats and dogs learning to open doors and gates by manipulating latches, handles, and door knobs. One of the more colorful of these featured a cat belonging to Romanes's coachman.

> Walking up to the door with a most matter-or-course kind of air, she used to spring at the half-hoop handle just below the thumb-latch. Holding on to the bottom of this half-hoop with one fore-paw, she then raised the other to the thumb-piece, and while depressing the latter, finally with her hind legs scratched and pushed the doorposts so as to open the door. . . . Of course in all such cases the cats must have previously observed that the doors are opened by persons placing their hands upon the handles, and, having observed this, the animals forthwith act by what may be strictly termed rational imitation. . . . First the animal must have observed that the door is opened by the hand grasping the handle and moving the latch. Next she must reason, by "the logic of feelings"—If a hand can do it, why not a paw? (Romanes, 1892, pp. 421–422)

"If a hand, why not a paw" captures very well what is cognitively distinctive about imitation. True imitation requires the observer to store a representation of a demonstrator's action and use it to generate an action of her own that matches the demonstrator's. Moreover, to be convincing evidence for imitation, the observer's action should be otherwise improbable. One animal performing a species-specific activity under the influence of another animal would not be said to be imitating. Thorndike (1911/1970) made this distinction with another anecdote.

> Some sheep were being driven on board ship one at a time. In the course of their progress they had to jump over a hurdle. On this being removed before all had passed it, the next sheep was seen to jump as if to get over a hurdle, and so on for five or six, apparently sure evidence that they imitated the action, each of the one in front. Now, it is again possible that among gregarious animals there may be elaborate connections in the nervous system which allow the sight of certain

particular acts in another animal to arouse the innervation leading to those acts, but that these connections are *limited*. The reactions on this view are specific responses to definite signals, comparable to any other instinctive or associational reaction. The sheep jumps when he sees other sheep jump, not because of a general ability to do what he sees done, but because he is furnished with the instinct to jump at such a sight, or because his experience of following the flock over boulders has got him into the habit of jumping at the spot where he sees one ahead of him jump. . . . (pp. 78–79)

What Thorndike emphasized still bears repeating (Galef, 1996a): by themselves, observations like those of cats opening latches or sheep all jumping in the same place cannot reveal how such behavior came about. Field data can be enormously suggestive, but experiments, or at least systematic observations of acquisition, are required to answer questions about how behavior develops. Thorndike's own experiments were based fairly directly on Romanes's stories about dogs and cats opening latches. But instead of letting animals open gates, Thorndike confined them in "puzzle boxes" that could be opened in various ways to allow the animal to escape and find food. In his experiments on imitation, a cat or a young chick was allowed to learn by itself, by trial and error, how to escape. Then a second, observer animal was allowed to watch. If observers learned faster than demonstrators, imitation may have occurred. Thorndike's experiments with cats and chicks provided no evidence for imitation, but he did leave open the possibility that monkeys would imitate, a possibility that is still being debated (see section 10.4).

Thorndike's conclusion—that animals learn gradually by trial and error rather than insightfully or through imitation—left the study of social learning very much in the background in psychology. In the foreground, as illustrated in the preceding chapters of this book, were studies of how isolated individuals learn about features of the physical environment—where things are, what follows what and when, and so on. Ethologists accumulated observations of socially influenced learning, but most of them were not analyzed very thoroughly. Systematic analysis was not helped by the fact that examples of animals apparently learning from one another were labeled with a bewildering variety of different terms (Galef, 1988; Heyes, 1994a; Whiten & Ham, 1992). The past 15 years or so have seen an increase in the systematic study of social learning (see Heyes & Galef, 1996). As we will see, the ways in which one animal may learn from another's behavior extend well beyond imitation. *Social learning* can be used to refer to all such learning, with *imitation* reserved for cases in which an animal performs an otherwise improbable action as a result of seeing another animal perform it.

10.2.2 An Example and Some Distinctions

Not so long ago, milk was delivered to the doors of homes in Great Britain and elsewhere in glass bottles sealed with foil or paper. The milk was not homogenized, so it had a thick layer of cream at the top. In the 1920s and '30s, blue tits (*Parus caeruleus*), small birds related to North American chickadees,

Figure 10.5. A blue tit peeling the top off a milk bottle and drinking the cream underneath. Redrawn from Gould and Gould (1994) with permission.

began puncturing the bottle tops and stealing the cream (figure 10.5). Milk bottle opening became relatively common in a few isolated areas rather than appearing randomly all over Britain, suggesting that it was being culturally transmitted—that is, transferred from one bird to another by some sort of social learning (Fisher & Hinde, 1949; Hinde & Fisher, 1951; Lefebvre, 1995a). However, a little thought reveals that there are numerous ways in which bottle-opening birds might have influenced others' behavior. Similar possibilities exist for the pigeons that learned to open food dishes in the last section.

First, pecking or tearing open a bottle top is clearly not imitation, since pecking and tearing at bark and seeds are prominent components of tits' foraging behavior. At most the birds might have been learning from one another what to direct these behaviors at. But this learning need not have been inherently social. Rather, the products of one individual's behavior—the opened bottles—could have provided the conditions under which another individual learned for itself. The naive tit drinking from an already-opened bottle would associate bottles with food. As a result, it might approach closed bottles and engage in food-related behaviors like pecking and tearing, which would then be reinforced (Hinde & Fisher, 1951). Sherry and Galef (1984, 1990) showed that indeed this kind of mechanism may have had a role in the spread of milk-bottle opening. They taught captive black-capped chickadees (*Parus atricapillus*) to open small cream tubs like those served in restaurants. Then some experimentally naive chickadees watched demonstrators opening cream tubs while chickadees in another experimental group simply learned to feed from opened tubs. Birds in both groups were subsequently more likely to open sealed tubs on their own than chickadees that had simply observed an empty cage containing a closed cream tub, but the proportion of opening individuals in the two groups did not differ.

The products of a conspecific's behavior may facilitate learning by naive individuals in a number of ways. Adult black rats of the Israeli pine forests, described at the beginning of this chapter, do not directly teach or demonstrate efficient pine cone stripping to their young. Rather, cones partially stripped by experienced rats have their scales exposed in such a way that a young rat gnawing at the cone can easily remove them in an efficient, spiral pattern and get at the seeds underneath. Naive rats encountering completely unopened cones gnaw them all over in an inefficient way (Aisner & Terkel, 1992; Zohar & Terkel, 1996). Thus efficient stripping of scales from pine cones, which these rats must develop in order to access their only food in the forest, is socially transmitted when the young rats follow adults around, steal partially opened cones, and continue the stripping themselves (Terkel, 1995).

In other cases, the products of one individual's behavior attract others to the same sites, allowing those individuals to learn something there. For instance, a place where rats have been feeding is scattered with their feces and urine. Other rats, given a choice of two places to feed, prefer the one surrounded with fresh rat excrement. This preference leads them to become familiar with the food they eat there and to prefer it over an unfamiliar food later on (Laland & Plotkin, 1991, 1993). This kind of social influence has been referred to as *local enhancement* or *stimulus enhancement* (Galef, 1988; Heyes, 1994a; Whiten & Ham, 1992). The demonstrator's behavior, or some product of its behavior like open milk bottles or fresh excrement, draws the observer's attention to a part of the environment, which it then learns about on its own. Features of the demonstrators themselves are not part of the conditions or content of this learning.

10.2.3 Observational Conditioning

In all three of the examples just described, behavior can be passed from one generation to another through mechanisms that are not essentially social. One animal simply creates conditions under which others learn for themselves in the demonstrator's absence. In other cases, however, one animal must actually observe another for learning to occur, and the demonstrator's actions or the affective state and behavior they arouse in the observer are associated with stimuli present at the time. The observer then performs similar behavior when it encounters those stimuli again by itself. One striking example is provided by the mobbing behavior that small birds direct toward predators. In mobbing, as the name suggests, birds approach a predator in a group, uttering special calls. This behavior functions to alert potential victims in the area to the location of the predator and may also drive the predator away. Some common predators, like owls, are mobbed even by naive birds, but mobbing other predators depends on social learning (Curio, 1988). Social transmission of enemy recognition has been studied in European blackbirds (*Turdus merula*) and other species in the apparatus depicted in figure 10.6. A "teacher" bird sees a stuffed owl in the central compartment. The "pupil" sees and hears the teacher mobbing the owl and is stimulated to engage in mobbing behavior itself. However, in its side of the central compartment the pupil sees not the owl but a harmless bird like a honeyeater or an owl-sized plastic bottle. When the pupil later encounters the training object by itself, it will mob it. The pupil can now "teach" naive blackbirds to mob bottles or honeyeaters. This "cul-

Figure 10.6. Setup for the experiments of Curio and his colleagues in which one black-bird (the one on the left) can "teach" another to mob a harmless object. Redrawn from Gould and Gould (1994) with permission.

turally transmitted" mobbing can be perpetuated across chains of up to six birds (Curio, Ernst, & Vieth, 1978).

This is evidently an example of Pavlovian conditioning. In effect, one blackbird is imitating another, but because the mobbing demonstrator elicits mobbing in the pupil, the pupil acquires an association between the bottle or honeyeater and its own mobbing behavior system (figure 10.7). However, to be sure that mobbing is indeed associated specifically with the training object, nonassociative controls are necessary. Experiments on acquired mobbing have generally begun with a phase in which the subjects are habituated to the bottle or the honeyeater, so later mobbing is clearly the result of having seen the teacher mob. However, it is also necessary to demonstrate that mobbing is enhanced selectively to the object that was mobbed by the teacher. For ex-ample, birds that have mobbed the honeyeater should not mob bottles as strongly, and *vice versa*, but this does not seem to have been tested (see Curio, 1988, for review).

Predator recognition might be expected to be transmitted socially in many species because individuals that must experience predators for themselves in order to learn they are dangerous may not survive those experiences. The best-analyzed example involves monkeys' fear of snakes (Mineka & Cook, 1988). Monkeys reared in captivity do not exhibit fear the first time they en-

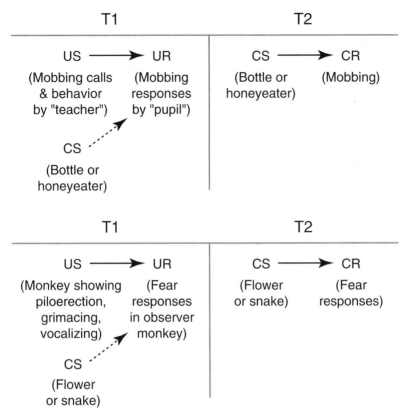

Figure 10.7. Observational conditioning of mobbing or fear as classical conditioning.

counter live or toy snakes. If they watch another monkey behaving fearfully toward a snake, they later do the same themselves. As with mobbing behavior, the naive observer exhibits behavior like the model's during the learning trial (responses such as withdrawal, vocalization, and piloerection). If naive monkeys observe a model behaving fearfully toward a snake and neutrally toward another object like a flower, they acquire the same discrimination. For example, if they are later offered raisins that are out of reach beyond a flower or a snake, they reach quickly over the flower but refuse to reach over the snake.

Selective acquisition of fear shows that the animals are not simply sensitized to behave fearfully to any and all relatively novel objects in the experimental situation. However, even though naive monkeys do not show fear to snakes or flowers, they acquire fear much more quickly to snakes than to flowers (Cook & Mineka, 1990). Subject monkeys that saw videotapes of demonstrators apparently reacting fearfully to snakes and nonfearfully to flowers acquired fear of snakes, just as if they had seen live demonstrators. However, subjects exposed to tapes edited to depict a monkey fearing flowers but not snakes did not learn to fear either stimulus. This comparison shows simultaneously that snake fear is acquired associatively (it depends on the specific pairing of demonstrator's behavior with a snake stimulus) and that the associative process is selective (not any initially neutral stimulus will be feared; see chapter 3). Selective learning about snakes seems to be specific to fear. Monkeys trained with video images of either snakes or flowers paired with food learned equally quickly in both conditions (Cook & Mineka, 1990, experiment 3). Unfortunately, however, the stimuli used and the discriminations to be learned were not exactly the same in this experiment as in those involving socially transmitted fear, so this conclusion must remain somewhat tentative (Heyes, 1994a).

Social learning about aversive events seems to be phylogenetically fairly general, as functional considerations suggest it should be. And at the same time, the events learned about are species-specific. Several species of birds learn to avoid aversive foods by watching others (Mason, 1988; but see Avery, 1994). Curio's paradigm (see figure 10.6) has been used to train New Zealand robins to recognize stoats, an introduced predator (Maloney & McLean, 1995). Predator recognition can be transmitted socially in fish as in birds and monkeys (Chivers & Smith, 1994; Suboski, et al., 1990). A naive fish exposed to an alarmed conspecific also exhibits alarm (*social facilitation*), and when later tested alone it shows that same behavior to a chemical or visual stimulus that was present at the time. Suboski (1990) has termed this form of learning *releaser-induced recognition learning* because at T1 a sign stimulus is present, eliciting behavior that classical ethologists would say reflects an innate releasing mechanism (see chapter 1). At T2, the animal reveals its recognition of a neutral stimulus that accompanied the releaser. Others have referred to the examples described here as *observational conditioning* (Heyes, 1994a). The interevent relationships necessary for learning seem to be the same as in Pavlovian conditioning, so it is not clear that any special term is needed.

In an example involving appetitive learning, young chicks peck at items they see another chicken, or even a motor-driven model beak, pecking at. In the wild or the farmyard, this behavior directs chicks to food being eaten by a mother hen. If a young chick simply watches a beaklike object selectively "pecking" dots of one color on the other side of a barrier, it pecks at that same color on its side and retains this discrimination when tested alone later on (Suboski & Bartashunas, 1984). The chick apparently does not need to peck for itself during training in order to learn the discrimination. When young junglefowl watched others pecking for food in a distinctively decorated bowl, they later pecked more in bowls decorated in the same way (McQuoid & Galef, 1992). The most important result of this experiment is that the socially acquired preference was weak and transitory if the bowls were empty in the test, but it was robust and long-lasting if the birds got food in the test. This might be typical of socially acquired preferences (Galef, 1995). Social learning about positive stimuli need only have a small effect to have important consequences because once the animal makes the socially induced choice, positive reinforcement can perpetuate the behavior. In contrast, socially acquired behavior toward predators should continue indefinitely without the need for each individual to be hurt by the predator.

To summarize, the social learning phenomena that have been referred to as observational conditioning (Heyes, 1994a) or releaser-induced recognition learning (Suboski, 1990) appear to be examples of simultaneous Pavlovian conditioning. At T1 the observer is aroused to behave like a conspecific by viewing that demonstrator's behavior in the presence of a relatively neutral stimulus, and later it engages in the same behavior to that stimulus. Some animals come to copy others' choice of mate through a process that may be similar (box 10.2). The process responsible for social transmission of food preferences in rats also appears similar in that rats have to experience the food odor together with carbon disulfide, but if it is genuine associative learning, it should show overshadowing and blocking, and in the one published test it did not (Galef & Durlach, 1993). There is clearly room for more detailed analyses of the learning involved in all of these examples.

Box 10.2. Do Animals Copy Others' Choice of Mate?

If females are actively choosing males, as indicated by the discussion of sexual selection in chapter 2, some males will receive more matings than others simply because they possess more of whatever characteristic females are basing their choices on. For instance, in species where males congregate and display together on leks, males controlling certain locations on the lek may get most of the matings (Hoglund, Alatalo, Gibson, & Lundberg, 1995). In the past few years there has been considerable interest in the idea that females might prefer males simply because other females have been seen mating with them—that is, they might copy others' mate choice (Kraak, 1996; Pruett-Jones, 1992). If assessing a potential mate's characteristics takes time, entails a risk of predation, or is otherwise costly, simply doing what others are doing would reduce the cost of assessment (review in Dugatkin, 1996). Of course, functional copying would result if females used cues that a male had been chosen previously, such as the presence of eggs in fish species where males guard a nest. But remembering the identity of males chosen by other females and later preferring those males might be an interesting new example of social learning. What is the evidence for it?

The most extensive relevant research has been done by Dugatkin and his collaborators, using guppies (review in Dugatkin, 1996). Figure B 10.2 depicts the design

⟶

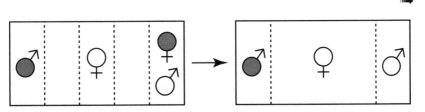

Figure B 10.2. Plan of experiments designed to see whether female guppies, quail, or other animals copy the mate choice of other females. Dashed lines represent transparent barriers.

Box 10.2. Do Animals Copy Others' Choice of Mate? (*continued*)

---

of a typical experiment. In the exposure or training phase, a female is confined equidistant from two males, one of whom is courting a female while the other is alone. Later—usually immediately afterwards—the subject female is released and the time she spends in defined areas of the tank near each male is recorded. "Preference" consists of spending more time near one male than the other. Consideration of figure B10.2 suggests a number of potential confounding variables whose effects need to be examined if the female were to prefer the previously courting male. She might simply prefer the place where more fish had been seen, the place where a courting male had been seen, a male that had been seen courting, or a male that showed signs of having courted recently, among other possibilities. Again, functionally such effects would result in mate copying, even though mechanistically they might not be described as copying (Kraak, 1996). Dugatkin (1992; review in Dugatkin, 1996) reported data consistent with mate copying by female guppies. However, an attempt to replicate his basic findings using somewhat improved methods and guppies from a different population revealed no evidence of mate copying (Lafleur, Lozano, & Sclafani, 1997). Mate copying in this species may not be very robust or may be confined to certain populations.

Other evidence of mate copying in fish has been reported in male sailfin mollies (Schlupp & Ryan, 1997). In birds, the nonrandom mate choice of female black grouse visiting a lek apparently reflects females' preference for males seen copulating. Stuffed females were placed in males' territories, either on the ground, where males could mount and copulate, or on sticks as if sitting in a bush, where males could not copulate. Subject females spent more time in the former than in the latter territories (Hoglund, Alatalo, Gibson, & Lundberg, 1995). Mate copying has recently been documented in laboratory experiments with Japanese quail using a design like that in figure B10.2, and a series of careful analytical studies has begun to isolate the factors involved (Galef & White, 1998).

10.2.4 Imitation: The "Two-Action Test"

The fact that one animal's behavior can come to resemble another's in so many different ways makes it very difficult to find unambiguous evidence for true imitation. Imitation seems to be what's left over when all other conceivable routes for social learning have been ruled out (Zentall, 1996). The most promising experimental design was pioneered by Thorndike (1911/1970). A puzzle box had two escape routes, and a chick watched one being used. If the chick was capable of imitating it should have used the method it had observed rather than the alternative, equally easy one. In the more refined version developed by Dawson and Foss (1965), this design has come to be known as the *two-action test* (Heyes, 1996a; Zentall, 1996). In their experiments, a budgerigar watched a conspecific remove the lid from a food bowl with its foot or by pecking or pulling with its beak. Observers tested alone were more likely to use the method they had seen than the alternative. However, when Galef, Manzig, and Field (1986) performed similar experiments with improved

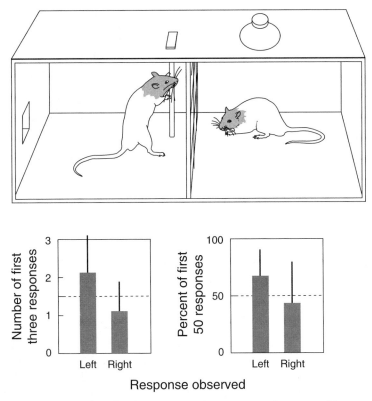

Figure 10.8. Setup and results of experiments demonstrating observational learning in rats. The "joystick " hanging from the roof of the cage could only be moved parallel to the partiton dividing the demonstrator from the observer, to the demonstrator's left or right. Apparatus redrawn from Heyes and Dawson (1990) with permission. Data from Heyes et al. (1992).

methods, they found only a small and transient effect of observation. Palameta (1989) also found very variable effects of exposing pigeons to demonstrators pulling vs. pecking a cork, but more recently other investigators have reported reliable effects with rats, pigeons, and quail in two-action tests.

Heyes and her collaborators (Heyes, 1996b; Heyes & Dawson, 1990; Heyes, Dawson, & Nokes, 1992) have performed an extensive series of experiments in which demonstrator rats are trained to push a hanging "joystick" either to the left or to the right (figure 10.8). Observer rats then reinforced for pushing a joystick in either direction tend to push in the direction they observed more often than in the other direction. This result is especially interesting because when the rats are watching, they see the joystick move in the opposite direction relative to their bodies from that in which they later push it. A rat observing a left-pushing demonstrator, for instance, sees the joystick move to its own right. Surprisingly, when the joystick was moved to the center of one side wall of the cage before observers were tested, they still pushed in the direction they had seen demonstrators pushing (Heyes et al., 1992). This suggests that they were not learning simply where to stand when pushing it but something about the spatial relationship between demonstrator and joystick. Furthermore, rats have to see other rats pushing the joystick; just watching a moving joystick that signals food delivery is not enough (Heyes, Jaldow, Nokes, & Dawson, 1994).

These findings are intriguing but problematical. Heyes herself (e.g., Heyes, 1993a) has been an outspoken critic of purported demonstrations of imitation in monkeys and apes, so it may not be surprising that the possible problems with her own results have attracted critical attention from investigators studying social learning in primates (Byrne & Tomasello, 1995; Whiten, Custance, Gomez, Teixidor, & Bard, 1996). One problem is that it is unclear how the motor patterns shown by left-pushing and right-pushing rats differ (see figure 10.8). Moreover, because behavior is recorded automatically as joystick movements in these experiments, there is no guarantee that observers are reproducing the motor patterns shown by their demonstrators anyway. Further criticism has been directed at the purported demonstration that seeing the joystick move automatically is ineffective in inducing rats to move the joystick in the same way. Observers may have attended less closely to the joystick when it moved by itself than when it was moved by another rat (Byrne & Tomasello, 1995). Any application of the two-action test in which, as in this one, the two actions move the manipulandum in different ways is open to the criticism that the animal learned to produce a certain kind of result in the environment rather than to make a certain motion (Zentall, 1996). A final problem is that although rats would be predicted to show social learning because they are social omnivores (section 10.1), one might wonder why, if imitation reflects a separable learning module that permits another's actions to be translated into one's own behavior (Heyes, 1993a; Whiten & Ham, 1992), it should have evolved in a nocturnal forager like a rat that may have little opportunity to benefit from seeing others performing complex actions to obtain food.

Such criticisms of their experiments notwithstanding, Heyes and her collaborators, among others, have had a salutary effect on researchers attempting to document imitation in primates. Until the last 10 years or so, the study of primate imitation suffered from a number of problems (Fragaszy & Visalberghi, 1996; Heyes, 1993a; Visalberghi & Fragaszy, 1990a; Whiten & Ham, 1992). The most fundamental stems from the assumption that because human children are supposedly good imitators our closest relatives must be good imitators too. Indeed, in many languages the the same word (e.g., *ape*) refers both to a nonhuman primate and to the act of imitating (Visalberghi & Fragaszy, 1990a). The assumption that apes *can* ape has led to a lack of skepticism about the evidence. And until recently most of the evidence consisted of anecdotes from the field or from captive animals reared in close association with humans. Both have the same weakness: no matter how improbable an animal's actions, it is impossible to assess from isolated observations the relative contributions of imitation vs. shaping and reinforcement. That requires a detailed analysis of the animal's history.

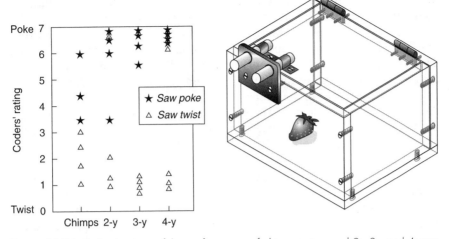

Figure 10.9. Coders' ratings of the performance of chimpanzees and 2-, 3-, and 4-year-old children presented with the artificial fruit at right as a function of whether the subjects had seen a human adult demonstrator poke or twist the bolts. Each data point represents one subject. Redrawn from Whiten et al. (1996) with permission.

In this context an experiment by Whiten et al. (1996; see also Nagell, Olguin, & Tomasello, 1993) is truly a breakthrough. Not only did these researchers give chimpanzees a two-action test of imitation, they also tested young children under the same conditions. Moreover, their task—opening an artificial "fruit" —resembled foraging behaviors chimpanzees in the wild have been said to learn by imitation. The artificial fruit was a transparent plastic box containing a food treat that could be opened by manipulating various handles or bolts (figure 10.9). In one version the lid was closed by two bolts that could be either poked or twisted out. Captive chimpanzees or 2-, 3-, or 4-year-old children saw a human adult poke or twist the bolts and then were given a similar "fruit" that could be opened using either action. Subjects' behavior was videotaped and scored independently by two observers ignorant of which action the subjects had witnessed. Subjects of both species were significantly more likely to use the action they had seen than the alternative (figure 10.9). The tendency to imitate was smallest in the chimpanzees and greatest in the 4-year-old children. The children were more likely than the chimpanzees to copy slavishly even nonfunctional parts of the demonstrator's acts, as if taking for granted that an adult's way of doing things is worth copying. The chimpanzees did direct their behavior at the correct part of the box even when they did not use the same actions they had seen. Such an effect of observation has been called *goal emulation* or simply *emulation*. The subject seems to learn from observation where to direct its behavior or what goal is to be achieved (in this case, removing the bolts) but does not copy precisely the actions of the demonstrator.

These results suggest that humans and chimpanzees differ in their tendency to imitate. In a sense, however, the chimpanzees in this experiment did not have a fair test because they were not given an opportunity to imitate a member of their own species as the children were. Moreover, although the task was equally novel for chimps and children, the subjects likely had very different histories of social and material rewards for imitating human adults. This is especially so because the chimps had been raised in laboratory colonies and zoos rather than "enculturated" by living in close association with people, like some of the chimps we will meet in chapter 11. Therefore, although this experiment clearly shows that chimpanzees *do* imitate in a foraging-like situation, it does not necessarily show that they imitate less faithfully than 2-year-old children. However, as we will see in section 10.4, several species of monkey have failed to imitate in a variety of tests of tool-use, suggesting that there are some genuine species differences among primates. Further evidence consistent with this conclusion comes from an experiment with orangutans very similar to that of Whiten et al. (1996). Orangutans watched either a human or an orangutan push, pull, or rotate the handle on a small box to cause food to be dispensed. Observers were not more likely to reproduce the action they had observed than the other actions (Call & Tomasello, 1995). These results lend support to suggestions that chimpanzees are the only great apes than can interpret events from another's point of view (Whiten & Ham, 1992; see also chapter 11). Indeed, to some a defining feature of imitation is that the observer understand what the demonstrator is trying to do (Heyes, 1996a; Tomasello, 1996). The difficulties in trying to infer intention in animals are discussed extensively in chapter 11. For the case of imitation, it is clear that, as Heyes (1993a, p. 1008) put it, "An imitator may represent the imitated animal's mental state, its point of view, or its beliefs and desires, but this kind of higher-order representational ability is not implied by the act of imitation. What is apparently essential for imitation is that the imitating animal represent what the demonstrator did, not what it thought."

It is still a mystery how animals imitate, but we can expect some progress in the near future with new two-action tests for pigeons (Kaiser, Zentall, & Galef, 1997; Zentall, Sutton, & Sherburne, 1996) and quail (Akins & Zentall, 1996). Both of these demonstrations involve a lever that can be depressed by pecking or stepping. Notice that although these two responses are very different in topography, they both cause the lever to move in the same way. The results for the quail were particularly striking. In a procedure generally similar to that used by Heyes and her colleagues for rats, each subject was trained to eat from the feeder in its demonstrator's compartment before 10 minutes of viewing a demonstrator either peck or step on the treadle and receive food reinforcers. Observers were placed in the response half of the chamber immediately after this experience. Every bird's first response to the treadle matched the responses it had observed. In the first five minutes of the reinforced test session, on average about 90% of the responses to the treadle were imitative responses (figure 10.10). To some (see Heyes, 1996a), this demonstration may not qualify as imitation because the motor patterns being copied are not novel and unusual behaviors for this species. Perhaps the cognitive process involved here or with Heyes's rats is no different from what Thorndike

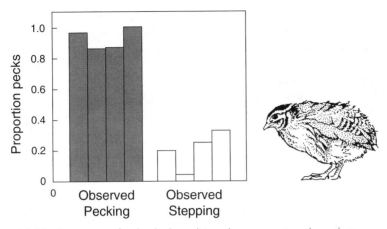

Figure 10.10. Proportion of individual quails' total responses to a lever that were pecks during the first 5 minutes of a two-action test. Redrawn from Akins and Zentall (1996) with permission.

hypothesized for the jumping sheep; imitation in primates could involve a different process. But because this demonstration involves clear effects with a species that is readily available in the laboratory, it opens the way for a more analytical program of research into the factors responsible for at least this form of social learning.

10.2.5 Other Candidates for Visual Imitation

The two-action test is the best controlled test of imitation, but it is also pretty convincing to see an animal do something like put on lipstick or use a tool in a way it has seen humans do. In a sense these are "multiple action tests" because there is a multitude of things the animal might do at the time. When what it does is very like what a person would do, it is hard not to be impressed. The literature on imitation by primates is full of accounts of these sorts of behaviors, mostly by chimpanzees and orangutans that have lived closely with people (see Whiten et al., 1996; Whiten & Ham, 1992). One of the first of these was the chimpanzee Viki, raised like a child by the psychologists Keith & Cathy Hayes (Hayes & Hayes, 1952). The Hayeses demonstrated that Viki had a fairly general ability to imitate novel actions by training her to obey the spoken command, "Do this." Custance, Whiten, & Bard (1995) trained two laboratory-reared chimpanzees in a similar way to the Hayes but documented the procedures and results more fully. The animals were reinforced for obeying "Do this" using a set of 15 actions, like raising the arms, stamping, and wiping one hand on the floor. After more than three months of intensive training, they reproduced these actions with 80% accuracy or better. Then they were tested with 48 other actions and their behavior videotaped and rated independently by two observers, who were required to classify the taped actions as imitations of one of the model actions. The chimps' actions could be classified at better than chance levels, but the agreement was far from perfect, suggesting that they were still not very good generalized imitators.

A host of accounts of orangutans reproducing complex human activities like using hammers and paintbrushes, constructing bridges out of logs, and making fires (!) comes from observations on formerly captive orangutans being rehabilitated for release in the Indonesian jungle (Russon & Galdikas, 1993, 1995). Observations of complex imitations are not confined to primates, either. Alex, the parrot we met in chapter 8, learned to talk by watching two people, one of whom played the role of parrot and was rewarded by the other for using words correctly (Pepperberg, 1993a, 1993b). This situation is thought to reproduce the social situation in which wild parrots acquire vocalizations. However, once Alex began to vocalize himself, he received attention, food, and/or access to the objects he was naming. Explicit reward was scrupulously avoided with another parrot, Okichoro, trained by Moore (1992) to vocalize and imitate associated movements. The bird lived alone in a large laboratory room and was visited several times a day by a keeper who performed various stereotyped behavior sequences such as waving while saying "ciao" or opening his mouth and saying "look at my tongue." Gradually, Okichoro began to imitate both the actions and the words of the keeper while he was alone and observed on closed-circuit TV (figure 10.11). Because each vocalization in effect labeled a specific movement, possible imitation could be isolated from the stream of nonimitative behavior. Eventually many cases of imitation were recorded, including examples of nonvocal mimicry of sounds. For instance, the parrot imitated the sound of someone rapping on the door by rapping its beak on a perch. Moore claims that this is a special category of imitative learning, of considerable evolutionary significance (see section 10.5).

Although they can be entertaining, all these examples suffer to some degree from the problems that afflict most anecdotal evidence. They are often based on a single subject, and a very special single subject at that. The reader can have no idea what proportion of animals exposed to these experiences would do the same thing—that is, we don't know how typical is the behavior being described. This is not a problem if one wants to know what animals of this species *can* do, but it is if we want to know what they *do* do, which is important in deciding whether the behaviors described could be of importance in the wild. Often, we do not know the animal's history. Was it reinforced for approximations to the purportedly imitated behavior or similar actions in the past? This lack of necessary background information very often applies to isolated observations in the field, but studying animals in captivity is not always the solution. As with Alex or Okichoro, lengthy and complex experience often precedes the behaviors of interest. Even if every effort was made to control this experience, the person wanting to evaluate the results rarely can know precisely what it was. It may also be difficult to determine how selective the observers were in recording the subject's behavior. For instance, in a "Do this" test, as opposed to a two-action test, the alternatives to reproducing the model's behavior may not be clearly specified nor is the time interval within

"Ciao"   "Look at my tongue"   "Nod"

Figure 10.11. Okichoro performing some of his imitations. Each action was accompanied by the vocalization indicated. After photographs in Moore (1992) with permission.

which the animal must imitate as opposed to doing something else (Zentall, 1996). Like the proverbial band of monkeys who would reproduce the works of Shakespeare if left long enough in a room full of typewriters, primates raised in homelike environments have many opportunities to perform humanlike actions, and those that are most humanlike and striking are most likely to be the ones reported. For example, how often did the formerly captive orangutans do something *inappropriate*, like bite a paintbrush, hold it by the bristles, or hit a nail with it? Finally, the observers—for the very reason they are living closely with the animals in the first place—may be biased like proud parents to anthropomorphize what they see their animals do. Another problem for long-term research with one or a few subjects is the possibility of Clever Hans effects (see section 8.4)—the possibility that the observer is unintentionally influencing the subjects to produce the desired behavior. Unfortunately, being aware that such effects can occur is not necessarily enough to prevent them, and if the relevant contingencies are not detected by the investigators themselves, they may be difficult or impossible for others to detect in published reports (see section 12.3).

The reports of imitation summarized here do not necessarily suffer from all, or even any, of these problems. For instance, Moore rigorously avoided Clever Hans effects by collecting data only over closed-circuit TV when the parrot was alone and by stopping data collection on any imitation once it had occurred in the presence of the experimenter. The rehabilitant orangutans imitated some elaborate sequences of behavior that were actively discouraged, like stealing boats and riding down the river (Russon & Galdikas, 1993). However, it is important always to keep the many possible problems in mind when assessing either anecdotes from the field or long-term work with a few subjects in captivity. Fortunately, the reappraisal of work on imitation in the last decade or so is leading to more and more sophisticated experiments. We can look forward to more well-controlled experiments in this area in the near future.

10.2.6 Future Directions

As should be evident from the foregoing sections, even though it has been going on for over a century, the study of imitation in animals is still at a stage where experimenters are seeking to demonstrate it. With just a few exceptions, research on nonimitative mechanisms for social learning is in an even more primitive state. It has been retarded by two things: confusion over terminology and a tendency to dismiss phenomena like local enhancement and observational conditioning as if they were at the same time uninteresting and well understood. With the notable exceptions of social transmission of flavor preferences in rats and food-getting behaviors in pigeons and doves, there is virtually no social learning phenomenon for which the conditions for learning, the content of learning, and/or the effects of learning on behavior have been clearly delineated. Until the mechanisms for imitation and other social learning phenomena are analyzed in more detail it will be impossible to say how possible different forms of social learning are related to the conventional categories of single-stimulus, S-S, and S-R learning (see Heyes, 1994a, for some suggestions).

An example of what such an analysis might entail is provided by one of the first experiments in which pigeons learned by watching others to peck through a paper cover on a food bowl (Palameta & Lefebvre, 1985). This study asked not simply whether the birds were influenced by seeing trained demonstrators but also exactly what they had to see. Accordingly, some pigeons saw demonstrators eating from an already-opened bowl; others saw demonstrators pecking through a paper cover but not eating; still others saw demonstrators both pierce the paper and eat from the bowl. Birds in the last group were more likely to pierce the paper by themselves than birds with no observational experience. Just seeing models pierce but not eat had no effect. That is, the pigeons did not show evidence of blind imitation like Moore's parrot, but of course they were treated very differently from the parrot, too. Very few other studies have analyzed the causal factors for any form of social learning in such detail (Laland & Plotkin's, 1990, studies of rats digging for buried carrots provide another example). Palameta and Lefebvre's (1985) approach could be a model for some powerful tests of the conditions for social learning.

10.3 Vocal Imitation: Bird Song Learning

It's easier to tell if you sound like the fellow you heard than to tell if you look the way he did when he was singing. That is to say, feedback from an observer's actions can be matched more closely to a stored representation of a model's actions when those actions produce sounds than when they are merely seen. This kind of reasoning explains why most discussions of social learning and imitation dismiss bird song learning as a special case. It is indeed special, in more ways than one. Song learning is a fascinating and instructive example of specialized developmental plasticity. It has probably been studied in more different species than has any other sort of learning. There are enormous species differences in song itself, in what aspects of song are learned, and how. Song learning is a functional category like imprinting, and so, as with imprinting, a central theoretical question is whether any single model of the process(es) involved in it can encompass all of its cross-species variations. Also, as with imprinting, research on song learning has been dominated until recently by a rather simple model arising from the results of early studies, a model that eventually turned out to be too simple. Its rationale and its limitations are most evident when species are compared. We therefore begin with brief accounts of song development in three contrasting species, the white-crowned sparrow (*Zonotrichia leucophrys*), the zebra finch (*Taeniopygia guttata*), and the brown-headed cowbird (*Molothrus ater*).

10.3.1 A Study in Species Differences

Song and How It Is Studied   Not all the sounds birds make are songs. Birds emit alarm calls and contact calls like the "tseeping" of a winter flock of chickadees moving through a forest. Some birds like roosters could hardly be said to sing at all. For the most part, bird song refers to species-typical musical vocalizations, usually emitted primarily by males in the breeding season. Depending on the species, males may sing from one to over a hundred distinct songs. Song functions variously in territory defense and advertisement and in attracting mates (Catchpole & Slater, 1995). Females, of course, must respond selectively to the features of song that identify males of their species, but the development of female sensitivity has been studied much less than the male ability to produce song (DeVoogd, 1994).

Evidence of vocal learning has been found in oscine birds (a suborder of passeriformes, or perching birds), parrots, and hummingbirds. Oscines make up 46% of the approximately 9,000 species of birds (Gill, 1995). In contrast to the oscines, suboscines (the other suborder of passeriformes) exhibit neither geographic variation in their song nor evidence of song learning. The species mainly discussed here are altricial—that is, unlike chickens and ducks, they hatch naked and helpless, dependent on their parents for warmth and food. Many such species develop very rapidly and are able to leave the nest, if not the protection of their parents, within two or three weeks. In temperate climates, home of most best-studied species, hatching takes place in spring or early summer, when adult males are still singing. Breeding, and hence singing by adults, ends by late summer. Many species then migrate for the winter and return to the breeding grounds the next spring, when the young males are ready to breed. First-year males do not produce full adult song all of a sudden, however. It may be preceded as early as the first summer by a period of subsong, quiet, rather formless vocalizations that may have few if any identifiable elements in common with adult song. Shortly before

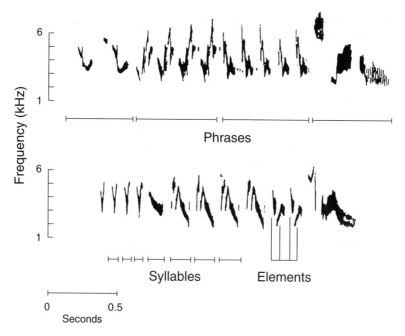

Figure 10.12. Example of a sound spectrogram, or sonagram, from the song of a male chaffinch, showing the sorts of units into which bird songs are typically analyzed. Redrawn from Catchpole and Slater (1995) with permission.

full song appears, there is a period of plastic song sometimes lasting only a few days. Plastic song includes many elements identifiable in adult song, but these may drop out as the bird comes to sing one or more (depending on species) crystallized adult songs that may remain in its repertoire for the rest of its life (Catchpole & Slater, 1995).

Birds' vocal output is normally studied by tape recording samples of song and turning them into sound spectrograms, or plots of frequency against time (figure 10.12). Distinctive vocal patterns are thereby turned into distinctive visual patterns that can be inspected for their similarity to the patterns to which the singer was exposed during development. Fortunately for students of bird song, songs are generally stereotyped and vary in a discontinuous manner, so that it is meaningful to say that one song or song element does come from one song tutor and not from another. However, computerized pattern recognition may increasingly be applied in this area to aid in detecting subtleties not readily evident to the unaided eye (Catchpole & Slater, 1995).

The White-crowned Sparrows   White-crowned sparrows are widely distributed in North America. Each male has a single, rather simple song, which he shares with his neighbors. Males in different geographical areas, some quite small, have different songs—that is, there are local dialects (Catchpole & Slater, 1995; Marler & Tamura, 1964). The fact that each male has a single,

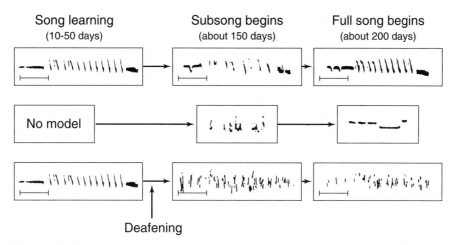

Figure 10.13. Comparison of song development in normal and isolated male white-crowned sparrows (top two rows) and in birds deafened after hearing normal song during the sensitive period for vocal learning. Left-most sonagrams in top and bottom sequences represent the songs heard by the subjects; others represent the songs they sang. After Marler (1970b) with permission.

loud, whistled song simplifies the analysis of song learning in this species — and the existence of dialects suggests that learning is likely to be important in its development.

White-crowned sparrows reared in isolation sing abnormal songs. Their songs still undergo some development, however. Each male progresses from a stage of disorganized and variable vocalizations to one in which he produces a single stereotyped song that still has some species-typical characteristics. Deafened birds also fail to develop normal song, but their vocalizations are much more abnormal. The contrast between isolated and early deafened birds (figure 10.13) indicates that the progression from subsong to crystallized but atypical song shown by isolates depends on auditory feedback from the bird's own vocalizations. White-crowned sparrows given normal early experience and then deafened as adults, however, continue to sing a species-typical song, indicating that auditory feedback may not play a role in maintaining the structure of crystallized song (Konishi, 1965; but see also Nordeen & Nordeen, 1992).

White-crowned sparrows taken from the nest at a few days of age and reared in isolation acquire normal song if they hear tape-recorded white-crowned sparrow songs between 10 and 50 days of age (Marler, 1970a). They acquire the song they hear even if it is not from the same dialect area where they were born. However, they do not learn the songs of other species from tape recordings. Since white-crowned sparrows do not start to sing until early in the spring after they hatch, effects of the experience of hearing song in the first two months of life must be retained for many months (Marler & Peters, 1981; see also box 6.1). Song learning in this species thus has two phases: a sensory phase, in which in which the bird stores auditory information; and a motor phase, in which this information guides development of the bird's own song.

Just as with imprinting, the sensitive phase for learning depends to some extent on the stimuli available for learning (ten Cate, 1989). For example, white-crowned sparrows learn from live tutors up to about 100 days of age, when tapes are no longer effective. They will also learn the songs of other species from live tutors (Petrinovich, 1988). Perhaps live birds draw more attention, their song may be more varied than a tape, or they may interact socially with the pupil (Petrinovich, 1988). The optimal stimulation for song learning could also depend on the age of the bird. For instance, social interaction may affect a young bird differently than an older one (Marler, 1987).

Zebra Finches   Zebra finches live in Australia and nearby islands (Slater, Eales, & Clayton, 1988). Permanent pairs form large flocks. Each male has a single song with 3–13 elements. The song is rather quiet, serving communication with nearby birds rather than the long-distance territorial advertisement of white-crowned sparrows. Breeding depends on rainfall and can take place at any time of year. Permanent monogamy facilitates this because males do not have to spend time setting up territories and wooing females before breeding can begin. The young are chased away by their parents about 35 days after hatching and join mixed-species flocks with other young birds and nonbreeding adults. They are ready to begin breeding themselves by the time they are 80 days old.

Like white-crowned sparrows, zebra finches raised in isolation do not sing a normal species-typical song. Unlike white-crowned sparrows, they do not learn from tape-recorded song in the laboratory, nor do they learn much, if anything, from live tutors in neighboring cages. They need direct social interaction, although they will also learn from tapes if they can perform an operant to turn the tape on (Adret, 1993). In normal rearing conditions, males begin to sing when they are around 30 days old and are well into plastic song by the age of 40 days. Song crystallizes by 60–80 days of age, before first breeding. Thus, the period of motor learning begins before young males leave their parents at 35 days of age but concludes later.

To find out how learning occurs normally in the wild, Slater and his colleagues (see Slater et al., 1988) separated young zebra finches from their parents and introduced them to an unrelated male zebra finch tutor when they were 35 days old. Under these conditions, the birds learn from the tutor with which they interact after 35 days. In contrast, males kept with their father until 65 days of age learn his song. Males introduced to the tutor at 50 days combine elements from the father's and the tutor's songs. These and other data indicate that song learning in zebra finches normally takes place between 35 and 65 days of age. However, birds deprived of song during this time retain the ability to learn from a live companion until adulthood. Song heard before 35 days of age is also learned to some extent and will be sung if later stimulation is inadequate. Indeed, males raised only by females produce a "song" made up of female call notes. Like white-crowned sparrows, zebra finches have a bias to learn the song of their own species.

Brown-headed Cowbirds Brown-headed cowbirds are nest parasites. Females lay their eggs in other birds' nests and leave the young to be raised by the hosts. After fledging, young cowbirds join into flocks, where they remain until breeding the next spring. Early exposure to its own species' song is unlikely to influence song development in a bird raised by another species. Indeed, it was long thought that song development in nest parasites is an example of a "closed motor program"—that is, closed rather than open to influences of experience (Mayr, 1974). On this notion, adult male cowbirds raised in isolation ought to sing normal species-typical song. And indeed they do sing a species-typical song; but far from being normal, it is a supernormal releaser of female copulatory behavior and male aggression. Released into a flock of cowbirds, a male with such a song is attacked by other males. Thus, aggression from male flock mates could serve to teach the young male to sing a less threatening song, one that is also less attractive to females. But it turns out that female cowbirds also have a role in shaping the male's vocalizations. An inexperienced male cowbird sings several different song types to females he encounters. The females appear at first to just sit and listen, but close observation reveals that a female listening to male song occasionally flips her wings slightly in a distinctive way. The male tends to repeat any song that elicits this "wing stroke" response (West & King, 1988). Songs that elicit wing strokes are also highly effective in releasing copulatory responses in the females. Cowbird subspecies from different geographic areas have somewhat different songs, which seem to result from shaping by different female song preferences (King & West, 1983).

10.3.2 The Template Model

The classic model of song learning is depicted in figure 10.14 (Konishi, 1965). It was based largely on studies with white-crowned sparrows in North America and chaffinches (*Fringilla coelebs*) in Europe. The bird behaves as if it hatches with a simple, rough representation of its species-typical song, an *auditory template*. The template plays different roles during the initial sensory or memorization phase of song learning and during the later motor phase. During the sensitive period for sensory learning, the template selects, in a species-specific way, what songs will be learned. For instance, swamp sparrows (*Melospiza georgiana*) selectively learn typical swamp sparrow syllables even if they hear them in a temporal pattern characteristic of song sparrows, whereas song sparrows (*M. melodia*) acquire a much wider range of syllable types but they must hear them in a song sparrow–like temporal pattern (Marler & Peters, 1989; see also figure 1.3). The hypothetical template is separate from general auditory selectivity: birds can perceive and memorize many songs that they never sing themselves (see box 6.1).

In the classic model, early experience hearing song is stored as modifica-

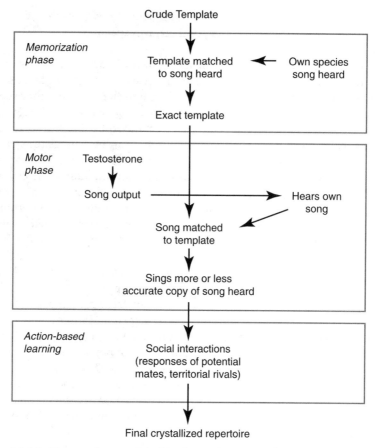

Figure 10.14. The template model of bird song learning. After Slater (1983) with permission.

tions of the template. Then, during the motor learning phase, the bird learns to sing songs it has heard by matching its own vocalizations to the refined template. A bird reared in isolation has only the rough, unmodified template to guide it during the motor phase of learning, as witnessed by the fact that its song has more species-typical characteristics than the song of a bird deafened before the onset of singing. Birds that are socially isolated during the motor learning phase do refine their songs during the period of plastic song, whereas deafened birds do not. Thus, social feedback is not necessary for song development in the motor phase. A bird that can hear himself sing spontaneously shapes his vocalizations to match those he has heard months earlier and stored as modifications of his auditory template. However, recent evidence from several sparrow species suggests that under natural conditions social factors do play a role at this stage. During the period of plastic song (i.e., the early part of the motor learning phase), the birds produce a number of different songs that are apparently later rejected from the repertoire. Among the songs produced in plastic song, the ones most likely to be retained in crystallized song are those being sung by their neighbors (Marler & Nelson, 1993). A young male field sparrow (*Spizella pusilla*) is most likely to retain songs that match those of his territorial rival (Nelson, 1992). This has been called *action-based learning* (Marler, 1991b; Marler & Nelson, 1993). More songs are generated than are eventually crystallized, and action-based learning selects which will be retained. Because the discarded songs become stereotyped before they are discarded, action-based learning is thought to select among existing songs, not shape their form. Furthermore, in field sparrows, a male will not match a neighbor's song if it is a type he was never exposed to in the sensory or memorization phase. Action-based learning appears to reflect a process of social reinforcement, but the details of the social interactions involved remain to be worked out.

The variations in song learning can be described within the framework provided by the template model in figure 10.14, with the processes in song learning divided into those responsible for producing species-typical song and those responsible for selecting what to sing from among the songs produced. Production may or may not require learning early in life: in sparrows and zebra finches it does, but in cowbirds it does not. The learning that does occur is well described by the classic template model as a memorization phase followed by a motor learning phase, with the addition of a possible third phase, action-based learning. The contrast between zebra finches and white-crowned sparrows shows how the optimal time and stimuli for learning vary across species. Purely acoustic features may be used to select what is to be learned, as in swamp and song sparrows, or features of the singer may be important, as in zebra finches. In cowbirds, there is very little if any selective learning in this phase, but regardless of how the young bird comes to produce his first songs, selection among them results from action-based learning. This is basically operant conditioning. Some of the reinforcers and punishers involved have been isolated for cowbirds, but different social experiences may be important in other species (Marler & Nelson, 1993).

10.3.3 Implications

Imitation requires matching one's own behavior to an acquired representation of another's actions. Song learning provides the best worked out example of such a process. Deafening after early exposure to song but before the sensorimotor phase breaks the feedback loop and proves that the bird must be able to match the output from its own behavior to its auditory template (Konishi, 1965). One role for social learning processes generally may be to allow the learner to generate new behaviors that can then be influenced by general processes of reinforcement and punishment (Galef, 1995). Action-based song learning provides an excellent example. Songs that have been retained from the memorization phase and produced in plastic song during the motor learning phase are selected to remain in the repertoire by their effects on other birds. Of course the propensity to be influenced by the effects of one's behavior on others is an aspect of social learning, too. The reinforcers and punishers are species-specific—for instance, the sight of a female cowbird wing-stroking is unlikely to have much effect on a male zebra finch—but they seem to act similarly to other reinforcers.

Song learning is found in a variety of species, not all of which are currently thought to be closely related (Gill, 1995). Among passerine birds, oscines and suboscines are closely related, yet no suboscine has been found to learn song or to possess the brain areas that subserve song learning (Kroodsma & Konishi, 1991). Yet parrots and hummingbirds, which are not passerines, do learn song and seem to have brain structures homologous to the song system in passerines. This distribution suggests that song learning has evolved more than once. Vocal mimicry differs from song learning in being less constrained by sensitive periods and by what can be learned. Parrots are the best known mimics, but starlings and some other passerines also mimic. The very restricted distribution of vocal mimicry suggests that it has evolved from song learning (Moore, 1992, 1996). Nonvocal mimicry, as illustrated by Okichoro's knocking with his beak in imitation of the experimenter's rapping on the door, appears to be even more restricted, suggesting that it evolved from vocal mimicry. Moore (1992) has speculated that movement imitation represents a further evolution. If these speculations are correct, then the ability to copy another's movements should be found only in groups of bird species that also show vocal and nonvocal mimicry of sounds. Movement imitation in mammals, if it exists, must have evolved separately.

The restricted distribution of song learning underlines the fact that it is an excellent example of cognitive modularity. Song learning has a specialized function, is subserved by a specialized area of the brain, and is fine-tuned in species-specific ways. Even if, in birds, it is an evolutionary precursor to a general mimetic ability, being able to imitate song does not imply being able to imitate arbitrary sounds, let alone actions. Moreover, memorizing songs that are later sung is apparently separate from memorizing songs for recognition (see box 6.1). The ability to recognize vocalizations of individual mates, young, or other social companions is present in species such as gulls that do not learn their songs (Gill, 1995).

Song learning has often been compared to imprinting, another specialized learning module (Baptista, Bell, & Trail, 1993; ten Cate, 1989; ten Cate, Vos, & Mann, 1993), and indeed there are many similarities. In both, exposure to a restricted range of stimuli during a restricted period in development has long-lasting effects (see chapter 4). Both are also restricted to certain species, generally different ones. For instance, chickens and ducks do not learn their vocalizations, but they do imprint. A few species, like zebra finches, show both sexual imprinting and song learning, and there are interesting relationships between them (ten Cate et al., 1993). Clearly, however, the details of how experience affects behavior differ markedly between song learning and imprinting. The template model would not do a good job of accounting for imprinting. There are good functional reasons for any similarities. In both song learning and imprinting, the young animal must learn about stimuli specific to its species, its geographic area, and/or its family, and a good way to ensure that this happens is to restrict learning to the period when the young animal is guaranteed to be in the presence of such stimuli and back this up by restricting sensitivity to species-relevant stimuli. — WHY PARENTS WHEN YOUNG

10.4 Tool Use and Teaching

10.4.1 What Is Tool Use?

Tool use has been defined as "the use of an external object as a functional extension of mouth or beak, hand or claw, in the attainment of an immediate goal" (van Lawick-Goodall, 1970). Making and using tools has been seen as a landmark in human evolution, but all sorts of animals use tools (Beck, 1980). Some crabs attach anenomes to their claws, where the anenomes' stings repel the crab's enemies. Sea otters break mollusk shells on stone "anvils" that they hold on their chests. Egyptian vultures throw stones at ostrich eggs to crack them, and chimpanzees use bunches of leaves as sponges to collect water from crevices. Some animals make the tools they use. New Caledonian crows nibble pieces off the stiff edges of pandanus leaves and use them to poke and pull insects out of holes (Hunt, 1996). Captive blue jays have been observed tearing strips of paper and using them to pull in food through the bars of their cages (Jones & Kamil, 1973). Chimpanzees make a variety of tools from sticks, leaves, and grass (McGrew, 1992).

As a functional category of behavior, tool use seems clear enough, but it is quite hazy around the edges. For instance, only from an anthropocentric viewpoint does it make sense to distinguish one gull's dropping stones onto mussels (tool use) from another's dropping mussels onto stones (not tool use; see Beck, 1980, 1982). Both birds are performing a food-reinforced chain of instrumental behavior involving stones. Such considerations forced Beck (1980, p. 133) to conclude, "tool use, in terms of topography, function, and causal dynamics, dovetails imperceptibly with other categories of behavior." Nevertheless, in humans, tool using involves not only performing complex instrumental behavior but also understanding how tools work. Furthermore, in early hominids and in chimpanzees, distinctive types of tools or uses of tools are observed in restricted geographic areas, suggesting that information about tool use is transmitted socially. Two of the more elaborate examples of tool using shown by wild chimpanzees are "fishing" for termites with twigs and grass blades and cracking nuts with stone "hammers" and anvils (McGrew, 1992). Not all populations of chimpanzees show these behaviors, even if they have access to the requisite materials. Another famous candidate for primate culture was described in box 10.1.

Suggestions that animals understand how tools work, that imitation is involved in learning to use tools, and that some animals may teach others to use tools are frankly anthropomorphic. Animals can use tools without any of these assumptions being correct. Lately, all of them have been questioned. Because it is generally difficult to be sure how wild animals learn to use tools and what they know about them, clever laboratory analogues of tool-using situations observed in the field have been presented to several primate species to allow a critical, controlled look at the extent to which simple associative learning vs. imitation and/or understanding may be involved. The results indicate that imitation and understanding are less important than has typically been assumed, but they may sometimes be shown by chimpanzees.

10.4.3 What Do Tool Users Know?

Capuchins (*Cebus spp.*) are small, active South American monkeys. They have only seldom been seen using tools in the wild, possibly because their tree-dwelling way of life makes them difficult to observe, but in captivity they readily make and use tools such as sticks, stones, and "sponges" (Visalberghi & Limongelli, 1996; Westergaard & Fragaszy, 1987). A foot-long horizontal transparent Plexiglas tube with a peanut in the middle was placed in the cage of a group of four capuchins. The tube was too narrow for a monkey's arm, but the peanut could be extracted by inserting a stick into one end of the tube and pushing out the nut. When sticks were provided, three of the four monkeys used them to obtain peanuts from the tube (Visalberghi & Trinca, 1989). To use sticks effectively, however, the monkeys need not have understood anything about the requirements of the situation, such as the length and thickness of effective sticks. Poking a stick into the tube could be a simple instrumental behavior, reinforced with food and acquired through trial and error. To test whether more is involved, and whether species differ, Visalberghi and her colleagues presented capuchins, apes, and human children with clever modifications of the tube task that were designed to differentiate simply learning "put in a stick, get out a peanut" from understanding why the tool worked (Visalberghi & Limongelli, 1996).

One series of tests involved a tube with a trap in the middle (figure 10.15; Visalberghi & Limongelli, 1994). The reward (a candy in this experiment) can be extracted from the trap tube only if the stick is inserted at the end farther from the candy. When the stick is inserted at the end closer to the candy, it pushes the candy into the trap. Three out of four capuchins given the trap tube never got the candy more than half the time in 140 presentations. The fourth began to succeed almost every time after 90 trials. But even this animal could have solved the task by simple discrimination learning, because the trap was always in the middle of the tube. The successful individual was therefore given further tests designed to probe its understanding. For instance, the tube was rotated so the trap was on top. Now the stick could be inserted on either end, but the monkey persisted in carefully selecting the end farther from the candy and frequently monitoring the movement of the candy as she slowly slid the stick into the tube. She did the same when the tube was covered with paper so the candy could be seen only by looking in at the end. Thus, even the successful animal did not understand the causal relationship between moving the stick and pushing reward out. It learned a simple distance-based associative rule.

Five captive chimpanzees were tested in a similar way to the capuchins

Figure 10.15. A capuchin monkey about to make an error in a trap tube task. After a photograph in Visalberghi and Limongelli (1994) with permission.

(Limongelli, Boysen, & Visalberghi, 1995). These animals, experienced in a variety of laboratory tasks, all solved the plain tube task right away. However, in 140 trials with the trap tube, only two of them ever performed above chance, and that not until after 70–80 trials. To see whether they were using a simple distance-based associative rule, these two animals were tested with a new trap tube that had the hole displaced from the center. Now, inserting the stick on the end away from the reward could push it into the trap. However, both animals were successful in this task almost from the beginning, showing that they took into account the position of the reward relative to the trap. One of the successful chimpanzees (Sheba, the counting chimpanzee we met in chapter 8) appeared to anticipate the effects of the stick on the reward, as she rarely even began by inserting it on the wrong side. The other animal was more likely to begin with the stick on the wrong side, then withdraw and reinsert it.

The results with the trap tube indicate that some chimpanzees understand the causal relationship between movements of the tool and production of the reward, whereas the capuchins learn a simple associative rule, if they master the tube task at all. The chimpanzees could still have learned a simple rule based on the position of the reward relative to the hole, something like "Insert the stick on the side of the trap away from the candy." However, the results of another series of tests are more consistent with the notion that the chimpanzees understand the physical requirements of the situation (notice, though, that these are different requirements than those of the trap tube). Capuchins, chimpanzees, bonobos (*Pan paniscus*), and an orangutan had the tube task with sticks that had to be modified in some way before use (Visalberghi, Fragaszy, & Savage-Rumbaugh, 1995). The sticks were tied into a bundle too thick to be inserted into the tube or a stick was present that had smaller sticks inserted into its ends, in an *H* shape. To obtain a suitable tool, the animals had to untie the bundle or remove one of the small sticks from the *H*. All the animals tested did so, but only the apes appeared to do so out of an understanding of the situation. The capuchins sometimes tried to push the whole bundle of sticks into the tube, but the apes never did. The monkeys also persistently tried to use the *H*-shaped stick, but the apes only tried this approach in their first block of trials.

This series of studies is unique so far as a careful and comparative analysis of the knowledge underlying successful tool using. Although it was done with captive animals, the tasks were based on information about primates' tool use in the wild. The results of several different tests all converge on the same conclusion, making it seem more likely that the differences in performance reflect genuine species differences. However, the species difference is not entirely clear-cut. Only one capuchin learned the distance-based associative rule, and three out of five chimpanzees tested performed as badly as the majority of the capuchins. Even though all the chimpanzees tested modified sticks for use as if they understood the requirements of the task, not all of them could avoid the trap. A further caution is that capuchins and chimpanzees were not equated in their past experience. All of the animals tested had lived in captivity for a long time, and many of them had participated in a variety of other tasks. Moreover, even within the experiments comparing capuchins with apes (Limongelli, Boysen, & Visalberghi, 1995), the animals had different amounts of experience with the plain tube before the critical tests. It would be very difficult to overcome such problems in any comparative study with primates, but this does not mean they can be overlooked entirely. A related point is that animals raised in captivity may have had a very impoverished experience compared to animals in the wild, and may show more stereotyped, less complex behavior and cognition than would animals raised in the wild (McGrew, 1992). Nevertheless, the results of this program of research clearly show how tool-using behavior can be underlain by different cognitive structures. Interestingly, children less than 3 years old perform like capuchins when tested with the trap tube, whereas older children are more likely to understand the structure of the situation and act as adults would (Visalberghi & Limongelli, 1996).

10.4.3 How Do Animals Learn to Use Tools?

Two alternatives to trial-and-error learning of tool use are insight and imitation. The idea that chimpanzees might have sudden insights about how to use sticks to rake in food or reach inaccessible places is an old one in psychology, but it is now considered suspect in the light of evidence about the importance of past experience with the objects to be used as tools (box 10.3). In any case,

Box 10.3. Insight in Chimpanzees and Pigeons?

"Aha, I've got it!" In people, this experience accompanies insight, sudden solution of a problem without apparent previous trial and error. The most famous cases of apparent insight in another species were described by Wolfgang Köhler (1959) in the chimpanzees he studied on the island of Tenerife during World War I. They used sticks, strings, and boxes in novel ways to obtain food placed out of reach. For instance, two sticks were joined together to rake bananas into the cage; a box was moved across the cage and animals climbed on it to reach fruit suspended high on the wall. When first confronted with such a problem, animals would usually try the direct solution, jumping up and down under a suspended banana or fruitlessly reaching arms and legs between cage bars. These attempts might be abandoned and the animal might start doing something else when suddenly it would jump up, grab the necessary tool, and immediately solve the problem, as if having experienced an insight into what was required.

Subsequent researchers have emphasized, however, that "insightful" behavior does not come out of nowhere but is built from species-typical motor patterns with the aid of past experience (review in Beck, 1980; Schiller, 1957). Chimpanzees spontaneously carry and climb on boxes, pull strings, play with sticks, and put two sticks together. Such experience contributes to solving problems like Köhler's, as does perceptual and motor maturation. Similarly, some species of birds appear to understand how to obtain food hanging below a perch on a string by pulling the string up bit by bit, holding it with a foot until the beak can reach the food, but closer observation reveals a central role for reinforcement of appropriate species-typical feeding motor patterns (Vince, 1961).

Experience with the elements of a solution definitely contributed to "insightful" behavior in pigeons trained by Epstein and his colleagues (Epstein, Kirshnit, Lanza, & Rubin, 1984). They trained three pigeons in two separate parts of a "banana and box" problem. In some sessions the birds were reinforced with grain for climbing onto a small stationary box and pecking a facsimile of a banana, wherever it was in the testing chamber. Jumping toward the banana in the absence of the box was extinguished. In separate sessions, carried on concurrently, the birds were trained to push the box toward a spot on the wall of the same chamber, without regard to where the spot and the box were placed. Other birds were trained to climb and peck the banana but did not learn to push the box toward a target. In the critical session, the banana was placed out of reach and the box was available in the chamber, without any spot being present. The birds trained to peck and to push directionally all behaved like Köhler's chimpanzees: at first they stretched beneath the banana and looked back and forth between banana and box, but within a minute or so they began to push the box into place under the banana. When the box was in place they climbed onto it and pecked the banana (figure B10.3). This sequence of behavior can be analyzed as resulting from the presence of two stimuli, banana and box, that elicit conflicting responses, pecking and directional pushing (Epstein, 1985). Hence the birds looked back and forth between banana and box at first. But since flying and jumping at the banana had already been extinguished, pushing the box quickly became the dominant response. Mediated generalization (chapter 5) could account for how the banana became the target of pushing in the absence of the spot because both

⟫

Box 10.3. Insight in Chimpanzees and Pigeons? (*continued*)

banana and spot had been associated with grain. Finally, the birds climbed onto the box when it was under the banana because this behavior had been reinforced in the past. Whether or not the comparable behavior of Köhler's chimpanzees can be accounted for in a similar way is impossible to say, since their histories were not known as completely as the pigeons'. However, films of the pigeons reportedly created in viewers a strong impression of humanlike thoughts and emotions (Epstein, Kirshnit, Lanza, & Rubin, 1984).

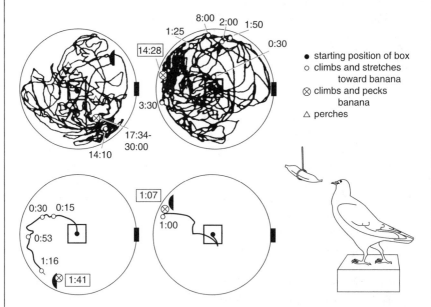

Figure B10.3. Movement of the box during the first 30 minutes of the test of insight in pigeons. Upper row: Data from two birds trained to push the box, but in no particular direction. Lower row: Data from two birds trained to push the box toward a spot on the wall, which was absent in this test. The arena was 69 cm in diameter. Times are minutes and seconds from the beginning of the test; time in a rectangle is the time to solution. Redrawn from Epstein et al. (1984) with permission.

insight might be expected only in species capable of understanding how tools operate, and we have just seen that this may be rare. As for imitation, we have already seen that there is very little good evidence for true imitation in any species. Nevertheless, even crude attempts at imitation could get tool using started, and then reinforcement contingencies could take over (Galef, 1995). Tool using is the sort of task that might favor evolution of imitation, or at least emulation, because it may involve a chain of behavior too complex to be acquired readily by a naive animal left to its own devices. For example, an animal breaking a nut or cracking a mussel shell on a stone anvil has to have a stone and a potential food item at the same time and place. It may be necessary to bring one and then the other to a suitable location. If the reward yielded by such a complex performance is too small to share, the observer will gain more by learning to do the task itself than by scrounging from a knowledgeable demonstrator (see section 10.5). Finally, when related animals live in close proximity in small social groups, demonstrators may tolerate observers who can learn from them. This condition is certainly met in chimpanzee development because the young stay with their mothers for many years.

The fact that termite fishing, nut cracking, and some other sorts of tool using appear to be transmitted socially in chimpanzees does not have to mean that they are learned by imitation, however (see Visalberghi & Fragaszy, in press). There are plenty of ways in which other sorts of social influence could work. For instance, mothers leave stones for cracking nuts lying around near anvils, thereby increasing the likelihood that an inexperienced individual will use both together (Boesch, 1991). The presence of knowledgeable individuals near a food source like a bees' nest full of honey may attract others who then employ species-typical behaviors to get the resource for themselves. The requirements of the situation may shape their initial crude attempts toward more effective actions. This sort of mechanism may make more functional sense than blind imitation (Galef, 1995).

Chimpanzees show the most widespread, elaborate, and varied tool use of any species in the wild. But precisely because their development is so protracted, it is almost impossible to draw firm conclusions about the learning that underlies their tool using (see McGrew, 1992), and there are similar problems with understanding the acquisition of naturally occuring tool use in other species (Beck, 1980). Therefore, we need to look to experimental studies of captive animals. Here there is little evidence for detailed imitation of tool-using behavior, though plenty of evidence for other forms of social influence. For example, naive capuchins exposed to others solving the tube task are very interested in their activities but show no evidence of learning specifically to poke sticks into the tube (Fragaszy & Visalberghi, 1989; Visalberghi & Fragaszy, 1990a). The one individual that did not solve the task in Visalberghi and Trinca's (1989) experiment was later exposed to knowledgeable solvers without effect, but after she had learned to dip a stick into a container to get sweet liquid, she began using sticks as tools in the tube task as well. Here, generalizing from individual experience seemed to be more powerful than learning from watching others.

Tomasello, Davis-Dasilva, Camak, and Bard (1987) allowed young captive chimpanzees to watch another chimpanzee raking food into its cage using a T-shaped metal bar. Chimps in a control group watched the same animal when it was not occupied with the tool. The observing animals subsequently learned to use the T-bar themselves more quickly than those that had not seen it being used, but they did not use the same technique as the demonstrator. They had apparently learned to *emulate* the demonstrator, not *impersonate* or imitate her (Byrne, 1995). A similar conclusion comes from a study in which chimps and children watched a human adult rake in a reward using one of two techniques (Nagell, Olguin, & Tomasello, 1993). All observers interacted with the tool more than individuals that had not seen it used, but just as in the study of "fruit opening" by Whiten et al. (1996), the children had a much greater tendency to copy details of the technique they had observed. Thus observation clearly facilitates learning to use the tool, but not always through strict imitation.

From data like those just reviewed, Tomasello (1996) has concluded that apes developing under species-typical conditions are no better at imitating than are monkeys—that is, apes don't really ape. He (e.g., Tomasello, 1994) has gone on to make the more controversial claim that chimpanzees cannot be said to have culture. By now, readers will recognize that this is one of those claims that is never going to be settled by evidence one way or the other. It seems unduly restrictive to claim that culture (whatever else may be meant by the term) has to be transmitted by imitation as distinct from other possible forms of social influence (McGrew, 1992). In the first place, it is very difficult to be sure that different populations of animals observed in the field really do have locale-specific behaviors or traditions—that is, any sort of behavior that might be called cultural (see Galef, 1996a). For instance, consider how many hundreds of hours tracking animals through the forest are needed to bestow reasonable confidence that chimps in one part of Africa *never* show a kind of tool use commonly observed elsewhere. Moreover, even if this conclusion is favored, it may be difficult to be sure that all the conditions conducive to the tool use in question are present *except* the availability of knowledgeable demonstrators. The cases where these conditions are fulfilled, which include termite fishing and nut cracking by chimpanzees, along with traditions of bower birds' decorating their bowers (Diamond, 1987), seem to qualify as well for the label "cultural" as any example of human behavior (McGrew, 1992). But animal culture is analogous to human culture, not homologous (Tomasello, 1994). Imitation does not necessarily have any role in it (Galef, 1996a; Heyes, 1993a).

10.4.4 Do Nonhuman Animals Teach?

Whether or not animals can learn by imitation, in some circumstances they clearly do learn from one another's activities or the products of those activities. So does that mean that any nonhuman species engage in behavior that could be called *teaching*? Obviously, to answer this question we have to begin by deciding what counts as teaching. To qualify as engaged in teaching, an animal has to modify its behavior in the presence of naive individuals in such a way as to facilitate their learning (Caro & Hauser, 1992) . The teacher should incur some immediate cost to itself, although for teaching to evolve, the teacher needs to reap some benefit in the long term, perhaps as increased inclusive fitness. The bird mobbing an owl in Curio's experiments on enemy recognition is therefore not teaching because, as far as is known, it would engage in mobbing whether or not naive individuals were present. Similarly, the demonstrator rats in the experiments on transmission of flavor preferences are not teaching other rats. They are the more or less passive vehicles for stimuli that other colony members encounter when engaging in routine mouth-to-mouth contact. In contrast are some provocative observations of adults apparently teaching their young what foods to eat or how to get them. In these cases, the parents appear to be postponing or inhibiting catching or ingesting prey in the presence of inexperienced offspring, with the effect that the clumsy youngsters have an opportunity to interact with the prey themselves. Thus, the putative teaching has an immediate cost in delayed feeding (sometimes the prey even escapes), and two potential later benefits. The parent will sooner be able to reduce the time it has to spend finding food for its offspring, and, in the longer term, the offspring may increase the teacher's inclusive fitness by becoming more efficient foragers and hence producing more grandchildren for the teacher. Unfortunately, however, almost none of the examples of apparent teaching that have been observed in the field or in captive animals have been accompanied by controlled demonstrations of the costs or benefits to the teacher, nor of the benefits to the pupil. If teaching is effective, pupils should later behave differently from untaught individuals, even if only by showing the taught behavior sooner than they would otherwise.

Teaching might be expected to evolve when the behaviors to be acquired are unusually difficult and complex, as in capturing large, swift prey or using tools. A number of carnivores behave in a way that apparently functions to teach their offspring what prey to catch and/or how to catch them (Caro & Hauser, 1992). Domestic cats with very young kittens at first eat prey away from the nest, where they caught it. Later, they bring dead birds and mice back to the nest and present them to the kittens. Then, as the kittens mature, mother cats carry back live prey and allow the kittens to play with it, but if the prey escapes the mother still catches it again. Finally, the kittens capture prey by themselves, with little intervention by the mother (Caro, 1980). Cheetahs behave in a similar way toward their cubs (Caro & Hauser, 1992), as do meercats toward their young (Ewer, 1969). Osprey, which snatch fish from the water in their talons, have been seen apparently teaching their fledglings to forage (see Caro & Hauser, 1992). These observations are all very suggestive, although demonstrations that the offspring are, in fact, profiting from their parents' behavior would be required to clinch the case for teaching. Ethology provides so many examples of complex motor patterns maturing without apparent practice that we should beware of assuming that experience plays much role here.

Some of the socially transmitted tool-using behaviors of chimpanzees are also candidates for taught behaviors. The best example is cracking coula nuts with stone hammers and anvils by chimpanzees in West Africa (Boesch, 1991; Boesch-Achermann & Boesch, 1993; Inoue-Nakamura & Matsuzawa, 1997). In over 10 years of field work, Boesch (1991, figure 10.16) observed hundreds of cases in which chimpanzee mothers "stimulated" or "facilitated" their infants' nut cracking and two cases in which they seemed to directly teach. Stimulation consisted of leaving stone hammers near anvils rather than carrying them off, as adults often do. Facilitation meant providing both hammers

Figure 10.16. Adult chimpanzees cracking and eating coula nuts as a young one watches. After a photograph in Boesch-Achermann and Boesch (1993) with permission.

and nuts to infants at anvils. Both of these kinds of behavior changed in apparently appropriate ways with the ages of the infants. In the two cases of apparent teaching, an infant was using a stone to pound at nuts resting on a stone anvil, but was not successful at breaking them because either the hammer or the nut was misoriented. In each case, the mother intervened and positioned the tool or the nut correctly. In contrast to these observations in which mothers were apparently sensitive to the ignorance of their offspring and took corrective action, no indications of teaching or of imitative learning were found in detailed analysis of the development of nut cracking in another area of West Africa (Inoue-Nakamura & Matsuzawa, 1997). There is also little or no evidence that chimpanzees teach their offspring how to "fish" for termites. Indeed, it appears that even though infants spend a lot of time watching their mothers extract termites and even get some of the insects to eat, as with nut cracking they need a good deal of individual practice to become efficient fishers themselves (see Visalberghi & Fragaszy, 1996). And in the next chapter we will see evidence that vervet monkeys do not take corrective action when their offspring are behaving in an ignorant way.

At the beginning of this section teaching was defined functionally, in terms of outcomes for the learner and the teacher, but some would say that true teaching requires that the teacher intend to modify the pupil's behavior or understanding. There are two problems with making the teacher's intention part of the definition of teaching. How can we measure the teacher's intention? And are any animals sensitive to one another's knowledge or understanding anyway? We will see in chapter 11 that intentions are very difficult to assess in nonverbal species, and when they can be there is little if any evidence for them. There is even less evidence that one animal understands what knowledge another has, a capacity referred to as having a theory of mind (chapter 11). Behavior that functions to teach can evolve whether or not the teachers have intentions or a theory of mind (Caro & Hauser, 1992). For instance, mother black rats tolerate their young taking partially opened pine cones from them, and this allows the young to learn on their own (Terkel, 1995).

An example that looks like teaching at first sight comes from the behavior of mother hens toward chicks. It is especially instructive because hens are often thought of as rather stupid animals, and even if they are not, they resemble humans so much less than chimpanzees do that they are unlikely to be anthropomorphized by being thought to teach intentionally (see Beck, 1982, for further examples). Like the mother cats and chimps described earlier in this section, hens present food to their offspring and behave in a way that facilitates their learning its characteristics. Both hens and roosters sometimes show food-calling, which consists of picking up a morsel of food in the beak and assuming a special posture with the breast lowered and the tail spread, while uttering a distinctive call. The food-calling animal repeatedly picks up and drops the food and pecks the ground while holding the morsel in her beak. Hens food-call in the presence of young chicks (Sherry, 1977). Food-calls attract the chicks, and because chicks tend to peck where they see another bird pecking, the hen's food-calling functions to cause the chicks to peck at the food, in effect teaching them what to peck at. Food-calling meets the functional definition of teaching. The hen incurs a cost in delaying her own feeding, and perhaps increasing her risk of predation by calling so loudly. Furthermore, data on observational conditioning referred to in section 10.2.3 (Suboski & Bartashunas, 1984) indicate that chicks do learn what to peck from pecking at the food presented by the hen. But the hen's behavior can be understood as a complex motor pattern controlled by the sight of chicks and her own internal state. Hens that cannot see chicks or that are not in the hormonal state necessary for brooding young do not food-call (Sherry, 1977). An intention by the hen to teach the chicks need not be postulated as a proximate cause of her food-calling. Moreover, the chicks do not learn from the hen through imitation—they already know how to peck—but through the process referred to earlier in the chapter as observational conditioning.

In summary, then, teaching can—and should—be defined as a functional category of behavior, without reference to intentions or theory of mind. There are some observations of animals apparently teaching their offspring, but few of them have been accompanied by clear evidence that the behaviors in question do actually function to teach. Even if they do, it is not clear that teaching merits attention as a special category of behavior. As Ewer (1969, p. 698) put it, "It is . . . misleading and anthropocentric to concentrate on the behaviour of the mother. Her responses and those of her young have been selectively tailored to complement each other. The responses of the mother are simply those which provide the correct situation for evoking the developing repertoire of responses of the young who are thus enabled to educate themselves."

10.5 Putting It All Together

> Animal social learning suffers from a lack of coherent theory, a relatively narrow empirical focus, and a lack of rigor in population level studies. (Laland, Richerson, & Boyd, 1993, p. 271)

> What, then are the advances generated by a century of research? On the one hand, the verdict must be "very few." When we survey the scene with hindsight, we must admit how little is firmly empirically established about which species can and do imitate and through what mechanisms. But the reason for this dull conclusion is an exciting revolution that has taken place in the last decade. (Whiten & Ham, 1992, p. 275)

10.5.1 Mechanisms for Social Learning

As a way of classifying learning or cognitive mechanisms, "social learning" has a lot in common with "spatial learning" (see chapter 7). Both are essentially functional categories, based on the kind of information acquired rather than on the way in which it is acquired; therefore, it should not be surprising to find that both encompass a variety of specific mechanisms. However, individual mechanisms of spatial learning such as path integration, landmark use, and sun compass orientation are relatively well defined and well studied, and there are at least the beginnings of theory and data about how their outputs combine. In both spatial learning and social learning, disproportionate interest has focused on a single, anthropomorphic Alfa Romeo of mechanisms, cognitive mapping in the one case and true imitation in the other. Thoughtful analysis of what these concepts entail, combined with careful experiments, have provided little, if any, unambiguous evidence that any animals possess either one. Instead, it appears that researchers are beginning to appreciate how species-specific fine-tuning and integration of numerous cognitively rather simpler mechanisms can lead to adaptive behavior in natural environments.

Among other phenomena, social learning includes stimulus enhancement, observational conditioning, and emulation. None of these sorts of learning is very well understood in terms of the conditions that bring it about, the contents of that learning, and the effects of learning on behavior. Heyes (1994a) suggests that each one is roughly analogous to a recognized category of associative or perceptual learning. In stimulus enhancement, the analogue of perceptual learning, the products of one animal's behavior attract conspecifics to interact with the same type of stimulus. Demonstrators don't even need to be present, only their traces, as in droppings or opened food containers. There seems to be no reason to think the learning done by the "observers" once they interact with the stimulus is anything other than Pavlovian or instrumental conditioning. In observational conditioning, however, direct contact with the demonstrator's behavior is one of the conditions of learning. Observers come to behave like demonstrators apparently through associating something about the observer's behavior or the affective state it arouses in them with other stimuli present at the time—that is, they engage in S-S learning. Examples include learned enemy recognition by birds and monkeys and recognition of food by rats and birds. Questions like the role of contingency and the possible occurrence of overshadowing and blocking have hardly begun to be asked here. But it is necessary to answer them to know whether social learning is distinctive in any way other than in the events that are learned about.

In Heyes's (1994a) scheme, emulation or imitation are the social learning analogues to instrumental conditioning, in that the conditions for learning include (by definition) exposure of the animal to a response of the demonstrator. But whether or not the observer must also see the demonstrator obtain a reinforcer contingent on that response is a question that has hardly been tackled. Some animals under some conditions engage in "blind imitation." Examples include song birds, Okichoro the parrot, chimpanzees trained to "do this," human-reared orangutans, and young children. But in other cases, as when one bird copies another opening a food container or one chimpanzee emulates another manipulating a tool, the role of demonstrator reward has been little studied (but see Giraldeau & Templeton, 1991). In summary, much remains to be done to understand how any form of social learning comes about in any species. Byrne (1995) suggests that much social learning consists of priming preexisting motor patterns or stimulus sensitivities rather than bringing new ones into being. This insight could also prove helpful in understanding how social learning works.

10.5.2 The Function and Evolution of Social Learning

Both individual and social learning can allow adaptation to changed conditions in advance of evolutionary adaptations. Social learning might be especially important for acquiring skills too complex or time-consuming for each individual to acquire on its own. The pine cone stripping of Israeli black rats is a good example. It is also a good example of how a complex skill that individuals do not acquire when left to their own devices is acquired but by much simpler mechanisms than imitation. A young black rat need never *see* another black rat stripping the scales off a cone; it need only be be provided with cones than have been partially stripped in the right way (Terkel, 1995). Even when observation of another's actions is a condition for learning, observation may function primarily to increase the range of variation of the observer's behavior. Reinforcement then does the job of selecting and perpetuating the successful variants. In most circumstances, there is no need for strict imitation. The job can be done by emulation and the other social learning processes that don't require storing a representation of the demonstrator's behavior as such. Indeed, a tendency to blindly imitate what others do regardless of the positive or negative outcomes for oneself would likely be maladaptive (Galef, 1995). Thus what may need to be explained is not why most species seem incapable of true imitation but why any *are* capable of it.

Is social learning an adaptive specialization for social life? As we have seen, there is very little relevant evidence here, and plenty of scope to collect more. Cross-species comparisons like those between pigeons and Zenaida doves are one way forward. If a convincing pattern of species differences were found, the next step would be to ask what is actually different about the species in question. Adaptive specializations for social transmission of information need not necessarily be in *learning*, but may be in motivation, perception, attention, or social structure. Rats learn about food by smelling other rats' breath because the smell of rat breath has motivational significance for them and because when rats greet each other the nose of one comes close to the mouth of another. Young mammals can learn to do what their mothers do in part because their mothers tolerate them nearby. In species where individuals live alone or in small groups for much of their lives, there is simply less chance to learn from conspecifics. Who an individual can learn from will depend on species-specific social structure and the individual's own place in it, as well as on other species characteristics like activity level and inquisitiveness (Coussi-Korbel & Fragaszy, 1995). Imitation might be favored, not when animals have extensive and prolonged interactions but when interactions are brief and the information to be acquired from conspecifics is of only temporary value (Laland, Richerson, & Boyd, 1993). In this view, it is not surprising that pigeons learn by observation how to open food containers just as chimpanzees do.

The revolution mentioned above has at least two aspects. One is the advance in critical thinking about the evidence for imitation in animals and, perhaps, in understanding the variety of forms of social learning and the many factors that contribute to it in nature. The other is the development of a few model research programs that combine theory and data about social transmission in the field with sophisticated analyses in the laboratory. If recent developments are any indication, the revolution is not over yet.

Further Reading

The books edited by Zentall and Galef (1988) and Heyes and Galef (1996) include reviews of all the major contemporary issues and research programs on social learning. A stimulating theoretical overview from a functional perspective is provided by Laland et al. (1993). The book by McGrew (1992) is a thoughtful critical summary of field work on chimpanzee cultures. It is highly recommended. Bird song in all its aspects is reviewed in the useful book by Catchpole and Slater (1995). A recent collection of chapters on specific issues in bird song is the volume edited by Kroodsma and Miller (1996). For teaching in animals, Caro and Hauser's (1992) review is recommended, along with the chapter by Visalberghi and Fragaszy (1996). The latter authors have also contributed a number of insightful and articulate discussions of tool use and imitation in monkeys and other primates (e.g., Visalberghi & Fragaszy, 1990a). The book by Beck (1980) remains the definitive review of tool use by all nonhuman species. The chapter by Galef (1976) was influential in stimulating more recent developments and is still a valuable review of earlier work. The more recent chapter by Whiten and Ham (1992), which brings the field up to date, also helped set the stage for the recent wave of experiments on imitation. Heyes (1993a) gives a critical and controversial examination of assumptions about the relationships between imitation and culture.

11

Cognitive Ethology and the Evolution of Mind

11.1 Cognitive Ethology

11.1.1 Three Vignettes

Among the sand dunes edging a Long Island beach, a plover guards her eggs. A fox comes into view, and the plover does a most curious thing. Rather than sitting tight on the nest guarding her eggs, she scuttles away, dragging one wing on the ground as if injured (figure 11.1). The fox follows the plover, and the bird keeps up her strange display till the fox is some way from the nest, at which point she suddenly takes to the air and flies back to her eggs. The fox prowls on, soon disappearing behind a dune. What is going on here? The plover's behavior has clearly functioned to deceive the fox, but did the plover intend to lead the fox away by pretending to be injured? Did she consciously plan to deceive him, or can her behavior be adequately characterized as a system of mindless, albeit complex and flexible responses to sign stimuli typical of predators?

In a laboratory not far from the plover's nesting ground, a researcher places a large mirror outside a chimpanzee's cage. Peering at its reflection, the chimp sees a spot of red dye on its eyebrow. The animal moves its hand toward its own head and touches the red spot. Why? Does the chimp in any sense understand that the image in the mirror is itself? And if showing mirror-

475

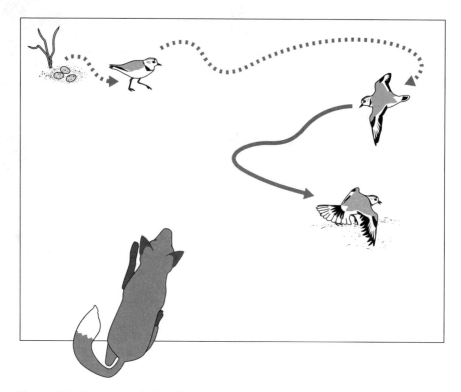

Figure 11.1. Distraction display of a piping plover.

guided inspection of its own body means it has a concept of self, does it have a similar concept of others? Does the chimpanzee, for example, understand that seeing things gives other organisms the same knowledge of those things that it, itself, would gain from seeing them? How could we possibly find out?

In a remote part of Africa, a troop of baboons moves slowly through the bush. The troop is large, so individuals on the edge of the group are often out of sight of others. However, the baboons are grunting softly as they move along, as if to tell one another where they are. But are they *really* communicating? Do the grunts actually function to allow animals at the periphery to follow the group? And do animals in the center of the group know their troop mates are in danger of getting lost and want to tell them which way to go? Once again, how could we tell?

11.1.2 Questions Cognitive Ethologists Ask

The questions about intentions, beliefs, plans, and the like raised by our three vignettes are typical of those asked by *cognitive ethologists* (Jamieson & Bekoff, 1993; Ristau, 1991a; Griffin, 1976, 1992). Cognitive ethologists are distinguished from traditional ethologists by their embrace of mentalistic terms as explanations for behavior. Most classical ethology is very behavioristic, in some ways not so different from Skinnerian psychology in its insistence on scrupulously objective descriptions of behavior. But in classical ethology, in contrast to Skinnerian psychology, describing behavior was just the beginning of an analysis of internal causal organization, function, evolution, or development (see chapter 1). In principle, wants, plans, beliefs, or intentions can be causes of behavior, but in fact the causal analyses of classical ethology did not include them. For instance, a causal analysis of hunger in chickens would be a summary of how factors like the sight of food and the length of time since eating combine to influence pecking, scratching the ground, walking about, and other motor patterns that function to get the chicken a meal. Similarly, a causal analysis of the plover's response to the fox would include specifying such things as what constitutes "predator" stimuli, how their distance and direction from the nest influence the plover's movement, and how her hormonal state and the presence of eggs in the nest determine whether she sits still, shows a broken wing display, or flies away from the fox. The chicken's subjective feeling of hunger, its possible plans or desires to find food, or the plover's possible intention to deceive the predator are irrelevant to these analyses.

In 1976, however, the distinguished ethologist Donald Griffin published a book called *The Question of Animal Awareness* (1976, 1981; see also Griffin, 1978, 1991, 1992), in which he argued that it was time to stop pushing questions about animals' internal subjective experiences under the rug, bring them out into the open, and try to investigate them empirically. He drew together a large number of examples of apparently clever, planful, or communicative behavior and asked whether any or all of them were evidence for conscious awareness. For example, are chickadees planning to come back for seeds when caching them? Are herons that drop bread crumbs on the water and prey upon the fish so attracted intending to "fish" with this "bait"? When bees dance in the hive after finding nectar, do they intend to tell their fellows about its location? Could an insightful ethologist figure out how to ask them what they think by mastering bee language?

Griffin really raised two classes of questions, and these need to be kept distinct: (1) Do animals show behavior that can be taken as evidence of intention, belief, deception, and the like? (2) If they do, do they have subjective states of awareness like those a person would experience while engaging in functionally similar behavior? As readers may recognize from the discussion of consciousness in chapter 1, the second question may be fundamentally unanswerable. The first may not be, as we will see. Even more than 20 years on, though, suggestions that scientists should tackle questions of either sort stir up violent opinions (Bekoff, 1995a; Kummer, Dasser, & Hoyningen-Huene, 1990; Ristau, 1991a; de Waal, 1991; Yoerg & Kamil, 1991; see also Further Reading for this chapter). On the one extreme, hard-nosed radical behaviorists see cognitive ethologists as the wooly-minded fringe, ignoring all the progress that has been made in the century since Romanes. On the other, proponents of Griffin-like interpretations of behavior see traditional ethologists and comparative psychologists as narrow-minded deniers of the true richness of animal mental life. In this chapter we will adopt a "try it and see" (Churchland, 1996) approach, the middle ground of the sceptics (Bekoff, 1995a) who find the questions intriguing but insist that they be addressed with rigorous behavioral methods.

Why wasn't Griffin's suggestion that ethologists should study animals' subjective thoughts immediately dismissed as no different from Romanes's suggestion (see chapter 10) that his coachman's cat opened the gate because she deduced, "If a hand why not a paw"? Of course, one reason was Griffin's sheer reputation as an ethologist. However, at least four other factors led to his ideas being taken seriously by some. For one, Griffin began writing at a time when other behavioral scientists were rejecting a narrow focus on behavior in favor of cognitive theorizing. However, as we have seen, the "cognitive revolution" in psychology was not about internal subjective states but about mechanisms of information processing that could be inferred from behavior. That is to say, cognitive psychologists are methodological behaviorists, in that they study behavior, but not radical behaviorists, in that they do not reject the study of internal psychological processes.

Within biology, the rise of behavioral ecology in the 1970s also helped to favor acceptance of Griffin's suggestions because behavioral ecologists often use very cognitive-sounding terms. Kin recognition, deception, sampling, and strategic decision making are examples of topics that suggest behavioral ecologists are depicting animals as consciously weighing alternatives and planning to achieve certain outcomes. No matter how strongly theorists emphasize (e.g., Krebs & Davies, 1997) that they are using these terms only as convenient labels for functional classes of behavior, cognitive interpretations of them are almost irresistible (Kennedy, 1992).

A third feature of the scientific environment that made it fertile ground for Griffin's suggestions was the outpouring of field studies on primates that began about 30 years ago (Kummer, Dasser, & Hoyningen-Huene, 1990). The complex social relationships among monkeys and apes, coupled with the fact that they look so much like us, seem to compel explanations of their behavior in terms of conscious thought and awareness. Maybe bees, birds, bats, fish, or snakes don't think or know what they are doing, but surely apes and monkeys do.

Finally, the questions raised in our three vignettes are expressions of a powerful human tendency to anthropomorphize other species that even professional observers of animal behavior cannot always resist (Kennedy, 1992). Its power is implicit in the titles of popular books like *When Elephants Weep*, *The Human Nature of Birds*, and *The Secret Life of Dogs*, and it is not the least among the factors encouraging cognitive ethologists. Understanding the behavior of other people as the expression of an underlying belief or intention is part of *folk psychology*, or plain intuitive common sense (Beer, 1991; Churchland, 1986). Folk psychology is a useful predictor of other people's behavior, and it may have evolved for that reason (Humphrey, 1976; Kennedy, 1992; McFarland, 1995). Generalizing to other species can be a useful informal way of predicting their behavior, too. A tendency to apply folk psychology to animals could be a human adaptation for hunting and evading predators. Indeed, it is very difficult for most beginning students of animal behavior, let alone the consumers of popular books, to conceive of the possibility that other species have a completely different way of understanding the world and behaving adaptively in it than we do. It takes a real leap of imagination to understand, for example, that a rat doesn't find its way home because it "knows where it is" but because it is unconsciously pushed and pulled by stimuli it encounters along the way. An analogous explanation of baboons' communicative behavior is even more difficult to grasp. Just as "clever" behavior in the physical world evokes explanations in terms of intelligence and conscious thought (Blumberg & Wasserman, 1995; see also chapter 1), so sophisticated behavior in the social world naturally evokes explanations in terms of sensitivity to others' needs and states of mind (box 11.1)

In this chapter we examine three issues in cognitive ethology that are implicit in the three vignettes at the start: intentionality, self- recognition, and theory of mind. There is much controversy in this area, and most research is still at the stage of attempts to demonstrate the phenomena of interest. Questions like, Which species have which elements of a theory of mind, and under what conditions do they show evidence of it? have hardly begun to be addressed. There are many more questions than answers, and so far the most progress has been made in understanding how to formulate the questions.

11.2 Intention, Intentionality, and the Intentional Stance

11.2.1 Whaaat?

"I'll pick up the children from school today," says Max as he leaves for work. We'd normally say that Max's statement conveys an intention. We can predict that he will drive from his office to the school by a certain route at a certain time and that he will change his behavior if the circumstances change. For instance, if he is working away from the office, he'll travel by a different route and start out at a different time; if the road is blocked, he'll make a detour; if the car breaks down, he may walk or take a taxi. That is to say, his behavior will be directed by the goal of being at the school on time.

A philosopher might say that Max exhibits *intentionality*, but in doing so she would mean much more than that Max has intentions in the everyday, folk psychological sense. Intention in the philosophical sense is the property of *aboutness* (Allen, 1995; Dennett, 1987, 1996). Intentionality, being about things, is perhaps the defining property of mental states. Beliefs and desires, plans, understandings and wishes, as well as intentions, are examples of *intentional states*. A belief, for instance, has to be a belief about something. A distinguishing feature of intentional statements is that they do not obey the usual logical rules of substitutability. For instance, Max is Susie's father, and Max is a man born in 1950. It follows logically that Susie's father is a man born in 1950. However, Susie can believe that Max is her father without necessarily believing that a man born in 1950 is her father. If we ask whether nonhumans

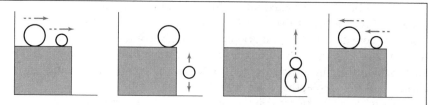

Figure B11.1. Four frames (from left to right) of a cartoon sequence that would be perceived as depicting intentional, as opposed to purely physical, interactions.

Box 11.1. The Perception of Intention

In section 8.4.4 we saw how human infants' and nonhuman primates' knowledge of arithmetical relations could be tested by showing them possible or impossible sequences of events and comparing the times they spent looking at these two kinds of sequences. In a similar experiment to investigate implicit knowledge of physical causality, infants or young children might be shown a cartoon in which, say, a red ball moves in from the left and collides with a green stationary ball. A physically impossible sequel to this event might be the red ball starting back toward the left upon contact with the green ball close behind it. In recent years an extensive body of research has established that even very young infants display considerable implicit knowledge of physical causality in tests of this sort (see Sperber, Premack, & Premack, 1995).

The hypothetical impossible sequence just described would likely be described by an adult as Red hitting Green and then being chased by Green. And in fact young children, too, attribute intentional states to very simple inanimate objects if they appear to be self-propelled and goal-directed (Premack, 1990). The sort of materials described as being used in the first study documenting this are sketched in figure B11.1 (Dasser, Ulbaek, & Premack, 1989). In an experimental sequence, the big ball and the small one entered the screen together, the smaller one "fell down the cliff" and bounced around frantically, the big one descended and "helped it up," and they left the screen together. A control sequence consisted of this series of events in reverse order. Children of about three years old looked longer at the experimental than at the control sequence. Furthermore, when the roles of the balls were reversed, children previously shown the experimental sequence looked longer than those previously shown control sequences.

Subsequent research has documented that even infants have a special set of expectations about self-propelled objects (Gergely, Nadasdy, Csibra, & Biro, 1995; Sperber, Premack, & Premack, 1995). Direct perception of intentionality may form the basis for theory of mind. The success of experiments using looking time to assess numerical concepts in nonhuman primates suggests similar experiments on theory of mind might be possible in other species (Hauser, 1996; Hauser & Carey, in press).

have intentions, beliefs, desires, or the like we are asking whether they are *intentional systems*. As we will see, asking this question means formulating clear operational criteria for what an animal with a certain sort of intentional state does.

Philosophers distinguish a hierarchy of orders of intentionality (Dennett, 1983). In terms of this hierarchy, an animal that does not have beliefs, desires—one that does not in fact have intentional states—is exhibiting zero-order intentionality. Systems of responses to stimuli have zero-order intentionality. A creature that has beliefs, desires, and the like about the real or imagined physical world or the behavior of others is a first-order intentional system. When its mental states concern the mental states of others, we have graduated to second-order intentionality. Thus, if Max *plans* to arrive at the school on time, he is exhibiting first-order intentionality. If he *believes* that the children *know* he is coming for them today, he is exhibiting second-order intentionality. If he *wants* them to *believe* that he *expects* them to be waiting for him, then he is exhibiting third-order intentionality. Level can be piled on level endlessly in this way, but in dealing with nonhuman intentional states, it is enough (usually more than enough) to wonder whether one individual is capable of having beliefs or desires regarding another's beliefs and desires (i.e., second-order intentionality), or just regarding others' behavior or physical states of the world (first-order intentionality).

In predicting what Max will do when circumstances change, we are taking the *intentional stance* (Dennett, 1983, 1987). That is, we are using the assumption that he is an intentional being—folk psychology, in other words—to predict and explain his behavior. The intentional stance is just that—a *stance*, a point of view assumed for the sake of argument and possibly increased understanding. We could just as well take a functional stance, a physical stance, a radical behaviorist stance, or some other kind of stance. Most of the time the intentional stance works very well in accounting for the behavior of other adult human beings. In an informal way it often appears to predict the behavior of other species, too. But even if the intentional stance provides useful rough and ready predictions of other species' behavior, it seldom provides detailed mechanistic explanations. Finding out whether or not it does is the point of experiments. The experimentalist's rule of thumb is Lloyd Morgan's canon (see chapter 1): accept the lowest level of intentional explanation that works. The philosophical case for this *modus operandi* is not necessarily so clear (Allen, 1995; Bennett, 1991b; Dennett, 1983). From the point of view of natural selection, what matters is that the animal achieves goals such as finding food, mates, and safety. Using Lloyd Morgan's canon to choose among alternative explanations assumes that natural selection has always produced the lowest level intentional system that can do the job.

11.2.2 Intentional Plovers?

Let us return to the displaying piping plover (*Charadrius melodus*) described at the beginning of the chapter and illustrated in figure 11.1 (Ristau, 1991b).

One way to account for broken-wing displays is to suggest that the plover is a first-order intentional system: the plover *plans* or *desires* to lead the fox away from the nest. A deceptive plover, capable of second-order intentionality, *wants* the fox to *believe* that she is easy prey and/or that she has no nest. Higher orders are conceivable, too, but here it will be enough to think about what kind of evidence could distinguish first-order from zero-order intentionality.

As suggested in the example of Max, one hallmark of intention (in its folk psychological sense) is that flexible behavior is used to achieve a goal. Accordingly, in one of the first ethological studies explicitly inspired by the intentional stance, Ristau (1991b) sought evidence that nesting plovers show flexible behavior toward human intruders approaching their nests, behavior expressing an intention to lead the intruder farther from the nest. Indeed, in 87% of staged encounters in which a person approached the nest, the plover moved in a direction that would not take a follower closer to the nest. Plovers should behave as if believing the intruder is dangerous, and indeed a "dangerous" intruder caused more arousal than a "nonthreatening" one. If the plover wants to lead the intruder away, it should also monitor the intruder's behavior. For instance, it should start to display when the intruder can see it, and that also seemed to be the case. If the intruder stops following, the plover might be expected to stop as well, and perhaps intensify its display or even approach the intruder as if to attract his attention. Indeed, all cases of reapproaching occurred when the intruder stopped following, but it is not clear from Ristau's (1991b) account exactly how many cases there were of each kind and how their other features compared.

There is a fundamental problem here, though, and that is that the nonintentional, classical ethological alternative is not specified very well. As a result, tests of the hypothesis that the broken-wing display is intentional (in both philosophical and folk psychological senses) rest on appeals to outdated assumptions that nonintentional systems of responses to stimuli are rigid and inflexible and therefore could not produce the observed behavior. But, as we have seen in earlier chapters, behavior that is conditional on combinations of external and internal stimuli can be very flexible indeed. For instance, it is clearly not the case that the sight of an intruder simply releases a broken-wing display in which the bird mindlessly moves in any random direction. The sign stimulus for the display could be more subtle, perhaps including the eyes (box 11.2) and learned signal value of the intruder. Moreover, the display itself is directed in a sophisticated way by the positions of the bird, the intruder, and the nest. The plover does not move directly away from the intruder if that path would take her closer to the nest. But we have seen in chapter 7 that animals commonly show evidence of implicitly computing distances and directions and adding vectors to locate themselves relative to goals, so there may be nothing very special here. What is needed is an explicit model that incorporates assumptions about what stimuli release the display and how its direction is determined. Is it, for instance, possible to formulate a set of if-then statements that completely describe the plover's behavior (Hauser, 1996)? Until such explicit models have been tested and found wanting, the verdict on the intentional interpretation of the plover's broken wing display must be, "provocative, but not proven."

Interestingly, an unrelated bird species, the greater honeyguide of Africa (*Indicator indicator*), also has a set of behavior patterns that can function to lead a member of another species, but in a motivationally and functionally very different situation. Honeyguides have special calls and flight patterns that African tribespeople use to find bees' nests in trees and termite mounds up to a kilometer or more away. A honeyguide encountering people in the vicinity of a bees' nest perches and calls in a distinctive way, then flies off in the direction of the nest, returning shortly and calling again and again. Such behavior is repeated as the honey hunters proceed toward the nest. The honeyguides benefit from investing time and energy in such guiding because they can feed on pieces of honeycomb left behind after people or honey badgers open the nest. Just as the native honey gatherers claim, the birds' behavior is related to the distance and direction from bees' nests in an informative way (Isack & Reyer, 1989).

11.2.3 Intention and Control Theory

Some light can be shed on the issues here by considering a control systems approach to classifying how systems reach goals (McFarland, 1995). The folk-

---

Box 11.2. The Cognitive Ethology of Vigilance: Sign Stimuli or Theory of Mind?

Individuals are less vigilant when in a group (Elgar, 1989; section 2.7.4). A functional explanation may be that any one individual is less likely to be attacked by a predator when in the midst of other potential prey. In addition, group mates can be relied on to some extent to detect predators. Existing data do not clearly distinguish this latter "many eyes" hypothesis from the hypothesis that the group dilutes the effect of a predator, perhaps through the confusion effect (see chapter 2), and in fact both could be correct (G. Roberts, 1996). But when an animal changes the degree to which it scans the environment in the presence of conspecifics, is it responding to their presence, to their behavior, or perhaps to their inferred states of knowledge?

Lima (1995) tested whether it is simply the presence of other individuals or their degree of vigilance that matters by releasing hungry juncos into different-sized flocks of juncos feeding in the field. In the first few minutes after being released, the hungry birds appeared oblivious to the size of the flock, feeding equally fast regardless of whether many or few other birds were present. More important, the only variable predicting vigilance—as measured by the inverse of pecking rate—in nondeprived individuals was total flock size. It didn't matter whether deprived nonvigilant birds were part of the flock or not. Thus, the birds monitored only the number of other individuals present and not their behavior. Evening grosbeaks, at least, appear to encode flock size in terms of the number of individuals they can see. Bekoff (1995b) manipulated the geometric arrangement of free-ranging flocks of grosbeaks by providing food on a square platform or along a long straight rail. Birds feeding in a row along the

⥅

Box 11.2. The Cognitive Ethology of Vigilance: Sign Stimuli or Theory of Mind? (*continued*)

---

rail, where they could not see many other birds at once, spent more time scanning and responded more slowly to changes in group size than did birds feeding on the platform, in circular arrays.

As a label for behavior, *vigilance* seems to imply that animals scanning the environment and monitoring what others are doing are consciously seeking information. But, contrary to some suggestions (e.g., Bekoff, 1995a, 1996), modifying behavior in response to what others know does not require a theory of mind. The orientation of the head and eyes is a good indicator of what visual information another animal is taking in. Accordingly, the eyes of conspecifics or predators are often powerful sign stimuli (Coss & Goldthwaite, 1995). For instance, when European jays are feeding in a group, subordinates are more intimidated by a binocular glance from a dominant than by being fixated monocularly (Bossema & Burgler, 1980). Binocular looking is, in fact, more likely to be followed by an attack. Sensitivity to the direction of gaze is also evident in reactions to predators. For instance, Hampton (1994) startled captive house sparrows by raising a mask (a model predator) with eyes in different positions or orientations. The birds were most startled by a mask with two eyes facing them. Responding was much less when the mask had only one eye or faced down or away from the birds (figure B11.2). The observations on predator avoidance in plovers and gaze-following in chimpanzees and monkeys described in the text suggest that these animals are also sensitive to stimuli correlated with the direction of another's gaze.

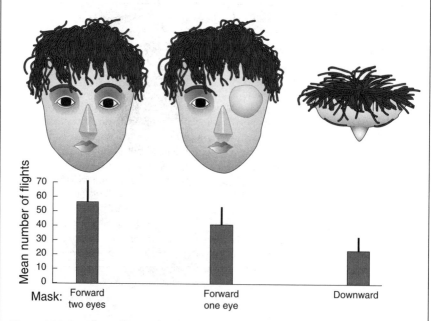

Figure B11.2. Effect of a simulated predator's direction of gaze (or number of eyes) on escape reactions by captive house sparrows measured as number of flights within an aviary. Data from Hampton (1994). Masks from photographs by Robert Hampton.

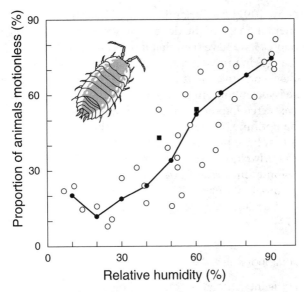

Figure 11.2. Proportion of wood lice inactive for 30 seconds as a function of humidity. Data redrawn from Gunn (1937) with permission.

psychological interpretation of intention implies continuous guidance by a representation of the goal of the behavior. It is this goal representation that conveys flexibility: Max doesn't just get into his car each day at 4:00 and start driving but modifies his behavior in a rational way to achieve his goal. However, within animal behavior, robotics, control theory, and cognitive science generally, it is well recognized that a system can be organized so as to achieve a given goal without containing any representation of the goal as such (Clark, 1997; McFarland, 1995). The behavior of wood lice (figure 11.2) provides a simple example of a *goal-achieving* system, which reaches a goal in a completely passive way. Wood lice, as most gardeners and house owners know, are found in dark damp places, but they don't get there by knowing where dark damp places are and intending to find them. Rather, wood lice that are dry and/or in the light move about randomly, whereas wood lice that are damp and in the dark move relatively little. As a result, wood lice wind up in damp dark places because they keep moving around if they're not in such a place, and they stop when they reach one (Fraenkel & Gunn, 1961).

It can be difficult, perhaps impossible, to tell whether a system that arrives at a goal is doing so in a passive or an active manner. Perhaps because we experience ourselves as acting in relation to explicit goals, many controversies in animal behavior revolve around the issue of active vs. passive control of goal-achieving behavior. For instance, a central issue in the study of body weight regulation is whether or not animals that exhibit a stable body weight are "defending a set point for body weight or fat" or simply arriving at a "settling point" where the various forces driving weight up and down are in equilibrium (see Kennedy, 1992; McFarland, 1995). The original notion of search image was of a mental image of the desired prey item that the forager tried to match, but in chapter 2 we have seen that it is not necessary to use this notion to account for changes in prey selection with experience. The issue of whether or not animals have cognitive maps (see chapter 7) is another controversy of this sort, as is the issue of how animals achieve optimal behavior (McFarland, 1995). As we have seen (chapter 9), behavior is not usually governed by a representation of the optimum as such but rather is the outcome of various simple mechanisms that have presumably been selected because in nature they lead to outcomes fairly close to the optimum most of the time. And, generalizing this discussion even further, evolution itself is not the product of any mind's design or intention but the inevitable, yet in the sense used here passive, outcome of inheritance, reproduction, and selection (see Dennett, 1995; also box 1.2).

11.2.4 Intentional Rats?

To say that an act is intentional in folk psychological terms implies that the actor has two intentional states: belief that the goal can be achieved through the given action and desire to achieve it (Bennett, 1991a). Thus, rather than look for flexibility as the hallmark of intentional behavior, one might look for evidence that behavior is underlain by belief and desire. By these criteria, rats trained to bar-press for food are showing intentional behavior (Heyes & Dickinson, 1990). Indeed, the rat does press the bar because it believes its action leads to desired food. Rats that have never experienced the action-food sequence or that have been exposed to extinction, in which the action no longer leads to food, do not press the bar—that is, they do not press in the absence of evidence that bar-pressing leads to food. This is one of the most basic facts of operant conditioning. Moreover, rats that do not desire the food because they are satiated or because they have learned that the offered food makes them ill do not press the bar, either. The studies supporting this claim are not quite so straighforward as simple demonstrations of acquisition and extinction. First, the rat must be trained to bar-press and then tested in extinction—that is, without actually presenting the reward. In this way, it is possible to assess what the rat learned earlier rather than new learning. Second, if the rat's state of hunger is to be changed in the test, it may be necessary first to allow the rat to experience the food when it is both hungry and sated so it learns that food can alleviate its hunger. Finally, to control for possible general effects of changes in hunger and reward value, a design should be used in which rats are trained on two responses, each for a different reinforcer (table 11.1; this design parallels those of the Pavlovian experiments discussed in section 3.4.2). When the value of one reward is changed, only the response it followed should be affected (figure 11.3). The results of a considerable body of research with rats make it difficult to resist the conclusion that the rat is behaving intentionally, since changing either its belief about the relationship between responding and food or its desire for

Table 11.1. Design of an experiment to test the roles of belief and desire in the control of instrumental behavior

Stage 1	Stage 2	Stage 3 (test)
Response 1 - Reward 1 (e.g., bar press for sucrose)	Revalue Reward 1 (e.g., poison sucrose)	Test responding in extinction
Response 2 - Reward 2 (e.g., chain pull for pellets)		

Note: The complete experiment would include four subgroups sampling all possible pairings of response, reward, and reward revaluation.

the food affects its bar-pressing (Colwill, 1994; Dickinson, 1994; Balleine & Dickinson, 1998).

This conclusion is not trivially true of any rewarded responding, but rather must be tested in each case. In fact, by the belief criterion, some of the pecking of pigeons at lighted keys is distinctly unintentional. The finding is this: As we already know from chapter 3, a pigeon will come to peck a lighted key if it reliably signals the arrival of food, in a so-called autoshaping procedure. This was originally a startling finding (Brown & Jenkins, 1968) because pecking at lighted keys was an archetypal Skinnerian operant. In effect, people assumed that pigeons pecked lighted keys only if they were given evidence that the response was required to produce food, whereas the autoshaping procedure is adequate to support only the belief that the lit key predicts food. Furthermore, once the bird begins pecking and getting food contingent on pecking, pecking still does not become intentional. If the food is omitted each time the pigeon pecks but presented after each lighting of the key without pecks (an *omission procedure*), pigeons peck anyway, though less than without omis-

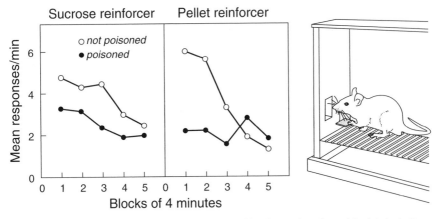

Figure 11.3. Results of stage 3 of an experiment like that outlined in table 11.1. In Stage 2 different groups of rats experienced mild poisoning following ingestion of either sucrose or pellets. Redrawn from Colwill and Rescorla (1985) with permission.

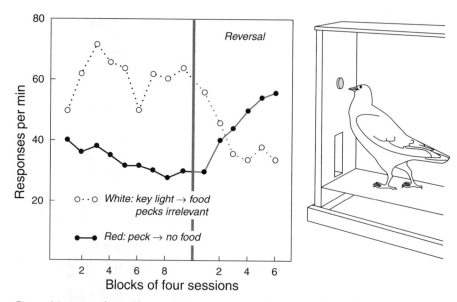

Figure 11.4. Autoshaped key pecking in pigeons and persistent, but reduced, pecking during omission training. Presentations of a white and a red key light were alternated. Food was presented occasionally during red except when the bird pecked. Food occurred during white at the same rate as during red regardless of whether the bird pecked or not. To the right of the vertical line, the significance of red and white was reversed. Data redrawn from Schwartz and Williams (1972) with permission.

sion (Williams & Williams, 1969; see figure 11.4). In its persistence in the face of nonreinforcement, the pigeons' autoshaped pecking is like the cases of "animal misbehavior" documented by the Brelands (1961; see also chapter 3). Like "misbehavior," autoshaped pecking in pigeons and other birds and its species- and reward-specific form (see Jenkins & Moore, 1973; Kamil & Mauldin, 1988) can be accommodated by the behavior systems account of Pavlovian conditioned responding (section 3.4.3). Pavlovian conditioning has traditionally been supposed to tap emotional, involuntary responses so, given that pecking appears to be largely Pavlovian, the conclusion that it is not as well controlled by belief and desire as the rat's bar-pressing perhaps should not be surprising. Pigeons also do not show evidence of encoding intentions to peck one response key rather than another in a delayed response procedure (Urcuioli & De Marse, 1997).

11.2.5 Conclusion

Our first case study in cognitive ethology is coming to a surprising conclusion. There is good evidence that rats press bars in operant chambers intentionally but no compelling evidence that the apparently much more "clever" and flexible distraction behavior shown by plovers in the field expresses an intention to lead away predators. However, the story is not all told yet. We will

Figure 11.5. A chimpanzee engaging in self-exploratory behavior while looking at itself in a mirror. From photographs in Povinelli and Preuss (1995) with permission.

consider intentions (in the folk psychological sense) again in chapter 12 when we ask whether any animals send signals to other animals because they intend to communicate. In the meanwhile, it is important to bear in mind that the two examples did not come to different conclusions just because intentional states can be convincingly demonstrated only in laboratory studies or artificial conditions (contra Allen & Bekoff, 1995). It may be much more difficult to engineer the situations required to collect convincing data in the field, but it can be done, as we will see.

11.3 Monkey in the Mirror

11.3.1 Data

The second vignette at the start of the chapter depicts a kind of experiment first reported by Gallup (1970). Young chimpanzees that had never seen mirrors before were isolated, and a mirror was placed just outside each one's cage for 10 days, during which time their behavior was sampled systematically. At first the animals, like many other mammals, birds, or fish confronted with mirrors, treated the reflection like a conspecific. That is, they directed threatening, greeting, and other social responses to it. Over a few days, however, the chimps' social responses waned and self-directed responses increased (figures 11.5 and 11.6). The latter included "grooming parts of the body which would otherwise be visually inaccessible without the mirror, picking bits of food from between the teeth while watching the mirror image, visually guided manipulation of anal-genital areas by means of the mirror . . . making faces at the mirror, blowing bubbles, and manipulating food wads with the lips by watching the reflection" (p. 86). Such observations suggested that the animals were referring the reflected image to themselves rather than to another animal, but to be sure Gallup devised what has come to be called the *mark test*. The chimps were anesthetized and marked on one eyebrow and the top of the opposite ear with an odorless, nonirritating red dye. When they had recovered from the anesthesia, the animals were watched for 30 minutes without a mirror; there was virtually no behavior directed at the marks during this time. But

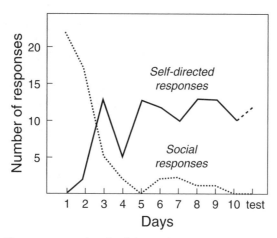

Figure 11.6. Changes in social and self-directed responses in four chimpanzees over successive days of exposure to a mirror. Redrawn from Gallup (1970) with permission.

when the mirror was reintroduced, the animals behaved as described in the vignette, touching and rubbing the marks, sometimes looking at their fingers or sniffing them in between touches.

This study included two other important sets of observations. First, two chimpanzees that had never seen mirrors before were also anesthetized, marked, and tested with mirrors. These controls did not direct any responses to the marks, indicating that indeed the experimental animals' behavior was a consequence of experience with mirrors. Second, a total of 10 monkeys of various species were exposed to mirrors, sometimes for much longer than the chimpanzees, and given the mark test. The monkeys all behaved socially to the mirrors throughout exposure, and none of them touched the marks above control levels during the tests. In the ensuing quarter-century, this latter finding has been repeated many times with a large number of different species of monkeys. Among other apes, orangutans behave like chimpanzees, the small amount of available evidence indicates bonobos do too, but gorillas generally do not (Parker & Mitchell, 1994; Povinelli & Cant, 1995; Tomasello & Call, 1997).

However, it would be premature to conclude that no monkeys react to marks seen in a mirror. Monkeys of many species treat staring from another individual as a threat and look away. Looking away could well interfere with the development of other responses to mirrors. In such cases, a very striking change in an individual's appearance might be required for it to react to a mark seen in a mirror. Stimulated by such reasoning, Hauser and his colleagues (Hauser, Kralik, Botto-Mahan, Garrett, & Oser, 1995) dyed the naturally white tufts of hair on the heads of cotton-top tamarins purple, green, or other colors. Marked monkeys that had previously been exposed to mirrors for three or four weeks stared in the mirror longer than monkeys with undyed hair or marked monkeys with little or no previous exposure to a mirror. They were also the only subjects that touched their hair during the test.

11.3.2 Interpretations

In his original report, Gallup (1970) offered a suitably cautious interpretation of his data. Noting that conventional comparative tests of learning had revealed no differences between monkeys and apes, he observed

> Recognition of one's own reflection would seem to require a rather advanced form of intellect; . . . Moreover, *insofar as self-recognition of one's mirror image implies a concept of self*, these data *would seem to qualify* as the first experimental demonstration of a self concept in a subhuman form. . . . Over and above simple self-recognition, self-directed and mark-directed behaviors would seem to require the ability to project, as it were, proprioceptive information and kinesthetic feedback onto the reflected visual image so as to coordinate the appropriate visually guided movements via the mirror. (p. 87, italics added)

Over the years, this work has been a source of controversy, mainly because Gallup himself (e.g., 1977, 1979) and then his critics focused on the italicized portion of the conclusions (Gallup et al., 1995; Heyes, 1994c, 1995, 1996c; Mitchell, 1996; Parker, Mitchell, & Boccia, 1994; W. P. Roberts & Fragaszy, 1995). For human beings, the sense of self goes way beyond a sense of the physical self. Among other things, the mirror confirms that the person reflected in it is both unique and like other people and thereby conveys a sense of one's own mortality and one's place in the universe. Clearly, it is unlikely that chimpanzees behave as they do in front of mirrors because they have a full humanlike sense of self, and critics like Heyes (1994c) are certainly justified in pointing this out. Their deflationary tactics have included a demonstration that pigeons can be trained, through normal procedures of shaping and positive reinforcement, to direct pecks at a spot on their breast that can be seen only in a mirror (Epstein, Lanza, & Skinner, 1981; but Thompson & Contie, 1994, found this result difficult to replicate). It certainly can be argued that the pigeons' behavior in Epstein et al.'s experiment does not capture the spontaneity and variability of chimpanzees' behavior in front of mirrors. Nevertheless, this little demonstration does make the point that investigators need to focus on what the animals actually *do* in front of mirrors, what experiences contribute to their doing it, and how. One way to advance in this direction is to refer to positive outcomes of the mark test by a more operational, less theoretically loaded term than "self-recognition." For instance, *mirror-guided body inspection* (Heyes, 1994c) describes what the animals do without any implications about why they do it.

The cognitive prerequisites for mirror-guided body inspection are something like the following (Gergely, 1994; see also Parker & Mitchell, 1994):

1. The animal has to be able to use a mirror to locate objects in the world. An object seen *in* the mirror is not inside a looking glass world but in a predictable position outside it. A variety of species including parrots (Pepperberg, Garcia, Jackson, & Marconi, 1995) and elephants (Povinelli, 1989) can be trained to use mirrors to locate objects without displaying any evidence of "self-recognition."

2. The animal must detect the relationship between its movements and the

movements of the "animal in the mirror." Again, a variety of species appear sensitive to a contingency between their own movements and those in a mirror or video image. For instance, rhesus monkeys can learn to manipulate a joystick that controls the movement of images on a TV screen, in a kind of simple video game (Rumbaugh, Richardson, & Washburn, 1989).

3. Experience with the mirror must allow the animal to form a visual representation of the parts of its body that it does not normally see, such as its face and ano-genital region. This representation allows it later to detect a mismatch, as when dye is applied to its face in the mark test.

4. The animal must be motivated to explore the altered parts of its body. Many animals will groom marks on their bodies that they can see or feel, although species differences in this tendency could contribute to differences in mirror-guided body inspection. However, where chimpanzees, orangutans, and people appear to be unique is in the ability underlying number 3. That is, the representation or body image based on the visual, tactile, and proprioceptive feedback that arises when touching and looking at normally visible parts of the body must be integrated with the representation based on tactile and proprioceptive feedback obtained while touching normally invisible parts of their bodies while looking in the mirror.

In this analysis, chimpanzees' behavior in front of mirrors is evidence of self-*perception*, not self-*conception*. Any animals must use some sort of sense of its own body to move around in the world without bumping into things. Pouncing on prey, leaping from branch to branch, flying through a forest, as well as scratching an itch, all require at least a limited perception of the body's extent. Some birds, for instance, are reluctant to fly through a narrow gap unless there is a big reward on the other side, as if sensing the extent of their wings (Cuthill & Guilford, 1990). Why, then, would the ability to integrate visual, tactile, and proprioceptive input obtained while in front of a mirror with the direct visual perception of self be confined to apes and humans? One suggestion is that their ancestral model of locomotion was distinctly different from that of other primates (Povinelli & Cant, 1995). Rather than being relatively small animals with relatively stereotyped locomotion—for example, walking along branches or swinging along underneath them—ape/human ancestors were more like modern orangutans. Orangutans are large, with adults weighing 40 kg or more, yet they live primarily in the trees and get around by *clambering* (figure 11.7). Clambering involves all sorts of motor patterns, climbing up and down tree trunks, swinging from branch to branch, using flexible tree trunks as slingshots to propel oneself across gaps. It is thus very variable in form and appears to require constant judgment as to the location of all the animal's limbs in relation to spatially complex surroundings. These judgments must be made very accurately because a fall is much more likely to damage a large than a smaller animal. Povinelli and Cant (1995) argue that effective clambering requires planning and a representation of oneself as a causal agent. This representation is a limited form of self-conception, and they suggest that it underlies behavior in front of mirrors and perhaps other behaviors soon to be discussed that are also unique to great apes and humans.

The clambering hypothesis is one among several accounts of the evolution

Figure 11.7. Arboreal clambering by an orangutan. Redrawn from Povinelli and Cant (1995) with permission.

of unique cognitive abilities in apes and humans. It may go further than is justified in the cognitive consequences it attributes to a clambering way of life. However, other discussions of the significance of behavior in front of mirrors have gone even further. In particular, Gallup (e.g., 1994) suggested that an animal that recognizes itself in front of mirrors not only has a conception of itself but also a conception of the minds of others, a *theory of mind*. As discussed in the next section of the chapter, having a theory of mind implies being able to understand the intentions and desires of others. A theory of mind is implied by correct attribution of knowledge and ignorance to others, deception, imitation, teaching, and intentional communication. If mirror-guided body inspection implies a theory of mind, then animals that "pass" the mark test should also "pass" very different sorts of tests of theory of mind. Evidence of dissociations among these sorts of behavior would be evidence against this sweeping proposal, and in fact there is considerable such evidence. For instance, autistic children appear deficient in their understanding of other people's mental states, but their behavior in front of mirrors develops normally (Povinelli, 1996).

11.3.3 Recent Developments

By now, some readers may be inclined to dismiss the vexing question of what animals do in front of mirrors as overblown and misguided. However, that would be to ignore some informative recent research, some of it stimulated by criticisms of earlier work. These recent developments are of four kinds.

The Mark Test   The original mark test can be criticized because whether or not the mirror was present was confounded with the time since the animals

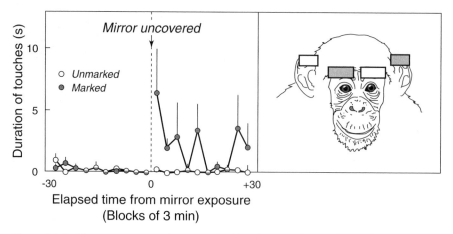

Figure 11.8. Chimpanzees' touches to marked (dark rectangles) and unmarked (white rectangles) facial areas for 30 minutes before and 30 minutes after a mirror was exposed. Redrawn from Povinelli et al. (1997) with permission.

were anesthetized (Heyes, 1994b, 1994c). Because only touches to the marked area were recorded, a general increase in self-grooming during recovery from anesthesia could not be distinguished from an increase in grooming the marked area resulting from presentation of the mirror. This criticism does not apply to a recent experiment in which touches to the marked eyebrow and ear were compared to touches to unmarked control areas on the opposite eyebrow and ear (Povinelli et al., 1997). Once the mirror was uncovered, the animals touched the marked areas much more than the unmarked ones (figure 11.8). However, what is also noteworthy here is that, consistent with other data (e.g., Swartz & Evans, 1997), only four of the seven animals "passed" the mark test; the others touched the marks very little whether the mirror was present or not.

Development   The seven animals in the preceding study were among 95 chimpanzees of all ages that were observed in front of mirrors (Povinelli, Rulf, Landau, & Bierschwale, 1993). The animals were observed in their normal social groups during five days of exposure to mirrors. Behavior in front of the mirror was classified in considerable detail, and behavior that might be evidence of self-recognition was divided into three categories: contingent body movements were repetitive movements made while apparently looking at the reflection; contingent facial movements consisted of an animal making "unusual facial contortions while it was judged to be looking at its own image"; and self-exploration consisted of manipulating parts of the body not otherwise visible while judged to be looking at the mirror image. As in other studies, the animals initially directed social behaviors toward the mirror. Here these waned within the first day or two. Twenty-one animals were classified as then showing compelling evidence of self-recognition because they exhibited high levels of self-exploration in front of the mirror along with substantial levels of contingent body and facial movements. When the subjects were grouped by age, the 1- to 5-year-olds had the smallest proportion of self-recognizing animals (1 out of 48), and the 8- to 15-year-olds had the highest, at 75%. Interestingly, the proportion of chimpanzees apparently recognizing themselves in mirrors after five days' exposure declined in older animals. Extra mirror exposure later on did not seem to have any effect on these animals, nor on the very young animals. Thirty of the chimpanzees Povinelli et al. (1993) had observed were later given a mark test to see whether self-exploratory behavior in front of the mirror would predict "passing" it. Half of the 18 animals classed as self-recognizers in their spontaneous behavior with mirrors passed the mark test, compared to 11% of the remaining animals. These data are hardly a perfect fit to the notion that all mirror-guided body inspection expresses a unitary self-concept.

Video Feedback   If self-exploration in front of a mirror results from an ability to integrate the mirror's special contingent visual feedback with a perception of one's own body, then video technology could be used to explore the effects of altered feedback. Chimpanzees do at least distinguish between seeing themselves in a mirror and seeing other chimpanzees on TV (Eddy, Gallup, & Povinelli, 1996). In front of the mirror they show more contingent facial and body movements and older ones show more self-exploration than in front of the TV. This kind of approach has been used successfully with young children to explore the development of the sense of the visible self, as seen in mirrors and video images, and its relationship to theory of mind (Povinelli, Landau, & Perilloux, 1996), but it remains to be more fully exploited with chimpanzees and other species (Gallup, 1994; Tomasello & Call, 1997). The best controlled approach would seem to be comparing the effects of "live" video to those of delayed showing of the same kind of videos to the same animals so that the images being viewed would be identical while the contingency between image and tactile plus proprioceptive inputs would differ. This was not done in the study by Eddy et al. (1996).

Comparisons to Children   As in research on theory of mind (section 11.4) and language development (chapter 12), research with chimpanzees and other nonhuman primates is proceeding side by side with research on young children (cf. Povinelli, 1995). There is a practical side to the interrelationships of these two kinds of research. In both cases researchers are dealing with organisms that have at best limited verbal abilities so they must devise behavioral tests of their cognitive capacities with the utmost care and insight. Sometimes techniques for testing animals can be adapted to children, and vice versa. There is also a theoretical side, in trying to compare the developmental trajectories of closely related species (Parker, 1996; Tomasello & Call, 1997; see box 11.3). Just how much overlap is there between the cognitive development of chimpanzees and that of human children, and what do the similarities and differences in how primate species develop tell us about how the human mind evolved?

Box 11.3. Object Permanence in Animals?

When a very young infant sees an attractive object disappear behind a barrier, she does not search for it: "out of sight is out of mind." An older infant searches for an object that disappears behind one barrier, but if it is moved to a second hiding place while the infant watches, it will be searched for in the first (an "A not B" error). Eventually, around two years of age, children will search for objects that are hidden and then displaced invisibly, while inside a container. If the object is removed and the child shown the empty container, she will search wherever the container was taken last. Such behavior is assumed to be accompanied by a concept of object permanence, knowledge that objects still exist when out of sight.

The description of the six stages through which object permanence develops is one of Jean Piaget's best-known contributions to psychology. But searching for hidden objects is useful for many animals. For instance, predators may continue tracking prey that have gone into cover, and nutcrackers dig up seeds they have buried. Clearly, however, there are a variety of ways in which animals could successfully search for disappearing objects without believing they exist when out of sight. The sight of an object disappearing behind an occluder could elicit search behaviors prefunctionally, or an animal might learn what to do by trial and error. For instance, when young domestic chicks watched a mealworm being pulled through a tube and disappearing behind a screen (figure B11.3), they did not immediately follow it, but they eventually learned by trial and error to find the hidden worm (Etienne, 1973; but see Regolin, Vallortigara, & Zanforlin, 1995). As in tests of other abstract concepts, immediate accurate performance in a novel situation is necessary to rule out simple stimulus generalization of previously reinforced behaviors (Doré & Dumas, 1987).

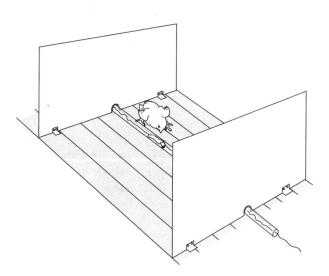

Figure B11.3. Test of object permanence for young chicks. Chicks do not spontaneously search for the mealworm behind the screen under which it disappears, but they eventually learn to do so. Redrawn from Etienne (1973) with permission.

Box 11.3. (*continued*)

A variety of species of birds and mammals have been tested to see what stage of object permanence they are capable of achieving (Doré & Dumas, 1987). Among birds, pigeons behave like Etienne's chicks, but mynahs immediately search for disappearing grapes in a novel situation (Plowright, Reid, & Kilian, 1998). Parrots search for invisibly displaced objects, a behavior characteristic of Piaget's stage 6 also seen in chimpanzees and other great apes (Pepperberg, Willner, & Gravitz, 1997). Domestic cats have been tested extensively by Doré, Dumas, and their colleagues (Dumas, 1992; Fiset & Doré, 1996; Goulet, Doré, & Rousseau, 1994). A predator like a cat that stalks moving prey might be expected to be skilled at finding prey that have hidden themselves. This proves to be the case in laboratory tests, but it usually depends on the cat seeing the displacement. Recently, however, this research, as well as research with other species (Plowright, Reid, & Kilian, 1998), has moved away from the tricky question of what animals believe about hidden objects to the likely more productive approach of studying search for disappearing objects as a task that taps working memory for the object's last location (e.g., Doré, Fiset, Goulet, Dumas, & Gagnon, 1996). In this approach, the focus is on whether and how the animal finds hidden objects and how this ability develops, not on whether or not the animal "passes" one anthropomorphic test or another.

11.3.4 Summary

What emerges from the controversy surrounding the extent and meaning of species differences in behavior in front of mirrors? It seems fair to say that the more extravagant claims for self-concept in chimpanzees have not been upheld. Some of them cannot be, in principle. The critics have stimulated more detailed analyses of what is going on when chimpanzees are confronted with mirrors, but it is not clear that we yet completely understand what is going on when an animal shows mirror-guided body inspection and why that behavior develops in some species and not others.

Although animals in the wild may occasionally see their reflections in pools of water, it is not clear that how they behave toward them has much adaptive significance. Normal associative learning could probably ensure that they don't confuse a reflected animal with the real thing and go plunging in after it. Although some intriguing connections have been made between mirror-guided body inspection and other aspects of cognition, it is not clear that watching animals' behavior in front of mirrors is the best way to see reflections of any fundamental cognitive processes.

11.4 Theory of Mind

11.4.1 What Is a Theory of Mind?

Like research on behavior in front of mirrors, research on theory of mind stems from a single innovative article (Premack & Woodruff, 1978) that has

inspired work in child development and primatology, in both the field and the laboratory. As introduced by Premack and Woodruff (1978), having a *theory of mind* means imputing mental states to oneself and others. Monkey A has a theory of mind if she eats a banana while out of monkey B's sight because she believes B wants the banana and will take it if he sees her eating it. If she does so only because eating bananas near B in the past has resulted in B's snatching the banana, her behavior is not based on a theory of mind but on associative learning. Theory of mind is evident not only in intentional deception but also in using others to gain information by imputing knowledge or belief to them, switching roles, and communicating with intent to inform, among other ways. In terms of the classification of intentional states, theory of mind implies second-order intentionality.

The basic issue in this area is how to distinguish responding to others' behavior from responding to others' mental states. As Premack and Woodruff (1978) put it, "Is the chimpanzee a behaviorist or a mentalist?" But the key to incisive research here is the realization that it is impossible to be only a mentalist. Inferences about mental states are based on behavior: we infer that B wants bananas not only because he looks avidly at A's banana, but also because he eats bananas whenever possible, he climbs tall trees to get bananas, and so on. The situation is exactly the same as that facing motivation theorists deciding, for example, when to describe a rat as thirsty as opposed to merely drinking in response to external stimuli (Whiten, 1996). In the traditional language of experimental psychology, a theory of mind or a motivational state is an intervening variable. The animal as psychologist and the human as animal psychologist have the same problem (Whiten, 1994, 1996). It becomes defensible to infer such a variable if behavior can be described more economically and predicted more effectively by doing so than by not doing so (figure 11.9). Thus, we cannot tell if monkey A is imputing desire and belief to B if all we observe is A concealing bananas from B. An animal that has a theory of mind should act appropriately in a variety of situations, including physically novel ones where simple stimulus generalization from past learning will not work. Such a device might be expected to evolve if it permits more fitness-increasing generalization from one social situation to another than does a set of associations (Seyfarth & Cheney, 1994; see section 11.5). For instance, seeing B climb tall trees for bananas and snatch bananas from others gives A the associationist no grounds to fear B as a banana thief because she cannot generalize from those physical situations to one in which B is watching when she is eating a banana. But if she infers from B's behavior that he wants bananas, she can infer that he will want her banana (figure 11.10).

If a theory of mind is a device that allows its possessor economically to encode information and generalize about others' behavior, it follows that any attempt to assess theory of mind in nonverbal organisms must use more than one behavioral test. Heyes (1993b) has called this method *triangulation* because it is designed to point to the same conclusion from different metaphorical angles. In triangulation, an animal trained in one set of conditions is tested in conditions that are conceptually but not physically similar. This

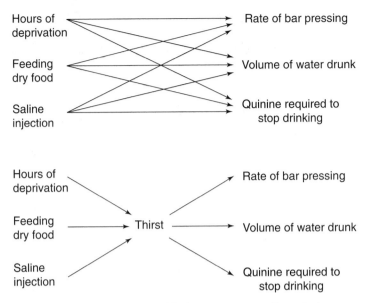

Figure 11.9. *Thirst* as an intervening variable that summarizes efficiently the pairwise relationships among each of three independent variables and three kinds of behavioral observations. If only, say, deprivation and rate of bar pressing had been looked at, the inference of a mediating internal state would complicate rather than simplify matters. Redrawn from Miller (1959) with permission.

makes it difficult for the animal to solve the new task by associative learning plus stimulus generalization. For instance, in their original article Premack and Woodruff (1978) described a series of tests of whether the chimpanzee Sarah imputed intentions to humans. Sarah, a very special animal with more than 10 years' experience in laboratory tests of cognition, watched short videos in which an actor was thwarted in accomplishing a goal like reaching a banana outside a cage, plugging in a heater, or washing a floor with a hose. The video was stopped and Sarah was allowed to choose between two photographs, one showing the actor about to reach the goal and one not. For instance, the actor might be picking up a long stick to reach the bananas or a short one, connecting an intact or a broken hose to a tap. More often than not, Sarah chose the picture showing the action and/or object appropriate to the goal, as if she imputed desires and beliefs to the actor. The fact that she did this in a variety of physically different situations is consistent with behavior arising from a theory of mind. An alternative "chimpanzee as behaviorist" account is that in each case she chose the picture that completed a familiar sequence. Because she had extensive experience watching people do all sorts of everyday tasks, that possibility could not be ruled out. Indeed, Premack and Woodruff's (1978) article was just the opening chapter in a continuing scientific detective story (Premack, 1988; see Carruthers & Smith, 1996; Povinelli, 1996, for reviews of further developments). Its main function was to for-

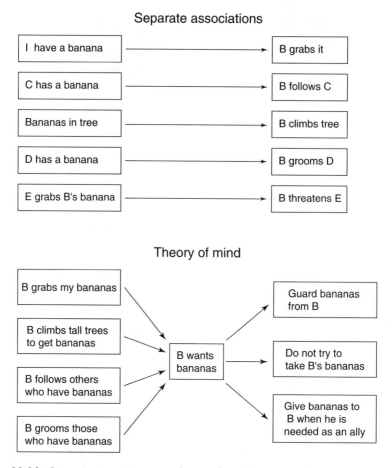

Figure 11.10. Separate associations vs. theory of mind as ways of storing and acting on information about another animal's behavior. Modified from Whiten (1994) with permission.

mulate the concept of theory of mind, raise the question of whether nonhumans have one, and suggest a variety of situations in which theory of mind might be tested.

11.4.2 Detecting Knowledge vs. Ignorance in Others

Premack and Woodruff sketched several methods for testing whether a creature's theory of mind extends to imputing knowledge and ignorance to others, but researchers in child development reported the first relevant data (Wimmer & Perner, 1983). In what has become a popular kind of paradigm, a young child is introduced to a puppet or a person, say a puppet clown. The child and the clown watch as the experimenter hides a treat or a toy (figure 11.11): "Where is the teddy? . . . In the green box." Then the clown leaves the scene and the child alone sees the experimenter move the object: "Now where

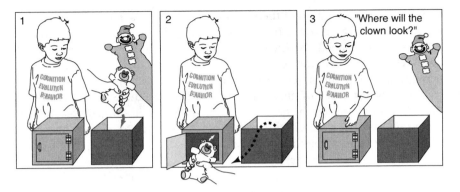

Figure 11.11. Steps in a typical test of theory of mind for 3- or 4-year-old children.

is the teddy? . . . In the purple box." Then the clown returns and the child is asked, "Where will he look for the teddy?" Surprisingly, until they are about 4 years old, children predict that the ignorant stooge will look where they themselves know the object is, as if they cannot separate their own representation of the situation from another's: "He will look in the purple box." This general type of finding appears in a variety of situations, and has stimulated much research and theorizing about the young child's theory of mind and how it develops (cf. Carruthers & Smith, 1996).

One way to test whether, like 4-year-olds, nonverbal organisms appreciate that seeing leads to knowing is to give them the choice of using information provided by two informants, one of whom has been observed getting access to that information while the other has not (Premack, 1988). Povinelli and his colleagues used a test of this kind with chimpanzees, rhesus monkeys, and children (Povinelli & deBlois, 1992; Povinelli, Nelson, & Boysen, 1990; Povinelli, Parks, & Novak, 1991). In the experiment with chimpanzees (Povinelli et al., 1990), there were four food containers, each provided with a handle that the animal could pull to get the food. As each trial began, the containers were hidden behind a screen, and the animal watched as one experimenter baited a single container in view of a confederate (the Knower), while a second confederate (the Guesser) was out of the room. Then the Guesser returned, and Knower and Guesser each pointed to a container as the chimpanzee was allowed to make a choice. A creature whose theory of mind encompasses the understanding that seeing conveys knowledge would obviously choose (correctly, in this case) the container indicated by the Knower, whereas one that does not would choose randomly. In fact, all four chimpanzees tested by Povinelli et al. (1990) chose the container indicated by the Knower significantly more often than that indicated by the Guesser, at least some of the time. However, the procedure just described went on for 300 trials, so the animals had plenty of opportunity to learn a conditional discrimination based on being rewarded for choosing the person who had been in the room when the container was baited. And, in accord with such an associationist interpretation of their behavior, the animals' tendency to choose the Knower increased across trials. This is clearly a case where triangulation is called for, and indeed, Povinelli et al. (1990) concluded their study with a novel test. Now both Knower and Guesser were in the room when the container was baited, but the Guesser had a paper bag over his head. Over all 30 trials of this test, three of the chimpanzees still chose the Knower. However, they chose randomly on the first two such trials (Povinelli, 1994), a result more consistent with the conclusion that they quickly learned to choose the person who had not worn a bag than with behavior based on knowledge attribution.

If the chimpanzees' behavior in such tests is based on associative learning, then the failure of monkeys to learn to choose the Knower more often than the Guesser after 400 trials in a similar experiment (Povinelli et al., 1991) is especially puzzling, since the monkeys should have been able to learn, too. In Povinelli et al.'s (1991) experiment with monkeys, the Knower even wore a red hat to make him more discriminable from the Guesser. However, the results of further trials with one monkey suggested that placing the cue on the Knower's hand, so it was close to the reward, would allow the monkeys to learn. At this stage, one might begin to wonder whether this sort of test is, in fact, a good test for knowledge attribution in children, but it does seem to be, as witnessed by the fact that more 4-year-olds than 3-year-olds consistently choose the Knower in a similar procedure (Povinelli & deBlois, 1992). One might also begin to worry that these experiments seem to be testing monkeys' and chimpanzees' theory of the *human* mind. Perhaps the animals would be sensitive to the states of knowledge of conspecifics in naturalistic situations. One investigation of this possibility was carried out by Cheney and Seyfarth (1990a) using Japanese and rhesus macaque mothers and their infants. Mothers watched from the side of an arena while a technician either hid pieces of apple there or brandished a net for catching monkeys and then hid in the arena. Half the mothers were together with their young offspring while watching; for the other half, the offspring was separated from her and from the arena by an opaque partition. If monkeys have a theory of mind, this latter group of mothers might be expected to behave in such a way as to inform their offspring about the presence of the food or the "predator." However, although the ignorant young monkeys behaved very differently from the knowledgeable ones, their mothers did not. These findings are consistent with the results of Povinelli et al.'s less naturalistic test and with other evidence reviewed in chapter 12 that monkeys' communicative behavior is not sensitive to the audience's need for information.

To summarize, then, tests of theory of mind based on seeing whether an animal can discriminate a knowledgeable from an ignorant individual provide no evidence that monkeys can do so, and the data for chimpanzees can be explained by associative learning as well as by a theory of mind. A recent experiment by Gagliardi, Kirkpatrick-Steger, Thomas, Allen, and Blumberg (1995) provides an instructive commentary on this line of work. They showed college students short videos depicting situations similar to those shown to the monkeys and chimpanzees in the Knower-Guesser experiments. The students were given 25 cents every time they responded correctly. However, for one group the Guesser, a person whose back was turned during the baiting procedure, aways pointed to the correct container. A second group was exposed to the natural contingency in which the Knower was correct. Even though associative learning was inconsistent with theory of mind for one group and consistent for the other, the two groups of students learned equally quickly to indicate the correct container. Since there can be no doubt that young adults have a theory of mind, these results serve as a reminder that subjects may use associative learning to solve a task even if they have the ability to use another solution. Placing the theory of mind solution in conflict with the associative solution or presenting subjects with a situation in which only theory of mind leads to efficient behavior might be a productive approach with other species.

11.4.3 Back to Square One: Detecting the Direction of Gaze

Attributing knowledge to the witness of an event implies three distinct cognitive activities. At the lowest level, it is necessary to discriminate the witness's gaze: was the witness actually looking at the event in question? Next, it is necessary to appreciate that looking at something implies attending to it, actually seeing it as opposed to just looking toward it. Finally, it is necessary to appreciate that seeing conveys knowledge, that what the witness saw yesterday she remembers today. This analysis implies that a theory of mind is not unitary but modular (Baron-Cohen, 1995). It suggests that a creature that does not correctly attribute knowledge or ignorance to others might lack a basic theory of mind module such as the ability to detect the direction of gaze or to appreciate seeing as attention. This approach to theory of mind has proved powerful in understanding the development of theory of mind in human infants and deficiencies in theory of mind in autistic children (Baron-Cohen, 1995). It also suggests that the behavior of nonhuman species should be analyzed more closely to see whether they differ from adult humans only in understanding seeing as knowledge or in some more basic theory of mind module. This is the approach taken by Povinelli and Eddy (1996a, 1996b, 1996c) in an exemplary series of experiments with young chimpanzees.

The subjects in these experiments were seven 4- to 5-year-old chimpanzees that had been born and raised in captivity in groups with other chimpanzees. Although they were used to people and had friendly relations with them, they were not "enculturated"—that is, they had not been raised like human children. All of Povinelli and Eddy's experiments exploited the animals' natural begging gesture, a gesture that humans readily interpret as intentional communication. They began by training the animals to enter a test room connected to their living area and gesture through a hole in a transparent Plexiglas wall toward an experimenter holding food on the other side (figure 11.12). The wall was provided with two holes, one on the left side and one on the right, and the experimenter was positioned in front of one or the other.

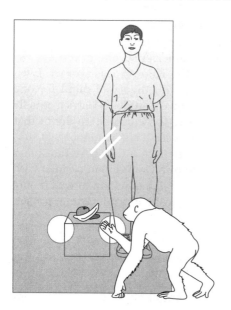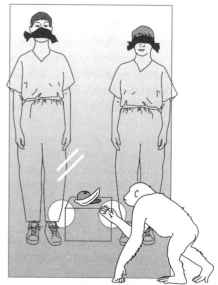

Figure 11.12. Setup for tests of theory of mind in chimpanzees. Left: Control condition. The animal is given the food for directing a begging gesture through the hole in front of the experimenter. Right: The animal will receive food for gesturing toward the experimenter that can see. After photographs in Povinelli and Preuss (1995) with permission.

The animal received the treat only for reaching through the hole closer to the experimenter. To be sure the animals were attending to what was being offered, occasional probe trials were administered in which one experimenter sat near each hole, one holding a block of wood and the other a food treat. Both experimenters looked straight ahead at the Plexiglas wall, not attempting to meet the chimpanzee's gaze. Once the animals discriminated very reliably between the two experimenters on the probe trials, Povinelli and Eddy started a series of tests in which both experimenters held out food but one could clearly see the chimpanzee, as before, whereas the other could not. For instance, the "nonattending" experimenter might be wearing a blindfold, have his hands or a cardboard screen over his eyes, or have his back to the chimpanzee. Controls for having something unusual on the face included the "attending" experimenter having a blindfold or hands over her mouth or a cardboard screen elsewhere near her face. All such tests were intermixed with normal trials and occasional probes offering a choice between a block of wood and food. The chimpanzee was always rewarded for begging from the experimenter who could see.

The surprising result of these experiments was that, in nearly every type of probe test, the chimpanzees gestured as often to the experimenter who could not see them as to the experimenter who could. This was despite the fact that the continuing regular trials and probes with the block of wood established that the animals still performed well in the basic task. The exception to random behavior in the probes occurred when one experimenter had her back to the animal. Here, the chimpanzees tended to choose the experimenter who was facing them. Even this result did not indicate an understanding of seeing as attention because when both experimenters turned their backs while one looked over her shoulder toward the subject, choice reverted to random. Over all trials of all kinds, however, the proportion of choices of the "attending" experimenter gradually crept above 50%, indicating that the chimpanzees were learning, perhaps to choose the person whose eyes were visible.

Povinelli and Eddy's conclusion, then, is that at least young chimpanzees do not understand seeing as attention but may learn through normal associative processes to direct behavior selectively to people who can see them. Perhaps predictably, this conclusion has not gone unchallenged. For instance, it appears to contradict reports that hand-raised chimpanzees respond appropriately to signs of people's attention in tests similar to Povinelli and Eddy's (Gomez, 1996). However, if chimpanzees can learn what behavior predicts rewarding responses from humans there is likely no real contradiction, since Gomez's animals had extensive close interactions with humans. Moreover, chimpanzees do respond to "body language" indicative of attention from humans (Povinelli & Eddy, 1996c). Similarly, reports (Gomez, 1996) that a young hand-reared gorilla learned to take people by the hand, lead them to a door she wanted opened, and move their hands toward the latch, while they are appealing, need not indicate that the gorilla understood the states of attention underlying her helpers' behavior.

Criticisms have also been directed at the nature of Povinelli and Eddy's (1996a) tests. For instance, maybe the animals gesturing toward the unseeing experimenters were trying to get their attention: the experimenters were behaving stupidly here, not the chimpanzees (Smith, 1996). Another possible explanation for Povinelli and Eddy's negative results is that their animals were not old enough to have developed a theory of mind. When chimpanzees do attain landmarks in cognitive development comparable to those in humans, they do so more slowly (Parker, 1996), so this possibility cannot be completely ruled out. Clearly, further tests with older animals would be very informative. Maybe chimpanzees have a theory of mind that includes understanding the intentionality of seeing, but it does not generalize to people. However, if chimpanzees have any aspect of a human theory of mind, it likely existed in a common ancestor to chimpanzees and humans. Humans readily generalize their "mindreading" tendencies to reading the minds of other species. (Indeed, Povinelli and Eddy's results indicate that they sometimes do so too readily.) It would be odd if chimpanzees had some of the same abilities but did not generalize them (Povinelli & Eddy, 1996a).

If young chimpanzees do not understand seeing as attention, what, if anything, do they respond to in another creature's gaze? Animals of many species respond to correlates of the the direction of another's gaze (see box 11.2), and this includes chimpanzees. For instance, when Povinelli and Eddy's animals were confronted with an experimenter looking at a spot on the wall behind them, they turned to look at it too. They also behaved appropriately when confronted with someone looking at a location they could not see directly, peering around a partition to get a view of it (Povinelli & Eddy, 1996b). This research is still going on and will doubtless stimulate further cycles of controversy and experiment for some time to come. A promising new approach to testing whether or not an animal follows the direction of gaze of an individual of its own species has been tried with rhesus monkeys. The subject views a video of a conspecific seated between two identical objects and looking toward one of them. Eye movement recordings show that the subject monkeys look more at the object apparently being attended to by the monkey on the video—that is, they not only follow the video monkey's gaze but appear to attend to the same object (Emery, Lorincz, Perrett, Oram, & Baker, 1997).

11.4.4 Deception

Functional deception is widespread in animals and plants. Mimicry and crypsis, as in the pattern matching flounder described in chapter 2, evidently evolved because their possessors fooled potential predators or pollinators into treating them like something they were not. However, mimicry and crypsis are relatively fixed species-typical characteristics that do not demand explanation in terms of intentional deception, especially not when they occur in plants. Other examples of functional deception are discussed in chapter 12 when we consider the idea that some communicative behaviors have evolved to convey false information. The plover's broken-wing display is a functionally deceptive behavior, but as we have seen there is little if any convincing evidence that it reflects an intention to lead intruders away. In any case, such behavior on the part of plovers is apparently specific to the domain of predators approaching the nest. Here we will be concerned with deceptive behavior possibly reflecting not only first-order but also second-order intentionality. That is, when monkey A hid the banana from monkey B, might she have done so because she wanted B to believe she did not have a banana?

The idea that monkeys and apes might be practicing deception on others in their social groups has attracted a good deal of attention from primatologists (Byrne, 1995; Quiatt & Reynolds, 1993), but the primary support for it comes from a large collection of anecdotes (Whiten & Byrne, 1988). In some of these anecdotes a subordinate animal appears to conceal sexual behavior or close social contact with others from a dominant animal by moving behind a rock or other obstruction as if able to interpret the situation from the visual perspective of the feared dominant (figure 11.13). In other cases, an animal appears to conceal its intentions from the target of its deception, approaching in a friendly manner and then suddenly attacking or snatching food. For example, in one much-discussed anecdote, a female baboon approached a male that was holding a desirable antelope carcass and began to groom him. When he relaxed and lolled back under her attentions, she snatched the meat and ran off with it (Jolly, 1985, quoted in Heyes, 1994b, p. 294). In still other cases, a subordinate animal knows the location of hidden food, but when a

Figure 11.13. Cartoon of the representations that might be implied by imputing intentional deception to a subordinate baboon that conceals its activities from a dominant. Here second-order intentionality is depicted: the subordinate, on the right, wants the dominant to believe that there is no other baboon behind the rock. After Byrne (1995) with permission.

rival is nearby it moves away from the food or appears to attend to something else, as if trying to distract the rival's attention so as to get all the food for itself.

These reports suffer from all the usual problems with anecdotes (Heyes, 1993b; Quiatt & Reynolds, 1993; see section 10.2.5). Apparently deceptive behavior could occur simply by chance. For instance, the subordinate baboon need not have planned to copulate out of sight of the dominant but just happened to be behind the rock when the opportunity for copulation arose. It is usually impossible to tell whether functionally deceptive behavior in the field reflects situation-specific learning about behavioral contingencies or inferences by the perpetrator about intentional states of its victim. A stable group of long-lived animals provides many opportunities for its members to learn from interactions with each other. The field worker witnessing one incident is unlikely to have access to all the relevant past history of the individuals involved. The problem of collecting adequate evidence for deception from free-living animals is exacerbated because by definition deception must be rare. If the baboon that snatched the antelope carcass always performed unfriendly acts after grooming, her troop mates would soon learn to avoid her. The great mass of anecdotes that has been collected and classified (Whiten & Byrne, 1988) includes reports from many different observers about many individuals of many species. A single individual practicing different kinds of deceptive acts might be convincing evidence of a theory of mind, but this is not the same thing as different acts by different individuals (Heyes, 1994b).

Experimental studies of deception are few. In one, the chimpanzee Sarah was exposed to a very contrived situation with a "good" and "bad" trainer to see if she would attempt to deceive the "bad" one (Premack, 1988). Two studies with captive monkeys show how the situations described in anecdotes from the field can be converted into controlled tests. Coussi-Korbel (1994) observed a captive group of seven mangabeys in a large enclosure with numerous boxes for hiding food. The two animals of most interest in her study were Boss, the dominant male, and Rapide, a juvenile male. Boss would threaten the other monkeys and displace them from baited food boxes if he didn't get there first. In baseline trials, all the monkeys could see the food being hidden and were then allowed to find it. Boss and Rapide both went directly toward the food in most of these trials, but Boss generally got much of it. In the next series of trials, peanuts were hidden in two of the boxes while Rapide watched and the rest of the group was confined out of sight. When all the animals were released into the enclosure shortly afterwards, Rapide went straight to the food on the first trial, with Boss close behind him, but from trial 2 of this condition onward, Rapide often began by going away from the food and then doubling back to a baited box after Boss had begun to search in other boxes. In later trials when Boss could also see the peanuts being hidden, Rapide no longer displayed this functionally deceptive behavior but again went straight to the food.

These observations, like earlier observations on chimpanzees by Menzel (1978), document the development of deceptive behavior, but they are far from conclusively showing that it reflects a theory of mind on the part of the deceiver. Moreover, like most anecdotes from the field, they deal with only one individual. Rapide's behavior of going only indirectly toward the food did not appear at once but developed over the first few trials. One can emphasize the fact that it did not appear without experience in the situation (Coussi-Korbel, 1994) or the fact that rather little experience was required (Byrne, 1995). There is no way of knowing whether Rapid's behavior reflected insight into Boss's intentions because there was no attempt at triangulation — that is, testing whether Rapide would lead Boss away from a goal in a physically novel situation at the first opportunity.

Kummer, Anzenberger, and Hemelrijk (1996) did incorporate such a test into their clever study of hiding behavior in captive long-tailed macaques (*Macaca fascicularis*). This experiment was an attempt to capture in a controlled situation the behavior of hiding one's activities from potentially threatening individuals. Long-tailed macaques were tested individually in a large cage where they could drink juice from either of two nipples at the front of the cage (figure 11.14). An experimenter standing just outside the cage threatened the occupant by staring and making a harsh sound resembling a long-tailed macaque threat vocalization whenever the monkey tried to drink. If the monkey still approached a nipple, the experimenter picked up a water hose used to chase monkeys into their cages. The monkeys could drink in peace when the experimenter's back was turned. Periods of two or three minutes with the experimenter looking and threatening alternated with equivalent periods in which he was not looking. Seven monkeys learned to do at least 90%

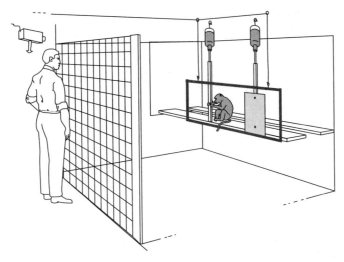

Figure 11.14. Setup for a test of deception in long-tailed macaques. Here the experimenter is looking at the monkey, which is drinking from an exposed position even though a hiding place is available behind the screen on the right. While the monkeys were being trained to avoid drinking within sight of the experimenter, the frame holding the screen (black rectangle) was kept lowered. Redrawn from Kummer et al. (1996) with permission.

of their drinking when the experimenter was not looking and needed only minimal threats to stop when the experimenter was looking. These animals then had a transfer test in which an opaque screen was raised in front of one of the juice nipples while the other nipple remained in the experimenter's view (figure 11.14). Would they attempt to deceive the experimenter by drinking behind the screen when he was looking? This question was clearly answered in the negative. The monkeys drank from the nipple behind the screen about half the time on average whether the experimenter was looking or not.

Interestingly, when macaques of the same species were provided with hiding places in their home enclosure, subordinate animals appeared to use them to conceal copulations from dominants (Gygax, 1995). There are obviously many differences between the situations confronting the animals in these two studies. Gygax's (1995) study was carried out over a considerable period of time, over which, as he points out, the monkeys could have learned by trial and error to use the hiding places. On the other hand, Kummer at al.'s (1996) study was less "natural" since it involved threat by a person rather than another macaque. Nevertheless, the subjects in that study did appear to treat the experimenter's threat as they would a macaque's. There are several other possible explanations of the different results of the two studies (Kummer et al., 1996), none of which can be completely ruled out without further research. Kummer et al.'s study is most important as a model experimental study of deception. Since chimpanzees have been suggested to have a theory of mind that monkeys lack, they would be good subjects for further studies of this kind. However, the data indicating that chimpanzees do not interpret gazing as attending predict that the results would be no different than these with macaques.

11.4.5 Do Other Species Have a Theory of Mind?

Our discussion of theory of mind began by saying that a creature with a theory of mind treats others as intentional beings, attributing to them knowledge, belief, wants, desires, and other intentional states. This description characterizes a possible theory of mind as a unitary psychological process from which flows recognizing oneself in mirrors, understanding when others are knowledgeable or ignorant, deceiving intentionally, taking another's point of view, imitating others' actions, and communicating with intent to inform, among other accomplishments. In the years since research on theory of mind began, however, it has become clear that theory of mind is better viewed as modular than unitary. Children develop the different skills attributed to a theory of mind at different times. For instance, they may understand that others have desires before they understand belief. Even the ability to appreciate another's point of view is itself modular (Baron-Cohen, 1995). Dissociations among different behaviors suggestive of theory of mind are also evident in nonhumans. For instance, rats and parrots apparently imitate (see chapter 10), but so far they have shown no evidence of self-recognition in mirrors. Thus, when it comes to considering the evolution of theory of mind, the question is not whether or not a particular species has a theory of mind but what aspects of theory of mind, if any, it has. Chimpanzees, for example, may have a weak or low-level theory of mind, attributing desire but not belief to others (Gomez, 1996; Premack & Woodruff, 1978; Whiten, 1996). Consistent with this suggestion, the Knower-Guesser experiments provide no evidence that chimpanzees understand others' knowledge. Similarly thorough investigations of the possible attribution of desire have yet to be reported. It has been suggested that a theory of mind is possible only with language (Smith, 1996). If A could tell us in words why she is hiding the banana from B, we would know whether she believed he wanted it or just knew that she would lose the banana if B could see it. Verbal labels for others' states of mind may be what allows information about their beliefs, desires, intentions, and so on to be transferred from one situation to another. However, in considering this possibility, one has to wonder where the inferences being so labeled came from in the first place (Whiten, 1996).

As this section has indicated, nearly all the research on theory of mind in nonhuman species has been done with monkeys and apes, primarily chimpanzees. Here, just as with the research on imitation and teaching reviewed in chapter 10, enthusiastic acceptance of the humanlike abilities suggested by field workers' anecdotes has given way to profound scepticism on the part of experimentalists. Such scepticism is still resisted in some quarters, especially by field workers who point out how contrived and "unnatural" are most tests of theory of mind in the laboratory (van Hooff, 1994; de Waal, 1991). It may always be possible to find a "bottom of the barrel, killjoy explanation" (Dennett, 1983) for any behavior. Some people have suggested that the most parsimonious alternative for species with a recent common ancestor to humans may be the more cognitively complex one—that is, chimpanzees should be assumed to be like humans unless the data unambiguously indicate otherwise (de Waal, 1991). Debate on such controversial issues is not likely to reach a conclusion any time soon (possible new directions are discussed by Heyes, 1998; Tomasello & Call, 1997). Some progress may be made by looking at field data and by considering why a theory of mind might evolve. The latter issue is addressed by the social theory of intellect, discussed next.

11.5 The Social Theory of Intellect and Evolutionary Psychology

11.5.1 The Social Theory of Intellect

In the 1960s and '70s, several people independently proposed that unique social conditions in primate social groups drove the evolution of general problem-solving ability. The impetus for this *social theory of intellect* came in part from the conclusion that monkeys and apes display qualitatively different abilities from other species in traditional comparative studies of concept formation, learning set, discrimination reversal, and the like. As we have seen in chapters 5 and 6, this conclusion should now be considered questionable because more recent research shows that, for example, some birds can perform like monkeys on such tests and that there may even be dramatic differences in performance within a species when the sensory features of the task are varied. Any social selection pressures that are supposed to account for primates' apparently unique intellectual abilities might well be present in highly social species of other genera, too.

The theory that social demands drive the evolution of general problem-solving abilities assumes that intelligence is general rather than modular. But the social theory of intellect is also compatible with the possibility that cognitive modules might originate for processing restricted sorts of information, such as those inherent in social relationships, and gradually become capable of processing other sorts of information, for instance, information about physical relationships (Rozin, 1976). Variations from extreme modularity to complete accessibility lead to a continuum of hypotheses about how social demands influence the evolution of cognition. As originally proposed by Jolly (1966) and Humphrey (1976), the social theory of intellect assumes that cognitive modularity is low and accessibility of cognitive adaptations for social life to problems with nonsocial content is high. Thus, the original version of the social theory of intellect implies that complex social organization and general problem-solving ability go together, while an extreme modular view implies they are independent. The intermediate possibility is that complex social cognition evolved first and the problem-solving abilities it entailed gradually became accessible in other realms, such as foraging or tool using. In principle, comparative and phylogenetic data can distinguish among these possibilities. For instance, lemurs have a complex social organization but perform more poorly on tests of physical intelligence than Old World monkeys (Jolly, 1966). Since lemurs are prosimians, closer to ancestral primates than monkeys, this comparison is consistent with the view that social intelligence preceded the evolution of equivalent physical intelligence.

An often-proposed alternative to the social theory of intellect might be called the foraging theory of intellect. For instance, temporal and spatial variation in a species' food supply might drive the evolution of superior spatial and temporal cognition (e.g., Milton, 1988). Tropical forests are a complex mosiac of hundreds or thousands of tree species, each with its own schedule of fruit and flower production. Because fruits are typically available for a shorter time than leaves, fruit-eating species appear to be faced with a harder environmental tracking problem than leaf-eating species. A primate troop of a given size needs a larger home range if they eat fruit than leaves since at any given time there may be less food available in it. The foraging theory of intellect therefore predicts that fruit eaters should show evidence of greater generalized learning ability than leaf eaters. Comparison of howler monkeys (leaf eaters) and spider monkeys (fruit eaters) on Barro Colorado Island yields evidence consistent with this hypothesis (Milton, 1988). More broadly based evidence that fruit vs. leaf eating is correlated with general cognitive differences comes from comparative data on brain size. In bats, rodents, and primates, fruit-eating species have heavier brains relative to their body weights than their leaf-eating relatives (Harvey & Krebs, 1990). Such evidence from three different groups of mammals is quite compelling. Nevertheless, some possible confounding factors should be recognized, especially if relatively few species are being compared (Byrne, 1995, chap. 14). For instance, it takes a longer gut to digest leaves than fruits, so a difference in brain:body ratios could arise because leaf eaters have relatively big bodies rather than relatively small brains. In species dependent on food sources that require more learning, the young may remain dependent on their natal social group for longer periods and thereby have more complex social relationships and/or increased opportunity for social learning. These and other factors do not seem to be important in these large-scale correlations (Harvey & Krebs, 1990). But what does overall brain size mean? It is a convenient standard measure on which to compare species, but specific cognitive demands are likely to be most strongly reflected in specific areas of the brain (chapter 1; see also Preuss, 1995). We need to know more about what brain areas are involved in learning about the physical vs. social environments and whether these are the same or different before neuroanatomical comparisons can be used as evidence for or against the social theory of intellect.

11.5.2 Solving Social Problems

So far we have taken for granted that living in a social group presents distinctive cognitive problems. But what do animals need to learn and remember about their social companions? Do any of these tasks require a distinctive *form* of cognition, as opposed to a distinctive social *use* of some more general cognitive ability?

Observations of primates in free-ranging social groups have suggested much about their social knowledge (see Byrne, 1995; Cheney & Seyfarth, 1990b; Kummer, 1995). In long-lasting, stable social groups, individuals treat one another differently depending on sex, age, dominance status, and relatedness to themselves and others. Knowledge of other individuals may be expressed in grooming partnerships and in the formation of alliances in aggressive interactions. In a few cases, intuitions about what the animals know have been put to the test in clever ways. For instance, we saw in chapter 5 how Dasser (1988a) used an operant category learning paradigm to test whether Java monkeys had a concept of the relationship *mother-offspring*. Monkeys' knowledge of social relationships has been tested extensively in the field by Cheney and Seyfarth (e.g., 1990b). Like Java monkeys, the vervets they studied show evidence of associating particular infants with their mothers. When vervets hear the cries of a familiar but temporarily unseen infant broadcast from a concealed speaker, they are more likely to look toward that infant's mother than toward some other monkey. Vervets also show various sorts of evidence that they are sensitive to more remote kinship relationships among troop members. For instance, a monkey that has recently been the subject of aggression is more likely to behave aggressively toward a relative of its attacker than toward an unrelated monkey. However, while all these observations reveal social knowledge, the processes by which it is acquired need not be specifically social. Mothers and infants are normally seen together and thereby may become associated in the minds of their companions. Relatives may look alike or become associated through proximity, promoting generalization from one to another.

Knowing who belongs with whom or what kind of behavior to expect from A as opposed to B may be explicable by simple associative learning, but animals sometimes seem to exhibit more complex forms of social knowledge. An ability to categorize observed interactions among specific individuals in terms of kinds of social relationships such as mother-offspring, ally, and so on might be especially valuable in species in which each individual repeatedly interacts with many others. Classifying interactions in terms of relationships, as opposed to brute force memorization, would enable ready generalization to completely new individuals as groups change, merge with other groups, and so on (Seyfarth & Cheney, 1994). A pioneer in designing experiments to tap such knowledge was the Swiss ethologist Hans Kummer (see Kummer, 1995), working with hamadryas baboons (*Papio hamadryas*) in Ethiopia. Hamadryas baboons live in large multi-male troops in which adult males have harems of females. Large numbers of males with their females and offspring gather to sleep and rest each day, but the powerful males seldom if ever appear to fight over access to females. One male's respect for another's possession of a female arises from observing the two interacting in a friendly manner, as Bachmann and Kummer (1980) showed in the experiment depicted in figure 11.15. The sub-

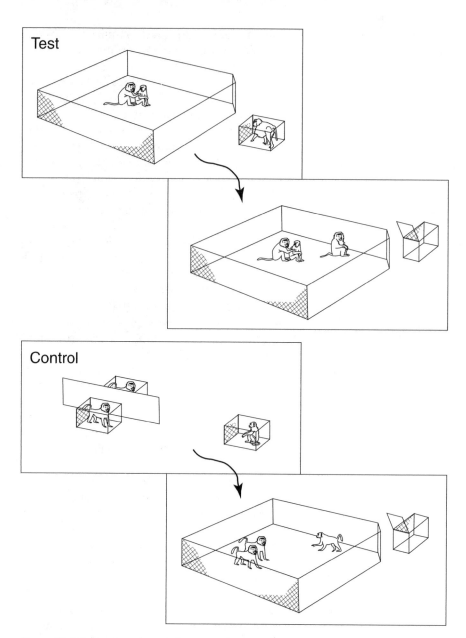

Figure 11.15. Setup and results for a test of male baboons' respect for another male's possession of a female. Redrawn from Kummer (1995) with permission.

jects were pairs of males from the same troop and females unfamiliar to them. What would the males do when placed together with a female if (a) one had previously seen the other interacting in a friendly manner with the female or if (b) they had both seen the female before but neither had interacted with her? In the first case, as little as 15 minutes observing the pair inhibited any attempt by the second male to interact with the "married" female and her partner. When introduced into the enclosure with them, he sat in the corner with his back turned and groomed himself or looked at the sky or into the bushes. In the control condition, however, both males tried to interact with the female and occasionally fought over her.

More subtle social knowledge—what could be referred to as causal reasoning in the social domain—was demonstrated by Cheney, Seyfarth, and Silk (1995) in females of another species of baboon (*Papio cyanocephalus*). Baboon females are very interested in each other's babies, as evidenced by the fact that one female will approach another who is holding an infant and attempt to hold the baby herself. When a dominant female approaches a subordinate, the dominant will often emit a grunt vocalization, and the subordinate may emit a fear bark. If instead a subordinate approaches a dominant, this sequence of vocalizations is never heard. Dominants do not give fear barks to more subordinate individuals. Cheney et al.'s experiment tested whether baboons understand the causal relationship between status of the approaching, grunting female and fear barking by the female being approached. They made use of the fact that many species of primates recognize their social companions by voice and react to sounds broadcast in the field by looking longer toward the source of anomalous or unfamiliar sounds than to the source of familiar ones. This information allowed Cheney et al. to test baboons' knowledge of social causation by comparing their reactions to causally consistent and inconsistent sequences of grunts and fear barks (figure 11.16). In inconsistent sequences, a grunt by a subordinate individual, say F, was followed by the fear bark of a female dominant to her, say C. A consistent sequence matched to this example would also contain F's grunt followed by C's fear bark, but in this case a grunt by an individual dominant to C, say A, followed C's fear bark. This sequence was causally consistent because C's fear bark could be caused by the approach of A. The consistent sequence contained more vocalizations, so it might be expected to be more salient and attract more looking than an inconsistent, or impossible, sequence.

Matched sets of consistent and inconsistent sequences were composed of vocalizations from a number of different troop members and played to subjects when the recorded individuals were out of sight. Each subject heard a consistent sequence on one occasion and an inconsistent sequence on another occasion. On average, subjects looked toward the speaker longer when an inconsistent sequence was played. Because the stimuli used were matched for possibly confounding features like the specific vocalizations they contained, these results seem to show that the baboons do recognize a kind of social causation in the sequences of grunts and fear barks. In order to do so, they need to recognize other individuals' calls and dominance ranks and to

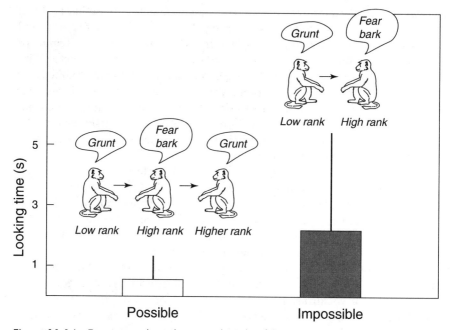

Figure 11.16. Experimental conditions and results of the experiment on social causal reasoning baboons. After Hauser (1996) with permission; data from Cheney et al. (1995) redrawn with permission.

know in some sense that fear barks only result from the approach of a dominant toward a less dominant animal. Another possibility, however, is that the subjects had simply heard the specific consistent sequence more often than the inconsistent sequence in the past. It would be difficult for a study of this kind to escape from such an objection, since it is only through exposure to the interactions of other individuals that a subject monkey would come to know their relative dominance ranks, and in the course of such exposure the individuals being learned about would almost certainly be interacting vocally, grunting and barking, in a way consistent with their ranks.

11.5.3 Comparing Social and Nonsocial Intelligence

The social theory of intellect implies not simply that animals have social intelligence but also that physical intelligence reflects mechanisms evolved to deal with social problems. Testing this notion requires comparing how animals solve social and physical problems with the same logical structure. If social intelligence is more highly developed than and incompletely accessible to physical intelligence, social problems should be solved more quickly or accurately than parallel physical problems. There are few examples of social problems that have a parallel in the physical domain. Transitive inference is one. In social groups with a linear dominance hierarchy, dominance relations form a transitive sequence: if A is dominant to B and B is dominant to C, then A will be dominant to C. Animals in such social groups must have to learn dominance relationships, but do they learn them more readily than the sort of physical transitive inference problems described in box 5.3? Clearly this question would be very difficult to answer because it assumes that physical and social problems can be equated for familiarity, motivation to perform correctly, salience of their contents, and so on. As discussed in box 5.3, pigeons solve physical transitive inference problems by associative value transfer whereas monkeys use a specifically inferential mechanism (see also box 8.1). This species difference could reflect a difference in demands for transitive inference in the social domain, but more species must be studied to find out.

Observations of vervet monkeys in the field suggest that they know much more about the social than the physical world (Cheney & Seyfarth, 1990b). Vervets seem to know all sorts of characteristics of individuals in their own and neighboring social groups—their voices, their relationships to self and others, where they are typically found—but their knowledge about other species in their environment seems to lack a similar degree of detail. For instance, although vervets are frightened of leopards, they show no evidence of alarm when encountering signs of a nearby leopard, such as a dead antelope hanging over a tree branch. Similarly, a vervet may have watched fearfully on many occasions as a snake slithered by, leaving a trail on dry ground, but show no apprehension on encountering a trail in the absence of a snake. In these cases, simple associative learning that might be expected does not seem to occur. Vervets appear to be good social psychologists but poor naturalists (Cheney & Seyfarth, 1985, 1990b). Once again, however, possible confounds such as greater familiarity or salience of social stimuli make it impossible to conclude that social and physical learning abilities differ, let alone in which direction. Similarly, one might suggest that baboons' subtle social reasoning is not matched by the physical reasoning ability of the tool-using capuchins described in chapter 10, but without careful within-species comparisons this is little more than speculation (Cheney, Seyfarth, & Silk, 1995).

Primates that form relatively large and stable social groups are usually assumed to have the most highly developed social cognition of any animals, so most discussions of the social theory of intellect focus on data from primates (see for example Dunbar, 1996). Long-term repeated interactions set the stage for individuals to learn one another's identity and to build up enduring altruistic or antagonistic relationships. But some nonprimate species also form long-lasting groups. These include elephants, social carnivores (e.g., wolves, lions), whales, and dolphins (see Cheney & Seyfarth, 1990b). In some bird species, such as pinyon jays, Florida scrub jays, and white-fronted bee eaters, individuals remain together for more than a year and develop complex and differentiated interactions with their companions. For instance, rather than dispersing and breeding on their own, young Florida scrub jays may stay with their parents and help to raise their younger siblings. Issues arising from the social theory of intellect have hardly begun to be addressed in nonprimates, but there are some interesting possibilities. For instance, among the

Table 11.2. The relationship between sociality and food storing in four species of corvids

		Reliance on Stored Food	
		low	high
Sociality (Relative Size of	low	scrub jay	Clark's nutcracker
Typical Group)	high	Mexican jay	pinyon jay

four species of food-storing corvids studied by Kamil, Balda, and their colleagues (see chapter 6), two are very reliant on stored food and two are less reliant. Within each of these pairs of species, one lives in social groups and the other does not (table 11.2). The social theory of intellect suggests that whereas pinyon jays and Clark's nutcrackers—the species most reliant on storing—perform better in tests of spatial memory than the other two species, pinyon jays and Mexican (or gray-breasted) jays—the more social species—should perform best on tests that tap social cognition (Balda, Kamil, & Bednekoff, 1996). Such tests might include the sort of fine visual discriminations required to learn individuals' identities.

11.5.4 Modularity and Humans' Reasoning Abilities

The largest body of evidence relevant to the social theory of intellect comes from studies of how people reason. This research is part of *evolutionary psychology*, the attempt to understand human cognition in terms of domain specific modules evolved to solve specific ecological problems that were important in early hominid society (Barkow, Cosmides, & Tooby, 1992; Cosmides & Tooby, 1994a, 1995). Evolutionary psychology has implications in all areas of psychology, but two kinds of findings have been taken as evidence for specifically social information processing that follows different rules from physical information processing. One of these was described in box 11.1. Even young infants identify certain very abstract kinds of motion as expressions of intentionality (i.e., as showing a kind of social causation). Other kinds of motion are identified with physical causality. Even with input as simple as two colored disks moving on a video screen, some patterns of interaction are perceived as social and intentional whereas others are not. Thus, people (and perhaps other species; Hauser, 1996) seem to divide the world into physical and social beings at a very primitive level of perception and development. This process may help to set the stage for other differences in processing social vs. nonsocial information.

In the last section we saw that comparing social to nonsocial cognition could be problematical because it is difficult to equate the input for such things as familiarity and salience and subjects' motivation to solve the tasks. Recent studies of how people solve the *Wason selection task* are largely free of this problem (see review by Cosmides & Tooby, 1992). As originally studied by the psychologist Peter Wason, this task requires people to look for viola-

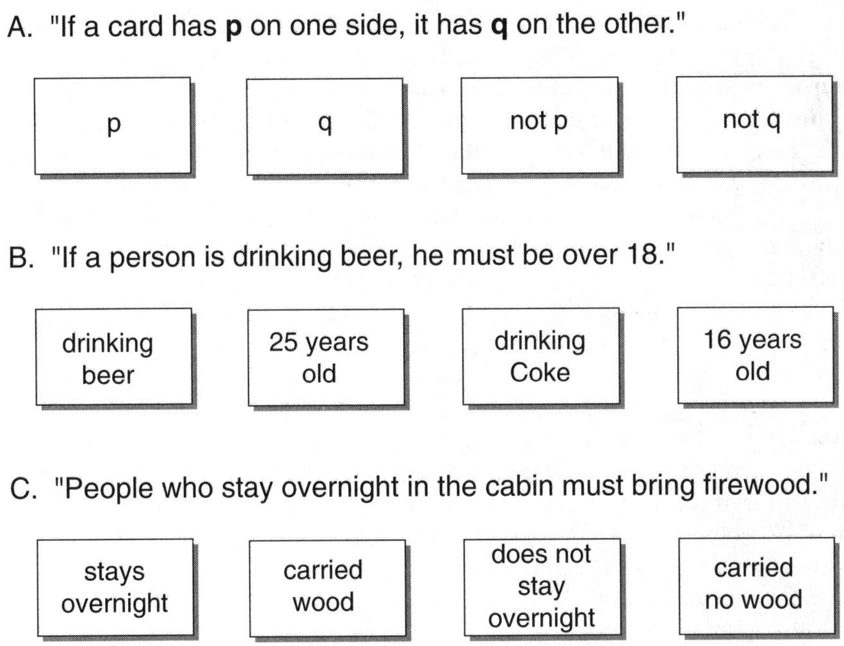

A. "If a card has **p** on one side, it has **q** on the other."

p	q	not p	not q

B. "If a person is drinking beer, he must be over 18."

drinking beer	25 years old	drinking Coke	16 years old

C. "People who stay overnight in the cabin must bring firewood."

stays overnight	carried wood	does not stay overnight	carried no wood

Figure 11.17. Three instantiations of the Wason selection task. In each case, the cards on the ends, and only those cards, need to be inspected to check the truth of the statement above them. A and B after Cosmides (1989) with permission.

tions of a logical rule of the form "If p, then q." In the most abstract version of this task, a subject would be given four cards with p's and q's as shown in figure 11.17A and asked which ones need to be turned over to detect violations of the rule, "If a card has p on one side, it has q on the other." Most people turn over the card with p on the front to see if it has q on the back. Very few turn over only the one necessary additional card, the one with *not q*. This same logical problem can be posed with less abstract content, but such familiar content doesn't always improve performance. An example of content that does elicit good performance is shown in figure 11.17B. As many as 75% of subjects can detect whether people are drinking illegally by turning over the correct cards. According to Cosmides and others (Cosmides & Tooby, 1992), reasoning ability evolved to detect cheaters on social contracts in early hominid society, and the drinking-age problem involves detecting violations of a social contract. Reciprocal altruism depends on participants obeying general rules of the form, "If you take a benefit, you pay a cost." For instance, "If I share my meat with you, you help me gather wood." Cheaters take the benefit without paying the cost—they satisfy the logical condition, "p and *not q*."

The view that reasoning in the Wason task reflects a cognitive adaptation for social exchange has been supported by the results of a series of clever experiments in which people are asked to reason about identical statements in a social context vs. another sort of context. To control for familiarity of content, Cosmides (1989) told Harvard students elaborate stories about fictitious tribes and their customs. When asked to solve the Wason task in this context, subjects were much more likely to give correct solutions when the basic "If p, then q" relation—for instance, "If a man eats cassava root, then he must have a tatoo on his face"—was framed as a social contract than when it was framed as a description of the customs or appearance of the fictitious tribe.

Solving the Wason task is facilitated specifically by a set to detect cheaters on a social contract rather than just by framing the problem as a social contract (figure 11.17C). Gigerenzer and Hug (1992) presented the same rule to two groups of subjects. In one, they were to imagine they were members of a Swiss mountain climbing club sent to enforce the club's rule that people staying overnight in a mountaintop hut had to bring their own firewood. Subjects in the other group were to imagine they were German mountain climbers visiting the Swiss mountaintop hut and trying to figure out whether the Swiss had the same rule about bringing firewood that they did. If framing a logical problem as a social contract simply facilitates clear thinking, the two groups should have performed the same. However, whereas a set to detect cheaters led to about 90% correct performance, people with a set to deduce the descriptive rule performed correctly only about 50% of the time.

Although the evolutionary psychologists' approach is basically the same as the approach to cognition taken in this book, it is still controversial when applied to human cognition (cf. Kacelnik & Krebs, 1997). Not surprisingly for a reasoning task that was already much studied before any evolutionary theorizing about it, some researchers claim that the data are most consistent with other explanations (e.g., Sperber, Cara & Girotto, 1995; Liberman & Klar, 1996). Nevertheless, the approach to human reasoning exemplified by studies of the Wason selection task has begun to be applied to reasoning in other areas as well, to see whether giving ecologically reasonable content to abstract problems facilitates correct solutions. Box 9.4 provided one example. Just as with the Wason task, it appears that common logical errors can be understood as reflecting the fact that reasoning evolved in a certain adaptive context and is incompletely accessible to content that might have been irrelevant in earlier evolutionary time.

11.5.5 Conclusions

Given the widespread evidence for cognitive modularity, it is perhaps not surprising that there is little support for the social theory of intellect as originally proposed. However, in fairness to the theory that the demands of a complex social life drive the evolution of general cognitive abilities, it has to be said that there have been few, if any, adequate comparative tests of it. If correct, the social theory of intellect should apply to all sorts of species, not just primates, or else it should be able to account for differences between primates (as well as among primate species) and other species in terms of differences in the nature or complexity of their social organization. Yet evidence for social intelligence has seldom been sought in species outside of primates.

Rather than promoting the evolution of general intelligence, living in a complex and long-lasting social group may promote the evolution of a number of forms of specifically social cognition. There are several examples in this section of the chapter. Humphrey (1976) suggested that, as well as promoting abstract reasoning, social life is necessary for the evolution of consciousness. He suggested animals that are aware of their own internal states and motives and that can infer that others have the same experiences under similar circumstances might be expected to behave differently from those that simply react to others' behavior. However, research on intentionality, self-recognition, and theory of mind provides little if any evidence for such processes in species other than humans.

11.6 Whither Cognitive Ethology?

Most of the questions discussed in this chapter are embraced by the research program of cognitive ethology. We considered in most detail three questions: Do any animals have intentions, recognize themselves in mirrors, or have a theory of mind? Contemporary interest in such questions was stimulated by the writings of Donald Griffin (1976), but they are evidence of an enduring human compulsion to anthropomorphize and apply folk psychology to other species. The philosophical analysis of intentionality has been helpful in understanding the special status of beliefs, desires, intentions, and other intentional states and thereby in formulating questions for research. The biggest challenge here, as in other investigations of cognition in nonverbal creatures, is how to get unambiguous behavioral evidence for the cognitive processes of interest.

Research in cognitive ethology has been fraught with controversy. If nothing else, the interplay of proponents and rigorous critics has led to progress in understanding how to formulate the questions in experimentally tractable ways. After an initial wave of excitement about evidence seeming to show that animals have intentional states similar to humans', there is currently a swing back to behaviorism. Sharp-eyed (and sharp-penned) behaviorist critics like Cecelia Heyes (e.g., 1993a, 1993b, 1994c) have begun to stimulate a new wave of better designed experiments. Although we can look forward to learning their results with interest, these experiments touch on such fundamental human beliefs about the nature of other living beings that it is unlikely the questions discussed in this chapter will be answered any time soon. We will consider some of them again in the next chapter, on the nature of communication.

Further Reading

A sense of the controversies surrounding cognitive ethology can be gotten from a series of "Target Articles" and accompanying commentaries in *The Behavioral and Brain Sciences*. These include Griffin on cognitive ethology (1978), Dennett (1983) on the intentional stance, Premack and Woodruff (1978) on theory of mind, Whiten and Byrne (1988) on tactical deception, and the discussions of Cheney and Seyfarth's book *How Monkeys See the World* (1990b, 1992). The book itself is highly recommended, as is Kummer's (1995) autobiographical account of studying the hamadryas baboons in Ethiopia. The books edited by Griffin (1982), Ristau (1991a), and Bekoff and Jamieson (1996) include a variety of perspectives from philosophers, ethologists, and psychologists. Marian Dawkins's (1993) book *Through Our Eyes Only?* includes a very balanced evaluation of some of the relevant data in this area. *Kinds of Minds* (Dennett, 1996) is a brief introduction to the philosophical issues here. Heyes (1994b) briefly evaluates research on a number of questions about primates' social cognition. Overviews of primate behavior from two different viewpoints can be found in Quiatt and Reynolds (1993) and Byrne (1995). *Primate Cognition* by Tomasello and Call (1997), which appeared as this book was going to press, is highly recommended for comprehensive and critical discussions of theory of mind, self-recognition, and most of the other issues in chapters 10 through 12 that arise so compellingly when the behavior of primates is studied. Several edited volumes deal with specific issues in cognitive ethology. These include Byrne and Whiten's (1988) *Machiavellian Intelligence*; the volume on self-recognition edited by Parker, Mitchell, and Boccia (1994); *Anthropomorphism, Anecdotes and Animals* (Mitchell, 1996), and Carruthers and Smith (1996) on theory of mind. *The Adapted Mind* (Barkow, Cosmides, & Tooby, 1992) provides an extended sample of research and theory in evolutionary psychology.

12

Communication and Language

12.1 Approaches to Studying Communication

12.1.1 Influencing Behavior vs. Influencing Understanding

Figure 12.1 depicts a classic ethological example of communication. A male stickleback in breeding condition, with a red belly, swims in a wavering path toward an egg-laden female. When she responds to this "zigzig dance" by swimming toward the male, he heads toward his nest, and she follows. Upon reaching the nest, a little tunnel of vegetation lying on the substrate, the male pokes his head into the entrance, "showing" it to the female. She enters, and a further series of mutual actions and reactions ends in her depositing eggs in the nest and the male releasing sperm over them.

Courtship and egg laying in sticklebacks, as in many other animals, involves communication. Behaviors and structures apparently specially designed by natural selection are used by one animal to influence the behavior of others. In effect, the male's red belly and the zigzag dance tell the female something like "I am a male of your species, I have good genes and good health, I am ready to mate, and I want you to mate with me." But, of course, it is unnecessary to attribute such thoughts to the male. As figure 12.1 shows, the courtship sequence can be understood as a chain of events in which one

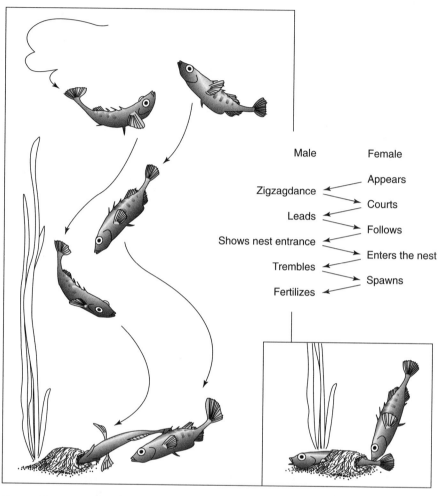

Figure 12.1. Courtship and spawning in the stickleback. After Tinbergen (1951) with permission.

animal provides the stimulus for its partner's response, which in turn provides the stimulus for the next response in the chain, and so on.

Figure 12.2 presents a rather different view of communication, one proposed by the philosopher Grice (1957) as an account of what goes on when people communicate with one another. People speaking to other people generally assume they are modifying not only their listeners' behavior but also their understanding. The young man in the figure is not just emitting sounds designed to cause the young woman to enter his car. Rather, he wants her to know that he is an attractive fellow who commands substantial resources and that he would like her to come. On this view, human communication, unlike the reaction chain of the sticklebacks, is a matter of at least third-order intentionality (Dennett, 1983; Gomez, 1994; see also chapter 11). In addition,

Figure 12.2. An example of human communication indicating the third-order intentionality assumed to accompany it. Modified from Gomez (1994) with permission.

it is referential. That is, unlike the stickleback's red belly, a Porsche is not a stimulus that by itself attracts all normal females of the species. In mentioning his Porsche, the young man in our example is referring to an object, and he intends to activate a representation of that object in his listener's mind. He evidently believes that his reference to it will enhance his attractiveness.

A cartoon of stickleback behavior might have the male saying "I'm a fit and sexy male. Come with me and lay your eggs in my lovely nest," but few, if any, students of animal behavior would seriously consider a Gricean analysis of the stickleback's courtship. There is no reason to think that the male's behavior is governed by a desire to cause the female to believe that he wants her to follow him, nor that his swimming toward the nest is a reference to a small tunnel of vegetation lying on the substrate. However, communicative behaviors in some other nonhuman species have raised the possibility that the senders of signals are referring to objects in the world and that they are intending to modify the signal receivers' behavior, perhaps even their beliefs. Figure 12.3 depicts probably the most discussed example. The basic finding is that vervet monkeys have three acoustically distinct alarm calls (Seyfarth, Cheney, & Marler, 1980a). One is given to snakes. Vervets hearing it stand up on their hind legs and look around at the ground. A second alarm call is given by a monkey sighting a leopard, and it causes nearby monkeys to run into the

a

| Monkey *A* | Monkey *B* |

sees leopard
↓
emits leopard alarm ──────────────────────→ hears leopard alarm
↓
runs to trees

b

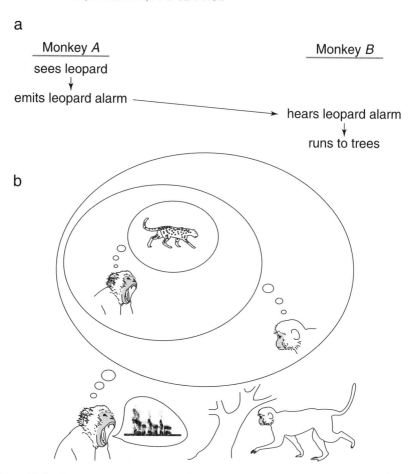

Figure 12.3. Two contrasting accounts of communication about predators by vervet monkeys. Vervets after Seyfarth and Cheney (1992) with permission.

trees, out of reach of leopards. The third alarm call is given to aerial predators like eagles that can snatch monkeys out of trees. Vervets hearing it seek shelter at ground level, in the bushes. We could describe the vervets' communication as sequences of stimulus and response, as shown in figure 12.3a, but would we be leaving out something important? Does an alarm-calling vervet intend to modify other monkeys' behavior in definite ways or is he simply emitting a response to a specific predator stimulus? Do the three calls refer to three different predators? How could we tell? Exploring the possibility of reference and intentionality has been an important thread in research on animal communication in recent years, and it will figure in the discussion of communication in bees, chickens, and monkeys that forms section 12.2.

As communications, the stickleback's approach to the female and the man's invitation to his date differ in another way than that depicted in figure 12.3. We would not be inclined to call the behavior sequence in figure 12.1

language because the stickleback is limited to a small number of species-typical communicative acts, put together in a rigid way. Yet some animal communication systems, such as the dancing of honeybees, have been referred to as languages. The vervets' alarm calls function somewhat like words. Discovering whether or in what way any animal communication systems share any properties of human language is part of the challenging enterprise of trying to unravel how human language evolved. Species phylogenetically closest to humans might be assumed to have the most humanlike capacities for communication, and this assumption has been behind a long history of attempts to teach forms of human language to chimpanzees. The results of these efforts have important implications for whether or not language should be attributed to a special cognitive module possessed only by humans. Section 12.3 reviews this research. But before discussing the details of some natural and artificial communication systems in animals, it will be helpful to consider a few more general issues. More extended discussions can be found in Hauser (1996), Halliday and Slater (1983), Krebs and Davies (1993), Krebs and Dawkins (1984), and the Further Readings for this chapter.

12.1.2 Elements of Communication

In communication, one animal influences the behavior of another animal through the transmission of *signals*. If my dog snarls and bares her teeth at your dog, she is clearly signaling hostility. If your dog runs away because he sees my dog sleeping in the yard, we would be unlikely to say any signaling has taken place. But, as we will see in a moment, the line between signaling and other kinds of information transmission is not always easy to draw. Classical ethologists studying communication focused on behavior patterns like the stickleback's zigzag dance that seemed selected specifically for a role in intraspecies interactions. Like other behavioral indices of motivational state, such behavior patterns are species-specific and occur in particular contexts. They also tend to be stereotyped in form. One dog encountering another dog that has defeated him in a recent fight is is more likely to adopt a submissive posture than an aggressive one (figure 12.4). Figure 12.4 also depicts an example of what Darwin (1872/1965) in *The Expression of the Emotions in Man and Animals* called the Principle of Antithesis: signals with opposing meanings tend to be opposite in form. Signals may have evolved this way because antithesis reduces ambiguity. Recording the behavioral context for a candidate signaling behavior and how other animals respond to it is necessary for deciding what, if anything, is being communicated. Observations of freely behaving animals often lead to questions about communication that can best be answered with experiments. For instance, Tinbergen discovered which parts of the courtship sequence function as signals by using dummies—crude model fish with only some of the features of live fish (see figure 5.1).

Instances of communication involve not only a physical signal, such as a sight, sound, or odor, but also a *sender* and a *receiver*. These terms all invite an interpretation of animal communication as an active process, involving be-

Figure 12.4. Contrast between aggressive and submissive postures, an example of the principle of antithhesis. After Darwin (1872/1965).

haviors and perhaps structures specifically selected to affect other animals' behavior. But animals may also transmit information about themselves in a more passive way. Red rain forest frogs or aposematic insects are often spoken of as signaling that they are unpalatable, and indeed their bright colors and conspicuous patterns are thought to have been selected to help predators avoid them (see box 5.1). As another example, the importance of being able to detect and respond to correlates of others' physical condition has been an important thread in recent discussions of communication in behavioral ecology (see Johnstone, 1997). Indeed, ragged fur, dull plumage, or the like may reveal an individual's poor physical condition to potential mates or predators, but it seems unlikely they have been specifically selected to do so. As these examples suggest, *signal* is another one of those terms whose application can be debatable.

As we saw in chapter 2, the physical properties of a signal and the receiver's perceptual sensitivity should be matched to each other, and both have to be suited to the transmission properties of the evironment. Observations of purported instances of communication also have to consider the message of a signal and its meaning to the receiver (Smith, 1977). The message is inferred from seeing what state of the sender and/or of the environment the signal is associated with. For instance, does an animal give different alarm calls in the presence of different kinds of threat or different levels of danger? The meaning of the signal, on the other hand, is inferred from the behavior of the receiver, so it may depend on the receiver's characteristics. For instance, in many species of birds, song is sung primarily by males in breeding condition while on their territories (see chapter 10). The song identifies the species of the singer, who he is, where he is, possibly something about his physical condition or the area he grew up in. These can all be considered part of its message. But the meaning of male territorial song is different for rival conspecific males (who may treat it either as a challenge for a territorial fight or as a signal to stay away), conspecific females (who may treat it as a signal to approach), and birds of other species (who are likely to be indifferent to it).

12.1.3 The Ethology and Behavioral Ecology of Communication

Let us return for a moment to the stickleback's courtship. The male's zigzag dance is a classic example of what ethologists call a *display*, a conspicuous stereotyped movement performed in a special context with an apparent communicative function. The zigzag dance is a example of a display arising from a motivational conflict, in this case between approaching the female and fleeing from her. Intention movements—the fragmentary beginnings of an activity that precede its full blown appearance—are the other main evolutionary source of displays. The male's behavior of "showing the nest" is one example here. In both cases, behaviors that normally occur in a given motivational context seem to have evolved into exaggerated and stereotyped, or *ritualized*, forms because exaggerated, stereotyped displays are less ambiguous, more likely to elicit responses. Special coloration and patterning may also have been selected because they make displays more noticeable to receivers.

These ideas about the evolution of displays are supported by numerous studies by ethologists from Lorenz (1941/1971) onward. Underlying many of them was the notion that communication is a matter of cooperation: signaling systems have evolved because both signaler and receiver benefit from sharing information. Male and female sticklebacks can both increase their fitness by getting fertile eggs into the nest. The dog that growls and bares its teeth and the dog that runs away both avoid a potentially damaging fight. In the past 20 years, however, discussions of the evolution and function of communication have been dominated by the idea that systems of animal communication evolve because animals benefit from manipulating one another. This view (R. Dawkins & Krebs, 1978) follows from behavioral ecologists' emphasis on individual selection. No animal would be selected to give a costly display, one that takes time, consumes energy, and that might even increase its conspicuousness to predators, simply to share information with a conspecific. Signals must have been selected because they cause the receiver to behave in a way that increases the sender's fitness. The receiver, on this view, doesn't have to receive any benefit. At the same time, of course, the receiver's response to the signal, along with her perceptual sensitivity to it, will be selected only if *her* net fitness is increased more by responding to the signal than by ignoring it or responding in some other way. Communication will most often be cooperative in cases of close genetic relatedness, as in the honeybee colonies discussed in section 12.2.

In contrast to the traditional ethological view, R. Dawkins and Krebs's (1978; Krebs & Dawkins, 1984) view of communication says that signals are not necessarily truthful indicators of the sender's state. It follows that signaler and receiver are engaged in an arms race. For instance, males may attract more mates and thereby increase their fitness by appearing to be bigger, stronger, and sexier than they really are. However, in species where fathers provide resources for their offspring, females will increase their fitness most by detecting the males that are truly healthy and good providers, since this will increase the chances that the bearers of their genes will be healthy and well provided for. Similarly, territory owners that can bluff challengers about their ability to win a fight may engage in fewer costly battles than individuals that signal honestly, but over generations rivals should get better and better at detecting bluffs. The predator-prey interactions in mimicry systems (see chapter 5) are a case of deceptive interspecific signaling in that palatable prey sport the appearance of unpalatable ones. Here the evolutionary arms race is responsible for the very close resemblances between model and mimic, as well as between cryptic prey and background (see chapter 2). In some cases however, honest rather than deceptive communication should evolve. Sexual selection favors signals like big tails and antlers because they handicap their owners (Zahavi, 1975). For instance, a peacock that can keep himself in good condition and display vigorously to females in spite of producing and carrying around a huge tail can hardly be bluffing about his quality. Although the handicap principle and associated ideas about honest advertising were originally hotly debated, they are now more generally accepted (M. S. Dawkins, 1995; Johnstone, 1997).

Receivers of signals can be thought of as engaged in "mindreading" (Krebs & Dawkins, 1984) in that they may benefit from being able to tell what the sender of a signal will do next. For instance, will the snarling dog attack or go back and lie down? Mindreading in this sense is no different from what ethologists do all the time—that is, use the regularities in sequences of behavior in a predictive fashion. But whereas ethologists have to learn the predictive significance of other species' behavior patterns, the animals themselves may respond appropriately to signals like red bellies and territorial songs without much, if any, experience. R. Dawkins and Krebs's (1978; Krebs & Dawkins, 1984) ideas about the evolution and function of communication have stimulated a large amount of new research and theorizing in behavioral ecology, as well as more than their share of controversy (M. S. Dawkins, 1995; Hinde, 1981; Krebs & Davies, 1993, chap. 14). This brief sketch hardly begins to do them justice. One point to take away is that although contemporary discussions of communication in behavioral ecology make much use of terms like *mindreading, manipulation* and *deception*, these have clear functional meanings. They are not meant to imply that any animals are thinking about manipulating or deceiving each other, any more than a gray moth resting on a gray tree trunk is thinking about deceiving hungry blue jays.

12.1.4 Language and Animal Communication

Since linguists and philosophers still debate the nature of language there is not much point in trying here to answer the question, "What is language?" More worthwhile is to try to identify important features of human language and ask which of them are shared by the communication system of any other species, an approach taken by Hockett (1960; see also Evans & Marler, 1995; Hauser, 1996; Roitblat, Harley, & Helweg, 1993). Some of the most important such features are the following.

Limited vs. Unbounded Signal Set   Most nonhuman species communicate about a very limited set of things: sex, aggression, predators, food. More to the point, their ways of doing so are generally limited to a relatively small set of signals. Even if some signals are graded in intensity, qualitatively different signals are still rather few in number. If Martians arrived on Earth, animals could not talk about them. In contrast, words — the elements of human language — and the ways in which they are put together make it essentially unbounded. *Outsourcing* and *e-mail* are words invented in the 1990s to communicate about contemporary phenomena. More important, words are put together using the rules of syntax. Our implicit knowledge of English grammar means that once we know what new words like *e-mail* and *outsource* mean, we can immediately talk about them in all sorts of ways. In English, word order is important in conveying meaning. "Sue sent an e-mail to John" and "John sent an e-mail to Sue" mean two quite different things despite the fact that they contain the same words. On the other hand, "Sue was sent an e-mail by John" means the same as "John sent an e-mail to Sue" even though as a chain of visual or auditory stimuli it is more like "Sue sent an e-mail to John." The order of elements can matter in some animal signals, most notably bird song, but it does not seem to be used to create new meaning.

Reference and Situational Freedom   In the examples with which we began the chapter, the male stickleback and the snarling dog are communicating their internal states. This information allows the receiver to predict what the signaler will do next and behave appropriately: the female approaching the zigzagging male will likely be shown the nest, an intruder approaching the snarling dog will likely be attacked. But, as indicated in figure 12.2, humans also communicate about objects and events in the world, very often referring to ones that are not even present at the time. Although we cannot tell an animal's subjective state when it gives or receives a signal, the essential behavioral implications of reference are clear. A signal that refers to a particular object or event is reliably given in its presence and not under other conditions. This criterion separates behavior patterns caused by, for example, generalized excitement or anxiety from those performed in the presence of specific exciting or anxiety-producing conditions. Equally important, the receiver of a referential signal behaves consistently in an appropriate manner, even in the absence of the object or event that elicited the sender's signaling behavior. Thus, an animal hearing a signal for, say, flight flees whether or not it can hear or see what it is fleeing from. Signals that meet these two criteria are *functionally referential* (Evans, 1997; Evans & Marler, 1995; Marler, Evans, & Hauser, 1992). We will consider candidate examples from bees, chickens, and monkeys in the next part of the chapter.

One concomitant of reference in human language is *situational freedom* or *displacement*. We can talk about food or danger that we have experienced in the past or might experience in the future. No food or danger need be present for us to refer to them. As readers may suspect from the examples presented so far in this chapter, most animal signals do not exhibit situational freedom.

The dance language of bees (see section 12.2.1) is sometimes cited as an exception. Besides allowing communication about objects and events in the past or future, situational freedom permits lying. Accordingly, there has been some interest in whether animals can lie. This question refers not to the possibility that some signals are designed by evolution to deceive but to the cognitively more complex possibility that a signal with a particular message and meaning is occasionally used intentionally in another context for the sender's benefit. On the whole, there is little if any convincing evidence that animals lie, for the same reasons that there is little evidence for other forms of intentional deceptive behavior (see section 11.4).

Communication and Intention   As in figure 12.2, we generally use language with the intent of informing, or changing the cognitive state of our receivers. Behaviorally, this means that we suit our communication to the audience: a professor gives different lectures to an introductory class than to a professional society. Further, what we say and how we say it is continuously modified according to whether our communication is having its intended effect. If the introductory students know nothing about evolution, the intended lecture on communication will be postponed, whereas if they reveal that they learned the basics of signaling systems in another course, the wise professor will move on to the next topic. The idea that, similarly, animals might communicate with intent to inform has been investigated in two ways. How the signaler's behavior may be influenced by what other animals are present, the so-called *audience effect*, has been analyzed in most detail in chickens and in ground squirrels (see section 12.2.2). And how signalers might alter their behavior depending on the response of receivers has been looked at in some detail in primates, as described in section 12.2.3. In discussing both sorts of investigations, we will have to consider whether sophisticated conditional control by the behavior of receivers can be distinguished from control by the sender's understanding of whether or not the receivers are understanding the intended message. Readers of earlier chapters will already suspect what the answer will be.

12.2 Some Natural Communication Systems

12.2.1 Dancing in Honeybees

The Waggle Dance   People have been collecting honey, and therefore observing honeybees' behavior, since prehistoric times (Gould & Gould, 1988), but Aristotle was one of the first to record his observations (Gould, 1976). Aristotle noticed that when a source of sugar water, attractive to bees, was set out at some distance from a hive, no bees might arrive for several days, but once one did arrive others came soon after, apparently following the discoverer to the food. The actual mechanism underlying recruitment was not elucidated, however, until relatively recently. In the first half of this century, von Frisch and his students perfected methods for training bees to artificial food

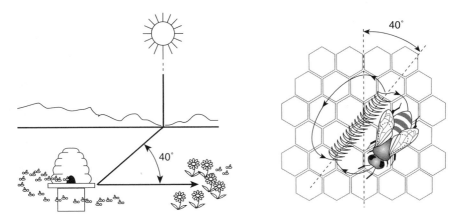

Figure 12.5. The waggle dance of the honeybee and the way in which its angle to the vertical is related to the angle between the path to the food and the sun's azimuth. Redrawn from Seeley (1985) with permission.

sources that permitted detailed study of their learning, orientation, and communication (see von Frisch, 1967; Gould & Gould, 1988). As we have already seen in chapters 3 and 7, the area of research opened up by von Frisch (for which he was awarded a Nobel Prize together with Konrad Lorenz and Niko Tinbergen) is still flourishing. Some of his conclusions, however, have not gone unchallenged.

In the 1940s von Frisch observed that when a bee returns from finding nectar 200 meters or more away, she may perform a *waggle dance* inside the dark hive on the surface of the vertical honeycomb. Bees returning from shorter distances perform a round dance. The waggle dance consists of a straight run in which the bee waggles her abdomen from side to side while vibrating her wings to make a buzzing sound. At the end of the straight run, she runs quickly back in a semicircle to begin another straight run. This return trip is made alternately to the left and to the right, tracing a figure-eight (figure 12.5). Bees that have not just been foraging successfully attend the dance, crowding round the forager and touching her with their anntennae. The waggle dance contains information about the distance and direction of the food source (or, equivalently, the flight just completed by the dancer). The angle of the straight run to the vertical corresponds to the angle of the food source to the sun's current azimuth (see section 7.1.6). If the food was located in a direct line from the hive toward the sun's azimuth, dancers' waggle runs will be oriented straight up on the vertical comb. If the sun is in the south and food is directly west of the hive, dances are oriented on average 90° to the right of vertical, and so on. The duration and length of the waggle run, together with the amount of buzzing accompanying it, corresponds to the distance to the food. This information could be conveyed to those attending the dance by the number of waggles, the amount of buzzing, and/or in other ways. The dancer also pauses from time to time and regurgitates a small drop of nectar. This

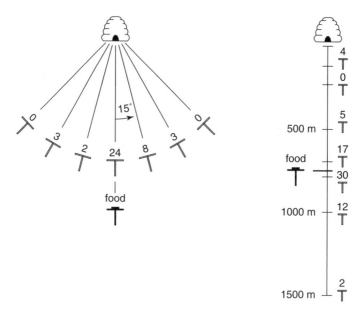

Figure 12.6. Arrangements of control feeders in von Frisch's "fan" and "step" experiments, showing the number of bees arriving at each one in the test. Redrawn from von Frisch (1953, 1967) with permission.

could provide information about the kind of food she has recently found. Whether dancing or not, the forager also carries information about the kind of food to be found in the form of odors picked up by waxy hairs on her body. Finally, returning foragers that have found a resource needed by the colony are most likely to dance, and the vigor with which they dance corresponds to the value of the resource. Bees dance not only after gathering nectar but also after finding pollen, water, tree sap, and potential new nest sites (see Seeley, 1995).

The waggle dance clearly carries information, but experiments were necessary to test whether other bees use it. The designs von Frisch used to test recruits' use of direction and distance information, respectively, are depicted in figure 12.6. In each case, marked foragers are first trained to come to a feeding platform that is gradually moved farther and farther from the hive. Because they are offered a relatively weak sugar solution at this stage, they do not yet dance and recruit other bees. (If they do, the recruits are removed from the colony.) Then, on the test day, the solution is made strong enough to elicit dancing, control platforms are set out along with the training platform, and arriving bees are counted (and, ideally, removed) upon arrival at each one. In the "fan experiment," designed to test the use of directional information, the control feeders in von Frisch's design were equidistant from the hive, spread out on both sides of the training feeder. In the "step experiment," designed to test for the use of distance information, the control feeders and the training feeder were in the same straight line from the hive, with control feeders both nearer and farther than the training feeder. In both cases, the majority of recruits turned up at the training location, though when there is a feeder close to the hive in a step experiment, many foragers turn up there as well.

The Dance Language Controversy   At first glance, the results of the fan and step experiments seem to be unambiguous evidence that recruits use the information in the dance. This is especially so when they are combined with observations of individual bees in other experiments. If foragers are returning to a hive from two sites in opposite directions from the hive, recruits tend to arrive most often at the site indicated by a dance they attended, not the alternative site (see Gould, 1976). However, a few cautions are necessary. First, it is definitely not the case that every bee attending a dance flies off immediately and unerringly in a beeline for the site being indicated. Far from it. Recruits are generally much slower to arrive than experienced foragers, and not all the bees attending a dance necessarily find the indicated site. Furthermore, long before he discovered the waggle dance, von Frisch established that bees can find sites recently visited by other bees by odor alone. They use not only the odor of the food itself, which may of course be quite distinctive in the case of flowers, but other distinctive odors at or near the site as well as odors deposited by successful foragers. In the late 1960s, the clear importance of odor together with the results of some experiments similar, but not identical in detail, to von Frisch's fan and step experiments led Wenner and others to reexamine the dance language hypothesis (Gould, 1976; Wenner & Wells, 1990). They concluded that the dance did not function as communication. All von Frisch's results, together with the results of their new experiments, could be explained by the bees' use of odor. In particular, in both the fan and the step designs, the target feeder—the one where most bees turn up—was in the center of a gradient of odor from the whole array of feeders. In addition, it was the location that had been most visited by bees. When different arrays were used, with the target feeder offset from the center, and controls instituted for past bee visits, most recruits still turned up in the center of the array.

Wenner's attack on the dance language hypothesis was answered by von Frisch himself, among others (see Gould, 1976; Gould & Gould, 1988), and in the early 1970s, the question of whether the waggle dance was communication or not was *the* controversial issue in ethology. It is still not universally regarded as entirely settled (Vadas Jr., 1994; Wenner, Meade, & Friesen, 1991). The experiments most generally accepted as having shown that the dance does function to communicate food locations have a logic that we will meet again in considering referential communication in chickens and monkeys. That logic is simple: if a given signal functions to communicate, then receivers must respond appropriately to it even in the absence of the environmental conditions that gave rise to it. Otherwise, it is impossible to be sure whether they have responded to the signal itself or directly to the state of the environment. James Gould, then a graduate student at Rockefeller University, saw that this could be accomplished by dissociating the direction signaled by

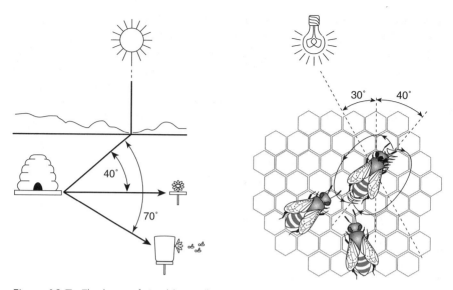

Figure 12.7. The logic of Gould's ocelli painting experiment. The dancer with painted ocelli has visited a food source at 40° to the right of the sun's azimuth°. She orients her waggle dance with respect to the vertical, but recruits attending the dance interpret it with respect to the light in the hive.

dancers from the actual location of the food (Gould, 1975). In effect, he caused dancing bees to lie and other bees to believe them. He did this by making use of the fact that although bees in the dark orient and interpret dances with respect to the vertical, bees in the light use the sun (figure 12.7). For instance, in the dark a dance elicited by food 90° to the right of the sun's azimuth will have a straight run 90° to the right of vertical, but if the hive is lighted, dancers arriving from the same place will orient 90° to the right of the light. Gould further made use of the fact that bees perceive the overall level of illumination with their ocelli, an array of photoreceptors on the top of the head. Bees with their ocelli covered with opaque paint behave as if in dim light. Most important, there are levels of hive illumination at which untreated bees reorient their dances and their interpretation of dances to the light while bees with painted ocelli do not. What Gould did, then, was to train some foragers with painted ocelli to a target feeder and cause them to dance in a lighted hive where the attendant bees had unpainted ocelli (figure 12.7). The dancers oriented their dance with respect to gravity while the potential recruits interpreted it with respect to the light. In this way Gould dissociated the location actually visited by the dancers, potentially detected by recruits via odor, and the location indicated by the dance. Contrary to the odor hypothesis, but consistent with the dance language hypothesis, most recruits arrived at the feeder indicated by the dance.

The traditional ethological tools for presenting signals at will, dissociated from the environmental conditions that normally elicit them, are dummies and playbacks. We will see examples shortly. The analogue for the dance language is a mechanical bee, and recently one has been produced that is successful in recruiting bees that attend its dances (Michelsen, Anderson, Storm, Kirchner, & Lindauer, 1992). Recruits use information about both distance and direction provided by the model. With the model, different components of the waggle dance, such as the duration of the waggle run and the amount of buzzing, can be dissociated. Like Gould's (1975) experiments, the experiments with the model bee indicate that the dance alone can function to communicate. However, this does not mean that odor is not important too, although it does not have the exclusive role attributed to it by Wenner and colleagues. As in many other controversies about what controls behavior, the answer is not just one thing or the other but "it depends," in this case perhaps on a variety of subtle aspects of the methods used to train bees to artificial foraging sites (Gould, 1976).

Evolution and Contents of the Dance   Although the honeybee's dance may be a unique form of communication, its elements have parallels in noncommunicative behaviors of other insects. Some insects translate direction relative to the sun into direction relative to gravity. If they are orienting to the sun on a horizontal surface they maintain their orientation, now relative to gravity, when the surface is tilted (see Gould & Towne, 1987). Many insects "wind down" after flight by vibrating their wings, more so after more effortful flights. Such observations suggest an evolutionary origin for the dancing behavior. On this hypothesis, the evolutionary innovation in the honeybees was mainly in the ability to decode the information in the dance and use it to direct foraging behavior (Dyer & Seeley, 1989). Interestingly, the different races of honeybees do so by slightly different rules for translating millimeters of straight run into meters flown (Dyer & Seeley, 1991).

In effect, dancing bees report about the flight they have just completed (or are just about to repeat), and bees that respond to the dance use it as a set of flying instructions. However, it has also been suggested that, contrary to this hypothesis, both the dancers' behavior and the recruits' response are mediated by their cognitive maps of the local environment (Gould & Towne, 1987). Two sorts of evidence seem especially consistent with this interpretation. One is that in some experiments returning foragers seem to "report" the straight line distance and direction of the food source rather than the distance and direction flown (von Frisch, 1953; Gould & Towne, 1987). But this observation need only mean that they use path integration to record the journey (Dyer & Seeley, 1989; see also chap. 7). It also seems inconsistent with observations indicating that when bees fly against the wind or carry small lead weights their dances correspond to longer distances than they have actually flown (see Kirchner & Braun, 1994). The cognitive map interpretation also does not fit readily with the notion that the waggle dance may have evolved from the more common insect behavior of "winding down" after a flight.

The second line of evidence cited in support of the cognitive mapping interpretation of dancing is an oft-described experiment the results of which can be interpeted in more than one way. In this experiment (Dyer & Seeley, 1989; Gould, 1990; Gould & Gould, 1988; Gould & Towne, 1987), forager bees were trained to come to a feeder on a boat in the middle of a lake. They were then induced to dance in the hive by suddenly increasing the sucrose concentration on the boat, and the arrival of recruits was monitored. But recruits did not arrive at the boat. Is this because they interpreted the dance as indicating a location that, in their experience, could not possibly contain food and therefore they never left the hive? Not necessarily (Dyer & Seeley, 1989). For one thing, bees tend to become disoriented when they fly over water and therefore are reluctant to do so. For another, when feeders were put out on the shore of the lake in this experiment, recruits arrived quickly, as if they had already left the hive in search of food but stopped at the edge of the lake. Better controlled experiments to differentiate the cognitive mapping and "flight instructions" hypotheses have been attempted (Gould, 1990; Gould & Gould, 1988). One approach consisted of familiarizing bees with a locale containing a lake, surreptitiously moving the hive away from any lakes, and arranging for foragers to signal two sites, one corresponding to the center of lake and one to its edge. If recruits use the dance as flight instructions (and if they are equally likely to attend equally effective dances signaling the two locations), they should turn up in both places. However, if they reference the location being signaled to their cognitive map of the area experienced around the hive before it was moved, they will turn up mostly at the "lake shore." Clearly, such a potentially important experiment needs to be replicated as well as done in reverse (start at the field, move to the lake). However, since the evidence reviewed in chapter 7 provides little evidence to think that bees have cognitive maps anyway, it has to be doubted whether the weight of evidence will eventually be on the side of the bees communicating about cognitive maps.

Conclusions   The dancing of bees appears to differ from the communication systems to be discussed next in that a continuously graded message signals a potentially infinite number of directions and distances. The dance has also (e.g., Roitblat, 1987) been claimed to be unique among animal communications in having the human-language property of displacement. This is obviously true in a trivial sense, since the dancer may be displaced in space several hundred meters from the food that caused her to dance. However, if the dance is seen as reporting on a just-completed journey, it is no more displaced than an alarm call given to a just-glimpsed snake. In both these cases, too, the communication is symbolic in that the signal bears an arbitrary relationship to the message. It has been suggested that "the dance-communication system of honey bees . . . is exceeded in complexity and information-carrying capacity only by human speech" (Gould & Towne, 1987, pp. 317–318). This conclusion seems over enthusiastic, to say the least, but perhaps such enthusiasm can be excused on the grounds that it predated the close analysis of functionally referential communication systems in other species, which are discussed next.

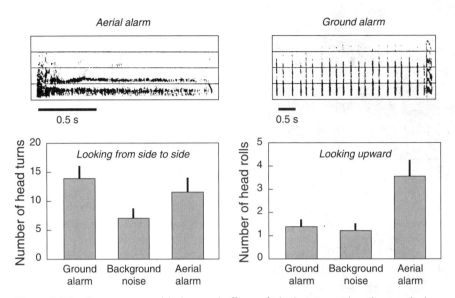

Figure 12.8. Sonagrams and behavioral effects of chickens' aerial and ground alarm calls, compared to effects of background noise. Redrawn from Evans, Evans, and Marler (1993) with permission.

12.2.2 Chickens Call about Food and Predators

In the mid 1980s, Peter Marler and a series of associates began an analysis of vocal communication in chickens, using various bantam strains that are closer to the ancestral jungle fowl than most domestic breeds. Originally, this work was strongly influenced by cognitive ethology, focusing on possible instances of intentional communication (Marler, Karakashian, & Gyger, 1991), but it has evolved into a careful operational analysis of functional reference, one of the most thorough so far for any species (Evans, 1997; Evans & Marler, 1995). This research program has been successful in part because chickens will court and alarm-call in the well-controlled conditions of the laboratory. Not only that, chickens also respond to video and audio tapes of predators and other chickens, facilitating experimental analysis of the critical features of these stimuli.

Chickens have two kinds of alarm calls (figure 12.8). Aerial predators like hawks elicit a scream or whistle, while ground predators like foxes and raccoons elicit a long series of pulses, "cut cut cut cut . . . cuuut." Behavior toward these two classes of predators differs in a functionally sensible way. A chicken sighting a hawk overhead may move toward cover; it crouches and repeatedly tilts its head to one side or the other, looking up at the sky. When a fox, dog, or raccoon approaches, on the other hand, the chicken stands erect and looks from side to side. Chickens' alarm calls satisfy the criteria for functional reference. Roosters were presented with video images of either a hawk on an overhead monitor or a raccoon on a monitor at the side of the cage (fig-

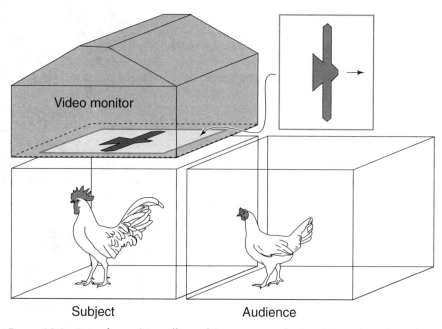

Figure 12.9. Setup for studying effects of the presence of a hen (the audience) on alarm calling by a rooster to a hawk's silhouette moved overhead. Redrawn from Evans and Marler (1992) and Evans, Macedonia, and Marler (1993) with permission.

ure 12.9). They gave aerial alarm calls to the hawk and ground alarm calls to the raccoon and behaved appropriately to each one (Evans, Evans, & Marler, 1993). Not only does each predator by itself elicit the appropriate alarm call, the first requirement for functional reference, but also each alarm by itself elicits appropriate behavior in receivers, the second requirement. Hens isolated in a laboratory cage heard either a ground alarm call, an aerial alarm call, or an equivalent period of recorded background noise. Hens moved toward cover only when hearing an aerial alarm, and they crouched and looked up most often in this condition (see figure 12.8). In contrast, hens hearing ground alarms did not seek cover, crouch, or look up any more than hens hearing background noise. Instead they stood in a tall sleeked posture and looked from side to side. The differences in behavior to aerial and ground predators reflect qualitative differences in the threat they signal, not quantitative differences in the predator's imminence. This was indicated, for example, by experiments in which the image overhead was varied in size and shape (Evans, Macedonia, & Marler, 1993). The number of alarm calls and nonvocal responses increased with the size of this "hawk," but their nature was always the same.

Alarm calling clearly makes sense only if other animals are around to get the message. Indeed, calling may have a cost for a solitary animal, by attracting a predator's attention. Section 4.4, on kin recognition and altruism, touched on the issue of when alarm calling should evolve and how the presence of other animals should affect it. For the cognitive ethology of communication, the issue is whether or not animals behave as if they intend to communicate to other animals about the presence of a predator. Operationally this means simply: is alarm calling affected by the presence vs. absence of an audience? This question has been answered affirmatively for aerial alarm calling by roosters (see Evans & Marler, 1995). Roosters alarm-call more when they can see a live or videotaped hen. The characteristics of the audience are also important: roosters alarm-call more when the audience is a conspecific than when it is a bobwhite quail (Karakashian, Gyger, & Marler, 1988). Just as with images of video predators, the features of the video audience can be manipulated to see what is critical in defining a suitable audience Notice, however, that the results of such experiments do not demand an intentional interpretation. What is being shown is that aerial alarm calling is affected by characteristics of both the predator and the audience.

A similar conclusion comes from studies of roosters' food calling. The courting rooster's food call is acoustically the same as the mother hen's food call, discussed in the section on teaching in chapter 10. As in many species of birds and insects, in chickens a behavior seen when mothers bring food to their young also appears in males offering food to potential mates. The food-calling rooster emits a food call in the presence of a tasty morsel of food, hens are attracted to it, are allowed to eat it, and may subsequently engage in other aspects of courtship with the rooster (Evans & Marler, 1994; Marler, Dufty, & Pickert, 1986a, 1986b). Again, we have a behavior that invites overinterpretation in terms of intentions to communicate, to attract the hen, and so on, but also what is going on can be understood as an example of conditional control of behavior by, among other things, the quality of food and kind of audience present.

12.2.3 Reference and Meaning in Vervet Monkeys

Vervet monkeys give different alarm calls to three classes of predator: eagles and other dangerous raptors, snakes, and leopards (figure 12.10). In effect, alarm calling and responding to alarms shows how vervets categorize predators, in much the same way as a pigeon's pecking a different one of four keys in the presence of slides of different kinds of objects shows that the pigeon is categorizing the images on the slides (see chapter 5). Vervets make finer discriminations among flying predators than chickens do (figure 12.11). Whereas chickens living outdoors in rural New York State gave a high proportion of their aerial alarms to harmless birds like doves and geese, and even to airplanes and falling leaves, adult vervets discriminate potentially harmful raptors (hawks and eagles) from equally large but harmless birds such as storks and vultures. Within each species, it seems likely that the degree of discrimination would be influenced to some extent by the caller's motivational state. A nervous animal may have a lower threshold for calling than a relaxed one. But since the observations summarized in figure 12.11 were collected over a period of time under a wide variety of conditions in the field, they likely

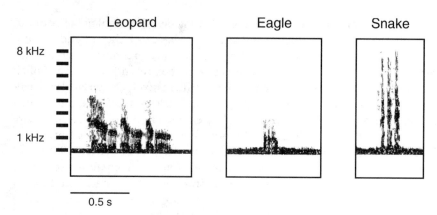

Figure 12.10. Sonagrams of one individual vervet's leopard, eagle, and snake alarms. From Seyfarth, Cheney, and Marler (1980b) with permission.

reflect a more basic species difference in discrimination. Species differences in alarm calling are discussed further in section 12.2.4.

The vervets' discrimination develops during the first four years or so of life (Seyfarth & Cheney, 1986). Infant vervets give the three types of alarms calls in a roughly appropriate manner—for example, eagle alarms to things in the air and snake alarms to long things on the ground. But at first infants do not show much discrimination among things in these classes. For instance, eagle alarms are as likely to nonraptors as to raptors. When juveniles begin to discriminate between the broad classes of raptors vs. nonraptors, they still include raptors that do not prey on monkeys, but later these are more or less ignored. Since these developmental changes take several years it is impossible to say exactly what experiences contribute to them and how they do so, but teaching by older vervets does not appear to be involved (Cheney & Seyfarth, 1990b). Adults do not, for example, correct infants when they call inappropriately. Observational learning, possibly like birds' and other monkeys' observational learning about predators (see section 10.2.3) may play a role.

The vervets' categorization of predators makes functional sense because each one demands a different kind of response. Eagles strike from above, so monkeys that are high in trees when an eagle is sighted should move down while monkeys on the ground should move into cover. Leopards, on the other hand, generally attack monkeys on the ground and can be escaped by climbing trees. Snakes approach along the ground and may be mobbed by the monkey troop. Monkeys spying a dangerous snake rear on their hind legs and peer down into the grass while alarm-calling. In opportunistic observations in the field, animals' responses to others' calls may be hard to distinguish from responses caused by their own sighting of the predator or other animals' behavior to it. But when Seyfarth, Cheney, and Marler (1980a) played the calls from concealed loudspeakers, alarms by themselves elicited appropriate responses in their hearers. For instance, animals that were on the ground when an alarm call was played were most likely to run into a tree to a leopard alarm,

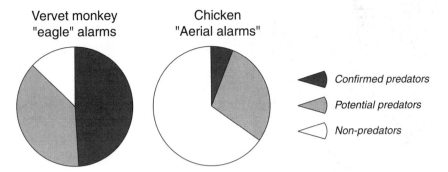

Figure 12.11. Comparison of the specificity of vervet eagle alarms and chicken aerial alarms, in terms of the proportions of calls given to confirmed predators vs. other things. Redrawn from Evans and Marler (1995) with permission.

look up and run into cover to an eagle alarm, and stand on their hind legs and look down upon hearing a snake alarm. For vervets already in a tree when the recordings were played, snake alarms elicited the most looking down, whereas eagle alarms elicited the most movement out of the tree.

The vervet alarm calls meet the criteria for functional reference, but do they have meaning for the monkeys? That is to say, do they simply elicit predator-appropriate responses or do they access a representation of a particular type of predator or response to a predator? And since different individuals have different voices, is something about the caller represented as well? To try to find out, Cheney and Seyfarth (1988) turned to habituation experiments (see chapter 4). These experiments also included vocalizations the vervets use in intergroup encounter. *Wrrs* are emitted when another group is approaching, as are *chutters*, but *chutters* are more frequent in direct aggressive interactions between groups (figure 12.12). Since vervets tend to look toward a calling animal, Cheney and Seyfarth filmed their subjects and then counted the number of seconds looking toward the speaker during and immediately after playbacks. Each experiment began with a playback of the target call to get a baseline measure of orienting toward it. On the next day, the subject heard a series of eight habituating calls about 30 minutes apart. Looking time generally declined during this series (figure 12.12). Then, about 30 minutes later, the target call was played again and looking time to it was compared to baseline looking time.

This design was used in two pairs of tests. Within each pair the same subjects were tested, some having one order of tests, some the other. The first pair tested whether habituation transferred from *wrrs* to an acoustically different call with similar meaning, *chutters*, and whether the identity of the caller mattered to any transfer of habituation. In effect this design asked, if animal A was unreliable because he repeatedly *wrr*'d from the bushes and no vervet group appeared, would he be treated as unreliable when he *chuttered*? The second series examined transfer between eagle and leopard alarms: would an animal habituated to an eagle alarm transfer this habituation to leopard alarms, and, again, would it matter if the same vs. different individuals had

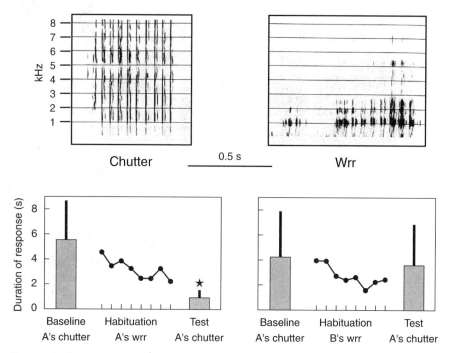

Figure 12.12. Sonagrams of *wrr* and *chutter* vocalizations of a single individual and data demonstrating cross-habituation between two calls from from the same caller. Redrawn from Cheney and Seyfarth (1988) with permission.

given the two different kinds of alarms? In both cases, the change in looking time from baseline to test was compared across tests with the same vs. a different caller. Regardless of the identity of the caller, habituation did not transfer between eagle and leopard alarms, nor did it transfer from one individual's *wrr* to another's *chutter*. However, habituation did transfer from a given individual's *wrrs* to that same individual's *chutters*, as if the vervets learned something like "Charlie is unreliable today when it comes to signaling the approach of another group" (figure 12.12). Comparing this case to the case in which the same individual was heard to signal two different predators suggests that habituation transfers between two acoustically different calls only if they have similar meaning. However, one might still worry that in some sense a *wrr* and a *chutter* from a single individual are more similar to each other as acoustic stimuli than are an eagle and a leopard alarm from one individual. But this doubt is laid to rest by a second set of studies showing that vervets treat another species' alarm calls as equivalent to their own.

Superb starlings (*Spreo superbus*) live with the vervets in Kenya and give acoustically distinctive "raptor alarms" to birds that attack them from the air. These seem equivalent to the vervets' eagle alarms because they are elicited by a similar class of predators. Superb starlings also give "terrestrial predator" alarms to a variety of species that attack from the ground, a wider variety of

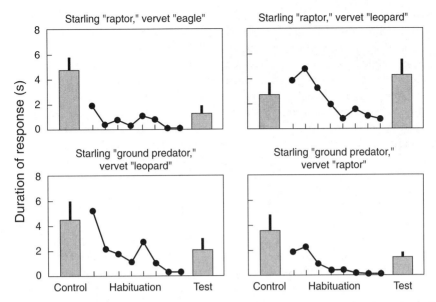

Figure 12.13. Duration of looking toward a speaker in vervets exposed to the indicated alarm calls recorded from vervets and starlings, demonstrating cross-habituation between calls with the same meaning. The call listed first above each panel was the habituating call; the second call was played in the control and test trials. Redrawn from Seyfarth and Cheney (1990) with permission.

predators than those that elicit the vervets' leopard alarms. Vervets respond to both of the starlings' alarm calls, apparently learning to do so (Hauser, 1988). This situation is perfect for testing whether habituation transfers from one call to an acoustically very different one with a similar meaning. Figure 12.13 summarizes the results of a series of habituation tests, this time with the call of one species used as the target, in baseline control and test, and the calls of the other species in the habituating series (Seyfarth & Cheney, 1990). The results were what would be expected if the vervets are responding to the meaning of the calls: habituation transferred between vervet and starling raptor alarms, whereas it did not transfer between vervet leopard alarms and starling raptor alarms. The starling raptor alarm is elicited by aerial predators and not by leopards. However, habituation to the much less specific starling terrestrial predator alarm transferred to both vervet leopard alarms and vervet eagle alarms. As Seyfarth and Cheney summarized the results of their playback experiments (1990, p. 764), "The results of these tests are difficult to explain without assuming that vervets have some representation of the objects and events denoted by different call types, and that they compare and respond to vocalizations on the basis of these representations." Notice, however, that this does not make vervet alarm calls unique. One could just as well say that the hamsters in Johnston and Jernigan's (1994) experiment treated odors of other hamsters in terms of their meaning ("female X") or that mediated generalization (see chapter 5) shows that arbitrary conditioned stimuli may be related to one another via their meanings—that is, via what they represent—just as the starling and vervet calls are treated as having similar meanings. Indeed, in recent discussions, Seyfarth and Cheney (1997) have emphasized that many of their findings are consistent with such associative explanations.

Cheney and Seyfarth's experiments are important and widely cited, but some authors have pointed to a few problems (Evans, 1997; Hauser, 1996). First, their experimental design does not conform to the idealized design for assessing learning discussed in chapter 3. Two groups should be compared at T2, the final presentation of the target stimulus, one group having been habituated to the stimulus of interest and one that had some sort of control treatment such as habituation to a completely unrelated stimulus. Unlike the before–after comparison used with the vervets, this comparison controls for possible unforseen generalized effects of the habituation treatment. However, this may not be such a problem as it first appears because the change from baseline looking time was generally compared across two treatments. For instance, change in response to *wrrs* was compared after habituation to the same vs. a different animal's *wrrs*. Any general changes in responsiveness over time could be presumed equal in the two groups. Another potential problem is so-called *pseudo-replication* (Hurlbert, 1984; Kroodsma, 1990). Conclusions about the effect of a certain call type should be based on systematic use of different examplars of that call, not repeated presentations of the same exemplar. The latter would be a case of pseudo-replication. It is not always clear from the published reports (Cheney & Seyfarth, 1988; Seyfarth & Cheney, 1990; see Hauser, 1996, for discussion) whether or not the eight presentations of a habituating stimulus were, in fact, eight different exemplars of the specified call type. Use of different instances of the same call would strengthen the conclusion that the animals are responding to them in terms of their meaning—that is, their semantic properties, rather than their acoustic structure alone. Finally, claims about the acoustic similarity or lack thereof between pairs of calls should ideally be based on tests of how the animals themselves classify calls, as in the experiments discussed in chapter 2, rather than of humans' assessments of sonagrams (Evans, 1997).

The results so far leave unclear what the calls actually mean. A leopard alarm, for instance, could mean "leopard" or it could mean "run to the trees if you're on the ground and stay in the trees if you're there already." This is the kind of issue that may be impossible ever to settle, but one way to tackle it might be to test whether habituation to a particular alarm call transfers to the sight of the predator it purportedly refers to (Evans, 1997). For instance, are animals habituated to a leopard alarm less responsive to the appearance of an actual leopard than animals habituated to, say, a snake alarm? Such experiments would be difficult and perhaps unethical to do in the field, but comparable manipulations might be possible with captive animals (see Hauser, 1996, chap. 8, for other ideas). But what is being suggested here is not very different from what Hollis (1984) showed in her experiments on Pavlovian conditioning of aggressive display in blue gouramis (see chapter 3). A male fish that had been exposed to pairings of a light with the appearance of a rival male showed an enhanced readiness to fight with an actual fish when the CS signaled his appearance. In a sense, then, the CS "meant" rival, in that it associatively elicited responses equivalent to the appearance of the rival himself.

Whatever the conclusion about the meaning of signals, it is a different question whether they are used with intent to inform. Like chickens, alarm-calling vervets show an audience effect. A solitary vervet is unlikely to alarm-call. However, there is no indication that an alarm-calling vervet takes into account the audience's need to know. The individual that first discovers the snake or the leopard should be more likely to call than one whose fellows are already calling or already safe from predation, but Cheney and Seyfarth's (1990b) extensive observations of vervets in the field yielded no evidence that this sort of thing was going on. Research on baboons' contact barks (Cheney, Seyfarth, & Palombit, 1996) and reconciliatory grunts (Cheney & Seyfarth, 1997) leads to the same conclusion. The evidence relevant to intentional communication in vervets and baboons might be summarized as showing that while callers are sensitive to some properties of their audience, they do not take other animals' understanding into account (for review see Seyfarth & Cheney, 1997). This conclusion is consistent with all the other indications in chapter 11 that monkeys do not have a theory of mind.

12.2.4 The Evolution of Functional Reference

The fact that an animal has specific alarm calls and responses for different predators does not necessarily mean the calls refer to qualitatively different predators. Some species of ground squirrels, for example, have different calls and behaviors for snakes and aerial predators, but these calls are better predicted by the immediacy of threat posed by the predator than by its qualitative nature (see Macedonia & Evans, 1993). For instance, an aerial predator sighted from a distance is responded to in the same way as a distant carnivore like a fox, whereas a carnivore appearing close by elicits the calls given to a nearby aerial predator. The imminence of predatory threat is reflected not only in the ground squirrels' calls but also in other behaviors such as whether or not they run into their burrows. Comparisons across several species of mammals suggests that the specificity of alarms reflects the specificity of evasive techniques available for different kinds of predators (Macedonia & Evans, 1993; Zuberbuhler, Noe, & Seyfarth, 1997). For instance, ground squirrels live in open grasslands where their only escape from predators is underground, in their burrows. The nearer the predator, the quicker they need to run in.

Some examples from birds are also consistent with this interpretation. Chickens' aerial alarm calls are fairly indiscriminate (see figure 12.11). This lack of specificity is clearly not due to birds or chickens in general being poor at discriminating and categorizing visual stimuli (see chapters 2 and 5). Three lapwing species in Africa and South America make finer discriminations among predators than chickens do (Walters, 1990). For instance, southern lapwings have three different antipredator responses, which include swooping and pecking at snakes and displaying with wings raised at cattle approaching a nest, presumably with the function of scaring off these predators. The birds' responses to raptors and other large birds depends on the species of predator, on whether the threatening bird was perching or flying, and on whether it had eggs or young in the nest. Walters (1990) studied only one side of possible functional reference in his birds; he did not report any experiments with playbacks. However, he suggests that the apparent difference in specificity of antipredator behavior between chickens and lapwings can be related to differences in their habitat and concomitant differences in the relative costs and benefits of correctly detecting predators vs. making false alarms (see chapter 2). Wild jungle fowl, the species ancestral to the chickens studied by Marler and associates, live—as their name suggests—in the jungle, where approaching predators are likely to be well concealed until they are nearby. In such a situation, it might be important to have a low threshold for alarm calling: any sign of a predator likely means attack is imminent. Making fine discriminations may not be worth the risk in possible decision time lost. In contrast, lapwings live in open habitat where predators can be sighted from afar. They have a wide field of view and are often seen in an upright, vigilant posture. If the birds reacted to anything remotely like a predator they might not have much time left for anything else, and, anyway, if an approaching bird or mammal can be seen from hundreds of meters away, there is plenty of time to take evasive action if the initial response is mistaken.

Similar comparisons among primates lead to the same sort of conclusion about the relationship between habitat and discrimination among predators. Macedonia (1990) used observations, playbacks, and experimental encounters with predators to compare the antipredator responses of two species of lemurs living in large enclosures. Ringtailed lemurs (*Lemur catta*) normally inhabit areas much like those inhabited by vervet monkeys and, because they are similar in size to vervets, they are menaced by similar categories of predators. Not surprisingly, then, they have different calls and different evasive behaviors for ground vs. aerial predators. Furthermore, playbacks of the aerial predator alarm cause ringtailed lemurs to look up, whereas if they are in the trees when they hear it, they tend to climb lower down. Ground predator alarms cause them to run into trees. Moreover, each type of behavior is characteristic of the type of threat, not its intensity. For instance, calls stimulated by a stuffed owl perched in the lemurs' enclosure or by a hawk silhouette pulled over the enclosure on wires were all aerial alarms, even though the "flying" hawk presumably represented a more immediate danger (Pereira & Macedonia, 1991). Ruffed lemurs (*Varecia variegata variegata*) are larger than ringtailed lemurs or vervet monkeys and spend much of their time in dense tree canopy. Although they have more than one alarm call, the responses to these calls are not well differentiated and, moreover, some of them are given in situations of high arousal not involving predators. Thus, their calls do not seem to be functionally referential (Macedonia, 1990; Macedonia & Evans, 1993). As with ground squirrels, imminence may be the only feature of predators that matters in the ruffed lemurs' habitat.

The foregoing comparisons among various birds and mammals suggest that the habitat of a species—for instance, whether or not it affords a view of predators from a distance—determines the variety of antipredator strategies available and, concomitantly, the specificity of alarm calls. A further important factor is social structure (see Hauser, 1996). The benefit of signaling will be a function of the degree to which the signal can influence kin or long-term companions that may reciprocate in future (see chapter 4). Since signaling may be costly if it attracts a predator's attention, we should expect alarm calling to evolve only when single individuals are likely to spot a source of danger before their companions and, in addition, be in a position to warn relatives or possible reciprocal altruists.

12.3 Trying to Teach Human Language to Other Species

It has been said (Snowdon, 1993) that ethologists who study natural communication differ from psychologists who try to teach human language to other species in the same way as anthropologists differ from missionaries. Anthropologists try to understand the natives whereas missionaries try to civilize them. Attempts to teach human language to chimpanzees and other animals have a long history (see Candland, 1993). To some extent, they are the expression of an enduring human wish to communicate with the silent minds of other species (Candland, 1993) or, as the title of one book (Bright, 1990) puts it, the "Dolittle Obsession." The last thirty years or so have seen a series of much-publicized and controversial attempts to teach various forms of human language to chimpanzees and a few other great apes. Although members of the public may be impressed by the apparent accomplishments of these animals when they are shown on television, as they frequently are, professionals still find much about them to debate. The various animal language projects have been extensively reviewed by both proponents and critics of their accomplishments (e.g., Ristau & Robbins, 1982; Rumbaugh & Savage-Rumbaugh, 1994; Wallman, 1992; see also Further Readings in this chapter). It is now generally accepted that the earliest projects had a number of serious flaws and, as a result, did not succeed in doing much more than teach chimpanzees a lot of clever tricks. More recent projects may or may not have overcome all of the problems of the earlier ones. One animal, Kanzi the bonobo, is reported to have reached a level of comprehension of spoken English comparable to that of a 2-year-old child. We begin, however, by considering what, in principle, it would mean if members of another species either did or did not acquire a form of human language.

12.3.1 What Can We Learn?

Can Any Animals Learn Language?   To begin with, "Can animals learn language?" is the wrong question (cf. Roitblat, Harley, & Helweg, 1993). Adult human language is a complex phenomenon with many distinct aspects (Hockett, 1960; Pinker, 1994). Since, as section 12.2 indicates, no other species communicates naturally in nearly such an elaborate way, the more reasonable question to ask is, "What aspect(s), if any, of human language can be acquired by members of another species?" Most features of language identified by Hockett (1960) are shared by the natural communication systems of some other species. The candidates for features uniquely characteristic of human languages include semanticity, displacement, productivity, and duality. As we have seen, the first two may be shared by the natural communication systems of vervets and bees, among possible others, but that does not necessarily mean that bees or vervets can be taught arbitrary "words" for anything in their world. Some recent research on language acquisition in chimpanzees has focused on whether chimpanzees can be.

A second key question has been whether the animals use the signs they learn productively. That is, do they combine signs to create new meanings? An ability to do so would imply an understanding of grammatical rules, or syntax. Much of the recent research to be discussed has used a system that potentially has duality—that is, in principle the language user could both comprehend and produce the words and sentences of the language. Thus, it is possible to ask whether subjects actually understand all that they can produce and vice versa. Focusing on comprehension equally with production liberates the seeker after animal syntax from waiting for the subject to produce novel utterances spontaneously. Rather, its knowledge of syntax can be tapped with tests of comprehension. However, to linguists grammar is more than discriminative responding to word order. It also entails knowledge of the interrelationships among structures in the language. For instance, the native speaker of English not only knows that "Tim gave the apple to Lana" means something different from "Lana gave the apple to Tim." She also knows the relationship of these statements to other grammatical sentences such as "To whom did Tim give the apple?" and "Was the apple given by Tim to Lana?"

Attempts to teach forms of human language to apes have been especially bedeviled by the problem of formulating clear behavioral criteria, for two reasons. One is that during the 30 years since the contemporary wave of such research by psychologists began, linguists and philosophers have also been busy debating and revising their ideas about the essence of language in humans. Within psychology, too, ideas have not stood still. In particular, there have been great advances in understanding language development in children and language use in deaf users of American Sign Language, which was taught to some of the apes we will shortly meet. Closer looks at what actually goes on as children acquire their first words and sentences have been stimulated to some extent by the ape language research (Seidenberg & Petitto, 1987). These developments have served to make the chimpanzee subjects of language training experiments look less like humans than they first appeared. But to the researchers and other proponents of apes' linguistic abilities, it has sometimes seemed as if they were chasing a moving target.

Another development with the same effect has been the Gricean approach to communication (see section 12.1) together with the increasing interest in consciousness on the part of psychologists and philosophers (see chapter 1). Hockett's (1960) features of language do not include the higher orders of intentionality implied by figure 12.2, but reference to them seems to underlie much of the controversy about whether any of the subjects of language training experiments "really have language." As Seidenberg & Pettito (1987) put it, the question is the same as the philosophical question of the Chinese room (Searle, 1980) or, equivalently in terms or artificial intelligence, the question of what, if anything, is the difference between a human and a computer that can answer any question put to it indistinguishably from a human. Intuitively, the human or the Chinese speaker in the Chinese room understands the questions and answers, whereas the computer or the non-Chinese speaker following rules for matching output with input does not. In a similar way, some linguists claim that the behavior of naming is not the same as understanding what naming is (Seidenberg & Petitto, 1987). As we have seen, students of animals' natural communication systems have finessed this issue (some might say, pushed it under the rug) by focusing on functional reference. Even if unavoidable, this sort of move is unlikely to be equally acceptable when it comes to the question of whether other species have human language.

Are Apes like Young Children?   We saw in chapter 11 that apes could profitably be compared with very young children in the nature and development of such capacities as theory of mind and self-concept. Similarly, even if animals cannot be taught to converse like human adults, some have thought they might at least have a childlike grasp of language. Thus, apes exposed to forms of human language might reasonably be compared to young children in their achievements and how they reach them, and this has been done in ape language projects from earlier in this century to the present day. The results of such comparisons parallel precisely the results of the comparisons of swamp sparrows and song sparrows mentioned in chapter 1 (see figure 1.3): when members of two species are exposed to an experience characteristic of the species typical development of one of them, they are influenced in very different ways. Each species of sparrow learns only its own song, and similarly, when child and chimpanzee are exposed to the child's species-typical experiences, the chimpanzee does not develop in the same way as the child.

Does Language Acquisition Reflect Some More General Learning Ability or a Specialized Module?   All hearing children, except those suffering extreme social deprivation, acquire the spoken language used by those around them. Moreover, children develop language in a way that is predictable across cultures and that is shown even in deaf children learning to sign (Pinker, 1994). For instance, even early two-word utterances obey simple grammatical rules. Children seem to develop the ability to speak and understand the language being used around them with very little direct teaching. Still, just as in other species, adults have some special ways of behaving around their young that provide conditions conducive to learning. For instance, mothers talk to their babies and toddlers in very simplified, repetitive language, or "motherese." Language development also depends on the ability to perceive the components of words (box 12.1) and on specifically social cognitive modules, in

Box 12.1. Categorical Perception: Adaptation for Language?

Categorical perception refers to a tendency to perceive stimuli that vary continuously as belonging to discrete categories. Discrimination is sharper at the category boundary than within categories, and stimuli on each side of the boundary are readily given a common verbal or behavioral label. Categorical perception was first studied in human speech (Evans & Marler, 1995; Hauser, 1996). For instance, as acoustic stimuli, /ba/ and /pa/ vary continuously, but adult listeners or young babies played these isolated elements of speech perceive them as belonging to one category or the other, rarely as something in between. Categorical perception of speech sounds would appear to help people recognize the same word when spoken by different speakers, and thus it originally appeared to be a module within the species-specific human language acquisition device. It turns out, though, that chinchillas or budgerigars taught a discrimination between specific exemplars of human speech sounds also behave as if perceiving them categorically. That is, in tests with intermediate sounds their responding does not vary continuously like that in the generalization gradients in figure 5.7. Rather responding shifts abruptly, defining an apparent category boundary.

Evidence for categorical perception is also found in animals' responses to species-relevant stimuli. Territorial male swamp sparrows respond categorically to continuous

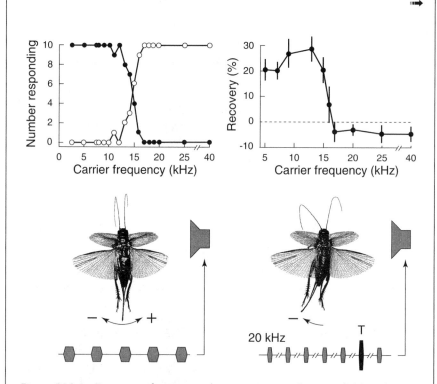

Figure B12.1. Two tests of categorical perception in Polynesian field crickets. Redrawn from Wyttenbach, May, and Hoy (1996) with permission.

Box 12.1. (*continued*)

variation in the duration of certain song notes (Nelson & Marler, 1989), and crickets respond categorically to continuous variation in the frequency of sound pulses (Wyttenbach, May, & Hoy, 1996). Polynesian field crickets (*Teleogryllus oceanicus*) should escape from sound pulses emitted at very high frequencies since they are likely to be emitted by bats, whereas they should approach low-frequency pulses, at 4-5 kHz, because these characterize the calls of conspecifics. Crickets tested in the lab did indeed turn toward sound pulses emitted at low frequencies and away from those at high frequencies, with a sharp break around 15 kHz (figure B12.1, left side). To test crickets' perception more directly, escape responses were habituated to a 20kHz train of pulses, then a test train of a different frequency was administered, followed by a final series at the original frequency. Escape was dishabituated on this final test only with dishabituating stimuli lower than about 15kHz—that is, on the other side of the cricket/bat category boundary (figure B12.1, right).

particular shared attention (see chapter 11). A child knows what an adult is talking about because she can perceive what the adult is attending to. The similarity of all human languages at the level of abstract structure together with the similarity in the way they are acquired led Chomsky (1968) to the idea of a species-specific Universal Grammar. This is the output of a species-specific Language Acquisition Device, or language module. This nativist view of language was opposed in the 1960s by Skinner's explanation of language as just another operant behavior, a view that is now largely discounted. The fact that language-trained apes, dolphins, or parrots do not learn more than rudimentary elements of linguistic behavior, at best, is one reason why it should be.

How Did Human Language Evolve?   The Chomskian view implies that language represents a major discontinuity in mental evolution. The issue of how something so complex, abstract, and specialized might have evolved is controversial and much discussed by brain anatomists, anthropologists, and human behavioral ecologists, among others (Bickerton, 1990; Dennett, 1995; Pinker, 1994; Pinker & Bloom, 1990; Hauser, 1996, chap. 2, provides a useful overview). For the present purposes, the issue is simply what, if anything, the effects of exposing apes or other species to language training can tell us about language evolution. A point often made (e.g., Rumbaugh & Savage-Rumbaugh, 1994) in support of ape language projects is that the results must be relevant to human language evolution because the great apes are our closest living relatives, and chimpanzees share 99% of their genes with humans. The problem with this line of reasoning (Pinker, 1994) is that "closest living relative" has no special status. If all extant primates went extinct tomorrow, some other mammal would be our closest living relative, but that would not mean that studying it would shed any special light on language evolution. Yet untold numbers of hominid species have come and gone since the last common ancestor of apes and humans. Language may have appeared first in a hominid species that is now extinct.

12.3.2 Recent Research, First Phase: Washoe, Nim, Sarah, and Lana

The immediate precursors of contemporary ape language projects were two projects in the 1930s and '40s in which husband-and-wife psychologists—the Kelloggs and later the Hayeses—raised a young chimpanzee like a child for periods of a few months to several years. Although both of these now-famous animals, Gua and Viki, could communicate and solve problems, sometimes better than children of the same age, they did not learn to talk. With great difficulty, Viki was shaped to make vocalizations that could be understood as "mama," "papa," and "cup." However, overall, the results led to the conclusion that chimpanzees could not actually talk, probably because they lacked the neural and anatomical requisites for speech. But clearly this does not mean that they might not be able to communicate linguistically using a medium more within their grasp, and that insight is behind all of the contemporary ape language training projects.

In the first of these, Beatrice and Allen Gardner attempted to teach American Sign Language (ASL) to the infant chimpanzee Washoe (Gardner & Gardner, 1969). As much research has revealed since the Gardners' work began, ASL, the sign language of the deaf, is a sophisticated natural language that is acquired and used like spoken language (see Pinker, 1994). Washoe was surrounded by people who signed but did not speak, in the hopes that she would acquire signing spontaneously, as deaf children do. Shaping and explicit instrumental reinforcement were also used. Washoe was prompted to sign in imitation of her trainers, and in some cases Washoe's hands were molded into the required positions. By the end of the 22nd month of the project, Washoe was judged to know 30 signs, and eventually she was reported to use over 100. Much of the data collection on which these numbers were based went on during the course of daily free behavior—going for walks, eating, looking at magazines, playing. Use of signs was recorded from memory after the event. Later on, Washoe was given structured vocabulary tests in which she signed the names of objects that were hidden from the person interpreting the signs. Later on, too, more emphasis was given to the question of whether combinations of signs constituted sentences. Particularly interesting was the possibility that Washoe combined her signs in novel but meaningful ways. For instance, she was reported to sign "water bird" for a swan. The ways in which this report might suffer from all the usual problems with anecdotes that were outlined in chapter 10 need hardly be mentioned here.

The Gardners' 1969 *Science* paper marked the beginning of an optimistic outpouring of projects with nonvocal languages. The optimism lasted until 1979, and the publication, also in the prominent *Science*, of a deflationary article by Terrace, Petitto, Sanders, and Bever (1979) entitled "Can an ape create a sentence?" These authors had trained an infant chimpanzee, Nim, in

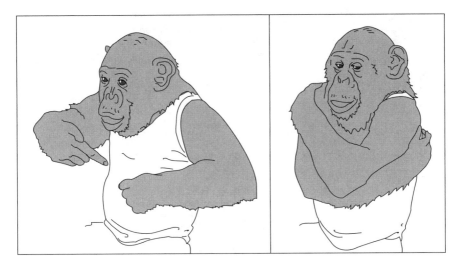

Figure 12.14. Nim signing "me" and "hug." From photographs in Terrace et al. (1979) with permission.

ASL using similar methods to the Gardners. Like Washoe, Nim learned to make many different signs and eventually produced them in combinations of two, three, or more (figure 12.14). His two-sign combinations did have structure rather than being random concatenations of signs. For instance, many combinations consisted of *me* or *Nim* as agent or object of an action, as in "me drink" or "hug Nim." Two-sign sequences like these had regularities that could not be accounted for in terms of the independent frequencies of their components, much like the early sentences of children. However, when it came to longer utterances, the resemblance to child language vanished. As a young child matures and acquires a larger vocabulary, the mean number of words per utterance increases dramatically. The same was not true of Nim. Even though his vocabulary increased to 125 signs by the end of the four-year project, the mean length of his "utterances" stayed about the same (figure 12.15). More important, when he did combine three or more signs, no syntactic rules were apparent. The added signs usually repeated signs already given, as in "play me Nim play" or "grape eat Nim eat." Longer strings of signs had added emphasis, not new information, as if the animal kept on signing till he got what he wanted.

Terrace et al.'s most devastating conclusion came from an analysis of 3.5 hours of filmed interaction between Nim and his trainers. The films revealed that very often Nim's signs were simple repetitions of signs that had just been made by the trainer. This same effect was evident in commercially available films of Washoe that Terrace et al. analyzed, much to the consternation of the Gardners (see Ristau & Robbins, 1982). These observations cast doubt on the possibility that even these animals' orderly two-word strings express an implicit knowledge of syntax. Moreover, the tendency simply to imitate what

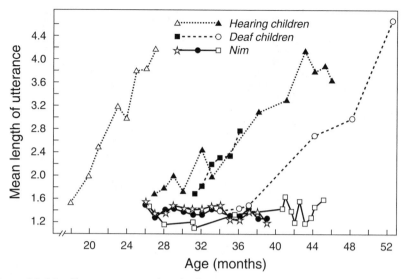

Figure 12.15. Changes in mean length of Nim's utterances over time compared to data from two hearing and two deaf children. Nim's data were recorded in three kinds of circumstances, represented by the three symbols. Redrawn from Terrace et al. (1979) with permission.

was just signed is but one of several ways in which the chimpanzees' use of signs is unlike the child's use of language. Children engage in conversation, which means taking turns to exchange (rather than merely repeat) information. Children also use language for more than getting what they want. They talk about the world, apparently for sheer pleasure in naming and commenting on things (see Pinker, 1994). In contrast, the signing apes tended to "talk out of turn" (Terrace et al., 1979) and seldom used signs other than as instrumental responses. In short, Terrace et al. concluded that the answer to the question posed in the title of their article was a resounding no.

Two other chimpanzee language training projects also got off the ground in the late 1960s. Both used invented nonvocal languages of visual symbols, thereby avoiding some of the methodological problems with signing (see Ristau & Robbins, 1982, for a thoughtful analysis of this issue). The chimpanzee Sarah was trained by Premack (e.g., 1971) to use a system of plastic shapes, and Lana was the first of a continuing series of apes trained by Rumbaugh, Savage-Rumbaugh, and associates to use "Yerkish" symbols on computer keys (Rumbaugh, 1977; Savage-Rumbaugh, 1986). When the animal communicates by touching plastic shapes or computer keys, it is no longer necessary to rely on trainers who sign, in some cases inexpertly and in nonstandardized ways. There is less ambiguity in the animal's "words" since there is less chance of overinterpreting the choice of a symbol than a movement of the animal's hands. With the computer system it is also possible in principle to record and analyze the subject's entire linguistic input and output. On the other hand, confining the animal's linguistic experience to sessions in front of

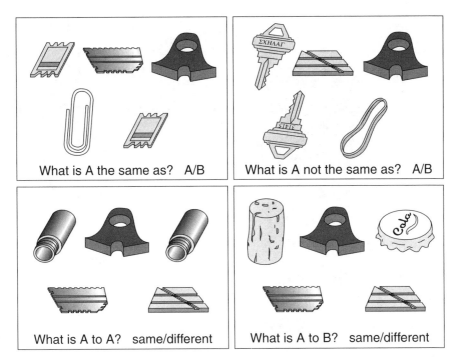

Figure 12.16. Questions about same/different relationships as represented in the system of tokens used to train the chimpanzee Sarah. In the two problems in the top row, Sarah had to choose the correct (matching or nonmatching) object. In the lower pair of questions, she had to choose the token corresponding to "same" or "different." From Premack and Premack (1983) with permission.

a keyboard limits the possibility for spontaneous use of language and makes more apparent the parallels between this form of "language training" and straightforward operant conditioning (see below). More recently, this problem has been overcome by using portable keyboards.

The chimpanzee Sarah was trained with standard operant conditioning methods to associate plastic tokens of various colors and shapes with the objects they "named." In effect she learned symbolic matching to sample. For instance, in the early phases, a piece of apple was placed out of reach and Sarah was required to put the token for *apple* onto a board before she was allowed to eat the apple (Premack, 1971). Once Sarah had acquired some vocabulary, the project focused on using the token system to probe her grasp of concepts like *same/different, color of, name of* (figure 12.16). Rather than a study of chimpanzee language learning it became a test of more general conceptual and problem-solving abilities, such as analogical reasoning (see Premack & Premack, 1983). It was claimed that language training had fostered Sarah's apparent abstract reasoning abilities. She is the same animal we have already met in studies of numerical competence (see chapter 8) and theory of mind (chapter 11).

Figure 12.17. Lana working at her keyboard. The inset shows four of the lexigrams. From the frontispiece of Rumbaugh (1977) with permission.

In the artificial communication system used first with Lana chimpanzee (named for the LANguage Analogue system), the "words" are geometric designs on plastic keys connected to a computer (figure 12.17; Rumbaugh, 1977). Like the animals in the other three early projects, Lana interacted with the symbol system primarily to get things she wanted. The computer was programmed to activate appropriate dispensers upon receipt of grammatical strings like "Please machine give apple" and "Please machine give drink." Not surprisingly, what Lana learned mirrored the contingencies built into this system. Her behavior could be accounted for as associations between actions, people, or objects and symbols that could be plugged into six stock sentences such as "please (person) (action)"(Thompson & Church, 1980). Terrace and others have subsequently demonstrated, in both pigeons and monkeys, the kind of sequence learning that might underlie learning such a stock sentence and studied some of its properties (see box 8.1). Because a very large number of stock sentences would be needed to describe them, some of Lana's later productions were less easily accounted for in this way. Nevertheless, even those who promoted the Lana project at the time now agree that any training regime in which "words" are used primarily as operants to obtain food and activities does not promote genuine linguistic competence, even if chimpanzees might be capable of it (e.g., Rumbaugh, Savage-Rumbaugh, & Sevcik, 1994).

12.3.3 Recent Research, Second Phase: Sherman and Austin, Jack and Jill

Lana continued to serve in studies of cognition, but as a student of Yerkish she was replaced by Sherman and Austin. They were initially trained like Lana, but the most important, later work with them emphasized the interrelationships of production and comprehension, the social use of language, and the possible acquisition of meaning. Syntax was less emphasized, perhaps correctly, given the difficulty of distinguishing simple syntax from sequence learning. Sherman and Austin were taught to name foods and other things by being rewarded with something other than the object being named. For instance, Sherman might be shown a banana and asked (in Yerkish symbols, or *lexigrams*) "What this?" If he selected the lexigram for banana in reply, he received praise or the opportunity to request a different food, but not a piece of banana (Savage-Rumbaugh, 1986). The animals, which already had a considerable vocabulary of lexigrams, took 100–200 trials to learn this skill. Notice that formally it is like symbolic matching to sample or category learning: the animal is exposed to a sample, selects a response, and is reinforced. To continue this analogy, Sherman and Austin were also trained in a form of delayed matching to sample, in which they were shown a food or other interesting object in one room and then led back to their keyboard in a different room and asked to describe or request what they had seen. At a later stage, they were encouraged to use lexigrams to specify what they were about to do or wanted to do (Savage-Rumbaugh, 1986; Savage-Rumbaugh, Pate, Lawson, Smith, & Rosenbaum, 1983). For instance, they were shown how to use a variety of tools such as wrenches and keys to open closed food containers. When presented with a problem that required a particular tool for its solution, Sherman or Austin could request that tool. To see if the requester "knew what he was saying" he might be presented with the whole tool kit to see if he chose the tool he had asked for, which he did at better than chance levels. Naming and requesting were combined with other skills in a situation described as demonstrating "Symbolic communication between two chimpanzees" (Savage-Rumbaugh, Rumbaugh, & Boyson, 1978). Sherman and Austin were induced, by a combination of shaping and simply being placed in a novel situation where they could use lexigrams, to request and share food with one another through the mediation of lexigrams. Now one animal "informed" the other of the contents of a food container, the second animal requested some of the contents, and if both were correct, they both got some of it to eat. There are obvious parallels here with the attempts to establish the functional reference of natural signals (section 12.2), in that the animals have to both produce and respond to the signal appropriately.

As the preceding summary implies, many of the elements of Sherman and Austin's behavior can be described as instrumental discriminations. This was underlined by a tongue-in-cheek report of a simulation of Sherman and Austin's performance by two pigeons, Jack and Jill (Epstein, Lanza, & Skinner, 1980). With conventional procedures of shaping and selective reinforcement,

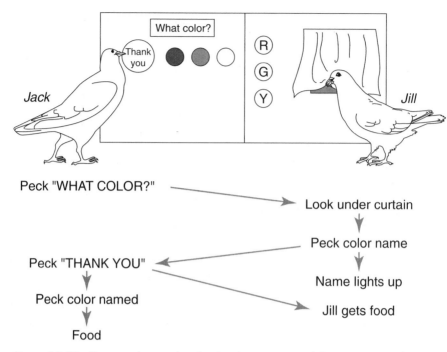

Figure 12.18. Setup and procedure for the demonstration of "communication between two pigeons." After Epstein, Lanza, and Skinner (1980) with permission.

Jack was trained to ask Jill the color of a light hidden under a curtain by peck-ing a "what color?" key, and she was trained to report it to him by pecking a color name. He evidenced his understanding of her report by pecking the se-lected color and then a "Thank you" key (figure 12.18). When both birds per-formed correctly, both were reinforced with grain. Borrowing the words of Savage-Rumbaugh et al. (1978), Epstein et al. (1980, p. 545) concluded, "We have thus demonstrated that pigeons can learn to engage in a sustained and natural conversation without human intervention, and that one pigeon can transmit information to another entirely through the use of symbols." The im-plication of this successful simulation of one aspect of Sherman and Austin's behavior is obviously that all of what they do can be accounted for by the con-tingencies of reinforcement. No special linguistic capacities need be invoked. The same can be said of a demonstration of vocal color naming and respond-ing to names in budgerigars (Manabe, Kawashima, & Staddon, 1995). Whether or not such demonstrations capture everything about the chimpanzees' be-havior and the processes that underlie it is of course debatable.

12.3.4 Kanzi the Bonobo

Just as when Thompson and Church (1980) reduced Lana's first lexigram strings to a few stock sentences, the proponents of the apes' language abilities replied to this attack by saying, in effect, that while part of what the animals do may be accounted for by relatively simple mechanisms, they are not the whole story (e.g., Rumbaugh & Savage-Rumbaugh, 1994). This assessment may or may not be correct for Sherman and Austin and other animals like them, but it is hard to deny for some animals studied more recently. Chief among them is Kanzi the bonobo. Bonobos are so-called pygmy chimpanzees (*Pan paniscus*); previous chimpanzee subjects of language-training projects had all been common chimpanzees (*Pan troglogytes*). Kanzi has two accomplishments that set him apart from previously trained chimpanzees. First, he learned to use and understand lexigrams through observing his foster mother being taught them (Savage-Rumbaugh, McDonald, Sevcik, Hopkins, & Rubert, 1986). Second, he understands human speech. When Savage-Rumbaugh and her colleagues realized Kanzi had evidently acquired his Yerkish and English comprehension skills simply through observation, much as young children initially comprehend more than they can produce, they turned to investigating how far he could go if treated more like a young child. He was allowed to roam a 55-acre wooded area where he could find food and all sorts of experiences, always accompanied by people who talked while communicating on portable keyboards about what was happening or about to happen.

Kanzi's understanding of spoken English sentences has been directly compared to that of a 2-year-old child in a carefully controlled way (Savage-Rumbaugh et al., 1993). Both Kanzi and Alia, the child, were asked to carry out instructions expressed by simple sentences like "Get the telephone that's outdoors" or "Make the doggie bite the snake." A variety of objects was present, and the two subjects were asked to do several actions with each one rather than just the obvious ones. Importantly, these tests employed some completely novel sentences (see Savage-Rumbaugh & Brakke, 1996). Precautions were taken against cuing by the person giving the instructions and selective recording by the raters. For instance, in some tests the other people present in the room with Kanzi to record data wore headphones broadcasting loud music so they would not know what he had been asked to do. The person talking to Kanzi was out of sight behind a one-way mirror, so as to avoid cues of gaze direction and the like. Kanzi performed comparably to Alia on these tests. In other tests, his competence at producing sentences with lexigrams was comparable to that of a 1 ½-year-old. These results can be taken to indicate that Kanzi has learned more than to perform complex operants to get what he wants but rather uses and understands words and sequences of words as representations of states of the world (Rumbaugh & Savage-Rumbaugh, 1994; Savage-Rumbaugh et al., 1993; but see Seidenberg & Petitto, 1987).

Does Kanzi's performance represent a species difference between bonobos and chimpanzees? Given the threat to both species in the wild, not to mention the expense and labor involved in raising them with a rich experience of spoken and symbolic language, it is unlikely that the data ideally required to answer this question will ever be collected. However, a few bonobos besides Kanzi have been studied, one in parallel with a similarly treated young chimpanzee, and it does appear that they have a greater propensity to acquire comprehension of spoken English than chimpanzees do (Rumbaugh & Savage-Rumbaugh, 1994). So far it is not at all clear why they would be expected to be especially likely to learn human language. Bonobos are not so well studied as chimpanzees in the wild, so it is not clear whether their natural communication system is more languagelike. Evolutionarily they are no more part of the hominid lineage than chimpanzees.

12.3.5 Conclusions

So much has been written about attempts to teach language to nonhuman species, and from so many conflicting points of view (see the Further Readings), that it is impossible to do more here than give this subject a brief look. In addition to the apes we have considered, a few orangutans and a gorilla have also been exposed to various forms of language training. Dolphins and a sea lion have been taught to obey complex systems of gestural or auditory commands (cf. chapters in Roitblat, Herman, & Nachtigall, 1993) Although these have some linguistic properties, the processes involved in learning to obey them can be analyzed as conditional discrimination learning and stimulus equivalence (Gisiner & Schusterman, 1992). And we have already met Alex the parrot in chapters 8 and 10. His ability to talk has been exploited more as a way to assess what nonlinguistic concepts he can acquire or express than for what it may reveal about language learning per se (Pepperberg, 1993b). The methods used to teach him through observational learning, mentioned in chapter 10, are unique in animal language-training projects. However, because they rely on shared attention they may have wider relevance (Pepperberg & McLaughlin, 1996).

Given how closely the results of animal language-training projects bear on ideas about what makes us human, controversy about them is likely to continue. As the reader may have noticed, however, most of the issues in this area are ones we have met in earlier chapters: the need for unambiguous behavioral criteria for an essentially human cognitive process in another species, the problems of Clever Hans and overinterpreted results, the shortcomings of anecdotes and single-subject studies, the relative roles of general processes of learning vs. modularity and species-specificity. In the context of an overview of animal cognition such as this one, animal language-training projects raise few if any issues that are unique. The main ones, in fact, have to do with what constitutes human language and how it develops in very young children, topics that are beyond the scope of this book.

Much of the controversy in this area boils down to disagreement over whether the subjects "really" have one aspect or another of linguistic competence—syntax, reference, etc.—or whether their behavior is "merely" instrumental responding. It is paradoxical that while experience of conditioning procedures is increasingly being said to lead to complex and subtle representations of the world (see chapters 3 and 5), interpreting animals' communicative behaviors as the results of associative learning is taken to rob them of interesting cognitive content. Consider, for example, the experiments of Holland and others reviewed in chapter 3 in which rats behave as if a Pavlovian CS evokes an image of its associated US, an image that can itself support new learning. Don't these findings mean the CS has acquired meaning for the rat?

Another anomaly is that any demonstration that linguistic output, whether it be vocal, pressing symbols, or responding to spoken commands, can be explained as simple discrimination learning is taken as showing that the subjects are not doing what a young child would do in similar circumstances. Yet simple associative learning may well explain some of the young child's early responses to speech, and some of the child's early sentences may be no more complex than Lana's stock sentences (Seidenberg & Petitto, 1987). One may note that Kanzi acquired his comprehension of spoken English only after intensive exposure and an extraordinary amount of attention from human companions, but such experience is the norm for young children. If language exposure changes apes' cognition as some claim (e.g., Premack, 1983; Savage-Rumbaugh & Brakke, 1996), then maybe some of the same changes are responsible for child language acquisition in the first place. Yet the difference remains that the child's early language rapidly develops into the elaborate and unique form of communication used, for example, in reading and writing books like this one, whereas even the bonobo's does not (Pinker, 1994).

12.4 Overview

The first part of this chapter, on natural communication systems, is but a brief survey of a major area of research in ethology, with vast literature of its own. Hauser (1996), for example, requires over 600 pages to review animal communication, and even then he leaves out almost everything about insects. However, many of the concepts and issues that arise in the study of communication have been considered already in this book. The contrast between ecological and anthropocentric approaches is apparent in the contrast between studies of natural communication systems and attempts to teach language to other species. Other issues introduced earlier in the book include how the properties of signals are matched to the receivers' perceptual systems (chapter 2), the immediate and long-term, selective costs and benefits of signaling and responding to signals (chapter 2), and how animals categorize stimuli and how such behavior can be studied (chapter 5). Issues relevant to the behavioral ecology and evolution of signalling were touched on in several places—for instance, in the discussion of reciprocal altruism and kin recognition in chapter 4. The cognitive ethological approach to communication suggests studying whether animals send signals with the intent to modify their receivers' behavior or perhaps even their understanding, abilities which require a theory of mind. Related issues include whether signals are used deceptively and whether adults teach young animals how and when to signal. Again, these questions involve more general issues in comparative cognition that have been discussed already, in chapters 10 and 11. Just as in the examples discussed in those chapters and elsewhere, a key issue is how to translate essentially anthropocentric concepts into predictions about observable behavior. In the context of natural communication systems, this has been done in the development of criteria for functional reference.

Demonstrations that bees, chickens, and vervet monkeys communicate with conspecifics about the state of the world contrast with the traditional ethological view of animal signals as expressions of motivational states like readiness to fight, flee, or mate. Clearly, that view was too limited. A more comprehensive view is that motivational and referential signaling are on a continuum (Marler, Evans, & Hauser, 1992). Nevertheless, there are important parallels among functional reference, attempts to study what "words" mean to language-trained apes, and phenomena in the study of what CSs represent in associative learning. The main difference may turn out to be that whereas the CS is produced by the experimenter and "understood" by the animal, signals are both produced by and received by animals.

What, then, are the concepts specific to the study of communication? Of course, the terminology of sender, receiver, message and meaning is new. In the comparison of animal communication to human language we have also encountered a variety of unique concepts having to do with the nature of language. One of the most contentious is whether or not any animals have acquired syntax, or, indeed, even semantics—that is, an understanding of the meanings of the elements in the system being taught. In that context it may be worth bearing in mind that none of the intensively studied systems of natural communication that we have reviewed provides any examples of syntax, or meaning derived from the ordering of elements. Bird song has sometimes been considered a possible exception, but although some birds sing many different songs (Catchpole & Slater, 1995; see also chapter 10), so far as is known these are used interchangeably rather than being put together in different ways to convey different messages.

Do honeybees have language? Can apes learn human language? The chapter began with the first of these questions and ended with the second. Research on communication in bees, apes, and other species has engendered controversy not because it is more difficult to do well than other kinds of research in comparative cognition but because its results seem to bear so much more directly on what makes us human. Darwin's (1871) claim of mental continuity between humans and other species has been severely tested when it comes to language. Macphail (1987) has suggested that there are essentially no qualitative differences among vertebrates in simple associative learning and all that flows from it, such as category learning, perceptual learning, and the like—everything reviewed in chapters 2 through 6. To that we might add spatial learning and timing, as reviewed in chapters 7 through 9. But what is unique about humans is the ability to acquire language. In that, Macphail joins the many linguists and evolutionary psychologists who see human language as the expression of a species-specific cognitive module. Apparently no amount of general intelligence, such as that exhibited by the subjects of ape language studies, suffices to allow other species to acquire more than a few rudiments of the behavior normally underlain by human language modules. And language may be what make possible self-recognition, theory of mind, and even consciousness.

Further Reading

Hauser's (1996) big book, *The Evolution of Communication*, is a thorough survey of animal communication and related issues from the same perspective as this book. Useful shorter reviews of the ethology and behavioral ecology of communication can be found in Halliday and Slater (1983) and Krebs and Davies (1993). Numerous detailed treatments of specific topics in this chapter are available. The well-illustrated book by Gould and Gould (1988) is a fine introduction to the lives of honeybees, with special attention to the dance language and spatial cognition. Seeley (1995) shows how communication helps regulate a hive's resources. Cheney and Seyfarth's research is described in their book *How Monkeys See the World*. A comprehensive recent review of their research on vervets and other species, emphasizing the role of associative learning is Seyfarth and Cheney (1997). Evans and Marler (1995) is a thoughtful overview of functional reference in chickens and other topics; Evans (1997) is a more detailed critical assessment. The book edited by Roitblat, Herman, and Nachtigall (1993) contains useful chapters representing most of the major contemporary research programs on natural and taught communication in species including parrots, vervets, and dolphins. Hockett (1960) remains a clear and useful comparison of animal communication and human language.

Pinker's (1994) *The Language Instinct* is a prize-winning account of all aspects of language, giving plenty of attention to evolutionary and comparative issues. Candland (1993) provides an illuminating and often entertaining account of the long history of attempts to talk with animals and feral human children. Few reviews of the animal language-training projects are not strongly biased one way or another. Ristau and Robbins (1982) is an exception. They thoughtfully analyze the methodology and results of all the early projects; many of their points still bear notice. Wallman's (1992) *Aping Language* is a useful but highly critical review of all the recent work. *Kanzi, the Ape at the Brink of the Human Mind* (Savage-Rumbaugh & Lewin, 1994) represents a different point of view. Briefer reviews are the chapters by Rumbaugh and Savage-Rumbaugh (1994) and Savage-Rumbaugh and Brakke (1996).

13

Summing Up and Looking Ahead

Weaving a tapestry, composing a symphony, making a journey—each requires continually shifting attention between an overall plan and a multitude of details. Our survey of how animals perceive, learn, and make decisions about the world is no different. A concern with the big issues stated in the preface and chapter 1 has constantly had to be traded off with discussions of how experiments were designed, how the results were interpreted, what theorists actually meant, and so on. This chapter briefly takes the longer view again, in an attempt to see what all the details signify. The first part of the chapter summarizes the evidence for modularity in animal cognition and contrasts some of the candidate parts of animal minds. It then asks what our survey suggests about how cognition might evolve. The issue of how animals represent the world has arisen in discussions of topics throughout the book, from associative learning to theory of mind. Section 13.3 tentatively summarizes what we can conclude about it. The final section once again argues for a synthetic program of research on comparative cognition.

13.1 Modularity and the Animal Mind

Our review of how animals perceive the world, learn about physical causation, recognize and categorize, time seconds and days, count, orient, imitate, relate to their conspecifics, and do other things makes clear that the animal mind contains a variety of adaptively specialized cognitive modules. As evolutionary psychologists are fond of saying, the mind is like a Swiss Army knife, a general-purpose tool made of many specialized parts. Cognitive modules were defined in chapter 1 as encapsulated information-processing mechanisms. Encapsulation means that a given module processes a restricted domain of information in a particular, functionally appropriate way but is impervious to other information. Some of the best examples of cognitive modularity are found in perception. Accordingly, chapter 2 set the stage for the remaining chapters by discussing examples of how sensory systems are tuned in species-specific ways to the most informative energies in the species' environment.

Cognitive modules are usually described as being domain-specific (Hirschfeld & Gelman, 1994), but this criterion is not necessarily easy to apply. What delimits a domain? Is visual information a single domain or is visual motion an appropriate domain to consider? All spatial information or distance and direction walked from home? *Domain* seems to be a fractal concept, in that any category of environmental information can be infinitely subdivided into smaller and smaller nested domains: visual information, then color, shape, motion, then the different wavelengths; spatial information, then vestibular motion sensations, visually localized landmarks, and so on. Similarly, how do we decide when we have more than one distinct cognitive module rather than a single module processing a variety of kinds of information? Clearly, these decisions are based on largely unstated assumptions about what kinds of differences are theoretically interesting.

One approach to resolving these problems is Sherry and Schacter's (1987) suggestion that different cognitive modules, or memory systems to use their term, have different rules of operation, matched to environmental requirements for functionally incompatible kinds of information processing. To take their example, song learning (chapter 10) and retrieving scatter hoarded food (box 1.4; chapter 6) must be subserved by different memory systems because in song learning a small amount of auditory information experienced repeatedly early in life is stored for months or years, whereas in food storing large amounts of spatial information, each experienced briefly, must be stored and later forgotten at various times throughout the bird's life. But these are quantitative differences, and differences in amount and durability of information storage are relatively weak evidence for cognitive modularity compared to evidence of qualitative differences in how information is processed, stored, or used—different rules of operation in Sherry and Schacter's terms.

So what examples of different rules of operation have we encountered? At various points in the book, explicit contrasts have been drawn between two or more qualitatively distinct ways of processing superficially rather similar information from related domains. For instance, in chapter 3 occasion setting (conditional control) was contrasted with the acquisition of excitation and inhibition. Chapter 7 presented evidence for a number of distinct spatial information-processing modules, including path integration, the sun compass, and landmark use. Not only do these differ among themselves in the kind of information that is used and the way in which it determines behavior but also none of them seems obviously to involve direct excitation and inhibition of behavior or motivational systems in the way associative learning does. To take other examples, in chapter 8 interval timing was contrasted with circadian timing, and chapter 10 discussed the distinct representational capacities presupposed by true imitation. These and other candidates for separable cognitive modules are distinguished from one another by domain, representational content, and possible distinctive rules of operation. Domain here is more abstract than categories of sensory information. For instance, associative learning can take place with all sorts of inputs, as long as they exemplify the abstract relationships typical of physical causation. Unambiguous evidence for different principles can be difficult to gather—as we have seen, for instance, in the discussion of overshadowing and blocking in spatial learning (chapter 7). There is still very little relevant data bearing on many of these distinctions, but in other cases the distinctions are clear. For instance, the ephemeris function (chapter 7) is intrisically part of a bee's sun compass system and has nothing do to with, say, learning what shape and color of flower has the most nectar.

The candidates for separate modules take different kinds of input and give output that serves different functions in an adaptive way: association formation tracks physical causation, circadian timing adjusts behavior to local day and night, dead reckoning tracks position relative to a starting point, and so on. However, adaptive differences in how information is acquired and operated on are not the same as adaptive uses of information (Sherry, 1988). In associative learning, for instance, inputs can be tactile, visual, auditory, olfactory, and gustatory; and outputs can serve social, sexual, feeding, defensive, and other behavior systems. But as far as is known, the way in which this diversity of information is acquired and put together to influence behavior is the same across sensory modalities and behavior systems. That is to say, associative learning has a variety of adaptive uses. In contrast, dead reckoning operates on very specific types of input—primarily vestibular in some mammals and primarily visual in some insects—and outputs instructions for locomotion relative to egocentric coordinates, though this locomotion may be motivated by more than one behavior system. But the concepts of excitation and inhibition simply do not seem relevant to understanding how the ant in the desert or the hamster in the dark relocates its nest, except possibly at the level of neural net models. Nevertheless, information acquisition has some general properties across many domains simply because of how the world works. Learning sometimes needs to be maximal after one trial—the ant or hamster that couldn't relocate its nest after a single trip on a unique path wouldn't survive to make other trips—but in general the more often something has been repeated, the more likely it comes from a stable property of the world, worth remembering and responding to (chapter 6). Hence, repeated trials generally have a greater effect than a single trial. Having acquired information, the animal must use it in an adaptive way. For instance, associating certain sounds or odors with the presence of a mate should not cause those cues to be attacked or fled from.

At the same time, however, differences among kinds of information dictate differences in how they should be processed. For instance, two weak physical causes of the same thing should produce an extra-big response when they occur together, whereas cues for two different time intervals don't add up to a cue to respond at an extra-long interval but to respond at each interval signaled, and two landmarks pointing to the same goal should lead to more precise localization of that goal. The competitive processing exemplified by blocking and overshadowing in associative learning is the most thoroughly documented principle for combining information from different sources, but we have seen examples of other possibilities. Different sources of information may be processed in parallel, treated as a unique configural entity, or one may give conditional information about the significance of the other in a hierarchical manner.

Discussions of modularity in cognition often emphasize that adaptive ways of processing different signals from the environment must be innate, like eyes, ears, and noses (e.g., Cosmides & Tooby, 1994; Shepard, 1994). Animals need an "innate schoolmarm" (Lorenz, 1965), an "instinct to learn" (Marler, 1991a). There simply is not time in most animals' life spans for appropriate ways of processing and using different kinds of information to develop from a system that is completely undifferentiated to start with. Prefunctional adaptive modularity is especially clear in sensory systems, in short-lived species like bees and ants, and in cases where learning has a crucial job to do early in life, long before correlates of its fitness consequences (as detected by evolved mechanisms of reinforcement) can feed back on cognitive organization. Imprinting (chapter 4) and song learning (chapter 10) provide exceptionally clear examples of prefunctional early learning. As another example, bees come prewired with a default ephemeris function, the ability to associate odor, color, shape, pattern, and time of day with nectar sources, and impressive navigational abilities—at least three separate and adaptively organized cognitive modules.

13.2 How Does Cognition Evolve?

The traditional, anthropocentric view of cognitive evolution can be summarized (or caricatured, depending on your point of view) roughly as follows (chapter 1). Species can be ranked on a phylogenetic scale from simplest to most complex. Animal intelligence consists of a hierarchy of learning processes (Mackintosh, 1994a; Macphail, 1996; Povinelli, 1994; Thomas, 1996). Habituation, the most elementary, is shared by all species. Next in the hierarchy and of similarly wide generality is associative learning, then various forms of more "complex" learning and problem solving, such as forming learning sets and acquiring abstract concepts. At the top of the hierarchy and unique to humans is language. In the light of the material in this book, such a view has an unjustifiably narrow behavioral and phylogenetic base. It sees animal intelligence as consisting of learning, primarily learning to solve problems said to require intellegence in people rather than problems that occur in the species own environment, and it focuses on data from socially isolated individuals of a few species solving problems about physical causation in the laboratory.

If, in contrast, intelligence is seen as solving problems of ecological relevance in the environment in which the species evolved, then all species still extant are equally intelligent in their own ways, and the question becomes what different species' intelligence consists of. Answering that question is part of the ecological program for comparative cognition. Just as species do not evolve in a linear way, neither does cognition. Because cognition is modular, it makes no more sense to propose a linear hierarchy of cognitive modules than it does to line up sensory systems from simplest and most general to most advanced. Echolocation, magnetoreception, electroreception, photoreception—all appear in diverse species whose lifestyle they particularly suit, and they are fine-tuned in each species. However, species do obviously differ in the number of states of the world they can discriminate—think of the difference between light-dark discrimination and color vision—and in the variety of ways they have available for acting on the world. Staddon (1983) makes this point very compellingly with the example of the one-celled organism *Stentor*, which can ingest, reject, or escape things that come its way in an appropriate and evolutionarily successful yet extremely simple manner.

In contrast to the traditional view of cognitive evolution as continuous improvement across the phylogenetic scale, the view of cognition as a collection of adaptively specialized modules suggests that some abilities will be widely shared while others will appear only on a few branches of the evolutionary tree, perhaps widely separated ones. Habituation (chapter 4) and associative learning (chapter 3) are examples of the former; true imitation (chapter 10) appears to be an example of the latter (Moore, 1996). Language and theory of mind may be among a constellation of abilities found in the human lineage alone (chapters 11 and 12). In addition to asking what kind of information processing occurs where in phylogeny and why, it might also be fruitful to ask whether new ways of combining existing modules also arise and why. For instance, desert ants seem to use dead reckoning and landmarks separately, in successive phases of their homeward journey, whereas hamsters may use them simultaneously, taking an average (chapter 7).

Although cognitive modules can be seen as adaptive specializations—evolved functionally appropriate ways of processing and using information—adaptive specialization does not necessarily result in separate cognitive modules. Evolution can produce quantitative fine-tuning of cognitive capacities general to many species, like the variations in birds' beaks illustrated in figure 1.15. These are also adaptive specializations. Again, sensory systems provide the paradigm examples: specialization on catching insects in the dark favors echolocation in bats, very refined hearing but not improved sensory abilities in general. Indeed, if for no other reason, the fact that an animal can carry around only just so much brain imposes tradeoffs.

Differences among cognitive modules seem to involve more than quantitative fine-tuning of an evolutionarily prior module. One suggestion here is that during evolution existing systems become accessible to a wider range of inputs (Rozin, 1976). We saw one possible example in chapter 7 in the way responding to environmental shape seemed to be the primary means of spatial orientation during human development, but that information from landmarks became accessible to spatial decision making later on. This means that when new cognitive requirements arise during evolution, existing mechanisms may turn out to be exaptations—that is, evolved under a different set of selection pressures but capable of being used to solve a new adaptive problem (Sherry & Schacter, 1987).

Accessibility and exaptation may not be the best ways to think about cognitive evolution, however. To take an example from perception, where modularity and species differences can be seen more clearly, would it make sense to think of electroreception in the platypus's bill as visual sensitivity extended to electric fields? Exaptation and accessibility may well be discernable in cognitive evolution, but to some extent this idea may be too much influenced by "boxes in the head" models of information processing like those discussed in chapters 4 and 8. Associative learning, for instance, is probably not localized to a single module in the brain that puts together any of a variety of inputs in the way described by the Rescorla-Wagner model and then produces outputs appropriate to the behavior system being served. Although it is easy to think of new inputs or outputs acquiring access to this sort of module, plasticity is more likely local to particular input-output systems, as habituation of the startle reflex is localized in the startle circuit. In this view, accessibility or exaptation might be expected at the level of cellular or subcellular mechanisms for neural plasticity.

In *The Origin of Species*, Darwin (1859) aimed to convince by sheer weight of evidence, by hundreds of examples from many phyla that all pointed to organic evolution. By contrast, there is little systematic data relevant to cognitive evolution at the level of detail required to draw conclusions on the issues touched on here. One way forward is comparisons of close relatives with divergent ecologies. By far the most detailed data relevant to a broadly based ecologically oriented comparative cognition come from the study of sensory systems (chapter 2), and this area is a good starting place for theorizing about how and why information-processing abilities evolve. Analyses of the mechanisms underlying cognitive differences among close relatives—as in responses to signals (chapter 2), song learning (chapter 10), or spatial memory (chapter 6)—are most likely to lead to insights into the mechanisms of cognitive evolution by eventually permitting comparisons at the level of fine-grained differences in neural circuitry and, ultimately, genetic mechanisms. Advances in theory and methods for tracing phylogenies are likely to make a contribution here, as are studies of molecular mechanisms of cognition—for instance, in manipulation of genes thought to be involved in specific aspects of cognition and behavior. Bringing molecular approaches together with the analysis of natural examples could be especially illuminating.

13.3 Anthropomorphism and Representational Explanations

Getting around, relating to other people, thinking about the past and planning for the future—most of us would find it difficult or impossible to describe what we do without reference to mental representations of the world. When members of other species do things that look like what people would do under analogous circumstances, whether it be carrying home a morsel of food or calling out at the sight of a dangerous predator, interpretations of their behavior in terms of analogous mental representations are almost irresistible (chapter 1, chapter 11). The animal was using its cognitive map, intending to warn its relatives, and so on. Cognitive ethology and cognitive science more generally encourage such interpretations, but as we have seen, many complex behaviors are apparently accomplished in the absence of explicit internal representations of their goals. In comparative psychology, anthropomorphic representational explanations of behavior are also encouraged by the tradition of looking for similarities between other animals and humans. But it is one thing to test whether other species share cognitive mechanisms with humans; it is another to assume those commonalities and fail to look for alternatives. Contributing to the confusion is the problem that many terms used by cognitive ethologists and behavioral ecologists have both functional and cognitive, folk psychological interpretations (Kennedy, 1992). Functional labels like "sampling," "optimizing," and "deceiving" too easily slip into use as causal explanations. For instance, the plover's broken-wing display may function to deceive the fox, in that the fox responds as he would to an injured bird, but this does not mean that the plover intends to deceive or that the fox is consciously thinking that the bird is injured and would therefore be easy prey (chapter 11). Similarly, animals may or may not behave in ways that function to teach others, but if they do they need not also have intentions to teach, let alone a theory of mind (chapter 10). Table 13.1 lists examples from throughout the book in which a piece of behavior has been taken as evidence for a more complex representational process than was warranted without further research. In some cases, such as spatial orientation in bees and transitive inference-like performance in pigeons, a simpler process has been shown to be doing the job.

The biggest pitfalls in this area can be avoided by trying to answer a few simple questions at the outset. The first is, What does an animal with cognitive capacity x do? Research on animal cognition has sometimes failed to specify adequately the behavioral evidence for the capacity being sought. This leads to a situation where evidence is presented by proponents of, say, cognitive mapping or intentional deception, and the sceptics' reaction is, "That's not what we meant; what about. . . ." Because research can take a long time and the rest of science is evolving in the meanwhile, what was agreed on at the outset of an investigation can come to seem oversimple by the time the data come in. Nowhere is this more evident than in the history of attempts to teach forms of human language to apes (chapter 12). Nevertheless, this possibility does not negate the importance of starting with some idea of what behavior

Table 13.1.

Behavior (Chapter)	Interpretation
Passing a test of transitive inference (5)	Understanding transitive inference
Discriminating natural stimulus categories (5)	Having a concept or a representation of the category prototype
Following a disappearing object (11)	Knowing an object exists when out of sight
Homing from a novel location (7)	Having a cognitive map
Maximizing overall net energy gain (9)	Adding numbers or amounts, adding times, computing and comparing rates
Copying another's behavior(10)	Taking the other's point of view
Using a tool(10)	Understanding how the tool works
Reacting to one's own mirror image (11)	Having a concept of self
Following another's gaze (11)	Having a theory of mind
Emitting an alarm or other call, exhibiting functional reference (12)	Intending to communicate

differentiates an animal that has x from one that doesn't. For example, if an animal has a general concept of number, it will be able to count novel objects in random arrays, whereas if it is memorizing responses to familiar stimuli, its proportion of correct responses will depend on the perceptual similarity of the test array to training arrays (chapter 8).

The next question is, What are alternative possibilities? How could a chimpanzee's behavior in front of a mirror be explained other than by its having a self-concept? Maybe the chimpanzee is engaging in normal species-specific grooming behavior and neither the mirror nor the mark has anything to do with its touching the mark. Maybe a rat is not using a cognitive map or comparing exemplars to a category prototype but memorizing and generalizing. In thinking about what hypotheses are worth entertaining, it can also help to ask whether it is reasonable to think that x has evolved rather than something cognitively simpler. What difference could it make to fitness for an animal to have conscious intentions, a theory of mind, a cognitive map, an explicit representation of a category prototype, or a concept of self? Of course, formulating unambiguous alternatives does not guarantee finding unambiguous answers. For example, some animals might show evidence of self-awareness or intentional behavior in some situations but not in others. The capacity in question may be multifaceted, so species may differ in how many attributes of it they possess. The results of language-training studies with chimpanzees provide many examples. Here, the best question turns out to be not, Do chimpanzees have language or not? but something like, What characteristics of linguistic behavior are chimpanzees capable of showing, and under what conditions? In this area, as in investigations of theory of mind in primates

(chapter 11), the expectation that there will be an all-or-nothing answer—for example, chimpanzees either are like humans or they are not—is being replaced by the notion that chimpanzees and perhaps other apes, but not monkeys, may have some of the same capabilities as very young children.

There are two issues here. One arises most pressingly in discussions of cognitive ethology, and that is whether or not behaviors of nonhuman species are governed by intentional states like those people would experience in similar circumstances—that is, plans, intentions, theory of mind, and the like. The other, partially independent issue is whether behavior is usefully thought of as governed by explicit representations at all. This is the question that arises, for example, when we ask whether an animal has a cognitive map as opposed to performing a chain of responses to successively encountered stimuli. This issue is sometimes, inappropriately it was argued in chapter 1, seen as that of whether animal behavior is "cognitive," on the one hand, or results from "mere associations," on the other. Paradoxically, even as accounts of animal (e.g., Gallistel, 1990) and human behavior in terms of explicit representations are being increasingly challenged (Clark, 1997), students of associative learning are increasingly emphasizing the power of "mere associations" to encode events in the world with great subtlety and sophistication (chapters 3–5).

The experimental strategy of triangulation (chapter 11) is nearly always required to distinguish representational from nonrepresentational, more robotlike interpretations of behavior or to distinguish one representational interpretation from another. Triangulation entails a series of tests designed to point to the same conclusion from different metaphorical angles. For example, an animal might be trained on an abstract concept in one set of conditions and then be given tests that are conceptually but not physically similar so that they cannot be solved by simple associative learning plus stimulus generalization. Researchers are increasingly aware that just because we see an experiment as a test of x doesn't ensure the animals do. From the animal's point of view, a test of theory of mind may be a conditioning experiment (chapter 11); a test of cognitive mapping may be an encounter with visual images that need to be matched with familiar views of the environment (chapter 7). As increasingly clever and sophisticated experiments are used to study cognitive processes of ecological importance, these methodological and conceptual issues are likely to remain in the fore.

13.4 Synthesizing the Ecological and Anthropocentric Programs

The ecological or adaptationist program for research on comparative cognition and the anthropocentric, traditional, or general-process program are distinguished from each other by the core questions they ask (chapter 1). In effect, the ecological program asks how animals acquire, process, and act on information in nature and why, in terms of evolution and ecology. The traditional program asks how animals perform on humanlike cognitive tasks and what cognitive mechanisms enable them to do so. In fact, of course, even if these two research traditions were that simple and one tracked, they could hardly be completely separate. Research within the ecological program frequently borrows procedures and ideas from the traditional or general-process program. For example, in research on spatial memory in food-storing birds (chapter 6), memory in chickadees, nutcrackers, and other species has been compared and analyzed in terms of list lengths, retention intervals, interference, item distinctiveness, and so on. Techniques for testing animals have been freely borrowed from laboratory studies of rats (radial mazes) and pigeons (operant delayed matching). On the flip side, the most thoughtful recent experiments on primate intelligence (chapters 10–12) have used information about phylogeny and natural history to try to illuminate differences and similarities among monkeys, apes, and humans. Productive research in these kinds of areas would be impossible without some sort of synthesis, even if not very explicit.

But what can be gained by more explicit syntheses of ecological/adaptationist and anthropocentric/traditional/general process traditions? In attempting to answer this question, it might be useful to distinguish between shallow and deep syntheses. Relatively shallow syntheses are those in which results or methods from one area are imported into another, without any real theoretical integration. Using results from laboratory studies of visual search to explain search image effects in the wild might be an example (chapter 2). This is a perfectly useful kind of integration, in that someone studying search images can save himself a lot of trouble by noticing that the effects of many of the variables he is interested in are already understood but labeled by psychologists as effects on visual search. Another example of a relatively shallow synthesis would be taking a capacity studied for anthropocentric reasons like counting or serial order learning and trying to account for why animals are capable of it with a "just so" story about behavior in the wild.

By contrast, deeper syntheses involve a genuine integration of theory and/or data from the two traditions. To take the example of search images a little further, the person using psychologists' data and theory about visual search to account for search image–like effects might find that some phenomena of importance in the wild remain unaccounted for. A gap in data could generate new mechanistic analyses that might lead on to a more comprehensive theory. To take another example, a deep synthesis of theory and data about simple discrimination learning in the laboratory with theory and data about mimicry systems (chapter 5) would entail, among other things, incorporating aspects of the Rescorla-Wagner model into models of the evolution of mimicry together with laboratory investigations of new questions about learning that might be generated by observations in the wild. In chapter 9, we saw several examples of how the principles of information use have been studied in the context of well-formulated adaptive problems such as response to risky foraging outcomes. The adaptive "what should they do and how do they do it" sets the agenda here. However, analysis of "how do they do it" has gone deeper than existing information as tests of risk sensitivity in the laboratory have generated new hypotheses about how animals assess and compare rates of reinforcement. In another example of a deep synthesis, information about species and sex differences in spatial behavior have been used to choose species for comparative study of brain areas related to spatial cognition (chapter 1).

A research program sets the agenda for a group of scientists by defining the important questions (see Kamil, 1998, for a discussion with respect to comparative cognition). In examples of shallow synthesis, researchers working within one program are forced to look outside it for answers to some of their questions, but the core questions of the program are not at issue. Deep syntheses, in contrast, are the beginnings of new research programs. New questions come to the fore; old data are reinterpreted in their light or simply become irrelevant. Regardless of whether or not a deep synthesis of the approaches to understanding comparative cognition is possible, let alone deserves to be called a new research program, there are many exciting questions about animal minds waiting to be tackled.

Further Reading

Other general discussions of the future of research on comparative cognition include the last chapter of Vauclair's (1996) text, articles in the symposium on comparative cognition published in the May 1993 issue of *Psychological Science*, Rozin and Schull (1988), Fetterman (1996), Gallistel (1995), Wasserman (1997), and the two articles by Kamil (1988, 1998).

References

Able, K. P. (1991). The development of migratory orientation mechanisms. In P. Berthold (Ed.), *Orientation in birds* (pp. 166–179). Basel: Brikhauser Verlag.

Able, K. P., & Able, M. A. (1990). Ontogeny of migratory orientation in the savannah sparrow, *Passerculus sandwichensis*: calibration of the magnetic compass. *Animal Behaviour, 39*, 905–913.

Able, K. P., & Able, M. A. (1996). The flexible migratory orientation system of the savannah sparrow (*Passerculus sandwichensis*). *Journal of Experimental Biology, 199*, 3–8.

Able, K. P., & Bingman, V. P. (1987). The development of orientation and navigation behavior in birds. *Quarterly Review of Biology, 62*, 1–29.

Adret, P. (1993). Vocal learning induced with operant techniques: an overview. *Netherlands Journal of Zoology, 43*, 125–142.

Adret, P. (1997). Discrimination of video images by zebra finches (*Taeniopygia guttata*): Direct evidence from song performance. *Journal of Comparative Psychology, 111*, 115–125.

Aisner, R., & Terkel, J. (1992). Ontogeny of pine cone opening behaviour in the black rat, *Rattus rattus*. *Animal Behaviour, 44*, 327–336.

Akins, C. K., & Zentall, T. R. (1996). Imitative learning in male Japanese quail (*Coturnix joponica*) using the two-action method. *Journal of Comparative Psychology, 110*, 316–320.

Alatalo, R. V., & Mappes, J. (1996). Tracking the evolution of warning signals. *Nature, 382*, 708–710.

Allan, L. G. (1993). Human contingency judgements: Rule based or associative? *Psychological Bulletin, 114*, 435–448.

Allen, C. (1995). Intentionality: Natural and artificial. In H. L. Roitblat & J.-A. Meyer (Eds.), *Comparative approaches to cognitive science* (pp. 93–110). Cambridge, MA: MIT Press.

Allen, C., & Bekoff, M. (1995). Cognitive ethology and the intentionality of animal behaviour. *Mind & Language, 10*, 313–328.

Allen, C., & Bekoff, M. (1997). *Species of mind: The philosophy and biology of cognitive ethology.* Cambridge, MA: MIT Press.

Amir, S., & Stewart, J. (1996). Resetting of the circadian clock by a conditioned stimulus. *Nature, 379*, 542–545.

Anderson, J. R. (1991). Is human cognition adaptive? *Behavioral and Brain Sciences, 14*, 471–517.

Anderson, J. R., & Milson, R. (1989). Human memory: An adaptive perspective. *Psychological Review, 96*, 703–719.

Anderson, J. R., & Schooler, L. J. (1991). Reflections of the environment in memory. *Psychological Science, 2*, 396–408.

Anderson, M. C., & Shettleworth, S. J. (1977). Behavioral adaptation to fixed-interval and fixed-time food delivery in golden hamsters. *Journal of the Experimental Analysis of Behavior, 27*, 33–49.

Andersson, M. (1994). *Sexual selection.* Princeton, NJ: Princeton University Press.

Andersson, M., & Krebs, J. (1978). On the evolution of hoarding behaviour. *Animal Behaviour, 26*, 707–711.

Arak, A., & Enquist, M. (1993). Hidden preferences and the evolution of signals. *Philosophical Transactions of the Royal Society B, 340*, 207–213.

Arolfo, M. P., Nerad, L., Schenk, F., & Bures, J. (1994). Absence of snapshot memory of the target view interferes with place navigation learning by rats in the water maze. *Behavioral Neuroscience, 108*(2), 308–316.

Aschoff, J. (1986). Anticipation of a daily meal: a process of 'learning' due to entrainment. *Monitore Zoologico Italiano, 20*, 195–219.

Aschoff, J. (1989). Temporal orientation: circadian clocks in animals and humans. *Animal Behaviour, 37*, 881–896.

Avery, M. L. (1994). Finding good food and avoiding bad food: does it help to associate with experienced flockmates? *Animal Behaviour, 48*, 1371–1378.

Bachmann, C., & Kummer, H. (1980). Male assessment of female choice in Hamadryas baboons. *Behavioral Ecology and Sociobiology, 6*, 315–321.

Baddeley, A. (1995). Working memory. In M. Gazzaniga (Ed.), *The cognitive neurosciences* (pp. 755–764). Cambridge, MA: MIT Press.

Baerends, G. P. (1982). Supernormality. *Behaviour, 82*, 358–363.

Baerends, G. P., & Kruijt, J. P. (1973). Stimulus selection. In R. A. Hinde & J. Stevenson-Hinde (Eds.), *Constraints on learning* (pp. 23–50). London: Academic Press.

Bakker, T. C. M., & Milinski, M. (1991). Sequential female choice and the previous male effect in sticklebacks. *Behavioral Ecology and Sociobiology, 29*, 205–210.

Balda, R. P., & Kamil, A. C. (1992). Long-term spatial memory in Clark's nutcracker, *Nucifraga columbiana. Animal Behaviour, 44*, 761–769.

Balda, R. P., Kamil, A. C., & Bednekoff, P. A. (1996). Predicting cognitive capacity from natural history. In V. Nolan Jr. & E. D. Ketterson (Eds.), *Current ornithology* (Vol. 13, pp. 33–66). New York: Plenum Press.

Balleine, B. W., & Dickinson, A. (1998.) The role of incentive learning in instrumental outcome revaluation by sensory-specific satiety. *Animal Learning & Behavior, 26*, 46–59.

Banaji, M. R., & Crowder, R. G. (1989). The bankruptcy of everyday memory. *American Psychologist, 44,* 1185–1193.

Baptista, L. F., Bell, D. A., & Trail, P. W. (1993). Song learning and production in the white-crowned sparrow: Parallels with sexual imprinting. *Netherlands Journal of Zoology, 43,* 17–33.

Barber, T. X. (1994). *The human nature of birds.* New York: Penguin Books.

Barker, L. M., & Smith, J. C. (1974). A comparison of taste aversions induced by radiation and lithium chloride in CS-US and US-CS paradigms. *Journal of Comparative and Physiological Psychology, 87,* 644–654.

Barkow, J. H., Cosmides, L., & Tooby, J. (Eds.). (1992). *The adapted mind.* New York: Oxford University Press.

Barlow, H. B. (1982). General principles: The senses considered as physical instruments. In H. B. Barlow & J. D. Mollon (Eds.), *The senses* (pp. 1–33). Cambridge: Cambridge University Press.

Barlow, H. B., & Mollon, J. D. (Eds.). (1982). *The senses.* Cambridge: Cambridge University Press.

Barnard, C. J. (1990). Kin recognition: Problems, prospects, and the evolution of discrimination systems. *Advances in the Study of Behavior, 19,* 29–81.

Barnard, C. J., & Aldhous, P. (1991). Kinship, kin discrimination and mate choice. In P. G. Hepper (Ed.), *Kin recognition* (pp. 125–147). Cambridge University Press.

Barnard, C. J., & Brown, C. A. J. (1981). Prey size selection and competition in the common shrew (*Sorex araneus* L.). *Behavioral Ecology and Sociobiology, 8,* 239–243.

Barnard, C. J., & Hurst, J. L. (1987). Time constraints and prey selection in common shrews *Sorex araneus* L. *Animal Behaviour, 35,* 1827–1837.

Barnet, R. C., Arnold, H. M., & Miller, R. R. (1991). Simultaneous conditioning demonstrated in second-order conditioning: Evidence for similar associative structure in forward and simultaneous conditioning. *Learning and Motivation, 22,* 253–268.

Barnet, R. C., Grahame, N. J., & Miller, R. R. (1993). Temporal encoding as a determinant of blocking. *Journal of Experimental Psychology: Animal Behavior Processes, 19,* 327–341.

Baron-Cohen, S. (1995). *Mindblindness.* Cambridge, MA: MIT Press.

Basolo, A. L. (1990a). Female preference predates the evolution of the sword in swordtail fish. *Science, 250,* 808–810.

Basolo, A. L. (1990b). Female preference for sword length in the green swordtail, *Xiphophorus helleri* (Pisces: Poeciliidae). *Animal Behaviour, 40,* 332–338.

Basolo, A. L. (1995a). A further examination of a pre-existing bias favouring a sword in the genus *Xiphophorus. Animal Behaviour, 50,* 365–375.

Basolo, A. L. (1995b). Phylogenetic evidence for the role of a pre-existing bias in sexual selection. *Proceedings of the Royal Society of London, B, 259,* 307–311.

Bateson, M., & Kacelnik, A. (1995). Preferences for fixed and variable food sources: variability in amount and delay. *Journal of the Experimental Analysis of Behaviour, 63,* 313–329.

Bateson, M., & Kacelnik, A. (1996). Rate currencies and the foraging starling: the fallacy of the averages revisited. *Behavioral Ecology, 7,* 341–352.

Bateson, M., & Kacelnik, A. (1997). Starlings' preferences for predictable and unpredictable delays to food. *Animal Behaviour, 53,* 1129–1142.

Bateson, M., & Kacelnik, A. (1998). Risk-sensitive foraging: decision-making in variable environments. In R. Dukas (Ed.), *Cognitive ecology* (pp. 297–341). University of Chicago Press.

Bateson, M., & Whitehead, S. C. (1996). The energetic costs of alternative rate currencies in the foraging starling. *Ecology, 77*, 1303–1307.

Bateson, P. P. G. (1966). The characteristics and context of imprinting. *Biological Review, 41*, 177–220.

Bateson, P. (1979). How do sensitive periods arise and what are they for? *Animal Behaviour, 27*, 470–486.

Bateson, P. P. G. (1981). The control of sensitivity to the environment during development. In K. Immelman, G. Barlow, M. Main, & L. Petrinovich (Eds.), *Behavioral development* (pp. 432–453). New York: Cambridge University Press.

Bateson, P. (1982). Preferences for cousins in Japanese quail. *Nature, 295*, 236–237.

Bateson, P. (1987). Imprinting as a process of competitive exclusion. In J. P. Rauschecker & P. Marler (Eds.), *Imprinting and cortical plasticity* (pp. 151–168). New York: John Wiley & Sons.

Bateson, P. P. G. (1988). Preferences for close relations in Japanese quail, *XIX Congressus Internationalis Ornithologici* (Vol. 1, pp. 961–972). Ottawa: University of Ottawa Press.

Bateson, P. (1990). Is imprinting such a special case? *Philosophical Transactions of the Royal Society of London B, 329*, 125–131.

Bateson, P., & Horn, G. (1994). Imprinting and recognition memory: a neural net model. *Animal Behaviour, 48*, 695–715.

Bateson, P. P. G., & Jaekel, J. B. (1976). Chicks' preferences for familiar and novel conspicuous objects after different periods of exposure. *Animal Behaviour, 24*, 386–390.

Bateson, P. P. G., & Reese, E. P. (1969). Reinforcing properties of conspicuous stimuli in the imprinting situation. *Animal Behaviour, 17*, 692–699.

Beatty, W. W., & Shavalia, D. A. (1980). Spatial memory in rats: Time course of working memory and effects of anesthetics. *Behavioral and Neural Biology, 28*, 454–462.

Beauchamp, G., & Kacelnik, A. (1991). Effects of the knowledge of partners on learning rates in zebra finches *Taeniopygia guttata. Animal Behaviour, 41*, 247–253.

Beck, B. B. (1980). *Animal tool behavior: The use and manufacture of tools by animals.* New York: Garland STPM Press.

Beck, B. B. (1982). Chimpocentrism: Bias in cognitive ethology. *Journal of Human Evolution, 11*, 3–17.

Beecher, M. D. (1990). The evolution of parent-offspring recognition in swallows. In D. A. Dewsbury (Ed.), *Contemporary issues in comparative psychology* (pp. 360–380). Sunderland, MA: Sinauer Associates.

Beecher, M. D., & Stoddard, P. K. (1990). The role of bird song and calls in individual recognition: contrasting field and laboratory perspectives. In W. C. Stebbins & M. A. Berkley (Eds.), *Comparative perception: Complex signals* (Vol. 2, pp. 375–408). New York: John Wiley and Sons.

Beer, C. G. (1991). From folk psychology to cognitive ethology. In C. A. Ristau (Ed.), *Cognitive ethology: the minds of other animals* (pp. 19–33). Hillsdale, NJ: Lawrence Erlbaum Associates.

Bekoff, M. (1995a). Cognitive ethology and the explanation of nonhuman animal behavior. In H. L. Roitblat & J.-A. Meyer (Eds.), *Comparative approaches to cognitive science* (pp. 119–150). Cambridge, MA: MIT Press.

Bekoff, M. (1995b). Vigilance, flock size, and flock geometry: Information gathering by western evening grosbeaks (*Aves, fringillidae*). *Ethology, 99*, 150–161.

Bekoff, M. (1996). Cognitive ethology, vigilance, information gathering, and representation: Who might know what and why? *Behavioural Processes, 35,* 225–237.

Bekoff, M., & Jamieson, D. (Eds.). (1996). *Readings in animal cognition.* Cambridge, MA: MIT Press.

Belke, T. W. (1992). Stimulus preference and the transitivity of preference. *Animal Learning and Behavior, 20,* 401–406.

Benhamou, S. (1996). No evidence for cognitive mapping in rats. *Animal Behaviour, 52,* 201–212.

Bennett, A. T. D. (1993). Spatial memory in a food storing corvid 1. Near tall landmarks are primarily used. *Journal of Comparative Physiology A, 173,* 193–207.

Bennett, A. T. D. (1996). Do animals have cognitive maps? *Journal of Experimental Biology, 199,* 219–224.

Bennett, A. T. D., & Cuthill, I. C. (1994). Ultraviolet vision in birds: What is its function? *Vision Research, 34,* 1471–1478.

Bennett, A. T. D., Cuthill, I. C., Partridge, J. C., & Maier, E. J. (1996). Ultraviolet vision and mate choice in zebra finches. *Nature, 380,* 433–435.

Bennett, J. (1991a). How is cognitive ethology possible? In C. A. Ristau (Ed.), *Cognitive ethology: the minds of other animals* (pp. 35–49). Hillsdale, NJ: Lawrence Erlbaum Associates.

Bennett, J. (1991b). How to read minds in behaviour: A suggestion from a philosopher. In A. Whiten (Ed.), *Natural theories of mind: Evolution, development and simulation of everyday mindreading* (pp. 97–108). Oxford: Basil Blackwell.

Berkley, M. A., & Stebbins, W. C. (Eds.). (1990). *Comparative perception.* New York: Wiley.

Berlyne, D. E. (1960). *Conflict, arousal, and curiosity.* New York: McGraw-Hill.

Bernays, E. A., & Wcislo, W. T. (1994). Sensory capabilities, information processing, and resource specialization. *Quarterly Review of Biology, 69,* 187–204.

Bernstein, C., Kacelnik, A., & Krebs, J. R. (1991). Individual decisions and the distribution of predators in a patchy environment. II. The influence of travel costs and structure of the environment. *Journal of Animal Ecology, 60,* 205–225.

Berridge, K. C., & Schulkin, J. (1989). Palatability shift of a salt-associated incentive during sodium depletion. *Quarterly Journal of Experimental Psychology, 41B,* 121–138.

Berthold, P. (1993). *Bird migration: A general survey* (Bauer, H.-G. Tomlinson, T., Trans.). Oxford: Oxford University Press.

Bhatt, R. S., Wasserman, E. A., Reynolds, W. F. J., & Knauss, K. S. (1988). Conceptual behavior in pigeons: Categorization of both familiar and novel examples from four classes of natural and artificial stimuli. *Journal of Experimental Psychology: Animal Behavior Processes, 14,* 219–234.

Bickerton, D. (1990). *Language and Species.* Chicago: University of Chicago Press.

Biebach, H., Falk, H., & Krebs, J. R. (1991). The effect of constant light and phase shifts on a learned time-place association in garden warblers (*Sylvia borin*): hourglass or circadian clock. *Journal of Biological Rhythms, 6,* 353–365.

Biebach, H., Gordijn, M., & Krebs, J. R. (1989). Time-and-place learning by garden warblers, *Sylvia borin. Animal Behaviour, 37,* 353–360.

Biegler, R., & Morris, R. G. M. (1993). Landmark stability is a prerequisite for spatial but not discrimination learning. *Nature, 361,* 631–633.

Biegler, R., & Morris, R. G. M. (1996a). Landmark stability: Studies exploring whether the perceived stability of the environment influences spatial representation. *Journal of Experimental Biology, 199,* 187–193.

Biegler, R., & Morris, R. G. M. (1996b). Landmark stability: Further studies pointing to a role in spatial learning. *Quarterly Journal of Experimental Psychology, 49B,* 307–345.

Bingman, V. P., & Jones, T.-J. (1994). Sun compass-based spatial learning impaired in homing pigeons with hippocampal lesions. *Journal of Neuroscience, 14,* 6687–6694.

Bischof, H.-J. (1994). Sexual imprinting as a two-stage process. In J. A. Hogan & J. J. Bolhuis (Eds.), *Causal mechanisms of behavioural development* (pp. 82–97). Cambridge: Cambridge University Press.

Bitterman, M. E. (1965). The evolution of intelligence. *Scientific American, 212*(1), 92–100.

Bitterman, M. E. (1975). The comparative analysis of learning. *Science, 188,* 699–709.

Bitterman, M. E. (1996). Comparative analysis of learning in honeybees. *Animal Learning and Behavior, 24,* 123–141.

Bizo, L. A., & White, K. G. (1994). Pacemaker rate in the behavioral theory of timing. *Journal of Experimental Psychology: Animal Behavior Processes, 20,* 308–321.

Bizo, L. A., & White, K. G. (1995). Reinforcement context and pacemaker rate in the behavioral theory of timing. *Animal Learning and Behaviour, 23,* 376–382.

Blaustein, A. R., & Porter, R. H. (1995). The ubiquitous concept of recognition with special reference to kin. In M. Bekoff & D. Jamieson (Eds.), *Readings in animal cognition* (pp. 169–184). Cambridge, MA: MIT Press.

Blough, D. S. (1967). Stimulus generalization as signal detection in pigeons. *Science, 158,* 940–941.

Blough, D. S. (1969). Attention shifts in a maintained discrimination. *Science, 166,* 125–126.

Blough, D. S. (1975). Steady state data and a quantitative model of operant generalization and discrimination. *Journal of Experimental Psychology: Animal Behavior Processes, 1,* 3–21.

Blough, D. S. (1979). Effects of number and form of stimuli on visual search in the pigeon. *Journal of Experimental Psychology: Animal Behavior Processes, 5,* 211–223.

Blough, D. S. (1992). Features of forms in pigeon perception. In W. C. Honig & J. G. Fetterman (Eds.), *Cognitive aspects of stimulus control* (pp. 263–277). Hillsdale, NJ: Erlbaum.

Blough, D. S. (1993a). Effects on search speed of the probability of target-distractor combinations. *Journal of Experimental Psychology: Animal Behavior Processes, 19,* 231–243.

Blough, D. S. (1993b). Reaction time drifts identify objects of attention in pigeon visual search. *Journal of Experimental Psychology: Animal Behavior Processes, 19,* 107–120.

Blough, D. S. (1996). Error factors in pigeon discrimination and delayed matching. *Journal of Experimental Psychology: Animal Behavior Processes, 22,* 118–131.

Blough, D., & Blough, P. (1977b). Animal psychophysics. In W. K. Honig & J. E. R. Staddon (Eds.), *Handbook of operant behavior.* Englewood Cliffs, NJ: Prentice-Hall.

Blough, D. S., & Blough, P. M. (1997a). Form perception and attention in pigeons. *Animal Learning & Behavior, 25,* 1–20.

Blough, P. M. (1984). Visual search in pigeons: Effects of memory set size and display variables. *Perception and Psychophysics, 35,* 344–352.

Blough, P. M. (1989). Attentional priming and visual search in pigeons. *Journal of Experimental Psychology: Animal Behavior Processes, 15,* 358–365.

Blough, P. M. (1991). Selective attention and search images in pigeons. *Journal of Experimental Psychology: Animal Behavior Processes, 17,* 292–298.

Blough, P. M. (1992). Detectibility and choice during visual search: Joint effects of sequential priming and discriminability. *Animal Learning and Behavior, 20,* 293–300.

Blumberg, M. S., & Wasserman, E. A. (1995). Animal mind and the argument from design. *American Psychologist, 50,* 133–144.

Boag, P. T. (1983). The heritability of external morphology in Darwin's ground finches *(Geospiza)* on Isla Daphne Major, Galápagos. *Evolution, 37,* 877–894.

Boag, P. T., & Grant, P. R. (1984). The classical case of character release: Darwin's finches *(Geospiza)* on Isla Daphne Major, Galápagos. *Biological Journal of the Linnean Society, 22,* 243–287.

Boakes, R. (1984). *From Darwin to behaviourism.* Cambridge: Cambridge University Press.

Boakes, R., & Panter, D. (1985). Secondary imprinting in the domestic chick blocked by previous exposure to a live hen. *Animal Behaviour, 33,* 353–365.

Boesch, C. (1991). Teaching among wild chimpanzees. *Animal Behaviour, 41A,* 530–532.

Boesch-Achermann, H., & Boesch, C. (1993). Tool use in wild chimpanzees: New light from dark forests. *Current Directions in Psychological Science, 2,* 18–21.

Boice, R., & Denny, M. R. (1965). The conditioned licking response in rats as a function of the CS-UCS interval. *Psychonomic Science, 3,* 93–94.

Bolhuis, J. J. (1991). Mechanisms of avian imprinting: A review. *Biological Review, 66,* 303–345.

Bolhuis, J. J. (1994). Neurobiological analyses of behavioural mechanisms in development. In J. A. Hogan & J. J. Bolhuis (Eds.), *Causal mechanisms of behavioural development* (pp. 16–46). Cambridge: Cambridge University Press.

Bolhuis, J. J. (1996). Development of perceptual mechanisms in birds: Predispositions and imprinting. In C. F. Moss & S. J. Shettleworth (Eds.), *Neuroethological studies of cognitive and perceptual processes* (pp. 158–184). Boulder, CO: Westview Press.

Bolhuis, J. J., & Bateson, P. (1990). The importance of being first: a primacy effect in filial imprinting. *Animal Behaviour, 40,* 472–483.

Bolhuis, J. J., de Vos, G. J., & Kruijt, J. P. (1990). Filial imprinting and associative learning. *Quarterly Journal of Experimental Psychology, 42B,* 313–329.

Bolhuis, J. J., & Trooster, W. J. (1988). Reversibility revisted: Stimulus-dependent stability of filial preference in the chick. *Animal Behaviour, 36,* 668–674.

Bolhuis, J. J., & van Kampen, H. S. (1988). Serial position curves in spatial memory in rats: primacy and recency effects. *Quarterly Journal of Experimantal Psychology, 40B,* 135–149.

Bolhuis, J. J., & van Kampen, H. S. (1992). An evaluation of auditory learning in filial imprinting. *Behaviour, 122,* 195–230.

Bolles, R. C. (1970). Species-specific defense reactions and avoidance learning. *Psychological Review, 77,* 32–48.

Bolles, R. C. (1985). The slaying of Goliath: What happened to reinforcement theory. In T. D. Johnston & A. T. Pietrewicz (Eds.), *Issues in the ecological study of learning* (pp. 387–399). Hillsdale, NJ: Lawrence Erlbaum Associates.

Bolles, R. C., & Beecher, M. D. (Eds.). (1988). *Evolution and learning.* Hillsdale, NJ: Lawrence Erlbaum Associates.

Bolles, R. C., & Moot, S. A. (1973). The rat's anticipation of two meals a day. *Journal of Comparative and Physiological Psychology, 83,* 510–514.

Bonardi, C., & Hall, G. (1996). Learned irrelevance: No more than the sum of CS and US preexposure effects? *Journal of Experimental Psychology: Animal Behavior Processes, 22,* 183–191.

Bond, A. B. (1983). Visual search and selection of natural stimuli in the pigeon: The attention threshold hypothesis. *Journal of Experimental Psychology: Animal Behavior Processes, 9,* 292–306.

Bonner, J. T. (1980). *The evolution of culture in animals.* Princeton, NJ: Princeton, University Press.

Bossema, I., & Burgler, R. R. (1980). Communication during monocular and binocular looking in European jays *(Garrulus g. glandarius). Behaviour, 74,* 274–283.

Bouton, M. E. (1993). Context, time, and memory retrieval in the interference paradigms of Pavlovian learning. *Psychological Bulletin, 114,* 80–99.

Bovet, J. (1992). Mammals. In F. Papi (Ed.), *Animal homing* (pp. 321–361). London: Chapman & Hall.

Bovet, J., & Oertli, E. F. (1974). Free-running circadian activity rhythms in free-living beaver *(Castor canadensis). Journal of Comparative Physiology, 92,* 1–10.

Boyse, E. A., Beauchamp, G. K., Yamazaki, K., & Bard, J. (1991). Genetic components of kin recognition in mammals. In P. G. Hepper (Ed.), *Kin recognition* (pp. 148–161). Cambridge: Cambridge University Press.

Boysen, S. T. (1993). Counting in chimpanzees: Nonhuman principles and emergent properties of number. In S. T. Boysen & E. J. Capaldi (Eds.), *The development of numerical competence* (pp. 39–59). Hillsdale, NJ: Lawrence Erlbaum Associates.

Boysen, S. T., & Berntson, G. G. (1989). Numerical competence in a chimpanzee *(Pan troglodytes). Journal of Comparative Psychology, 103,* 23–31.

Boysen, S. T., & Berntson, G. G. (1995). Responses to quantity: Perceptual versus cognitive mechanisms in chimpanzees *(Pan Troglodytes). Journal of Experimental Psychology: Animal Behavior Processes, 21,* 82–86.

Boysen, S. T., Berntson, G. G., Hannan, M. B., & Cacioppo, J. T. (1996). Quantity-based interference and symbolic representations in chimpanzees *(Pan troglodytes). Journal of Experimental Psychology: Animal Behavior Processes, 22,* 76–86.

Boysen, S. T., & Capaldi, E. J. (Eds.). (1993). *The development of numerical competence.* Hillsdale, NJ: Lawrence Erlbaum Associates.

Breland, K., & Breland, M. (1961). The misbehavior of organisms. *American Psychologist, 16,* 681–684.

Brennan, P., Kaba, H., & Keverne, E. B. (1990). Olfactory recognition: A simple memory system. *Science, 250,* 1223–1226.

Breukelaar, J. W. C., & Dalrymple-Alford, J. C. (1998). Timing ability and numerical competence in rats. *Journal of Experimental Psychology: Animal Behavior Processes, 24,* 84–97.

Bright, M. (1990). *The Dolittle obsession.* London: Robson Books.

Broadbent, H. A. (1994). Periodic behavior in a random environment. *Journal of Experimental Psychology: Animal Behavior Processes, 20,* 156–175.

Brodbeck, D. R. (1994). Memory for spatial and local cues: A comparison of a storing and a nonstoring species. *Animal Learning & Behavior, 22,* 119–133.

Brodbeck, D. R. (1997). Picture fragment completion: Priming in the pigeon. *Journal of Experimental Psychology: Animal Behavior Processes, 23,* 461–468.

Brodbeck, D. R., Burack, O. R., & Shettleworth, S. J. (1992). One-trial associative memory in black-capped chickadees. *Journal of Experimental Psychology: Animal Behavior Processes, 18,* 12–21.

Brodbeck, D. R., & Shettleworth, S. J. (1995). Matching location and color of a compound stimulus: Comparison of a food-storing and a non-storing bird species. *Journal of Experimental Psychology: Animal Behavior Processes, 21,* 64–77.

Brodin, A. (1994). The disappearance of caches that have been stored by naturally foraging willow tits. *Animal Behaviour, 47,* 730–732.

Brooks, D. R., & McLennan, D. A. (1991). *Phylogeny, ecology, and behavior.* Chicago: University of Chicago Press.

Brower, L. P. (Ed.). (1988). *Mimicry and the evolutionary process.* Chicago: University of Chicago Press.

Brown, C. H., Sinnott, J. M., & Kressley, R. A. (1994). Perception of chirps by Sykes's monkeys (*Cercopithecus albogularis*) and humans (*Homo sapiens*). *Journal of Comparative Psychology, 108,* 243–251.

Brown, M. F., & Bing, M. N. (1997). In the dark: Spatial choice when access to spatial cues is restricted. *Animal Learning & Behavior, 25,* 21–30.

Brown, M. F., Wheeler, E. A., & Riley, D. A. (1989). Evidence for a shift in the choice criterion of rats in a 12-arm radial maze. *Animal Learning & Behavior, 17,* 12–20.

Brown, P. L., & Jenkins, H. M. (1968). Auto-shaping of the pigeon's key-peck. *Journal of the Experimental Analysis of Behavior, 11,* 1–8.

Brown, S. D., & Dooling, R. J. (1992). Perception of conspecific faces by budgerigars (*Melopsittacus undulatus*): I. Natural faces. *Journal of Comparative Psychology, 106,* 203–216.

Brown, S. D., & Dooling, R. J. (1993). Perception of conspecific faces by budgerigars (*Melopsittacus undulatus*): II. Synthetic models. *Journal of Comparative Psychology, 107,* 48–60.

Bruce, D. (1985). The how and why of ecological memory. *Journal of Experimental Psychology: General, 114,* 78–90.

Brunner, D., Fairhurst, S., Stolovitzky, G., & Gibbon, J. (1997). Mnemonics for variability: Remembering food delay. *Journal of Experimental Psychology: Animal Behavior Processes, 23,* 68–83.

Brunner, D., & Gibbon, J. (1995). Value of food aggregates: parallel versus serial discounting. *Animal Behaviour, 50,* 1627–1634.

Brunner, D., Kacelnik, A., & Gibbon, J. (1992). Optimal foraging and timing processes in the starling, *Sturnus vulgaris*: effect of inter-capture interval. *Animal Behaviour, 44,* 597–613.

Brunner, D., Kacelnik, A., & Gibbon, J. (1996). Memory for inter-reinforcement interval variability and patch departure decisions in the starling, *Sturnus vulgaris*. *Animal Behaviour, 51,* 1025–1045.

Burley, N., Minor, C., & Strachan, C. (1990). Social preference of zebra finches for siblings, cousins, and non-kin. *Animal Behaviour, 39,* 775–784.

Byrne, R. (1995). *The Thinking Ape.* Oxford: Oxford University Press.

Byrne, R. W., & Tomasello, M. (1995). Do rats ape? *Animal Behaviour, 50,* 1417–1420.

Byrne, R. W., & Whiten, A. (Eds.). (1988). *Machiavellian intelligence: Social expertise and the evolution of intellect in monkeys, apes, and humans.* Oxford: Clarendon Press.

Cabeza de Vaca, S., Brown, B. L., & Hemmes, N. S. (1994). Internal clock and memory processes in animal timing. *Journal of Experimental Psychology: Animal Behavior Processes, 20,* 184–198.

Call, J., & Tomasello, M. (1995). Use of social information in the problem solving of orangutans (*Pongo pygmaeus*) and human children (*Homo sapiens*). *Journal of Comparative Psychology, 109,* 308–320.

Campbell, C. B. G., & Hodos, W. (1991). The *scala naturae* revisited: Evolutionary scales and anagenesis in comparative psychology. *Journal of Comparative Psychology*, *105*, 211–221.

Candland, D. K. (1993). *Feral children and clever animals*. New York: Oxford University Press.

Capaldi, E. J. (1993). Animal number abilites: Implications for a hierarchical approach to instrumental learning. In S. T. Boysen & E. J. Capaldi (Eds.), *The development of numerical competence* (pp. 191–209). Hillsdale, NJ: Lawrence Erlbaum Associates.

Capaldi, E. J., & Miller, D. J. (1988). Counting in rats: Its functional significance and the independent cognitive processes that constitute it. *Journal of Experimental Psychology: Animal Behavior Processes*, *14*, 3–17.

Caraco, T., Blanckenhorn, W. U., Gregory, G. M., Newman, J. A., Recer, G. M., & Zwicker, S. M. (1990). Risk sensitivity: ambient temperature affects foraging choice. *Animal Behaviour*, *39*, 338–345.

Caraco, T., Martindale, S., & Whittam, T. S. (1980). An empirical demonstration of risk-sensitive foraging preferences. *Animal Behaviour*, *28*, 820–830.

Carew, T. J., Pinsker, H. M., & Kandel, E. R. (1972). Long-term habituation of a defensive withdrawal reflex in aplysia. *Science*, *175*, 451–454.

Carlier, P., & Lefebvre, L. (1996). Differences in individual learning between group-foraging and territorial Zenaida doves. *Behaviour*, *133*, 1197–1207.

Carlier, P., & Lefebvre, L. (1997). Ecological differences in social learning between adjacent mixing populations of Zenaida doves. *Ethology*, *103*, 772–784.

Caro, T. M. (1980). Predatory behaviour in domestic cat mothers. *Behaviour*, *74*, 128–148.

Caro, T. M., & Hauser, M. D. (1992). Is there teaching in nonhuman animals? *Quarterly Review of Biology*, *67*, 151–174.

Carr, J. A. R., & Wilkie, D. M. (1997a). Rats use an ordinal timer in a daily time-place learning task. *Journal of Experimental Psychology: Animal Behavior Processes*, *23*, 232–247.

Carr, J. A. R., & Wilkie, D. M. (1997b). Ordinal, phase, and interval timing. In C. M. Bradshaw & E. Szabadi (Eds.), *Time and behaviour: Psychological and neurobiological analyses* (pp. 267–327). Amsterdam: Elsevier Science.

Carr, J. A. R., & Wilkie, D. M. (1998). Characterization of the strategy used by rats in an interval time-place learning task. *Journal of Experimental Psychology: Animal Behavior Processes*, *24*, 151–162.

Carruthers, P., & Smith, P. K. (Eds.). (1996). *Theories of theories of mind*. Cambridge: Cambridge University Press.

Cartwright, B. A., & Collett, T. S. (1983). Landmark learning in bees. *Journal of Comparative Physiology*, *151*, 521–543.

Cartwright, B. A., & Collett, T. S. (1987). Landmark maps for honeybees. *Biological Cybernetics*, *57*, 85–93.

Catchpole, C. K., & Slater, P. J. B. (1995). *Bird song: Biological themes and variations*. Cambridge: Cambridge University Press.

Cerella, J. (1979). Visual classes and natural categories in the pigeon. *Journal of Experimental Psychology: Human Perception and Performance*, *5*, 68–77.

Chalmers, D. J. (1995). The puzzle of conscious experience. *Scientific American*, *273*, 80–86.

Chantrey, D. F. (1972). Enhancement and retardation of discrimination learning in chicks after exposure to the discriminanda. *Journal of Comparative and Physiological Psychology*, *81*, 256–281.

Chantrey, D. F. (1974). Stimulus pre-exposure and discrimination learning by domestic chicks: Effects of varying interstimulus time. *Journal of Comparative and Physiological Psychology, 87,* 517–525.

Chappell, J., & Guilford, T. (1995). Homing pigeons primarily use the sun compass rather than fixed directional visual cues in an open-field arena food-searching task. *Proceedings of the Royal Society (London) B, 260,* 59–63.

Charnov, E. L. (1976). Optimal foraging: attack strategy of a mantid. *American Naturalist, 110,* 141–151.

Chater, N., & Heyes, C. (1994). Animal concepts: Content and discontent. *Mind and Language, 9,* 209–247.

Chelazzi, G. (1992). Invertebrates (excluding Arthropods). In F. Papi (Ed.), *Animal homing* (pp. 19–43). London: Chapman and Hall.

Chelazzi, G., & Francisci, F. (1979). Movement patterns and homing behaviour of *Testudo hermanni gmelin* (*Reptilia Testudinidae*). *Monitore Zoologica Italiano, 13,* 105–127.

Cheney, D., & Seyfarth, R. (1985). The social and non-social world of non-human primates. In R. A. Hinde, A. Perret-Clermont, & J. Stevenson-Hinde (Eds.), *Relationships and cognitive development* (pp. 23–44). Oxford: Oxford University Press.

Cheney, D. L., & Seyfarth, R. M. (1988). Assessment of meaning and the detection of unreliable signals by vervet monkeys. *Animal Behaviour, 36,* 477–486.

Cheney, D., & Seyfarth, R. (1990a). Attending to behaviour versus attending to knowledge: examining monkeys' attribution of mental states. *Animal Behaviour, 40,* 742–753.

Cheney, D. L., & Seyfarth, R. M. (1990b). *How monkeys see the world.* Chicago: University of Chicago Press.

Cheney, D. L., & Seyfarth, R. M. (1992). Precis of *How monkeys see the world. Behavioral and Brain Sciences, 15,* 135–182.

Cheney, D. L., & Seyfarth, R. M. (1997). Reconcilitatory grunts by dominant female baboons influence victims' behavior. *Animal Behaviour, 54,* 409–418.

Cheney, D. L., Seyfarth, R. M., & Palombit, R. A. (1996). The function and mechanisms underlying baboon 'contact' barks. *Animal Behaviour*(52), 507–518.

Cheney, D. L., Seyfarth, R. M., & Silk, J. B. (1995). The responses of female baboons (*Papio cynocephalus ursinus*) to anomalous social interactions: Evidence for causal reasoning? *Journal of Comparative Psychology, 109,* 134–141.

Cheng, K. (1986). A purely geometric module in the rat's spatial representation. *Cognition, 23,* 149–178.

Cheng, K. (1989). The vector sum model of pigeon landmark use. *Journal of Experimental Psychology: Animal Behavior Processes, 15,* 366–375.

Cheng, K. (1992). Three psychophysical principles in the processing of spatial and temporal information. In W. K. Honig & J. G. Fetterman (Eds.), *Cognitive aspects of stimulus control* (pp. 69–88). Hillsdale, NJ: Lawrence Erlbaum Associates.

Cheng, K. (1994). The determination of direction in landmark-based spatial search in pigeons: A further test of the vector sum model. *Animal Learning & Behavior, 22,* 291–301.

Cheng, K. (1995). Landmark-based spatial memory in the pigeon. *Psychology of Learning and Motivation, 33,* 1–21.

Cheng, K., Collett, T. S., Pickhard, A., & Wehner, R. (1987). The use of visual landmarks by honeybees: Bees weight landmarks according to their distance from the goal. *Journal of Comparative Physiology, 161,* 469–475.

Cheng, K., & Sherry, D. F. (1992). Landmark-based spatial memory in birds (*Parus atricapillus* and *Columba livia*): The use of edges and distances to represent spatial positions. *Journal of Comparative Psychology, 106,* 331–341.

Cheng, K., & Spetch, M. L. (1998). Mechanisms of landmark use in mammals and birds. In S. Healy (Ed.), *Spatial Representation in Animals* (pp. 1–17). Oxford: Oxford University Press.

Cheng, K., Spetch, M. L., & Johnston, M. (1997). Spatial peak shift and generalization in pigeons. *Journal of Experimental Psychology: Animal Behavior Processes, 23,* 469–481.

Cheng, K., Spetch, M. L., & Miceli, P. (1996). Averaging temporal duration and spatial position. *Journal of Experimental Psychology: Animal Behavior Processes, 22,* 175–182.

Cheng, K., & Westwood, R. (1993). Analysis of single trials in pigeons' timing performance. *Journal of Experimental Psychology: Animal Behavior Processes, 19,* 56–67.

Cheng, K., Westwood, R., & Crystal, J. D. (1993). Memory variance in the peak procedure of timing in pigeons. *Journal of Experimental Psychology: Animal Behavior Processes, 19,* 68–76.

Chittka, L., & Geiger, K. (1995a). Honeybee long-distance orientation in a controlled environment. *Ethology, 99,* 117–126.

Chittka, L., & Geiger, K. (1995b). Can honey bees count landmarks? *Animal Behaviour, 49,* 159–164.

Chittka, L., Geiger, K., & Kunze, J. (1995). The influences of landmarks on distance estimation of honey bees. *Animal Behaviour, 50,* 23–31.

Chittka, L., Shmida, A., Troje, N., & Menzel, R. (1994). Ultraviolet as a component of flower reflections, and the colour perception of hymenoptera. *Vision Research, 34,* 1489–1508.

Chitty, D., & Southern, H. N. (Eds.). (1954). *Control of rats and mice.* Oxford: Clarendon Press.

Chivers, D. P., & Smith, R. J. F. (1994). Fathead minnows, *Pimephales promelas,* acquire predator recognition when alarm substance is associated with the sight of unfamiliar fish. *Animal Behaviour, 48,* 597–605.

Chomsky, N. (1968). *Language and mind.* New York: Harcourt, Brace & World.

Christie, J. (1996). Spatial contiguity facilitates Pavlovian conditioning. *Psychonomic Bulletin and Review, 3,* 357–359.

Church, R. M. (1993). Human models of animal behavior. *Psychological Science, 4,* 170–173.

Church, R. M., & Broadbent, H. A. (1990). Alternative representations of time, number, and rate. *Cognition, 37,* 55–81.

Church, R. M., & Deluty, M. Z. (1977). Bisection of temporal intervals. *Journal of Experimental Psychology: Animal Behavior Processes, 3,* 216–228.

Church, R. M., & Gibbon, J. (1982). Temporal generalization. *Journal of Experimental Psychology: Animal Behavior Processes, 8,* 165–186.

Church, R. M., & Meck, W. H. (1984). The numerical attribute of stimuli. In H. L. Roitblat, T. G. Bever, & H. S. Terrace (Eds.), *Animal Cognition* (pp. 445–464). Hillsdale, NJ: Lawrence Erlbaum Associates.

Church, R. M., Meck, W. H., & Gibbon, J. (1994). Application of scalar timing theory to individual trials. *Journal of Experimental Psychology: Animal Behavior Processes, 20,* 135–155.

Churchland, P. M. (1995). *The engine of reason, the seat of the soul.* Cambridge, MA: MIT Press.

Churchland, P. S. (1986). *Neurophilosophy.* Cambridge, MA: MIT Press.

Churchland, P. S. (1996). *Towards a neurobiology of awareness*. Paper presented to the Program in Neuroscience, University of Toronto.

Clark, A. (1997). *Being there*. Cambridge, MA: MIT Press.

Clark, D. L., & Uetz, G. W. (1990). Video image recognition by the jumping spider, *Maevia inclemens* (Araneae: Salticidae). *Animal Behaviour, 40*, 884–890.

Clark, R. E., & Squire, L. R. (1998). Classical conditioning and brain systems: The role of awareness. *Science, 280*, 77–81.

Clayton, N. S. (1995). Development of memory and the hippocampus: Comparison of food-storing and non-storing birds on a one-trial associative memory task. *Journal of Neuroscience, 15*, 2796–2807.

Clayton, N. S., & Krebs, J. R. (1994). Memory for spatial and object-specific cues in food-storing and non-storing birds. *Journal of Comparative Physiology A, 174*, 371–379.

Clutton-Brock, T. H., & Harvey, P. (1977). Primate ecology and social organization. *Journal of Zoology, 183*, 1–39.

Clutton-Brock, T. H., & Harvey, P. H. (1984). Comparative approaches to investigating adaptation. In J. R. Krebs & N. B. Davies (Eds.), *Behavioural ecology: An evolutionary approach* (pp. 7–29). Oxford: Blackwell Scientific.

Clutton-Brock, T. H., & Parker, G. A. (1995). Punishment in animal societies. *Nature, 373*, 209–216.

Cole, P. D., & Honig, W. K. (1994). Transfer of a discrimination by pigeons (*Columba livia*) between pictured locations and the represented environments. *Journal of Comparative Psychology, 108*, 189–198.

Cole, R. P., Barnet, R. C., & Miller, R. R. (1995). Temporal encoding in trace conditioning. *Animal Learning and Behavior, 23*, 144–153.

Cole, S., Hainsworth, F. R., Kamil, A. C., Mercier, T., & Wolf, L. L. (1982). Spatial learning as an adaptation in hummingbirds. *Science, 217*, 655–657.

Collett, T. S., & Baron, J. (1994). Biological compasses and the coordinate frame of landmark memories in honeybees. *Nature, 368*, 137–140.

Collett, T. S., Cartwright, B. A., & Smith, B. A. (1986). Landmark learning and visuospatial memories in gerbils. *Journal of Comparative Physiology A, 158*, 835–851.

Collett, T. S., Dillmann, E., Giger, A., & Wehner, R. (1992). Visual landmarks and route following in desert ants. *Journal of Comparative Physiology A, 170*, 435–442.

Collett, T. S., & Kelber, A. (1988). The retrieval of visuo-spatial memories by honeybees. *Journal of Comparative Physiology A, 163*, 145–150.

Collett, T. S., & Lehrer, M. (1993). Looking and learning: a spatial pattern in the orientation flight of the wasp *Vespula vulgaris*. *Proceedings of the Royal Society of London B, 252*, 129–134.

Collett, T. S., & Zeil, J. (1996). Flights of learning. *Current Directions in Psychological Science, 5*, 149–155.

Collier, G. H. (1983). Life in a closed economy: The ecology of learning and motivation. In M. D. Zeiler & P. Harzem (Eds.), *Advances in analysis of behaviour* (Vol. 3. Biological factors in learning, pp. 223–274). Chichester: John Wiley & Sons Ltd.

Collier, G., Hirsch, E., & Hamlin, P. H. (1972). The ecological determinants of reinforcement in the rat. *Physiology and Behavior, 9*, 705–716.

Collier, G., & Johnson, D. F. (1997). Who's in charge? Animal vs. experimenter control. *Appetite, 29*, 159–180.

Collins, S. A. (1995). The effect of recent experience on female choice in zebra finches. *Animal Behaviour, 49*, 479–486.

Colwill, R. M. (1993). An associative analysis of instrumental learning. *Current Directions in Psychological Science, 2,* 111–116.

Colwill, R. M. (1994). Associative representations of instrumental contingencies. *Psychology of Learning and Motivation, 31,* 1–72.

Colwill, R. M. (1996). Detecting associations in Pavlovian conditioning and instrumental learning in vertebrates and in invertebrates. In C. F. Moss & S. J. Shettleworth (Eds.), *Neuroethological studies of cognitive and perceptual processes* (pp. 31–62). Boulder, CO: Westview Press.

Colwill, R. M., & Motzkin, D. K. (1994). Encoding of the unconditioned stimulus in Pavlovian conditioning. *Animal Learning and Behavior, 22,* 384–394.

Colwill, R. M., & Rescorla, R. A. (1985). Postconditioning devaluation of a reinforcer affects intrumental responding. *Journal of Experimental Psychology: Animal Behavior Processes, 11,* 120–132.

Commons, M. L., Kacelnik, A., & Shettleworth, S. J. (Eds.). (1987). *Quantative analyses of behavior (Vol. 6) (Foraging).* Hillsdale, NJ: Lawrence Erlbaum Associates.

Cook, A., Bamford, O. S., Freeman, J. D. B., & Teideman, D. J. (1969). A study of the homing habit of the limpet. *Animal Behaviour, 17,* 330–339.

Cook, M., & Mineka, S. (1990). Selective associations in the observational conditioning of fear in rhesus monkeys. *Journal of Experimental Psychology: Animal Behavior Processes, 16,* 372–389.

Cook, R. G. (1992a). Dimensional organization and texture discrimination in pigeons. *Journal of Experimental Psychology: Animal Behavior Processes, 18,* 354–363.

Cook, R. (1992b). Acquisition and transfer of visual texture discriminations by pigeons. *Journal of Experimental Psychology: Animal Behavior Processes, 18,* 341–353.

Cook, R. G., Brown, M. F., & Riley, D. A. (1985). Flexible memory processing by rats: Use of prospective and retrospective information in the radial maze. *Journal of Experimental Psychology: Animal Behavior Processes, 11,* 453–469.

Cook, R. G., Cavoto, K. K., & Cavoto, B. R. (1995). Same-different texture discrimination and concept learning by pigeons. *Journal of Experimental Psychology: Animal Behavior Processes, 21,* 253–260.

Cook, R. G., Cavoto, K. K., & Cavoto, B. R. (1996). Mechanisms of multidimensional grouping, fusion, and search in avian texture discrimination. *Animal Learning and Behavior, 24,* 150–167.

Cook, R. G., & Wixted, J. T. (1997). Same-different texture discrimination in pigeons: Testing competing models of discrimination and stimulus integration. *Journal of Experimental Psychology: Animal Behavior Processes, 23,* 401–416.

Cook, S. B. (1969). Experiments on homing in the limpet *Siphonaria normalis. Animal Behaviour, 17,* 679–682.

Cooke, F., & Davies, J. C. (1983). Assortative mating, mate choice, and reproductive fitness in Snow Geese. In P. Bateson (Ed.), *Mate choice* (pp. 279–295). Cambridge: Cambridge University Press.

Corballis, M. C., & Roldan, C. E. (1975). Detection of symmetry as a function of angular orientation. *Journal of Experimental Psychology: Human Perception and Performance, 1,* 221–230.

Cosmides, L. (1989). The logic of social exchange: Has natural selection shaped how humans reason? Studies with the Wason selection task. *Cognition, 31,* 187–276.

Cosmides, L., & Tooby, J. (1992). Cognitive adaptations for social exchange. In J. Barkow, L. Cosmides, & J. Tooby (Eds.), *The adapted mind: Evolutionary psychology and the generation of culture* (pp. 163–228). New York: Oxford University Press.

Cosmides, L., & Tooby, J. (1994). Origins of domain specificity: The evolution of functional organization. In L. A. Hirschfeld & S. A. Gelman (Eds.), *Mapping the mind* (pp. 85–116). Cambridge: Cambridge University Press.

Cosmides, L., & Tooby, J. (1995). From function to structure: The role of evolutionary biology and computational theories in cognitive neuroscience. In M. Gazzaniga (Ed.), *The cognitive neurosciences* (pp. 1199–1210). Cambridge, MA: MIT Press.

Cosmides, L., & Tooby, J. (1996). Are humans good intuitive statisticians after all? Rethinking some conclusions from the literature on judgement under uncertainty. *Cognition, 58,* 1–73.

Coss, R. G., & Goldthwaite, R. O. (1995). The persistence of old designs for perception. In N. S. Thompson (Ed.), *Perspectives in ethology* (Vol. 11, pp. 83–148). New York: Plenum Press.

Coussi-Korbel, S. (1994). Learning to outwit a competitor in mangabeys (*Cercocebus torquatus torquatus*). *Journal of Comparative Psychology, 108,* 164–171.

Coussi-Korbel, S., & Fragaszy, D. M. (1995). On the relation between social dynamics and social learning. *Animal Behaviour, 50,* 1441–1453.

Couvillon, P. A., Arakaki, L., & Bitterman, M. E. (1997). Intramodal blocking in honeybees. *Animal Learning and Behavior, 25,* 277–282.

Couvillon, P. A., Leiato, T. G., & Bitterman, M. E. (1991). Learning in honeybees (*Apis mellifera*) on arrival at and departure from a feeding place. *Journal of Comparative Psychology, 105,* 177–184.

Cowey, A., & Stoerig, P. (1995). Blindsight in monkeys. *Nature, 373,* 247–249.

Cowey, A., & Stoerig, P. (1997). Visual detection in monkeys with blindsight. *Neuropsychologia, 35,* 929–939.

Cowie, R. J. (1977). Optimal foraging in great tits (*Parus major*). *Nature, 268,* 137–139.

Cowie, R. J., Krebs, J. R., & Sherry, D. F. (1981). Food storing by marsh tits. *Animal Behaviour, 29,* 1252–1259.

Cramer, A. E., & Gallistel, C. R. (1997). Vervet monkeys as travelling salesmen. *Nature, 387,* 464.

Crawford, C. B. (1993). The future of sociobiology: Counting babies or studying proximate mechanisms. *Trends in Ecology and Evolution, 8,* 183–186.

Cristol, D. A., & Switzer, P. V. (in press). Avian prey-dropping behavior II: American crows and walnuts. *Behavioral Ecology.*

Cristol, D. A., Switzer, P. V., Johnson, K. L., & Walke, L. S. (1997). Crows do not use automobiles as nutcrackers: Putting an anecdote to the test. *Auk, 114,* 296–298.

Croze, H. (1970). Searching image in carrion crows. *Zietschrift fur Tierpsychologie, Supplement 5,* 1–85.

Crystal, J. D., Church, R. M., & Broadbent, H. A. (1997). Systematic nonlinearities in the memory representation of time. *Journal of Experimental Psychology: Animal Behavior Processes, 23,* 267–282.

Crystal, J. D., & Shettleworth, S. J. (1994). Spatial list learning in black-capped chickadees. *Animal Learning and Behavior, 22,* 77–83.

Cullen, E. (1957). Adaptations in the kittiwake to cliff nesting. *Ibis, 99,* 275–302.

Curio, E. (1988). Cultural transmission of enemy recognition by birds. In T. R. Zentall & B. G. Galef Jr. (Eds.), *Social learning: Psychological and biological perspectives* (pp. 75–97). Hillsdale, NJ: Lawrence Erlbaum Associates.

Curio, E., Ernst, U., & Vieth, W. (1978). The adaptive significance of avian mobbing. *Zeitschrift fur Tierpsychologie, 48,* 184–202.

Custance, D. M., Whiten, A., & Bard, K. A. (1995). Can young chimpanzees (*Pan troglodytes*) imitate arbitrary actions? Hayes & Hayes (1952) revisited. *Behaviour, 132*, 837–859.

Cuthill, I. C., & Bennett, A. T. D. (1993). Mimicry and the eye of the beholder. *Proceedings of the Royal Society of London B, 253*, 203–204.

Cuthill, I., & Guilford, T. (1990). Perceived risk and obstacle avoidance in flying birds. *Animal Behaviour, 40*, 188–190.

Cuthill, I. C., Haccou, P., & Kacelnik, A. (1994). Starlings (*Sturnus vulgaris*) exploiting patches: Response to long-term changes in travel time. *Behavioral Ecology, 5*, 81–90.

Cuthill, I. C., Kacelnik, A., Krebs, J. R., Haccou, P., & Iwasa, Y. (1990). Starling exploiting patches: the effect of recent experience on foraging decisions. *Animal Behaviour, 40*, 625–640.

Cynx, J., & Nottebohm, F. (1992). Testosterone facilitates some conspecific song discriminations in castrated zebra finches (*Taeniopygia guttata*). *Proceedings of the National Academy of Sciences (USA), 89*, 1376–1378.

D'Amato, M. R., & Columbo, M. (1988). Representation of serial order in monkeys (*Cebus apella*). *Journal of Experimental Psychology: Animal Behavior Processes, 14*, 131–139.

D'Amato, M. R., Salmon, D. P., & Colombo, M. (1985). Extent and limits of the matching concept in monkeys (*Cebus apella*). *Journal of Experimental Psychology: Animal Behavior Processes, 11*, 35–51.

D'Amato, M. R., & Van Sant, P. (1988). The person concept in monkeys. *Journal of Experimental Psychology: Animal Behavior Processes, 14*, 43–55.

Dale, S., & Slagsvold, T. (1996). Mate choice on multiple cues, decision rules and sampling strategies in female pied flycatchers. *Behaviour, 133*, 903–944.

Daly, M., Rauschenberger, J., & Behrends, P. (1982). Food aversion learning in kangaroo rats: A specialist-generalist comparison. *Animal Learning and Behavior, 10*, 314–320.

Darwin, C. (1859). *The origin of species*. London: John Murray.

Darwin, C. (1871). *The descent of man and selection in relation to sex*. London: John Murray.

Darwin, C. (1872/1965). *The expression of the emotions in man and animals*. Chicago: University of Chicago Press.

Dasser, V. (1987). Slides of group members as representations of the real animals (*Macaca fascicularis*). *Ethology, 76*, 65–73.

Dasser, V. (1988a). A social concept in Java monkeys. *Animal Behaviour, 36*, 225–230.

Dasser, V. (1988b). Mapping social concepts in monkeys. In R. W. Byrne & A. Whiten (Eds.), *Machiavellian intelligence: Social expertise and the evolution of intellect in monkeys, apes, and humans* (pp. 85–93). Oxford: Clarendon Press.

Dasser, V., Ulbaek, I., & Premack, D. (1989). The perception of intention. *Science, 243*, 365–367.

Davey, G. C. L. (1995). Preparedness and phobias: Specific evolved associations or a generalized expectancy bias? *Behavioral and Brain Sciences, 8*, 289–325.

Davies, N. B. (1977). Prey selection and the search strategy of the spotted flycatcher (*Muscicapa striata*): a field study on optimal foraging. *Animal Behaviour, 25*, 1016–1033.

Davies, N. B., & Brooke, M. de L. (1988). Cuckoos versus reed warblers: adaptations and counteradaptations. *Animal Behaviour, 36*, 262–284.

Davies, N. B., Brooke, M. de L., & Kacelnik, A. (1996). Recognition errors and probability of parasitism determine whether reed warblers should accept or reject mimetic cuckoo eggs. *Proceedings of the Royal Society of London B, 263*, 925–931.

Davies, N. B., & Houston, A. I. (1981). Owners and satellites: The economics of territory defence in the pied wagtail, *Motacilla alba. Journal of Animal Ecology, 50*, 157–180.

Davis, H. (1984). Discrimination of the number three by a racoon. *Animal Learning and Behaviour, 12*, 409–413.

Davis, H. (1993). Numerical competence in animals: Life beyond clever Hans. In S. T. Boysen & E. J. Capaldi (Eds.), *The development of numerical competence* (pp. 109–125). Hillsdale, NJ: Lawrence Erlbaum Associates.

Davis, H., & Bradford, S. A. (1986). Counting behaviour by rats in a simulated natural environment. *Ethology, 73*, 265–280.

Davis, H., & Memmott, J. (1982). Counting behaviour in animals: A critical evaluation. *Psychological Bulletin, 92*(3), 547–571.

Davis, H., & Perusse, R. (1988). Numerical competence in animals: Definitional issues, current evidence, and a new research agenda. *Behavioral and Brain Sciences, 11*, 561–615.

Davis, M. (1970). Effects of interstimulus interval length and variability on startle-response habituation in the rat. *Journal of Comparative and Physiological Psychology, 72*, 177–192.

Davis, M., Falls, W. A., Campeau, S., & Kim, M. (1993). Fear-potentiated startle: a neural and pharmacological analysis. *Behavioural Brain Research, 58*, 175–198.

Davis, M., & File, S. E. (1984). Intrinsic and extrinsic mechanisms of habituation and sensitization: Implications for the design and analysis of experiments. , *Habituation, Sensitization and Behavior* (pp. 287–323). New York: Academic Press.

Davis, M., & Wagner, A. R. (1969). Habituation of startle response under incremental sequence of stimulus intensities. *Journal of Comparative and Physiological Psychology, 67*, 486–492.

Dawkins, M. (1971a). Perceptual changes in chicks: Another look at the 'search image' concept. *Animal Behaviour, 19*, 566–574.

Dawkins, M. (1971b). Shifts of 'attention' in chicks during feeding. *Animal Behaviour, 19*, 575–582.

Dawkins, M. S. (1989). The future of ethology: How many legs are we standing on? *Perspectives in Ethology, 8*, 47–54.

Dawkins, M. S. (1993). *Through our eyes only?* Oxford: W. H. Freeman.

Dawkins, M. S. (1995). *Unravelling animal behaviour.* (2nd ed.). Harlow, Essex: Longman Scientific and Technical.

Dawkins, M. S., & Guilford, T. (1994). Design of an intention signal in the bluehead wrasse (*Thalassoma bifasciatum*). *Proceedings of the Royal Society of London, B, 257*, 123–128.

Dawkins, M. S., & Guilford, T. (1995). An exaggerated preference for simple neural network models of signal evolution? *Proceedings of the Royal Society of London B, 261*, 357–360.

Dawkins, M. S., Guilford, T., Braithwaite, V. A., & Krebs, J. R. (1996). Discrimination and recognition of photographs of places by homing pigeons. *Behavioural Processes, 36*, 27–38.

Dawkins, M. S., & Woodington, A. (1997). Distance and the presentation of visual stimuli to birds. *Animal Behaviour, 54*, 1019–1025.

Dawkins, R. (1976). *The selfish gene.* Oxford: Oxford University Press.

Dawkins, R. (1986). *The blind watchmaker*. Harlow, Essex: Longman Scientific and Technical.

Dawkins, R. (1995). God's utility function. *Scientific American, 273*(11), 80–85.

Dawkins, R., & Krebs, J. R. (1978). Animal signals: Information or manipulation? In J. R. Krebs & N. B. Davies (Eds.), *Behavioural ecology: An evolutionary approach* (pp. 282–309). Sunderland, MA: Sinauer Associates.

Dawson, B. V., & Foss, B. M. (1965). Observational learning in budgerigars. *Animal Behaviour, 13,* 470–474.

de Ruiter, L. (1952). Some experiments on the camouflage of stick caterpillars. *Behaviour, 4,* 222–232.

de Vos, G. J., & Bolhuis, J. J. (1990). An investigation into blocking of filial imprinting in the chick during exposure to a compound stimulus. *Quarterly Journal of Experimental Psychology, 42B,* 289–312.

de Waal, F. B. M. (1991). Contemporary methods and convergent evidence in the study of primate social cognition. *Behaviour, 118,* 297–320.

Deacon, T. W. (1990). Rethinking mammalian brain evolution. *American Zoologist, 30,* 629–705.

Deacon, T. W. (1995). On telling growth from parcellation in brain evolution. In E. Alleva, A. Fasolo, H.-P. Lipp, L. Nadel, & L. Ricceri (Eds.), *Behavioural brain research in naturalistic and semi-naturalistic settings* (pp. 37–62). Dordrecht: Kluwer Academic Publishers.

DeCola, J. P., & Fanselow, M. S. (1995). Differential inflation with short and long CS-US intervals: Evidence of a nonassociative process in long-delay taste avoidance. *Animal Learning and Behavior, 23,* 154–163.

Delius, J. D., Thompson, G., Allen, K. L., & Emmerton, J. (1972). Colour mixing and colour preferences in neonate gulls. *Experientia, 10,* 1244–1246.

Dennett, D. C. (1983). Intentional systems in cognitive ethology: The "Panglossian paradigm" defended. *Behavioral and Brain Sciences, 6,* 343–390.

Dennett, D. C. (1987). *The intentional stance*. Cambridge, MA: MIT Press.

Dennett, D. C. (1995). *Darwin's dangerous idea*. New York: Simon & Schuster.

Dennett, D. C. (1996). *Kinds of minds*. New York: Basic Books.

Denniston, J. C., Miller, R. R., & Matute, H. (1996). Biological significance as a determinant of cue competition. *Psychological Science, 7,* 325–331.

Devenport, J. A., & Devenport, L. D. (1993). Time-dependent decisions in dogs (*Canis familiaris*). *Journal of Comparative Psychology, 107,* 169–173.

Devenport, L. (1989). Sampling behavior and contextual change. *Learning and Motivation, 20,* 97–114.

Devenport, L. D., & Devenport, J. A. (1994). Time-dependent averaging of foraging information in least chipmunks and golden-mantled ground squirrels. *Animal Behaviour, 47,* 787–802.

Devenport, L., Hill, T., Wilson, M., & Ogden, E. (1997). Tracking and averaging in variable environments: A transition rule. *Journal of Experimental Psychology: Animal Behavior Processes, 23,* 450–460.

DeVoogd, T. J. (1994). The neural basis for the acquisition and production of bird song. In J. A. Hogan & J. J. Bolhuis (Eds.), *Causal mechanisms of behavioral development* (pp. 49–81). Cambridge: Cambridge University Press.

Diamond, J. (1987). Bower building and decoration by the bowerbird *Amblyornis inornatus*. *Ethology, 74,* 177–204.

Dickinson, A. (1980). *Contemporary animal learning theory*. Cambridge: Cambridge University Press.

Dickinson, A. (1994). Instrumental conditioning. In N. J. Mackintosh (Ed.), *Animal learning and cognition* (pp. 45–79). San Diego, CA: Academic Press.

Dickinson, A., & Balleine, B. (1994). Motivational control of goal-directed action. *Animal Learning and Behavior, 22,* 1–18.

Diez-Chamizo, V., Sterio, D., & Mackintosh, N. J. (1985). Blocking and overshadowing between intra-maze and extra-maze cues: A test of the independance of locale and guidance learning. *Quarterly Journal of Experimental Psychology, 37B,* 235–253.

Dingle, H. (1996). *Migration: The biology of life on the move.* New York: Oxford University Press.

Dolman, C. S., Templeton, J., & Lefebvre, L. (1996). Mode of foraging competition is related to tutor preference in *Zenaida aurita. Journal of Comparative Psychology, 110,* 45–54.

Domjan, M. (1983). Biological constraints on instrumental and classical conditioning: Implications for general process theory. *Psychology of Learning and Motivation, 17,* 215–277.

Domjan, M. (1994). Formulation of a behavior system for sexual conditioning. *Psychonomic Bulletin and Review, 1,* 421–428.

Domjan, M. (1998). *The principles of learning and behavior.* (4th ed.). Belmont, CA: Brooks/Cole.

Domjan, M., & Burkhard, B. (1986). *The principles of learning and behavior.* (2nd ed.). Monterey, CA: Brooks/Cole.

Domjan, M., & Galef, Jr., B.G. (1983). Biological constraints on instrumental and classical conditioning: Retrospect and prospect. *Animal Learning & Behavior, 11,* 151–161.

Domjan, M., & Hollis, K. L. (1988). Reproductive behavior: A potential model system for adaptive specialization in learning. In R. C. Bolles & M. D. Beecher (Eds.), *Evolution and learning* (pp. 213–237). Hillsdale, NJ: Lawrence Erlbaum Associates.

Domjan, M., & Wilson, N. E. (1972). Specificity of cue to consequence in aversion learning in the rat. *Psychonomic Science, 26,* 143–145.

Dooling, R. J., Brown, S. D., Klump, G. M., & Okanoya, K. (1992). Auditory perception of conspecific and heterospecific vocalizations in birds: Evidence for special processes. *Journal of Comparative Psychology, 106,* 20–28.

Dooling, R. J., Brown, S. D., Manabe, K., & Powell, E. F. (1996). The perceptual foundations of vocal learning in Budgerigars. In C. F. Moss & S. J. Shettleworth (Eds.), *Neuroethological studies of cognitive and perceptual processes* (pp. 113–137). Boulder, CO: Westview Press.

Dooling, R. J., Brown, S. D., Park, T. J., & Okanoya, K. (1990). Natural perceptual categories for vocal signals in budgerigars *(Melopsittacus undulatus).* In W. C. Stebbins & M. A. Berkley (Eds.), *Comparative perception* (Vol. 2, pp. 345–374). New York: Wiley.

Doré, F. Y., & Dumas, C. (1987). Psychology of animal cognition: Piagetian studies. *Psychological Bulletin, 102,* 219–233.

Doré, F. Y., Fiset, S., Goulet, S., Dumas, M.-C., & Gagnon, S. (1996). Search behavior in cats and dogs: Interspecific differences in working memory and spatial cognition. *Animal Learning & Behavior, 24,* 142–149.

Driessen, G., Bernstein, C., Van Alphen, J. J. M., & Kacelnik, A. (1995). A count-down mechanism for host search in the parasitoid *Ventura canescens. Journal of Animal Ecology, 64,* 117–125.

Dudchenko, P. A., Goodridge, J. P., Seiterle, D. A., & Taube, J. S. (1997). Effects of repeated disorientation on the acquisition of spatial tasks in rats: Dissociation between the appetitive radial arm maze and aversive water maze. *Journal of Experimental Psychology: Animal Behavior Processes, 23,* 194–210.

Dugatkin, L. A. (1992). Sexual selection and imitation: Females copy the mate choice of others. *American Naturalist, 139,* 1384–1389.

Dugatkin, L. A. (1996). Copying and mate choice. In C. M. Heyes & B. G. Galef Jr. (Eds.), *Social learning in animals: The roots of culture* (pp. 85–105). San Diego: Academic Press.

Dukas, R. (Ed.). (1998). *Cognitive ecology.* Chicago: University of Chicago Press.

Dukas, R., & Clark, C. W. (1995). Sustained vigilance and animal performance. *Animal Behaviour, 49,* 1259–1267.

Dukas, R., & Real, L. A. (1991). Learning foraging tasks by bees: A comparison between social and solitary species. *Animal Behaviour, 42,* 269–276.

Dukas, R., & Waser, N. M. (1994). Categorization of food types enhances foraging performance of bumblebees. *Animal Behaviour, 48,* 1001–1006.

Dumas, C. (1992). Object permanence in cats (*Felis catus*): An ecological approach to the study of invisible displacements. *Journal of Comparative Psychology, 106,* 404–410.

Dunbar, R. I. M. (1996). Determinants of group size in primates: A general model. *Proceedings of the British Academy, 88,* 33–57.

Dusenbery, D. B. (1992). *Sensory ecology.* New York: W. H. Freeman and Company.

Dyer, F. C. (1987). Memory and sun compensation by honey bees. *Journal of Comparative Physiology A, 160,* 621–633.

Dyer, F. C. (1991). Bees acquire route-based memories but not cognitive maps in a familiar landscape. *Animal Behaviour, 41*(2), 239–246.

Dyer, F. C. (1994). Spatial cognition and navigation in insects. In L. Real (Ed.), *Behavioral mechanisms in evolutionary ecology* (pp. 66–98). Chicago: Chicago University Press.

Dyer, F. C. (1996). Spatial memory and navigation by honeybees on the scale of the foraging range. *Journal of Experimental Biology, 199,* 147–154.

Dyer, F. C. (1998). Cognitive ecology of navigation. In R. Dukas (Ed.), *Cognitive ecology* (pp. 201–260). Chicago: University of Chicago Press.

Dyer, F. C., & Dickinson, J. A. (1994). Development of sun compensation by honeybees: How partially experienced bees estimate the sun's course. *Proceedings of the National Academy of Science USA, 91,* 4471–4474.

Dyer, F. C., & Dickinson, J. A. (1996). Sun-compass learning in insects: Representation in a simple mind. *Current Directions in Psychological Science, 5,* 67–72.

Dyer, F. C., & Seeley, T. D. (1989). On the evolution of the dance language. *American Naturalist, 133,* 580–590.

Dyer, F. C., & Seeley, T. D. (1991). Dance dialects and foraging range in three Asian honey bee species. *Behavioral Ecology and Sociobiology, 28,* 227–233.

Eddy, T. J., Gallup, G. G. Jr., & Povinelli, D. J. (1996). Age differences in the ability of chimpanzees to distinguish mirror-images of self from video images of others. *Journal of Comparative Psychology, 110,* 38–44.

Edhouse, W. V., & White, K. G. (1988). Sources of proactive interference in animal memory. *Journal of Experimental Psychology: Animal Behavior Processes, 14,* 56–70.

Eichenbaum, H., Fagan, A., & Cohen, N. J. (1986). Normal olfactory discrimination learning set and facilitation of reversal learning after medial-temporal damage in rats: Implications for an account of preserved learning abilities in amnesia. *Journal of Neuroscience, 6,* 1876–1884.

Eiserer, L. A. (1978). Maltreatment effects and learning processes in infantile attachment. *Behavioral and Brain Sciences, 3,* 445–446.

Eiserer, L. A. (1980). Development of filial attachment to static visual features of an imprinting object. *Animal Learning & Behavior, 8,* 159–166.

Eiserer, L. A., & Hoffman, H. S. (1973). Priming of ducklings' responses by presenting an imprinted stimulus. *Journal of Comparative and Physiological Psychology, 82,* 345–359.

Elgar, M. A. (1989). Predator vigilance and group size in mammals and birds: A critical review of the emprical evidence. *Biological Review, 64,* 13–33.

Ellard, C. G., & Bigel, M. G. (1996). The use of local features and global spatial context for object recognition in a visuomotor task in the Mongolian gerbil. *Animal Learning & Behavior, 24,* 310–317.

Ellen, P., Soteres, B. J., & Wages, C. (1984). Problem solving in the rat: Piecemeal acquisition of cognitive maps. *Animal Learning & Behavior, 12,* 232–237.

Elner, R. W., & Hughes, R. N. (1978). Energy maximization in the diet of the shore crab, *Carcinus maenas. Journal of Animal Ecology, 47,* 103–116.

Emery, N. J., Lorincz, E. N., Perrett, D. I., Oram, M. W., & Baker, C. I. (1997). Gaze following and joint attention in rhesus monkeys (*Macaca mulatta*). *Journal of Comparative Psychology, 111,* 286–293.

Emlen, S. T. (1970). Celestial rotation: Its importance in the development of migratory orientation. *Science, 170,* 1198–1201.

Emlen, S. T., Wiltschko, W., Demong, N. J., Wiltschko, R., & Bergman, S. (1976). Magnetic direction finding: Evidence for its use in migratory indigo buntings. *Science, 193,* 505–508.

Endler, J. A. (1986). *Natural selection in the wild.* Princeton, NJ: Princeton University Press.

Endler, J. A. (1991). Variation in the appearance of guppy color patterns to guppies and their predators under different visual conditions. *Vision Research, 31,* 587–608.

Endler, J. A. (1992). Signals, signal conditions, and the direction of evolution. *American Naturalist, 139, supplement,* S125–S153.

Endler, J. A., & Basolo, A. L. (in press). Neuroecology, perceptual biases and sexual selection. *Trends in Ecology and Evolution.*

Endler, J. A., & Théry, M. (1996). Interacting effects of lek placement, display behavior, ambient light, and color patterns in three neotropical forest-dwelling birds. *American Naturalist, 148,* 421–452.

Enquist, M., & Arak, A. (1994). Symmetry, beauty and evolution. *Nature, 372,* 169–172.

Epstein, R. (1985). Animal cognition as the praxist views it. *Neuroscience & Biobehavioral Reviews, 9,* 623–630.

Epstein, R., Kirshnit, C. E., Lanza, R. P., & Rubin, L. C. (1984). 'Insight' in the pigeon: antecedents and determinants of an intelligent performance. *Nature, 308,* 61–62.

Epstein, R., Lanza, R. P., & Skinner, B. F. (1980). Symbolic communication between two pigeons (*Columba livia domestica*). *Science, 207,* 543–545.

Epstein, R., Lanza, R. P., & Skinner, B. F. (1981). "Self-awareness" in the pigeon. *Science, 212,* 695–696.

Estes, W. K. (1950). Towards a statistical theory of learning. *Psychological Review, 57,* 94–107.

Etienne, A. S. (1973). Developmental stages and cognitive structures as determinants of what is learned. In R. A. Hinde & J. Stevenson-Hinde (Eds.), *Constraints on learning* (pp. 371–395). New York: Academic Press.

Etienne, A. S. (1992). Navigation of a small mammal by dead reckoning and local cues. *Current Directions in Psychological Science, 1,* 48–52.

Etienne, A. S., Maurer, R., & Saucy, F. (1988). Limitations in the assessment of path dependent information. *Behaviour, 106,* 81–111.

Etienne, A. S., Maurer, R., Saucy, F., & Teroni, E. (1986). Short-distance homing in the golden hamster after a passive outward journey. *Animal Behaviour, 34*(3), 696–715.

Etienne, A. S., Teroni, E., Hurni, C., & Portenier, V. (1990). The effect of a single light cue on homing behaviour of the golden hamster. *Animal Behaviour, 39,* 17–41.

Evans, C. S. (1997). Referential signals. *Perspectives in Ethology, 12,* 99–143.

Evans, C. S., Evans, L., & Marler, P. (1993). On the meaning of alarm calls: Functional reference in an avian vocal system. *Animal Behaviour, 46,* 23–38.

Evans, C. S., Macedonia, J. M., & Marler, P. (1993). Effects of apparent size and speed on the response of chickens, *Gallus gallus,* to computer-generated simulations of aerial predators. *Animal Behaviour, 46,* 1–11.

Evans, C. S., & Marler, P. (1992). Female appearance as a factor in the responsiveness of male chickens during anti-predator behaviour and courtship. *Animal Behaviour, 43,* 137–145.

Evans, C. S., & Marler, P. (1994). Food calling and audience effects in male chickens, *Gallus gallus:* Their relationships to food availability, courtship and social facilitation. *Animal Behaviour, 47,* 1159–1170.

Evans, C. S., & Marler, P. (1995). Language and animal communication: Parallels and contrasts. In H. L. Roitblat & J.-A. Meyer (Eds.), *Comparative approaches to cognitive science* (pp. 342–382). Cambridge, MA: MIT Press.

Ewer, R. F. (1969). The "instinct to teach." *Nature, 222,* 698.

Falk, H., Biebach, H., & Krebs, J. R. (1992). Learning a time-place pattern of food availability: a comparison between an insectivorous and a granivorous weaver species (*Ploceus bicolor* and *Euplectes hordeaceus*). *Behavioral Ecology and Sociobiology, 31,* 9–15.

Falls, B., & Brooks, R. J. (1975). Individual recognition by song in white-throated sparrows. II. Effects of location. *Canadian Journal of Zoology, 53,* 1412–1420.

Falls, J. B. (1982). Individual recognition by sounds in birds. In D. E. Kroodsma & E. H. Miller (Eds.), *Acoustic communication in birds* (Vol. 2, pp. 237–278). New York: Academic Press.

Fanselow, M. S. (1994). Neural organization of the defensive behavior system responsible for fear. *Psychonomic Bulletin and Review, 1,* 429–438.

Fanselow, M. S., & Lester, L. S. (1988). A functional behavioristic approach to aversively motivated behavior: Predatory imminence as a determinant of the topography of defensive behavior. In R. C. Bolles & M. D. Beecher (Eds.), *Evolution and learning* (pp. 185–212). Hillsdale, NJ: Lawrence Erlbaum Associates.

Fantino, E., & Abarca, N. (1985). Choice, optimal foraging, and the delay-reduction hypothesis. *Behavioral and Brain Sciences, 8,* 315–330.

Farber, I. B., & Churchland, P. S. (1995). Consciousness and the neurosciences: Philosophical and theoretical issues. In M. Gazzaniga (Ed.), *The cognitive neurosciences* (pp. 1295–1306). Cambridge, MA: MIT Press.

Felton, M., & Lyon, D. O. (1966). The post-reinforcement pause. *Journal of the Experimental Analysis of Behavior, 9,* 131–134.

Fetterman, J. G. (1993). Numerosity discrimination: Both time and number matter. *Journal of Experimental Psychology: Animal Behavior Processes, 19*, 149–164.

Fetterman, J. G. (1996). Dimensions of stimulus complexity. *Journal of Experimental Psychology: Animal Behavior Processes, 22*, 3–18.

Fetterman, J. G., Dreyfus, L. R., & Stubbs, D. A. (1996). Judging relative duration: The role of rule and instructional variables. *Journal of Experimental Psychology: Animal Behavior Processes, 22*, 350–361.

Fetterman, J. G., & Killeen, P. R. (1995). Categorical scaling of time: Implications for clock-counter models. *Journal of Experimental Psychology: Animal Behavior Processes, 21*, 43–63.

Finger, E., & Burkhardt, D. (1994). Biological aspects of bird colouration and avian colour vision including utraviolet range. *Vision Research, 34*, 1509–1514.

Fiset, S., & Doré, F. Y. (1996). Spatial encoding in domestic cats (*Felis catus*). *Journal of Experimental Psychology: Animal Behavior Processes, 22*, 420–437.

Fisher, J., & Hinde, R. A. (1949). The opening of milk bottles by birds. *British Birds, 42*, 347–357.

Fisher, J. A. (1995). The myth of anthropomorphism. In M. Bekoff & D. Jamieson (Eds.), *Readings in animal cognition* (pp. 3–16). Cambridge, MA: MIT Press.

FitzGerald, R. E., Isler, R., Rosenberg, E., Oettinger, R., & Battig, K. (1985). Maze patrolling by rats with and without food reward. *Animal Learning and Behavior, 13*, 451–462.

Fleishman, L. J. (1988). Sensory influences on physical design of a visual display. *Animal Behaviour, 36*, 1420–1424.

Fleming, A. S., Morgan, H. D., & Walsh, C. (1996). Experiential factors in postpartum regulation of maternal care. *Advances in the Study of Behavior, 25*, 295–332.

Fodor, J. A. (1983). *The modularity of mind*. Cambridge, MA: MIT Press.

Foree, D. D., & LoLordo, V. M. (1973). Attention in the pigeon: Differential effects of food-getting versus shock-avoidance procedures. *Journal of Comparative and Physiological Psychology, 85*, 551–558.

Fraenkel, G. S., & Gunn, D. L. (1961). *The orientation of animals*. New York: Dover Publications.

Fragaszy, D. M., & Visalberghi, E. (1989). Social influences on the acquisition of tool-use behaviors in tufted capuchin monkeys (*Cebus apella*). *Journal of Comparative Psychology, 103*, 159–170.

Fragaszy, D. M., & Visalberghi, E. (1996). Social learning in monkeys: Primate primacy reconsidered. In B. G. Galef & C. Heyes (Eds.), *Social learning: the roots of culture* (pp. 65–84). San Diego: Academic Press.

Francis, R. C. (1995). Evolutionary neurobiology. *Trends in Ecology and Evolution, 10*, 276–281.

Freeberg, T. M., King, A. P., & West, M. J. (1995). Social malleability in cowbirds (*Molothrus ater artemisiae*): Species and mate recognition in the first 2 years of life. *Journal of Comparative Psychology, 109*, 357–367.

Frisch, B., & Aschoff, J. (1987). Circadian rhythms in honeybees: entrainment by feeding cycles. *Physiological Entomology, 12*, 41–49.

Funayama, E. S., Couvillon, P. A., & Bitterman, M. E. (1995). Compound conditioning in honeybees: Blocking tests of the independence assumption. *Animal Learning & Behavior, 23*, 429–437.

Gaffan, E. A. (1992). Primacy, recency, and the variability of data in studies of animals' working memory. *Animal Learning & Behavior, 20*, 240–252.

Gaffan, E. A., Hansel, M. C., & Smith, L. E. (1983). Does reward depletion influence spatial memory performance? *Learning and Motivation, 14*, 58–74.

Gagliardi, J. L., Kirkpatrick-Steger, K. K., Thomas, J., Allen, G. J., & Blumberg, M. S. (1995). Seeing and knowing: Knowledge attribution versus stimulus control in adult humans (*Homo sapiens*). *Journal of Comparative Psychology, 109*, 107–114.

Galea, L. A. M., Kavaliers, M., Ossenkopp, K.-P., Innes, 'D., & Hargreaves, E. L. (1994). Sexually dimorphic spatial learning varies seasonally in two populations of deer mice. *Brain Research, 635*, 18–26.

Galef, B. G., Jr. (1976). Social transmission of acquired behavior: A discussion of tradition and social learning in vertebrates. *Advances in the Study of Behavior, 6*, 77–100.

Galef, B. G., Jr. (1988). Imitation in animals: History, definition, and interpretation of data from the psychological laboratory. In T. R. Zentall & B. G. Galef Jr. (Eds.), *Social learning: Psychological and biological perspectives* (pp. 3–28). Hillsdale, NJ: Lawrence Erlbaum Associates.

Galef, B. G., Jr. (1991). Information centres of Norway rats: sites for information exchange and information parasitism. *Animal Behaviour, 41*, 295–301.

Galef, B. G., Jr. (1995). Why behaviour patterns that animals learn socially are locally adaptive. *Animal Behaviour, 49*, 1325–1334.

Galef, B. G. (1996a). Tradition in animals: Field observations and laboratory analyses. In M. Bekoff & D. Jamieson (Eds.), *Readings in animal cognition* (pp. 91–105). Cambridge, MA: MIT Press.

Galef, B. G., Jr. (1996b). Social enhancement of food preferences in Norway rats: A brief review. In C. M. Heyes & B. G. Galef, Jr. (Eds.), *Social learning and imitation in animals: The roots of culture* (pp. 49–64). New York: Academic Press.

Galef, B. G., Jr., & Allen, C. (1995). A new model system for studying behavioural traditions in animals. *Animal Behaviour, 50*, 705–717.

Galef, B. G., Jr., & Durlach, P. J. (1993). Absence of blocking, overshadowing, and latent inhibition in social enhancement of food preferences. *Animal Learning & Behavior, 21*, 214–220.

Galef, B. G., Jr., Manzig, L. A., & Field, R. M. (1986). Imitation learning in budgerigars: Dawson and Foss (1965) revisited. *Behavioural Processes, 13*, 191–202.

Galef, B.G., Jr., & Osborne, B. (1978). Novel taste facilitation of the association of visual cues with toxicosis in rats. *Journal of Comparative and Physiological Psychology, 92*, 907–916.

Galef, B. G., Jr., & White, D. J. (1998). Mate-choice copying in Japanese quail, *Coturnix coturnix japonica*. *Animal Behaviour, 55*, 545–552.

Galef, B. G., Jr., & Wigmore, S. W. (1983). Transfer of information concerning distant foods: A laboratory investigation of the 'Information-centre' hypothesis. *Animal Behaviour, 31*, 748–758.

Gallagher, J. G. (1977). Sexual imprinting: A sensitive period in Japanese quail (*Coturnix cortunix japonica*). *Journal of Comparative and Physiological Psychology, 91*, 72–78.

Gallistel, C. R. (1990). *The organization of learning*. Cambridge, MA: MIT Press.

Gallistel, C. R. (1992). Classical conditioning as an adaptive specialization: A computational model. *Psychology of Learning and Motivation, 28*, 35–67.

Gallistel, C. R. (1993). A conceptual framework for the study of numerical estimation and arithmetic reasoning in animals. In S. T. Boysen & E. J. Capaldi (Eds.), *The development of numerical competence* (pp. 211–223). Hillsdale, NJ: Lawrence Erlbaum Associates.

Gallistel, C. R. (1994). Space and time. In N. J. Mackintosh (Ed.), *Animal Learning and Cognition* (pp. 221–253). San Diego: Academic Press.

Gallistel, C. R. (1995). The replacement of general-purpose theories with adaptive specializations. In M. Gazziniga (Ed.), *The cognitive neurosciences* (pp. 1255–1267). Cambridge, MA: MIT Press.

Gallistel, C. R., & Cramer, A. E. (1996). Computations on metric maps in mammals: Getting oriented and choosing a multi-destination route. *Journal of Experimental Biology, 199*, 211–217.

Gallup, G. G., Jr. (1970). Chimpanzees: Self-recognition. *Science, 167*, 86–87.

Gallup, G. G., Jr. (1977). Self recognition in primates: A comparative approach to the bidirectional properties of consciousness. *American Psychologist, 32*, 329–338.

Gallup, G. G., Jr. (1979). Self-awareness in primates. *American Scientist, 67*, 417–421.

Gallup, G. G., Jr. (1994). Self-recognition: Research strategies and experimental design. In S. T. Parker, R. W. Mitchell, & M. L. Boccia (Eds.), *Self-awareness in animals and humans: Developmental perspectives* (pp. 35–50). Cambridge: Cambridge University Press.

Gallup, G. G., Jr., Povinelli, D. J., Suarez, S. D., Anderson, J. R., Lethmate, J., & Menzel, E. W., Jr. (1995). Further reflections on self-recognition in primates. *Animal Behaviour, 50*, 1525–1532.

Gamberale, G., & Tullberg, B. S. (1996). Evidence for a more effective signal in aggregated aposematic prey. *Animal Behaviour, 52*, 597–601.

Gamzu, E., & Williams, D. R. (1971). Classical conditioning of a complex skeletal response. *Science, 171*, 923–925.

Garcia, J., Ervin, F. R., & Koelling, R. A. (1966). Learning with prolonged delay of reinforcement. *Psychonomic Science, 5*, 121–122.

Garcia, J., & Koelling, R. A. (1966). Relation of cue to consequence in avoidance learning. *Psychonomic Science, 4*, 123–124.

Garcia, J., McGowan, B. K., & Green, K. F. (1972). Biological constraints on conditioning. In A. H. Black & W. F. Prokasy (Eds.), *Classical conditioning II: Current theory and research* (pp. 3–27). New York: Appleton-Century-Crofts.

Gardner, R. A., & Gardner, B. T. (1969). Teaching sign language to a chimpanzee. *Science, 165*, 664–672.

Gaulin, S. J. C. (1995). Does evolutionary theory predict sex differences in the brain? In M. Gazzaniga (Ed.), *The cognitive neurosciences* (pp. 1211–1225). Cambridge, MA: MIT Press.

Gaulin, S. J. C., & Fitzgerald, R. W. (1989). Sexual selection for spatial-learning ability. *Animal Behavior, 37*, 322–331.

Gaulin, S. J. C., Fitzgerald, R. W., & Wartell, M. S. (1990). Sex differences in spatial ability and activity in two vole species (*Microtus ochrogaster* and *M. pennsylvanicus*). *Journal of Comparative Psychology, 104*, 88–93.

Geary, D. C. (1996). Sexual selection and sex differences in mathematical abilities. *Behavioral and Brain Sciences, 19*, 229–284.

Geiger, K., Kratzsch, D., & Menzel, R. (1995). Target-directed orientation in displaced honeybees. *Ethology, 101*, 335–345.

Gendron, R. P., & Staddon, J. E. R. (1983). Searching for cryptic prey: The effect of search rate. *American Naturalist, 121*, 172–186.

Gergely, G. (1994). From self-recognition to theory of mind. In S. T. Parker, R. W. Mitchell, & M. L. Boccia (Eds.), *Self-awareness in animals and humans: Developmental perspectives* (pp. 51–60). Cambridge: Cambridge University Press.

Gergely, G., Nadasdy, Z., Csibra, G., & Biro, S. (1995). Taking the intentional stance at 12 months of age. *Cognition, 56,* 165–193.

Gerhardt, H. C. (1983). Communication and the environment. In T. R. Halliday & P. J. B. Slater (Eds.), *Animal behaviour* (Vol. 2, pp. 82–113). New York: W.H. Freeman and Company.

Gerlai, R. (1996). Gene-targeting studies of mammalian behavior: Is it the mutation or the background genotype? *Trends in Neurosciences, 19,* 177–181.

Getty, T. (1995). Search discrimination, and selection: Mate choice by pied flycatchers. *American Naturalist, 145,* 146–154.

Getty, T., Kamil, A. C., & Real, P. C. (1987). Signal detection theory and foraging for cryptic or mimetic prey. In A. C. Kamil, J. R. Krebs, & H. R. Pulliam (Eds.), *Foraging behavior* (pp. 525–548). New York: Plenum Press.

Gibbon, J. (1991). Origins of scalar timing. *Learning and Motivation, 22,* 3–38.

Gibbon, J. (1995). Dynamics of time matching: Arousal makes better seem worse. *Psychonomic Bulletin and Review, 2,* 208–215.

Gibbon, J., & Allan, L. (Eds.). (1984). *Timing and time perception. Annals of the New York Academy of Sciences, 423.* New York: New York Academy of Sciences.

Gibbon, J., Baldock, M. D., Locurto, C., Gold, L., & Terrace, H. S. (1977). Trial and intertrial durations in autoshaping. *Journal of Experimental Psychology: Animal Behavior Processes, 3,* 264–284.

Gibbon, J., & Church, R. M. (1981). Time left: Linear versus logarithmic subjective time. *Journal of Experimental Psychology: Animal Behavior Processes, 7,* 87–108.

Gibbon, J., & Church, R. M. (1990). Representation of time. *Cognition, 37,* 23–54.

Gibbon, J., Church, R. M., Fairhurst, S., & Kacelnik, A. (1988). Scalar expectancy theory and choice between delayed rewards. *Psychological Review, 95,* 102–114.

Gibson, E. J., & Walk, R. D. (1956). The effect of prolonged exposure to visually presented patterns on learning to discriminate them. *Journal of Comparative and Physiological Psychology, 49,* 239–242.

Gibson, J. J. (1966). *The senses considered as perceptual systems.* Boston: Houghton Mifflin.

Gibson, J. J. (1979). *The ecological approach to visual perception.* Boston: Houghton Mifflin.

Gibson, R. M., & Langen, T. A. (1996). How do animals choose their mates? *Trends in Ecology and Evolution, 11,* 468–470.

Gigerenzer, G., & Hoffrage, U. (1995). How to improve Bayesian reasoning without instruction: Frequency formats. *Psychological Review, 102,* 684–704.

Gigerenzer, G., & Hug, K. (1992). Domain-specific reasoning: Social contracts, cheating, and perspective change. *Cognition, 43,* 127–171.

Gill, F. B. (1988). Trapline foraging by hermit hummingbirds: Competition for an undefended, renewable resource. *Ecology, 69,* 1933–1942.

Gill, F. B. (1995). *Ornithology.* (2nd ed.). New York: W.H. Freeman.

Gillan, D. J. (1981). Reasoning in the chimpanzee: II. Transitive inference. *Journal of Experimental Psychology: Animal Behavior Processes, 7,* 150–164.

Giraldeau, L.-A., Caraco, T., & Valone, T. J. (1994). Social foraging: individual learning and cultural transmission of innovations. *Behavioral Ecology, 5,* 35–43.

Giraldeau, L.-A., & Lefebvre, L. (1986). Exchangeable producer and scrounger roles in a captive flock of feral pigeons: a case for the skill pool effect. *Animal Behaviour, 34,* 797–803.

Giraldeau, L.-A., & Lefebvre, L. (1987). Scrounging prevents cultural transmission of food-finding behaviour in pigeons. *Animal Behaviour, 35,* 387–394.

Giraldeau, L.-A., & Templeton, J. J. (1991). Food scrounging and diffusion of foraging skills in pigeons, *Columba livia*: The importance of tutor and observer rewards. *Ethology, 89,* 63–72.

Gisiner, R., & Schusterman, R. J. (1992). Sequence, syntax, and semantics: Responses of a language-trained sea lion (*Zalophus californianus*) to novel sign combinations. *Journal of Comparative Psychology, 106,* 78–91.

Giurfa, M., Eichmann, B., & Menzel, R. (1996). Symmetry perception in an insect. *Nature, 382,* 203–210.

Godard, R. (1991). Long-term memory of individual neighbours in a migratory songbird. *Nature, 350,* 228–229.

Godin, J.-G. J., & Keenleyside, M. H. (1984). Foraging on patchily distributed prey by a cichlid fish (*Teleostei, cichlidae*): a test of the ideal free distribution theory. *Animal Behaviour, 32,* 120–131.

Godin, J.-G. J., & Smith, S. A. (1988). A fitness cost of foraging in the guppy. *Nature, 333,* 69–71.

Goldsmith, T. H. (1990). Optimization, constraint, and history in the evolution of eyes. *Quarterly Review of Biology, 65,* 281–322.

Goldsmith, T. H. (1994). Ultraviolet receptors and color vision: Evolutionary implications and a dissonance of paradigms. *Vision Research, 34,* 1479–1487.

Goldsmith, T. H., Collins, J. S., & Perlman, D. L. (1981). A wavelength discrimination function for the hummingbird *Archilochus alexandri*. *Journal of Comparative Physiology, 143,* 103–110.

Gomez, J.-C. (1994). Mutual awareness in primate communication: A Gricean approach. In S. T. Parker, R. W. Mitchell, & M. L. Boccia (Eds.), *Self-awareness in animals and humans: Developmental perspectives* (pp. 61–80). Cambridge: Cambridge University Press.

Gomez, J.-C. (1996). Non-human primate theories of (non-human primate) minds: some issues concerning the origins of mind-reading. In P. Carruthers & P. K. Smith (Eds.), *Theories of theories of mind* (pp. 330–343). Cambridge: Cambridge University Press.

Gonzalez-Mariscal, G., & Rosenblatt, J. (1996). Maternal behavior in rabbits. *Advances in the Study of Behavior, 25,* 333–360.

Goodale, M. A., & Milner, A. D. (1992). Separate visual pathways for perception and action. *Trends in Neurosciences, 15,* 20–25.

Gordon, W. C., & Klein, R. L. (1994). Animal memory: The effects of context change on retention performance. In N. J. Mackintosh (Ed.), *Animal learning and cognition* (pp. 255–279). San Diego, CA: Academic Press.

Goss-Custard, J. D. (1977). Optimal foraging and the size selection of worms by redshank, *Tringa totanus*, in the field. *Animal Behaviour, 25,* 10–29.

Gotceitas, V., & Colgan, P. (1991). Assessment of patch profitability and ideal free distribution: The significance of sampling. *Behaviour, 119,* 65–76.

Gottlieb, G. (1978). Development of species identification in ducklings: IV. Change in species-specific perception caused by auditory deprivation. *Journal of Comparative and Physiological Psychology, 92,* 375–387.

Gould, J. L. (1975). Honey bee recruitment: The dance-language controversy. *Science, 189,* 685–693.

Gould, J. L. (1976). The dance-language controversy. *Quarterly Review of Biology, 51,* 211–244.

Gould, J. L. (1986). The locale map of honey bees: Do insects have cognitive maps? *Science, 232,* 861–863.

Gould, J. L. (1990). Honey bee cognition. *Cognition, 37,* 83–103.

Gould, J. L. (1996). Specializations in honey bee learning. In C. F. Moss & S. J. Shettleworth (Eds.), *Neuroethological studies of cognitive and perceptual processes* (pp. 11–30). Boulder, CO: Westview Press.

Gould, J. L., & Gould, C. G. (1988). *The honey bee.* New York: Scientific American Library.

Gould, J. L., & Gould, C. G. (1994). *The animal mind.* New York: Scientific American Library.

Gould, J. L., & Towne, W. F. (1987). Evolution of the dance language. *American Naturalist, 130,* 317–338.

Gould, S. J., & Lewontin, R. C. (1979). The spandrels of San Marco and the Panglossian paradigm: a critique of the adaptationist program. *Proceedings of the Royal Society of London B, 205,* 581–598.

Gould-Beierle, K. L., & Kamil, A. C. (1996). The use of local and global cues by Clark's nutcracker, *Nucifraga columbiana. Animal Behaviour, 52,* 519–528.

Goulet, S., Doré, F. Y., & Rousseau, R. (1994). Object permanence and working memory in cats *(Felis catus). Journal of Experimental Psychology: Animal Behavior Processes, 20,* 347–365.

Grafen, A. (1990). Do animals really recognize kin? *Animal Behaviour, 39,* 42–54.

Grammer, K., & Thornhill, R. (1994). Human *(Homo sapiens)* facial attractiveness and sexual selection: The role of symmetry and averageness. *Journal of Comparative Psychology, 108,* 233–242.

Grant, D. S. (1976). Effect of sample presentation time on long-delay matching in pigeons. *Learning and Motivation, 7,* 580–590.

Grant, D. S. (1981). Short-term memory in the pigeon. In N. E. Spear & R. R. Miller (Eds.), *Information processing in animals: Memory mechanisms.* Hillsdale, NJ: Lawrence Erlbaum Associates.

Grant, D. S. (1982). Prospective versus retrospective coding of samples of stimuli, responses, and reinforcers in delayed matching with pigeons. *Learning and Motivation, 13,* 265–280.

Grant, D. S., Brewster, R. G., & Stierhoff, K. A. (1983). "Surprisingness" and short-term retention in pigeons. *Journal of Experimental Psychology: Animal Behavior Processes, 9,* 63–79.

Grant, D. S., & Soldat, A. S. (1995). A postsample cue to forget does initiate an active forgetting process in pigeons. *Journal of Experimental Psychology: Animal Behavior Processes, 21,* 218–228.

Grant, D. S., & Spetch, M. L. (1994). Mediated transfer testing provides evidence for common coding of duration and line samples in many-to-one matching in pigeons. *Animal Learning & Behavior, 22,* 84–89.

Grant, P. R. (1986). *Ecology and evolution of Darwin's finches.* New Jersey: Princeton University Press.

Gray, R. D. (1994). Sparrows, matching and the ideal free distribution: can biological and psychological approaches be synthesized? *Animal Behaviour, 48,* 411–423.

Gray, R. D., & Kennedy, M. (1994). Perceptual constraints on optimal foraging: a reason for departures from the ideal free distribution. *Animal Behaviour, 47,* 469–471.

Green, P. R. (1982). Problems in animal perception and learning and their implications for models of imprinting. *Perspectives in Ethology, 5,* 243–273.

Greenberg, R. (1984). A comparison of foliage discrimination learning in a specialist and a generalist species of migrant wood warbler (Aves: Parulidae). *Canadian Journal of Zoology, 63,* 773–776.

Greene, S. L. (1983). Feature memorization in pigeon concept formation. In M. L. Commons, R. J. Herrnstein, & A. R. Wagner (Eds.), *Quantitative analyses of behaviour* (Vol. 4, pp. 209–229). Cambridge, MA: Ballinger.

Grice, H. P. (1957). Meaning. *Philosophical Review, 66,* 377–388.

Griffin, D. R. (1976). *The question of animal awareness.* New York: Rockefeller University Press.

Griffin, D. R. (1978). Prospects for a cognitive ethology. *The Behavioral and Brain Sciences, 4,* 527–538.

Griffin, D. R. (1981). *The question of animal awareness.* (Revised and enlarged edition.) New York: Rockefeller University Press.

Griffin, D. R. (Ed.). (1982). *Animal mind - Human mind.* Heidelberg: Springer-Verlag.

Griffin, D. R. (1991). Progress toward a cognitive ethology. In C. A. Ristau (Ed.), *Cognitive ethology: the minds of other animals* (pp. 3–17). Hillsdale, NJ: Lawrence Erlbaum Associates.

Griffin, D. R. (1992). *Animal minds.* Chicago: University of Chicago Press.

Griswold, D. A., Harrer, M. F., Sladkin, C., Alessandro, D. A., & Gould, J. L. (1995). Intraspecific recognition by laughing gull chicks. *Animal Behaviour, 50,* 1341–1348.

Grobecker, D. B., & Pietsch, T. W. (1978). Crows use automobiles as nutcrackers. *Auk, 95,* 760–761.

Groves, P. M., & Thompson, R. F. (1970). Habituation: A dual-process theory. *Psychological Review, 77,* 419–450.

Guilford, T. (1988). The evolution of conspicuous coloration. In L. P. Brower (Ed.), *Mimicry and the evolutionary process* (pp. 7–21). Chicago: University of Chicago Press.

Guilford, T. (1989). Studying warning signals in the laboratory. In R. J. Blanchard, P. F. Brain, D. C. Blanchard, & S. Parmigiani (Eds.), *Ethoexperimental approaches to the study of behavior* (pp. 87–103). Dordrecht: Kluwer Academic Publishers.

Guilford, T., & Dawkins, M. S. (1987). Search images not proven: A reappraisal of recent evidence. *Animal Behaviour, 35,* 1838–1845.

Guilford, T., & Dawkins, M. S. (1991). Receiver psychology and the evolution of animal signals. *Animal Behaviour, 42,* 1–14.

Gunn, D. L. (1937). The humidity reactions of the woodlouse, *Porcellio scaber* (Latreille). *Journal of Experimental Biology, 14,* 178–186.

Gutierrez, G., & Domjan, M. (1996). Learning and male-male sexual competition in Japanese quail (*Coturnix japonica*). *Journal of Comparative Psychology, 110,* 170–175.

Gwinner, E. (1996). Circadian and circannual programmes in avian migration. *Journal of Experimental Biology, 199,* 39–48.

Gygax, L. (1995). Hiding behaviour of longtailed macaques (*Macaca fascicularis*). I. Theoretical background and data on mating. *Ethology, 101,* 10–24.

Hailman, J. P. (1967). The ontogeny of an instinct: The pecking response in chicks of the laughing gull (*Larus atricilla* L.) and related species. *Behaviour, Supplement 15.*

Hall, G. (1991). *Perceptual and associative learning.* Oxford: Clarendon Press.

Hall, G. (1994). Pavlovian conditioning: Laws of association. In N. J. Mackintosh (Ed.), *Animal learning and cognition* (pp. 15–43). San Diego, CA: Academic Press.

Hall, G. (1996). Learning about associatively activated stimulus representations: Implications for acquired equivalence and perceptual learning. *Animal Learning and Behavior, 24,* 233–255.

Hall, G., & Honey, R. (1989). Perceptual and associative learning. In S. B. Klein & R. R. Mowrer (Eds.), *Contemporary learning theories* (pp. 117–147). Hillsdale, NJ: Lawrence Erlbaum Associates.

Halliday, T. R., & Slater, P. J. B. (Eds.). (1983). *Animal Behavior* (Vol. 2). Oxford: Blackwell Scientific Publications.

Hamilton, W. D. (1963). The evolution of altruistic behavior. *American Naturalist, 97,* 354–356.

Hamm, S. L., & Shettleworth, S. J. (1987). Risk aversion in pigeons. *Journal of Experimental Psychology: Animal Behavior Processes, 13,* 376–383.

Hampton, R. R. (1994). Sensitivity to information specifying the line of gaze of humans in sparrows (*Passer domesticus*). *Behaviour, 130,* 41–51.

Hanson, H. M. (1959). Effects of discrimination training on stimulus generalization. *Journal of Experimental Psychology, 58,* 321–334.

Harper, D. G. C. (1982). Competitive foraging in mallards: 'ideal free' ducks. *Animal Behaviour, 30,* 575–584.

Harper, D. N., McLean, A. P., & Dalrymple-Alford, J. C. (1993). List item memory in rats: Effects of delay and delay task. *Journal of Experimental Psychology: Animal Behavior Processes, 19,* 307–316.

Harris, J. D. (1943). Habituatory response decrement in the intact organism. *Psychological Bulletin, 40,* 385–422.

Hartling, L. K., & Plowright, R. C. (1979). Foraging by bumble bees on patches of artificial flowers: a laboratory study. *Canadian Journal of Zoology, 57,* 1866–1870.

Harvey, P. H., & Krebs, J. R. (1990). Comparing brains. *Science, 249,* 140–146.

Harvey, P. H., & Pagel, D. (1991). *The comparative method in evolutionary biology.* Oxford: Oxford University Press.

Harvey, P. H., & Purvis, A. (1991). Comparative methods for explaining adaptations. *Nature, 351,* 619–624.

Hauser, M. D. (1988). How infant vervet monkeys learn to recognize starling alarm calls: The role of experience. *Behaviour, 105,* 187–201.

Hauser, M. (1996). *The evolution of communication.* Cambridge, MA: MIT Press.

Hauser, M., & Carey, S. (in press). Building a cognitive creature from a set of primitives: Evolutionary and developmental insights. In C. Allen & D. Cummins (Eds.), *The evolution of mind.* New York: Oxford University Press.

Hauser, M. D., Kralik, J., Botto-Mahan, C., Garrett, M., & Oser, J. (1995). Self-recognition in primates: Phylogeny and the salience of species-typical features. *Proceedings of the National Academy of Sciences (USA), 92,* 10811–10814.

Hauser, M. D., MacNeilage, P., & Ware, M. (1996). Numerical representations in primates. *Proceedings of the National Academy of Sciences (USA), 93,* 1514–1517.

Hayes, K. J., & Hayes, C. (1952). Imitation in a home-raised chimpanzee. *Journal of Comparative and Physiological Psychology, 45,* 450–459.

Healy, S. (Ed.). (1998). *Spatial Representation in Animals.* Oxford: Oxford University Press.

Healy, S. D., Clayton, N. S., & Krebs, J. R. (1994). Development of hippocampal specialisation in two species of tit (*Parus spp.*). *Behavioural Brain Research, 61,* 23–28.

Healy, S. D., & Hurly, T. A. (1995). Spatial memory in rufous hummingbirds (*Selasphorus rufus*): A field test. *Animal Learning & Behavior, 23,* 63–68.

Healy, S. D., & Krebs, J. R. (1993). Development of hippocampal specialisation in a food-storing bird. *Behavioural Brain Research, 53,* 127–131.

Heiligenberg, W. (1974). Processes governing behavioral states of readiness. *Advances in the Study of Behavior, 5,* 173–200.

Heinrich, B. (1995). Neophilia and exploration in juvenile common ravens, *Corvus corax*. *Animal Behaviour, 50*, 695–704.

Heinrich, B., & Collins, S. L. (1983). Caterpillar leaf damage, and the game of hide-and-seek with birds. *Ecology, 64*, 592–602.

Helbig, A. J. (1994). Genetic basis and evolutionary change of migratory directions in a European passerine migrant *Sylvia atricapilla*. *Ostrich, 65*, 151–159.

Helbig, A. J. (1996). Genetic basis, mode of inheritance and evolutionary changes of migratory directions in palearctic warblers (Aves: sylviidae). *Journal of Experimental Biology, 199*, 49–55.

Hepper, P. G. (1986). Kin recognition: Functions and mechanisms: a review. *Biological Review, 61*, 63–93.

Hepper, P. G. (Ed.). (1991). *Kin recognition*. New York: Cambridge University Press.

Hermer, L., & Spelke, E. S. (1994). A geometric process for spatial reorientation in young children. *Nature, 370*, 57–59.

Hermer, L., & Spelke, L. (1996). Modularity and development: the case of spatial reorientation. *Cognition, 61*, 195–232.

Herrnstein, R. J. (1961). Relative and absolute strength of response as a function of frequency of reinforcement. *Journal of the Experimental Analysis of Behavior, 4*, 267–272.

Herrnstein, R. J. (1964). Aperiodicity as a factor in choice. *Journal of the Experimental Analysis of Behavior, 7*, 179–182.

Herrnstein, R. J. (1979). Acquisition, generalization, and discrimination reversal of a natural concept. *Journal of Experimental Psychology: Animal Behavior Processes, 5*, 116–129.

Herrnstein, R. J. (1990). Levels of stimulus control: A functional approach. *Cognition, 37*, 133–166.

Herrnstein, R. J., & de Villiers, P. A. (1980). Fish as a natural category for people and pigeons. *Psychology of Learning and Motivation, 14*, 59–97.

Herrnstein, R. J., Loveland, D. H., & Cable, C. (1976). Natural concepts in pigeons. *Journal of Experimental Psychology: Animal Behavior Processes, 2*, 285–311.

Heyes, C. M. (1993a). Imitation, culture and cognition. *Animal Behaviour, 46*, 999–1010.

Heyes, C. M. (1993b). Anecdotes, training, trapping and triangulating: do animals attribute mental states? *Animal Behaviour, 46*, 177–188.

Heyes, C. M. (1994a). Social learning in animals: Categories and mechanisms. *Biological Review, 69*, 207–231.

Heyes, C. M. (1994b). Social cognition in primates. In N. J. Mackintosh (Ed.), *Animal learning and cognition* (pp. 281–305). San Diego: Academic Press.

Heyes, C. M. (1994c). Reflections on self-recognition in primates. *Animal Behaviour, 47*, 909–919.

Heyes, C. M. (1995). Self-recognition in primates: further reflections create a hall of mirrors. *Animal Behaviour, 50*, 1533–1542.

Heyes, C. M. (1996a). Introduction: Identifying and defining imitation. In C. M. Heyes & B. G. Galef Jr. (Eds.), *Social learning in animals: The roots of culture* (pp. 211–220). San Diego: Academic Press.

Heyes, C. M. (1996b). Genuine imitation? In C. M. Heyes & B. G. Galef Jr. (Eds.), *Social learning in animals: The roots of culture* (pp. 371–389). San Diego: Academic Press.

Heyes, C. M. (1996c). Self-recognition in primates: irreverence, irrelevance and irony. *Animal Behaviour, 51*, 470–473.

Heyes, C. M. (1998). Theory of mind in nonhuman primates. *Behavioral and Brain Sciences, 21,* 101–148.

Heyes, C. M., & Dawson, G. R. (1990). A demonstration of observational learning in rats using a bidirectional control. *Quarterly Journal of Experimental Psychology, 42B,* 59–71.

Heyes, C. M., Dawson, G. R., & Nokes, T. (1992). Imitation in rats: Initial responding and transfer evidence. *Quarterly Journal of Experimental Psychology, 45B,* 229–240.

Heyes, C., & Dickinson, A. (1990). The intentionality of animal action. *Mind & Language, 5,* 87–104.

Heyes, C. M., & Galef, B. G., Jr. (Eds.). (1996). *Social learning in animals: The roots of culture.* San Diego: Academic Press.

Heyes, C. M., Jaldow, E., Nokes, T., & Dawson, G. R. (1994). Imitation in rats (*Rattus norvegicus*): The role of demonstrator action. *Behavioural Processes, 32,* 173–182.

Hinde, R. A. (1970a). *Animal Behaviour.* (2nd ed.). New York: McGraw-Hill.

Hinde, R. A. (1970b). Behavioural habituation. In G. Horn & R. A. Hinde (Eds.), *Short-term changes in neural activity and behaviour* (pp. 3–40). London: Cambridge University Press.

Hinde, R. A. (1981). Animal signals: Ethological and games-theory approaches are not incompatible. *Animal Behaviour, 29,* 535–542.

Hinde, R. A. (1982). *Ethology.* Glasgow: William Collins & Sons.

Hinde, R. A., & Fisher, J. (1951). Further observations on the opening of milk bottles by birds. *British Birds, 44,* 392–396.

Hinde, R. A., & Stevenson-Hinde, J. (Eds.). (1973). *Constraints on learning.* London: Academic Press.

Hirschfeld, L. A., & Gelman, S. A. (1994). Toward a topography of mind: An introduction to domain specificity. In L. A. Hirschfeld & S. A. Gelman (Eds.), *Mapping the mind* (pp. 3–35). Cambridge: Cambridge University Press.

Hockett, C. F. (1960). Logical considerations in the study of animal communication. In W. E. Lanyon & W. N. Tavolga (Eds.), *Animal sounds and communication* (pp. 392–430). Washington, DC: American Institute of Biological Sciences.

Hodos, W., & Campbell, C. B. G. (1969). *Scala naturae:* Why there is no theory in comparative psychology. *Psychological Review, 76,* 337–350.

Hoffman, H. S. (1978). Experimental analysis of imprinting and its behavioral effects. *The Psychology of Learning and Motivation, 12,* 1–37.

Hoffman, H. S., & Ratner, A. M. (1973). A reinforcement model of imprinting: Implications for socialization in monkeys and men. *Psychological Review, 80,* 527–544.

Hoffman, H. S., Searle, J. L., Toffey, S., & Kozma, F., Jr. (1966). Behavioral control by an imprinted stimulus. *Journal of the Experimental Analysis of Behavior, 9,* 177–189.

Hogan, J. A. (1974). Responses in Pavlovian conditioning studies. *Science, 186,* 156–157.

Hogan, J. A. (1988). Cause and function in the development of behavior systems. In E. M. Blass (Ed.), *Handbook of behavioral neurobiology* (Vol. 9, pp. 63–106). New York: Plenum Publishing.

Hogan, J. A. (1994a). The concept of cause in the study of behavior. In J. A. Hogan & J. J. B. Bolhuis (Eds.), *Causal mechanisms of behavioral development* (pp. 3–15). Cambridge: Cambridge University Press.

Hogan, J. A. (1994b). Structure and development of behavior systems. *Psychonomic Bulletin and Review, 1,* 439–450.

Hogan, J. A., & Bolhuis, J. J. (Eds.). (1994). *Causal mechanisms of behavioural development.* Cambridge: Cambridge University Press.

Hogan, J., Kruijt, J. P., & Frijlink, J. H. (1975). "Supernormality" in a learning situation. *Zeitschrift für Tierpsychologie, 38,* 212–218.

Hoglund, J., Alatalo, R. V., Gibson, R. M., & Lundberg, A. (1995). Mate-choice copying in black grouse. *Animal Behaviour, 49,* 1627–1633.

Holland, P. C. (1977). Conditioned stimulus as a determinant of the form of the Pavlovian conditioned response. *Journal of Experimental Psychology: Animal Behavior Processes, 3,* 77–104.

Holland, P. C. (1984). Origins of behavior in Pavlovian conditioning. *Psychology of Learning and Motivation, 18,* 129–174.

Holland, P. C. (1990). Event representation in Pavlovian conditioning: Image and action. *Cognition, 37,* 105–131.

Holland, P. C. (1992). Occasion setting in Pavlovian conditioning. *Psychology of Learning and Motivation, 28,* 69–125.

Holland, P. C., & Rescorla, R. A. (1975). The effect of two ways of devaluing the unconditioned stimulus after first- and second-order appetitive conditioning. *Journal of Experimental Psychology: Animal Behavior Processes, 1,* 355–363.

Holland, P. C., & Straub, J. J. (1979). Differential effects of two ways of devaluing the unconditioned stimulus after Pavlovian appetitive conditioning. *Journal of Experimental Psychology: Animal Behavior Processes, 1,* 65–78.

Hollis, K. L. (1982). Pavlovian conditioning of signal-centered action patterns and autonomic behavior: A biological analysis of function. *Advances in the Study of Behavior, 12,* 1–64.

Hollis, K. L. (1984). The biological function of Pavlovian conditioning: The best defence is a good offence. *Journal of Experimental Psychology: Animal Behavior Processes, 10,* 413–425.

Hollis, K. L. (1990). The role of Pavlovian conditioning in territorial aggression and reproduction. In D. A. Dewsbury (Ed.), *Contemporary issues in comparative psychology* (pp. 197–219). Sunderland, MA: Sinauer Associates.

Hollis, K. L., Cadieux, E. L., & Colbert, M. M. (1989). The biological function of Pavlovian conditioning: A mechanism for mating success in the blue gourami (*Trichogaster trichopterus*). *Journal of Comparative Psychology, 103,* 115–121.

Hollis, K. L., Dumas, M. J., Singh, P., & Fackelman, P. (1995). Pavlovian conditioning of aggressive behavior in blue gourami fish (*Trichogaster trichopterus*): Winners become winners and losers stay losers. *Journal of Comparative Psychology, 109,* 123–133.

Hollis, K. L., Pharr, V. L., Dumas, M. J., Britton, G. B., & Field, J. (1997). Classical conditioning provides paternity advantage for territorial male blue gouramis (*Trichogaster trichopterus*). *Journal of Comparative Psychology, 111,* 219–225.

Hollis, K. L., ten Cate, C., & Bateson, P. (1991). Stimulus representation: A subprocess of imprinting and conditioning. *Journal of Comparative Psychology, 105,* 307–317.

Holmes, W. G. (1986a). Kin recognition by phenotype matching in female Belding's ground squirrels. *Animal Behaviour, 34,* 38–47.

Holmes, W. G. (1986b). Identification of paternal half-siblings by captive Belding's ground squirrels. *Animal Behaviour, 34,* 321–327.

Holmes, W. G., & Sherman, P. W. (1982). The ontogeny of kin recognition in two species of ground squirrels. *American Zoologist, 22,* 491–517.

Honey, R. C., Bateson, P., & Horn, G. (1994). The role of stimulus comparison in perceptual learning: An investigation with the domestic chick. *Quarterly Journal of Experimental Psychology, 47B*, 83–103.

Honey, R. C., Horn, G , & Bateson, P. (1993). Perceptual learning during filial imprinting: Evidence from transfer of training studies. *Quarterly Journal of Experimental Psychology, 46B*, 253–269.

Honig, W. K. (1978). Studies of working memory in the pigeon. In S. H. Hulse, H. Fowler, & W. K. Honig (Eds.), *Cognitive processes in animal behavior* (pp. 211–248). Hillsdale, NJ: Lawrence Erlbaum Associates.

Honig, W. K., & Fetterman, J. G. (Eds.). (1992). *Cognitive aspects of stimulus control.* Hillsdale, NJ: Lawrence Erlbaum Associates.

Honrado, G. I., & Mrosovsky, N. (1991). Interactions between periodic socio-sexual cues and light-dark cycles in controlling the phasing of activity rhythms in golden hamsters. *Ethology Ecology and Evolution, 3*, 221–231.

Hopkins, C. D. (1983). Sensory mechanisms in animal communication. In T. R. Halliday & P. J. B. Slater (Eds.), *Animal behaviour* (Vol. 2, pp. 114–155). New York: W. H. Freeman and Company.

Horn, G. (1967). Neuronal mechanisms of habituation. *Nature, 215*, 707–711.

Horn, G. (1985). *Memory, imprinting, and the brain.* Oxford: Clarendon Press.

Houston, A. (1986). The matching law applies to wagtails' foraging in the wild. *Journal of the Experimental Analysis of Behavior, 45*, 15–18.

Houston, A. I. (1987). The control of foraging decisions. In M. L. Commons, A. Kacelnik, & S. J. Shettleworth (Eds.), *Quantitative analyses of behavior* (Vol. 6, pp. 41–61). Hillsdale, NJ: Lawrence Erlbaum Associates.

Houston, A. I., & McNamara, J. (1981). How to maximize reward rate on two variable-interval paradigms. *Journal of the Experimental Analysis of Behavior, 35*, 367–396.

Houston, A. I., & McNamara, J. M. (1989). The value of food: effects of open and closed economies. *Animal Behaviour, 37*, 546–562.

Houston, A. I., & McNamara, J. M. (1990). Risk-sensitive foraging and temperature. *Trends in Ecology and Evolution, 5*, 131–132.

Huber, L., & Lenz, R. (1993). A test of the linear feature model of polymorphous concept discrimination with pigeons. *Quarterly Journal of Experimental Psychology, 46B*, 1–18.

Huber, L., & Lenz, R. (1996). Categorization of prototypical stimulus classes by pigeons. *Quarterly Journal of Experimental Psychology, 49B*, 111–133.

Huheey, J. E. (1988). Mathematical models of mimicry. In L. P. Brower (Ed.), *Mimicry and the evolutionary process* (pp. 22–41). Chicago: University of Chicago Press.

Hulse, S. H. (1993). The present status of animal cognition: An introduction. *Psychological Science, 4*, 154–155.

Hulse, S. H., Fowler, H., & Honig, W. K. (Eds.). (1978). *Cognitive processes in animal behavior.* Hillsdale, NJ: Lawrence Erlbaum Associates.

Hultsch, H. (1992). Time window and unit capacity: Dual constraints on the acquisition of serial information in songbirds. *Journal of Comparative Physiology A, 170*, 275–280.

Hultsch, H. (1993). Tracing the memory mechanisms in the song acquisition of nightingales. *Netherlands Journal of Zoology, 43*, 155–171.

Hultsch, H., & Todt, D. (1989). Memorization and reproduction of songs in nightingales (*Luscinia megarhynchos*): Evidence for package formation. *Journal of Comparative Physiology A, 165*, 197–203.

Humphrey, N. K. (1976). The social function of intellect. In P. P. G. Bateson & R. A. Hinde (Eds.), *Growing points in ethology* (pp. 303–317). Cambridge: Cambridge University Press.

Hunt, G. R. (1996). Manufacture and use of hook-tools by New Caledonian crows. *Nature, 379,* 249–251.

Hunt, R. R. (1995). The subtlety of distinctiveness: What von Restorff really did. *Psychonomic Bulletin & Review, 2,* 105–112.

Hunter, W. S. (1913). The delayed reaction in animals and children. *Behavior Monographs, 2,* 1–86.

Huntingford, F. A. (1993). Behavioral mechanisms in evolutionary perspective. *Trends in Ecology and Evolution, 8,* 81–84.

Hurlbert, S. H. (1984). Pseudoreplication and the design of ecological field experiments. *Ecological Monographs, 54,* 187–211.

Hursh, S. R. (1980). Economic concepts for the analysis of behavior. *Journal of the Experimental Analysis of Behavior, 34,* 219–238.

Immelmann, K. (1972). Sexual and other long-term aspects of imprinting in birds and other species. *Advances in the Study of Behavior, 4,* 147–174.

Immelmann, K., Prove, R., Lassek, R., & Bischof, H.-J. (1991). Influence of adult courtship experience on the development of sexual preferences in zebra finch males. *Animal Behaviour, 42,* 83–89.

Inman, A., & Shettleworth, S. J. (1996). Metamemory in the pigeon? Talk given at the Meetings of the Psychonomic Society, November.

Inoue-Nakamura, N., & Matsuzawa, T. (1997). Development of stone tool use by wild chimpanzees (*Pan troglodytes*). *Journal of Comparative Psychology, 111,* 159–173.

Isack, H. A., & Reyer, H.-U. (1989). Honeyguides and honey gathers: Interspecific communication in a symbiotic relationship. *Science, 243,* 1343–1346.

Jacobs, L. F. (1995). The ecology of spatial cognition. In E. Alleva, A. Fasolo, H.-P. Lipp, L. Nadel, & L. Ricceri (Eds.), *Behavioural brain research in naturalistic and semi-naturalistic settings* (pp. 301–322). Dordrecht: Kluwer Academic Publishers.

James, W. (1890). *The principles of psychology.* New York: Henry Holt.

Jamieson, D., & Bekoff, M. (1993). On aims and methods of cognitive ethology. *Philosophy of Science Association, 2,* 110–124.

Janetos, A. C. (1980). Strategies of female mate choice: A theoretical analysis. *Behavioral ecology and sociobiology, 7,* 107–112.

Jarman, P. J. (1974). The social organisation of antelope in relation to their ecology. *Behaviour, 48,* 215–267.

Jarvik, M. E., Goldfarb, T. L., & Carley, J. L. (1969). Influence of interference on delayed matching in monkeys. *Journal of Experimental Psychology, 81,* 1–6.

Jasselette, P., Lejeune, H., & Wearden, J. H. (1990). The perching response and the laws of animal timing. *Journal of Experimental Psychology: Animal Behavior Processes, 16,* 150–161.

Jenkins, H. M. (1979). Animal learning and behavior theory. In E. Hearst (Ed.), *The first century of experimental psychology* (pp. 177–228). Hillsdale, NJ: Lawrence Erlbaum Associates.

Jenkins, H. M., Barnes, R. A., & Barrera, F. J. (1981). Why autoshaping depends on trial spacing. In C. M. Locurto, H. S. Terrace, & J. Gibbon (Eds.), *Autoshaping and conditioning theory* (pp. 255–284). New York: Academic Press.

Jenkins, H. M., Barrera, F. J., Ireland, C., & Woodside, B. (1978). Signal-centered action patterns of dogs in appetitive classical conditioning. *Learning and Motivation, 9,* 272–296.

Jenkins, H. M., & Moore, B. R. (1973). The form of the autoshaped response with food or water reinforcers. *Journal of the Experimental Analysis of Behavior, 20*, 163–181.

Jitsumori, M. (1996). A prototype effect and categorization of artificial polymorphous stimuli in pigeons. *Journal of Experimental Psychology: Animal Behavior Processes, 22*, 405–419.

Johnson, M. H., & Horn, G. (1988). Development of filial preferences in dark-reared chicks. *Animal Behaviour, 36*, 675–683.

Johnston, R. E., Derzie, A., Chiang, G., Jernigan, P., & Lee, H.-C. (1993). Individual scent signatures in golden hamsters: Evidence for specialization of function. *Animal Behaviour, 45*, 1061–1070.

Johnston, R. E., & Jernigan, P. (1994). Golden hamsters recognize individuals, not just individual scents. *Animal Behaviour, 48*, 129–136.

Johnston, T. D. (1982). Selective costs and benefits in the evolution of learning. *Advances in the Study of Behavior, 12*, 65–106.

Johnston, T. D., & Gottlieb, G. (1981). Development of visual species identification in ducklings: What is the role of imprinting? *Animal Behaviour, 29*, 1082–1099.

Johnstone, R. (1994). Female preference for symmetrical males as a by-product of selection for mate recognition. *Nature, 372*, 172–175.

Johnstone, R. A. (1995). Sexual selection, honest advertisement and the handicap principle: Reviewing the evidence. *Biological Reviews, 70*, 1–65.

Johnstone, R. A. (1997). The evolution of animal signals. In J. R. Krebs & N. B. Davies (Eds.), *Behavioural ecology* (pp. 155–178). Oxford: Blackwell Science.

Jolly, A. (1966). Lemur social behavior and primate intelligence. *Science, 153*, 501–506.

Jones, T. B., & Kamil, A. C. (1973). Tool-making and tool-using in the northern blue jay. *Science, 180*, 1076–1078.

Jouventin, P., & Weimerskirch, H. (1990). Satellite tracking of wandering albatrosses. *Nature, 343*, 746–748.

Kaba, H., Rosser, A. E., & Keverne, E. B. (1988). Hormonal enhancement of neurogenesis and its relationship to the duration of olfactory memory. *Neuroscience, 24*, 93–98.

Kacelnik, A. (1984). Central place foraging in starlings (*Sturnus vulgaris*). I. Patch residence time. *Journal of Animal Ecology, 53*, 283–299.

Kacelnik, A. (1993). Leaf-cutting ants tease optimal foraging theorists. *Trends in Ecology and Evolution, 8*, 346–348.

Kacelnik, A. (1997). Normative and descriptive models of decision making: Time discounting and risk sensitivity. In G. R. Bock & G. Cardew (Eds.), *Characterizing human psychological adaptations* (pp. 51–70). London: John Wiley & Sons Ltd.

Kacelnik, A., & Bateson, M. (1996). Risky theories-the effects of variance on foraging decisions. *American Zoologist, 36*, 402–434.

Kacelnik, A., Brunner, D., & Gibbon, J. (1990). Timing mechanisms in optimal foraging: some applications of scalar expectancy theory. In R. N. Hughes (Ed.), *Behavioural mechanisms of food selection* (NATO ASI series, Vol. G20, pp. 61–82). Berlin: Springer-Verlag.

Kacelnik, A., & Cuthill, I. C. (1987). Starlings and optimal foraging theory: Modelling in a fractal world. In A. C. Kamil, J. R. Krebs, & H. R. Pulliam (Eds.), *Foraging behavior* (pp. 303–333). New York: Plenum Press.

Kacelnik, A., & Krebs, J. R. (1997). Yanomamo dreams and starling payloads: The logic of optimality. In L. Betzig (Ed.), *Human nature* (pp. 21–35). New York: Oxford University Press.

Kacelnik, A., Krebs, J. R., & Bernstein, C. (1992). The ideal free distribution and predator-prey populations. *Trends in Ecology and Evolution, 7*, 50–55.

Kacelnik, A., Krebs, J. R., & Ens, B. (1987). Foraging in a changing environment: An experiment with starlings (*Sturnus vulgaris*). In M. L. Commons, A. Kacelnik, & S. J. Shettleworth (Eds.), *Quantitative analyses of behavior* (Vol. 6: Foraging, pp. 63–87). Hillsdale, NJ: Lawrence Erlbaum Associates.

Kacelnik, A., & Todd, I. A. (1992). Psychological mechanisms and the Marginal Value Theorem: Effect of variability in travel time on patch exploitation. *Animal Behaviour, 43*, 313–322.

Kahneman, D., Slovic, P., & Tversky, A. (Eds.). (1982). *Judgement under uncertainty: Heuristics and biases*. Cambridge: Cambridge University Press.

Kaiser, D. H., Zentall, T. R., & Galef, B. G., Jr. (1997). Can imitation in pigeons be explained by local enhancement together with trial-and-error learning? *Psychological Science, 8*, 459–460.

Kamil, A. C. (1978). Systematic foraging by a nectar-feeding bird, the amakihi (*Loxops virens*). *Journal of Comparative and Physiological Psychology, 92*, 388–396.

Kamil, A. C. (1985). *The evolution of higher learning abilities in birds*. Paper presented at the XVIII International Ornithological Congress.

Kamil, A. C. (1988). A synthetic approach to the study of animal intelligence. In D. W. Leger (Ed.), *Nebraska Symposium on Motivation, Volume 35.* (pp. 257–308). Lincoln: University of Nebraska Press.

Kamil, A. C. (1998). On the proper definition of cognitive ethology. In I. Pepperberg, R. Balda, & A. C. Kamil (Eds.), *Animal cognition in nature*. San Diego: Academic Press.

Kamil, A. C., Balda, R. P., & Olson, D. J. (1994). Performance of four seed-caching corvid species in the radial-arm maze analog. *Journal of Comparative Psychology, 108*, 385–393.

Kamil, A. C., & Jones, J. E. (1997). The seed-storing corvid Clark's nutcracker learns geometric relationships among landmarks. *Nature, 390*, 276–279.

Kamil, A. C., Krebs, J. R., & Pulliam, H. R. (Eds.). (1987). *Foraging behavior*. New York: Plenum.

Kamil, A. C., & Mauldin, J. E. (1988). A comparative-ecological approach to the study of learning. In R. C. Bolles & M. D. Beecher (Eds.), *Evolution and learning* (pp. 117–133). Hillsdale, NJ: Lawrence Erlbaum Associates.

Kamil, A. C., & Sargent, T. D. (1981). *Foraging behavior*. New York: Garland STPM Press.

Kamil, A. C., & Yoerg, S. I. (1982). Learning and foraging behavior. *Perspectives in Ethology, 5*, 325–364.

Kamil, A. C., Yoerg, S. I., & Clements, K. C. (1988). Rules to leave by: Patch departure in foraging blue jays. *Animal Behaviour, 36*, 843–853.

Kamin, L. J. (1969). Predictability, surprise, attention, and conditioning. In B. A. Campbell & R. M. Church (Eds.), *Punishment and aversive behavior* (pp. 279–296). New York: Appleton-Century-Crofts.

Karakashian, S. J., Gyger, M., & Marler, P. (1988). Audience effects on alarm calling in chickens (*Gallus gallus*). *Journal of Comparative Psychology, 102*, 129–135.

Keeton, W. T. (1974). The orientational and navigational basis of homing in birds. *Advances in the Study of Behavior, 5*, 47–132.

Keith, J. R., & McVety, K. M. (1988). Latent place learning in a novel environment and the influences of prior training in rats. *Psychobiology, 16*, 146–151.

Keith-Lucas, T., & Guttman, N. (1975). Robust-single-trial delayed backward conditioning. *Journal of Comparative and Physiological Psychology, 88*, 468–476.

Kendrick, K. M., Atkins, K., Hinton, M. R., Broad, K. D., Fabre-Nys, C., & Keverne, B. (1995). Facial and vocal discrimination in sheep. *Animal Behaviour, 49,* 1665–1676.

Kendrick, K. M., Levy, F., & Keverne, E. B. (1992). Changes in the sensory processing of olfactory signals induced by birth in sheep. *Science, 256,* 833–836.

Kennedy, J. S. (1992). *The new anthropomorphism.* Cambridge: Cambridge University Press.

Kennedy, M., & Gray, R. D. (1993). Can ecological theory predict the distribution of foraging animals? A critical analysis of experiments on the Ideal Free Distribution. *Oikos, 68,* 158–166.

Kent, J. P. (1987). Experiments on the relationship between the hen and chick (*Gallus gallus*): The role of the auditory mode in recognition and the effects of maternal separation. *Behaviour, 102,* 1–14.

Kesner, R. P., & DeSpain, M. J. (1988). Correspondence between rats and humans in the utilization of retrospective and prospective codes. *Animal Learning & Behavior, 16,* 299–302.

Kiernan, M. J., & Westbrook, R. F. (1993). Effects of exposure to a to-be-shocked environment upon the rat's freezing response: Evidence for facilitation, latent inhibition, and perceptual learning. *Quarterly Journal of Experimental Psychology, 46B,* 271–288.

Killeen, P. R., & Fetterman, J. G. (1988). A behavioral theory of timing. *Psychological Review, 95,* 274–295.

Kim, S. D., Rivers, S., Bevins, R. A., & Ayres, J. J. B. (1996). Conditioned stimulus determinants of conditioned response form in Pavlovian fear conditioning. *Journal of Experimental Psychology: Animal Behavior Processes, 22,* 87–104.

King, A. P., & West, M. J. (1983). Epigenesis of cowbird song—A joint endeavour of males and females. *Nature, 305,* 704–706.

Kirchner, W. H., & Braun, U. (1994). Dancing honey bees indicate the location of food sources using path integration rather than cognitive maps. *Animal Behaviour, 48,* 1437–1441.

Klopfer, P. H. (1961). Observational learning in birds: The establishment of behavioral modes. *Behaviour, 17,* 71–79.

Koehler, J. J. (1996). The base rate fallacy reconsidered: Descriptive, normative, and methodological challenges. *Behavioral and Brain Sciences, 19,* 1–53.

Koehler, O. (1951). The ability of birds to "count." *Bulletin of Animal Behaviour, 9,* 41–45.

Kohler, W. (1959). *The mentality of apes* (Winter, E., Trans.). New York: Vintage Books.

Konishi, M. (1965). The role of auditory feedback in the control of vocalization in the white-crowned sparrow. *Zeitschrift für Tierpsychologie, 22,* 770–783.

Konorski, J. (1967). *Integrative activity of the brain.* Chicago: University of Chicago Press.

Kraak, S. B. M. (1996). 'Copying mate choice': Which phenomena deserve this term? *Behavioural Processes, 36,* 99–102.

Kraemer, P. J., Mazmanian, D. S., & Roberts, W. A. (1987). Simultaneous processing of visual and spatial stimuli in pigeons. *Animal Learning & Behavior, 15,* 417–422.

Kraemer, P. J., & Roberts, W. A. (1985). Short-term memory for simultaneously presented visual and auditory signals in the pigeon. *Journal of Experimental Psychology: Animal Behavior Processes, 11,* 137–151.

Krakauer, D. C. (1995). Groups confuse predators by exploiting perceptual bottlenecks: A connectionist model of the confusion effect. *Behavioral Ecology and Sociobiology, 36,* 421–429.

Krakauer, D. C., & Rodriguez-Girones, M. A. (1995). Searching and learning in a random environment. *Journal of Theoretical Biology, 177,* 417–429.

Krebs, J. R., & Biebach, H. (1989). Time-place learning by garden warblers (*Sylvia borin*): route or map? *Ethology, 83,* 248–256.

Krebs, J. R., & Davies, N. B. (1981). *An introduction to behavioural ecology.* (1st ed.). Oxford: Blackwell Scientific.

Krebs, J. R., & Davies, N. B. (1993). *An Introduction to behavioural ecology.* (3rd ed.). Oxford: Blackwell Scientific.

Krebs, J. R., & Davies, N. B. (1997). The evolution of behavioural ecology. In J. R. Krebs & N. B. Davies (Eds.), *Behavioural ecology* (4th Ed.) (pp. 3–18). Oxford: Blackwell Science.

Krebs, J. R., & Dawkins, R. (1984). Animal signals: Mind-reading and manipulation. In J. R. Krebs & N. B. Davies (Eds.), *Behavioural ecology: An evolutionary approach* (2nd Ed.) (pp. 380–402). Oxford: Blackwell Scientific.

Krebs, J. R., Erichsen, J. T., Webber, M. I., & Charnov, E. L. (1977). Optimal prey selection in the great tit (*Parus major*). *Animal Behaviour, 25,* 30–38.

Krebs, J. R., & Inman, A. J. (1994). Learning and foraging: Individuals, groups, and populations. In L. A. Real (Ed.), *Behavioral mechanisms in evolutionary ecology* (pp. 46–65). Chicago: University of Chicago Press.

Krebs, J. R., Kacelnik, A., & Taylor, P. (1978). Test of optimal sampling by foraging great tits. *Nature, 275,* 27–31.

Krebs, J. R., Ryan, J. C., & Charnov, E. L. (1974). Hunting by expectation or optimal foraging? A study of patch use by chickadees. *Animal Behaviour, 22,* 953–964.

Kroodsma, D. E. (1990). Using appropriate experimental designs for intended hypotheses in 'song' playbacks, with examples for testing effects of song repertoire sizes. *Animal Behaviour, 40,* 1138–1150.

Kroodsma, D. E., & Konishi, M. (1991). A suboscine bird (Eastern phoebe, *Sayornis phoebe*) develops normal song without auditory feedback. *Animal Behaviour, 42,* 477–487.

Kroodsma, D. E., & Miller, E. H. (1996). *Ecology and evolution of acoustic communication in birds.* Ithaca, NY: Comstock Publishing Associates.

Kroodsma, D. E., & Pickert, R. (1980). Environmentally dependent sensitive periods for avian vocal learning. *Nature, 288,* 477–479.

Kruijt, J. P. (1985). On the development of social attachments in birds. *Netherlands Journal of Zoology, 35,* 45–62.

Kruijt, J. P., & Meeuwissen, G. B. (1991). Sexual preferences of male zebra finches: Effects of early and adult experience. *Animal Behaviour, 42,* 91–102.

Krushinskaya, N. L. (1966). Some complex forms of feeding behavior of nutcrackers after removal of their old cortex. *Journal of Evolutionary Biochemistry and Physiology, 11,* 564–568.

Kummer, H. (1995). *In quest of the sacred baboon* (Biederman-Thorson, M. A., Trans.). Princeton, NJ: Princeton University Press.

Kummer, H., Anzenberger, G., & Hemelrijk, C. K. (1996). Hiding and perspective taking in long-tailed macaques (*Macaca fascicularis*). *Journal of Comparative Psychology, 110,* 97–102.

Kummer, H., Dasser, V., & Hoyningen-Huene, P. (1990). Exploring primate social cognition: some critical remarks. *Behaviour, 112,* 84–98.

Lafleur, D. L., Lozano, G. A., & Sclafani, M. (1997). Female mate-choice copying in guppies, *Poecilia reticulata*: a re-evaluation. *Animal Behaviour, 54*, 579–586.

Laland, K. N., & Plotkin, H. C. (1990). Social learning and social transmission of foraging information in Norway rats (*Rattus norvegicus*). *Animal Learning & Behavior, 18*, 246–251.

Laland, K. N., & Plotkin, H. C. (1991). Excretory deposits surrounding food sites facilitate social learning of food preferences in Norway rats. *Animal Behaviour, 41*, 997–1005.

Laland, K. N., & Plotkin, H. C. (1993). Social transmission of food preferences among Norway rats by marking of food sites and by gustatory contact. *Animal Learning & Behavior, 21*, 35–41.

Laland, K. N., Richerson, P. J., & Boyd, R. (1993). Animal social learning: Toward a new theoretical approach. *Perspectives in Ethology, 10*, 249–277.

Land, M. F. (1990). The design of compound eyes. In C. Blakemore (Ed.), *Vision: Coding and efficiency* . Cambridge: Cambridge University Press.

Landeau, L., & Terborgh, J. (1986). Oddity and the "confusion effect" in predation. *Animal Behaviour, 34*, 1372–1380.

Langley, C. M. (1996). Search images: Selective attention to specific visual features of prey. *Journal of Experimental Psychology: Animal Behavior Processes, 22*, 152–163.

Langley, C. M., & Riley, D. A. (1993). Limited capacity information processing and pigeon matching-to-sample: Testing alternative hypotheses. *Animal Learning & Behavior, 21*, 226–232.

Langley, C. M., Riley, D. A., Bond, A. B., & Goel, N. (1996). Visual search and natural grains in pigeons (*Columba livia*): Search images and selective attention. *Journal of Experimental Psychology: Animal Behavior Processes, 22*, 139–151.

Lauder, G. V., & Reilly, S. M. (1996). The mechanistic bases of behavioral evolution: A multivariate analysis of musculoskeletal function. In E. P. Martins (Ed.), *Phylogenies and the comparative method in animal behavior* (pp. 104–137). New York: Oxford University Press.

Laverty, T. M. (1994). Bumble bee learning and flower morphology. *Animal Behaviour, 47*, 531–545.

Lawrence, E. S. (1984). Vigilance during 'easy' and 'difficult' foraging tasks. *Animal Behavior, 33*, 1373–1374.

Lea, S. E. G. (1981). Correlation and contiguity in foraging behaviour. In P. Harzem & M. D. Zeiler (Eds.), *Predictability, correlation and contiguity* (pp. 355–406). New York: John Wiley & Sons Ltd.

Lea, S. E. G., & Dow, S. M. (1984). The integration of reinforcements over time. *Annals of the New York Academy of Sciences, 423*, 269–277.

Lea, S. E. G., Lohmann, A., & Ryan, C. M. E. (1993). Discrimination of five-dimensional stimuli by pigeons: Limitations of feature analysis. *Quarterly Journal of Experimental Psychology, 46B*, 19–42.

Leak, T. M., & Gibbon, J. (1995). Simultaneous timing of multiple intervals: Implications of the scalar property. *Journal of Experimental Psychology: Animal Behavior Processes, 21*, 3–19.

Lefebvre, L. (1986). Cultural diffusion of a novel food-finding behaviour in urban pigeons: an experimental field test. *Ethology, 71*, 295–304.

Lefebvre, L. (1995a). The opening of milk bottles by birds: Evidence for accelerating learning rates, but against the wave-of-advance model of cultural transmission. *Behavioural Processes, 34*, 43–54.

Lefebvre, L. (1995b). Culturally-transmitted feeding behaviour in primates: Evidence for accelerating learning rates. *Primates, 36*, 227–239.

Lefebvre, L., & Giraldeau, L.-A. (1994). Cultural transmission in pigeons is affected by the number of tutors and bystanders present. *Animal Behaviour, 47*, 331–337.

Lefebvre, L., & Giraldeau, L.-A. (1996). Is social learning an adaptive specialization? In C. M. Heyes & B. G. Galef Jr. (Eds.), *Social learning in animals: The roots of culture* (pp. 107–128). San Diego, CA: Academic Press.

Lefebvre, L., & Palameta, B. (1988). Mechanisms, ecology, and population diffusion of socially learned, food-finding behavior in feral pigeons. In T. R. Zentall & B. G. Galef Jr. (Eds.), *Social learning: Psychological and biological perspectives* (pp. 141–164). Hillsdale, NJ: Lawrence Erlbaum Associates.

Lefebvre, L., Palameta, B., & Hatch, K. K. (1996). Is group-living associated with social learning? A comparative test of a gregarious and a territorial columbid. *Behaviour, 133*, 241–261.

Lehrer, M. (1991). Bees which turn back and look. *Naturwissenschaften, 78*, 274–276.

Lehrer, M. (1993). Why do bees turn back and look? *Journal of Comparative Physiology A, 172*, 549–563.

Lehrman, D. S. (1970). Semantic and conceptual issues in the nature-nurture problem. In L. R. Aronson, E. Tobach, D. S. Lehrman, & J. S. Rosenblatt (Eds.), *Development and evolution of behavior* (pp. 17–52). San Francisco: Freeman.

Lejeune, H., & Wearden, J. H. (1991). The comparative psychology of fixed interval responding: Some quantitative analyses. *Learning and Motivation, 22*, 84–111.

Lemon, W. C. (1991). Fitness consequences of foraging behaviour in the zebra finch. *Nature, 352*, 153–155.

Leonard, B., & McNaughton, B. L. (1990). Spatial representation in the rat: Conceptual, behavioral, and neurophysiological perspectives. In R. P. Kesner & D. S. Olton (Eds.), *Neurobiology of comparative cognition* (pp. 363–422). Hillsdale, NJ: Lawrence Erlbaum Associates.

Lévy, F., Porter, R. H., Kendrick, K. M., Keverne, E. B., & Romeyer, A. (1996). Physiological, sensory, and experiential factors of parental care in sheep. *Advances in the Study of Behavior, 25*, 385–422.

Lewis, A. C. (1986). Memory constraints and flower choice in *Pieris rapae*. *Science, 232*, 863–865.

Liberman, N., & Klar, Y. (1996). Hypothesis testing in Wason's selection task: Social exchange cheating detection or task understanding. *Cognition, 58*, 127–156.

Lima, S. L. (1995). Back to the basics of anti-predatory vigilance: the group-size effect. *Animal Behaviour, 49*, 11–20.

Limongelli, L., Boysen, S. T., & Visalberghi, E. (1995). Comprehension of cause-effect relations in a tool-using task by chimpanzees (*Pan troglodytes*). *Journal of Comparative Psychology, 109*, 18–26.

Loesche, P., Stoddard, P. K., Higgins, B. J., & Beecher, M. D. (1991). Signature versus perceptual adaptations for individual vocal recognition in swallows. *Behaviour, 118*, 15–25.

Loftus, E. F. (1991). The glitter of everyday memory . . . and the gold. *American Psychologist, 46*, 16–18.

LoLordo, V. M. (1979). Constraints on learning. In M. E. Bitterman, V. M. LoLordo, J. B. Overmier, & M. E. Rashotte (Eds.), *Animal learning: Survey and analysis* (pp. 473–504). New York: Plenum Press.

LoLordo, V. M., & Droungas, A. (1989). Selective associations and adaptive specializations: Taste aversions and phobias. In S. B. Klein & R. R. Mowrer (Eds.), *Con-*

temporary learning theories: Instrumental conditioning theory and the impact of biological constraints on learning (pp. 145–179). Hillsdale, NJ: Lawrence Erlbaum Associates.

LoLordo, V. M., Jacobs, W. J., & Foree, D. D. (1982). Failure to block control by a relevant stimulus. *Animal Learning & Behavior, 10,* 183–193.

Lorenz, K. (1935/1970). Companions as factors in the bird's environment. In R. Martin (Trans.), *Studies in animal and human behavior* (Vol. 1, pp. 101–258). London: Methuen & Co.

Lorenz, K. Z. (1941/1971). Comparative studies of the motor patterns of Anatinae (1941). In R. Martin (Trans.), *Studies in animal and human behaviour* (Vol. 2, pp. 14–114). London: Methuen.

Lorenz, K. Z. (1952). *King Solomon's ring* (Wilson, M. K., Trans.). New York: Thomas Y. Crowell.

Lorenz, K. (1965). *Evolution and modification of behavior.* Chicago: University of Chicago Press.

Lorenz, K. (1970). Notes. In R. Martin (Trans.), *Studies in animal and human behavior* (pp. 371–380). London: Methuen.

Losey, G. S. Jr. (1979). Fish cleaning symbiosis: Proximate causes of host behaviour. *Animal Behaviour, 27,* 669–685.

Lotem, A. (1993). Learning to recognize nestlings is maladaptive for cuckoo (*Cuculus canorus*) hosts. *Nature, 362,* 743–745.

Lotem, A., Nakamura, H., & Zahavi, A. (1995). Constraints on egg discrimination and cuckoo-host co-evolution. *Animal Behaviour, 49,* 1185–1209.

Lucas, J. R. (1983). The role of foraging time constraints and variable prey encounter in optimal diet choice. *American Naturalist, 122,* 191–209.

Lythgoe, J. N. (1979). *The ecology of vision.* Oxford: Clarendon Press.

MacDougall-Shackleton, S. A., & Hulse, S. (1996). Concurrent absolute and relative pitch processing by European starlings (*Sturnus vulgaris*). *Journal of Comparative Psychology, 110,* 139–146.

Macedonia, J. M. (1990). What is communicated in the antipredator calls of lemurs: Evidence from playback experiments with ringtailed and ruffed lemurs. *Ethology, 86,* 177–190.

Macedonia, J. M., & Evans, C. S. (1993). Variation among mammalian alarm call systems and the problem of meaning in animal signals. *Ethology, 93,* 177–197.

Machado, A. (1997). Learning the temporal dynamics of behavior. *Psychological Review, 104,* 241–265.

Mackintosh, N. J. (1973). Stimulus selection: Learning to ignore stimuli that predict no change in reinforcement. In R. A. Hinde & J. Stevenson-Hinde (Eds.), *Constraints on learning* (pp. 75–100). London: Academic Press.

Mackintosh, N. J. (1974). *The psychology of animal learning.* New York: Academic Press.

Mackintosh, N. J. (1978). Cognitive or associative theories of conditioning; implications of an analysis of blocking. In S. H. Hulse, H. Fowler, & W. K. Honig (Eds.), *Cognitive processes in animal behavior* (pp. 155–175). Hillsdale, NJ: Lawrence Erlbaum Associates.

Mackintosh, N. J. (1983). *Conditioning and associative learning.* Oxford: Clarendon Press.

Mackintosh, N. J. (1988). Approaches to the study of animal intelligence. *British Journal of Psychology, 79,* 509–525.

Mackintosh, N. J. (1994a). Intelligence in evolution. In J. Khalfa (Ed.), *What is Intelligence?* (pp. 27–48). New York: Cambridge University Press.

Mackintosh, N. J. (Ed.). (1994b). *Animal learning and cognition*. San Diego, CA: Academic Press.

Mackintosh, N. J. (1995). Categorization by people and by pigeons: The twenty-second Bartlett memorial lecture. *Quarterly Journal of Experimental Psychology, 48B*, 193–214.

Mackintosh, N. J., Kaye, H., & Bennett, C. H. (1991). Perceptual learning in flavor aversion conditioning. *Quartarly Journal of Experimental Psychology, 43B*, 297–322.

Mackintosh, N. J., McGonigle, B., Holgate, V., & Vanderver, V. (1968). Factors underlying improvement in serial reversal learning. *Canadian Journal of Psychology, 22*, 85–95.

Macmillan, N. A., & Creelman, C. G. (1991). *Detection theory: A user's guide*. Cambridge: Cambridge University Press.

Macphail, E. M. (1982). *Brain and Intelligence in Vertebrates*. Oxford: Clarendon Press.

Macphail, E. M. (1987). The comparative psychology of intelligence. *Behavioral and Brain Sciences, 10*, 645–695.

Macphail, E. M. (1993). *The neuroscience of animal intelligence*. New York: Columbia University Press.

Macphail, E. M. (1996). Cognitive function in mammals: the evolutionary perspective. *Cognitive Brain Research, 3*, 279–290.

Macphail, E. M. (1998). The evolution of consciousness. Oxford: Oxford University Press.

Macphail, E. M., Good, M., & Honey, R. C. (1995). Recognition memory in pigeons for stimuli presented repeatedly: Perceptual learning or reduced associative interference? *Quarterly Journal of Experimental Psychology, 48B*, 13–31.

Macphail, E. M., Good, M., Honey, R. C., & Willis, A. (1995). Relational learning in pigeons: The role of perceptual processes in between-key recognition of complex stimuli. *Animal Learning & Behavior, 23*, 83–92.

Macphail, E. M., & Reilly, S. (1989). Rapid acquisition of a novelty versus familiarity concept by pigeons (*Columba livia*). *Journal of Experimental Psychology: Animal Behavior Processes, 15*, 242–252.

Macuda, T., & Roberts, W. A. (1995). Further evidence for hierarchical chunking in rat spatial memory. *Journal of Experimental Psychology: Animal Behavior Processes, 21*, 20–32.

Magurran, A. E. (1990). The adaptive significance of schooling as an anti-predator defence in fish. *Annales Zoologici Fennici, 27*, 51–66.

Maier, N. R. F. (1932a). A study of orientation in the rat. *Journal of Comparative Psychology, 14*, 387–399.

Maier, N. R. F. (1932b). Cortical destruction of the posterior part of the brain and its effect on reasoning in rats. *Journal of Comparative Neurology, 56*, 179–214.

Maier, N. R. F., & Schneirla, T. C. (1935/1964). *Principles of Animal Psychology*. New York: McGraw-Hill/Dover reprint 1964.

Maki, W. S. (1987). On the nonassociative nature of working memory. *Learning and Motivation, 18*, 99–117.

Maki, W. S., Moe, J. C., & Bierley, C. M. (1977). Short-term memory for stimuli, responses, and reinforcers. *Journal of Experimental Psychology: Animal Behavior Processes, 3*, 156–177.

Maloney, R. F., & McLean, I. G. (1995). Historical and experimental learned predator recognition in free-living New Zealand robins. *Animal Behaviour, 50*, 1193–1201.

Manabe, K., Kawashima, T., & Staddon, J. E. R. (1995). Differential vocalization in budgerigars: Towards an experimental analysis of naming. *Journal of the Experimental Analysis of Behavior, 63,* 111–126.

Mangel, M. (1990). Dynamic information in uncertain and changing worlds. *Journal of Theoretical Biology, 146,* 317–332.

Mangel, M., & Roitberg, B. D. (1989). Dynamic information and host acceptance by a tephritid fruit fly. *Ecological Entomology, 14,* 181–189.

Manger, P. R., & Pettigrew, J. D. (1995). Electroreception and the feeding behavior of platypus (*Ornithorhynchus anatinus*: Monotremata: Mammalia). *Philosophical Transactions of the Royal Society, B, 347,* 359–381.

March, J., Chamizo, V. D., & Mackintosh, N. J. (1992). Reciprocal overshadowing between intra-maze and extra-maze cues. *Quarterly Journal of Experimental Psychology, 45B,* 49–63.

Marchetti, K. (1993). Dark habitats and bright birds illustrate the role of the environment in species divergence. *Nature, 362,* 149–152.

Marcus, E. A., Nolen, T. G., Rankin, C. H., & Carew, T. J. (1988). Behavioral dissociation of dishabituation, sensitization, and inhibition in *Aplysia. Science, 241,* 210–213.

Margolis, R. L., Mariscal, S. K., Gordon, J. D., Dollinger, J., & Gould, J. L. (1987). The ontogeny of the pecking response of laughing gull chicks. *Animal Behaviour, 35,* 191–202.

Margules, J., & Gallistel, C. R. (1988). Heading in the rat: Determination by environmental shape. *Animal Learning & Behavior, 16,* 404–410.

Mark, T. A., & Gallistel, C. R. (1994). Kinetics of matching. *Journal of Experimental Psychology: Animal Behavior Processes, 20,* 79–95.

Marler, P. (1970a). A comparative approach to vocal learning: Song development in white-crowned sparrows. *Journal of Comparative and Physiological Psychology, 71,* 1–25.

Marler, P. (1970b). The origin of speech from animal sounds. In J. F. Kavanaugh & J. E. Cutting (Ed.), The role of speech in language (pp. 11–37). Cambridge, MA: MIT Press.

Marler, P. (1987). Sensitive periods and the roles of specific and general sensory stimulation in birdsong learning. In J. P. Rauschecker & P. Marler (Eds.), *Imprinting and cortical plasticity* (pp. 99–135). New York: John Wiley & Sons.

Marler, P. (1991a). The instinct to learn. In S. Carey & R. Gelman (Eds.), *The Epigenesis of Mind* (pp. 37–66). Hillsdale, NJ: Lawrence Erlbaum Associates.

Marler, P. (1991b). Song-learning behavior: the interface with neuroethology. *Trends in Neuroscience, 14,* 199–206.

Marler, P., Dufty, A., & Pickert, R. (1986a). Vocal communication in the domestic chicken: I. Does a sender communicate information about the quality of a food referent to a receiver? *Animal Behaviour, 34,* 188–193.

Marler, P., Dufty, A., & Pickert, R. (1986b). Vocal communication in the domestic chicken: II. Is a sender sensitive to the presence and nature of a receiver? *Animal Behaviour, 34,* 194–198.

Marler, P., Evans, C. S., & Hauser, M. D. (1992). Animal signals: Motivational, referential, or both? In H. Papousek, U. Jurgens, & M. Papousek (Eds.), *Nonverbal vocal communication* (pp. 66–86). Cambridge: Cambridge University Press.

Marler, P., Karakashian, S., & Gyger, M. (1991). Do animals have the option of withholding signals when communication is inappropriate? The audience effect. In C. Ristau (Ed.), *Cognitive ethology* (pp. 187–208). Hillsdale, NJ: Lawrence Erlbaum Associates.

Marler, P., & Nelson, D. A. (1993). Action-based learning: a new form of developmental plasticity in bird song. *Netherlands Journal of Zoology, 43*, 91–103.

Marler, P., & Peters, S. (1981). Sparrows learn adult song and more from memory. *Science, 213*, 780–782.

Marler, P., & Peters, S. (1989). Species differences in auditory responsiveness in early vocal learning. In R. J. Dooling & S. H. Hulse (Eds.), *The comparative psychology of audition: Perceiving complex sounds* (pp. 243–273). Hillsdale, NJ: Lawrence Erlbaum Associates.

Marler, P., & Tamura, M. (1964). Culturally transmitted patterns of vocal behavior in sparrows. *Science, 146*, 1483–1486.

Marr, D. (1982). *Vision*. New York: W. H. Freeman.

Marston, H. M. (1996). Analysis of cognitive function in animals, the value of SDT. *Cognitive Brain Research, 3*, 269–277.

Martin, G. M., Harley, C. W., Smith, A. R., Hoyles, E. S., & Hynes, C. A. (1997). Spatial disorientation blocks reliable goal location on a plus maze but does not prevent goal location in the Morris maze. *Journal of Experimental Psychology: Animal Behavior Processes, 23*, 183–193.

Martins, E. P., & Hansen, T. F. (1996). The statistical analysis of interspecific data: A review and evaluation of phylogenetic comparative methods. In E. P. Martins (Ed.), *Phylogenies and the comparative method in animal behavior* (pp. 22–75). New York: Oxford University Press.

Marzluff, J. M., Heinrich, B., & Marzluff, C. S. (1996). Raven roosts are mobile information centres. *Animal Behaviour, 51*, 89–103.

Mason, J. R. (1988). Direct and observational learning by redwinged blackbirds (*Agelaius phoeniceus*): The importance of complex visual stimuli. In T. R. Zentall & B. G. Galef Jr. (Eds.), *Social learning: Psychological and biological perspectives* (pp. 99–115). Hillsdale, NJ: Lawrence Erlbaum Associates.

Masson, J. M., & McCarthy, S. (1995). *When Elephants Weep*. New York: Delacorte.

Maurer, R., & Seguinot, V. (1995). What is modelling for? A critical review of the models of path integration. *Journal of Theoretical Biology, 175*, 457–475.

Mayford, M., Abel, T., & Kandel, E. R. (1995). Transgenic approaches to cognition. *Current Opinion in Neurobiology, 5*, 141–148.

Mayr, E. (1974). Behavior programs and evolutionary strategies. *American Scientist, 62*, 650–659.

Mazur, J. E. (1981). Optimization theory fails to predict performance of pigeons in a two-response situation. *Science, 214*, 823–825.

Mazur, J. E. (1992). Choice behavior in transition: Development of preference with ratio and interval schedules. *Journal of Experimental Psychology: Animal Behavior Processes, 18*, 364–378.

Mazur, J. E. (1995). Development of preference and spontaneous recovery in choice behavior with concurrent variable-interval schedules. *Animal Learning & Behavior, 23*, 93–103.

Mazur, J. E. (1996). Past experience, recency, and spontaneous recovery in choice behavior. *Animal Learning & Behavior, 24*, 1–10.

McClelland, J. L., Rumelhart, D. E., & the PDP Research Group (1987). *Parallel distributed processing*. Cambridge, MA: MIT Press.

McComb, K., Packer, C., & Pusey, A. (1994). Roaring and numerical assessment in contests between groups of female lions, *Panthera leo*. *Animal Behaviour, 47*, 379–387.

McDonald, R. J., & White, N. M. (1993). A triple dissociation of memory systems:

Hippocampus, amygdala, and dorsal striatum. *Behavioral Neuroscience, 107,* 3–22.

McDonald, R. J., & White, N. M. (1994). Parallel information processing in the water maze: Evidence for independent memory systems involving dorsal striatum and hippocampus. *Behavioral and Neural Biology, 61,* 260–270.

McFarland, D. (1991). Defining motivation and cognition in animals. *International Studies in the Philosophy of Science, 5,* 153–170.

McFarland, D., & Bösser, T. (1993). *Intelligent behavior in animals and robots.* Cambridge, MA: MIT Press.

McFarland, D. J. (1995). Opportunity versus goals in robots, animals, and people. In H. L. Roitblat & J.-A. Meyer (Eds.), *Comparative approaches to cognitive science* (pp. 415–433). Cambridge, MA: MIT Press.

McGonigle, B. O., & Chalmers, M. (1977). Are monkeys logical? *Nature, 267,* 694–696.

McGregor, P. K., & Avery, M. I. (1986). The unsung songs of great tits (*Parus major*): Learning neighbours' songs for discrimination. *Behavioral Ecology and Sociobiology, 18,* 311–316.

McGregor, P. K., & Westby, G. W. M. (1992). Discrimination of individually characteristic electric organ discharges by a weakly electric fish. *Animal Behaviour, 43,* 977–986.

McGrew, W. C. (1992). *Chimpanzee material culture: Implications for human evoluton.* Cambridge: Cambridge University Press.

McLaren, I. P. (1994). Representation development in associative systems. In J. A. Hogan & J. J. Bolhuis (Eds.), *Causal mechanisms of behavioural development* (pp. 377–402). Cambridge: Cambridge University Press.

McLaren, I. P. L., Kaye, H., & Mackintosh, N. J. (1989). An associative theory of the representation of stimuli: applications to perceptual learning and latent inhabition. In R. G. M. Morris (Ed.), *Parallel distributed processing* (pp. 102–130). Oxford: Clarendon Press.

McNamara, J. M., & Houston, A. I. (1992). Risk-sensitive foraging: a review of the theory. *Bulletin of Mathematical Biology, 54,* 355–378.

McNaughton, B. L., Barnes, C. A., Gerrard, J. L., Gothard, K., Jung, M.W., Knierim, J. J., Kudrimoti, H., Qin, Y., Skaggs, W. E., Suster, M., & Weaver, K. L. (1996). Deciphering the hippocampal polyglot: The hippocampus as a path integration system. *Journal of Experimental Biology, 199,* 173–185.

McNaughton, B. L., Knierim, J. J., & Wilson, M. A. (1995). Vector encoding and the vestibular foundations of spatial cognition: Neurophysiological and computational mechanisms. In M. Gazzaniga (Ed.), *The cognitive neurosciences* (pp. 585–595). Cambridge, MA: MIT Press.

McQuoid, L. M., & Galef, B. G., Jr. (1992). Social influences on feeding site selection by burmese fowl (*Gallus gallus*). *Journal of Comparative Psychology, 106,* 137–141.

Meck, W. H. (1996). Neuropharmacology of timing and time perception. *Cognitive Brain Research, 3,* 227–242.

Meck, W. H., & Church, R. M. (1983). A mode control model of counting and timing processes. *Journal of Experimental Psychology: Animal Behavior Processes, 9,* 320–334.

Menzel, E. W. (1978). Cognitive mapping in chimpanzees. In S. H. Hulse, H. Fowler, & W. K. Honig (Eds.), *Cognitive processes in animal behavior.* Hillsdale, NJ: Lawrence Erlbaum Associates.

Menzel, R., Geiger, K., Chittka, L., Joerges, J., Kunze, J., & Müller, U. (1996). The knowledge base of bee navigation. *Journal of Experimental Biology, 199*, 141–146.

Menzel, R., & Müller, U. (1996). Learning and memory in honeybees: From behavior to neural substrates. *Annual Review of Neuroscience, 19*, 379–404.

Meyer, A., Morrissey, J. M., & Schartl, M. (1994). Recurrent origin of a sexually selected trait in *Xiphophorous* fishes inferred from a molecular phylogeny. *Nature, 368*, 539–542.

Michelsen, A., Anderson, B. B., Storm, J., Kirchner, W. H., & Lindauer, M. (1992). How honeybees perceive communication dances, studied by means of a mechanical model. *Behavioral Ecology and Sociobiology, 30*, 143–150.

Miles, R. C. (1971). Species differences in "transmitting" spatial location information. In L. E. Jarrard (Ed.), *Cognitive processes of nonhuman primates*. New York: Academic Press.

Milinski, M. (1984). A predator's cost of overcoming the confusion effect. *Animal Behaviour, 32*, 1157–1162.

Milinski, M. (1990). Information overload and food selection. In R. N. Hughes (Ed.), *Behavioral mechanisms in food selection* (pp. 721–736). Berlin: Springer-Verlag.

Milinski, M., & Heller, R. (1978). Influence of a predator on the optimal foraging behaviour of sticklebacks (*Gasterosteus aculeatus* L.). *Nature, 275*, 642–644.

Milinski, M., & Parker, G. A. (1991). Competition for resources. In J. R. Krebs & N. B. Davies (Eds.), *Behavioural ecology* (3rd ed.) (pp. 137–168). Oxford: Blackwell Scientific.

Miller, D. J. (1993). Do animals subitize? In S. T. Boysen & E. J. Capaldi (Eds.), *The development of numerical competence* (pp. 149–169). Hillsdale, NJ: Lawrence Erlbaum Associates.

Miller, N. E. (1959). Liberalization of basic S-R concepts: Extensions to conflict behavior, motivation, and social learning. In S. Koch (Ed.), *Psychology: A study of a science* (Vol. 2). New York: McGraw-Hill.

Miller, N. E. (1985). The value of behavioral research on animals. *American Psychologist, 40*, 423–440.

Miller, R. C. (1922). The significance of the gregarious habit. *Ecology, 3*, 122–126.

Miller, R. R., & Barnet, R. C. (1993). The role of time in elementary associations. *Current Directions in Psychological Science, 2*, 106–111.

Miller, R. R., Barnet, R. C., & Grahame, N. J. (1995). Assessment of the Rescorla-Wagner model. *Psychological Bulletin, 117*, 363–386.

Milton, K. (1988). Foraging behaviour and the evolution of primate intelligence. In R. P. Bryne & A. Whiten (Eds.), *Machiavellian intelligence* (pp. 285–305). Oxford: Clarendon Press.

Mineka, S., & Cook, M. (1988). Social learning and the acquisition of snake fear in monkeys. In T. R. Zentall & B. G. Galef Jr. (Eds.), *Social learning: Psychological and biological perspectives* (pp. 51–73). Hillsdale, NJ: Lawrence Erlbaum Associates.

Mistlberger, R. E. (1993). Circadian food-anticipatory activity: formal models and physiological mechanisms. *Neuroscience and Biobehavioral Reviews, 18*, 171–195.

Mistlberger, R. E., & Marchant, E. G. (1995). Computational and entrainment models of circadian food-anticipatory activity: Evidence from non-24-hr feeding schedules. *Behavioral Neuroscience, 109*, 790–798.

Mitchell, R. W. (1996). Self-recognition, methodology and explanation: a comment on Heyes (1994). *Animal Behaviour, 51*, 467–469.

Mittelstaedt, H., & Mittelstaedt, M. L. (1982). Homing by path integration. In F. Papi

& H. G. Wallraff (Eds.), *Avian navigation* (pp. 290–297). New York: Springer-Verlag.

Møller, A. P. (1992). Female swallow preference for symmetrical male sexual ornaments. *Nature, 357,* 238–240.

Møller, A. P., & Pomiankowski, A. (1993a). Fluctuating asymmetry and sexual selection. *Genetica, 89,* 267–279.

Møller, A. P., & Pomiankowski, A. (1993b). Why have birds got multiple sexual ornaments? *Behavioral Ecology and Sociobiology, 32,* 167–176.

Montague, P. R., Dayan, P., Person, C., & Sejnowski, T. J. (1995). Bee foraging in uncertain environments using predictive hebbian learning. *Nature, 377,* 725–728.

Moody, A. L., & Houston, A. I. (1995). Interference and the ideal free distribution. *Animal Behaviour, 49,* 1065–1072.

Moore, B. R. (1992). Avian movement imitation and a new form of mimicry: Tracing the evolution of a complex form of learning. *Behaviour, 122,* 231–263.

Moore, B. R. (1996). The evolution of imitative learning. In C. M. Heyes & B. G. Galef Jr. (Eds.), *Social learning in animals: The roots of culture* (pp. 245–265). San Diego: Academic Press.

Moore-Ede, M. C., Sulzman, F. M., & Fuller, C. A. (1982). *The clocks that time us.* Cambridge, MA: Harvard University Press.

Morris, R. G. M. (1981). Spatial localization does not require the presence of local cues. *Learning and Motivation, 12,* 239–260.

Moss, C. F., & Schnitzler, H.-U. (1989). Accuracy of target ranging in echolocating bats: Acoustic information processing. *Journal of Comparative Physiology A, 165,* 383–393.

Moss, C. F., & Shettleworth, S. J. (Eds.). (1996). *Neuroethological studies of cognitive and perceptual processes.* Boulder, CO: Westview Press.

Mrosovsky, N., Reebs, S. G., Honrado, G. I., & Salmon, P. A. (1989). Behavioural entrainment of circadian rhythms. *Experientia, 45,* 696–702.

Muller, M., & Wehner, R. (1988). Path integration in desert ants, *Cataglyphis fortis. Proceedings of the National Academy of Science, 85,* 5287–5290.

Muntz, W. R. A. (1974). Behavioural studies of vision in a fish and possible relationships to the environment. In M. A. Ali (Ed.), *Vision in fishes* (pp. 705–717). New York: Plenum Press.

Nadel, L. (1995). The psychobiology of spatial behavior: The hippocampal formation and spatial mapping. In E. Alleva, A. Fasolo, H.-P. Lipp, L. Nadel, & L. Ricceri (Eds.), *Behavioural brain research in naturalistic and semi-naturalistic settings* (pp. 245–258). Dordrecht, The Netherlands: Kluwer Academic Publishers.

Nagel, T. (1974). What is it like to be a bat? *Philosophical Review, 83,* 435–450.

Nagell, K., Olguin, R. S., & Tomasello, M. (1993). Processes of social learning in the tool use of chimpanzees (*Pan troglodytes*) and human children (*Homo sapiens*). *Journal of Comparative Psychology, 107,* 174–186.

Nalbach, H. O., Wolf-Oberhollenzer, F., & Remy, M. (1993). Exploring the image. In H. P. Zeigler & H.-J. Bischof (Eds.), *Vision, brain, and behavior in birds* (pp. 25–46). Cambridge, MA: MIT Press.

Neisser, U. (1978). Memory: What are the important questions? In M. M. Gruneberg, P. Morris, & R. H. Sykes (Eds.), *Practical aspects of memory* (pp. 3–24). New York: Academic Press.

Nelson, D. A. (1992). Song overproduction and selective attrition lead to song sharing in the field sparrow (*Spizella pusilla*). *Behavioral Ecology and Sociobiology, 30,* 415–424.

Nelson, D. A., & Marler, P. (1989). Categorical perception of a natural stimulus continuum: Birdsong. *Science, 244*, 976–978.

Nelson, D. A., & Marler, P. (1990). The perception of birdsong and an ecological concept of signal space. In W. C. Stebbins & M. A. Berkley (Eds.), *Comparative perception: Complex signals* (Vol. 2, pp. 443–477). New York: John Wiley and Sons.

Nicol, C. J., & Pope, S. J. (1994). Social learning in small flocks of laying hens. *Animal Behaviour, 47*, 1289–1296.

Nishida, T. (1987). Local traditions and cultural transmission. In B. B. Smuts, D. L. Cheney, R. M. Seyfarth, R. W. Wrangham, & T. T. Struhsaker (Eds.), *Primate societies* (pp. 462–474). Chicago: University of Chicago Press.

Nordeen, K. W., & Nordeen, E. J. (1992). Auditory feedback is necessary for the maintenance of stereotyped song in adult zebra finches. *Behavioral and Neural Biology, 57*, 58–66.

O'Brien, W. J., Browman, H. I., & Evans, B. I. (1990). Search strategies of foraging animals. *American Scientist, 78*, 152–160.

Oden, D. L., Thompson, R. K. R., & Premack, D. (1988). Spontaneous transfer of matching by infant chimpanzees. *Journal of Experimental Psychology: Animal Behavior Processes, 14*, 140–145.

Oetting, S., Pröve, E., & Bischof, H.-J. (1995). Sexual imprinting as a two-stage process: mechanisms of information storage and stabilization. *Animal Behaviour, 50*, 393–403.

O'Keefe, J., & Nadel, L. (1978). *The hippocampus as a cognitive map*. Oxford: Clarendon Press.

Olson, D. J. (1991). Species differences in spatial memory among Clark's nutcrackers, scrub jays, and pigeons. *Journal of Experimental Psychology: Animal Behavior Processes, 17*, 363–376.

Olson, D. J., Kamil, A. C., Balda, R. P., & Nims, P. J. (1995). Performance of four seed-caching corvid species in operant tests of nonspatial and spatial memory. *Journal of Comparative Psychology, 109*, 173–181.

Olson, D. J., & Maki, W. S. (1983). Characteristics of spatial memory in pigeons. *Journal of Experimental Psychology: Animal Behavior Processes, 9*, 266–280.

Olthof, A., Iden, C. M., & Roberts, W. A. (1997). Judgements of ordinality and summation of number symbols by squirrel monkeys (*Saimiri sciureus*). *Journal of Experimental Psychology: Animal Behavior Processes, 23*, 325–339.

Olton, D. S. (1978). Characteristics of spatial memory. In S. H. Hulse, H. Fowler, & W. K. Honig (Eds.), *Cognitive processes in animal behavior* (pp. 341–373). Hillsdale, NJ: Lawrence Erlbaum Associates.

Olton, D. S., & Samuelson, R. J. (1976). Remembrance of places passed: Spatial memory in rats. *Journal of Experimental Psychology: Animal Behavior Processes, 2*, 97–116.

Ostfeld, R. S. (1990). The ecology of territoriality in small mammals. *Trends in Ecology and Evolution, 5*, 411–415.

Ostfeld, R. S., Pugh, S. R., Seamon, J. O., & Tamarin, R. H. (1988). Space use and reproductive success in a population of meadow voles. *Journal of Animal Ecology, 57*, 385–394.

Palameta, B. (1989). *The importance of socially transmitted information in the acquisition of novel foraging skills by pigeons and canaries*. PhD. thesis, Cambridge University.

Palameta, B., & Lefebvre, L. (1985). The social transmission of a food-finding technique in pigeons: what is learned? *Animal Behaviour, 33*, 892–896.

Papi, F. (Ed.). (1992a). *Animal homing*. London: Chapman and Hall.

Papi, F. (1992b). General aspects. In F. Papi (Ed.), *Animal homing* (pp. 2–18). London: Chapman and Hall.

Papi, F., & Wallraff, H. G. (1992). Birds. In F. Papi (Ed.), *Animal homing* (pp. 263–319). London: Chapman and Hall.

Papini, M. R., & Bitterman, M. E. (1990). The role of contingency in classical conditioning. *Psychological Review, 97,* 396–403.

Parker, G. A. (1978). Searching for mates. In J. R. Krebs & N. B. Davies (Eds.), *Behavioural ecology* (pp. 214–244). Sunderland, MA: Sinauer Associates.

Parker, G. A., & Maynard Smith, J. (1990). Optimality theory in evolutionary biology. *Nature, 348,* 27–33.

Parker, S. T. (1996). Using cladistic analysis of comparative data to reconstruct the evolution of cognitive development in hominids. In E. P. Martins (Ed.), *Phylogenies and the comparative method in animal behavior* (pp. 361–398). New York: Oxford University Press.

Parker, S. T., & Mitchell, R. W. (1994). Evolving self-awareness. In S. T. Parker, R. W. Mitchell, & M. L. Boccia (Eds.), *Self-awareness in animals and humans: Developmental perspectives* (pp. 413–428). Cambridge: Cambridge University Press.

Parker, S. T., Mitchell, R. W., & Boccia, M. L. (Eds.). (1994). *Self-awareness in animals and humans: Developmental perspectives* . Cambridge: Cambridge University Press.

Partridge, B. L., & Pitcher, T. J. (1979). Evidence against a hydrodynamic function for fish schools. *Nature, 279,* 418–419.

Patterson-Kane, E., Nicol, C. J., Foster, T. M., & Temple, W. (1997). Limited perception of video images by domestic hens. *Animal Behaviour, 53,* 951–963.

Pavlov, I. P. (1927). *Conditioned reflexes.* Oxford: Oxford University Press.

Pearce, J. M. (1987). A model for stimulus generalization in Pavlovian conditioning. *Psychological Review, 94,* 61–73.

Pearce, J. M. (1988). Stimulus generalization and the acquisition of categories by pigeons. In L. Weiskrantz (Ed.), *Thought without language* (pp. 133–155). Oxford: Clarendon Press.

Pearce, J. M. (1989). The acquisition of an artificial category by pigeons. *Quarterly Journal of Experimental Psychology, 41B,* 381–406.

Pearce, J. M. (1994a). Similarity and discrimination: A selective review and a connectionist model. *Psychological Review, 101,* 587–607.

Pearce, J. M. (1994b). Discrimination and categorization. In N. J. Mackintosh (Ed.), *Animal learning and cognition* (pp. 109–134). San Diego, CA: Academic Press.

Pepperberg, I. M. (1987). Evidence for conceptual quantitative abilities in the African grey parrot: Labeling of cardinal sets. *Ethology, 75,* 37–61.

Pepperberg, I. M. (1993a). A review of the effects of social interaction on vocal learning in African grey parrots (*Psittacus erithacus*). *Netherlands Journal of Zoology, 43,* 104–124.

Pepperberg, I. M. (1993b). Cognition and communication in an African grey parrot (*Psittacus erithacus*): Studies on a nonhuman, nonprimate, nonmammalian subject. In H. L. Roitblat, L. M. Herman, & P. E. Nachtigall (Eds.), *Language and communication: Comparative perspectives* (pp. 221–248). Hillsdale, NJ: Lawrence Erlbaum Associates.

Pepperberg, I. M. (1994). Numerical competence in an African gray parrot (*Psittacus erithacus*). *Journal of Comparative Psychology, 108,* 36–44.

Pepperberg, I. M., Garcia, S. E., Jackson, E. C., & Marconi, S. (1995). Mirror use by African grey parrots (*Psittacus erithacus*). *Journal of Comparative Psychology, 109,* 182–195.

Pepperberg, I. M., & McLaughlin, M. A. (1996). Effect of avian-human joint attention on allospecific vocal learning by grey parrots (*Psittacus erithacus*). *Journal of Comparative Psychology, 110*, 286–297.

Pepperberg, I. M., Willner, M. R., & Gravitz, L. B. (1997). Development of Piagetian object permanence in a grey parrot (*Psittacus erithacus*). *Journal of Comparative Psychology, 111*, 63–75.

Pereira, M. E., & Macedonia, J. M. (1991). Ringtailed lemur anti-predator calls denote predator class, not response urgency. *Animal Behaviour, 41*, 543–544.

Petrie, M., & Halliday, T. (1994). Experimental and natural changes in the peacock's (*Pavo criststus*) train can affect mating success. *Behavioral Ecology and Sociobiology, 35*, 213–217.

Petrinovich, L. (1988). The role of social factors in white-crowned sparrow song development. In T. R. Zentall & B. G. Galef Jr. (Eds.), *Social learning: Psychological and biological perspectives* (pp. 255–278). Hillsdale, NJ: Lawrence Erlbaum Associates.

Petrinovich, L., & Patterson, T. L. (1979). Field studies of habituation: I. Effect of reproductive condition, number of trials, and different delay intervals on responses of the white-crowned sparrow. *Journal of Comparative and Physiological Psychology, 93*, 337–350.

Pfungst, O. (1965). *Clever hans (The horse of Mr. Von Osten)*. New York: Holt, Rinehart and Winston.

Phelps, M. T., & Roberts, W. A. (1994). Memory for pictures of upright and inverted primate faces in humans (*Homo sapiens*), squirrel monkeys (*Saimiri sciureus*), and pigeons (*Columba livia*). *Journal of Comparative Psychology, 108*, 114–125.

Pietrewicz, A. T., & Kamil, A. C. (1981). Search images and the detection of cryptic prey: An operant approach. In A. C. Kamil & T. D. Sargent (Eds.), *Foraging behavior: Ecological, ethological, and psychological approaches* (pp. 311–331). New York: Garland STPM Press.

Pinel, J. P. J., & Treit, D. (1978). Burying as a defensive response in rats. *Journal of Comparative and Physiological Psychology, 92*, 708–712.

Pinker, S. (1994). *The language instinct*. New York: William Morrow.

Pinker, S., & Bloom, P. (1990). Natural language and natural selection. *Behavioral and Brain Sciences, 13*, 707–784.

Plaisted, K. (1997). The effect of interstimulus interval on the discrimination of cryptic targets. *Journal of Experimental Psychology: Animal Behavior Processes, 23*, 248–259.

Plaisted, K. C., & Mackintosh, N. J. (1995). Visual search for cryptic stimuli in pigeons: implications for the search image and search rate hypotheses. *Animal Behaviour, 50*, 1219–1232.

Platt, M. L., Brannon, E. M., Briese, T. L., & French, J. A. (1996). Differences in feeding ecology predict differences in performance between golden lion tamarins (*Leontopithecus rosalia*) and Wied's marmosets (*Callithrix kuhli*) on spatial and visual memory tasks. *Animal Learning & Behavior, 24*, 384–393.

Plowright, C. M. S. (1996). Simultaneous processing of short delays and higher order temporal intervals within a session by pigeons. *Behavioural Processes, 38*, 1–9.

Plowright, C. M. S., Reid, S., & Kilian, T. (1998). How mynah birds (*Gracula religiosa*) and pigeons (*Columba livia*) find hidden food: A study in comparative cognition. *Journal of Comparative Psychology, 112*, 13–25.

Plowright, C. M. S., & Shettleworth, S. J. (1990). The role of shifting in choice behavior of pigeons on a two-armed bandit. *Behavioural Processes, 21*, 157–178.

Plowright, C. M. S., & Shettleworth, S. J. (1991). Time horizon and choice by pigeons in a prey selection task. *Animal Learning & Behavior, 19,* 103–112.

Podos, J. (1996). Memory constraints on vocal development in a song bird. *Animal Behaviour, 51,* 1061–1070.

Pomiankowski, A. (1994). Swordplay and sensory bias. *Nature, 368,* 494–495.

Posner, M. I., & Nissen, M. J. (1976). Visual dominance: An information-processing account of its origins and significance. *Psychological Review, 83,* 157–171.

Poucet, B. (1993). Spatial cognitive maps in animals: New hypotheses on their structure and neural mechanisms. *Psychological Review, 100,* 163–182.

Poucet, B., Chapuis, N., Durup, M., & Thinus-Blanc, C. (1986). A study of exploratory behavior as an index of spatial knowledge in hamsters. *Animal Learning & Behavior, 14,* 93–100.

Povinelli, D. J. (1989). Failure to find self-recognition in Asian elephants (*Elephas maximus*) in contrast to their use of mirror cues to discover hidden food. *Journal of Comparative Psychology, 103,* 122–131.

Povinelli, D. J. (1994). Comparative studies of animal mental state attribution: A reply to Heyes. *Animal Behaviour, 48,* 239–341.

Povinelli, D. J. (1995). The unduplicated self. In P. Rochat (Ed.), *The self in infancy: Theory and research* (pp. 161–191): Amsterdam: North Holland-Elsevier.

Povinelli, D. J. (1996). Chimpanzee theory of mind? The long road to strong inference. In P. Carruthers & P. K. Smith (Eds.), *Theories of theories of mind* (pp. 293–329). Cambridge: Cambridge University Press.

Povinelli, D. J., & Cant, J. G. H. (1995). Arboreal clambering and the evolution of self-conception. *Quarterly Review of Biology, 70,* 393–421.

Povinelli, D. J., & deBlois, S. (1992). Young children's (*Homo sapiens*) understanding of knowledge formation in themselves and others. *Journal of Comparative Psychology, 106,* 228–238.

Povinelli, D. J., & Eddy, T. J. (1996a). What young chimpanzees know about seeing. *Monographs of the Society for Research in Child Development, 61*(247), 1–152.

Povinelli, D. J., & Eddy, T. J. (1996b). Chimpanzees: Joint visual attention. *Psychological Science, 7,* 129–135.

Povinelli, D. J., & Eddy, T. J. (1996c). Factors influencing young chimpanzees' (*Pan troglodytes*) recognition of attention. *Journal of Comparative Psychology, 110,* 336–345.

Povinelli, D. J., Gallup, G. G., Jr., Eddy, T. J., Bierschwale, D. T., Engstrom, M. C., Perilloux, H. K., & Toxopeus, I. B. (1997). Chimpanzees recognize themselves in mirrors. *Animal Behaviour, 53,* 1083–1088.

Povinelli, D. J., Landau, K. R., & Perilloux, H. K. (1996). Self-recognition in young children using delayed versus live feedback: Evidence of a developmental asynchrony. *Child Development, 67,* 1540–1544.

Povinelli, D. J., Nelson, K. E., & Boysen, S. T. (1990). Inferences about guessing and knowing by chimpanzees (*Pan troglodytes*). *Journal of Comparative Psychology, 104,* 203–210.

Povinelli, D. J., Parks, K. A., & Novak, M. A. (1991). Do rhesus monkeys (*Macaca mulatta*) attribute knowledge and ignorance to others? *Journal of Comparative Psychology, 105,* 318–325.

Povinelli, D. J., & Preuss, T. M. (1995). Theory of mind: evolutionary history of a cognitive specialization. *Trends in Neurosciences, 18,* 418–424.

Povinelli, D. J., Rulf, A. B., Landau, K. R., & Bierschwale, D. T. (1993). Self-recognition in chimpanzees (*Pan troglodytes*): Distribution, ontogeny, and patterns of emergence. *Journal of Comparative Psychology, 107,* 347–372.

Powell, G. V. N. (1974). Experimental analysis of the social value of flocking by starlings (*Sturnus vulgaris*) in relation to predation and foraging. *Animal Behaviour, 22*, 501–505.

Premack, D. (1971). Language in chimpanzee? *Science, 172*, 808–822.

Premack, D. (1983). Animal cognition. *Annual Review of Psychology, 34*, 351–362.

Premack, D. (1988). 'Does the chimpanzee have a theory of mind?' revisited. In R. W. Byrne & A. Whiten (Eds.), *Machiavellian intelligence: Social expertise and the evolution of intellect in monkeys, apes, and humans* (pp. 160–179). Oxford: Clarendon Press.

Premack, D. (1990). The infant's theory of self-propelled objects. *Cognition, 36*, 1–16.

Premack, D., & Premack, A. J. (1983). *The mind of an ape*. New York: W.W. Norton & Company.

Premack, D., & Woodruff, G. (1978). Does the chimpanzee have a theory of mind? *Behavioral and Brain Sciences, 4*, 515–526.

Preuss, T. M. (1995). The argument from animals to humans in cognitive neuroscience. In M. Gazzaniga (Ed.), *The cognitive neurosciences* (pp. 1227–1241). Cambridge, MA: MIT Press.

Proctor, H. C. (1992). Sensory exploitation and the evolution of male mating behaviour: a cladistic test using water mites (*Acari: Parasitengona*). *Animal Behaviour, 44*, 745–752.

Pruett-Jones, S. (1992). Independent versus nonindependent mate choice: Do females copy each other? *American Naturalist, 140*, 1000–1009.

Pulliam, H. R., & Caraco, T. (1984). Living in groups: Is there an optimal gorup size? In J. R. Krebs & N. B. Davies (Eds.), *Behavioural Ecology* (2nd ed.) (pp. 122–147). Oxford: Blackwell Scientific.

Pyke, G. H. (1979). Optimal foraging in bumblebees: Rule of movement between flowers within inflorescences. *Animal Behavior, 27*, 1167–1181.

Quiatt, D., & Reynolds, V. (1993). *Primate behaviour*. Cambridge: Cambridge University Press.

Rajecki, D. W. (1973). Imprinting in precocial birds: Interpretation, evidence, and evaluation. *Psychological Bulletin, 79*, 48–58.

Ramachandran, V. S., Tyler, C. W., Gregory, R. L., Rogers-Ramachnadran, D., Duensing, S., Pillsbury, C., & Ramachandran, C. (1996). Rapid adaptive camouflage in tropical flounders. *Nature, 379*, 815–818.

Real, L. A. (1991). Animal choice behaviour and the evolution of cognitive architecture. *Science, 253*, 980–986.

Real, L. A. (1993). Toward a cognitive ecology. *Trends in Ecology and Evolution, 8*, 413–417.

Real, P. G., Iannazzi, R., Kamil, A. C., & Heinrich, B. (1984). Discrimination and generalization of leaf damage by blue jays *(Cyanocitta cristata)*. *Animal Learning & Behavior, 12*, 202–208.

Reboreda, J. C., Clayton, N. S., & Kacelnik, A. (1996). Species and sex differences in hippocampus size in parasitic and non-parasitic cowbirds. *Neuroreport, 7*, 505–508.

Reboreda, J. C., & Kacelnik, A. (1991). Risk sensitivity in starlings: variability in food amount and food delay. *Behavioral Ecology, 2*, 301–308.

Rechten, C., Avery, M., & Stevens, A. (1983). Optimal prey selection: Why do great tits show partial preferences? *Animal Behaviour, 31*, 576–584.

Redhead, E. S., Roberts, A., Good, M., & Pearce, J. M. (1997). Interaction between piloting and beacon homing by rats in a swimming pool. *Journal of Experimental Psychology: Animal Behavior Processes, 23*, 340–350.

Reebs, S. G. (1996). Time place learning in golden shiners (Pisces: Cyprinidae). *Behavioral Processes, 36,* 253–262.

Reeve, H. K. (1989). The evolution of conspecific acceptance thresholds. *American Naturalist, 133,* 407–435.

Reeve, H. K., & Sherman, P. W. (1993). Adaptation and the goals of evolutionary research. *Quarterly Review of Biology, 68,* 1–32.

Regolin, L., Vallortigara, G., & Zanforlin, M. (1995). Object and spatial representations in detour problems by chicks. *Animal Behaviour, 49,* 195–199.

Reid, P. J., & Shettleworth, S. J. (1992). Detection of cryptic prey: Search image or search rate? *Journal of Experimental Psychology: Animal Behavior Processes, 18,* 273–286.

Rescorla, R. A. (1967). Pavlovian conditioning and its proper control procedures. *Psychological Review, 74,* 71–80.

Rescorla, R. A. (1969). Pavlovian conditioned inhibition. *Psychological Bulletin, 72,* 77–94.

Rescorla, R. A. (1986). Extinction of facilitation. *Journal of Experimental Psychology: Animal Behavior Processes, 12,* 16–24.

Rescorla, R. A. (1987). Facilitation and inhibition. *Journal of Experimental Psychology: Animal Behavior Processes, 13,* 250–259.

Rescorla, R. A. (1988a). Pavlovian conditioning: It's not what you think it is. *American Psychologist, 43,* 151–160.

Rescorla, R. A. (1988b). Behavioral studies of Pavlovian conditioning. *Annual Review of Neuroscience, 11,* 329–352.

Rescorla, R. A. (1996). Spontaneous recovery after training with multiple outcomes. *Animal Learning & Behavior, 24,* 11–18.

Rescorla, R. A., & Cunningham, C. L. (1979). Spatial contiguity facilitates Pavlovian second-order conditioning. *Journal of Experimental Psychology: Animal Behavior Processes, 5,* 152–161.

Rescorla, R. A., & Durlach, P. J. (1981). Within-event learning in Pavlovian conditioning. In N. E. Spear & R. R. Miller (Eds.), *Information processing in animals: Memory mechanisms* (pp. 81–111). Hillsdale, NJ: Lawrence Erlbaum Associates.

Rescorla, R. A., & Furrow, D. R. (1977). Stimulus similarity as a determinant of Pavlovian conditioning. *Journal of Experimental Psychology: Animal Behavior Processes, 3,* 203–215.

Rescorla, R. A., & Holland, P. C. (1976). Some behavioral approaches to the study of learning. In M. R. Rosenzweig & E. L. Bennett (Eds.), *Neural mechanisms of learning and memory* (pp. 165–192). Cambridge, MA: MIT Press.

Rescorla, R. A., & Solomon, R. L. (1967). Two-process learning theory: Relationships between Pavlovian conditioning and instrumental learning. *Psychological Review, 74,* 151–182.

Rescorla, R. A., & Wagner, A. R. (1972). A theory of Pavlovian conditioning: Variations in the effectiveness of reinforcement and nonreinforcement. In A. H. Black & W. F. Prokasy (Eds.), *Classical conditioning II: Current theory and research* (pp. 64–99). New York: Appleton-Century-Crofts.

Richards, R. J. (1987). *Darwin and the emergence of evolutionary theories of mind and behavior.* Chicago: University of Chicago Press.

Richner, H., & Heeb, P. (1995). Is the information center hypothesis a flop? *Advances in the Study of Behavior, 24,* 1–45.

Ridley, M. (1993). *Evolution.* Oxford: Blackwell Scientific.

Rijnsdorp, A., Daan, S., & Dijkstra, C. (1981). Hunting in the kestrel, *Falco tinnunculus,* and the adaptive significance of daily habits. *Oecologia, 50,* 391–406.

Riley, D. A., & Langley, C. M. (1993). The logic of species comparisons. *Psychological Science, 4,* 185–189.

Riley, D. A., & Leith, C. R. (1976). Multidimensional psychophysics and selective attention in animals. *Psychological Bulletin, 83,* 138–160.

Rilling, M. (1993). Invisible counting animals: A history of contributions from comparative psycholgy, ethology and learning theory. In S. T. Boysen & E. J. Capaldi (Eds.), *The development of numerical competence* (pp. 3–37). Hillsdale, NJ: Lawrence Erlbaum Associates.

Ristau, C. A. (Ed.). (1991a). *Cognitive ethology.* Hillsdale, NJ: Lawrence Erlbaum Associates.

Ristau, C. A. (1991b). Aspects of the cognitive ethology of an injury-feigning bird, the piping plover. In C. A. Ristau (Ed.), *Cognitive ethology* (pp. 91–126). Hillsdale, NJ: Lawrence Erlbaum Associates.

Ristau, C. A., & Robbins, D. (1982). Language in the great apes: A critical review. *Advances in the Study of Behavior, 12,* 141–255.

Roberts, A. D. L., & Pearce, J. M. (1998). Control of spatial behavior by an unstable landmark. *Journal of Experimental Psychology: Animal Behavior Processes, 24,* 172–184.

Roberts, G. (1996). Why individual vigilance declines as group size increases. *Animal Behaviour, 51,* 1077–1086.

Roberts, S. (1981). Isolation of an internal clock. *Journal of Experimental Psychology: Animal Behavior Processes, 7,* 242–268.

Roberts, W. A. (1980). Distribution of trials and intertrial retention in delayed matching to sample with pigeons. *Journal of Experimental Psychology: Animal Behavior Processes, 6,* 217–237.

Roberts, W. A. (1981). Retroactive inhibition in rat spatial memory. *Animal Learning & Behavior, 9,* 566–574.

Roberts, W. A. (1984). Some issues in animal spatial memory. In H. L. Roitblat, T. G. Bever, & H. S. Terrace (Eds.), *Animal cognition.* Hillsdale, NJ: Lawrence Erlbaum Associates.

Roberts, W. A. (1998). *Principles of Animal Cognition.* New York: McGraw-Hill.

Roberts, W. A., Cheng, K., & Cohen, J. S. (1989). Timing light and tone signals in pigeons. *Journal of Experimental Psychology: Animal Behavior Processes, 15,* 23–35.

Roberts, W. A., & Grant, D. S. (1974). Short-term memory in the pigeon with presentation time precisely controlled. *Learning and Motivation, 5,* 393–408.

Roberts, W. A., & Grant, D. S. (1978). An analysis of light-induced retroactive inhibition in pigeon short-term memory. *Journal of Experimental Psychology: Animal Behavior Processes, 4,* 219–236.

Roberts, W. A., & Mitchell, S. (1994). Can a pigeon simultaneously process temporal and numerical information? *Journal of Experimental Psychology: Animal Behavior Processes, 20,* 66–78.

Roberts, W. A., & Phelps, M. T. (1994). Transitive inference in rats: A test of the spatial coding hypothesis. *Psychological Science, 5,* 368–374.

Roberts, W. A., Phelps, M. T., Macuda, T., Brodbeck, D. R., & Russ, T. (1996). Intraocular transfer and simulantaneous processing of stimuli presented in different visual fields of the pigeon. *Behavioral Neuroscience, 110,* 290–299.

Roberts, W. P., & Fragaszy, D. M. (1995). Self-awareness in animals and humans: developmental perspectives. *Animal Behaviour, 50,* 571–572.

Rodrigo, T., Chamizo, V. D., McLaren, I. P. L., & Mackintosh, N. J. (1994). Effects of pre-exposure to the same or different pattern of extra-maze cues on subsequent extra-maze discrimination. *Quarterly Journal of Experimental Psychology*, *47B*, 15–26.

Rodrigo, T., Chamizo, V. D., McLaren, I. P., & Mackintosh, N. J. (1997). Blocking in the spatial domain. *Journal of Experimental Psychology: Animal Behavior Processes*, *23*, 110–118.

Rodriguez-Girones, M. A. (1995). *Processes of behavioural timing and their implications for foraging theory*. PhD. thesis, Oxford University.

Roitblat, H. L. (1987). *Introduction to comparative cognition*. New York: W.H. Freeman.

Roitblat, H. L., Bever, T. G., & Terrace, H. S. (Eds.). (1984). *Animal cognition* . Hillsdale, NJ: Lawrence Erlbaum Associates.

Roitblat, H. L., Harley, H. E., & Helweg, D. A. (1993). Cognitive processing in artificial language research. In H. L. Roitblat, L. M. Herman, & P. E. Nachtigall (Eds.), *Language and communication: Comparative perspectives* (pp. 1–44). Hillsdale, NJ: Lawrence Erlbaum Associates.

Roitblat, H. L., Herman, L. M., & Nachtigall, P. E. (Eds.). (1993). *Language and communication: Comparative perspectives*. Hillsdale, NJ: Lawrence Erlbaum Associates.

Romanes, G. J. (1892). *Animal intelligence*. New York: D. Appleton and Company.

Roper, K. L., Kaiser, D. H., & Zentall, T. R. (1995). True directed forgetting in pigeons may occur only when alternative working memory is required on forget-cue trials. *Animal Learning & Behavior*, *23*, 280–285.

Roper, K. L., & Zentall, T. R. (1993). Directed forgetting in animals. *Psychological Bulletin*, *113*, 513–532.

Rowland, W. J. (1989). The ethological basis of mate choice in male threespine sticklebacks, *Gasterosteus aculeatus*. *Animal Behaviour*, *38*, 112–120.

Rozin, P. (1976). The evolution of intelligence and access to the cognitive unconscious. *Progress in Psychobiology and Physiological Psychology*, *6*, 245–280.

Rozin, P., & Kalat, J. W. (1971). Specific hungers and poison avoidance as adaptive specializations of learning. *Psychological Review*, *78*, 459–486.

Rozin, P., & Schull, J. (1988). The adaptive-evolutionary point of view in experimental psychology. In R. Atkinson, R. J. Herrnstein, G. Lindzey, & R. D. Luce (Eds.), *S. S. Stevens' handbook of experimental psychology* (pp. 503–546). New York: Wiley.

Rumbaugh, D. M. (Ed.). (1977). *Language learning by a chimpanzee*. New York: Academic Press.

Rumbaugh, D. M., & Pate, J. L. (1984). The evolution of cognition in primates: A comparative perspective. In H. L. Roitblat, T. G. Bever, & H. S. Terrace (Eds.), *Animal cognition* (pp. 569–587). Hillsdale, NJ: Lawrence Erlbaum Associates.

Rumbaugh, D. M., Richardson, W. K., & Washburn, D. A. (1989). Rhesus monkeys (*Macaca mulatta*), video tasks, and implications for stimulus-response spatial contiguity. *Journal of Comparative Psychology*, *103*, 32–38.

Rumbaugh, D. M., & Savage-Rumbaugh, E. S. (1994). Language in comparative perspective. In N. J. Mackintosh (Ed.), *Animal learning and cognition* (pp. 307–333). San Diego: Academic Press.

Rumbaugh, D. M., Savage-Rumbaugh, E. S., & Hegel, M. T. (1987). Summation in the chimpanzee (*Pan troglodytes*). *Journal of Experimental Psychology: Animal Behavior Processes*, *13*, 107–115.

Rumbaugh, D. M., Savage-Rumbaugh, E. S., & Pate, J. L. (1988). Addendum to "Summation in the chimpanzee (*Pan troglodytes*)." *Journal of Experimental Psychology: Animal Behavior Processes*, *14*, 118–120.

Rumbaugh, D. M., Savage-Rumbaugh, E. S., & Sevcik, R. A. (1994). Biobehavioral roots of language: A comparative perspective of chimpanzee, child, and culture.

In R. W. Wrangham, W. C. McGrew, F. B. M. de Waal, P. G. Heltne, & L. A. Marquardt (Eds.), *Chimpanzee cultures* (pp. 319–334). Cambridge, MA: Harvard University Press.

Rumbaugh, D. M., Savage-Rumbaugh, E. S., & Washburn, D. A. (1996). Toward a new outlook on primate learning and behavior: complex learning and emergent processes in comparative perspective. *Japanese Psychological Research, 38*, 113–125.

Russon, A. E., & Galdikas, B. M. F. (1993). Imitation in free-ranging rehabilitant orangutans (*Pongo pygmaeus*). *Journal of Comparative Psychology, 107*, 147–161.

Russon, A. E., & Galdikas, B. M. F. (1995). Constraints on great apes' imitation: model and action selectivity in rehabilitant orangutan (*Pongo pygmaeus*) imitation. *Journal of Comparative Psychology, 109*, 5–17.

Ryan, C. M. E., & Lea, S. E. G. (1990). Pattern recognition, updating, and filial imprinting in the domestic chicken (*Gallus gallus*). In M. L. Commons, R. J. Herrnstein, S. M. Kosslyn, & D. B. Mumford (Eds.), *Quantitative analyses of behavior: Behavioral approaches to pattern recognition and concept formation* (pp. 89–110). Hillsdale, NJ: Lawrence Erlbaum Associates.

Ryan, M. J. (1994). Mechanisms underlying sexual selection. In L. A. Real (Ed.), *Behavioral mechanisms in evolutionary ecology* (pp. 190–215). Chicago: University of Chicago Press.

Ryan, M. J. (1996). Phylogenetics in behavior: Some cautions and expectations. In E. P. Martins (Ed.), *Phylogenies and the comparative method in animal behavior* (pp. 1–21). New York: Oxford University Press.

Ryan, M. J., & Keddy-Hector, A. (1992). Directional patterns of female mate choice and the role of sensory biases. *American Naturalist, 139, supplement*, s4–s35.

Ryan, M. J., & Rand, A. S. (1993). Sexual selection and signal evolution: the ghost of biases past. *Philosophical Transactions of the Royal Society B, 340*, 187–195.

Ryan, M. J., & Rand, A. S. (1995). Female responses to ancestral advertisement calls in Tungara frogs. *Science, 269*, 390–392.

Saffran, J. R., Aslin, R. N., & Newport, E. L. (1996). Statistical learning by 8-month-old infants. *Science, 274*, 1926–1928.

Saint Paul, U. v. (1982). Do geese use path integration for walking home? In F. Papi & H. G. Wallraff (Eds.), *Avian navigation* (pp. 298–307). New York: Springer-Verlag.

Savage-Rumbaugh, E. S. (1986). *Ape language: From conditioned response to symbol.* New York: Columbia University Press.

Savage-Rumbaugh, E. S., & Brakke, K. E. (1996). Animal language: Methodological and interpretive issues. In M. Bekoff & D. Jamieson (Eds.), *Readings in animal cognition* (pp. 269–288). Cambridge, MA: MIT Press.

Savage-Rumbaugh, E. S., & Lewin, R. (1994). *Kanzi, the ape at the brink of the human mind.* New York: John Wiley & Sons.

Savage-Rumbaugh, E. S., McDonald, K., Sevcik, R. A., Hopkins, W. D., & Rubert, E. (1986). Spontaneous symbol acquisition and communicative use by a pygmy chimpanzee (*Pan paniscus*). *Journal of Experimental Psychology: General, 115*, 211–235.

Savage-Rumbaugh, E. S., Murphy, J., Sevcik, R. A., Brakke, K. E., Williams, S. L., & Rumbaugh, D. M. (1993). Language comprehension in ape and child. *Monographs of the Society for Research in Child Development, 58*, 1–256.

Savage-Rumbaugh, E. S., Pate, J. L., Lawson, J., Smith, S. T., & Rosenbaum, S. (1983). Can a chimpanzee make a statement? *Journal of Experimental Psychology: General, 112*, 457–492.

Savage-Rumbaugh, E. S., Rumbaugh, D. M., & Boyson, S. (1978). Symbolic communication between two chimpanzees (*Pan troglodytes*). *Science, 201,* 641–644.

Save, E., Granon, S., Buhot, M. C., & Thinus-Blanc, C. (1996). Effects of limitations on the use of some visual and kinaesthetic information in spatial mapping during exploration in the rat. *Quarterly Journal of Experimental Psychology, 49B,* 134–147.

Sawrey, D. K., Keith, J. R., & Backes, R. C. (1994). Place learning by three vole species (*Microtus ochrogaster, M. montanus, and M. pennsylvanicus*) in the Morris swim task. *Journal of Comparative Psychology, 108,* 179–188.

Schacter, D. L. (1987). Implicit memory: History and current status. *Journal of Experimental Psychology: Learning, Memory, and Cognition, 13,* 501–518.

Schacter, D. L. (1995a). Introduction. In M. Gazzaniga (Ed.), *The cognitive neurosciences* (pp. 1291–1293). Cambridge, MA: MIT Press.

Schacter, D. L. (1995b). Implicit memory: A new frontier for cognitive neuroscience. In M. Gazzaniga (Ed.), *The cognitive neurosciences* (pp. 815–824). Cambridge, MA: MIT Press.

Schacter, D. L. (1998). Memory and awareness. *Science, 280,* 59–60.

Schacter, D. L., & Tulving, E. (1994). What are the memory systems of 1994? In D. L. Schacter & E. Tulving (Eds.), *Memory systems 1994* (pp. 1–38). Cambridge, MA: MIT Press.

Schatz, B., Beugnon, G., & Lachaud, J.-P. (1994). Time-place learning by an invertebrate, the ant *Ectatomma ruidum* Roger. *Animal Behaviour, 48,* 236–238.

Schenk, F., Grobety, M. C., Lavenex, P., & Lipp, H.-P. (1995). Dissociation between basic components of spatial memory in rats. In E. Alleva, A. Fasolo, H.-P. Lipp, L. Nadel, & L. Ricceri (Eds.), *Behavioural brain research in naturalistic and seminaturalistic settings* (pp. 277–300). Dordrecht, The Netherlands: Kluwer Academic Publishers.

Schiffrin, R. M. (1988). Attention. In R. C. Atkinson, R. J. Herrnstein, G. Lindzey, & R. D. Luce (Eds.), *Stevens' handbook of experimental psychology* (Vol. 2, pp. 739–811). New York: John Wiley.

Schiller, P. H. (1957). Innate motor action as a basis of learning. In C. H. Schiller (Ed.), *Instinctive behavior* (pp. 264–287). New York: International Universities Press.

Schlupp, I., & Ryan, M. J. (1997). Male sailfin mollies (*Poecilia latipinna*) copy the mate choice of other males. *Behavioral Ecology, 8,* 104–107.

Schmajuk, N. A., Lam, Y.-W., & Gray, J. A. (1996). Latent inhibition: A neural network approach. *Journal of Experimental Psychology: Animal Behavior Processes, 22,* 321–349.

Schöne, H. (1984). *Spatial orientation: The spatial control of behavior in animals and man.* Princeton: Princeton University Press.

Schwagmeyer, P. L. (1995). Searching today for tomorrow's mates. *Animal Behviour, 50,* 759–767.

Schwartz, B., & Williams, D. R. (1972). The role of the response-reinforcer contingency in negative automaintenance. *Journal of the Experimental Analysis of Behavior, 17,* 351–357.

Searcy, W. A., Coffman, S., & Raikow, D. F. (1994). Habituation, recovery and the similarity of song types within repertoires in red-winged blackbirds (*Agelaius phoeniceus*) (Aves, Emberizdae). *Ethology, 98,* 38–49.

Searle, J. R. (1980). Minds, brains, and programs. *The Behavioral and Brain Sciences, 3,* 417–424.

Seeley, T. D. (1985). *Honey bee ecology.* Princeton, NJ: Princeton University Press.

Seeley, T. D. (1995). *The wisdom of the hive.* Cambridge, MA: Harvard University Press.

Seguinot, V., Maurer, R., & Etienne, A. S. (1993). Dead reckoning in a small mammal: The evaluation of distance. *Journal of Comparative Physiology A, 173,* 103–113.

Seidenberg, M. S., & Petitto, L. A. (1987). Communication, symbolic communication, and language: Comment on Savage-Rumbaugh, McDonald, Sevcik, Hopkins, and Rupert (1986). *Journal of Experimental Psychology: General, 116,* 279–287.

Seligman, M. E. P. (1970). On the generality of the laws of learning. *Psychological Review, 77,* 406–418.

Seyfarth, R. M., & Cheney, D. L. (1986). Vocal development in vervet monkeys. *Animal Behaviour, 34,* 1640–1658.

Seyfarth, R., & Cheney, D. (1990). The assessment by vervet monkeys of their own and another species' alarm calls. *Animal Behaviour, 40,* 754–764.

Seyfarth, R. M., & Cheney, D. L. (1992). Meaning and mind in monkeys. *Scientific American, 62*(12), 122–128.

Seyfarth, R. M., & Cheney, D. L. (1994). The evolution of social cognition in primates. In L. A. Real (Ed.), *Behavioral mechanisms in evolutionary ecology* (pp. 371–389). Chicago: University of Chicago Press.

Seyfarth, R. M., & Cheney, D. (1997). Behavioral mechanisms underlying vocal communication in nonhuman primates. *Animal Learning and Behavior, 25,* 249–267.

Seyfarth, R. M., Cheney, D. L., & Marler, P. (1980a). Monkey responses to three different alarm calls: Evidence of predator classification and semantic communication. *Science, 210,* 801–803.

Seyfarth, R. M., Cheney, D. L., & Marler, P. (1980b). Vervet monkey alarm calls: Semantic communication in a free-ranging primate. *Animal Behaviour, 28,* 1070–1094.

Shanks, D. R. (1994). Human associative learning. In N. J. Mackintosh (Ed.), *Animal learning and cognition* (pp. 335–374). San Diego, CA: Academic Press.

Shaw, K. (1995). Phylogenetic tests of the sensory exploitation model of sexual selection. *Trends in Ecology and Evolution, 10,* 117–120.

Shepard, R. N. (1984). Ecological constraints on internal representation: Resonant kinematics of perceiving, imagining, thinking, and dreaming. *Psychological Review, 91,* 417–447.

Shepard, R. N. (1987). Toward a universal law of generalization for psychological science. *Science, 237,* 1317–1323.

Shepard, R. N. (1994). Perceptual-cognitive universals as reflections of the world. *Psychonomic Bulletin and Review, 1,* 2–28.

Sherman, P. W., Reeve, H. K., & Pfennig, P. W. (1997). Recognition systems. In J. R. Krebs & N. B. Davies (Eds.), *Behavioural ecology* (4th ed.) (pp. 69–96). Oxford: Blackwell Scientific.

Sherry, D. F. (1977). Parental food-calling and the role of the young in the Burmese red junglefowl (*Gallus gallus spadiceus*). *Animal Behaviour, 25,* 594–601.

Sherry, D. (1984). Food storage by black-capped chickadees: Memory for the location and contents of caches. *Animal Behaviour, 32,* 451–464.

Sherry, D. F. (1988). Learning and adaptation in food-storing birds. In R. C. Bolles & M. D. Beecher (Eds.), *Evolution and learning* (pp. 79–95). Hillsdale, NJ: Lawrence Erlbaum Associates.

Sherry, D. F., & Duff, S. J. (1996). Behavioural and neural bases of orientation in food-storing birds. *Journal of Experimental Biology, 199,* 165–171.

Sherry, D. F., Forbes, M. R. L., Khurgel, M., & Ivy, G. O. (1993). Females have a larger hippocampus than males in the brood-parasitic brown-headed cowbird. *Proceedings of the National Academy of Sciences, 90,* 7839–7843.

Sherry, D. F., & Galef, B. G., Jr. (1984). Cultural transmission without imitation: Milk bottle opening by birds. *Animal Behaviour, 32,* 937–938.

Sherry, D. F., & Galef, B. G., Jr. (1990). Social learning without imitation: More about milk bottle opening by birds. *Animal Behaviour, 40,* 987–989.

Sherry, D. F., Jacobs, L. F., & Gaulin, S. J. C. (1992). Spatial memory and adaptive specialization of the hippocampus. *Trends in Neurosciences, 15,* 298–303.

Sherry, D. F., & Schacter, D. L. (1987). The evolution of multiple memory systems. *Psychological Review, 94,* 439–454.

Sherry, D., & Vaccarino, A. L. (1989). Hippocampus and memory for food caches in black-capped chickadees. *Behavioral Neuroscience, 103,* 308–318.

Sherry, D., Vaccarino, A. L., Buckenham, K., & Herz, R. S. (1989). The hippocampal complex of food-storing birds. *Brain, Behavior and Evolution, 34,* 308–317.

Shettleworth, S. J. (1972). Constraints on learning. *Advances in the Study of Behavior, 4,* 1–68.

Shettleworth, S. J. (1975). Reinforcement and the organization of behavior in golden hamsters: Hunger, environment, and food reinforcement. *Journal of Experimental Psychology: Animal Behavior Processes, 104,* 56–87.

Shettleworth, S. J. (1983). Function and mechanism in learning. In M. D. Zeiler & P. Harzem (Eds.), *Advances in analysis of behaviour* (Vol. 3. Biological Factors in Learning, pp. 1–39). Chichester: Wiley.

Shettleworth, S. J. (1984). Learning and behavioral ecology. In J. R. Krebs & N. B. Davies (Eds.), *Behavioural ecology* (2nd Ed.) (pp. 170–194). Oxford: Blackwell Scientific.

Shettleworth, S. J. (1985). Handling time and choice in pigeons. *Journal of the Experimental Analysis of Behavior, 44,* 139–155.

Shettleworth, S. J. (1987). Learning and foraging in pigeons: Effects of handling time and changing food availability on patch choice. In M. L. Commons, A. Kacelnik, & S. J. Shettleworth (Eds.), *Quantative analyses of behavior* (Vol. 6, pp. 115–132). Hillsdale, NJ: Lawrence Erlbaum Associates.

Shettleworth, S. J. (1988). Foraging as operant behavior and operant behavior as foraging: what have we learned? *Psychology of Learning and Motivation, 22,* 1–49.

Shettleworth, S. J. (1989). Animals foraging in the lab: problems and promises. *Journal of Experimental Psychology: Animal Behavior Processes, 15,* 81–87.

Shettleworth, S. J. (1993a). Varieties of learning and memory in animals. *Journal of Experimental Psychology: Animal Behavior Processes, 19,* 5–14.

Shettleworth, S. J. (1993b). Where is the comparison in comparative cognition? Alternative research programs. *Psychological Science, 4,* 179–184.

Shettleworth, S. J. (1994a). Commentary: What are behavior systems and what use are they? *Psychonomic Bulletin and Review, 1,* 451–456.

Shettleworth, S. J. (1994b). The varieties of learning in development: toward a common framework. In J. A. Hogan & J. J. Bolhuis (Eds.), *Causal mechanisms of behavioural development* (pp. 358–376). Cambridge: Cambridge University Press.

Shettleworth, S. J. (1995). Comparative studies of memory in food storing birds: From the field to the Skinner box. In E. Alleva, A. Fasolo, H. P. Lipp, L. Nadel, & L. Ricceri (Eds.), *Behavioral brain research in naturalistic and semi-naturalistic settings.* Dordrecht: Kluwer Academic Press.

Shettleworth, S. J., & Hampton, R. H. (1998). Adaptive specializations of spatial cognition in food storing birds? Approaches to testing a comparative hypothesis. In I. Pepperberg, R. Balda, & A. Kamil (Eds.), *Animal cognition in nature* (pp. 65–98). San Diego: Academic Press.

Shettleworth, S. J., & Juergensen, M. R. (1980). Reinforcement and the organization of behavior in golden hamsters: Brain stimulation reinforcement for seven action patterns. *Journal of Experimental Psychology: Animal Behavior Processes, 6,* 352–375.

Shettleworth, S. J., & Krebs, J. R. (1982). How marsh tits find their hoards: The roles of site preference and spatial memory. *Journal of Experimental Psychology: Animal Behavior Processes, 8,* 354–375.

Shettleworth, S. J., Krebs, J. R., Stephens, D. W., & Gibbon, J. (1988). Tracking a fluctuating environment: a study of sampling. *Animal Behaviour, 36,* 87–105.

Shettleworth, S. J., & Plowright, C. M. S. (1992). How pigeons estimate rates of prey encounter. *Journal of Experimental Psychology: Animal Behavior Processes, 18,* 219–235.

Shettleworth, S. J., Reid, P. J., & Plowright, C. M. S. (1993). The psychology of diet selection. In R. N. Hughes (Ed.), *Diet selection* (pp. 56–77). Oxford: Blackwell Scientific.

Shillito, E. E. (1963). Exploratory behaviour in the short-tailed vole, *Microtus agrestis. Behaviour, 21,* 145–154.

Shorten, M. (1954). The reaction of the brown rat towards changes in its environment. In D. Chitty & H. N. Southern (Eds.), *Control of rats and mice* (Vol. 2, pp. 307–334). Oxford: Clarendon Press.

Siegel, S., & Allan, L. G. (1996). The widespread influence of the Rescorla-Wagner model. *Psychonomic Bulletin and Review, 3,* 314–321.

Silver, R. (1990). Biological timing mechanisms with special emphasis on the parental behavior of doves. In D. A. Dewsbury (Ed.), *Contemporary issues in comparative psychology* (pp. 252–277). Sunderland, MA: Sinauer Associates.

Slater, P. J. B. (1983). The development of individual behaviour. In T. R. Halliday & P. J. B. Slater (Eds.), *Animal behaviour* (Vol. 3, *Genes, development and learning*) (pp. 82–113). Oxford: Blackwell Scientific Publications.

Slater, P. J. B., Eales, L. A., & Clayton, N. S. (1988). Song learning in zebra finches (*Taeniopygia guttata*). *Advances in the Study of Behavior, 18,* 1–33.

Slater, P. J. B., & Halliday, T. R. (Eds.). (1994). *Behaviour and evolution* . Cambridge: Cambridge University Press.

Sluckin, W. (1962). Perceptual and associative learning. *Symposia of the Zoological Society of London, 8,* 193–198.

Sluckin, W., & Salzen, E. A. (1961). Imprinting and perceptual learning. *Quarterly Journal of Experimental Psychology, 13,* 65–77.

Smith, J. D., Shields, W. E., Schull, J., & Washburn, D. A. (1997). The uncertain response in humans and animals. *Cognition, 62,* 75–97.

Smith, J. N. M., & Dawkins, R. (1971). The hunting behaviour of individual great tits in relation to spatial variations in their food density. *Animal Behaviour, 19,* 695–706.

Smith, M. C., Coleman, S. R., & Gormezano, I. (1969). Classical conditioning of the rabbit's nictitating membrane response at backward, simultaneous, and forward CS-US intervals. *Journal of Comparative and Physiological Psychology, 69,* 226–231.

Smith, P. K. (1996). Language and the evolution of mind-reading. In P. Carruthers & P. K. Smith (Eds.), *Theories of theories of mind* (pp. 344–354). Cambridge: Cambridge University Press.

Smith, W. J. (1977). *The behavior of communicating.* Cambridge, MA: Harvard University Press.

Snowdon, C. T. (1993). Linguistic phenomena in the natural communication of animals. In H. L. Roitblat, L. M. Herman, & P. E. Nachtigall (Eds.), *Language and communication: Comparative perspectives* (pp. 175–194). Hillsdale, NJ: Lawrence Erlbaum Associates.

Sokolov, E. N. (1963). *Perception and the conditioned reflex.* Oxford: Pergamon Press.

Spence, K. W. (1937). The differential response in animals to stimuli varying within a single dimension. *Psychological Review, 44,* 430–444.

Sperber, D., Cara, F., & Girotto, V. (1995). Relevance theory explains the selection task. *Cognition, 57,* 31–95.

Sperber, D., Premack, D., & Premack, A. J. (Eds.). (1995). *Causal cognition.* Oxford: Clarendon Press.

Spetch, M. L. (1995). Overshadowing in landmark learning: Touch-screen studies with pigeons and humans. *Journal of Experimental Psychology: Animal Behavior Processes, 21*(2), 166–181.

Spetch, M. L., Cheng, K., & MacDonald, S. E. (1996). Learning the configuration of a landmark array: I. Touch-screen studies with pigeons and humans. *Journal of Comparative Psychology, 110,* 55–68.

Spetch, M. L., Cheng, K., MacDonald, S. E., Linkenhoker, B. A., Kelly, D. M., & Doerkson, S. R. (1997). Use of landmark configuration in pigeons and humans: II. Generality across search tasks. *Journal of Comparative Psychology, 111,* 14–24.

Spetch, M. L., & Honig, W. K. (1988). Characteristics of pigeons' spatial working memory in an open-field task. *Animal Learning & Behavior, 16,* 123–131.

Spetch, M. L., Wilkie, D. M., & Pinel, J. P. J. (1981). Backward conditioning: A reevaluation of the empirical evidence. *Psychological Bulletin, 89,* 163–175.

Squire, L. R. (1992). Memory and the hippocampus: A synthesis from findings with rats, monkeys, and humans. *Psychological Review, 99,* 195–231.

Staddon, J. E. R. (1975). A note on the evolutionary significance of "supernormal" stimuli. *American Naturalist, 109,* 541–545.

Staddon, J. E. R. (1983). *Adaptive behavior and learning.* Cambridge: Cambridge University Press.

Staddon, J. E. R. (1989). The tyranny of anthropocentrism. *Perspectives in Ethology, 8,* 123–135.

Staddon, J. E. R., & Higa, J. J. (1996). Multiple time scales in simple habituation. *Psychological Review, 103,* 720–733.

Staddon, J. E. R., & Reid, A. K. (1987). Adaptation to reward. In A. C. Kamil, J. R. Krebs, & H. R. Pulliam (Eds.), *Foraging behavior* (pp. 497–523). New York: Plenum Press.

Stahl, J., & Ellen, P. (1974). Factors in the resoning performance of the rat. *Journal of Comparative and Physiological Psychology, 87,* 598–604.

Stamps, J. A. (1991). Why evolutionary issues are reviving interest in proximate behavioral mechanisms. *American Zoologist, 31,* 338–348.

Stamps, J. A. (1995). Motor learning and the value of familiar space. *American Naturalist, 146,* 41–58.

Stanhope, K. J. (1989). Dissociation of the effect of reinforcer type and response strength on the force of a condtioned response. *Animal Learning & Behavior, 17,* 311–321.

Stephens, D. W. (1981). The logic of risk-sensitive foraging preferences. *Animal Behaviour, 29,* 628–629.

Stephens, D. W. (1987). On economically tracking a variable environment. *Theoretical Population Biology, 32*, 15–25.

Stephens, D. W. (1991). Change, regularity, and value in the evolution of animal learning. *Behavioral Ecology, 2*, 77–89.

Stephens, D. W., & Krebs, J. R. (1986). *Foraging theory*. Princeton, NJ: Princeton University Press.

Stevens, T. A., & Krebs, J. R. (1986). Retrieval of stored seeds by marsh tits, *Parus palustris*, in the field. *Ibis, 128*, 513–525.

Stoddard, P. K., Beecher, M. D., Loesche, P., & Campbell, S. E. (1992). Memory does not constrain individual recognition in a bird with song repertoires. *Behaviour, 122*, 274–287.

Storey, A. E., Anderson, R. E., Porter, J. M., & Maccharles, A. M. (1992). Absence of parent-young recognition in kittiwakes: A re-examination. *Behaviour, 120*, 302–323.

Suboski, M. D. (1990). Releaser-induced recognition learning. *Psychological Review, 97*, 271–284.

Suboski, M. D., Bain, S., Carty, A. E., McQuoid, L. M., Seelen, M. I., & Seifert, M. (1990). Alarm reaction in acquisition and social transmission of simulated-predator recognition by zebra danio fish (*Brachydanio rerio*). *Journal of Comparative Psychology, 104*, 101–112.

Suboski, M. D., & Bartashunas, C. (1984). Mechanisms for social transmission of pecking preferences to neonatal chicks. *Journal of Experimental Psychology: Animal Behavior Processes, 10*, 182–194.

Sullivan, K. A. (1988). Age-specific profitability and prey choice. *Animal Behaviour, 36*, 613–615.

Sutherland, N. S., & Mackintosh, N. J. (1971). *Mechanisms of animal discrimination learning*. New York: Academic Press.

Sutherland, R. J., Chew, G. L., Baker, J. C., & Linggard, R. C. (1987). Some limitations on the use of distal cues in place navigation by rats. *Psychobiology, 15*, 48–57.

Sutherland, R. J., & Linggard, R. (1982). Being there: A novel demonstration of latent spatial learning in the rat. *Behavioral and Neural Biology, 36*, 103–107.

Swaddle, J. M. (1996). Reproductive success and symmetry in zebra finches. *Animal Behaviour, 51*, 203–210.

Swaddle, J. P., & Cuthill, I. C. (1994). Preference for symmetric males by female zebra finches. *Nature, 367*, 165–166.

Swartz, K. B., Chen, S., & Terrace, H. S. (1991). Serial learning by Rhesus monkeys: I. Acquisition and retention of mulitiple four-item lists. *Journal of Experimental Psychology: Animal Behavior Processes, 17*, 396–410.

Swartz, K. B., & Evans, S. (1997). Anthropomorphism, anecdotes, and mirrors. In R. W. Mitchell, N. S. Thompson, & H. L. Miles (Eds.), *Anthropomorphism, anecdotes, and animals* (pp. 296–310). Albany: State University of New York Press.

Swartzentruber, D. (1995). Modulatory mechanisms in Pavlovian conditioning. *Animal Learning and Behavior, 23*, 123–143.

Switzer, P. V., & Cristol, D. A. (in press). Avian prey-dropping behavior I: Effects of prey characteristics and social environment. *Behavioral Ecology*.

Tegeder, R. W., & Krause, J. (1995). Density dependence and numerosity in fright stimulated aggregation behaviour of shoaling fish. *Philosophical Transactions of the Royal Society of London, B, 350*, 381–390.

Templeton, J. J., & Giraldeau, L.-A. (1995). Patch assessment in foraging flocks of european starlings: evidence for the use of public information. *Behavioral Ecology, 6,* 65–72.

ten Cate, C. (1986). Sexual preferences in zebra finch (*Taeniopygia guttata*) males raised by two species (*Lonchura striata* and *Taeniopygia guttata*): I. A case of double imprinting. *Journal of Comparative Psychology, 100,* 248–252.

ten Cate, C. (1987). Sexual preferences in zebra finch males raised by two species: II. The internal representation resulting from double imprinting. *Animal Behaviour, 35,* 321–330.

ten Cate, C. (1989). Behavioral development: Towards understanding processes. *Perspectives in Ethology, 8,* 243–269.

ten Cate, C. (1994). Perceptual mechanisms in imprinting and song learning. In J. A. Hogan & J. J. Bolhuis (Eds.), *Causal mechanisms of behavioural development* (pp. 116–146). Cambridge: Cambridge University Press.

ten Cate, C., Los, L., & Schilperood, L. (1984). The influence of differences in social experience on the development of species recognition in zebra finch males. *Animal Behaviour, 32,* 852–860.

ten Cate, C., Vos, D. R., & Mann, N. (1993). Sexual imprinting and song learning; two of one kind? *Netherlands Journal of Zoology, 43,* 34–45.

Terkel, J. (1995). Cultural transmission in the black rat: Pine cone feeding. *Advances in the Study of Behavior, 24,* 119–154.

Terrace, H. S. (1984). Animal cognition. In H. L. Roitblat, T. G. Bever, & H. S. Terrace (Eds.), *Animal cognition* (pp. 7–28). Hillsdale, NJ: Lawrence Erlbaum Associates.

Terrace, H. S. (1991). Chunking during serial learning by a pigeon: I. Basic evidence. *Journal of Experimental Psychology: Animal Behavior Processes, 17,* 81–93.

Terrace, H. S. (1993). The phylogeny and ontogeny of serial memory: List learning by pigeons and monkeys. *Psychological Science, 4,* 162–169.

Terrace, H. S., Chen, S., & Newman, A. B. (1995). Serial learning with a wild card by pigeons (*Columba livia*): Effect of list length. *Journal of Comparative Psychology, 109,* 162–172.

Terrace, H. S., Pettito, L. A., Sanders, R. J., & Bever, T. G. (1979). Can an ape create a sentence? *Science, 206,* 891–902.

Thinus-Blanc, C. (1995). Spatial information processing in animals. In H. L. Roitblat & J.-A. Meyer (Eds.), *Comparative approaches to cognitive science* (pp. 241–269). Cambridge, MA: MIT Press.

Thinus-Blanc, C., Bouzouba, L., Chaix, K., Chapuis, N., Durup, M., & Poucet, B. (1987). A study of spatial parameters encoded during exploration in hamsters. *Journal of Experimental Psychology: Animal Behavior Processes, 13,* 418–427.

Thomas, D. R., Mood, K., Morrison, S., & Wiertelak, E. (1991). Peak shift revisited: A test of alternative interpretations. *Journal of Experimental Psychology: Animal Behavior Processes, 17,* 130–140.

Thomas, R. K. (1996). Investigating cognitive abilities in animals: unrealized potential. *Cognitive Brain Research, 3,* 157–166.

Thompson, C. R., & Church, R. M. (1980). An explanation of the language of a chimpanzee. *Science, 208,* 313–314.

Thompson, E., Palacios, A., & Varela, F. J. (1992). Ways of coloring: Comparative color vision as a case study for cognitive sciences. *Behavioral and Brain Sciences, 15,* 1–74.

Thompson, N. S. (1969). Individual identification and temporal patterning in the cawing of common crows. *Communications in Behavioral Biology, 4,* 29–33.

Thompson, R. F., & Spencer, W. A. (1966). Habituation: A model phenomenon for the study of neuronal substrates of behavior. *Psychological Review, 73*, 16–43.

Thompson, R. K. R. (1995). Natural and relational concepts in animals. In H. L. Roitblat & J.-A. Meyer (Eds.), *Comparative approaches to cognitive science* (pp. 175–224). Cambridge, MA: MIT Press.

Thompson, R. K. R., & Contie, C. L. (1994). Further reflections on mirror usage by pigeons: Lessons from Winnie-the-Pooh and Pinocchio too. In S. T. Parker, R. W. Mitchell, & M. L. Boccia (Eds.), *Self-awareness in animals and humans: Developmental perspectives* (pp. 392–409). Cambridge: Cambridge University Press.

Thompson, R. K. R., Oden, D. L., & Boysen, S. T. (1997). Language-naive chimpanzees (*Pan trogodytes*) judge relations between relations in a conceptual matching-to-sample task. *Journal of Experimental Psychology: Animal Behavior Processes, 23*, 31–43.

Thorndike, E. L. (1911/1970). *Animal intelligence*. Darien, CT: Hafner Publishing.

Thorpe, W. H. (1956). *Learning and instinct in animals*. London: Methuen.

Timberlake, W. (1983). The functional organization of appetitive behavior: Behavior systems and learning. In M. D. Zeiler & P. Harzem (Eds.), *Advances in analysis of behaviour* (Vol. 3, pp. 177–221). Chichester: John Wiley & Sons.

Timberlake, W. (1984). A temporal limit on the effect of future food on current performance in an analogue of foraging and welfare. *Journal of the Experimental Analysis of Behavior, 41*, 117–124.

Timberlake, W. (1990). Natural learning in laboratory paradigms. In D. A. Dewsbury (Ed.), *Contemporary issues in comparative psychology* (pp. 31–54). Sunderland, MA: Sinauer Associates.

Timberlake, W. (1994). Behavior systems, associationism, and Pavlovian conditioning. *Psychonomic Bulletin and Review, 1*, 405–420.

Timberlake, W., & Grant, D. L. (1975). Auto-shaping in rats to the presentation of another rat predicting food. *Science, 190*, 690–692.

Timberlake, W., & Peden, B. F. (1987). On the distinction between open and closed economies. *Journal of the Experimental Analysis of Behavior, 48*, 35–60.

Timberlake, W., & Washburne, D. L. (1989). Feeding ecology and laboratory predatory behavior toward live and artificial moving prey in seven rodent species. *Animal Learning & Behavior, 17*, 2–11.

Tinbergen, L. (1960). The natural control of insects in pine woods I. Factors influencing the intensity of predation by songbirds. *Archives Neerlandaises de Zoologie, 13*, 265–343.

Tinbergen, N. (1951). *The study of instinct*. Oxford: Oxford University Press.

Tinbergen, N. (1959). Comparative studies of the behaviour of gulls (Laridae): A progress report. *Behaviour, 15*, 1–70.

Tinbergen, N. (1972). *The animal in its world* (Vol. 1). Cambridge, MA: Harvard University Press.

Tinbergen, N., Broekhuysen, G. J., Feekes, F., Houghton, J. C. W., Kruuk, H., & Szulc, E. (1963). Egg shell removal by the black-headed gull, *Larus ridibundus L.*; A behaviour component of camouflage. *Behaviour, 19*, 74–117.

Tinbergen, N., & Kruyt, W. (1938/1972). On the orientation of the digger wasp *Philanthus triangulum* Fabr. (1938): III. Selective learning of landmarks. In N. Tinbergen (Ed.), *The Animal in its World* (Vol. 1, pp. 146–196). Cambridge, MA: Harvard University Press.

Tinbergen, N., & Kuenen, D. J. (1939/1957). Feeding behavior in young thrushes. In

C. H. Schiller (Ed.), *Instinctive behavior* (pp. 209–238). New York: International Universities Press.

Tinbergen, N., & Perdeck, A. C. (1950). On the stimulus situation releasing the begging response in the newly hatched herring gull chick (*Larus argentatus argentatus* Pont). *Behaviour*, *3*, 1–39.

Tinklepaugh, O. L. (1928). An experimental study of representative factors in monkeys. *Journal of Comparative Psychology*, *8*, 197–236.

Todd, I. A., & Kacelnik, A. (1993). Psychological mechanisms and the Marginal Value Theorem: dynamics of scalar memory for travel time. *Animal Behaviour*, *46*, 765–775.

Tolman, E. C. (1948). Cognitive maps in rats and men. *Psychological Review*, *55*, 189–208.

Tolman, E. C. (1949). There is more than one kind of learning. *Psychological Review*, *56*, 144–155.

Tomasello, M. (1994). The question of chimpanzee culture. In R. W. Wrangham, W. C. McGrew, F. B. M. de Waal, & P. G. Heltne (Eds.), *Chimpanzee cultures* (pp. 301–317). Cambridge, MA: Harvard University Press.

Tomasello, M. (1996). Do apes ape? In C. M. Heyes & B. G. Galef Jr. (Eds.), *Social learning in animals: The roots of culture* (pp. 319–346). San Diego: Academic Press.

Tomasello, M., & Call, J. (1997). *Primate cognition*. New York: Oxford University Press.

Tomasello, M., Davis-Dasilva, M., Camak, L., & Bard, K. (1987). Observational learning of tool-use by young chimpanzees. *Human Evolution*, *2*, 175–183.

Tooby, J., & Cosmides, L. (1995). Mapping the evolved functional organization of mind and brain. In M. Gazzaniga (Ed.), *The cognitive neurosciences* (pp. 1185–1197). Cambridge, MA: MIT Press.

Treichler, F. R., & Van Tilburg, D. (1996). Concurrent conditional discrimination tests of transitive inference by macaque monkeys: List linking. *Journal of Experimental Psychology: Animal Behavior Processes*, *22*, 105–117.

Treisman, A. (1988). Features and objects: The fourteenth Bartlett Memorial lecture. *Quarterly Journal of Experimental Psychology*, *40B*, 201–223.

Treisman, A. M., & Gelade, G. (1980). A feature integration theory of attention. *Cognitive Psychology*, *12*, 97–136.

Trivers, R. L. (1971). The evolution of reciprocal altruism. *Quarterly Review of Biology*, *46*, 35–57.

Tulving, E. (1985). How many memory systems are there? *American Psychologist*, *40*, 385–398.

Tulving, E. (1995). Organization of memory: Quo vadis? In M. Gazzaniga (Ed.), *The cognitive neurosciences* (pp. 839–847). Cambridge, MA: MIT Press.

Tulving, E., & Schacter, D. L. (1990). Priming and human memory systems. *Science*, *247*, 301–306.

Tulving, E., Schacter, D. L., & Stark, H. A. (1982). Priming effects in word-fragment completion are independent of recognition memory. *Journal of Experimental Psychology: Learning, Memory, and Cognition*, *8*, 336–342.

Tversky, A., & Kahneman, D. (1974). Judgement under uncertainty: Heuristics and biases. *Science*, *185*, 1124–1131.

Tversky, A., & Kahneman, D. (1982). Evidential impact of base rates. In D. Kahneman, P. Slovic, & A. Tversky (Eds.), *Judgement under uncertainty: Heuristics and biases* (pp. 153–160). Cambridge: Cambridge University Press.

Ugolini, A. (1987). Visual information acquired during displacement and initial orientation in *Polistes gallicus* (L.) (Hymenoptera, Vespidae). *Animal Behaviour*, 35(2), 590–595.

Urcuioli, P. J., & DeMarse, T. B. (1997). Memory processes in delayed spatial discriminations: Response intentions or response mediation? *Journal of the Experimental Amalysis of Behavior*, 67, 323–336.

Urcuioli, P. J., & Zentall, T. R. (1992). Transfer across delayed discriminations: Evidence regarding the nature of prospective working memory. *Journal of Experimental Psychology: Animal Behavior Processes*, 18, 154–173.

Vadas Jr., R. L. (1994). The anatomy of an ecological controversy: honey-bee searching behavior. *Oikos*, 69, 158–166.

Vallortigara, G., Zanforlin, M., & Pasti, G. (1990). Geometric modules in animals' spatial representations: A test with chicks (*Gallus gallus domesticus*). *Journal of Comparative Psychology*, 104, 248–254.

van Hest, A., & Steckler, T. (1996). Effects of procedural parameters on response accuracy: Lessons from delayed (non-) matching procedures in animals. *Cognitive Brain Research*, 3, 193–203.

van Hooff, J. A. R. A. M. (1994). Understanding chimpanzee understanding. In R. W. Wrangham, W. C. McGrew, F. B. M. de Waal, P. G. Heltne, & L. A. Marquardt (Eds.), *Chimpanzee cultures* (pp. 267–284). Cambridge, MA: Harvard University Press.

van Kampen, H. (1996). A framework for the study of filial imprinting and the development of attachment. *Psychonomic Bulletin & Review*, 3, 3–20.

van Kampen, H. S., & de Vos, G. J. (1995). A study of blocking and overshadowing in filial imprinting. *Quarterly Journal of Experimental Psychology*, 48B, 346–356.

van Lawick-Goodall, J. (1970). Tool-using in primates and other vertebrates. *Advances in the Study of Behavior*, 3, 195–249.

Vander Wall, S. B. (1982). An experimental analysis of cache recovery in Clark's nutcracker. *Animal Behaviour*, 30, 84–94.

Vander Wall, S. B., & Balda, R. P. (1981). Ecology and evolution of food-storage behavior in conifer-seed -caching corvids. *Zeitschrift für Tierpsychologie*, 56, 217–242.

Vauclair, J. (1996). *Animal cognition*. Cambridge, MA: Harvard University Press.

Vaughan, W., Jr. (1988). Formation of equivalence sets in pigeons. *Journal of Experimental Psychology: Animal Behavior Processes*, 14, 36–42.

Vaughan, W., Jr., & Greene, S. L. (1984). Pigeon visual memory capacity. *Journal of Experimental Psychology: Animal Behaviour Processes*, 10, 256–271.

Vidal, J.-M. (1980). The relations between filial and sexual imprinting in the domestic fowl: Effects of age and social experience. *Animal Behaviour*, 28, 880–891.

Viitala, J., Korpimaki, E., Palokangas, P., & Koivula, M. (1995). Attraction of kestrals to vole scent marks visible in ultraviolet light. *Nature*, 373, 425–427.

Vince, M. A. (1961). "String-pulling" in birds. III. The successful response in greenfinches and canaries. *Behaviour*, 17, 103–129.

Visalberghi, E. (1994). Learning processes and feeding behavior in monkeys. In B. G. Galef, M. Mainardi, & P. Valsecchi (Eds.), *Behavioral aspects of feeding. Basic and applied research on mammals* (pp. 257–270). Chur (Switzerland): Harwood Academic Publisher.

Visalberghi, E., & Fragaszy, D. M. (1990a). Do monkeys ape? In S. T. Parker & K. R. Gibson (Eds.), *"Language" and intelligence in monkeys and apes: Comparative developmental perspectives* (pp. 247–273). Cambridge: Cambridge University Press.

Visalberghi, E., & Fragaszy, D. M. (1990b). Food-washing behaviour in tufted capuchin monkeys, *Cebus apella*, and crabeating macaques, *Macaca fascicularis. Animal Behaviour, 40,* 829–836.

Visalberghi, E., & Fragaszy, D. M. (1996). Pedagogy and imitation in monkeys: Yes, no, or maybe? In D. Olson (Ed.), *Handbook of psychology and education. New models of learning, teaching and schooling* (pp. 277–301). London: Blackwell.

Visalberghi, E., Fragaszy, D. M., & Savage-Rumbaugh, S. (1995). Performance in a tool-using task by common chimpanzees (*Pan troglodytes*), bonobos (*Pan paniscus*), an orangutan (*Pongo pygmaeus*), and capuchin monkeys (*Cebus apella*). *Journal of Comparative Psychology, 109,* 52–60.

Visalberghi, E., & Limongelli, L. (1994). Lack of comprehension of cause-effect relations in tool-using capuchin monkeys (*Cebus apella*). *Journal of Comparative Psychology, 108,* 15–22.

Visalberghi, E., & Limongelli, L. (1996). Acting and understanding: Tool use revisited through the minds of capuchin monkeys. In A. Russon, K. Bard, & S. Parker (Eds.), *Reaching into thought. The minds of the great apes* (pp. 57–79). Cambridge: Cambridge University Press.

Visalberghi, E., & Trinca, L. (1989). Tool use in capuchin monkeys: Distinguishing between performing and understanding. *Primates, 30,* 511–521.

von Fersen, L., Wynne, C. D. L., Delius, J. D., & Staddon, J. E. R. (1991). Transitive inference formation in pigeons. *Journal of Experimental Psychology: Animal Behavior Processes, 17,* 334–341.

von Frisch, K. (1953). *The dancing bees* (Dora Ilse, Trans.). New York: Harcourt Brace.

von Frisch, K. (1967). *The dance language and orientation of bees.* Cambridge: Belknap Press of Harvard University Press.

von Uexküll, J. (1934/1957). A stroll through the worlds of animals and men. In C. H. Schiller (Ed.), *Instinctive behavior* (pp. 5–80). New York: International Universities Press.

Vos, D. R., Prijs, J., & ten Cate, C. (1993). Sexual imprinting in zebra finch males: A differential effect of successive and simultaneous experience with two colour morphs. *Behaviour, 126,* 137–154.

Voyer, D., Voyer, S., & Bryden, M. P. (1995). Magnitude of sex differences in spatial abilities: A meta-analysis and consideration of critical variables. *Psychological Bulletin, 117,* 250–270.

Waage, J. K. (1979). Foraging for patchily-distributed hosts by the parasitoid, *Nemeritis canescens. Journal of Animal Ecology, 48,* 353–371.

Waddington, C. H. (1966). *Principles of development and differentiation.* New York: Macmillan.

Wagner, A. R. (1978). Expectancies and the priming of STM. In S. H. Hulse, H. Fowler, & W. K. Honig (Eds.), *Cognitive processes in animal behavior* (pp. 177–209). Hillsdale, NJ: Lawrence Erlbaum Associates.

Wagner, A. R. (1981). SOP: A model of automatic memory processing in animal behavior. In N. E. Spear & R. R. Miller (Eds.), *Information processing in animals: Memory mechanisms* (pp. 5–47). Hillsdale, NJ: Lawrence Erlbaum Associates.

Wagner, A. R., Logan, F. A., Haberlandt, K., & Price, T. (1968). Stimulus selection in animal discrimination learning. *Journal of Experimental Psychology, 76,* 171–180.

Waldbauer, G. P. (1988). Asynchrony between Batesian mimics and their models. In L. P. Brower (Ed.), *Mimicry and the evolutionary process* (pp. 103–121). Chicago: University of Chicago Press.

Waldbauer, G. P., & LaBerge, W. E. (1985). Phenological relationships of wasps, bumblebees, their mimics and insectivorous birds in northern Michigan. *Ecological Entomology, 10,* 99–110.

Waldman, B., Frumhoff, P. C., & Sherman, P. W. (1988). Problems of kin recognition. *Trends in Ecology and Evolution, 3,* 8–13.

Wallman, J. (1992). *Aping language.* Cambridge: Cambridge University Press.

Walters, J. R. (1990). Anti-predatory behavior of lapwings: Field evidence of discriminative abilities. *Wilson Bulletin, 102,* 49–70.

Ward-Robinson, J., & Hall, G. (1996). Backward sensory preconditioning. *Journal of Experimental Psychology: Animal Behavior Processes, 22,* 395–404.

Warren, J. M. (1965). Primate learning in comparative perspective. In A. M. Schrier, H. F. Harlow, & F. Stollnitz (Eds.), *Behavior of nonhuman primates* (Vol. 1, pp. 249–281). New York: Academic Press.

Wasserman, E. A. (1973). Pavlovian conditioning with heat reinforcement produces stimulus-directed pecking in chicks. *Science, 181,* 875–877.

Wasserman, E. A. (1984). Animal intelligence: Understanding the minds of animals through their behavioral "ambassadors." In H. L. Roitblat, T. G. Bever, & H. S. Terrace (Eds.), *Animal cognition* (pp. 45–60). Hillsdale, NJ: Lawrence Erlbaum Associates.

Wasserman, E. A. (1986). Prospection and retrospection as processes of animal short term memory. In D. F. Kendrick, M. E. Rilling, & M. R. Denny (Eds.), *Theories of animal memory* (pp. 53–75). Hillsdale, NJ: Lawrence Erlbaum Associates.

Wasserman, E. A. (1993). Comparative cognition: Beginning the second century of the study of animal intelligence. *Psychological Bulletin, 113,* 211–228.

Wasserman, E. A. (1997). The science of animal cognition: Past, present, and future. *Journal of Experimental Psychology: Animal Behavior Processes, 23,* 123–135.

Wasserman, E. A., & Astley, S. L. (1994). A behavioral analysis of concepts: Its application to pigeons and children. *Psychology of Learning and Motivation, 31,* 73–132.

Wasserman, E. A., DeVolder, C. L., & Coppage, D. J. (1992). Non-similarity-based conceptualization in pigeons via secondary or mediated generalization. *Psychological Science, 3,* 374–379.

Wasserman, E. A., Hugart, J. A., & Kirkpatrick-Steger, K. (1995). Pigeons show same-different conceptualization after training with complex visual stimuli. *Journal of Experimental Psychology: Animal Behavior Processes, 21,* 248–252.

Watanabe, M. (1996). Reward expectancy in primate prefrontal neurons. *Nature, 382,* 629–632.

Watanabe, S. (1993). Object-picture equivalence in the pigeon: An analysis with natural concept and pseudoconcept discriminations. *Behavioural Processes, 30,* 225–232.

Watanabe, S. (1997). Visual discrimination of real objects and pictures in pigeons. *Animal Learning & Behavior, 25,* 185–192.

Watanabe, S., Lea, S. E. G., & Dittrich, W. H. (1993). What can we learn from experiments on pigeon concept discrimination? In H. P. Zeigler & H.-J. Bischof (Eds.), *Vision, brain, and behavior in birds* (pp. 351–376). Cambridge, MA: MIT Press.

Watson, P. J., & Thornhill, R. (1994). Fluctuating asymmetry and sexual selection. *Trends in Ecology and Evolution, 9,* 21–25.

Wearden, J. H., & Doherty, M. F. (1995). Exploring and developing a connectionist model of animal timing: Peak procedure and fixed-interval simulations. *Journal of Experimental Psychology: Animal Behavior Processes, 21,* 99–115.

Weary, D. M. (1996). How birds use frequency to recognize their songs. In C. F. Moss

& S. J. Shettleworth (Eds.), *Neuroethological studies of cognitive and perceptual processes* (pp. 138–157). Boulder, CO: Westview Press.

Weary, D. M., Guilford, T. C., & Weisman, R. G. (1993). A product of discriminative learning may lead to female preferences for elaborate males. *Evolution, 47,* 333–336.

Weary, D. M., & Krebs, J. R. (1992). Great tits classify songs by individual voice characteristics. *Animal Behaviour, 43,* 283–287.

Wehner, R. (1992). Arthropods. In F. Papi (Ed.), *Animal homing* (pp. 45–144). London: Chapman and Hall.

Wehner, R., & Lanfranconi, B. (1981). What do the ants know about the rotation of the sky? *Nature, 293,* 731–733.

Wehner, R., & Menzel, R. (1990). Do insects have cognitive maps? *Annual Review of Neuroscience, 13,* 403–414.

Wehner, R., & Srinivasan, M. V. (1981). Searching behaviour of desert ants, genus *Cataglyphis* (Formicidae, Hymenoptera). *Journal of Comparative Physiology A, 142,* 315–338.

Weindler, P., Wiltschko, R., & Wiltschko, W. (1996). Magnetic information affects the stellar orientation of young bird migrants. *Nature, 383,* 158–160.

Weiner, J. (1994). *The beak of the finch.* New York: Knopf.

Weiner, J. (1995). Evolution made visible. *Science, 267,* 30–33.

Weiskrantz, L. (1986). *Blindsight.* Oxford: Clarendon Press.

Welty, J. C. (1963). *The life of birds.* New York: WB Saunders.

Wenger, D., Biebach, H., & Krebs, J. R. (1991). Free-running circadian rhythm of a learned feeding pattern in starlings. *Naturwissenschaften, 78,* 87–89.

Wenner, A. M., Meade, D. E., & Friesen, L. J. (1991). Recruitment, search behavior, and flight ranges of honey bees. *American Zoologist, 31,* 768–782.

Wenner, A. M., & Wells, P. H. (1990). *Anatomy of a controversy.* New York: Columbia University Press.

West, M. J., & King, A. P. (1988). Female visual displays affect the development of male song in the cowbird. *Nature, 334,* 244–246.

Westergaard, C. G., & Fragaszy, D. M. (1987). The manufacture and use of tools by capuchin monkeys (*Cebus apella*). *Journal of Comparative Psychology, 101,* 159–168.

White, K. G., Ruske, A. C., & Colombo, M. (1996). Memory procedures, performance and processes in pigeons. *Cognitive Brain Research, 3,* 309–317.

Whiten, A. (1994). Grades of mindreading. In C. Lewis & P. Mitchell (Eds.), *Children's early understanding of mind: Origins and development* (pp. 47–70). Hove, UK: Lawrence Erlbaum Associates.

Whiten, A. (1996). When does smart behaviour-reading become mind-reading? In P. Carruthers & P. K. Smith (Eds.), *Theories of theories of mind* (pp. 277–292). Cambridge: Cambridge University Press.

Whiten, A., & Byrne, R. W. (1988). Tactical deception in primates. *The Behavioral and Brain Sciences, 11,* 233–273.

Whiten, A., Custance, D. M., Gomez, J.-C., Teixidor, P., & Bard, K. A. (1996). Imitative learning of artificial fruit processing in children (*Homo sapiens*) and chimpanzees (*Pan troglodytes*). *Journal of Comparative Psychology, 110,* 3–14.

Whiten, A., & Ham, R. (1992). On the nature and evolution of imitation in the animal kingdom: Reappraisal of a century of research. *Advances in the Study of Behavior, 21,* 239–283.

Whitlow, J. W. Jr. (1975). Short-term memory in habituation and dishabituation. *Journal of Experimental Psychology: Animal Behavior Processes, 104,* 189–206.

Whitlow, J. W. Jr., & Wagner, A. R. (1984). Memory and habituation. In L. Petrinovich & H. V. S. Peeke (Eds.), *Habituation, sensitization, and behavior* (pp. 103–153). New York: Academic Press.

Wiegmann, D. D., Real, L. A., Capone, T. A., & Ellner, S. (1996). Some distinguishing features of models of search behavior and mate choice. *American Naturalist, 147*, 188–204.

Wiley, R. H. (1994). Errors, exaggeration, and deception in animal communication. In L. A. Real (Ed.), *Behavioral mechanisms in evolutionary ecology* (pp. 157–189). Chicago: University of Chicago Press.

Wiley, R. H., & Richards, D. G. (1982). Adaptations for acoustic communication in birds: Sound transmission and signal detection. In D. E. Kroodsma & R. H. Miller (Eds.), *Acoustic communication in birds* (pp. 131–181). New York: Academic Press.

Wilkie, D. M. (1995). Time-place learning. *Current Directions in Psychological Science, 4*, 85–89.

Wilkie, D. M., & Summers, R. J. (1982). Pigeons' spatial memory: Factors affecting delayed matching of key location. *Journal of the Experimental Analysis of Behavior, 37*, 45–56.

Wilkie, D. M., Willson, R. J., & Kardal, S. (1989). Pigeons discriminate pictures of a geographic location. *Animal Learning & Behavior, 17*, 163–171.

Wilkinson, G. S. (1984). Reciprocal food sharing in the vampire bat. *Nature, 308*, 181–184.

Williams, B. A. (1988). Reinforcement, choice, and response strength. In R. C. Atkinson (Ed.), *Stevens handbook of experimental psychology* (pp. 167–244).

Williams, B. A. (1994). Reinforcement and choice. In N. J. Mackintosh (Ed.), *Animal learning and cognition* (pp. 81–108). New York: Academic Press.

Williams, D. A., & LoLordo, V. M. (1995). Time cues block the CS, but the CS does not block time cues. *Quarterly Journal of Experimental Psychology, 48B*, 97–116.

Williams, D. A., Overmier, J. B., & LoLordo, V. M. (1992). A reevaluation of Rescorla's early dictums about Pavlovian conditioned inhibition. *Psychological Bulletin, 111*, 275–290.

Williams, D. R., & Williams, H. (1969). Auto-maintenance in the pigeon: Sustained pecking despite contingent non-reinforcement. *Journal of the Experimental Analysis of Behavior, 12*, 511–520.

Williams, G. C. (1966). *Adaptation and natural selection.* Princeton, NJ: Princeton University Press.

Wilson, B., Mackintosh, N. J., & Boakes, R. A. (1985). Transfer of relational rules in matching and oddity learning by pigeons and corvids. *Quarterly Journal of Experimental Psychology, 37B*, 313–332.

Wilson, E. O. (1975). *Sociobiology.* Cambridge, MA: Belknap Press.

Wiltschko, W., & Balda, R. P. (1989). Sun compass orientation in seed-caching scrub jays (*Aphelocoma coerulescens*). *Journal of Comparative Physiology A, 164*, 717–721.

Wimmer, H., & Perner, J. (1983). Beliefs about beliefs: Representation and constraining function of of wrong beliefs in young children's understanding of deception. *Cognition, 13*, 103–128.

Wixted, J. T. (1993). A signal detection analysis of memory for nonoccurence in pigeons. *Journal of Experimental Psychology: Animal Behavior Processes, 19*, 400–411.

Wixted, J. T., & Ebbesen, E. E. (1991). On the form of forgetting. *Psychological Science, 2*, 409–415.

Woolfenden, G. E., & Fitzpatrick, J. W. (1984). *The Florida scrub jay: Demography of a cooperatively breeding vird.* Princeton, NJ: Princeton University Press.

Wright, A. A. (1972). Psychometric and psychophysical hue discrimination functions for the pigeon. *Vision Research, 12,* 1447–1464.

Wright, A. A. (1989). Memory processing by pigeons, monkeys, and people. *Psychology of Learning and Motivation, 24,* 25–70.

Wright, A. A. (1991). A detection and decision process model of matching to sample. In M. L. Commons, J. A. Nevin, & M. C. Davison (Eds.), *Signal detection: Mechanisms, models, and applications* (pp. 191–219). Hillsdale, NJ: Lawrence Erlbaum Associates.

Wright, A. A. (1994). Primacy effects in animal memory and human nonverbal memory. *Animal Learning & Behavior, 22,* 219–223.

Wright, A. A., Cook, R. G., & Rivera, J. J. (1988). Concept learning by pigeons: Matching-to-sample with trial-unique video picture stimuli. *Animal Learning & Behavior, 16,* 436–444.

Wright, A. A., Cook, R. G., Rivera, J. J., Shyan, M. R., Neiworth, J. J., & Jitsumori, M. (1990). Naming, rehearsal, and interstimulus interval effects in memory processing. *Journal of Experimental Psychology: Learning, Memory, and Cognition, 16,* 1043–1059.

Wright, A. A., & Rivera, J. J. (1997). Memory of auditory lists by rhesus monkeys (*Macaca mulatta*). *Journal of Experimental Psychology: Animal Behavior Processes, 23,* 441–449.

Wright, A. A., Santiago, H. C., Sands, S. F., Kendrick, D. F., & Cook, R. G. (1985). Memory processing of serial lists by pigeons, monkeys, and people. *Science, 229,* 287–289.

Wright, A. A., Urcuioli, P. J., & Sands, S. F. (1986). Proactive interference in animal memory. In D. F. Kendrick, M. E. Rilling, & M. R. Denny (Eds.), *Theories of animal memory* (pp. 101–125). Hillsdale, NJ: Lawrence Erlbaum Associates.

Wright, A. A., & Watkins, M. J. (1987). Animal learning and memory and their relation to human learning and memory. *Learning and Motivation, 18,* 131–146.

Wynn, K. (1992). Addition and subtraction by human infants. *Nature, 358,* 749–750.

Wynn, K. (1995). Infants possess a system of numerical knowledge. *Current Directions in Psychological Science, 4,* 172–177.

Wynne, C. D. L. (1995). Reinforcement accounts for transitive inference performance. *Animal Learning & Behavior, 23,* 207–217.

Wyttenbach, R. A., May, M. L., & Hoy, R. R. (1996). Categorical perception of sound frequency by crickets. *Science, 273,* 1542–1544.

Yerkes, R. M., & Morgulis, S. (1909). The method of Pawlow in animal psychology. *Psychological Bulletin, 6,* 257–273.

Yoerg, S. I. (1991). Ecological frames of mind: The role of cognition in behavioral ecology. *Quarterly Review of Biology, 66,* 287–301.

Yoerg, S. I., & Kamil, A. C. (1991). Integrating cognitive ethology with cognitive psychology. In C. A. Ristau (Ed.), *Cognitive ethology: the minds of other animals* (pp. 273–289). Hillsdale, NJ: Lawrence Erlbaum Associates.

Young, M. E. (1995). On the origin of personal causal theories. *Psychonomic Bulletin and Review, 2,* 83–104.

Young, M. E., & Wasserman, E. A. (1997). Entropy detection by pigeons: Response to mixed visual displays after same-different discrimination training. *Journal of Experimental Psychology: Animal Behavior Processes, 23,* 157–170.

Zach, R. (1979). Shell dropping: decision making and optimal foraging in northwestern crows. *Behaviour, 68,* 106–117.

Zahavi, A. (1975). Mate selection—a selection for a handicap. *Journal of Theoretical Biology, 67*, 603–605.

Zahavi, A. (1996). The evolution of communal roosts as information centers and the pitfall of group selection: A rejoinder to Richner and Heeb. *Behavioral Ecology, 7*, 118–119.

Zeldin, R. K., & Olton, D. S. (1986). Rats acquire spatial learning sets. *Journal of Experimental Psychology: Animal Behavior Processes, 12*, 412–419.

Zentall, T. R. (1996). An analysis of imitative learning in animals. In C. M. Heyes & B. G. Galef Jr. (Eds.), *Social learning in animals: The roots of culture* (pp. 221–243). San Diego: Academic Press.

Zentall, T. R., & Galef, B. G., Jr. (Eds.). (1988). *Social learning: Psychological and biological perspectives* . Hillsdale, NJ: Lawrence Erlbaum Associates.

Zentall, T. R., & Sherburne, L. M. (1994). Transfer of value from S+ to S- in a simultaneous discrimination. *Journal of Experimental Psychology: Animal Behavior Processes, 20*, 176–183.

Zentall, T. R., Sherburne, L. M., Roper, K. L., & Kraemer, P. J. (1996). Value transfer in a simultaneous discrimination appears to result from within-event Pavlovian conditioning. *Journal of Experimental Psychology: Animal Behavior Processes, 22*, 68–75.

Zentall, T. R., Steirn, J. N., & Jackson-Smith, P. (1990). Memory strategies in pigeons' performance of a radial-arm-maze analog task. *Journal of Experimental Psychology: Animal Behavior Processes, 16*, 358–371.

Zentall, T. R., Sutton, J. E., & Sherburne, L. M. (1996). True imitative learning in pigeons. *Psychological Science, 7*, 343–346.

Zentall, T. R., Urcuioli, P. J., Jagielo, J. A., & Jackson-Smith, P. (1989). Interaction of sample dimension and sample-comparison mapping on pigeons' performance of delayed conditional discriminations. *Animal Learning & Behavior, 17*, 172–178.

Zohar, O., & Terkel, J. (1996). Social and environmental factors modulate the learning of pine-cone stripping techniques by black rats, *Rattus rattus*. *Animal Behaviour, 51*, 611–618.

Zoladek, L., & Roberts, W. A. (1978). The sensory basis of spatial memory in the rat. *Animal Learning & Behavior, 6*, 77–81.

Zolman, J. F. (1982). Ontogeny of learning. *Perspectives in Ethology, 5*, 295–323.

Zuberbuhler, K., Noe, R., & Seyfarth, R. M. (1997). Diana monkey long-distance calls: Messages for conspecifics and predators. *Animal Behaviour, 53*, 589–604.

Credits

Chapter 1

1.2 Boag, P. T. (1984). The heritability of external morphology in Darwin's ground finches (*Geospiza*) on Isla Daphne Major, Galapagos. *Evolution, 37*, 877–894. Redrawn with permission from the journal *Evolution*.

1.2 Boag, P. T., & Grant, P. R. (1984). The classical case of character release: Darwin's finches (*Geospiza*) on Isla Daphne Major, Galapagos. *Biological Journal of the Linnean Society, 22*, 243–287.

1.3 Marler, P., & Peters, S. (1989). Species differences in auditory responsiveness in early vocal learning. In R. J. Dooling & S. H. Hulse (eds.), *The Comparative Psychology of Audition: Perceiving Complex Sounds*, 243–373. Hillsdale, NJ: Erlbaum.

1.5. Clutton-Brock, T. H., & Harvey, P. H. (1984). Comparative approaches to investigating adaptation. J. R. Krebs & N. B. Davies, *Behavioral Ecology: An Evolutionary Approach*, 7–29.

1.6 Sherry, D. F., Vaccarino, A. L., Buckenham, K., & Herz, R. S. (1989). The hippocampal complex of food-storing birds. *Brain, Behavior and Evolution, 34*, 308–317. Redrawn with permission of S. Karger AG, Basel.

1.7 Ridley, M. (1993). *Evolution*, 365.

1.8 Ridley, M. (1993). *Evolution*, 475.

1.9 Brooks, D. R., & McLennan, D. A. (1991). *Phylogeny, Ecology, and Behavior*, 163. Published by University of Chicago Press. Copyright © 1991 by University of Chicago Press.

1.10 Hogan, J. A. (1988). Cause and function in the development of behavior systems. E. M. Blass, *Handbook of Behavioral Neurobiology, 9*, 63–106.

1.11 Shettleworth, S. J. (1987). Learning and foraging in pigeons: Effects of handling time and changing food availability on patch choice. M. L. Commons, A. Kacelnik, & S. J. Shettleworth, *Quantitative Analysis of Behavior (Foraging)*, 6, 115–132.

1.12 Healy, S. D., Clayton, N. S., & Krebs, J. R. (1994). Development of hippocampal specialisation in two species of tit (*Parus spp.*). *Behavioural Brain Research*, 61, 23–38.

1.13 Gaulin, S. J. C. (1995). Does evolutionary theory predict sex differences in the brain? In M. Gazzaniga (ed.), *The Cognitive Neurosciences*, 1211–1225, published by MIT Press. Copyright © 1995 by MIT Press.

1.14 Gaulin, S. J. C. (1995). Does evolutionary theory predict sex differences in the brain? In M. Gazzaniga (ed.), *The Cognitive Neurosciences*, 1211–1225, published by MIT Press. Copyright © 1995 by MIT Press.

1.15 Welty, J. C. (1963). *The Life of Birds*. Copyright © 1963 by W. B. Saunders Company Ltd.

B1.1 Redrawn with permission from *Nature*, 373, Cowey, A. & Stoerig, P., Blindsight in monkeys, 247–249. Copyright © 1995. Macmillan Magazines Limited.

B1.3 Redrawn with permission from *Science, 188*, Bitterman, M. E., The comparative analysis of learning, 699–709. Copyright © 1975 American Association for the Advancement of Science.

T1.1 Krebs, J. R. & Davies, N. B. (1981). *An Introduction to Behavioural Ecology*, 34.

Chapter 2

2.1 von Uexkull, J. (1934/1957). A stroll through the worlds of animals and men. In C. H. Schiller (ed.), *Instinctive Behavior*, 5–80. Published by International Universities Press, Inc.

2.2 Endler, J. A. (1992a). Signals, signal conditions, and the direction of evolu-

tion. *American Naturalist, 139,* Supplement, S125–S153. Published by University of Chicago Press. Copyright © 1992 by University of Chicago Press.

2.3 Welty, J. C. (1963). *The Life of Birds*. Copyright © 1963 by W. B. Saunders Company, Ltd.

2.4 Redrawn from *Animal Behaviour, 45,* Johnstone, R. E., Derzie, A., Chiang, G., Jernigan, P., & Lee, H.-C, Inividual scent signatures in golden hamsters: evidence for specialization of function, 1061–1070, Copyright 1993, by permission of the publisher Academic Press.

2.5 Moss, C. F., & Schnitzler, H.-U. (1989). Accuracy of target ranging in echolocating bats: Acoustic information processing. *Jounal of Comparative Physiology A, 165,* 383–393. Copyright © 1989 by Springer-Verlag.

2.6 Muntz, W. R. A. (1974). Behavioural studies of vision in a fish and possible relationships to the environment. M. A. Ali, *Vision in Fishes*, 705–717.

2.7 Redrawn with permission from *Nature, 379,* Ramachandran, V. S., Tyler, C. W., Gregory, R. L., Rogers-Ramachandran, D., Duensing, S., Pillsbury, C., & Ramachandran, C., Rapid adaptive camouflage in tropical flounders, 815–818. Copyright © 1996. Macmillan Magazines Limited.

2.8 Wiley, R. H. (1994). Errors, exaggeration, and deception in animal communication. In L. A. Real (ed.), *Behavioral Mechanisms in Evolutionary Biology*, 157–189. Published by University of Chicago Press. Copyright © 1994 by University of Chicago Press.

2.9a Redrawn from *Vision Research, 12,* Wright, A. A., Psychometric and psychophysical hue discrimination functions for the pigeon, 1447–1464. Copyright © 1972, with kind permission from Elsevier Science Ltd., The Boulevard, Langford Lane, Kidlington 0x5 1GB, UK.

2.9b Redrawn with permission from Blough, D. S., Stimulus generalization as signal detection in pigeons. *Science, 158*, 940–941. Copyright © 1967 American Association for the Advancement of Science.

2.11 Dawkins, M. S., & Guilford, T., (1994). Design of an intention signal in the bluehead wrasse (*Thalassoma bifacsciatum*). *Proceeds of the Royal Society of London, B, 257*, 123–128. Published by The Royal Society.

2.12 Basolo, A. L. (1995). A further examination of a pre-existing bias favouring a sword in the genus *Xiphophorus. Animal Behaviour, 50*, 366.

2.13 Redrawn from *Animal Behaviour, 19*, Dawkins, M., Perceptual changes in chicks: Another look at the 'search image' concept, 566–574, 1971a, by permission of the Academic Press.

2.14 Treisman, A. M., & Gelade, G. (1980). A feature integration theory of attention. E. Hunt, *Cognitive Psychology, 12*, 97–36.

2.15 Cook, R. G. (1992). Dimensional organization and texture discrimination in pigeons. *Journal of Experimental Psychology: Animal Behavior Processes, 18*, 354–363. Copyright © 1992 by the American Psychological Association. Adapted with permission.

2.16a Blough, P. M. (1992b). Detectibility and choice during visual search: Joint effects of sequential priming and discriminability. *Animal Learning and Behavior, 20*, 293–300, Redrawn by permission of the Psychonomic Society, Inc.

2.16b Blough, P. M. (1989). Attentional priming and visual search in pigeons. *Journal of Experimental Psychology: Animal Behavior Processes, 15*, 358–365. Copyright © 1989 by the American Psychological Association. Adapted with permission.

2.17 von Uexkull, J. (1934/1957). A stroll through the worlds of animals and men. In C. H. Schiller (ed.), *Instinctive Behavior*, 5–80. Published by International Universities Press, Inc.

2.18 Bond, A. B. (1983). Visual search and selection of natural stimuli in the pigeon: The attention threshold hypothesis. *Journal of Experimental Psychology: Animal Behavior Processes, 9*, 292–306. Copyright © 1983 by the American Psychological Association. Adapted with permission.

2.19 Pietrewicz, A. T., & Kamil, A. C. (1981). Search images and the detection of cryptic prey: An operant approach. A. C. Kamil & T. G. Sargent, *Foraging Behavior: Ecological, ethological and psychological approaches*, 311–331.

2.20 Reid, P. J., & Shettleworth, S. J. (1992). Detection of cryptic prey: Search image or search rate? *Journal of Experimental Psychology: Animal Behavior Processes, 18*, 273–286. Copyright © 1992 by the American Psychological Association. Adapted with permission.

2.21 Langley, C. M. (1996). Search images: Selective attention to specific visual features of prey. *Journal of Experimental Psychology: Animal Behavior Processes, 22*, 152–163. Copyright © 1996 by the American Psychological Association. Adapted with permission.

2.22 Redrawn with permission from *Nature, 333*, Godin, J.-G. & Smith, S. A., A fitness cost of foraging in the guppy, 69–71. Copyright © 1988. Macmillan Magazines Limited.

B2.1 Redrawn with permission from *Nature, 357*, Moller, A. P., Female swallow preference of symmetrical male sexual ornaments, 238–240. Copyright © 1992. Macmillan Magazines Limited.

Chapter 3

3.2 Cheng, K. (1986). A purely geometric module in the rat's spatial representation. *Cognition, 23,* 149–178.

3.5b Colwill, R. M. (1996). Detecting associations in Pavlovian conditioning and instrumental learning in vertebrates and in invertebrates. C. F. Moss & S. J. Shettleworth, *Neuroethological Studies of Cognitive and Perceptual Processes,* 31–62.

3.6b Rescorla, R. A. (1988a). Pavlovian conditioning: It's not what you think it is. *American Psychologist, 43,* 151–160. Copyright © 1988 by the American Psychological Association. Adapted with permission.

3.10 Rescorla, R. A. & Furrow, D. R. (1977). Stimulus similarity as a determinant of Pavlovian conditioning. *Journal of Experimental Psychology: Animal Behavior Processes, 3,* 203–215. Copyright © 1977 by the American Psychological Association. Adapted with permission.

3.11 From *Psychonomic Science, 3,* Boice, T., & Denny, M. R. The conditioned licking response in rats as a function of the CS-UCS interval. 93–94, 1965. Redrawn by permission of Psychonomic Society, Inc.

3.11 Rescorla, R. A. (1988b). Behavioral studies of Pavlovian conditioning. *Annual Review of Neuroscience, 11,* 329–352. With permission, from the Annual Review of Neuroscience, vol. 11, © 1988, by Annual Reviews Inc.

3.11 Smith, M. C., Coleman, S. R., & Gormezano, I. (1969). Classical conditioning of the rabbit's nictitating membrane response at backward, simultaneous, and forward CS-US intervals. *Journal of Comparative and Psychological Psychology, 69,* 226–231. Copyright © 1969 by the American Psychological Association. Adapted with permission.

3.11 From *The Principles of Learning and Behavior* by M. Domjan. Copyright © 1998, 1993, 1986, 1982 Brooks/Cole Publishing Company,

Pacific Grove, CA 93950, a division of International Thomson Publishing Inc. By permission of the publisher.

3.12 Barnet, R. C., Arnold, H. M., & Miller, R. R. (1991). Simultaneous conditioning demonstrated in second-order conditioning: Evidence for similar associative structure in forward and simultaneous conditioning. *Learning and Motivation, 22,* 261–262.

3.14 Timberlake, W. (1994). Behavior systems, associationism, and Pavlovian conditioning. *Psychonomic Bulletin and Review, 1,* 405–420, Redrawn by permission of the Psychonomic Society, Inc.

3.15 Hollis, K. L. (1984). The biological function of Pavlovian conditioning: The best defense is a good offense. *Journal of Experimental Psychology: Animal Behavior Processes, 10,* 413–425. Copyright © 1984 by the American Psychological Association. Adapted with permission.

B3.1 From *Psychonomic Science, 26,* Domjan, M. & Wilson, N. E. Specificity of cue to consequence in aversion learning in the rat, 143–145, 1972. Redrawn by permission of Psychonomic Society, Inc.

B3.2a Lehrer, M. (1993) Why do bees turn back and look? *Journal of Comparative Pysiology A, 172,* 549–563. Copyright © 1993 by Springer-Verlag.

B3.2b Redrawn from *Animal Behaviour, 47,* Laverty, T. M., Bumble bee learning and flower morphology, 531–545, 1994, by permission of the publisher Academic Press Limited London.

Chapter 4

4.1 Groves, P. M., & Thompson, R. F. (1970). Habituation: A dual-process theory. *Psychological Review, 77,* 419–450. Copyright © 1970 by the American Psychological Association. Adapted with permission.

4.2 Davis, M., & File, S. E. (1984).

Intrinsic and extrinsic mechanisms of habituation and sensitization: Implications for the design and analysis of experminents. *Habituation, Sensitization, and Behavior*, 287–323.

4.3 Davis, M. (1970). Effects of interstimulus interval length and variability on startle-response habituation in the rat. *Journal of Comparative and Psychological Psychology, 72*, 177–192. Copyright © 1970 by the American Psychological Association. Adapted with permission.

4.4 Redrawn with permission from *Science, 175,* Carew, T., Pinsker, H. M., & Kandel, E. R. Long-term habituation of a defensive withdrawal reflex in aplysia, 451–454. Copyright © 1972 American Association for the Advancement of Science.

4.5 From: *Introduction to Comparative Cognition* by Roitblat, © 1987 by W. H. Freeman and Company. Used with permission.

4.7 McLaren, I. P. L., Kaye, H., & Mackintosh, N. J. (1989). An associative theory of the representation of stimuli: Applications of perceptual learning and latent inhibition. R. G. M. Morris, *Parallel distributed processing*, 102–103. Redrawn by permission of Oxford University Press.

4.8 Horn, G. (1985). *Memory, Imprinting, and the Brain*, 38–167. Redrawn by permission of Oxford University Press.

4.9 Eiserer, L. A. & Hoffman, H. S. (1973). Priming of ducklings' responses by presenting an imprinted stimulus. *Journal of Comparative and Psychological Psychology, 82*, 345–359. Copyright © 1973 by the American Psychological Association. Adapted with permission.

4.10 Eiserer, L. A. (1980). Development of filial attachment to static visual features of an imprinting object. *Animal Learning & Behavior, 8*, 159–166, Redrawn by permission of the Psychonomic Society, Inc.

4.11 Bateson, P. (1990). Is imprinting such a special case? *Philosophical Transactions of the Royal Society of London, B, 329*, 125–131. Published by The Royal Society.

4.12 Bateson, P. (1979). How do sensitive periods arise and what are they for? *Animal Behaviour, 27*, 481.

4.13 Redrawn from *Animal Behaviour, 28,* Vidal, J.-M., The relations between filial and sexual imprinting in the domestic fowl: Effects of age and social experience, 880–891, 1980, by permission of the publisher Academic Press.

4.14 Redrawn with permission from *Nature, 295*, Bateson, P., Preferences for cousins in Japanese quail, 236–237. Copyright © 1982. Macmillan Magazines Limited.

4.15 Redrawn from *Animal Behaviour, 35*, ten Cate, C. Sexual preferences in zebra finch males raised by two species: II. The internal representation resulting from double imprinting, 321–330, 1987, by permission of the publisher Academic Press.

4.16 Immelmann, K., Prove, R., Lassek, R., & Bischof, H.-J. (1991). Influence of adult courtship experience on the development of sexual preferences in zebra finch males. *Animal Behaviour, 42*, 83–89.

4. 17 Redrawn from *Trends in Ecology and Evolution, 3,* Waldman, B., Frumhoff, P. C., & Sherman, P. W., Problems of kin recognition. 8–13. Copyright © 1988, with permission from Elsevier Science.

4.18 Redrawn from *Animal Behaviour, 34,* Holmes, W. G., Kin recognition by phenotype matching in female Belding's ground squirrels, 38–47, 1986a, by permission of the publisher Academic Press.

4.18 Redrawn from *Animal Behaviour, 34,* Holmes, W. G., Identification of paternal half-siblings by captive Belding's ground squirrels, 321–327, 1993, by permission of the publisher Academic Press.

4.18 Krebs, J. R. & Davies, N. B. (1993). *An Introduction to Behavioural Ecology*. (3 ed.).

B4.1 Falls, B., & Brooks, R. J. (1975). Individual recognition by song in white-throated sparrows. II. Effects of location. *Canadian Journal of Zoology*, 53, 1412–1420.

B4.2a Davies, N. B., Brooke, M. D. L., & Kacelnik, A. (1996). Recognition errors and probability of parasitism determine whether reed warblers should accept or reject mimetic cuckoo eggs. *Proceedings of the Royal Society of London B, 263*, 925–931. Published by The Royal Society.

B4.2b Redrawn with permission from *Nature, 362*, Lotem, A., Learning to recognize nestlings is maladaptive for cuckoo, *Cuculus canorus*, hosts, 743–745. Copyright © 1993, Macmillan Magazines Limited.

B4.3 Redrawn with permission from *Science, 250*, Brennan, P., Kaba, H., & Keverne, E. B., Olfactory recognition: A simple memory system, 1223–1226. Copyright © 1990 American Association for the Advancement of Science.

Chapter 5

5.1 Tinbergen, N. (1951). *The Study of Instinct*, 28–39. Redrawn by permission of Oxford University Press.

5.2 Heiligenberg, W. (1974). Processes governing behavioral states of readiness. *Advances in the Study of Behavior, 5*, 173–200.

5.3 Behaviour Supplement 15, 1967. Published by Brill, Leiden, the Netherlands.

5.4 Nelson, D. A. & Marler, P. (1990). The perception of birdsong and the ecological concept of signal space. In W. C. Stebbins & M. A. Berkely (eds.). *Comparative Perception: Complex Signals* (Vol. 2, pp. 443–477). Copyright © 1990 by John Wiley and Sons,

Inc. Adapted by permission of John Wiley and Sons, Inc.

5.5 Dooling, R. J., Brown, S. D., Klump, G. M., & Okanoya, K. (1992). Auditory perception of conspecific and heterospecific vocalizations in birds: Evidence for special processes. *Journal of Comparative Psychology, 106*, 20–28. Copyright © 1992 by the American Psychological Association. Adapted with permission.

5.6 Brown, S. D. & Dooling, R. J. (1993). Perception of conspecific faces by budgerigars (*Melopsittacus undulatus*): II. Synthetic models. *Journal of Comparative Psychology, 107*, 48–60. Copyright © 1993 by the American Psychological Association. Adapted with permission.

5.7 Hanson, H. M. (1959). Effects of discrimination training on stimulus generalization. *Journal of Experimental Psychology, 58*, 321–324.

5.9 Spence, K. W. (1937). The differential response in animals to stimuli varying within a single dimension. *Psychological Review, 44*, 430–444.

5.10 Blough, D. S. (1975). Steady state data and a quantitative model of operant generalization and discrimination. *Journal of Experimental Psychology: Animal Behavior Processes, 1*, 3–21. Copyright © 1975 by the American Psychological Association. Adapted with permission.

5.11 Mackintosh, N. J., McGonigle, B., Holgate, V., & Vanderver, V. (1968). Factors underlying improvement in serial reversal learning. *Canadian Journal of Psychology, 22*, 85–95. Copyright © 1968 Canadian Psychological Association. Redrawn with permission.

5.12 Warren, J. M. (1965). Primate learning in comparative perspective. A. M. Schrier, H. F. Harlow, & F. Stollnitz, *Behavior of Nonhuman Primates, 1*, 249–281.

5.13 Redrawn with permission from

Science, 166, Attention shifts in a maintained discrimination, 125–126. Copyright © 1969 American Association for the Advancement of Science.

5.14 Bhatt, R. S., Wasserman, E. A., Reynolds, W. F., & Knauss, K. S. (1988). Conceptual behavior in pigeons: Categorization of both familiar and novel examples from four classes of natural and artificial stimuli. *Journal of Experimental Psychology: Animal Behavior Processes, 14,* 219–234. Copyright © 1988 by the American Psychological Association. Adapted with permission.

5.15 Lea, S. E. G., Lohmann, A., & Ryan, C. M. E. (1993). Discrimination of five-dimensional stimuli by pigeons: Limitations of feature analysis. *Quarterly Journal of Experimental Psychology, 46B,* 19–42. Redrawn by permission of Psychology Press Ltd. Copyright © 1993 by Psychology Press Ltd.

5.16 Pearce, J. M. (1989). The acquisition of artificial category by pigeons. *Quarterly Journal of Experimental Psychology, 41B,* 381–406. Redrawn by permission of Psychology Press Ltd. Copyright © 1989 by Psychology Press Ltd.

5.17 Mackintosh, N. J. (1995). Categorization by people and pigeons: The twenty-second Bartlett memorial lecture. *Quarterly Journal of Experimental Psychology, 48B,* 193–214. Redrawn by permission of Psychology Press Ltd. Copyright © 1995 by Psychology Press Ltd.

5.18 Wasserman, E. A., Hugart, J. A., & Kirkpatrick-Steger, K. (1995). Pigeons show same-different conceptualization after training with complex visual stimuli. *Journal of Experimental Psychology: Animal Behavior Processes, 21,* 248–252. Copyright © 1995 by the American Psychological Association. Adapted with permission.

5.19 Real, P. G., Iannazzi, R., Kamil, A. C., & Heinrich, B. (1984). Discrimination and generalization of leaf damage by blue jays (*Cyanocitta cristata*). *Animal Learning and Behavior, 12,* 202–208, Redrawn by permission of Psychonomic Society, Inc.

B5.1 Waldbauer, G. P. (1988). Asynchrony between Batesian mimics and their models. In L. P. Brower (Ed.), *Mimicry and the Evolutionary Process,* 103–121, published by University of Chicago Press. Copyright © 1988 by University of Chicago Press.

B5.1 Waldbauer, G. P., & LaBerge, W. E. (1985). Phenological relationships of wasps, bumblebees, their mimics and insectivorous birds in northern Michigan. *Ecological Entomology, 10,* 99–110, published by Blackwell Science Ltd.

T5.1 Mackintosh, N. J. (1995). Categorization by people and by pigeons: The twenty-second Bartlett memorial lecture. *Quarterly Journal of Experimental Psychology, 48B,* 193–214. Copyright © 1995. Reprinted by permission of Psychology Press Ltd.

Chapter 6

6.1 Anderson, J. R., & Schooler, L. J. (1991). Reflections of the environment in memory. *Psychological Science,* 2, 405–406. Redrawn with permission of Cambridge University Press.

6.2 Baddeley, A. (1995). Working memory. In M. Gazzaniga (ed.), *The Cognitive Neurosciences,* 755–764. Published by MIT Press. Copyright © 1995 by MIT Press.

6.3 Maier, N. R. F., & Schneirla, T. C. (1935/1964). *Principles of Animal Psychology.* Published by Dover Publications, Inc.

6.4a Wright, A. A. (1991). A detection and decision process model of matching to sample. In M. L. Commons, J. A. Nevin, & M. C. Davison (eds.),

Signal Detection Mechanisms, Models and Applications, 191–219.

6.4b Grant, D. S. (1976). Effect of sample presentation time on long-delay matching in pigeons. *Learning and Motivation*, 7, 580–590.

6.5a From *Introduction to Comparative Cognition* by Herbert L. Roitblat. Copyright © 1987 by W.H. Freeman and company. Redrawn with permission.

6.5b Beatty, W. W., & Shavalia, D. A. (1980). Spatial memory in rats: Time course of working memory and effects of anesthetics. *Behavioral and Neural Biology*, 28, 454–462.

6.7 Olton, D. S. (1978). Characteristics of spatial memory. In S. H. Hulse, H. Fowler, & W. K. Honig (eds.), *Cognitive Processes in Animal Behavior*, 341–373.

6.8 Langley, C. M. & Riley, D. A. (1993). Limited capacity information processing and pigeon matching-to-sample: Testing alternative hypotheses. *Animal Learning & Behavior*, 21, 226–232. Redrawn by permission of Psychonomic Society, Inc.

6.9 Whitlow, J., J. W. (1975). Short-term memory in habituation and dishabituation. *Journal of Experimental Psychology: Animal Behavior Processes*, 104, 189–206. Copyright © 1975 by the American Psychological Association. Adapted with permission.

6.10 Redrawn from *Animal Behaviour*, 47, Brodin, A., The disappearance of caches that have been stored by naturally foraging willow tits, 730–732, 1994, by permission of the publisher Academic Press.

6.11 Miles, R. C. (1971). Species differences in "transmitting" spatial location information. L. E. Jarrard, *Cognitive Processes of Nonhuman Primates*, 169.

6.12 Kamil, A. C., Balda, R. P., & Olson, D. J. (1994). Performace of four seed-caching corvid species in the radial-arm maze analog. *Journal of Comparative Psychology*, 108, 385–393. Copyright © 1994 by the American Psychological Association. Adapted with permission.

6.13 Olson, D. J., Kamil, A. C., Balda, R. P., & Nims, P. J. (1995). Performance of four seed-caching corvid species in operant tests of nonspatial and spatial memory. *Journal of Comparative Psychology*, 109, 173–181. Copyright © 1995 by the American Psychological Association. Adapted with permission.

6.14 Wright, A. A., Santiago, H. C., Sands, S. F., Kendrick, D. F., & Cook, R. G., Memory processing of serial lists by pigeons, monkeys, and people, *Science 229*, 287–289.

6.15 Roper, K. L., & Zentall, T. R. (1993). Directed forgetting in animals. *Psychological Bulletin, 113*, 513–532. Copyright © 1993 by the American Psychological Association. Adapted with permission.

6.16 Roper, K. L., Kaiser, D. H., & Zentall, T. R. (1995). True directed forgetting in pigeons may occur only when alternative working memory is required on forget-cue trials. *Animal Learning & Behavior, 23*, 280–285, Redrawn by permission of the Psychonomic Society, Inc.

6.17 Tulving, E., Schacter, D. L., & Stark, H. A. (1982). Priming effects in word-fragment completion are independent of recognition memory. *Journal of Experimental Psychology: Learning, Memory, and Cognition, 8*, 336–342. Copyright © 1982 by the American Psychological Association. Adapted with permission.

B6.2b Shettleworth, S. J., & Krebs, J. R. (1982). How marsh tits find their hoards: The roles of site preference and spatial memory. *Journal of Experimental Psychology: Animal Behavior Processes, 8*, 354–375. Copyright © 1982 by the American Psychological Association. Adapted with permission.

Chapter 7

7.1 Chelazzi, G., & Francisci, F. (1979). Movement patterns and homing behaviour of Testudo hermanni gmelin (*Reptilia Testudinidae*). *Monitore Zoologico Italiano 13*, 105–127.

7.1 Papi, F., (1992b). General aspects. In F. Papi (ed.), *Animal Homing*, 2–45. Courtesy of P. Dalla Santina.

7.1 Jouventin, P., & Weimerskirch, H. (1990). Satellite tracking of wandering albatrosses. *Nature*, 343, 746–748. Courtesy of P. Dall' Antonia.

7.2a,b Wehner, R., & Srinivasan, M. V. (1981). Searching behaviour of desert ants, genus *Cataglyphis* (Formicidae, Hymenoptera. *Journal of Comparative Physiology A, 142*, 315–338. Copyright © 1981 by Springer-Verlag.

7.2c Wehner, R. (1992). Arthropods. In F. Papi (ed.), *Animal Homing*, 45–144.

7.3 Muller, M., & Wehner, R. (1988). Path integration in desert ants, *Cataglyphis fortis. Proceedings of the National Academy of Science, 85*, 5287–5290.

7.4 Morris, R. G. M. (1981). Spatial localization does not require the presence of local cues. *Learning and Motivation, 12*, 239–260.

7.5 Tinbergen, N. (1951). *The Study of Instinct*, 147–148. Redrawn by permission of Oxford University Press.

7.7b Cheng, K. (1994). The determination of direction in landmark-based spatial search in pigeons: A further test of the vector sum model. *Animal Learning & Behavior, 22*, 291–301, Redrawn by permission of Psychonomic Society, Inc.

7.8 Cartwright, B. A., & Collett, T. S. (1987). Landmark maps for honeybees. *Biological Cybernetics,57*, 85–93. Copyright © 1987 by Springer-Verlag.

7.9 Redrawn with permission form *Nature, 370*, Hermer, L., & Spelke,

E. S. A geometric process for spatial reorientation in young children, 57–59. Copyright 1994. Macmillan Magazines Limited.

7.10 Spetch, M. L., Cheng, K., MacDonald, S. E., Linkenhoker, B. A., Kelly, D. M., Doerkson, S. R. (1997). Use of landmark configuration in pigeons and humans: II. Generality accross search tasks. *Journal of Comparative Psychology, 111*, 14–24. Copyright © 1997 by the American Psychological Association. Adapted with permission.

7.11 Wehner, R. (1992). Arthropods. In F. Papi (ed.), *Animal Homing*, 45–144.

7.13 Redrawn from *Animal Behaviour*, 30(1), Vander Wall, S. B., An experimental analysis of cache recovery in Clark's nutcracker, 84–94. Copyright © 1982, by permission of the publisher Academic Press.

7.14 From *Animal Learning and Behavior, 22*, 119–133, Brodbeck, D. R. (1994). Memory for spatial and local cues: A comparison of a storing and a nonstoring species, Redrawn by permission of Psychonomic Society, Inc.

7.15 Chittka, L., & Geiger, K. (1995). Honeybee long-distance orientation in a controlled environment. *Ethology*, 99, 117–126.

7.16 Dyer, F. C. (1996). Spatial memory and navigation by honeybees on the scale of the foraging range. *The Journal of Experimental Biology, 199*, 147–154. Redrawn with permission from Company of Biologists Limited.

7.17a Menzel, E. W. (1978). Cognitive mapping in chimpanzees. In S. H. Hulse, H. Fowler, & W. K. Honig (eds.), *Cogniive Processes in Animal Behavior*.

7.17b Gallistel, C. R., & Cramer, A. E. (1996). Computations on metric maps in mammals: Getting oriented and choosing a multi-destination route. *The Journal of Experimental Biology, 199*, 211–217. Redrawn with permission from Company of Biologists Limited.

7.18 Gallistel, C. R., & Cramer, A. E. (1996). Computations on metric maps in mammals: Getting oriented and choosing a multi-destination route. *The Journal of Experimental Biology, 199*, 211–217. Redrawn with permission from Company of Biologists Limited.

7.19 Maier, N. R. F. (1932b). Cortical destruction of the posterior part of the brain and its effect on reasoning in rats. *The Journal of Comparative Neurology, 56*, 179–214. Copyright © 1932 by John Wiley & Sons, Inc. Redrawn by permission of Wiley-Liss, Inc., a subsidiary of John Wiley & Sons.

7.19b From *Animal Learning and Behavior, 12(2)*, 232–237, Ellen, P., Soteres, B. J., & Wages, C. (1984). Problem solving in the rat: Piecemeal acquistion of cognitive maps, Redrawn by permission of Psychonomic Society, Inc.

7.20 Biegler, R., & Morris, R. G. M. (1996b). Landmark stability: Further studies pointing to a role in spatial learning. *Quarterly Journal of Experimental Psychology, 49B*, 307–345. Redrawn by permission of Psychology Press, Ltd. Copyright © 1996 by Psychology Press, Ltd.

7.21 Able, K. P., & Able, M. A. (1990). Ontogeny of migratory orientation in the savannah sparrow, *Passerculus sandwichensis*: calibration of the magnetic compass. *Animal Behaviour, 39*, 908.

B7.1 Dyer, F. C., & Dickinson, J. A. (1994). Development of sun compensation by honeybees: How partially experienced bees estimate the sun's course. *Proceedings of the National Academy of Science USA, 91*, 4471–4474.

B7.2 Helbig, A. J. (1996). Genetic basis and evolutionary change of migratory directions in a European passerine migrant *Sylvia atricapilla*. *Ostrich, 65*, 150–159.

T7.1 O'Keefe, J., & Nadel, L. (1978). *The Hippocampus as a Cognitive Map.*

T7.2 O'Keefe, J., & Nadel, L. (1978). *The Hippocampus as a Cognitive Map.*

Chapter 8

8.1 Moore-Ede, M. C., Sulzman, F. M., & Fuller, C. A. (1982). *The Clocks that Time Us.* Published by Harvard University Press. Copyright © 1982 by Harvard University Press.

8.3 Moore-Ede, M. C., Sulzman, F. M., & Fuller, C. A. (1982). *The Clocks that Time Us.* Published by Harvard University Press. Copyright © 1982 by Harvard University Press.

8.4 Bolles, R. C. & Moot, S. A. (1973). The rat's anticipation of two meals a day. *Journal of Comparative and Psyiological Psychology, 83*, 510–514. Copyright © 1973 by the American Psychological Association. Adapted with permission.

8.5 Redrawn from *Animal Behaviour, 47*, Biebach, H., Gordijn, M., & Krebs, J. R., Time-and-place learning by garden warblers, *Sylvia borin*, 353–360, 1989, by permission of the publisher Academic Press.

8.6 Roberts, S. (1981a). Isolation of an internal clock. *Journal of Experimental Psychology: Animal Behavior Processes, 7*, 242–268. Copyright © 1981 by the American Psychological Association. Adapted with permission.

8.7 Church, R. M., & Deluty, M. Z. (1977). Bisection of temporal intervals. *Journal of Experimental Psychology: Animal Behavior Processes, 3*, 216–228. Copyright © 1977 by the American Psychological Association. Adapted with permission.

8.8 Gibbon, J., & Church, R.M. (1981). Time left: Linear versus logarithmic subjective time. *Journal of Experimental Psychology: Animal Behavior Process, 7*, 87–108. Copyright © 1981

by the American Psychological
Association. Adapted with permission.

8.9 Cabeza de Vaca, S., Brown, B. L., &
Hemmes, N. S. (1994). Internal clock
and memory processes in animal
timing. *Journal of Experimental
Psychology: Animal Behavior Processes,
20*, 184–198. Copyright © 1994 by
the American Psychological Association. Adapted with permission.

8.10 Church, R. M., Meck, W. H., &
Gibbon, J. (1994). Application of
scalar timing theory to individual
trials. *Journal of Experimental
Psychology: Animal Behavior Processes,
20*, 135–155. Copyright © 1994 by
the American Psychological Association. Adapted with permission.

8.12 Anderson, M. C. & Shettleworth,
S. J. (1977). Behavioural adaptation
to fixed-interval and fixed-time food
delivery in golden hamster. *Journal of
the Experimental Analysis of Behavior,
27*, 33–49. Copyright © 1977 by the
Society for the Experimental Analysis
of Behavior, Inc.

8.12 Shettleworth, S. J. (1975). Reinforcement and the organization of
behavior in golden hamsters: Hunger,
environment, and food reinforcement.
*Journal of Experimental Psychology:
Animal Behavior Processes, 104*, 56–87.
Copyright © 1975 by the American
Psychological Association. Adapted
with permission.

8.13 Cheng, K., Spetch, M. L., &
Miceli, P. (1996). Averaging temporal
duration and spatial position. *Journal
of Experimental Psychology: Animal
Behavior Processes, 22*, 175–182.
Copyright © 1996 by the American
Psychological Association. Adapted
with permission.

8.14 Meck, W. H., & Church, R. M.
(1983). A mode control model of
counting and timing processes.
*Journal of Experimental Psychology:
Animal Behavior Processes, 9*, 320–
334. Copyright © 1983 by the Ameri-

can Psychological Association.
Adapted with permission.

8.15 Roberts, W. A., & Mitchell, S.
(1994). Can a pigeon simultaneously
process temporal and numerical information? *Journal of Experimental
Psychology: Animal Behavior Processes,
20*, 66–78. Copyright © 1994 by the
American Psychological Association.
Adapted with permission.

8.16 Capaldi, E. J., & Miller, D. J.
(1988). Counting in rats: its functional significance and the independent cognitive processes that
constitute it. *Journal of Experimental
Psychology: Animal Behavior Processes,
14*, 3–17. Copyright © 1988 by the
American Psychological Association.
Adapted with permission.

8.17 Boysen, S. T., & Berntson, G. G.
(1989). Numerical competence in a
chimpanzee (*Pan troglodytes*). *Journal
of Comparative Psychology, 103*, 23–31.
Copyright © 1989 by the American
Psychological Association. Adapted
with permission.

8.18 Redrawn with permission from
Nature, 358, Wynn, K., Addition and
subtraction by human infants, 749–
750. Copyright © 1992. Macmillan
Magazines Limited.

8.18 Wynn, K. (1995). Infants possess
a system of numerical knowledge.
*Current Directions in Psychological
Science, 4*, 172–177. Redrawn with the
permission of Cambridge University
Press.

8.19 Hauser, M. D., MacNeilage, P.,
& Ware, M. (1996). Numerical
representations in primates. *Proceedings of the National Academy of
Sciences USA, 93*, 1514–1517. Copyright © 1996 National Academy of
Sciences, U.S.A..

B8.1 D'Amato, M. R., & Columbo, M.
(1988). Representation of serial order
in monkeys (*Cebus apella*). *Journal of
Experimental Psychology: Animal
Behavior Processes, 14*(2), 131–139.
Copyright © 1988 by the American

Psychological Association. Adapted with permission.

B8.2 Redrawn from *Animal Behaviour,* *47*, McComb, K., Packer, C., & Pusey, A., Roaring and numerical assessment in contests between groups of female lions, *Panthera leo,* 379–387, by permission of the publisher Academic Press Limited London.

Chapter 9

9.1 Redrawn with permission from *Nature, 348,* Parker, G. A., & Maynard Smith, J., Optimality theory in evolutionary biology, 27–33. Copyright © 1990. Macmillan Magazines Limited.

9.2 Redrawn with permission from *Nature, 275,* Krebs, J. R., Kacelnik, A., & Taylor, P., Test of optimal sampling by foraging great tits, 27–31. Copyright © 1978. Macmillan Magazines Limited.

9.3 Redrawn from *Animal Behaviour,* 36, Shettleworth, S. J., Krebs, J. R., Stephens, D. W., & Gibbon, J., Tracking a fluctuating environment: a study of sampling, 87–105, 1988, by permission of the publisher Academic Press.

9.4 Bateson, M., & Kacelnik, A. (1995). Preferences for fixed and variable food sources: variability in amount and delay. *Journal of the Experimental Analysis of Behaviour, 63,* 313–329. Copyright © 1995 by the Society for the Experimental Analysis of Behavior, Inc.

9.5 Herrnstein, R. J. (1961). Relative and absolute strength of response as a function of frequency of reinforcement. *Journal of the Experimental Analysis of Behavior, 4,* 267–272. Copyright © 1961 by the Society for the Experimental Analysis of Behavior, Inc.

9.6 Mark, T. A., & Gallistel, C. R. (1994). Kinetics of matching. *Journal*

of Experimental Psychology: Animal Behavior Processes, 20, 79–95. Copyright © 1994 by the American Psychological Association. Adapted with permission.

9.8 Kennedy, M., & Gray, R. D. (1993). Can ecological theory predict the distribution of foraging animals? A critical analysis of experiments on the Ideal Free Distribution. *Oikios, 68,* 158–166. Copyright © 1993.

9.9 Redrawn from *Animal Behaviour,* *30,* Harper, D. G. C., Competitive foraging in mallards: 'ideal free' ducks, 575–584, 1982, by permission of the publisher Academic Press.

9.11 Redrawn from *Animal Behaviour,* 22, Krebs, J. R., Ryan, J. C., & Charnov, E. L., Hunting by expectation or optimal foraging? A study of patch use by chickadees, 953–964, 1974, by permission of the publisher Academic Press.

9.12 Waage, J. K. (1979). Foraging for patchily-distributed hosts by the parasitoid, *Nemeritis canescens. Journal of Animal Ecology, 49,* 353–371.

9.13 Krebs, J. R., & Davies, N. B. (1993). *An Introduction to Behavioural Ecology* (3 ed.), originally appearing in A. Kacelnik (1984), *Journal of Animal Ecology, 53,* 283–299.

9.14 Redrawn from *Animal Behaviour,* *39,* Brunner, D., Kacelnik, A., and Gibbon, J., Optimal foraging and timing processes in the starling, *Sturnus vulgaris*: effect of inter-capture interval, 597–613, 1996, by permission of the publisher Academic Press.

9.15 Redrawn from *Cognition, 37,* Gibbon, J., & Church, R. M., Representation of time, 23–54, Copyright © 1990, with kind permission of Elsevier Science-NL, Sara Burgerhartstraat 25, 1055 KV Amsterdam, The Netherlands.

9.17 Shettleworth, S. J., & Plowright, C. M. S. (1992). How pigeons estimates rates of prey encounter. *Journal of Experimental Psychology:*

Animal Behavior Processes, 18, 219–235. Copyright © 1992 by the American Psychological Association. Adapted with permission.

9.18 Bateson, M., & Kacelnik, A. (1996). Rate currencies and the foraging starling: the fallacy of the averages revisted. *Behavioral Ecology, 7*, 341–352, by permission of Oxford University Press.

9.19 Redrawn from *Animal Behaviour, 53*, Bateson, M. & Kacelnik, A., Starlings preferences for predictable and unpredictable delays to food, 1129–1142, 1997, by permission of the publisher Academic Press.

B9.2 Redrawn from *Pysiology and Behavior, 9*, Collier, G., Hirsch, E., & Hamlin, P. H., The ecological determinants of reinforcement in the rat, 705–716, 1972, Elsevier Science, Inc.

B9.2 Hursh, S. R. (1980). Economic concepts for the analysis of behavior. *Journal of the Experimental Analysis of Behavior, 34*, 219–238. Copyright © 1980 by the Society for the Experimental Analysis of Behavior, Inc.

Chapter 10

10.1 Terkel, J. (1995). Cultural transmission in the black rat: Pine cone feeding. *Advances in the Study of Behavior, 24*, 119–154.

10.2 Redrawn from *Animal Behaviour, 31*, Galef, B. G., Jr., and Wigmore, S. W., Transfer of information concerning distant foods: A laboratory investigation of the 'Information-centre' hypothesis, 748–758, 1983, by permission of the publisher Academic Press.

10.3 Redrawn from *Animal Behaviour, 35*, Giraldeau, L.-A. and Lefebvre, L., Scrounging prevents cultural transmission of food-finding behaviour in pigeons, 387–394, 1987, by permission of the publisher Academic Press.

10.5 From: *The Animal Mind* by Gould and Gould, © 1994 by Scientific American Library. Used with permission of W. H. Freeman and Company.

10.6 From: *The Animal Mind* by Gould and Gould, © 1994 by Scientific American Library. Used with permission of W. H. Freeman and Company.

10.8 Heyes, C. M., & Dawson, G. R. (1990). A demonstration of observational learning in rats using a bidirectional control. *The Quarterly Journal of Experimental Psychology, 42B*, 59–71. Redrawn by permission of Psychology Press Ltd. Copyright © 1990 by Psychology Press Ltd.

10.9 Whiten A., Custance, D. M., Gomez, J.-C., Teixidor, P., & Bard, K. A. (1996). Imitative learning of artificial fruit processing in children (*Homo sapiens*) and chimpanzees (*Pan troglodytes*). *Journal of Comparative Psychology, 110*, 3–14. Copyright © 1996 by the American Psychological Association. Adapted with permission.

10.10 Akins, C. K., & Zentall, T. R. (1996). Imitative learning in male Japanese quail (*Coturnix joponica*) using the two-action method. *Journal of Comparative Psychology, 110*, 316–320. Copyright © 1996 by the American Psychological Association. Adapted with permission.

10.11 Behaviour, 1992. Published by Brill, Leiden, the Netherlands. With permission from Bruce R. Moore.

10.12 Catchpole, C. K., & Slater, P. J. B. (1995). *Bird Song: Biological Themes and Variations*. Redrawn with the permission of Cambridge University Press.

10.13 Marler, P. (1976). Sensory template in species-specific behavior. In J. C. Fentress (ed.), *Simpler Networks and Behavior*, 314–329. Published by MIT Press. Copyright © 1976 by MIT Press.

10.14 Slater, P. J. B. (1983). The development of individual behaviour.

T. R. Halliday and P. J. B. Slater, *Animal Behaviour (Genes,Development and Learning)*, *3*, 82–113.

10.15 Visalberghi, E., & Limongelli, L. (1994). Lack of comprehension of cause-effect relations in tool-using capuchin monkeys (*Cebus apella*). *Journal of Comparative Psychology, 108*, 15–22.

10.16 Boesch-Acherman, H. & Boesch, C. (1993). Tool use in wild chimpanzees: New light from dark forests. *Current Directions in Psychological Science, 2*, 19. Redrawn by permission of Cambridge University Press.

B10.1 Galef, B. G. (1996a). Tradition in animals: Field observations and laboratory analyses. In M. Bekoff & D. Jamieson (eds.), *Readings in Animal Cognition*, 91–105. Published by MIT Press. Copyright © 1996 by MIT Press.

B10.3 Redrawn with permission from *Nature, 308*, Epstein, R., Kirshnit, C. E., Lanza, R. P., & Rubin, L. C., Insight in the pigeon: antecendents and determinants of an intelligent performance, 61–62. Copyright © 1984. Macmillan Magazines Limited. Original Drawing by Robert Epstein. Reprinted with permission.

Chapter 11

11.2 Gunn, D. L. (1937). The humidity reactions of the woodlouse, *Porcellio scaber* (Latrielle). *The Journal of Experimental Biology, 14*, 178–186. Redrawn with permission from Company of Biologists, Ltd.

11.3 Colwill, R. M., & Rescorla, R. A. (1985). Postconditioning devaluation of a reinforcer affects instrumental responding. *Journal of Experimental Psychology: Animal Behavior Processes, 11*, 120–132. Copyright © 1985 by the American Psychological Association. Adapted with permission.

11.4 Schwartz, B., & Williams, D. R. (1972). The role of the response-reinforcer contingency in negative automaintenance. *Journal of the Experimental Analysis of Behavior, 17*, 351–357. Copyright © 1972 by the Society for the Experimental Analysis of Behavior, Inc.

11.5 Redrawn from *Trends in Neurosciences, 18*, Povinelli, D. J., & Preuss, T. M. Theory of mind: evolutionary history of cognitive specialization, 418–424, Copyright 1995, with kind permission from Elsevier Science Ltd., The Boulevard, Langford lane, Kidlington 0X5 1GB, UK.

11.6 Redrawn with permission from *Science, 167*, Gallup, G. G., Jr. Chimpanzees: Self-recognition, 86–87. Copyright © 1970 American Association for the Advancement of Science.

11.7 Povinelli, D. J., & Cant, J. G. H. (1995). Arboreal clambering and the evolution of self-conception. *The Quarterly Review of Biology, 70*, 393–421. Published by the University of Chicago Press. Copyright © 1995 by University of Chicago Press.

11.8 Redrawn from *Animal Behaviour, 53*, Povinelli, D. J., Gallup, G. G., Jr., Eddy, T. J., Bierschwale, D. T., Engstrom, M. C., Perillous, H. K., & Toxopeus, I. B., Chimpanzees recognize themselves in mirrors, 1083–1088, 1997, by permission of the publisher Academic Press.

11.9 Miller, N. E. (1959). Liberalization of basic S-R concepts: Extensions to conflict behavior, motivation, and social learning. In S. Koch (ed.), *Psychology: A Study of a Science* (vol. 2). Copyright © 1959. Published by The McGraw-Hill Companies. Redrawn with permission from The McGraw-Hill Companies.

11.10 Whiten, A. (1994). Grades of mindreading. In C. Lewis & P. Mitchell (eds.), *Children's Early Understanding of Mind: Origins and Development*, 47–70. Reprinted by permission of Psychology Press Limited, Hove, UK.

11.12 Redrawn from *Trends in Neuro-sciences, 18*, Povinelli, D. J., & Preuss, T. M. Theory of mind: evolutionary history of cognitive specialization. 418–424. Copyright 1995, with kind permission from Elsevier Science Ltd., The Boulevard, Langford lane, Kidlington 0X5 1GB, UK.

11.13 Byrne, R. (1995). *The Thinking Ape*. Redrawn by permission of Oxford University Press and R. Byrne. Original drawing by David Bygolt.

11.14 Kummer, H., Anzenberger, G., & Hemelrijk, C. K. (1996). Hiding and perspective taking in long-tailed macaques (*Macaca fascicularis*). *Journal of Comparative Psychology, 110*, 97–102. Copyright © 1996 by the American Psychological Association. Adapted with permission.

11.15 Kummer, H. (1995). *In Quest of the Sacred Baboon*. (Biederman-Thorson, M. A., trans.). Copyright © 1995 by Princeton University Press. Redrawn by permission of Princeton University Press.

11.16 Hauser, M. (1996). *The Evolution of Communication*. Published by MIT Press. Copyright © 1996 by MIT Press.

11.16 Cheney, D. L., Seyfarth, R. M., & Silk, J. B. (1995). The responses of female baboons (*Papio cynocephalus ursinus*) to anomalous social interactions: Evidence for causal reasoning? *Journal of Comparative Psychology, 109*, 134–141. Copyright © 1995 by the American Psychological Association. Adapted with permission.

11.17 Reprinted from *Cognition, 31*, Cosmides, L., The logic of social exchange: Has natural selsction shaped how humans reason? Studies with the Wason selection task, 187–276. Copyright 1989, with kind permission from Elsevier Science-NL Sara Bugerhartstraat 25, 1055 KV Amsterdam, The Netherlands.

B11.3 Redrawn from *Constraints on*

Learning, R. A. Hinde & Stevenson-Hinde (eds.), Etienne, A. S., Developmental stages and cognitive structures as determinants of what is learned, 371–395, 1973, by permission of the publisher Academic Press Limited London.

Chapter 12

12.1 Tinbergen, N. (1951). *The Study of Instinct*, 28–39. Redrawn by permission of Oxford University Press.

12.2 Gomez, J.-C. (1994). Mutual awareness in primate communication: A Gricean approach. In S. T. Parker, R. W. Mitchell, & M. L. Boccia (eds.), *Self-awareness in animals and humans: Developmental perspectives*, 61–80.

12.3 Seyfarth, R. M., Cheney, D. L., & Wynn, P. J. (1992). Meaning and mind in monkeys. *Scientific American*, 122–128.

12.5 Seeley, T. D. (1985). *Honey Bee Ecology*. Princeton: Princeton University Press. Redrawn by permission of Princeton University Press.

12.6 Reprinted by permission of the Publisher from *Dance Language and Orientation of Bees* by Karl von Frisch, Cambridge, Mass.: Harvard University Press, Copyright © 1967 by the President and Fellows of Harvard College.

12.8 Redrawn from *Animal Behaviour, 46*, Evans, C. S., Evans, L., & Marler, P., On the meaning of alarm calls: functional reference in an avian vocal system, 23–38, 1993, by permission of the publisher Academic Press Limited London.

12.9 Redrawn from *Animal Behaviour, 43*, Evans, C. S. & Marler, P., Female appearance as a factor in the responsiveness of male chickens during anti-predator behaviour and courtship, 137–145, 1992, by permission of the publisher Academic Press Limited London.

12.9 Redrawn from *Animal Behaviour,*

Index of Subjects

Index of Names

Able, K. P., 327
Able, M. A., 327
Allen, C., 431
Allen, G. J., 502
Anderson, J. R., 235
Anzenberger, G., 508
Aristotle, 532

Bachmann, C., 513–14
Baerends, G. P., 67
Balda, R. P., 265, 518
Bard, K. A., 449, 467
Basolo, A. L., 73–74
Bateson, M., 416, 418, 419, 420
Bateson, P. P. G., 156, 162
Beck, B. B., 461
Beecher, M. D., 70, 71, 174
Behrends, P., 105
Bekoff, M., 483
Belke, T. W., 394
Bennett, A. T. D., 311, 317, 326
Bernstein, C., 402
Berntson, G. G., 374
Bever, T. G., 554–56
Biebach, H., 345
Biegler, R., 324, 326
Bingman, V. P., 300
Bitterman, M. E., 18–20, 116
Blough, D. S., 64–65, 81, 208, 213,
    214, 269
Blough, P. M., 83
Blumberg, M.S., 502
Boesch, C., 469
Bolhuis, J. J., 161
Bolles, R. C., 340
Bond, A. B., 84, 86
Boysen, S. T., 373, 374

Bradford, S. A., 370
Breland, K., 98, 488
Breland, M., 98, 488
Broadbent, H. A., 359
Brodbeck, D. R., 275, 305
Brown, S. D., 194, 196
Brunner, D., 408, 420
Byrne, R., 473

Camak, L., 467
Cant, J. G. H., 492
Capaldi, E. J., 370
Caraco, T., 415
Carew, T. J., 147
Carr, J. A. R., 345
Chantrey, D. F., 165
Charnov, E. L., 403–4
Cheney, D. L., 502, 513, 515, 542–47
Cheng, Ken, 99, 293, 294, 363
Chiang, G., 54
Chittka, L., 306, 371
Chomsky, N., 553
Church, R. M., 359, 366, 560
Clements, K. C., 410
Colgan, P., 401
Collett, T. S., 303, 326
Collins, J. S., 56–57
Colwill, R. M., 111
Cook, R., 80
Coppage, D. J., 224
Cosmides, L., 42, 44, 519, 520
Coussi-Korbel, S., 508
Cramer, A. E., 315–16
Cristol, D. A., 3–4
Crystal, J. D., 359
Custance, D. M., 449
Cynx, J., 196

685